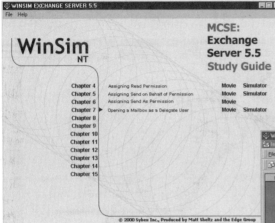

Prepare for Microsoft's tough simulation questions with the brand-new WinSim NT program!

✔ Use the simulators to guide you through real-world tasks step-by-step, or watch the movies to see the "invisible hand" perform the tasks for you.

Network Press MCSE Study Guide Sampler

✔ Preview chapters from the best-selling line of MCSE study guides from Sybex. We've also included a copy of Adobe Acrobat Reader, which you'll need to view the various preview chapters. From the core requirements to the most popular electives, you'll see why Sybex MCSE Study Guides have become the self-study method of choice for hundreds of thousands seeking certification.

Get a jump with LearnKey's Exchange Server 5.5 #1 CD-ROM (a $100 Value)!

✔ The second CD in this study guide is part of LearnKey's world-renowned *Exchange Server 5.5* course, providing interactive computer-based training on key topics for the Microsoft exam. Study with expert video instruction, then use the interactive exercises to test your knowledge.

I wanted to take this opportunity to let you know what outstanding products your MCSE study guides have been in assisting me on my certification track to becoming an MCSE. I have found the information contained in them to be invaluable. It is not often that I take the time to express my pleasure with any product, but I just had to say how impressed I am with the Sybex books.

Gina Pierson
PC LAN Specialist

Less than a month after I bought the MCSE Core Requirements books, I passed the first test with flying colors, and am currently about to take the NT Workstation test. The book's explanation of these difficult topics was extremely clear, and it let me work around what I already knew and focus on what I didn't. The practice exams, both in the book and on the accompanying CD-ROMs, were incredibly helpful in my preparation. I've recommended these materials to everyone I know pursuing these certifications.

Jonathan Disher
Network Engineer

Since I ordered the Sybex MCSE Core Requirements study guides, I have been on a confident and direct course to MCSE certification. The guides are very well written, at times humorous, and always reinforcing a necessary learning point. A "must buy" for every aspiring MCSE!

Phil Withers, MCP
Assistant Combat Information Systems Officer
USS George Washington (CVN-73)

I found the Sybex study guides to be extremely informative and very thorough. Before picking up the Sybex study guides, I had never been exposed to networking or Windows NT. I was able to pass the MCSE exams within a three-and-half month period simply by studying the Sybex study guides.

Patrick Sean Massey, MCSE
Software Technical Support,
Sparrow Systems Consultants

MCSE: Exchange Server 5.5
Study Guide
Third Edition

Richard Easlick
with James Chellis

San Francisco • Paris • Düsseldorf • Soest • London

Associate Publisher: Neil Edde

Contracts and Licensing Manager: Kristine O'Callaghan

Acquisitions & Developmental Editor: Neil Edde

Associate Developmental Editor: Dann McDorman

Editors: Kelly Winquist, Ben Miller, Lori Ash

Technical Editor: Rob Sanfilippo

Book Designers: Bill Gibson, Patrick Dintino

Graphic Illustrators: Steve Brooks, Andrew Benzie, Mike Taylor

Electronic Publishing Specialists: Cyndy Johnsen, Kate Kaminski, Bill Gibson, Robin Kibby

Project Team Leaders: Jennifer Durning, Amy Eoff

Proofreader: Jennifer Campbell

Production Assistant: Rebecca Rider

Indexer: Ted Laux

CD Coordinator: Kara Schwartz

CD Technician: Keith McNeil

Cover Design: Archer Design

Cover Illustrator/Photographer: FGP International

SYBEX, Network Press, and the Network Press logo are registered trademarks of SYBEX Inc.

Screen reproductions produced with Collage Complete.

Collage Complete is a trademark of Inner Media Inc.

The CD Interface music is from GIRA Sound AURIA Music Library © GIRA Sound 1996.

Microsoft® Internet Explorer © 1996 Microsoft Corporation. All rights reserved. Microsoft, the Microsoft Internet Explorer logo, Windows, Windows NT, and the Windows logo are either registered trademarks or trademarks of Microsoft Corporation in the United States and/or other countries.

Use of the Microsoft Approved Study Guide logo on this product signifies that it has been independently reviewed and approved in compliance with the following standards:

- acceptable coverage of all content related to Microsoft exam number 70-081, entitled Implementing and Supporting Microsoft Exchange Server 5.5;

- sufficient performance-based exercises that relate closely to all required content; and

- technically accurate content, based on sampling of text.

SYBEX is an independent entity from Microsoft Corporation, and not affiliated with Microsoft Corporation in any manner. This publication may be used in assisting students to prepare for a Microsoft Certified Professional Exam. Neither Microsoft Corporation, its designated review company, nor SYBEX warrants that use of this publication will ensure passing the relevant exam. Microsoft is either a registered trademark or trademark of Microsoft Corporation in the United States and/or other countries.

TRADEMARKS: SYBEX has attempted throughout this book to distinguish proprietary trademarks from descriptive terms by following the capitalization style used by the manufacturer.

First edition copyright © 1997 SYBEX Inc.
Second edition copyright © 1998 SYBEX Inc.

Library of Congress Card Number: 99-69045
ISBN: 0-7821-2726-6

Manufactured in the United States of America

10 9 8 7 6 5 4 3 2 1

SYBEX®

To our valued readers:

From the start, Sybex has made every effort to publish high quality MCSE study guides, working closely with Microsoft, our authors, and technical reviewers to ensure the accuracy and relevance of our texts. We realize, however, that readers such as yourself require more than accurate text; you need software that offers you the opportunity to reinforce your understanding of the subject matter, test your knowledge, and gain hands-on experience with the NT computing environment. With Microsoft's recent introduction of adaptive and simulative exam formats, it's become even more critical that exam candidates possess a comprehensive understanding of NT and other Microsoft programs. It was with these points in mind that we decided to publish these new editions of our best-selling MCSE study guides.

Along with the highly acclaimed courseware on the pages that follow, you'll now find enhanced CD content that includes the following:

Program Simulators Not a mock-up, but a program that shows you how Windows NT really looks and operates. In addition to video walk-throughs of the exercises in the book, we also provide a number of hands-on simulation exercises that require your input, just as it will be required on a simulative format exam!

Electronic Flashcards for PCs and Palm Devices With each study guide, we now provide hundreds of flashcard-style questions that you can use to reinforce your understanding of key concepts. And we provide these flashcard questions in two formats—one that can be run off a standard PC and another that can be run off a Palm device. Now you can study anywhere, anytime!

Sample Adaptive Exams Now a standard feature in our test engine, the adaptive testing component gives you an opportunity to experience the pressure of taking an adaptive test, one that will quickly determine if you're ready or not.

Bonus Exam-style Questions We've added hundreds of additional exam-style questions to our test engine, so you can test and re-test yourself before sitting for the actual exam.

We value your opinion and encourage you to e-mail us at Support@Sybex.com if you encounter any problems with the study guide you purchased. You can also e-mail me directly at JGold@Sybex.com with suggestions for improvements for future study guides.

Thank you for supporting Sybex and good luck in pursuit of your MCSE!

Sincerely,

Jordan Gold
Vice President/Publisher
Sybex, Inc.

SYBEX INC. 1151 MARINA VILLAGE PARKWAY, ALAMEDA, CA 94501
TEL: 510/523-8233   FAX: 510/523-2373   HTTP://WWW.SYBEX.COM

Acknowledgments

My thanks to Ben Miller and Lori Ash, editors, and to Rob Sanfilippo, technical editor, for all their hard work and contributions. I also appreciate the great work from all the people at Sybex: Guy Hart-Davis, Neil Edde, Amy Eoff, Robin Kibby, Jennifer Durning, Bill Gibson, Cyndy Johnsen, Kate Kaminski, Keith McNeil, Kara Schwartz, Dann McDorman, Jennifer Campbell, and Kelly Winquist. And finally, thanks to Louise for letting me use her green room as my office and lab. Thanks to all of you!

Contents at a Glance

Table of Contents

Table of Exercises

Introduction

The Microsoft Certified Systems Engineer (MCSE) certification is *the* hottest ticket to career advancement in the computer industry today. Hundreds of thousands of corporations and organizations worldwide are choosing Windows NT for their networks. This means that there is a tremendous need for qualified personnel and consultants to help implement NT and related products, such as Exchange Server 5.5. The MCSE certification is your way to show these corporations and organizations that you have the professional abilities they need.

This book has been developed in alliance with Microsoft Corporation to give you the knowledge and skills you need to prepare for one of the key elective exams of the MCSE certification program: Implementing and Supporting Microsoft Exchange Server 5.5. Certified by Microsoft, this book presents the information you need to acquire a solid foundation in Exchange Server 5.5, to prepare for the Implementing and Supporting Microsoft Exchange Server 5.5 exam, and to take a big step toward MCSE certification.

Is This Book for You?

If you want to learn how Microsoft Exchange 5.5 works, this book is for you. You'll find clear explanations of the fundamental and advanced concepts you need to grasp.

If you want to become certified as a Microsoft Certified Systems Engineer (MCSE), this book is also for you. As the Microsoft exams continue to change, the need for true skills and understanding is becoming more and more important for certification. This book will give you what you need to become truly prepared for the challenge of MCSE certification.

Microsoft Certified Professional Magazine's recent surveys reveal the average MCSE is earning a base salary of more than $65,000 (U.S.) per year, while the average MCSE+I is earning a base salary of more than $74,000 per year. If you want to acquire the knowledge base you need to pass Exchange Server 5.5 MCSE exam, take a step closer to your MCSE, and boost your career efforts, this book will serve you well.

What Does This Book Cover?

Think of this book as your guide to Microsoft Exchange Server 5.5. It begins by covering key technologies that make up Exchange, such as the following:

- Client/server messaging

- MAPI and RPC

- X.400 and X.500

Next it covers the architecture of Exchange, including the following:

- Core components

- Optional components

- Component communication

Then it continues with the following important topics:

- Installing Exchange Server

- Creating recipients

- The architecture, installation, and configuration of Microsoft Exchange clients

- Forms, public folders, and advanced security

- Internet clients for Exchange Server

Finally, a number of advanced topics are included:

- Managing an Exchange environment

- Connecting sites

- Internet mail and Exchange

- Microsoft Mail and Exchange

- Migrating other mail systems to Exchange

- Planning an Exchange environment

How Do You Become an MCSE?

Attaining MCSE or MCSE+I status is a serious challenge. The exams cover a wide range of topics and require dedicated study and expertise. This is, however, why the MCSE certificate is so valuable. If achieving the MCSE was too easy, the market would be quickly flooded by MCSEs and the certification would become meaningless. Microsoft, keenly aware of this fact, has taken steps to ensure that the certification means its holder is truly knowledgeable and skilled.

Exam Requirements

Successful candidates have to pass a minimum set of exams that measure technical proficiency and expertise:

- Candidates for the MCSE must pass four core requirements and two electives.

- Candidates for the MCSE+Internet must pass seven core requirements and two electives.

Exam	Title	MCSE	MCSE+Internet
70-058	Networking Essentials	Required	Required
70-067	Windows NT Server 4.0	Required	Required
70-068	Windows NT Server 4.0 in the Enterprise	Required	Required
70-073 *or*	Windows NT Workstation 4.0	Required	Required
70-064 *or*	Windows 95		
70-098	Windows 98		
70-059	Internetworking with TCP/IP on Windows NT 4.0	Elective	Required
70-077 *or*	Internet Information Server 3.0 and Index Server 1.1	Elective	Required
70-087	Internet Information Server 4.0		
70-079	Internet Explorer Administration Kit	Elective	Required
70-076 *or*	Exchange Server 5.0	Elective	Elective
70-081	**Exchange Server 5.5**	**Elective**	**Elective**
70-026 *or*	System Administration for SQL Server 7.0	Elective	Elective
70-028	Administering Microsoft SQL Server 7.0		

Exam	Title	MCSE	MCSE+Internet
70-088	Proxy Server 2.0	Elective	Elective
70-085	SNA Server 4.0	Elective	Elective
70-018 *or* 70-086	Systems Management Server 1.2 Systems Management Server 2.0	Elective	Elective

For a more detailed description of the Microsoft certification programs, go to www.microsoft.com/train_cert.

This book is a part of a series of Network Press MCSE study guides, published by Sybex, that covers the four core requirements as well as the electives you need to complete your MCSE track.

What Types of Questions Are There?

Until recently, the formats of the MCSE exams were rather straightforward, consisting almost entirely of multiple-choice questions appearing in a few different sets. Prior to taking an exam, you knew how many questions you would see and what type of questions would appear. If you had purchased the right third-party exam preparation products, you could even be quite familiar with the pool of questions you would be asked. All of this is changing.

In an effort to both refine the testing process and protect the quality of its certifications, Microsoft has recently begun introducing adaptive testing and new exam elements. These innovations add new challenges for individuals taking the exams. Most importantly, they make it much more difficult for someone to pass an exam after simply "cramming" for it.

Microsoft is taking steps to make it more difficult for third-party companies, or individuals participating in online "brain dumps," to acquire all of the test questions in any exam pool. It will be accomplishing this by regularly adding and removing exam questions, limiting the number of questions that any individual sees in a beta exam, limiting the number of questions delivered to an individual by using adaptive testing (more about that follows), and adding new exam elements.

Real skills and in-depth knowledge are now needed much more than they were before. Because Microsoft has a policy of not stating in advance what type of format you will see, let's take a look at adaptive testing and the new exam question types so you can be aware of all the possibilities.

Adaptive Exams

Microsoft is in the process of converting exams to a new "adaptive" format. This format is radically different from the conventional format previously used for Microsoft certification exams. If you have never taken an adaptive test, there are a few things you should know.

Conventional tests and adaptive tests are different in that conventional tests are static, containing a fixed number of questions, while adaptive tests change or "adapt," depending on your answers to the questions presented. The number of questions presented in your adaptive test will depend on how long it takes the exam to "figure out" what your level of ability is (according to the statistical measurements upon which the exam questions are ranked).

To "figure out" a test-taker's level of ability, the exam will present questions in increasing or decreasing orders of difficulty. By presenting sequences of questions with determined levels of difficulty, the exam is supposed to be able to determine your level of understanding.

For example, we have three test-takers, Herman, Sally, and Rashad. Herman doesn't know much about the subject, Sally is moderately informed, while Rashad is an expert. Herman answers his first question incorrectly, so the exam gives him a second, easier question. He misses that, so the exam gives him a few more easy questions, all of which he misses. Shortly thereafter, the exam ends, and he receives his failure report. Sally, meanwhile, answers her first question correctly, so the exam gives her a more difficult question, which she answers correctly. She then receives an even more difficult question, which she answers incorrectly, so the exam gives her a somewhat easier question, as it tries to gauge her level of understanding. After numerous questions of varying levels of difficulty, Sally's exam ends, perhaps with a passing score, perhaps not. Her exam included far more questions than Herman's included, because her level of understanding needed to be more carefully tested to determine whether or not it was at a passing level. When Rashad takes his exam, he answers his first question correctly, so he's given a more difficult question, which he also answers correctly. He's given an even more difficult question, which he also answers correctly. He then is given a few more very difficult questions, all of which he answers correctly. Shortly thereafter, his exam ends. He passes. His exam was short, about as long as Herman's.

Microsoft has begun moving to adaptive testing for several reasons:

- It saves time by focusing only on the questions needed to determine a test-taker's abilities. This way an exam that, in the conventional format, took $1^1/_2$ hours can be completed in less than half that time. The number of questions presented can be far less than the number required by a conventional exam.

- It protects the integrity of the exams. By exposing a fewer number of questions at any one time, it makes it more difficult for individuals to collect the questions in the exam pools with the intent of facilitating exam "cramming."

- It saves Microsoft and/or the test delivery company money by cutting down on the amount of time it takes to deliver a test.

Unlike the previous test format, the adaptive format will not allow you to go back to see a question again. The exam only goes forward. Once you enter your answer, that's it; you cannot change it. Be very careful before entering your answer. There is no time limit for each individual question (only for the exam as a whole). As your exam may be shortened by correct answers (and lengthened by incorrect answers) there is no advantage to rushing through questions.

Select-and-Place Exam Questions

Select-and-place exam questions involve graphical elements that the test-taker must manipulate in order to successfully answer a question. For example, a question could present a diagram of a computer network as shown in Figure 1.

In the diagram are several computers next to boxes that read "Place Here." There are also several labels representing different computer roles on network, such as Print Server, File Server, etc. Based upon information given for each computer, you are asked to drag and drop each label to the correct box.

You need to correctly drag the correct labels to *all* correct boxes in order to get credit for the question. No credit is given if you correctly label only some of the boxes.

F I G U R E 1

A "Quick Drop" screen
from a Select-and-Place
exam question

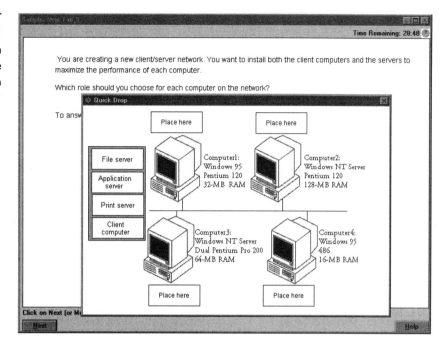

Simulations

Simulations are the kinds of questions that most closely represent and test the actual skills you use while working with Microsoft software interfaces. These types of exam questions include a mock or imitation interface on which you must perform certain actions according to a given scenario. The simulated interfaces look nearly identical to what you see in the actual product, as shown in Figure 2.

Simulations are by far the most complex element introduced into Microsoft exams to date. Because of the number of possible errors that can be made on simulations, it is worthwhile to consider the following recommendations from Microsoft:

- Do not change any simulation settings that don't pertain to the solution directly.

- Assume default settings when related information has not been provided because it is non-critical.

- Be sure entries are spelled correctly.

■ Close all simulation application windows after completing the set of tasks in the simulation.

■ Most important, however, is that you spend time working with the operating system.

The best preparation for this type of exam is to work with the graphical interface of the product on which you will be tested. By completing the exercises in this study guide, and by working with the WinSim software we have included on the first CD, you can greatly improve your level of preparation for this type of exam question.

Case Study–Based Questions

Case Study–based questions first appeared in the Microsoft Certified Solution Developer program (Microsoft's certification for programmers). The basic idea of the Case Study–based exam item is that you have a scenario with a range of requirements. Based on the information provided, you need to answer a series of multiple-choice questions. The interface for Case Study–based questions has a number of tabs with the information about the scenario appearing under each tab. The net result is that you have a rather lengthy description of a scenario, with several multiple-choice questions.

What the Implementing and Supporting Microsoft Exchange Server 5.5 Exam Covers

The Implementing and Supporting Microsoft Exchange Server 5.5 exam covers concepts and skills required for the support of Microsoft Exchange Server 5.5. It emphasizes the following areas of Exchange Server support:

- Internet protocols
- Managing Exchange Servers and clients
- Backing up and restoring Exchange Servers
- Configuring and managing site-to-site communication
- Microsoft Exchange coexistence with foreign systems
- Migrations to Exchange
- Troubleshooting Exchange

The exam focuses on fundamental concepts relating to Microsoft Exchange Server operation. But it can also be quite specific about operational settings and troubleshooting situations. Careful study of this book, along with hands-on experience with Exchange Server, will be especially helpful in preparing you for the exam. The Microsoft Exchange Server Resource Guide is another good reference for preparing for the exam.

Microsoft provides exam objectives to give you a very general overview of possible areas of coverage of the Microsoft exams. For your convenience, we have added in-text objectives listings at the points in the text where specific Microsoft exam objectives are covered.

Exam objectives are subject to change at any time without prior notice and at Microsoft's sole discretion. Please visit Microsoft's Training & Certification Web site (www.microsoft.com/Train_Cert) for the most current exam objectives listing.

How Does Microsoft Develop the Exam Questions?

Microsoft follows an exam development process consisting of eight mandatory phases. The process takes an average of seven months and contains more than 150 specific steps. The phases of Microsoft Certified Professional exam development follow:

1. Job analysis

2. Objective domain definition

3. Blueprint survey

4. Item development

5. Alpha review and item revision

6. Beta exam

7. Item selection and cut-score setting

8. Exam live

Microsoft describes each phase as follows.

Phase 1: Job Analysis

Phase 1 is an analysis of all the tasks that make up a specific job function, based on tasks performed by people who are currently performing that job function. This phase also identifies the knowledge, skills, and abilities that relate specifically to the performance area to be certified.

Phase 2: Objective Domain Definition

The results of the job analysis provide the framework used to develop objectives. The development of objectives involves translating the job function tasks into a comprehensive set of more specific and measurable knowledge, skills, and abilities. The resulting list of objectives—the *objective domain*—is the basis for the development of both the certification exams and the training materials.

Phase 3: Blueprint Survey

The final objective domain is transformed into a blueprint survey in which contributors—technology professionals who are performing the applicable job function—are asked to rate each objective. Contributors may be selected from lists of past Microsoft Certified Professional (MCP) candidates, from appropriately skilled exam development volunteers, and from within Microsoft itself. Based on the contributors' input, the objectives are prioritized and weighted. The actual exam items are written according to the prioritized objectives. Contributors are queried about how they spend their time on the job, and if a contributor doesn't spend an adequate amount of time actually performing the specified job function, his or her data is eliminated from the analysis.

The blueprint survey phase helps determine which objectives to measure, as well as the appropriate number and types of items to include on the exam.

Phase 4: Item Development

A pool of items is developed to measure the blueprinted objective domain. The number and types of items to be written are based on the results of the blueprint survey. During this phase, items are reviewed and revised to ensure that they are

- Technically accurate

- Clear, unambiguous, and plausible

- Not biased for any population subgroup or culture

- Not misleading or tricky

- Testing at the correct level

- Testing for useful knowledge, not obscure or trivial facts

Items that meet these criteria are included in the initial item pool.

Phase 5: Alpha Review and Item Revision

During this phase, a panel of technical and job function experts reviews each item for technical accuracy, then answers each item, reaching consensus on all technical issues. Once the items have been verified as technically accurate, they are edited to ensure that they are expressed in the clearest language possible.

Phase 6: Beta Exam

The reviewed and edited items are collected into beta exams. During the beta exam, each participant has the opportunity to respond to all the items in this beta exam pool. Based on the responses of all beta participants, Microsoft performs a statistical analysis to verify the validity of the exam items and to determine which items will be used in the certification exam. Once the analysis has been completed, the items are distributed into multiple parallel forms, or *versions*, of the final certification exam.

Phase 7: Item Selection and Cut-Score Setting

The results of the beta exams are analyzed to determine which items should be included in the certification exam based on many factors, including item difficulty and relevance. During this phase, a panel of job function experts determines the *cut score* (minimum passing score) for the exams. The cut score differs from exam to exam because it is based on an item-by-item determination of the percentage of candidates who answered the item correctly and who would be expected to answer the item correctly. The cut score is set in a group session to increase the reliability among the experts.

Phase 8: Exam Live

The exams hit the street. Microsoft Certified Professional exams are administered by Sylvan Prometric and VUE (Virtual University Enterprises).

Tips for Taking the Exchange Server 5.5 Exam

Here are some general tips for taking the exams successfully:

- Arrive early at the exam center so you can relax and take one last review of your study materials, particularly tables and lists of exam-related information.

- Read the questions carefully. Don't be tempted to jump to an early conclusion. Make sure you know *exactly* what the question is asking.

- Answer all questions.

- On simulations, do not change settings that are not directly related to the question. Also, assume default settings if the question does not specify or imply what they might be.

- Use a process of elimination to get rid of the obviously incorrect answers first on questions that you're not sure about. This method will improve your odds of selecting the correct answer if you need to make an educated guess.

- A reminder: The adaptive format will *not* allow you to go back to see a question again. Be very careful before entering your answer. Because your exam may be shortened by correct answers (and lengthened by incorrect answers) there is no advantage to rushing through questions.

Where Do You Take the Exams?

You may take the exams at any of more than 1,000 Authorized Prometric Testing Centers (APTCs) and VUE Testing Centers available around the world. For the location of a testing center near you, call 800-755-EXAM (755-3926) or call VUE at 888-837-8616. Outside the United States and Canada, contact your local Sylvan Prometric or VUE registration center.

To register for a Microsoft Certified Professional exam:

1. Determine the number of the exam you want to take.

2. Register with the Sylvan Prometric or VUE registration center that is nearest to you. At this point you will be asked for advance payment for the exam—as of December 1999 the exams are $100 each. Exams must be taken within one year of payment. You can schedule exams up to six weeks in advance or as late as one working day prior to the date of the exam. You can cancel or reschedule your exam if you contact the center at least two working days prior to the exam. Same-day registration is available in some locations, subject to space availability. Where same-day registration is available, you must register a minimum of two hours before test time.

You may also register for your exams online at www.sylvanprometric .com/ or www.vue.com/ms/.

When you schedule the exam, you'll be provided with instructions regarding appointment and cancellation procedures, ID requirements, and information about the testing center location. In addition, you will receive a registration and payment confirmation letter from Sylvan Prometric or VUE.

Microsoft requires certification candidates to accept the terms of a Non-Disclosure Agreement before taking certification exams.

What Software Products Are on the CDs?

With this third edition of our best-selling MCSE Study Guides, we are including quite an array of training resources. On the first CD are numerous simulations, practice exams, and flashcards to help you study for the exam. On the second CD is a training video from LearnKey. These are outlined in the following sections.

The Sybex WinSim NT

We developed WinSim NT to provide readers with multimedia and interactive experiences of Exchange Server 5.5 in operation. Nothing beats observing and working with the graphical interfaces and products that run on NT, such as Exchange Server 5.5. This product provides both audio/video files and hands-on experiences with key features of Exchange 5.5. Built around the exercises in this study guide, WinSim NT can give you knowledge and hands-on skills that are invaluable for understanding Exchange 5.5 and passing the exam. Figure 3 shows a sample screen from WinSim NT.

FIGURE 3

Interactive experiences based upon the exercises in this book help you understand Exchange Server.

The Sybex MCSE EdgeTests

The EdgeTests are a collection of multiple-choice questions that can help you prepare for your exam. They consist of:

- 150 questions specially prepared for this edition of the study guide.

- An adaptive test simulator that will give the feel for how adaptive testing works.

- All of the questions from the study guide presented in a test engine for your review.

Figure 4 is a screen capture from the Sybex MCSE EdgeTests.

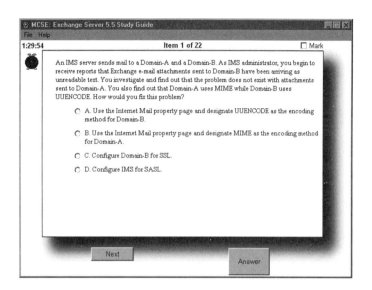

The Sybex MCSE Flashcards

The "flashcard" style of exam question offers an effective way to quickly and efficiently test your understanding of fundamental concepts covered in the Exchange Server 5.5 exam. The Sybex MCSE Flashcards consists of 100 questions presented in a special engine developed specifically for this study guide series. Figure 5 shows the Sybex MCSE Flashcards interface.

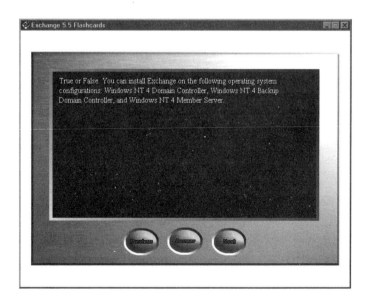

The Sybex Flashcards for Palm Devices

After receiving much demand for such a product, we developed, in conjunction with Land-J Technologies, a version of the flashcard questions that you can take with you on your 3COM Palm device.

Multimedia Windows Exchange Server 5.5 Training from LearnKey

Included on the second CD that accompanies the study guide is an Exchange Server 5.5 video from one of the leading video production companies, LearnKey. This LearnKey video covers important topics that can help you with your studies. This product, the first of three in LearnKey's Exchange Server 5.5 set, has a retail value of $99.95. The full set of Exchange Server 5.5 videos may be purchased directly from LearnKey. Figure 6 shows a screen capture from the LearnKey Exchange Server 5.5 video included with this study guide.

How to Use This Book

This book can provide a solid foundation for the serious effort of preparing for the Exchange Server 5.5 exam. To best benefit from this book, you may wish to use the following study method:

1. Study each chapter carefully. Do your best to fully understand the information.

2. Complete all hands-on exercises in the chapters, referring back to the text as necessary so that you understand each step you take. If you do not have access to a lab environment in which you can complete the exercises, install and work with the exercises available in the WinSim software included with this study guide.

3. Answer the review questions at the end of each chapter. (You will find the answers to these questions in Appendix A.) We've included the chapter questions in the EdgeTests on the first CD. If you would prefer to answer the questions in a timed and graded format, install the EdgeTests and answer the chapter questions there instead of in the book.

4. Note which questions you did not understand and study the corresponding sections of the book again.

5. Make sure you complete the entire book.

6. Before taking the exam, go through the Sybex MCSE EdgeTests included on the first CD that comes with this book. Be sure to try the adaptive version of the EdgeTests that is included with the Sybex MCSE EdgeTest. Lastly, review and sharpen your knowledge with the MCSE Flashcards.

F I G U R E 6

The LearnKey video

If you prefer to use this book in conjunction with classroom or online training, you have many options. Both Microsoft-authorized training and independent training are widely available. CyberState University is a Microsoft Certified Technical Education Center offering excellent online MCSE programs across the Internet, using the Sybex materials. Their program also includes an online NT lab where you can practice many of the exercises in this book, as well as videos, exam preparation software, chat forums, and lectures, all centered around the Sybex MCSE Study Guide series. You can reach CyberState at 888-GET-EDUCated (888-438-3382) or www.cyberstateu.com.

In order to completely run the exercises in this book, there are certain minimum hardware requirements, as detailed in Tables 1, 2, and 3.

T A B L E I

Server Requirements

Resource	Minimum	Recommended
CPU	Pentium 60	Pentium 133 or higher
RAM	24MB	32MB or higher
Free disk space	250MB	Depends on user storage
Network adapter/ cable/etc.	Almost anything (e.g. Ethernet, Token Ring, etc.)	N/A
Operating system	Windows NT Server v3.51 Service Pack 5 or above	Windows NT Server 4 (need Service Pack 2 if installing the Active Server Components.)

T A B L E 2	Resource	Minimum	Recommended
Windows 95/NT Client Requirements (Using Microsoft Outlook)	CPU	486/33	Pentium 100 or higher
	RAM	8MB for Win95 16MB for NT	16MB or higher
	Free disk space	26MB	46MB
	Network adapter/ cable/etc.	Ethernet, Token Ring, etc.	N/A
	Operating system	Windows 95 Windows NT Workstation 3.51 or 4	N/A

T A B L E 3	Resource	Minimum	Recommended
Windows 3.x Client Requirements (Using Microsoft Exchange Client)	CPU	N/A	N/A
	RAM	8MB	12 or 16MB
	Free disk space	12MB	22MB
	Network adapter/ cable/etc.	Ethernet, Token Ring, etc.	N/A
	Operating system	Windows 3.x	N/A

If you do not have access to such equipment, be sure to work with the WinSim NT product included with this book!

To learn all the material covered in this book, you will need to study regularly and with discipline. Try to set aside the same time every day to study and select a comfortable and quiet place in which to do it. If you work hard, you will be surprised at how quickly you learn this material. Good luck!

Contact Information

To find out more about Microsoft Education and Certification materials and programs, to register with Sylvan Prometric or VUE, or to get other useful information, check the following resources.

Resource	Contact Information	Description
Microsoft Training and Certification Home Page	www.microsoft.com/ train_cert	Visit the MCP for information about the Microsoft Certified Professional program and exams, and to order the latest Microsoft Roadmap to Education and Certification.
Sylvan Prometric testing centers	(800) 755-EXAM or www.sylvanprometric .com	To register to take a Microsoft Certified Professional exam at any of more than 800 Sylvan Prometric testing centers around the world, contact Sylvan Prometric.
VUE testing centers	(888) 837-8616 or www.vue.com	To register to take a Microsoft Certified Professional exam at a VUE testing centers, call the VUE registration center.
Microsoft Certification Development Team—Web	www.microsoft.com/ Train_Cert/mcp/ examinfo/certsd.htm	Contact the Microsoft Certification Development Team through their Web site to volunteer for one or more exam development phases or to report a problem with an exam. Address written correspondence to: Certification Development Team; Microsoft Education and Certification; One Microsoft Way; Redmond, WA 98052.

Resource	Contact Information	Description
Microsoft TechNet Technical Information Network	(800) 344-2121 or www.microsoft.com/ technet/subscription/ about.htm	Use this Web site or number to contact support professionals and system administrators. Outside the United States and Canada, instead of using the telephone number, contact your local Microsoft subsidiary for information.
Palm Training Product Development: Land-J	(407) 359-2217 or www.land-j.com	Land-J Technologies is a consulting and programming business currently specializing in application development for the 3Com Palm Personal Digital Assistant. Land-J developed the Palm version of the Edge Tests which is included with this study guide.
Training Resources: CyberState University	(888) 438-3382 or www.cyberstateu.com	CyberState University is a Microsoft Certified Technical Education Center that offers online MCSE certification training from virtually anywhere in the world, using a curriculum centered around the Sybex MCSE Study Guides.

CHAPTER

1

Introduction to Microsoft Exchange

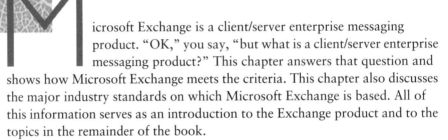

icrosoft Exchange is a client/server enterprise messaging product. "OK," you say, "but what is a client/server enterprise messaging product?" This chapter answers that question and shows how Microsoft Exchange meets the criteria. This chapter also discusses the major industry standards on which Microsoft Exchange is based. All of this information serves as an introduction to the Exchange product and to the topics in the remainder of the book.

In this chapter, we will address the following subjects:

- Messaging systems

- The client/server model

- Enterprise-wide computing

- Industry standards used by Exchange

The first three items relate to our previous question, "What is a client/server enterprise messaging product?" Messaging systems relate to *what* Exchange does, client/server models relate to *how* it does it, and enterprise-wide computing relates to the *context* in which it does it.

Messaging Systems

An enterprise needs information in order to get work done. Information is its oxygen. Frequently information *is* the work *and* the product (for example, a consulting company). In this context electronic messaging has become a mission-critical function in most organizations. While electronic mail (e-mail) is still the core ingredient, other applications are now included in this category. The category of messaging can be divided into the following subcategories:

- E-mail

- Workflow

- Electronic forms

- Groupware

- Other messaging applications

Each of these categories, and how Exchange addresses them, are briefly discussed in the following text.

 Due to the multiple functionality of some of the client programs, a single program could fit into more than one of the previous categories. For example, Microsoft Outlook includes e-mail functions and groupware functions like group scheduling.

E-Mail

An e-mail program allows a user to create, send, read, store, and manipulate electronic messages and attachments. E-mail is an example of *push-style* communication, meaning that the sender initiates the communication. Because of the importance of e-mail in the overall communication of organizations, these programs have evolved from merely creating and sending text messages, into multifeatured programs.

Microsoft Exchange ships with the Outlook client applications for Microsoft Windows 3.*x*, Windows 95 and Windows NT, and Macintosh. Also included is an Exchange client application for MS DOS.

Microsoft also has server components that enable Internet clients to be Exchange e-mail clients. Those Internet clients include:

- Web browsers

- Internet e-mail programs with the Post Office Protocol version 3 (POP3)

- Internet e-mail programs with Internet Message Access Protocol version 4 (IMAP4) support

Figure 1.1 illustrates these e-mail client applications.

F I G U R E   1.1

E-mail clients to Exchange
Server

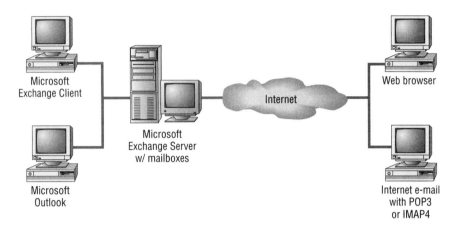

Microsoft Exchange Client

The Exchange Client is a feature-rich e-mail program. Some of its features include the following:

- **Universal inbox (mailbox)**   This central storage area can hold not only e-mail messages, but other data such as word processing documents, spreadsheet files, faxes, electronic forms, even voice mail files.

Two terms refer to a user's mailbox, *mailbox* and *inbox*. The most common usage in this book will be mailbox. This is our primary term for two reasons. One, Microsoft divides a mailbox into folders, one of which is labeled the inbox. Using the term inbox for only the folder helps prevent confusion. The other reason is that the Exchange object name for a mailbox is *mailbox*.

- **Hierarchical data storage**   The Exchange Client organizes the client's mailbox into four default folders: Inbox, Outbox, Deleted Items, and Sent Items. Users can also create their own folders, thereby creating a personalized organization of their data.

- **Customized views**   Users have the ability to determine what and how data is presented to them on their screens. Messages can be ordered by sender, date, priority, subject, and other properties.

- **Search tool**   Users can search and retrieve messages in their mailboxes using a variety of search criteria, such as sender, date, and subject.

- **AutoAssistants**   Exchange includes software routines that can automatically carry out actions based upon rules the user defines. This functionality is referred to as AutoAssistants. Some of the actions AutoAssistants can perform are alerting, deleting, moving, copying, forwarding, and replying.

- **Rich-text message content**   Historically, most e-mail content was simple text. The Exchange Client message editor enables the creation of rich-text message content which can include multiple fonts, sizes, colors, alignments, and other formatting controls.

- **Microsoft Word as message editor**   Even though the Exchange Client includes a rich message editor, it can be configured to use Microsoft Word as its message editor.

- **Compound messages and drag-and-drop editing**   The Exchange Client program is OLE 2.0 (Object Linking and Embedding) compliant, and therefore allows the creation of compound documents. For example, a user could drag-and-drop a group of cells from a spreadsheet into an e-mail message.

- **Secure messages**   Digital signatures and message encryption are advanced security features built into the Exchange Client.

- **Remote mail**   Because more and more workers spend some of their work time outside of the office, special features relating to remote mail have been incorporated. One example is the ability to remotely access a mailbox and selectively download new mail to the remote computer, and to send out all outgoing mail that was created on the remote computer.

- **Delegate access**   Some users need to allow other users to access their mailbox. For example, a manager might want a secretary to read meeting request messages in order to handle the manager's schedule. In many mail systems, this would be accomplished by having the secretary log on as the manager. This creates an obvious security hole. Microsoft solves this problem by allowing the manager to grant the secretary permission to access the manager's mailbox. This permission can be restricted to certain folders. The secretary can also be granted permission to send messages "on behalf of" the manager, or even send messages as the manager, called "send as."

- **Send/Receive electronic forms**   Users can send and receive electronic forms through the Exchange Client application.

These are just some of the many features of the Exchange Client program. Chapters 6 and 7 discuss these features in greater detail.

Microsoft includes versions of this e-mail program for the following operating system platforms:

- MS-DOS

- Microsoft Windows 3.*x*

- Microsoft Windows for Workgroups

- Microsoft Windows 95

- Microsoft Windows NT

- Apple Macintosh

Microsoft Outlook

Outlook is a new e-mail client that ships with Exchange Server and Microsoft Office 97 as a stand-alone product. It has a 32-bit version designed for Windows 95 and Windows NT, as well as versions that run on Windows 3.x and Macintosh. Outlook is referred to as a desktop information manager because it is more than just an e-mail client. It also performs such tasks as calendaring, scheduling, and task and contact management. Outlook is intended to be a central program for client management of data.

Microsoft Outlook includes the feature set listed previously for the Exchange Client, but also adds some additional advanced features. Some of them that specifically relate to e-mail are listed here:

- **MessageFlags**   These tags can be associated with e-mail messages to help the user prioritize follow-up action. MessageFlags include reply, read, and "for your information." Users can sort their messages by these MessageFlags, which helps with task management.

- **Voting**   Outlook has the ability to add voting buttons in the header of a mail message and to collect the responses. This allows surveys to be conducted through e-mail.

- **MessageRecall**   Permits a sent message to be recalled, provided the recipient has not opened the message. Users can also replace a sent message with a new message.

- **AutoPreview**   Outlook can automatically display the first three lines of a mail message so users can quickly decide which messages to read or delete.

- **AutoCreate**   Outlook can automatically convert one Outlook item into another. For example, a mail message may contain an action item which the user can simply drag-and-drop into the Task folder. Outlook would automatically convert the mail message into a task. This saves the user from retyping.

- **Recover deleted items**   Enables users of Outlook version 8.03 to recover deleted items in a mailbox or public folder.

- **Expanded storage capacity**   Users can store up to 64,000 items in their personal folder or an offline folder.

These are just some of the e-mail features of Microsoft Outlook. This client program will be discussed further in Chapters 6 and 7.

Web Browsers

Exchange Server 5.5 ships with a component called Outlook Web Access that can run on Microsoft Internet Information Server (IIS) and enable Web browsers to access Exchange resources such as mailboxes. Any standard Web browser can be used, such as Microsoft Internet Explorer or Netscape Navigator. This Exchange functionality permits users of other operating system platforms, such as UNIX or IBM's OS/2, to also be Exchange clients. Chapter 11 covers the Exchange components required for web browser clients.

Internet E-Mail Programs with POP3

Exchange has built-in support for the Post Office Protocol version 3 (POP3). POP enables mail clients to retrieve mail messages stored on a remote mail server. Exchange's support for this protocol allows Internet e-mail programs that support POP3 to access their Exchange mailbox and download their messages. Chapter 11 will cover POP in the Exchange environment.

Internet E-Mail Programs with IMAP4

Exchange also has built-in support for the Internet Message Access Protocol version 4 (IMAP4). IMAP is similar to POP in that it is a mail retrieval protocol. But IMAP has more features than POP, such as the ability to select the messages to download rather than having to download all new messages. Chapter 11 will provide further details on IMAP.

Electronic Forms

Electronic forms are electronic messages with built-in fields. They can be used instead of paper-based forms to automate and streamline organizational processes. Items such as expense reports, order entry, and purchase requests can all be implemented with electronic forms.

The two Exchange e-mail clients—Exchange Client and Outlook—can send and receive electronic forms. Exchange also ships with two programs that can be used to create customized electronic forms:

- Microsoft Exchange Forms Designer

- Microsoft Outlook Forms Designer

Microsoft Exchange Forms Designer

The Exchange Forms Designer is a visual, nonprogrammatic design and creation tool for electronic forms. Users simply draw a form's appearance and choose its behavior. The Forms Designer program is actually a special version of Microsoft's Visual Basic development tool. Because of this, forms created in the Forms Designer environment can be further modified in Visual Basic.

Electronic forms can be used with two types of applications:

- Stand-alone form applications

- Folder-based applications

Stand-alone form applications are electronic forms that are going to be sent from one person to another person or persons. An example is an expense report form that would be filled out and sent to the user's manager.

Folder-based applications utilize *public folders* and can have electronic forms associated with them. Both public folders and the way in which electronic forms relate to them will be discussed in the Groupware section that follows. Chapter 8 will cover the topic of forms in detail.

Microsoft Outlook Forms Designer

The Outlook Forms Designer is a program that can create 32-bit forms. It contains the basic functionality of the Exchange Forms Designer, and adds some powerful new functions. One of those new functions is the ability to use Microsoft Office 97 applications to create templates for Outlook forms. Chapter 8 will cover the topic of the Microsoft Outlook Forms Designer.

Workflow

Microsoft Exchange Server 5.5 makes it possible to create simple workflow applications using the Microsoft Exchange Scripting Agent. This capability enables developers to create event- or time-based workflow applications using VBScript or JavaScript that run on the server. For example, a user could submit a purchase request via an electronic form that is sent to a designated public folder. Once the form reaches the public folder, a script could activate, which would examine the value in the cost field of the form. If the amount is less than $100, the request is sent to the purchasing department. If the amount is greater than $100, the request is sent to a manager for approval. Chapter 9 will examine creating workflow applications with public folders and the Microsoft Exchange Scripting Agent.

Groupware

A simple definition of *groupware* is any application (the *ware* in groupware) that allows *groups* to store and share information. That is a very broad definition, and one that includes applications like e-mail and electronic forms. And indeed, as you will see, they are important ingredients in groupware. But the emphasis in groupware is collaboration, not merely sending something—but enabling many people to collaborate.

Microsoft Schedule+, which comes with the Exchange Server, is a straightforward groupware application. One of its functions is to enable many people to share calendar and scheduling information. A user, with the necessary permissions, can view the schedule of another user. This allows people to collaborate on their schedules. Microsoft Outlook also incorporates many groupware functions, such as the ability to share a calendar, schedule, task list, and contact list.

Another example of groupware is *folder-based* applications. These applications utilize public folders. A public folder is a special storage area for group access. Various types of information can be contained in a public folder, such as documents, spreadsheets, graphics, e-mail messages, forms, and many other types of information. Along with storing information, a public folder can be assigned security, so that only selected users or groups can access the public folder. Other features like views and rules can be assigned to a public folder. A simple folder-based application would be where a sales department places all their sales letters in a specified sales public folder. Only the employees in the sales department would be given permission to access this public folder.

Folder-based applications can also utilize electronic forms. A specific electronic form or forms can be associated with a public folder. Users can then fill out and "post" the form to the public folder. Other users can access the public folder and view the posted information. An example of this type of application is a discussion-and-response application. A product manager could create a public folder for discussion about a product under development. That manager could also create customized electronic forms that people could use to enter their comments and then send, through e-mail, to the public folder. The product manager and product developers could then access the public folder to read the comments. It is even possible to set up customized views of the content in the public folder in order to view only data on a specific topic. A marketing person might want to see only comments relating to the possible market for the product. Folder-based applications are examples of *pull-style* communication, because users go to the information and decide what is relevant to them. See Chapter 9 for more on the topic of public folders. Figure 1.2 illustrates folder-based applications.

FIGURE 1.2

Folder-based applications

Another groupware element of Exchange is the Microsoft Exchange Chat Service. The Chat Service enables users to conduct online meetings, discussions, or collaborate on documents or projects online and in real time. The Chat Service is based on the Internet protocol Internet Relay Chat (IRC). Chapter 11 will discuss this service.

Other Messaging Applications

Along with e-mail, electronic forms, and groupware, there are many other types of messaging applications. Exchange provides an open platform that encourages the integration of other types of applications, some of which include:

- **Workflow**   While Exchange includes some basic workflow capabilities, some third-party workflow solutions that work with Exchange are also available, such as Keyflow from Keyfile Corporation.

- **Fax**   Fax software can be integrated with the Exchange clients so that e-mail and faxes can be sent and received from the same location, as well as share the same address book.

- **Paging**   Some paging products can enable an Exchange client to send an electronic page through an Exchange server, to a wireless paging service, and to another person's pager.

- **Video conferencing**   Products like Microsoft's NetMeeting can be integrated with the Exchange clients to provide video conferencing, as well as other features like *whiteboard conferencing* (i.e., collaborative drawing) and text-based chatting.

- **Voice mail**   There are various voice mail products that integrate with Exchange and store their messages in an Exchange mailbox.

Client/Server Model

Microsoft Exchange uses a client/server computing model to implement its messaging system. To better understand the client/server model, two other models will be briefly discussed to provide a contrast to the client/server model. The three models discussed in this section are:

- Host-based computing
- LAN-based shared-file computing
- Client/server computing

Host-Based Computing

Host-based computing consists of a powerful host computer, such as a mainframe computer or minicomputer, and numerous input-output devices attached to the host, such as terminals, printers, and personal computers running terminal emulation software. The advantages of this architecture are the powerful, centralized computing processing, administration, and backup. These features permit a large number of users on these systems. The disadvantages are that these features incur high costs, that personal computing power and applications are not leveraged, and that most of these systems have a proprietary architecture. Examples of messaging systems that use this type of model are IBM PROFS (Professional Office System) and OfficeVision.

Figure 1.3 illustrates the host-based computing model.

LAN-Based Shared-File Computing

This network computing model works in a local area network (LAN) context. At least one powerful personal computer is used as a server computer to store files. Users, working on their own networked personal computers, access and share the files on the server computer. Microsoft Mail is a messaging system that uses this type of architecture.

Using this model, a shared-file mail system has *active clients* and *passive servers*. Each mail user is assigned a mailbox. A mailbox is actually a directory on the server where mail messages will be placed. The server software is passive in that its main task is to store mail messages.

The client software is said to be active because it performs almost all mail activities. Along with the normal mail activities of creating and reading mail, the client software is also responsible for sending mail to mailboxes and checking for new mail (this is referred to as *polling).*

This could be compared to a postal system where people must take their outgoing mail to the post office and place it in the respective recipients' mail slots. They must also visit the post office to check their mail slots for any new mail. The primary duty of the post office is to store the mail. This is analogous to the shared-file mail system in that the clients are active and the server is passive.

The advantages of shared-file mail systems include the following:

- **Minimal server requirements**   Because the server has a passive role, it does not need to run on a high-end hardware platform.

- **Minimal server configuration in a single-server environment**   Because the server is mainly a storage location, it does not need a lot of configuration.

FIGURE 1.3

Host-based computing
model

Terminals

Mainframe

Printers

Personal computers with
terminal emulation software

The disadvantages of shared-file mail systems include the following:

- **Limited security**   Because the client software is responsible for sending
  mail to a recipient's mailbox, each client must have write permissions on
  each mail directory. Each client must also have read permissions on the
  entire mail directory structure in order to read forwarded or copied messages. From a security standpoint, this is considered an excessive level of
  permissions.

- **Increased network traffic** The periodic client polling of mailboxes for new mail increases network traffic.

- **Increased client load** The active clients do almost all of the processing work.

- **Limited scalability** These systems cannot accommodate large numbers of users due to the shared-file model. Users must access common files that can be opened by only one process at a time.

Figure 1.4 illustrates a shared-file mail system.

FIGURE 1.4

Shared-file mail system

Mail Clients (active)

Mail Server (passive)

Server Role:
Store messages

Client Role:
– Poll mail directory for new mail
– Read mail (necessitates read permission over entire mail directory structure)
– Create mail
– Send mail (necessitates write permission over entire mail directory structure)

Client/Server Computing

Client/server computing is where a computer task is divided between the client processes and server processes. Each side, while performing specific parts of the task, works to accomplish the task. The two processes are usually running on separate computers and are communicating over a network. The communication is in the form of requests and replies passed back and forth through messages.

The client side includes a user's personal computer or workstation and client software. The client software provides the interface to the user for manipulating data and making requests to and receiving replies from the server. The processing power to carry out those tasks is provided by the client's computer.

The server side includes the server computer and server software. The server software receives and processes client requests, provides storage capabilities, implements security, provides for administrative functions, and performs many more duties. The server's processor, or processors, power these functions.

When this model is applied to a mail system, both the client side and the server side are active participants. Mail activities are divided between the two sides in a way that takes advantage of both parties. The client software enables users to initiate mail activities like creating, sending, reading, storing, and forwarding mail and attachments.

The server software also has an active role. Some of its tasks are implementing security, placing messages in mailboxes (as opposed to the client software doing it), notifying clients of new mail (which eliminates clients polling their mailboxes), and performing specified actions on mail, such as applying rules, rerouting messages, along with many other tasks. Many of the mail activities that are initiated by the client software are actually implemented on the server. For example, when a client initiates the reading of a message, the client software sends a read request to the server where the message physically resides. The server software receives this request, processes it (for example, checks security to see if this user is permitted to read this message), and then sends the message to the client. The user can then use the client software and processor to manipulate the message (edit the message, for example). This illustrates how both sides are active.

In this model, the software running on the client machine is frequently referred to as the *front-end* program, while the software running on the server is referred to as the *back-end* program.

The advantages of the client/server model include the following:

- **Distributed computer processing**   The computer processing power of both the client and server machines are utilized. The client processor handles the end-user mail activities, such as creating, reading, and manipulating mail, while the server processor (or processors) handles the security, routing, and special handling of mail. This spreads the processing load over a multitude of client processors, while still utilizing the powerful processing of the server machine.

The Big Ox Fallacy

Grace Hopper, one of the developers of the COBOL programming language, once told a story about a farmer who came upon a huge tree that had fallen across his road. The farmer brought out his ox and some rope and tried in vain to move the tree. The farmer's next act was to take the ox and breed it with another big ox hoping to produce an even bigger ox. He figured he would do this until he had bred an ox big enough to move that huge tree. Grace Hopper's commentary was that obviously the farmer's logic was flawed. What the farmer should have done was simply go get all his neighbors' oxen and hook them up to the tree and pull the tree off the road. This story illustrates the need to utilize the distributed processing power of all the machines on a network.

- **Tight security**   The server software is responsible for the security of the mail system. The server software is the entity that actually places messages in mailboxes. The clients therefore do not need permissions to all mailboxes. This creates a much more secure mail system.

- **Reduced network traffic**   Because the server software informs clients of new mail, the client software does not have to poll the server, thus reducing network traffic.

- **Scalable**   The term *scalable* relates to the ability to grow easily. A client/server mail system can scale to any size organization.

The primary disadvantage of the client/server model is the following:

- **Increased server hardware requirements**   Because the server has an active role in the messaging environment, there are greater requirements for the server hardware platform. This should not be seen as much of a disadvantage in light of the advantages of scalability, central administration, backup, and other advantages.

Figure 1.5 illustrates the client/server mail system.

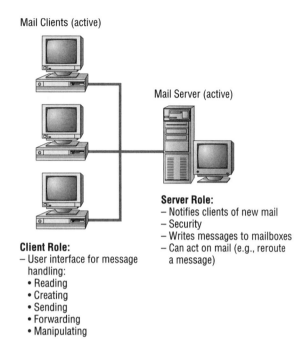

Exchange is a client/server messaging system. The Exchange Server software runs as an application on a Windows NT Server. It provides server-side messaging functions for the client applications. Exchange also ships with the client applications noted earlier in this chapter. These programs, along with third-party applications like Web browsers, provide the client-side functions such as making requests to the server and creating and manipulating data.

So far we have learned *what* features make up Exchange 5, and *how* the system is implemented, namely the client/server model. Now we need to turn our attention to the context or scale in which Exchange can be implemented.

Enterprise-Wide Computing

Microsoft Exchange was designed to be an *enterprise* messaging system, meaning one that spans an entire organization. While an enterprise can be of small or medium size with straightforward requirements, it can also be very large and have very complex requirements. For Exchange to be an enterprise messaging system, a large number of technologies had to be included or leveraged from other products (such as Microsoft Windows NT Server). This section briefly discusses the technologies that make Exchange a true enterprise messaging system. Those technologies fall into six categories:

- Enterprise-quality application platform

- Scalability

- Interoperability

- Performance

- Administration

- Reliability

Enterprise-Quality Application Platform

Before a determination can be made as to whether or not a product can scale to the size an organization needs, it must be determined that the product can do the things it needs to do. Exchange provides the necessary application platform to meet the requirements of almost any organization. The following are some of the elements of the Exchange application platform:

- **Supports large number of messaging services** E-mail, electronic forms, groupware, and add-on products for fax, paging, video conferencing, voice mail, and many services are supported.

- **Supports large number of client platforms** There is client software that runs on MS-DOS, Windows 3.*x,* Windows 95, Windows NT Workstation, Apple Macintosh, UNIX, and IBM OS/2.

- **Integrates with other client applications** The Exchange client programs that ship with Exchange have very tight integration with the most popular application suite on the market, Microsoft Office.

- **Provides open architecture/extensibility** Exchange is based on an open architecture, meaning that the specifications of many of its protocols are available in the public domain. Examples of published protocols include the Messaging Application Programming Interface (MAPI), Internet protocols, and various CCITT protocols. Developers can use this openness to create additional applications and programs that work with or extend Exchange. That is what is meant by *extensible.* One example of the way Microsoft encourages this is by including a single-user version of the

Microsoft Visual InterDev product with Exchange Server. Developers can use Visual InterDev to create Web-based applications that enable Web clients to access Exchange resources. Chapter 11 will briefly cover this topic.

- **Based on industry standards** The Exchange protocols, along with being open and extensible, are based on industry standards (protocols can be open and extensible but not industry standards). The MAPI protocol is considered an industry standard. Some of the industry standard Internet and CCITT protocols used in Exchange are:

    Internet mail Simple Mail Transfer Protocol (SMTP), Post Office Protocol 3 (POP3), and Internet Message Access Protocol version 4 (IMAP4). See Chapter 11.

    Internet Chat Internet Relay Chat (IRC). See Chapter 11.

    Internet directory access Lightweight Directory Access Protocol (LDAP). See Chapter 11.

    Internet news services Network News Transfer Protocol (NNTP). See Chapter 11.

    Internet management Simple Network Management Protocol (SNMP). See Chapter 12.

    Internet security Secure MIME (S/MIME), Secure Sockets Layer version 3 (SSL), and Simple Authentication and Security Layer (SASL).

    Internet Web protocols HyperText Transfer Protocol (HTTP) and HyperText Markup Language (HTML). See Chapter 11.

    CCITT message transfer (International Telegraph and Telephone Consultative Committee): X.400. See the section "Industry Standards" later in this chapter.

    CCITT directory X.500. See the section "Industry Standards" later in this chapter.

- **Security features** Using the Internet security protocols listed above, along with other protocols, Exchange can provide advanced security features. For example, messages can be sent with a digital signature to confirm the identity of the sender, and message content can be encrypted to prevent unauthorized viewing. Chapters 10 and 11 discuss the protocols and administration of advanced security in Exchange. Further security features, and ones that are leveraged from Microsoft Windows NT Server, include:

Mandatory logon   A user must have a domain account and password to log on to a Windows NT Server domain.

Discretionary access control   An Exchange administrator can use NT security to control access to Exchange resources. For example, one administrator could have security to manage one particular Exchange server, but not other servers.

Auditing   Windows NT can be configured to monitor and record certain events. This can help diagnose security events. The audit information is written to the Windows NT Event Log.

Scalability

Once a product has been determined to accomplish the types of things you need to get done, then you must find out if it can do it on the scale you need. Exchange is extremely scalable due to the following features:

- **Software scalable**   Exchange can be implemented with a single Exchange server, or dozens of servers, depending on the message requirements. Even with multiple Exchange servers, a single enterprise messaging system exists. This is due to the Exchange features that enable communication between servers. Some of those features include message routing, directory replication, and data replication. This functionality permits Exchange to scale from a single server to multiple server implementations. Microsoft itself uses Exchange for its worldwide messaging system.

- **Hardware scalable**   Scalability is also evidenced by the maximum hardware specifications that Exchange can utilize.

  - **CPUs**   Scalable from 1–8 processors.

  - **RAM**   Maximum is 4 gigabytes.

- **Disk Storage**   Storage is limited only by hardware capacity. The Standard edition of Microsoft Exchange Server 5.5 has a 16GB storage limit on each of the Exchange databases. The Enterprise edition has a 16TB (i.e., terabyte; trillion bytes) limit on each of those databases.

Interoperability

For a product to fit into an enterprise, it might need to work with an existing messaging system. This is called *interoperability* or coexistence. An organization might need to move all its existing messaging data to a new messaging product. This is called a *migration*. Exchange addresses both of these issues.

To interoperate with various non-Exchange systems, referred to as *foreign systems*, Microsoft had to write special software programs called *connectors*. Connectors are similar to translators who understand both Exchange and the foreign system and translate between them. Third-party companies also have written similar programs. Microsoft refers to these programs as *gateways*. Some of the messaging systems that Exchange can interoperate with include:

- Internet mail

- X.400 mail systems

- Microsoft Mail

- Lotus cc:Mail

- Lotus Notes

- IBM PROFS and OfficeVision

- Digital Equipment Corporation (DEC) All-IN-1

- Verimation MEMO

The Standard edition of Exchange Server 5.5 ships with connectors for Internet mail, Microsoft Mail, Lotus cc:Mail, and Lotus Notes. The Enterprise edition adds to that list connectors for X.400 systems, and IBM OfficeVision/PROFS and IBM SNADS–based systems. Connectivity to other systems, such as DEC ALL-IN-1 or Verimation MEMO, is provided through third-party gateway products.

For Exchange to interoperate with some of the previous systems, third-party software is required. Chapters 14 and 15 discuss interoperability in more detail.

Some of the messaging systems that Exchange can perform a migration with include:

- Microsoft Mail

- Lotus cc:Mail

- Novell GroupWise

- Netscape Collabra

- IBM PROFS and OfficeVision

- DEC All-IN-1

- Verimation MEMO

For Exchange to perform a migration with some of the previous systems, third-party software is required. Migration is discussed in Chapter 16.

Performance

A messaging system requires adequate performance to be used on an enterprise scale. Exchange meets that requirement by being a 32-bit, multithreaded program running on a high-performance operating system, Microsoft Windows NT Server. Exchange also ships with a program to help optimize performance, called the Exchange Optimizer. Another Exchange program that relates to performance is Load Simulator. This program can simulate load on the system and predict the system's performance.

Administration

An important element of any enterprise application is the ability to effectively and efficiently administer it. Exchange meets this need by including powerful administration programs, one of which is the Exchange Administrator program. This program provides a single point of administration for an entire Exchange organization. Exchange servers anywhere in the enterprise can be managed from this program, and such activities as creating mailboxes, configuring a server, and managing connections to foreign systems, can all be managed from this program. The Exchange Administrator program also enables the creation of mailboxes in a batch process, and provides for the tracking of messages. The Exchange Administrator program includes these administrative utilities:

- **Link Monitor**   Examines the link between two servers.

- **Server Monitor**   Examines the status of a particular server.

Exchange Server 5.5 has also added support for the Simple Network Management Protocol (SNMP). This enables third-party SNMP monitor programs to collect various management information about an Exchange server, such as performance information collected by NT Performance Monitor. The topic of Exchange Server administration is covered in Chapter 12.

Along with its own administrative utilities, Exchange can leverage the administrative capabilities of the Windows NT Server operating system. Exchange integrates with Windows NT Server utilities like Performance Monitor and Event Viewer.

Reliability

Because of the importance of a messaging system to an enterprise, it must be reliable. Exchange provides reliability through the following:

- **Transaction log files**   Data that is to be written to an Exchange database is first written to these log files (which can be done very fast). The data is later written to the appropriate database, which takes longer because of the structured nature of a database. If for whatever reason, a server has an unintended shutdown, data that has not been written to the database is not lost; it can be automatically reconstructed from the transaction log files. Chapter 12 will discuss this topic further.

- **Windows NT Backup program**   When Exchange is installed, it adds extensions to the Windows NT Backup program, allowing that program to backup Exchange information.

- **Replicas**   Exchange can be configured to have multiple copies, called *replicas*, of a single public folder on different servers. This prevents a single point of failure in terms of data access.

- **Intelligent message routing**   This feature allows multiple routes to a destination, thereby preventing a single point of failure for message delivery.

- **Windows NT Server fault tolerance** Exchange takes advantage of the many fault tolerant features of the Windows NT Server operating system, such as disk mirroring and disk striping with parity. The Enterprise Edition of Exchange Server 5.5 supports Microsoft's Cluster Server product. Cluster Server provides fault tolerance in the event of an NT server malfunction. If a server fails, another server can take its place, thereby providing uninterrupted service to users.

Industry Standards

Microsoft Exchange is based on industry standard technologies. Someone once joked that the best thing about standards was that there were so many of them from which to choose. But being a standards-based product ensures an open architecture and therefore extensibility (i.e., the ability to easily add on to the product). An adequate understanding of the standards used in Exchange will help in utilizing it. This section presents a brief coverage of the following standards:

- Messaging Application Programming Interface (MAPI)

- The Remote Procedure Call (RPC) protocol

- CCITT X.400

- CCITT X.500

The Internet standards are also very important in Exchange, and they will be discussed in Chapters 11 and 14.

Messaging Application Programming Interface (MAPI)

To understand MAPI, you must first understand what an application programming interface is. At the code level, a program's functions are invoked through specific instructions. The collection of those instructions are referred to as an application programming interface (API). That phrase is appropriate because the API allows a programmer to interface with the functions of a program. For example, if a program has the ability to read a message, there is a specific API instruction, also called a *function call*, that can invoke that ability. If two programs need to interact, they must do so with an API they both understand. For example, if program A sends the instruction Read_Message 4 to program B, but program B only understands the instruction Message_4_Read then the instruction will not be understood. Humans can use slightly different grammar and still understand one another, but computers are not that forgiving.

In the past, many client/server messaging products had their own APIs for the client/server interaction. If someone wrote a client program, it would only work with the messaging system whose API it used. If a user needed to connect to multiple messaging systems, multiple client programs were needed (see Figure 1.6).

FIGURE 1.6

Multiple messaging APIs require multiple programs

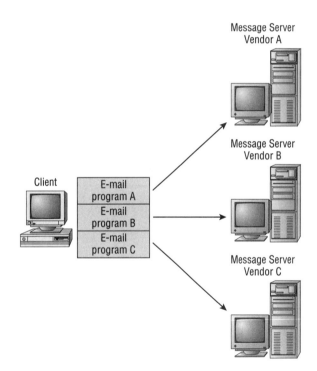

Microsoft decided to remedy that situation by creating a standard messaging architecture, referred to as the Messaging API (MAPI). MAPI accomplishes two broad goals. One, it provides a standard API for client/server messaging interaction. This role makes MAPI a type of *middleware*, meaning that it stands in the middle between clients and servers. Some authors refer to middleware as the slash (/) between the words client and server. MAPI makes it possible for a single client application to access different messaging servers (see Figure 1.7 for an illustration).

FIGURE 1.7

Accessing different
messaging servers
through MAPI

The second broad goal of MAPI is to provide a standard set of services to client messaging applications. These services include address books, message storage, and transport mechanisms. Even when using different types of MAPI applications, like e-mail, fax, and voice mail, a user can access a single address book (universal address book) and store different data types in the same folder (universal inbox). The transport mechanisms relate to a single client application connecting to different messaging systems. A single MAPI e-mail application can access a Exchange server, a Microsoft Mail post office, an Internet mail server, and others. Chapter 6 examines the MAPI services in more detail.

Although MAPI includes individual API instructions, it most often communicates those instructions in an object-oriented manner. An object is a container: in this context, it functions as a container of API instructions. The Microsoft specification for object-oriented programming is called the Component Object Model (COM). MAPI, OLE, ActiveX, and other technologies are part of the COM standard.

The original version of MAPI (called Simple MAPI) was developed by Microsoft. But in the subsequent version (MAPI 1.0), Microsoft worked with over 100 different vendors to develop an industry standard. Microsoft has also turned over the vast majority of the MAPI specification to standards organizations, while still taking a leadership role by including the core MAPI component with the Microsoft Windows 95 and Windows NT operating systems.

While MAPI deals with instructions, the next section discusses the protocols that enable those instructions to be passed between clients and servers.

Procedure Calls

We now know the instruction standard used by the Exchange client/server messaging applications, namely MAPI. But client/server applications are divided across physical machines. When a client issues a read instruction for a message, that message could be on the server. The server could understand that instruction and could send the message, but the instruction has to get to the server and the message has to get back to the client. MAPI does not handle those procedures. From MAPI's perspective, the physical distinction of the client and the server does not exist, it is transparent. Microsoft uses the Remote Procedure Call protocol (RPC) to pass instructions and data between machines. Before discussing the RPC protocol, we will first define what a procedure call is, and discuss the two types of procedure calls, local and remote.

Procedure calls handle the transfer of instructions and data between a program and processor, or processors. When a program issues an instruction, that instruction is passed to the processor for execution, and the results of the execution are passed back to the program. There are two main types of procedure calls:

- Local procedure calls

- Remote procedure calls

Local Procedure Calls

When a program issues an instruction that is executed on the same computer as the program executing the instruction, the procedure is referred to as a *local procedure call*. When Exchange Server components perform activities on that server, they issue instructions that are executed by that server's CPU or CPUs. That is an example of a local procedure call. Exchange uses a Microsoft protocol called the Local Procedure Call (LPC) to implement this mechanism. Examples of how Exchange uses LPCs will be forthcoming in Chapter 2.

Remote Procedure Calls

A *remote procedure call* is similar to a local procedure call in that it relates to the transfer of instructions and data between a program and processor. But unlike a local procedure call, a remote procedure call enables an instruction issued on one computer to be sent over the network to another computer for execution, with the results being sent back to the first computer. The computer making the instruction and the computer performing the execution are remote from each other. The transfer of instructions and data between the computers is totally transparent to the original program and to the user. To the program issuing the instruction, all its instructions appear to be locally executed. Remote procedure calls are a key ingredient in distributed processing and client/server computing.

The RPC mechanism permits the optimizing of different computers for specific tasks. For example, some programs require lots of processor power, memory, storage, or all three. It would be impractical to give every computer running these applications those level of resources. But one specialized computer could be given, for example, 4 processors, 512MB of RAM, and 16GB of storage. Clients could use those resources through the RPC mechanism.

Because the request/reply aspect of RPC is intended to be transparent to the client program and user, the speed of network communication is a factor. The computers involved in a RPC session need to have a high-speed permanent link between them, such as a local area network (LAN) or a high-speed wide area network (WAN).

Exchange uses remote procedure calls in many of its communications. The protocol that Exchange uses to implement remote procedure calls is also called Remote Procedure Call (RPC). This protocol is discussed in the following section.

Remote Procedure Call (RPC) Protocol

As previously stated, the protocol that Exchange uses to implement remote procedure calls is also called Remote Procedure Call (RPC). It is based on a protocol created by the standards group Open Software Foundation (OSF) and is part of the OSF's Distributed Computing Environment (DCE) protocol suite. Microsoft includes the RPC protocol with their Windows NT operating system, and this is what Exchange uses for much of its communication.

When a user chooses to read a message, the Exchange client program issues a MAPI instruction (MAPIReadMail). The RPC protocol on the client transfers this instruction to the Exchange server where the message physically resides. This is called a *request*. The RPC protocol on the server receives this request, has it executed, and sends the message back to the client's screen. The is called a *reply*. RPC clients make requests, and RPC servers make replies. RPC is sometimes referred to as a request/reply protocol. RPCs are also used in some Exchange server-to-server communications. Figure 1.8 illustrates the RPC mechanism.

FIGURE 1.8

The Remote Procedure Call protocol

CCITT X.400

For most of the history of electronic messaging in the private sector, there were no widely accepted messaging standards. Different messaging products used vastly different messaging protocols. This prevented, or made difficult and costly, interoperability between different systems. To address this situation, different standards organizations began to develop what they hoped would become internationally recognized messaging standards. One of those standards organizations was the Comité Consultatif International Telegraphique et Telephonique (CCITT). This is translated in English as the International Telegraph and Telephone Consultative Committee. One of the standards they developed was the X.400 Message Handling System (MHS) standard. Exchange uses some of the technologies of the X.400 standard.

The CCITT is now a subdelegation of the International Telegraph Union (ITU), which is an agency of the United Nations. The State Department is the voting member from the United States.

The different versions of the X.400 standard are referred to by the year they were officially published and by a specified color. Versions to date are:

- 1984 "Red Book"

- 1988 "Blue Book"

- 1992 "White Book"

The Message Handling System (MHS) discussed in this section is not the same standard as the Novell-related Message Handling System (MHS).

X.400 is a set of standards relating to the exchange of electronic messages (messages can be e-mail, fax, voice mail, telex, etc.). The goal of X.400 is to enable the creation of a global electronic messaging network. Just as you can make a telephone call from almost anywhere in the world to almost anywhere in the world, X.400 hopes to make that a reality for electronic messaging. X.400 only defines application-level protocols and relies on other standards for the physical transportation of data (e.g., X.25, and others).

X.400 Addressing: Originator/Recipient Address

Try to imagine the American telephone system if different parts of the country used different numbering schemes: different number lengths, different placement of the area code, etc. Obviously that would lead to a lot of complexity and problems: hence a standard numbering scheme exists. Electronic messaging also needs a standard addressing scheme to avoid the same sort of chaos.

One might think that you could simply list people's names in alphabetical order. But there are many problems with that scheme. The addressing scheme needs to potentially scale to the entire world's population. An alphabetical list would be quite long. There is also the problem of what constitutes a last name, different countries have different methods (e.g., Anwar el-Sadat, Willem de Kooning). A truly global address scheme needs to be totally unambiguous.

The address scheme that X.400 uses is called the Originator/Recipient Address (O/R Address). It is similar to a postal address in that it uses a hierarchical format. While a postal address hierarchy is country, zip code, state, city, street, and recipient's name, the O/R address hierarchy consists of countries, communication providers (like AT&T), companies or organizations, and other categories. Figure 1.9 and Table 1.1 present some of these categories, called *fields*.

FIGURE 1.9

X.400 Originator/
Recipient address example

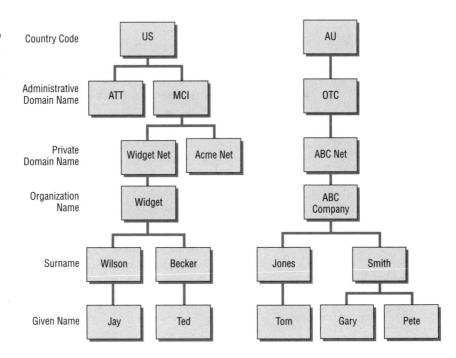

Field	Abbreviation/ Example	Description
Country code	c=us	Country
Administrative Management Domain (ADMD)	a=mci	The third-party networking system used (e.g., ATT, MCI, Sprint, etc.)
Private Management Domain (PRMD)	p=WidgetNet	Subscriber to the ADMD (company name)
Organization	o=Widget	Name of company or organization
Surname	s=Wilson	Last name
Given name	g=Jay	First name

T A B L E   1.1

Some X.400 Originator/ Recipient address fields

The O/R Address specifies an unambiguous path to where the recipient is located in the X.400 network (it does not specify a path the message might take, only the path to where the recipient is located).

In actual practice, this addressing scheme is not as standardized as Table 1.1 seems to indicate, nor is it used in the standardized way. Although the address fields have always been specified, the order in which to write them was not specified until 1993. Consequently, you will see them written in different ways. Some X.400 implementations have modified the standard.

X.400 Message Format: Interpersonal Messaging (IPM)

X.400 also specifies the protocols for formatting messages. The most common one is called Interpersonal Messaging (IPM), and is used for e-mail messages. There are other protocols for other types of messaging, such as electronic data interchange (EDI).

X.400 Message Routing: Message Transfer Agent (MTA)

Another very important X.400 protocol is Message Transfer Agent (MTA). MTA is the protocol that runs in the message routing machines (i.e., routers). MTA is like a local post office, in that it receives and routes messages to their ultimate destinations. And just like a postal system (a snail mail system), electronic messages can go through several MTAs before they arrive at their ultimate destinations. This type of delivery method is called *store and forward.* An MTA machine receives a message, stores it so it can calculate its next route, and then forwards it either to another MTA machine or its ultimate destination. This method eliminates the need for the sender's application and the recipient's application to perform any simultaneous actions in order to exchange data. A sender's message is simply packaged with all the necessary addressing information, and is sent to the next store-and-forward MTA machine (i.e., router). That MTA can route it to the next MTA, and so on, until it reaches it final destination.

Other X.400 Information

While the X.400 standard does not define the protocols for the physical transporting of messages, it does specify what other standards it can use. They include the following OSI (Open Systems Interconnection) protocols:

- TP0/X.25

- TP4 (CLNP)

- TP0/RPC 1006 to TCPIP

 TP stands for Transport Protocol.

Third-party X.400 networks that can be subscribed to include: AT&T Mail, AT&T EasyLink, MCI Mail, Sprintmail, Atlas 400 (France), Envoy 100 (Canada), Telebox 400 (Germany), and Telecom Australia. Microsoft Exchange is an X.400 messaging product.

CCITT X.500

The CCITT X.500 standard defines the protocols for a global directory service. A directory service is a database of information about resources. Resources can be user accounts, user groups, mailboxes, printers, fax machines, and many other items. These resources are officially referred to as objects. The information about an object, such as a mailbox, can include the owner of the mailbox, the owner's title, phone number, fax number, and many other types of information. The information about an object is referred to as its *properties* or *attributes*. A directory enables objects and their properties to be made available to users and administrators.

The directory's importance cannot be overstated. To use a telephone analogy, imagine the current global telephone system without telephone directories. The technology to make a call would be in place, but you would have a hard time locating a person's number to call. The creation of a global, electronic yellow pages could go a long way toward solving the "I know it's out there, I just can't find it" problem.

To create a directory service, X.500 addresses two main areas:

- **Directory structure**   How resources should be organized.

- **Directory access**   How one is able to read, query, and modify a directory.

X.500 Directory Structure

The X.500 directory structure is hierarchical, which facilitates a logical organization of information, which leads to finding information easier. Figure 1.10 illustrates the X.500 directory structure, and Table 1.2 explains it.

FIGURE 1.10

X.500 directory structure example

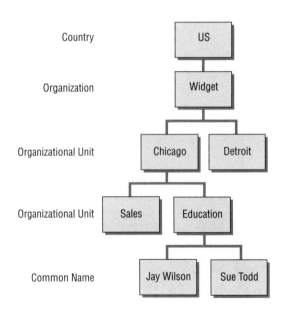

Country — US
Organization — Widget
Organizational Unit — Chicago, Detroit
Organizational Unit — Sales, Education
Common Name — Jay Wilson, Sue Todd

	X.500 Object	Abbreviation/Example	Description
TABLE 1.2 Descriptions of X.500 objects	Country	c=us	Country of the organization
	Organization	o=Widget	Name of the organization
	Organization Unit	ou=Chicago ou=Detroit	Subcategory of the organization
	Organization Unit	ou=Sales ou=Education	Subcategories under the ou=Chicago
	Common Name	cn=JayWilson	Name of a specific resource (username, fax name, printer name, etc.)

The X.500 terminology for the structure of a directory is the Directory Information Tree (DIT). The term for the information in the directory is Directory Information Base (DIB).

To communicate the location of an object in the directory hierarchy, list the path to that object, starting at the top and moving down. This is called a Distinguished Name (DN). The DN of the example in Figure 1.10 is:

c=us; o=widget; ou=Chicago; ou=Education; cn=jaywilson

The differences between an X.500 address, the distinguished name (DN), and an X.400 address are due to their different purposes. A DN is the location of an object in the directory, whereas the X.400 address is the location of an object in a message system. Getting back to the telephone analogy, a DN is the location of a person in the phone book, and an X.400 address is where they are in the physical telephone system. This is illustrated by the fact that an X.400 address can include information about third-party messaging networks used to physically deliver a message, some examples being AT&T, MCI, and Sprint.

The 1988 release of X.400 incorporated the use of a DN address instead of, or along with, an O/R address. Some implementations of X.400 also incorporated some of the X.500 fields, like ou= and cn=.

A directory also puts a more natural interface to network resources. Many communication objects have long numeric identifiers that are hard to remember. A directory allows objects to be presented to users by a natural descriptive term. The directory then maps the descriptive term to the numeric.

X.500 has a 1988 version and a 1993 version.

Directory Access

Having a directory is only half the equation. Users and administrators must also be able to access it to read, query, and write to it. A user might query the directory for a printer in the sales department, fourth floor, and the directory could respond with the needed information about the printer. Other issues that must be addressed are security (e.g., who can access an object and modify its properties) and directory replication (a true global directory would need to be on more than one machine). These issues are addressed by directory access protocols.

The standard access protocol in the X.500 recommendations is the Directory Access Protocol (DAP). DAP is considered more of a model than a real-world protocol. This is because DAP is very computer-resource intense (i.e., heavy) on client machines, and the few implementations of it were proprietary. But a newer access protocol that is getting a lot of attention today is the Lightweight Directory Access Protocol (LDAP). LDAP is an Internet protocol derived from the X.500 DAP. One of the reasons LDAP is called lightweight is because it requires fewer computer resources on the client. While LDAP is an Internet protocol, it is designed to enable access to an X.500-type directory. Almost every major software vendor has pledged support for LDAP.

Summary

The Exchange product is a powerful client/server enterprise messaging product.

The types of applications in an Exchange environment are:

- Electronic mail (e-mail)

- Electronic forms

- Workflow

- Groupware

- Other applications, such as fax, paging, video conferencing, and voice mail

The client applications that are shipped with Exchange are:

- Exchange Client

- Exchange Forms Designer

- Schedule+ 7.5

- Outlook

- Outlook Forms Designer

The network computing model that Exchange uses to implement its messaging system is the client/server model. This model utilizes the computing power of both client computers and server computers.

Exchange was designed for enterprise-wide implementations and consequently meets the following requirements:

- Enterprise-quality application services

- Scalability

- Interoperability

- Performance

- Administration

- Reliability

The following industry standards are used by Exchange:

- Messaging Application Programming Interface (MAPI)

- Internet protocols (e.g., POP3, IMAP4, LDAP, SNMP, and others)

- Remote Procedure Call (RPC)

- X.400

- X.500

Review Questions

1. The type of utility that would allow you to transfer data from a foreign message system to Exchange is:

   A. Administrative tool

   B. Security utility

   C. X.500

   D. Migration tool

2. This type of mail system has a passive server:

   A. Shared-file mail system

   B. Client/server mail system

   C. Host-based mail system

   D. Exchange server

3. Which of the following is NOT a feature of a client/server messaging system?

   A. Distributed processing

   B. Tight security

   C. Passive client application

   D. Reduced network traffic

4. Microsoft Outlook is a desktop information manager application that runs on the following operating system:

   A. Windows 3.*x*

   B. Windows for Workgroups

   C. Windows NT

   D. 32-bit UNIX

5. The following types of components can be used to connect Exchange to a foreign messaging system:

   A. Gateway

   B. Connector

   C. Groupware

   D. Key Management

6. The universal inbox is part of this software:

   A. Exchange Client

   B. SMTP clients

   C. POP3 clients

   D. LDAP clients

7. The following is an e-mail protocol:

   A. LDAP

   B. PNP

   C. PPP

   D. POP3

8. Which of the following could NOT be used as an Exchange e-mail client?

    A. Word processing program

    B. Web browser

    C. Internet e-mail program

    D. Microsoft Outlook

9. Which Exchange Client feature enables e-mail content to include multiple format types, such as fonts, sizes, and colors?

    A. WordPerfect

    B. This software cannot do this

    C. Richman message content

    D. Rich-text message content

10. This Microsoft technology enables the Exchange Client to create compound documents using drag-and-drop:

    A. OLE

    B. OOP

    C. DLL

    D. SNADS

11. Recalling a sent, but unopened, message is a feature of what program or programs?

    A. Outlook

    B. Exchange Client

    C. Public folders

    D. Forms

12. Which of the following relate to the performance of Exchange?

   A. Load Simulator

   B. 32-bit program

   C. Multithreaded

   D. Auditing

13. Since Exchange is scalable, it cannot be used in small to medium environments.

   A. True

   B. False

14. Exchange could use the Internet as part of its WAN design.

   A. True

   B. False

15. The following feature enables a Exchange client to create rules for processing incoming mail:

   A. Search tool

   B. Customized views

   C. Universal inbox

   D. AutoAssistants

16. What is the name of the mechanism when two Exchange components on the same machine pass instructions and data?

   A. Remote procedure call

   B. Remote instruction call

   C. Local instruction call

   D. Local procedure call

17. What is the name of the mechanism when a client-read instruction is sent to an Exchange server for execution?

    A. Local procedure call

    B. Local instruction call

    C. Remote instruction call

    D. Remote procedure call

CHAPTER

2

Microsoft Exchange Architecture

An *architecture* is a description of the structure of something. A structure can be something physical, like a building or bridge, or something abstract, like the principles of a philosophy. When applied to a software product, an architecture is a description of the software components of the product, what they are, what they do, and how they relate to each other. Part of what software components do is create and manage *objects* (i.e., resources) like servers, mailboxes, public folders, address books, etc. How those objects are structured or organized is also part of a software architecture.

There are many practical benefits to understanding the architecture of Microsoft Exchange. It will aid a person in designing, installing, administering, and troubleshooting an Exchange system. For example, understanding component functionality will assist in deciding what optional components, if any, to choose during an installation. Troubleshooting can frequently benefit from a good understanding of an architecture; just understanding some error messages requires this knowledge. This chapter also serves as a good conceptual background for the topics in the remainder of the book.

In this chapter, we will address the following issues:

- The organization of Microsoft Exchange objects

- Core components of Microsoft Exchange

- Optional components of Microsoft Exchange

Microsoft Exchange Object Organization

Many of the Microsoft Exchange components create and manage objects. Objects, as stated earlier, are resources such as servers, mailboxes, public folders, and address books. The organization of these objects is part of the architecture of Microsoft Exchange. Finding an object in the Exchange directory requires understanding object organization and object management. As you will learn, if a number of objects need the same configuration, and those objects are all grouped under a single object, the configuration can be given to the single object and then inherited by the objects underneath it.

Exchange is organized hierarchically. A *hierarchy* is the grouping and arrangement of items by rank, order, class, etc. A family tree is a good example of a hierarchy. At the top of the tree are the family patriarch and matriarch. Below them are their children, and their children below them, and so on. The family tree shows the relationships between people. One of these relationships is the parent-child relationship. Inherent to that relationship is the passing of traits from parent to children. A person can be both a parent and a child. A person will always be a child in reference to their parents, and that person can have children, making them also a parent. All of these concepts will relate to Microsoft Exchange.

Three objects constitute the main structures in the Exchange hierarchy:

- Organization

- Sites

- Servers

These objects contain other objects, but these three form the major structure of the hierarchy. Later in this chapter, under "Core Components" and "Directory Service," additional information will be given on them, as well as the other objects contained in them. Figure 2.1 illustrates the three main structures.

Organization

The largest unit, and the one at the top of the Exchange hierarchy, is the organization. All other Exchange structures are contained under this unit. The organization is the parent to the sites. This relationship permits an administrator to configure something at the organization level and have it apply or be available at all the sites (its children).

Because an organization encompasses an entire Exchange system, each company or business should create only one organization.

FIGURE 2.1

Three main structures of
the Microsoft Exchange
hierarchy

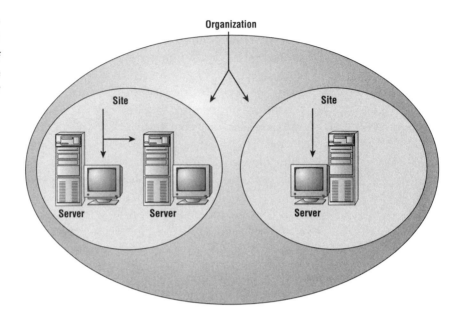

Sites

Sites are logical groupings of one or more Exchange servers. Even though resources reside on different servers in the site, the site groups all those resources without reference to their locations. This grouping makes using resources in the site very easy. For example, let us say that a certain mailbox physically resides on site server A. That site server is called the mailbox's *home server*. Senders do not need to know the physical location of the mailbox in order to send messages to it. They simply see the mailbox in the site listing, and send it a message. The same principle applies to public folders in a site. The particular server a public folder is stored on is of no concern to the users wanting to access it. They simply see the public folder listed in their site and access it. This is called *location transparency*. From the user's perspective, a site creates a transparent messaging environment.

A site also creates a smaller, more manageable Exchange network within the larger network of the organization. Administrators can assign a setting to the site (the parent), and it will be inherited by its site servers (the children).

There are two primary prerequisites for a site to be created:

- **Permanent, high-speed connections between the site servers** All communication that takes place within a site is done with RPCs. As you learned earlier, the RPC protocol transfers instructions issued at one machine to another machine for execution, and waits for the data to be sent back (a request/reply mechanism). For this to work efficiently, there must be a relatively high-speed connection between all the machines in the site. The connection also needs to be permanent. It is strongly recommended that all site servers be within a local area network (LAN) or high-speed wide area network (WAN) with permanent links.

- **All the site servers must be in the same Windows NT security context** (*context* **relates to location**)   When an Exchange component on one site server initiates communication with a component on another site server, the initiating component logs on to the other site server. The Windows NT account that is used for logging on is called the Site Services Account (the actual name of the account could be anything, Jane, Steve, etc., but it is referred to as the Site Services Account). This means all the site servers must be in the same Windows NT domain or domains with trust relationships.

Servers

Exchange servers comprise the final main structure in the Exchange hierarchy. These computers run the Windows NT Server operating system and the Exchange Server software. The Exchange servers are the physical location for mailboxes, folders, and other data and information for the site. Individual servers, while inheriting certain configuration parameters from the site (the parent), can also be individually configured. For example, even though recipients can be managed at the site level, they can also be managed at the server they were created on, their home server. All Exchange objects, as well as all related processes, are created and managed by the software components that make up the Exchange product. These components are divided into two main groups, core components and optional components, which are covered in the following discussion.

Core Components

The Exchange components are executable programs that perform the Exchange functions. Some are in the form of EXE files, others are in the form of Dynamic Link Libraries (DLLs). They are referred to as core components because they are necessary for Exchange to be operational. They are also referred to as services, because they run as services on the Microsoft Windows NT Server operating system. The core components include:

- Directory Service (DS)

- Information Store (IS)

- Message Transfer Agent (MTA)

- System Attendant (SA)

Table 2.1 uses a post office analogy to illustrate the functions of the core components.

	Exchange Core Component	Post Office Service
TABLE 2.1 Post office analogy for core components	Directory Service	Creation of a comprehensive address book
	Information Store	Storage and delivery of mail
	Message Transfer Agent	Routing decisions for mail to be sent between post offices
	System Attendant	Post office management

Directory Service (DS)

The Directory Service (DS) creates and manages the storage of all information about Exchange objects, such as the organization, site, servers, mailboxes, distribution lists, and public folders. The characteristics of these objects are called *properties* or *attributes*. The DS organizes all this information into a hierarchical database called the Directory, which is contained in the file DIR.EDB. The Directory hierarchy is patterned after the X.500 standard.

Structure and Objects of the Directory

This section provides additional details about the main objects in the Directory—organization, site, and server— and information on the other objects in the Directory. Figure 2.2 and Table 2.2 illustrate an X.500 directory structure along with the corresponding Exchange structures.

As can be seen in Figure 2.2 and Table 2.2, the Exchange Directory uses the same basic hierarchical structure as X.500. A minor difference is the naming

FIGURE 2.2

The Exchange Directory
and X.500

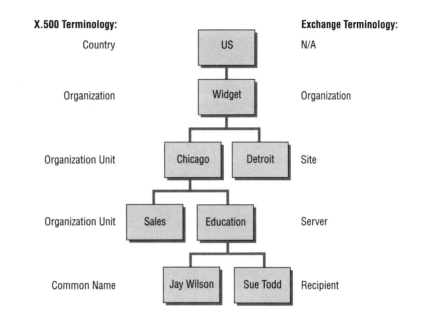

FIGURE 2.2

The Exchange Directory
and X.500

X.500 Object	Example	Description	Mapping to Exchange
Country	c=US	Country of the organization	N/A
Organization	o=Widget	Name of the organization	Organization name
Organization Unit	ou=Chicago ou=Detroit	Subcategory of the organization	Site name
Organization Unit	ou=Sales ou=Education	Subcategories under the ou=Chicago	Server names
Common Name	cn=Jay Wilson cn=Sue Todd	Name of a specific resource (e.g., username, fax name, printer name, etc.)	Recipient (e.g., mailbox, public folder)

TABLE 2.2

The Exchange Directory
and X.500

conventions. For example, the Exchange Directory refers to site names and X.500 refers to organization units, but they are easily mapped to each other.

The Exchange Directory, like X.500, contains objects. Objects are the representation, or abstraction, of a resource. That resource can be a person (e.g., Jay Wilson), or even an entire Exchange organization (e.g., Widget). Objects have properties, which are the characteristics of the object. The Jay Wilson object can have *properties* such as first name, last name, job title, telephone number, e-mail address, and many others. Properties are also called *attributes*. Figure 2.3 illustrates the properties of an object.

FIGURE 2.3

Properties of an object

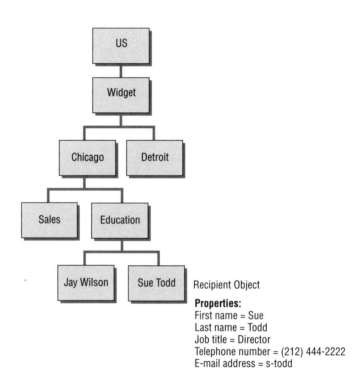

Recipient Object

Properties:
First name = Sue
Last name = Todd
Job title = Director
Telephone number = (212) 444-2222
E-mail address = s-todd

While the Exchange Directory objects map to the main structures in the X.500 hierarchy, Exchange also adds some additional objects. The three main structures (organization, site, server) are discussed next, along with the other objects within them.

Organization Object   As stated earlier, the organization encompasses all the Exchange objects of a company or other enterprise. The organization structure is an object and, as an object, it has properties. The primary property is *permissions,* which determine what functions the specified people can perform at the organization level. For example, one Exchange administrator can be given permission to create child objects under the organization, such as additional sites.

Because other objects are contained under the organization object, it is considered a container object. Along with site objects, two other objects are under the organization object:

- **Global Address List (GAL)**   The GAL object contains a comprehensive list of all the published mail addresses in the organization. Client software can access this list in order to send information to anybody in the organization. The global address list is considered a *container object* because it contains other objects, in this case, message recipients. These objects include mailboxes, distribution lists (multiple addresses grouped as one), and public folders. Each of these objects are considered *leaf objects*, because they do not have any other objects contained in them.

- **Folders**   The folders object contains public and system folders. An example of a public folder could be a folder named Technical Help containing a listing of all the people who provide technical help on the network. Examples of system folders are the organization forms and offline address book. An example of a folder property is replicas, which are the Exchange servers that contain a copy of that folder.

See Figure 2.4 for a depiction of the organization container.

Site Object   A site is a logical grouping of Exchange servers. The purpose of the grouping is to create a transparent messaging environment (users do not need to know on which server a resource is located). The properties of a site are the same type as with the organization object, the main one being permissions. Permissions can be assigned to a particular administrator allowing that administrator to create or modify child objects (like mailboxes) in the site. The difference between permissions granted at the organization object versus the site object is the *context* (i.e., the location in the hierarchy). Permissions granted at a site only apply to objects in that site, not to other sites and not to the organization.

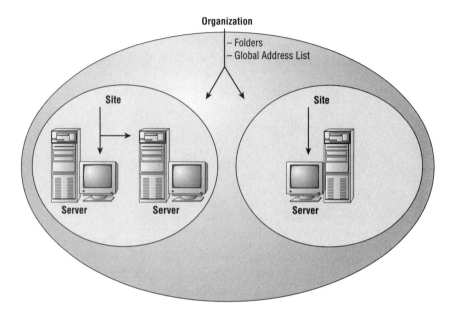

Sites are also container objects with the following objects under them:

- **Configuration** This container object holds seven additional container objects that pertain to numerous aspects of a site configuration. There are also four non-container objects under Configuration. These eleven objects are listed here (each item will be discussed in Chapter 12):

  - **Add-Ins** (container object)

  - **Addressing** (container object)

  - **Connections** (container object)

  - **Directory Replication** (container object)

  - **Monitors** (container object)

  - **Protocols** (container object)

  - **Servers** (container object)

  - **DS Site Configuration**

  - **Information Store Site Configuration**

  - **MTA Site Configuration**

  - **Site Addressing**

- **Recipients**   These are objects to which Exchange users can send messages. Recipient objects include:

  - **Mailboxes**   A location from which messages can be received, sent, stored, etc. Also stores other types of data.

  - **Distribution lists**   A grouping of individual recipients.

  - **Public folders**   A storage container for group access.

  - **Custom recipients**   E-mail addresses that represent a foreign mail system address.

See Figure 2.5 for an illustration of the site container.

FIGURE 2.5

The site container object

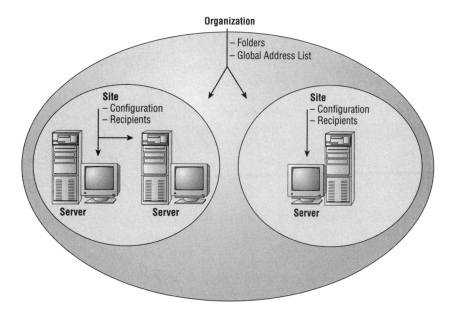

Servers Object Configuration   The Servers' container object is under the Configuration container. This object contains a listing of all the servers in the selected site. Each particular server object can be managed individually and contains the following two container objects:

- **Protocols**   This object contains the protocols, such as LDAP, NNTP, IMAP4, and POP3, that can be configured on the selected server. (These protocols will be discussed in Chapter 11.)

- **Server Recipients**   This object contains all the recipient objects (mailboxes, distribution lists, public folders, and custom recipients) stored on the selected server.

Figure 2.6 illustrates the server container and its objects.

Directory Replication

All Exchange servers in a site contain a complete copy of the directory information of that site. This is accomplished by automatic directory replication between servers of a site. When an Exchange object, for example a mailbox, is created on a particular Exchange server, that mailbox information is automatically copied to all the other servers in that site. This is an important factor in creating a transparent messaging environment. Users see all site recipients in their site address book. And while users do not need to know the physical location of a recipient, each Exchange server can route a message to the correct server because it has a copy of the site directory which contains this information.

There can also be directory replication between sites. This is not an automatic process, and must be configured by an administrator. This ability allows administrators to decide what resources to share with other sites. But directory replication between sites can be used to create an enterprise messaging environment. More on the topic of directory replication appears in Chapter 13.

Directory Access to the DS Directory

The DS component supports directory access through the MAPI interface and through the LDAP interface. This enables both Microsoft Exchange Client software and Internet LDAP-enabled applications to access the Exchange directory. Administrators access the directory through the Microsoft Exchange Administrator program, which is a MAPI program.

Benefits of the DS

There are many benefits to having an object-oriented hierarchical directory like the one the DS creates and manages. Because all Exchange configuration information is stored in the directory, the other Exchange components know where to go to reference information. Exchange administrators benefit from a graphical view of the Exchange environment, which helps in creating and managing Exchange resources. Administrators manage the Exchange environment by configuring the properties of objects in the directory. Users also benefit from a graphical view of resources, such as public folders and mailboxes, which makes it much easier to find resources. See Figure 2.7 for a review of the main points of the Directory Service.

Information Store (IS)

The Information Store (IS) provides the storage for Exchange message data. The IS is the back-end component for mailboxes, public folders, and their data. Many features of the Exchange client applications, such as folders, permissions, rules, and views, are made possible by the IS. It is also responsible for delivering messages to users on the same server as the sender, as well as notifying users of new messages in their mailboxes.

One of the powerful storage techniques used by the IS is single-instance storage. This means that a message sent to multiple users on the same server is stored only once. Each user would see the message in their mailbox, even though the message is not physically stored in the mailbox. Each of those mailboxes would have a pointer to the physical location of the message. This technique helps minimize storage levels.

FIGURE 2.7

Directory Service (DS)

Microsoft
Exchange Server

Core Components

DS			

DS Main Functions, Characteristics, Benefits:

Creates and manages directory

Characteristics of directory:
• Directory contains objects
• Objects have properties
• Directory structure is hierarchical
• Main hierarchy structures are:
– Organization
– Sites
– Servers

Benefits of the directory:
• Central location of all Exchange information
• Easy to find information because of the hierarchical structure

In addition to supporting access by MAPI clients, the IS also supports access by Internet clients using the Post Office Protocol 3 (POP3) and the Internet Message Access Protocol 4 (IMAP4). Those two Internet protocols are built into the IS.

Even though POP3 is built into the Information Store, it is still sometimes referred to as the Microsoft Exchange POP3 Service.

The IS storage consists of two databases: the Public Information Store, which contains all the Exchange public folders; and the Private Information Store, which contains all the Exchange mailboxes. By default, the IS creates both of these databases on an Exchange server. However, an administrator can choose to have only one of those databases on a server; this will be discussed later in this chapter under the heading "Dedicated Servers."

Public Information Store

The Public Information Store contains all the public folders of a particular server. Public folders are containers for shared information. In a sense, they are like a public mailbox. Different types of data can be stored in a public folder, such as e-mail messages, word processing documents, graphic files, and many other types. Public folders are used to create groupware applications. The Public Information Store is contained in the file PUB.EDB and stored on an Exchange server.

Private Information Store

The Private Information Store contains all user mailboxes. Security makes mailboxes accessible only to their owners and to others who have been given access permission. This database is contained in the file PRIV.EDB and stored on an Exchange server.

By default, a user's messages are stored in their mailbox in this database. Although mailboxes are always located in the Private Information Store on an Exchange server, messages do not have to be stored there. A user can specify a personal location for message storage. This type of folder is called a personal folder and has a PST file extension. A personal folder can be located on a user's local computer or on a server. Even when a user is using a personal folder for message storage, their mailbox is still on their Exchange server and in the Private Information Store. When they are sent a message, the message still first goes to their mailbox in the Private Information Store, and then is rerouted to a personal folder (the message would then physically reside only in the personal folder). The advantage of storing messages in a personal folder, especially if it is on a local computer, is that the user can access it without logging on to the server. The advantages of keeping message storage in the Private Information Store, which is the default, are centralized backup and fault tolerance.

Dedicated Servers

By default, an Exchange server contains both the Public and Private databases. But Exchange servers can also be configured to store only one of the two. If only the Private Information Store were configured, that server would act as a dedicated mailbox server. A dedicated folder server would only have the Public Information Store configured. Dedicated servers are created to improve the performance of information access.

Information Store Management Properties

Before we can begin a discussion of IS management, we need to introduce some IS properties that relate to management issues:

- **Replication**   Public folders can be configured to be replicated (copied) to other Exchange servers. This can be done for different reasons, including locating folders for easier network access and fault tolerance.

- **Storage limits**   The IS can be configured to set a storage limit for each mailbox.

- **Aging**   Folders can be configured to mark and delete information that has been in them for a specified length of time.

- **Views of resource usage**   An administrator can view the resources used by a user in the IS. An administrator can view resources by either mailbox or public folder. Resources viewed include disk space, number of stored items, log on time, and last log off time.

 Chapter 9 discusses the management of public folders. Chapter 12 discusses the overall management of an Exchange server, which includes managing the IS.

As an analogy, the IS as a service can be compared to a postal worker who stores letters and packages. If a letter's destination is that post office, this person will place the letter in the correct mailbox. The IS as a database is like the mailboxes and other storage at the post office. Figure 2.8 depicts the Information Store and some of its features.

Message Transfer Agent (MTA)

The Message Transfer Agent (MTA) manages the *routing* of messages between servers in a site, between servers in different sites, and between Exchange and some non-Exchange systems, such as Microsoft Mail. The MTA uses other components, called *connectors,* to manage the transfer of data, while the MTA handles the routing functions. The MTA could be compared to a post office that receives mail and routes it to another post office. The MTA component is based on the CCITT 1984 and 1988 X.400 standard.

FIGURE 2.8

Information Store (IS)

Microsoft
Exchange Server

Core Components

DS	**IS**		

IS Main Functions:

Creates and manages information storage
• Public Information Store (e.g., public folders)
• Private Information Store (e.g., mailboxes)

Notifies clients of new messages

Delivers message when sender and recipient are
on the same server

The main routing functions of the MTA component include:

- Addressing messages: O/R Addresses

- Translating message formats

- Making routing decisions

Addressing Messages: O/R Addresses

Because the MTA component is based on X.400, it also uses an Originator/
Recipient Address (O/R Address). Chapter 1 discussed the X.400 addressing
scheme. Figure 2.9 and Table 2.3 provide a review of the O/R Address and
how Exchange information is applied to this addressing scheme.

The example in Figure 2.9 and Table 2.3 could be written the following way:

c=us; a=mci; p=widget; o=Chicago; s=wilson; g=jay

If you compare the way Exchange uses the X.400 address format (Figure 2.9
and Table 2.2) and the X.500 name format (Figure 2.2 and Table 2.2), you will
notice a difference in how Exchange uses the organization field. In the X.400

Country Code — US

Administrative Domain Name — MCI

Private Domain Name — Widget

Organization Name — Chicago

Surname — Wilson

Given Name — Jay

organization field, Exchange places the site name rather than the Exchange organization name. This is probably due to the fact that the 1984 X.400 standard, which predated the X.500 standard, did not include the organization unit field. But when X.500 was published in 1988, the X.400 standard was revised to include X.500 names, such as organization unit and common name. Microsoft Exchange adheres to both the 1984 and 1988 X.400 standard. Exchange by default places the Exchange site name in the organization field. This value can be left in place, or the administrator can easily change it to the Exchange organization name. The administrator can also include an organization unit (ou=) field, placing the site name as its value. Using this format, the X.400 address would look like the following:

c=us; a=mci; p=widget; o=widget; ou=chicago; s=wilson; g=jay

The directory location to modify these addresses is Site/Configuration/Site Addressing.

	Field	Abbreviation	Description	Mapping to Exchange
TABLE 2.3 An X.400 addressing scheme and Microsoft Exchange	Country code	c=us	Country	Country
	Administrative Management Domain (ADMD)	a=mci	The third-party networking system used (e.g., ATT, MCI, Sprint, etc.)	Abbreviation of third-party network, or if not using one, leave field with a space
	Private Management Domain (PRMD)	p=Widget	Subscriber to the ADMD (i.e., company name)	Exchange organization name
	Organization	o=Chicago	Name of company or organization	Exchange site name
	Surname	s=Wilson	Last name	Last name attribute field for a mailbox
	Given name	g=Jay	First name	First name attribute field for a mailbox

Translating Message Content Format

If a message is being routed from Exchange to an X.400 message system, the MTA translates the message from the Exchange format, called the Microsoft Database Exchange Format (MDBEF) to the X.400 message format, called the Interpersonal Message (IPM) format.

This translation ability allows Microsoft Exchange clients to exchange mail with X.400 mail users, or use an X.400 network as a backbone to another Exchange environment and a user on that system. Figure 2.10 illustrates this latter scenario.

Making Routing Decisions

When the MTA receives a message to be forwarded, it first stores that message to determine its next route. This process involves comparing the message

F I G U R E   2.10

An X.400 network as a
backbone for Exchange
networks

recipient's address (either DN or O/R) to the routing table. The routing table, called the Gateway Address Routing Table (GWART), is the list of reachable destinations. If the MTA finds a route to the message recipient's address, it sends the message to the next location in that route. Because there could be multiple routes to a destination, an administrator can assign *costs* to different routes. Costs allow priorities to be given to different routes. The MTA will choose the lowest cost route when selecting a route. If the MTA cannot forward a message, a Non-Delivery Report (NDR) is sent to the message originator. Chapter 13 discusses message routing in greater detail. Figure 2.11 depicts the role of the MTA.

F I G U R E   2.11

Message Transfer
Agent (MTA)

Microsoft
Exchange Server

Core Components

| DS | IS | **MTA** | |

MTA Main Functions:

Addressing messages

Translating message content format
(only if a message is moving from Exchange
to an X.400 mail system)

Making routing decisions

The Microsoft Exchange MTA is based on the 1984 and 1988 versions of X.400 standards.

System Attendant (SA)

This service monitors and logs information about the other Exchange services. It also builds and maintains the routing tables for the site. The primary functions of the System Attendant are as follows:

- **Monitoring**   Two Exchange features, Link Monitor and Server Monitor, use the SA component to monitor. The Link Monitor sends test messages between servers to see if there is a connection between them. The Server Monitor checks the status of Exchange or other NT services on a server by sending test messages to that server. Both of these features use the SA component to send and receive the test messages.

- **Verifying information**   The SA verifies the accuracy of a server's directory replication information. If it is incorrect, the SA will repair the inconsistencies.

- **Logging**   The SA writes message tracking information to the message tracking log. Information tracked includes the route a message took, and if the message arrived at its destination.

- **Building routing tables**   The SA builds the routing tables of a site. The MTA references these tables when making routing decisions. By default, the routing table is automatically rebuilt once per day. This process can be configured and can be manually initiated through the properties of the MTA (even though it is carried out by the SA).

- **Generating e-mail addresses**   When new recipients are created by the DS, the SA ensures that their e-mail addresses are generated.

- **Assisting with advanced security**   The SA accepts client requests for advanced security initialization and passes those requests on to the Exchange server advanced security components. Advanced security relates to digital signatures and data encryption. Advanced security will be introduced later in this chapter under the "Optional Exchange Components" section. It is also covered in more detail in Chapter 10.

Figure 2.12 illustrates the main functions of the SA component.

FIGURE 2.12

System Attendant (SA)

Microsoft
Exchange Server

Core Components

DS	IS	MTA	**SA**

SA Main Functions:

Monitoring
• Link Monitor
• Server Monitor

Logging
• Message tracking log

Building routing tables

Generating e-mail addresses

Optional Exchange Components

Optional components, as the name implies, are not necessary for the basic operation of Exchange. But these components could be needed for additional functionality in your Exchange environment. Optional components include:

- Connectors or gateways

- Outlook Web Access

- Chat Service

- Scripting Agent

- Key Management

Individual gateways will not be covered because they are documented in their own third-party literature.

Connectors or Gateways

Most of the optional components are connectors or gateways. These are components that enable Exchange to interoperate with non-Exchange systems, sometimes referred to as foreign systems. Connectors are developed by Microsoft, whereas gateways are developed by third-party companies (i.e., not Microsoft). Examples of foreign message systems that have connectors include the following:

- Internet Mail Service (IMS)
- Microsoft Mail Connector
- Schedule+ Free/Busy Connector
- Lotus cc:Mail Connector
- Lotus Notes Connector
- IBM OfficeVision/VM

Internet Mail Service (IMS)

The Internet Mail Service (IMS) connector enables an Exchange system to interoperate with an SMTP mail system. SMTP, Simple Mail Transfer Protocol, is the standard mail exchange protocol for the TCP/IP protocol suite. It is used in many intranet mail systems (inside a company or organization), as well as on the Internet. The IMS permits Exchange users and SMTP mail users to send and receive mail to each other. Organizations that already have an SMTP mail system can add Microsoft Exchange, gaining its rich feature set, and yet still have enterprise messaging because of the interoperability through the IMS. The IMS connector also permits an organization with geographically disperse locations to use the Internet as a messaging backbone. Messages can be sent from one Exchange user, through the Internet, to the Exchange recipient. Figure 2.13 illustrates the IMS component. Chapter 14 provides further information on the IMS.

Internet News Service (INS)

The Internet News Service (INS) connector permits an Exchange system to interoperate with USENET newsgroups. USENET is a network of host machines containing posted discussions on various topics. A discussion area is referred to as a newsgroup. Users can access a newsgroup and read the text of a discussion or post their own comments. The USENET uses the Internet, as well as other networks. USENET uses Network News Transport Protocol (NNTP) to replicate newsgroup information between hosts.

FIGURE 2.13

Internet Mail Service (IMS)

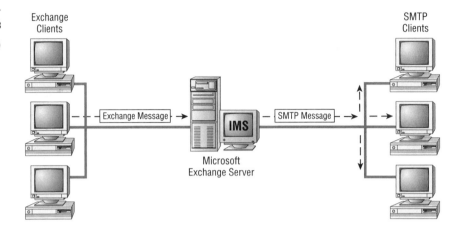

The Microsoft Internet News Service includes the NNTP protocol and can download newsgroup information from the USENET into an Exchange public folder, and vice versa. The Internet New Service is discussed in more detail in Chapter 11.

Microsoft Mail Connector

An Exchange system can interoperate with a Microsoft Mail system through the Microsoft Mail Connector. Microsoft Mail is a mail product for PC or AppleTalk networks. The Microsoft Mail Connector can translate Exchange messages to and from the Microsoft Mail format. This permits Exchange users and Mail users to exchange mail. You will find more on the Microsoft Mail Connector in Chapter 15.

If an Exchange system and a Microsoft Mail system want to interoperate, they must share their directory information (e.g., listings of mailboxes, distribution lists, and folders). This involves Exchange exporting its directory information to Microsoft Mail, and importing directory information from Microsoft Mail. The Exchange component that performs this is the Directory Synchronization Agent (DXA). Chapter 15 will provide more information on the DXA.

Schedule+ Free/Busy Connector

Microsoft Schedule+ performs personal and group calendaring, scheduling, and task management. The group scheduling feature allows a user who wants to schedule a meeting to view the schedules of other users. The user scheduling the meeting can see if a particular time period is unscheduled for the other users, called *free*, or if it is already scheduled, called *busy*.

Microsoft Exchange ships with Schedule+ 7.5, while Microsoft Mail ships with the earlier version 1.0. These two versions are incompatible in terms of viewing each others free/busy status. To solve this incompatibility, Microsoft Exchange ships with the Schedule+ Free/Busy Connector which allows the two versions to share their free/busy information. This connector requires the Microsoft Mail Connector. Further information on the Schedule+ Free/Busy Connector is found in Chapter 15.

Connector Lotus cc:Mail

This connector permits Exchange to interoperate with a Lotus cc:Mail system. Users of each system can exchange mail with the other system. As with the other connectors, this connector permits organizations to implement Exchange with another messaging system and still have interoperability. Chapter 15 provides further discussion on the Connector for Lotus cc:Mail.

Lotus Notes Connector

Both the Standard and Enterprise editions of Exchange Server 5.5 include the connector for Lotus Notes. This connector provides message exchange and directory synchronization between Exchange and Lotus Notes or Domino. The Lotus Notes system must be version 3 or 4, or Domino version 4.x. Through this connector, Exchange users can send rich-text (colors, fonts, italic, etc.) to Notes users, receive status messages about message delivery, or read receipts, and non-delivery reports (NDRs). Exchange users can even receive Notes document links. This connector, however, does not provide a connection between Exchange public folders and Lotus Notes databases.

IBM OfficeVision/VM Connector

The Microsoft Exchange Connector for IBM OfficeVision/VM provides connectivity between Exchange and two IBM host-based messaging applications, OfficeVision/VM (Virtual Machine) and PROFS (Professional Office System). Because of the large number of users of IBM host-based systems, this connector can help provide true enterprise messaging in an environment with both Microsoft and IBM. This connector features support for the IBM Network Job Entry (NJE) protocol, the exchange of PROFS and CMS notes and documents, mapping between the IBM host and Exchange status messages, and the ability of the host-based users to send mail to the Internet through Exchange.

This connector requires the Microsoft SNA Server for basic connectivity to the IBM host system. This connector is only shipped with the Enterprise Edition of Exchange Server 5.5.

Outlook Web Access

Outlook Web Access, formerly called *Active Server Components* in version 5.0 of Exchange, are ActiveX programs that ship with Microsoft Exchange Server, but that run on a Microsoft Internet Information Server 3.0 (IIS). Outlook Web Access enables users of any standard Web browser to connect through an IIS server and access Exchange resources, such as mailboxes, public folders, and schedules. Because of the popularity of Web browsers, Exchange Outlook Web Access greatly expands the number of clients for Exchange Server. Chapter 11 provides more extensive coverage on Outlook Web Access.

Chat Service

The Microsoft Exchange Chat Service permits Exchange users and users of the Internet Relay Chat (IRC) protocol to interact through an online, real-time, text-based, conversation. The Chat Service is an example of a groupware feature of Exchange.

Scripting Agent

The Microsoft Exchange Scripting Agent adds some workflow capabilities to Exchange. Developers can write JScript and Visual Basic scripts that add customized functions to an Exchange public folder. The Scripting Agent component executes these scripts. For example, a script could be written to read a value in a purchase request form sent to a public folder, and then based upon that value route the form to the relevant party.

Key Management

The key management components provide additional security features such as encryption and digital signatures. Encryption prevents unauthorized people from reading messages as they are being sent over the network. Digital signatures ensure that the person whose name appears in the From field is the actual sender of the message. Chapter 10 covers the topic of key management.

Summary

The three main objects (structures) of the Exchange hierarchy are the organization, sites, and servers. Each company or enterprise defines one Exchange organization object. The organization object encompasses all the other objects of an Exchange implementation. Two of the objects contained within the organization object are the Global Address List (GAL) and Folders. The GAL is a comprehensive listing of all e-mail addresses of the organization. The folders object contains public folders and systems folders.

Sites are logical groupings of Exchange servers. They create a transparent messaging environment. Site users can use Exchange resources in the site without regard to the physical location of those resources. Two of the objects contained within the site object are the Configuration object and the Recipients object. The Recipients object holds all the recipients created in that site. Examples of recipients are mailboxes, distribution lists, public folders, and custom recipients.

Servers are the computers running the Exchange Server components. They are the physical location of the Exchange mailboxes, public folders, and other information.

Exchange Server is made up of various software components. The components that are required for Exchange to be operational are called core components. The following are the four core components:

- Directory service

- Information store

- Message transfer agent

- System attendant

Other components, called optional components, provide additional functionality that could be needed depending on the particular implementation.

Review Questions

1. The following is NOT a core component of Exchange:

A. Internet Mail Service

B. System Attendant

C. Message Transfer Agent

D. Information Store

2. The Information Store is made up of these two databases:

A. SQL and ODBC

B. Message tracking log

C. Private and public information store

D. MTA and SA databases

3. This component generates new e-mail addresses:

A. Directory Service

B. System Attendant

C. Global Address List

D. Client components

4. This component is involved in advanced security:

A. Directory Service

B. Information Store

C. Key Management

D. Message Transfer Agent

5. This component builds routing tables:

    A. System Attendant

    B. Key Management

    C. Information Store

    D. Internet Mail Service

6. This component notifies clients of new mail:

    A. Directory Service

    B. Microsoft Mail Connector

    C. Information Store

    D. System Attendant

7. The Internet Mail Service relates to which protocol?

    A. X.400

    B. RPC

    C. OSF

    D. SMTP

8. Which of the following is NOT an example of a foreign system?

    A. An Exchange server in a different site

    B. IBM SNADS

    C. SMTP system

    D. Microsoft Mail system

9. This component calculates the route a message could take to its destination:

   A. System Attendant

   B. Message Transfer Agent

   C. Information Store

   D. Internet Mail Service

10. This standard is used as the pattern of the Exchange Directory:

    A. X.400

    B. SMTP

    C. LDAP

    D. X.500

11. The following object creates a transparent messaging environment for Exchange users:

    A. Site

    B. System Attendant

    C. Protocols

    D. INS

12. The Global Address List is contained in this object:

    A. Site

    B. Server

    C. Enterprise

    D. Organization

13. Users must know the name of the server on which a public folder is homed in order to access the public folder.

    A. True

    B. False

14. This component enables World Wide Web users to access Exchange resources:

    A. Outlook Web Access

    B. SNMP

    C. X.400

    D. X.500

15. The Message Transfer Agent is based on this standard:

    A. SNMP

    B. SMTP

    C. X.500

    D. X.400

CHAPTER

3

Component Communication

hapter 2 explained that no single Exchange component does all the messaging operations, but that each component specializes in some aspect of messaging. All of the components working together create a messaging system. For those components to work together, they must communicate between themselves. Within a single Exchange site, component communication falls into two basic categories:

- Component communication within a single Exchange server

- Component communication between Exchange servers in a site

In this chapter, you will learn about both categories (see Figure 3.1).Understanding component communication is as beneficial as understanding the architecture. It will aid you in designing, installing, administering, and troubleshooting an Exchange system.

Component communication between sites will be covered in Chapter 13.

Component Communication within a Single Exchange Server

Components within an Exchange server communicate with each other. This communication is necessary for the server to carry out messaging operations, including receiving, sending, and storing messages. This section will show what components communicate with what other components. First, we will discuss the core components, then some of the optional components. The final part of this section will outline some common messaging operations (e.g., sending a message) and will explain how component communication accomplishes those operations.

FIGURE 3.1

The two basic categories of component communication within a single site

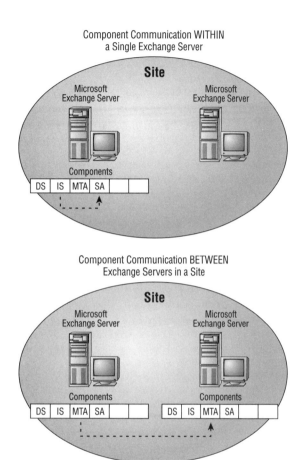

Core Component Communication

The core components and their communication is obviously very important because an Exchange server cannot be operational without them. Almost all component communication is *event driven*. That means when a specific event occurs, such as when the IS receives a message from a client, the relevant components communicate in order to accomplish the message operation, such as delivering a message. The following text explains the events that involve the specific core components and the associated component communication.

Directory Service (DS)

For the most part, other components initiate communication with the DS; the DS does not initiate communication with them. This makes sense in light of the DS role (keeper of directory information). The only time the DS initiates communication with another component is during directory replication. As Chapter 2 mentioned, directory replication is the copying of an Exchange directory to other Exchange servers. If the servers are in the same site, the DS on one server communicates with the DS on the other server. This will be discussed later in this chapter (see "Component Communication between Exchange Servers in a Site"). If the servers are in different sites, the DS uses the MTA for the replication. This scenario will be covered in Chapter 13.

Information Store (IS)

As Chapter 2 explained, the IS manages the storage of data on an Exchange server. This data includes mail messages and public folder content. Four primary operations that require the IS to initiate communication with other components are:

- Local delivery of a message

- Remote delivery of a message

- Transfer of messages to local connector or gateway

- Creation of a new folder

Local Message Delivery When the IS receives a message for delivery, the IS references the DS to determine the physical location of the recipient's mailbox. This process is referred to as *resolving* an address. If the recipient's mailbox is located on the same server the IS is on, the IS will potentially deliver the message to that mailbox. This is called a *local delivery*. The phrase "potentially deliver" was used because after resolving the address, the IS then references the properties of that mailbox. The mailbox could have properties that determine whether or not the message should be delivered, such properties as message rejection and rules that would refuse the message. The mailbox could also have properties that determine how the message should be delivered, such as an alternate recipient who is supposed to get any messages for this mailbox instead of, or along with, the mailbox owner.

A message recipient can be a distribution list (DL). A DL is a grouping of recipients. DLs make it easy for users to communicate with a group of recipients. Instead of creating and sending a message to every individual recipient, a user can send a single message to the DL. Exchange then processes and sends the message to each member of the DL. When the IS receives a message addressed to a DL, it passes the DL to the Message Transfer Agent (MTA) which determines the individual members of the DL. This is called expanding a distribution list (there is more on this in the "MTA" section). Once the DL has been expanded, the IS delivers the message to those recipients.

When a mailbox receives a new message, the IS notifies the mailbox owner, through the client application, of the new message. The user can configure the client application for the type of notification, be it a sound, a changing cursor, or a pop-up message to the user's screen.

If IS message tracking is enabled, the last component that the IS communicates with is the SA. Whenever the IS is involved in a messaging operation, such as a message delivery, the IS notifies the SA of this event in order for the SA to write the event to the log files.

Remote Message Delivery   If after referencing the DS when resolving an address, the IS learns from the DS that the message recipient's mailbox is located on another server, the IS passes the message to the MTA for routing. The IS also notifies the SA of the event for logging purposes.

Transfer of Messages to a Local Connector or Gateway   When an Exchange user sends a message destined for a foreign system, the message is routed by the MTA to the Exchange server that the foreign connector or gateway is homed on. The IS then notifies the connector or gateway that a message is queued and holds the message until the connector or gateway retrieves the message for processing and delivery to the foreign system.

New Folder Creation   Whenever a user creates a new folder in the IS, the IS communicates this information to the DS. The DS then creates a new directory entry for that folder. Table 3.1 and Figure 3.2 summarize and illustrate this information.

1 Resolve addresses
Read mailbox properties

2 Remote mail delivery to an Exchange Server
Expand distribution lists

3 Remote mail delivery to a foreign mail system

4 Notification for logging purposes

5 Notification of new messages

Component	Purpose of Communication
Directory Service	• Resolve addresses • Read mailbox properties • Create new directory entries for folders
Message Transfer Agent	• Deliver remote messages • Expand distribution lists
Local Connector or Gateways	• Deliver remote messages to a foreign system
System Attendant	▪ Write events to tracking log files
Client Applications	• Notify of new messages

Message Transfer Agent (MTA)

The MTA manages the routing of messages. The first step in making a routing decision is for the MTA to reference the DS to resolve the address of the message. If the message recipient is a distribution list, the MTA will reference the DS in order to expand the distribution list, and then resolve the addresses. If the message is destined for a remote Exchange server, the MTA will deliver the message to the remote server's MTA. If the message is destined for a foreign system, the MTA routes the message to the home server of the connector. If the message is received from a remote MTA, it is delivered to the IS. The MTA will then inform the SA of this event for its inclusion in the tracking log files.

If while referencing the DS, the MTA learns that the message is destined for that server, the MTA passes the message to the IS for delivery. As with a remote delivery, the MTA then communicates its actions to the SA for tracking logging purposes. Figure 3.3 and Table 3.2 summarize and illustrate this information.

FIGURE 3.3

Message Transfer Agent initiated communication with other components

Microsoft
Exchange Server

| DS | IS | MTA | SA | Connector | Gateway |

1. Resolve addresses
Expand distribution lists

2. Write events to tracking log files

3. Deliver locally
Store messages for pick up by connector or gateway

	Component	Purpose of Communication
TABLE 3.2 Message Transfer Agent initiated communication with other components	Directory Service	■ Resolve addresses ■ Expand distribution list
	Information Store	■ Local delivery of messages ■ Store message for pick up by connector or gateway
	Connectors or Gateways	■ Delivery to remote Exchange Server ■ Delivery to connector or remote Exchange Server
	System Attendant	■ Write events to tracking log files

The MTA handles some additional processes itself, such as route calculation, but the preceding scenarios describe the other components with which the MTA communicates. For a more complete description of message routing, see Chapter 13.

System Attendant (SA)

The SA has many functions, but primarily initiates communication with three other components, the DS, IS, and Key Management components. Whenever a recipient object is created in the DS, the SA manages the generation of its e-mail addresses. By default, the addresses created are for Microsoft Mail, X.400, Lotus cc:Mail, and SMTP. The e-mail addresses allow an Exchange recipient to receive messages from a foreign mail system (there would have to be a connector or gateway set up also). The SA generates these addresses and communicates the information to the DS for inclusion in the directory. More information on this topic appears in Chapter 5, which covers Exchange recipients.

One of the functions of the SA is to build a site's routing tables that will be used by the MTA. To do this, the SA references server information contained in the DS.

The SA is involved in Link Monitors and Server Monitors. The Link Monitors test the link between Exchange servers by sending a test message. Link Monitors use the SA to send the test message. To have the message delivered, the SA places it in the IS. The IS then passes it to the MTA for routing. The Server Monitor program tests the Exchange services of a server. It also uses the SA to send messages to the server to be tested. Again, the SA places the test message in the IS for delivery. In the course of addressing either of these types of test messages, the SA might need to access the DS to resolve an address.

Another process that requires the SA to communicate with another component is directory replication. The SA monitors the status of various processes. One of the most important processes it monitors is directory replication. The SA accesses the DS to verify that directory information is correct, and if it is not, it corrects inconsistencies.

Although the Key Management components are the primary programs for advanced security, the SA is also involved. The SA retrieves user requests for the initialization of advanced security features. The SA also assists in managing *security keys*. A key is a number used in encrypting data. Figure 3.4 and Table 3.3 summarize and illustrate this information.

FIGURE 3.4

System Attendant initiated communication with other components

1 Create e-mail addresses
   Check on directory replication status
   Resolve addresses for sending test messages
   Reference information for building routing tables

2 Send Link Monitor test messages
   Send Server Monitor test messages

TABLE 3.3

System Attendant initiated communication with other components

Component	Purpose of Communication
Directory Service	■ Writes e-mail addresses ■ Resolve addresses for sending test messages ■ Monitor directory replication status ■ Reference information to build routing tables
Information Store	■ Send Link Monitor test messages ■ Send Server Monitor test messages
Key Management	■ Assist in collecting and managing security keys

Chapter 10 covers advanced security.

Optional Components Communication

The Exchange optional components provide additional messaging functionality. Most of these components are connectors or gateways and therefore provide interoperability with foreign messaging systems. Because connectors, gateways, and other related components are involved in the same type of events and communicate with the same components, we will group them together. The other optional components are discussed under their own headings.

Components That Communicate with Foreign Systems

All of the components discussed in this section help to enable Exchange to interoperate with a foreign messaging system. The following components use the same component communication:

- Internet Mail Service (IMS)

- Microsoft Mail Connector

- Connector for Lotus cc:Mail

- Connector for Lotus Notes

- Connector for IBM OfficeVision/VM

- Connector for SNADS

Third-party gateways are also included in this discussion. Two primary events initiate component communication for a connector/gateway:

- Receiving a foreign message for local delivery

- Receiving and routing a foreign message (remote delivery)

Receiving a Foreign Message for Local Delivery When a connector/gateway receives a foreign message, it passes the message to the IS for local delivery.

Receiving and Routing a Foreign Message (Remote Delivery) Connectors pick up outbound messages from the IS. Figure 3.5 and Table 3.4 summarize and illustrate this information.

F I G U R E 3.5

Connectors/Gateways
initiated communication
with other components

Microsoft
Exchange Server

| DS | IS | MTA | SA | Connectors/Gateways |

① Deliver inbound messages
Pick up outbound messages

T A B L E 3.4

Connector/Gateway
initiated communication
with other components

Component	Purpose of Communication
Information Store	■ Submit inbound messages ■ Pick up outbound messages

You will learn about two other components and how they relate to interoperability with a foreign system under the following two headings:

- Directory Synchronization Agent (DXA)

- Schedule+ Free/Busy Connector

Directory Synchronization Agent (DXA) The Directory Synchronization Agent (DXA) handles the *exporting* and *importing* of directory information between Exchange and an MS Mail or compatible foreign directory. When a change is made to the Exchange directory, such as the creation of a recipient, the DXA communicates the new information to the foreign system. This is called exporting directory information.

If a foreign system sends directory information to the DXA, which is referred to as importing directory information, the DXA communicates this information to the DS. Figure 3.6 and Table 3.5 summarize and illustrate this information.

The Directory Synchronization Agent (DXA) is also sometimes referred to as "DX," for Directory eXchange.

FIGURE 3.6

Directory Synchronization Agent initiated communication with other components

① Communicating imported foreign directory information

② Routing Exchange directory information to be exported to a foreign system

TABLE 3.5

Directory Synchronization Agent initiated communication with other components

Component	Purpose of Communication
Directory Services	■ Communicate imported foreign directory information
Foreign System	■ Export new changes to foreign system

For the DXA component to communicate with a foreign message system directory, the foreign system must use the Microsoft Mail directory synchronization protocol.

Schedule+ Free/Busy Connector   Microsoft Schedule+ performs personal and group calendaring, scheduling, and task management. Microsoft Exchange ships with version 7.5 of Schedule+, while Microsoft Mail ships with version 1.0. In order to interoperate with the two versions, Microsoft created the Schedule+ Free/Busy Connector.

This connector communicates with the Microsoft Mail Connector in order to send and receive free/busy information. It also stores free/busy information that it receives from the Microsoft Mail users in the IS. The Schedule+ Free/Busy Connector also interfaces with the DS. It references the DS to resolve addresses. Figure 3.7 and Table 3.6 summarize and illustrate this information.

FIGURE 3.7

Schedule+ Free/Busy Connector initiated communication with other components

TABLE 3.6

Schedule+ Free/Busy Connector initiated communication with other components

Component	Purpose of Communication
Directory Service	■ Resolve addresses
Information Store	■ Store free/busy information
MS Mail Connector	■ Send Exchange users' free/busy information to Mail users

Key Management

Key Management provides an Exchange system with additional security, such as message encryption and digital signatures. The DS and SA are the other primary Exchange components with which Key Management communicates. Key Management uses the SA to assist in collecting and managing security key information. It uses the DS to store various security information. Chapter 10 covers Key Management in more detail. Figure 3.8 and Table 3.7 summarize and illustrate this information.

FIGURE 3.8

Key Management initiated communication with other components

Component	Purpose of Communication
Directory Service	■ Store various security information
System Attendant	■ Collect and manage security keys

TABLE 3.7

Key Management initiated communication with other components

Internet News Service (INS)

The Internet News Service enables the publishing of USENET newsgroup content to Exchange public folders. Exchange public folders can also be published to USENET newsgroups. The primary component that the INS communicates with is the IS. Communication is straightforward because public folders are part of the IS. Figure 3.9 and Table 3.8 summarize this information.

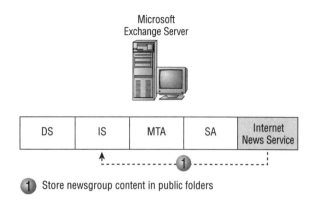

DS	IS	MTA	SA	Internet News Service

1 Store newsgroup content in public folders

Component	Purpose of Communication
Information Service	■ Store newsgroup content in public folders

Outlook Web Access

The Outlook Web Access components are shipped with Microsoft Exchange but run on a Microsoft Internet Information Server (IIS) 3.0. These components make Exchange resources available to Web browser clients. They accomplish this by translating MAPI services to a HyperText Markup Language (HTML) format.

Web users, through Outlook Web Access, communicate with the IS to send and receive messages and to access public folders. They also access the DS to look up directory information, such as the Global Address List. Figure 3.10 and Table 3.9 summarize and illustrate this information.

Component	Purpose of Communication
Directory Service	■ Look up directory information
Information Store	■ Send messages ■ Receive messages ■ Access public folders

Common Messaging Operations

We will now discuss several common messaging operations and how the various Exchange components enable those operations. By starting with a real-world operation and then explaining how the various components enable that operation, we will tie our earlier discussions together. The operations that will be discussed are two of the most common in a site. They are:

- Local message delivery
- Reading mail

Local Message Delivery

The following steps trace the sending of a message to another Exchange user on the same Exchange server. Steps 1, 2, and 3 correspond to Figure 3.11.

1. Client A looks up client B's address by accessing the Global Address List in the Directory. The RPC protocol is used for the client/server interaction.

2. Client A creates a message to be sent to client B.

3. Client A sends this message. The message is received on the Exchange server by the IS.

Steps 4 and 5 correspond to Figure 3.12.

FIGURE 3.11

Sending mail:
Steps 1, 2, and 3

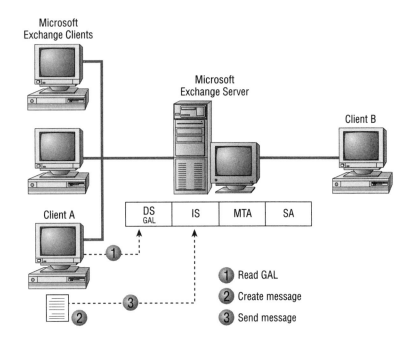

FIGURE 3.11

Sending mail:
Steps 1, 2, and 3

1 Read GAL
2 Create message
3 Send message

FIGURE 3.12

Sending mail:
Steps 4 and 5

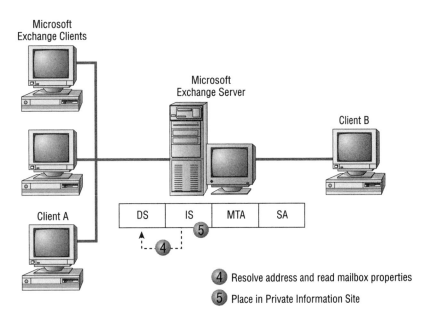

FIGURE 3.12

Sending mail:
Steps 4 and 5

4 Resolve address and read mailbox properties
5 Place in Private Information Site

4. In order to deliver the message, the IS accesses the Directory to determine the physical location of the recipient's mailbox (using a local procedure call, LPC). In this scenario, the recipient's mailbox is on the same server. The IS also references the properties of the destination mailbox, some of which are stored in the Directory. For example, the mailbox could have forwarding rules, reject messages from, and other properties.

5. The IS places the message in the recipient's mailbox.

Reading Mail

The following steps trace the way a message is read on an Exchange server. Steps 1 and 2 correspond to Figure 3.13.

FIGURE 3.13

Reading mail:
Steps 1 and 2

1. IS notifies Client B of new message

2. Client issues a read request that is executed as an RPC request sent to the server

1. The IS notifies client B of the new message.

2. Client B, using an RPC, sends a read request to the IS.

Step 3 corresponds to Figure 3.14.

3. The IS sends the message to client B (in response to client B's RPC in Step 2).

FIGURE 3.14

Reading mail:
Step 3

Microsoft
Exchange Server

Microsoft
Exchange
Client A

| DS | IS | MTA | SA |

Client B

③ IS sends message through a RPC reply

Component Communication between Exchange Servers in a Site

An Exchange site, by grouping messaging functions, presents a single messaging environment to users and administrators. For example, although mailboxes can be created and reside on different home servers, they all appear in the address book without reference to their physical location. Users do not need to know the physical location of a recipient. They simply create and send messages. If a message recipient is on another server, the various Exchange components transparently deliver the message to that server.

The underlying mechanism that creates this single messaging environment is component communication between Exchange servers in a site. This server-to-server communication within a site is called *intrasite* communication.

Communication between sites, called intersite communication, will be covered in Chapter 13.

Two main components implement the transfer of all information between Exchange servers within a site, they are:

- Directory Service (DS)

- Message Transfer Agent (MTA)

The DS and MTA run under the security context of the site service account. Each Exchange site must have a single, designated user account that serves this purpose. This allows Windows NT security to ensure no unauthorized access is made to Exchange services. The use of a single designated account means that all the Exchange components are under the same security context.

As with client/server interactions, the server-to-server interactions also use the RPC protocol. A server sending a request to another server is in the client role, and the server sending the reply is in the server role.

Three main communication processes take place within a site; they are:

- Directory replication

- Mail message transfer

- Link Monitor message transfer

The following sections cover each process by discussing the Exchange components and steps involved in each process.

Directory Replication

Directory replication is the mechanism by which Exchange servers in an organization share directory information. For instance, when a directory object, such as a mailbox, is created, modified, or deleted on a server, that information will be communicated with all the other Exchange servers in its site. Each Exchange server is responsible for updating the other Exchange servers in its site. The result is that each server contains a comprehensive copy of all the resources in the site. This scheme is sometimes called the *multimaster* model because each server contains the entire site directory, rather than one central server maintaining the directory and the other servers having to collect information from the central server.

Directory replication within a site takes place automatically and does not need the intervention of an administrator (there are some parameters that can be set, but they are optional). Directory replication between sites (intersite) does require configuration by the administrator (this topic will be covered in Chapter 13).

The Directory Service component implements the directory replication mechanism. A DS component on one server transfers directory information to the DS component on another server. For intrasite replication, this process does not use the MTA component.

Directory replication includes a tracking method that ensures all new changes to a directory are replicated throughout the site. This tracking method is called the *update sequence number* (USN). Each Exchange server is automatically assigned a unique number for its USN value. Each server also contains a list of the last known USN values for all the other servers in the site.

USNs allow the directory service to copy only modified information during directory replication. If USNs were not used, directory replication would have to copy entire directories between servers, rather than only the modifications. USNs also contribute to the fault tolerance features of Exchange by ensuring a current and accurate directory throughout a site.

Directory Replication Procedure

The following steps occur during the directory replication process. Steps 1 and 2 are illustrated in Figure 3.15, and Steps 3, 4, and 5 are illustrated in Figure 3.16.

FIGURE 3.15

Directory replication: Steps 1 and 2

1. On Server A, which contains a modified directory, the DS will delay starting the replication process for a period of 300 seconds (5 minutes). This allows the DS to replicate changes in a batch manner (i.e., all at once) rather than one at a time. This delay is referred to as the *replication latency* and can be configured in the Registry at the following location:

   ```
   HKEY_LOCAL_MACHINE

   System

   CurrentControlSet

   Services

   MSExchangeDS

   Parameters

   Replicator notify pause after modify(secs)
   ```

2. At the end of the replication latency, the DS on Server A starts to send notifications to the other servers in the site. It knows what servers to notify because it has a list of the other Exchange servers in the site. This replication list is discussed later in this chapter. From Server A's perspective, the other servers are referred to as *remote servers*.

   The notification that is sent does not contain the actual changes, but only a notice that changes have been made. The DS sends this notification to one remote server at time, pausing after each notification before continuing with the next remote server. This pause allows the notified server to perform some actions (Step 3). The default pause period is 30 seconds and can be modified in the Registry at the following location:

   ```
   HKEY_LOCAL_MACHINE

   System

   CurrentControlSet

   Services

   MSExchangeDS

   Parameters

   Replicator notify pause between

   DSAs (secs)
   ```

FIGURE 3.16

Directory replication:
Steps 3, 4, and 5

3 Reads USN value. Requests new information

4 Sends requested directory information

5 Adds information to Directory

3. When a remote server receives the notification, it compares the USN value in the notification with the value it has recorded for Server A. If Server A's (i.e., the server sending the notice) USN is greater than what the remote server has recorded for it, the remote server knows there are changes to Server A's directory. The remote server then requests that Server A send it all of its directory objects with a USN higher than the remote server's last known USN for Server A.

4. The DS on Server A then uses the RPC mechanism to transfer the requested information to the DS on the remote server.

5. The DS on the remote server adds the new information to its directory.

Directory Replication Fault Tolerance Features

Because directory information is so important, Microsoft has included various fault tolerance features for directory replication. The three main fault tolerance features are:

- Update Sequence Numbers (USNs)

- Replication lists

- Knowledge Consistency Checker (KCC)

Update Sequence Numbers (USNs) As stated earlier, directory replication includes a tracking method that ensures that all new changes to a directory are replicated throughout a site. This tracking method is called update sequence numbers (USNs).

Replication Lists Each Exchange server directory contains lists of other Exchange servers in its site. REPS-TO is a list of the servers that are to receive directory updates. REPS-FROM is a list of the servers from which directory updates can be accepted. These lists are *cached* (i.e., stored) in a server's memory.

Replication lists provide fault tolerance by ensuring that each server knows the other servers that should be involved in directory replication.

Knowledge Consistency Checker (KCC) The knowledge consistency checker (KCC) runs on every Exchange server. The KCC on each server compares its replication lists to the replication lists on other servers. It makes sure there are no Exchange servers in the site that are not on its replication lists. That situation is called a *mismatch*. If there is a mismatch, the KCC updates its lists by requesting replication lists from another server. This ensures that an Exchange server's replication lists are accurate.

The KCC process runs by default every 3 hours. It can also be manually started through the Directory Service.

The KCC process is also involved in intersite directory replication, which will be discussed in Chapter 13.

Events That Trigger Fault Tolerance Features

The fault tolerance features of directory replication are operational during normal operation of Microsoft Exchange. However, there are certain circumstances under which these features are especially relevant:

- When a server has been offline and is now back online

- When there is failed communication because a server is down, removed, or reconfigured

- When installing an Exchange server to an existing site

In the first two circumstances, the fault tolerant features of directory replication work in a straightforward manner. The third circumstance, when a new server is added to a site, warrants a short discussion.

Directory Replication for a New Server in a Site   When a new Exchange server has been added to a site, it must collect the directory information for that site. During setup, the installer is prompted for the name of an existing Exchange server. This existing server will be the one that the SETUP program connects to and copies its directory information. The steps are outlined here:

1. The SETUP program adds the name of the new server to the existing server's directory. This event also notifies the existing server that it needs to send its Directory to the new server.

2. The existing server sends a modified directory, without the site recipients, to the new server. This directory without recipients is referred to as the STUB directory. Using the STUB allows the SETUP program to efficiently finish its installation process because it does not need to spend time copying all the recipients to the new server. Instead, SETUP can efficiently copy the essential parts of the site directory and then finish its installation functions. Recipients are copied to the new server during Step 4.

3. Using the STUB directory, the new server builds its replication lists.

4. The new server can now connect to the other site servers and instruct them to begin directory replication. This is how the new server receives a copy of the recipients list.

Directory replication ensures that accurate information needed for messaging is distributed throughout a site. It serves as a foundation for the next communication process to be discussed, the transferring of mail messages.

Message Transfer

All communication within a site, with the exception of directory replication, uses the MTA component. That includes the two most common types of communication, transferring of mail messages and the updating of public folder data. Both forms of communication use mail messages to send their content, and both use the MTA to deliver messages to other servers. In this section, you will learn about:

- Formatting mail messages: X.400 interpersonal messages (IPMs)

- Addressing mail messages: X.400 and X.500

- Transferring messages within a site

- Expanding a distribution list

Formatting Mail Messages: X.400 (IPMs)

When a user of the Microsoft Exchange Client application creates a mail message, that message is created in the X.400 interpersonal message (IPM) format. An IPM message is comprised of two main parts, the message content and the message envelope (see Figure 3.17).

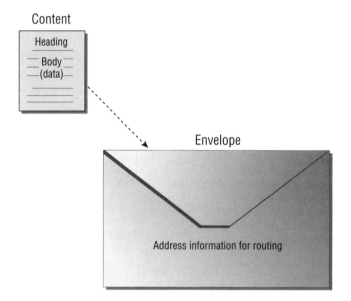

F I G U R E   3 . 1 7

The interpersonal
message (IPM) format

Message Content   This is the information that the user is sending. It is similar in concept to an office memo in that it is subdivided into two parts:

- **Heading**   The heading, also called the header, contains information such as the originator of the message (the sender), the recipient (or recipients) of the message, and information about how the message is to be handled (such as an expiration time).

- **Body**   The body contains the actual data of the IPM. Common types of data are text and graphics. Other types of data include facsimile (fax), telex, and voice.

Message Envelope   Message content, like memos or a letter, must be placed in an envelope in order to be mailed. The protocol used by Microsoft Exchange to accomplish this is the X.400 P1 protocol. The X.400 envelope, just like a postal envelope, is used to route a message to its destination. Some of the information on the X.400 envelope is the same as on the mail message header, such as the originator and recipient of the message. The delivery priority of the message can also be on the envelope.

X.400 and X.500 Addressing

Exchange uses both X.400 and X.500 addresses to address and route messages. The X.500 address, called a Distinguished Name (DN), is the path to the location of an object in the directory hierarchy. An example DN is:

   o=Widget; ou=Chicago; cn=Recipients; cn=JayWilson

Whenever a user creates and addresses a message, Exchange uses a DN as the address format. The Exchange MTA component uses DNs for all routing within an Exchange organization.

But Exchange also generates an X.400 address, called an Originator/Recipient Address (O/R Address), for each message. This is in case the message will be sent outside the organization to, or through, an X.400 network. The Exchange MTA will always first try to resolve a route with the DN, and failing, will then use the O/R Address. An example of an O/R Address is:

   c=us; a=mci; p=WidgeNet; o=Widget; s=Wilson; g=Jay

Transferring Mail Messages within a Site

A mail message can be used to send an e-mail message to another server and to update public folder data on another server. The following process transfers a message within a site from one Exchange server to another Exchange server. Even though we are focusing on the role of the MTA component, other steps are included to provide a better context to the mail message transfer process.

1. A user, through an Exchange client application, creates and sends an e-mail message, or edits data inside a public folder (an e-mail message will be used for the rest of this example). To do this, the user must:

   - Choose recipients for the message.

   - Create the content of the mail message.

Then Exchange must:

- Format the message in the IPM format.

- Assign addresses to the message in the form of a distinguished name (DN) and an Originator/Recipient (O/R).

2. When a message is created, it is initially stored in the IS. The IS performs the following actions:

- Resolves the recipient's address by referencing the DS.

- If the recipient's mailbox is on this Exchange server, the IS delivers the message to the recipient's mailbox and notifies the recipient that they have new mail. This is a local delivery.

- If the recipient's mailbox is on another Exchange server in the site, the IS passes the message to the MTA. (This option is used in the example.) This is a remote delivery.

3. The MTA accesses the DS to learn the recipient's home server.

4. The MTA uses the RPC protocol under the context of the site service account to open a session with the MTA on the recipient's home server.

5. The MTA transfers the message to the MTA on the recipient's home server.

6. The MTA on the recipient's server temporarily stores the message and notifies the IS that a message has arrived.

7. The IS retrieves the message from the MTA and notifies the client application of the recipient that there is new mail.

If the MTA cannot deliver the message, the message is sent back to the sender in a nondelivery report (NDR).

If the MTA on the sender's server (Steps 3, 4, and 5) receives a message that has multiple recipients, and those recipients reside on different servers, the MTA will create an individual message for each of the destination servers. You will learn more about this in the next section.

Expanding a Distribution List

A distribution list is a grouping of recipients. One of the functions of the MTA is to expand a distribution list recipient into its individual members. The following are the steps involved in this process:

1. The IS receives a message addressed to a distribution list recipient.

2. The IS passes this message to the MTA.

3. The MTA determines the individual members of the distribution list. These members can be any Exchange recipient, such as mailboxes, custom recipients, public folders, and other distribution lists. The process of determining the members is also referred to as *expanding* or *resolving* the distribution list.

4. The MTA creates an individual message for each destination server MTA containing members of the distribution list.

Link Monitor Messages

One of the administrative features of Exchange is the testing of connections between Exchange servers within a site. This is done through the Link Monitor utility, which sends test messages between Exchange Servers.

The Link Monitor utility uses the System Attendant to create and receive test messages (test messages are actually mail messages used for these purposes). The SA uses the MTA to send the test messages. The following steps explain this process:

1. An administrator configures the Link Monitor to send test messages from one Exchange server, the local server, to other Exchange servers, referred to as the monitored servers.

2. At the specified intervals, the SA creates test messages addressed to the monitored servers.

3. The MTA delivers the test messages to the MTAs on the monitored servers.

4. The MTAs on the monitored servers pass the test messages to their respective SAs.

5. The SA on a monitored server responds to the test message by sending back a reply message.

The use of Link Monitor messages can help administrators continually test connections and therefore assist in providing a high level of network service. More information on this topic, including exercises, appears in Chapter 12.

Summary

Because no single Exchange component performs all messaging services, components must communicate amongst themselves to create a messaging system. Component communication takes place within a single Exchange server and between Exchange servers in a site. The latter is called intrasite communication.

Component communication is involved in such activities as accessing the Global Address List, sending and reading a message, and delivering local messages. Component communication between servers involves activities like directory replication, message transfer, and Link Monitor messages.

Review Questions

1. The IS communicates with this component to perform a remote delivery:

A. SA

B. IS on other server

C. Key Manager

D. MTA

2. This component is referenced by other components when resolving an address:

A. DS

B. IS

C. MTA

D. SA

3. Intrasite Directory replication uses the MTA to route directory information.

   A. True

   B. False

4. The IS notifies clients of new messages.

   A. True

   B. False

5. This component assists in the implementation of advanced security:

   A. IS

   B. SA

   C. MTA

   D. DXA

6. The Outlook Web Access runs on this system:

   A. Microsoft Exchange server

   B. Web client

   C. Internet router

   D. Microsoft IIS server

7. The INS communicates with this component for the storing of USENET content:

   A. Microsoft IIS server

   B. DS

   C. SA

   D. IS

8. Connectors, such as the Connector for Lotus cc:Mail, CANNOT place foreign messages in the IS.

   A. True

   B. False

9. When routing a message, the MTA may communicate with this component for the physical transfer of the message:

   A. Connector or gateway

   B. MTA on another server

   C. Key Manager

   D. SA

10. The DS uses this information when performing a directory replication:

   A. Site number

   B. Update Sequence Number (USN)

   C. Server DS number

   D. Combination site and server number

11. The Link Monitor utility uses this component to send test messages:

   A. LDAP

   B. INS

   C. Key Security

   D. SA

12. To expand a distribution list, the MTA references this component:

   A. IS

   B. DS

   C. Key security

   D. SA

13. When addressing messages for delivery within an Exchange organization, this address format is used:

   A. Distinguished Name

   B. MS Mail name

   C. Exchange lengthwise address

   D. cc:Mail name

14. This component enables Web browser users to access Exchange resources.

   A. MTA

   B. Key Management

   C. Web Browser Component

   D. Outlook Web Access

15. The Information Store holds messages destined for foreign systems for transfer to this type of component:

   A. Connector or gateway

   B. DXA

   C. DS

   D. SA

16. This component is responsible for the delivery of messages when the recipient is homed on the same server as the sender.

  A. Connector or gateway

  B. MTA

  C. DS

  D. IS

17. When performing a directory replication with another Exchange server in the same site, a DS communicates with what component on the other server?

  A. MTA

  B. DS

  C. Directory Synchronization Agent (DXA)

  D. IS

18. This component is involved in e-mail address generation and the logging of Exchange message tracking events.

  A. MTA

  B. DS

  C. SA

  D. IS

CHAPTER

4

Installing Microsoft Exchange Server

ecause Exchange is a Microsoft Windows NT application, it has a straightforward installation process. But there are still some issues that need to be dealt with in a careful manner. In this chapter, you will learn the necessary steps to install Microsoft Exchange Server in a single-site organization. The main subjects of this chapter are:

- Standard Edition vs. Enterprise Edition of Microsoft Exchange Server 5.5

- Preinstallation considerations

- Installing Microsoft Exchange Server

- Postinstallation considerations

- Troubleshooting a Microsoft Exchange installation

- Upgrading Microsoft Exchange Server

- Installing Exchange Server on clustered servers

Planning would be a normal step to perform before executing an installation. But the topic of planning cannot be covered at this time because the necessary prerequisite knowledge has not been covered. However, by the end of this book you will have that knowledge. Consequently, the last chapter in this book, Chapter 17, is on planning.

Microsoft ✓ Exam Objective **Install an Exchange Server computer.**

Exchange Server 5.5: Standard Edition vs. Enterprise Edition

Microsoft Exchange Server 5.5 is available in two editions: the Standard edition or the Enterprise edition. The main difference between them is the connectors that are bundled with each.

Standard Edition Connectors

The Standard edition ships with the following connectors:

- Internet Mail Service

- Microsoft Mail Connector

- Connector for Lotus cc:Mail

- Connector for Lotus Notes

Additional Enterprise Edition Connectors

The Enterprise edition adds to this list the following connectors:

- Connector for IBM OfficeVision/VM

- Connector for SNADS

- X.400 Connector

In addition, the Enterprise edition can work with Microsoft Cluster Server. Cluster Server logically groups servers into an interdependent system, called a cluster, for fault tolerance. The installation of Exchange in a cluster environment will be discussed later in this chapter.

The Enterprise edition also increases the storage limit to 16TB for each of the Exchange databases, namely the DS, Private IS, and Public IS databases.

Preinstallation Considerations

Several important issues must be dealt with before you install Exchange Server. Having the correct information and making the right decisions about these issues will go a long way to ensuring a successful installation. The pre-installation issues that will be covered in this section are:

- Minimum system requirements
- The NT user accounts related to the Exchange installation
- Licensing issues
- The relationship between Exchange sites and NT domains
- Installation scenarios
- Other preinstallation steps

Minimum System Requirements

This section lists the minimum requirements for the computer system upon which Exchange is to be installed. These minimums are valid when you install only the core components. Using additional Exchange components, and depending on your particular performance demands, could require more resources than the following minimum requirements.

Hardware Requirements

The minimum hardware requirements for installing Exchange are listed below:

Microprocessor	Intel Pentium 90 MHz or higher (recommended: Pentium 166MHz or higher), or RISC microprocessor such as Digital Alpha 4/275 (recommended: Digital alpha 5/500)
Random Access Memory (RAM)	24MB RAM for Intel platform; 32MB RAM for RISC platform (recommended: 32MB for Intel and 48MB for RISC)
Hard Disk Space	250MB free disk space; 300MB for RISC (recommended: 500MB for all platforms)

The Microsoft Exchange Server software comes on a compact disc. If the machine intended to be the Exchange Server has no compact disc drive, the administrator may copy the necessary files from the compact disc to a shared hard disk or share a compact disc drive on another machine.

Software Requirements

The software requirements for an Exchange installation are listed below:

Operating System	Microsoft Windows NT Server version 4.0 Service Pack 3. The operating system needs to be configured for a page file size equal to 50MB of disk space plus the amount of RAM in the machine. (For example, if the machine has 48MB of RAM, the page file size should be 50 plus 48, equaling 98MB. The recommended size is 100 MB of disk space plus the amount of physical RAM.)
Apple Macintosh clients (optional)	Windows NT Services for Macintosh is needed if Macintosh Exchange clients will access the Exchange server or if the Microsoft Mail Connector will be installed for interoperability with clients using MS Mail for AppleTalk.
Novell NetWare clients (optional)	The Microsoft Gateway Services for NetWare (GSNW) is required on the Exchange server. If the NetWare clients are using IPX/SPX, then the Exchange server will also require Microsoft NWLink.
SMTP/POP/IMAP clients (optional)	Windows NT Transmission Control Protocol/Internet Protocol (TCP/IP) is required if the Internet Mail Service will be installed for Internet client connectivity.
Web browser clients (optional)	If you want Web browser clients to access your Exchange server, Microsoft Internet Information Server (IIS) 3 must be installed, and it must be running the Exchange Outlook Web Access components.
IBM messaging (e.g. OfficeVision/VM or PROFS) connectivity (optional)	The Microsoft SNA Server is required for host connectivity if the Exchange Connector for IBM OfficeVision/VM or Connector for SNADS will be used.
Advanced fault tolerance (optional)	As stated earlier, the Enterprise edition of Exchange Server 5.5 can work with Microsoft Cluster Server. Cluster Server ships with Windows NT Server 4.0 Enterprise Edition.

Remember that the minimum requirements probably will not provide the optimal operational performance, or take into account the requirements for any future growth of system demand. The actual system requirements of any installation will depend on the particulars of that specific environment. To determine your real-world requirements, refer to the *Microsoft Exchange Server Concepts and Planning Guide*.

NT User Accounts Related to the Exchange Installation

Both during and after installation, Microsoft Exchange utilizes the following Windows NT user accounts:

- Windows NT administrator account

- Site services account

Windows NT Administrator Account

To install Exchange Server on a Windows NT Server, a user must log on to that computer with a *user account* that has administrator privileges (i.e., an account that is in the local administrator's group). This level of privileges is needed because during installation services will be started, files will be copied to the \<winnt_root>\SYSTEM32 directory, and rights will be granted to the site services account.

Site Services Account

The Exchange Server components, also called services, need an NT user account to operate. This account is referred to as the *site services account*. The Exchange services use this account to log on to the NT system and carry out their functions. The following facts and parameters relate to the site services account:

- It must be created before performing the Exchange Server installation. The Exchange Server installation will prompt you for the account name and password to use for this account. You should configure this account so that the "User Cannot Change Password," and that the "Password Never Expires," and you need to clear the check box for "User Must Change Password at Next Logon."

- The Exchange Server installation program will automatically grant the following rights to the account you specify as the site services account:

  - Act as part of the operating system

  - Log on as a Service

  - Restore files and directories

For security reasons do not use a user account that has administrator privileges as the site services account.

Licensing Issues

Licensing issues relate to matters of legality (specifically, the number of servers Exchange can be loaded on and the number of clients that can access a server).

Four main licenses pertain to the various Microsoft Exchange product packages:

- Server License

- Connector License

- Client Access License (CAL)

- Client Pack License

Server License

The basic server license provides the legal right to install and operate Microsoft Exchange Server on a single-server machine. A couple of specific components can be installed on additional machines without additional licenses. These components are the Microsoft Exchange Administrator Program and the Source Extractor software contained in the Microsoft Exchange Migration Utilities. The license for the Source Extractor software permits the migration of data only to a Microsoft Exchange system.

Connector License

X.400 software is licensed for installation and use on a single Microsoft Exchange Server. In addition other Exchange servers that do not have the X.400 connector installed, but are utilizing the X.400 connector on another Exchange server, will also need a license. This scenario is illustrated in Figure 4.1.

FIGURE 4.1

Connector licenses

Since many licensing policies can change over time, always check for the latest policy to ensure your compliance.

Client Access License (CAL)

A Client Access License (CAL) gives a user the legal right to access an Exchange server. An organization designates the number of (CALs) it needs when a Microsoft Exchange server is purchased. Each CAL provides a user the legal right to access the Exchange Server. Any client software that has the ability to be a client to Microsoft Exchange Server is legally required to have a CAL purchased for it. Microsoft Exchange Client, Microsoft Outlook, as well as third-party client messaging programs, require a CAL. Microsoft Exchange Server 5.5 uses only a "per seat" licensing mode, unlike earlier versions which allowed either a per seat or per server licensing mode.

Client Access Licenses are NOT included in any version of Microsoft Windows or in Microsoft Office. For example, the Microsoft Exchange Inbox in the Windows 95 operating system legally requires a CAL.

Client Pack License

The Client Pack License includes both Exchange client software and 20 CALs. The Client Pack is offered primarily for using the Exchange client software to connect to non-Exchange back-ends, such as Microsoft Mail.

Microsoft	Configure server locations.
Exam	
Objective	Manage site security.

Exchange Sites and Windows NT Domain

A Windows NT *domain* is a logical grouping of NT Servers and clients which use the same security accounts manager (SAM). The SAM is a database containing information on the resources and configurations of a domain, such as users, groups, permissions, and rights. The domain creates a logical network. Users log on to a particular domain by using an account from that domain's SAM. This is called being *authenticated*. Once logged on from the domain, a user has access to the resources of that domain, depending on the permissions granted.

An organization can have more than one domain. The domains can be totally separate, or they can work with each other. This is done by creating a *trust relationship* between the domains. While there are multiple implementations of trust relationships between domains, the following describes one straightforward implementation for the purpose of review. If Domain B wanted to allow the users of Domain A to use its resources, Domain B could "trust" Domain A. To trust another domain means to allow its SAM (e.g., its users and groups) to have access to your domain. Even though there are two domains, each with its own SAM, from the perspective of Domain B there is one virtual SAM which includes Domain B and Domain A. See Figure 4.2 for an illustration of this concept.

FIGURE 4.2

A trust relationship between domains

A *Microsoft Exchange site* is a logical grouping of Exchange Servers and clients (it must include at least one Exchange Server). Exchange sites and NT domains relate to two different environments. They are not the same thing. But while different, there is an operational connection between the two.

Microsoft Exchange sites utilize NT domain SAMs. For example, for Exchange services to operate they must use a site service account, which is contained in a domain SAM. If an Exchange site has multiple Exchange Servers, they must all use the same site services account in order to communicate with each other. There are two ways to accomplish this. The easiest is to have the Exchange site map directly to the NT domain (see Figure 4.3). All the Exchange Servers would have direct access to the same SAM, and therefore to the same site service account.

FIGURE 4.3

An Exchange site mapping directly to an NT domain

But imagine an Exchange site planned to encompass multiple domains with the Exchange Servers located in the different domains (see Figure 4.4).

The Exchange site servers need to use the same site service account, but there are multiple domains and therefore multiple SAMs. The solution is to establish trust relationships between the domains. This would allow domains to access each other's SAMs and, in effect, create one single, virtual SAM. The Exchange site servers could then use the same site service account. See Figure 4.5 for an illustration of one way to implement this concept.

For communication between sites, not within a site but between sites, the Exchange Servers do not have to use the same site service account. See Figure 4.6 for an illustration of this concept. The logical boundaries between sites are called *site boundaries*.

A single Exchange site and
multiple domains

An Exchange site and
multiple trusted NT
domains

FIGURE 4.6

Communication between sites

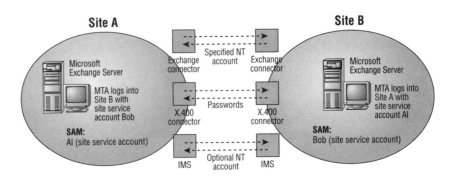

If an organization plans to have multiple Exchange sites (which they do not have to have, they could have only one site), there are many factors relating to the Exchange organization design. Some are logical factors, like the previous situation with domains and the site service account. Some are physical, like the speed of the connections between the Exchange Servers. Because Exchange Servers within a site communicate through RPCs, there needs to be a permanent, high-speed connection between all the Exchange Servers. There is more information on multiple site networks in Chapter 13.

Designing the number of sites and the location of the site boundaries is important for numerous reasons, some of which are performance, security, and access to NT accounts. Another reason is that if you later want to redesign your Exchange organization, you will have to reinstall and reconfigure the Exchange Servers.

Installation Scenarios

During the Exchange Server installation, you will have the option of having this new server create a new site, or having it join an existing site. Both scenarios are discussed in the following text.

Creating a New Site

While executing the SETUP program, one of the dialog boxes (shown in Figure 4.7) will present the installer with the option to create a new site. This would be the choice for the first installation of Exchange in an organization, or when an existing Exchange implementation requires a new site to be added to the organization.

If you choose the Create a New Site option, you will be prompted to enter information on the following topics:

- **Exchange organization name**   The organization is at the top of the Exchange hierarchy. This case-sensitive field can be up to 64 characters in length. The organization name is associated with every object in the Exchange directory, such as mailboxes, public folders, and distribution lists. The organization name cannot be modified after the installation.

- **Exchange site name**   Site names distinguish between multiple sites, and are also associated with directory objects within the site. They must be unique names within the organization and can be up to 64 characters in length and are also case-sensitive.

- **Name of the directory for installation**   The default directory location and name is C:\EXCHSRVR, but this can be modified by the installer.

- **Site Service account and password**   When creating a new site, the default site service account will be the account currently logged in during the installation. This can be changed by the installer.

FIGURE 4.7

Setup dialog box for creating or joining a site

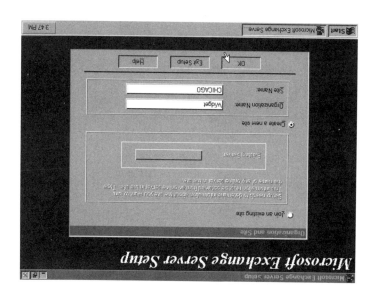

- **CD Key** The setup program will present you with a dialog box requesting the CD Key or product ID number (PID). The CD Key is a unique 11-digit number found on the Exchange Server compact disc case.

Joining an Existing Site

There are many reasons to add an Exchange server to an existing site. The primary reasons are for performance, capacity and scaling, and fault tolerance. Each is briefly discussed below.

- **Performance** An organization could place certain Exchange services on additional Exchange Servers, making those servers dedicated to those functions. Examples are:

  - **Public and/or private information stores** These databases could be located on an additional Exchange Server dedicated to those functions.

  - **Connector software** The same principle relates to running connector software on a dedicated Exchange Server.

- **Capacity and scaling** If the physical limits of a particular system are being approached, Exchange services and their related physical resources (e.g., disk space) can be spread out among multiple Exchange servers. This issue also relates to performance issues.

- **Fault tolerance through redundancy** Many Exchange services and resources are replicated throughout an Exchange organization. This redundancy implements a built-in level of fault tolerance. For example, all the Exchange servers within a site share the same directory information through replication. If one particular Exchange server were taken offline, when it came back online its directory information would be automatically updated by another Exchange server through the replication mechanism.

To join an existing site, the installer must know the name of an existing Exchange server in the site, as well as the password of the site service account. After the installer supplies the existing server name, SETUP will search the

Exchange directory of that server and then automatically supply the name of the Exchange organization and site to this new installation. It will also auto-matically supply the site service account.

Adding a server to an existing site will create a new object under the Con-figuration container in the Exchange hierarchy. This requires the installer's user account to have certain Exchange permissions at the site object and con-figuration object. Those permissions are granted by assigning the user with one of the following security roles:

- Admin.
- Permissions Admin.
- Service Account Admin.

These roles give the installer the ability to create a new server object under the Configuration container in the Exchange hierarchy. These roles are assigned through the Microsoft Exchange Administrator program and the Permissions tab of the site object and Configuration object. As with creating a new server, the installer must also have NT adminis-trator privileges.

Other Preinstallation Steps

Prior to installing the Exchange Server software, you should consider these additional steps:

- Verify that the Windows NT Server primary domain controller (PDC) is operational.
- Close any messaging-aware applications.
- Back up your existing Exchange installation, if you will be performing an upgrade.
- Verify that your Cluster Server is installed, if you will be installing Exchange in that environment.

Installing Exchange Server

T his section explains the installation options and then walks you through an actual installation. So boot up your Windows NT Server, grab your Exchange CD, and get ready to rumble... that is, do an installation.

Installation Options

The Exchange Server setup can be initiated by simply inserting the Exchange Server compact disc into the CD-ROM drive. This will automatically cause a Web-like page to load that contains the option to setup Exchange Server 5.5. Another way to initiate setup is to execute the file SETUP.EXE found on the Exchange Server CD. This file is found in the \Setup\<processor>\ directory. For example, if you are using an Intel processor, the directory path would be \Setup\I386\.

When SETUP runs, it checks for a current installation of Exchange on that machine. If it finds one, it goes into maintenance mode and lets you add or remove components, reinstall, or remove all components. If it does not find one, it prompts you for the type of installation to undertake. There are three installation options:

- Typical

- Complete/Custom

- Minimum

After a brief explanation of these three options, you can take an exercise through an actual installation.

Typical Installation

The Typical Installation option installs the Microsoft Exchange Server software and the Exchange Administrator program. No connectors, client software, or online documentation are installed. Those items can be installed from CD at a later time.

Complete/Custom Installation

This option provides the ability to install all the Exchange software, including the following:

- Microsoft Exchange Server software with the following options:
  - MS Mail Connector
  - Connector for Lotus cc:Mail
  - Connector for Lotus Notes
  - Microsoft Exchange Scripting Agent
  - Microsoft Exchange Administrator program
  - Books Online
  - Outlook Web Access

NOTE   While you will not see the Internet Mail Service, Internet News Service, and the Dynamic RAS Connector components as options on the setup screen, they will be automatically installed through the Complete/Custom option.

The Enterprise Edition of Exchange Server 5.5 also allows the option to install the Connector for Lotus Notes, X.400 Connector, Connector for IBM OfficeVision/VM, and Connector for SNADS. These connectors have their own Setup program found on the Exchange Server CD in the EXCHCONN directory.

This is also the option used when installing the Microsoft Exchange Administrator program on an administrator's Microsoft Windows NT workstation. The installer deselects all the options, except the Microsoft Exchange Administrator program, and then continues with the installation.

Minimum Installation

The Minimum installation option installs only the Microsoft Exchange Server software. This option does not install the Administrator program or connectors. You would use this option to install an additional Exchange Server in a site when the server does not need the Administrator program. Not every Exchange Server needs the Administrator program because all servers can be centrally managed from one machine running the Administrator program.

Microsoft √ Exam Objective	Optimize Exchange Server. Tasks include:
	• Hardware optimization
	• Operating system optimization

The Microsoft Exchange Performance Optimizer Program

One of the options available during initial setup is the Microsoft Exchange Performance Optimizer. This is a Windows NT-based application that analyzes the hard disk and memory of the server machine to determine the best place to locate Exchange files and databases.

The Exchange components and files for which a change in directory location may be recommended are:

- Information Store
- Directory Service database
- Message Transfer Agent
- Transaction log files

Performance Optimizer will also recommend the amount of memory for caching data from the Information Store and Directory Service. This program can also be run at any time after installation; it can be found in the Microsoft Exchange Server program group. It is recommended that you run Performance Optimizer after any major hardware change to your server, such as adding RAM or a hard disk.

Performing the Installation

The following exercises provide the actual steps to install Microsoft Exchange Server. Exercise 4.1 outlines the steps for creating and configuring the site services account that will be used in the installation and operation of Microsoft Exchange. Exercise 4.2 provides the installation steps, using the Complete/Custom option and the Create a New Site option, and discusses the Join an Existing Site option.

EXERCISE 4.1

Creating the Site Service Account for Microsoft Exchange Server

1. In the Administrative Tools program group, start User Manager for Domains.

2. Select the New User option from the User menu.

3. In the Username field type **SiteAcct.** We will use this user account for the Exchange site service account. This could be any legal NT name you choose.

4. In the Full Name field, enter **Site Service Account.** This is an optional field and is for your information only.

5. In the Description field, enter **Site Service Account for Exchange Server.** This is also an optional field and is for your information.

6. Enter the password **12*12** in the Password and Confirm Password fields.

7. Clear the check box for the option User Must Change Password At Next Logon.

8. Check the box for User Cannot Change Password, and also the checkbox for Password Never Expires.

9. Click Add to finish creating the site service account.

10. Click Close to exit from User Manager for Domains.

Now that the site services account is created and configured, you may begin the installation steps for Microsoft Exchange Server. Those steps are outlined in Exercise 4.2.

 NOTE Please review the system requirements needed by your lab computer to perform these exercises. Those requirements are found in the Introduction of this book in Table A.1 in the section "How to Use This Book."

EXERCISE 4.2

Installing Microsoft Exchange Server

1. Insert the Microsoft Exchange Server CD into the server's compact disc drive. This will automatically cause a Web-like page to load that contains the option to setup Exchange Server 5.5. (Other options are to share the CD on another machine on the network and then connect to that share, or to copy the CD to the server's hard drive.)

2. Click on the words Server Setup.

3. Click on the setup option for your particular language. For example, "Set up English language Exchange Server."

4. The End-User License Agreement page will appear next. If you agree with the license then click on Accept.

5. The Microsoft Exchange Server dialog box lists the installation options, as well as the option to choose the directory into which Exchange Server will be installed. This latter option is accessed through the Change Directory button. For this exercise, we will assume the installation directory is C:\EXCHSRVR. The installation option we will use for this exercise is the Complete/Custom option. If you would like to see the components that will be installed with the Exchange Server option, highlight that option and click on the Change Option button. For this exercise, use the defaults, which are all the components. To continue this setup, click on the Continue button on the Complete/Custom screen.

6. The next screen will contain an information message stating that the Internet Information Server services will be stopped temporarily. Click on OK.

7. A licensing screen will appear explaining the need for you to purchase client access licenses before clients can access this Exchange server. Exchange Server 5.5 only supports the "per seat" licensing mode. Once you have read and agreed to this licensing, click on the "I agree that" checkbox. Then click OK.

8. The Organization and Site dialog box appears next. This is where you either join an existing site, or create a new site. If joining a site, you will select the Join an Existing Site option, and then enter the name of an existing Exchange server in that site in the Existing server field. SETUP will communicate with that server and automatically insert the name of the Exchange organization and site. If you are creating a new site, you will need to choose the option Create a New Site. You then must supply the name of the organization and site. For this exercise, click on Create a New Site, and then enter a name in the Organization Name field, like **Widget**, and a name in the Site Name field, like **Chicago**. (The names Widget and Chicago will be used throughout the remainder of this book, so you should use them for consistency). After entering this information, click OK.

9. A message will now appear prompting you to confirm the creation of a new site. Click Yes.

10. The Site Services Account dialog box appears. Click Browse and pick the SiteAcct account you created in Exercise 4.1 from the list provided. Then enter the password **12*12** and click the OK button.

11. A message screen will appear stating that the user account you just entered has been granted the rights to "Log on as a service," "Restore files and directories," and "Act as part of the operating system." Click OK. The SETUP program will now create Exchange directories and download files from the Exchange CD to those directories.

12. The next screen will give you the ability to run the Microsoft Exchange Performance Optimizer program. Click on Run Optimizer button. A Welcome screen will appear. Click on Next.

EXERCISE 4.2 (CONTINUED FROM PREVIOUS PAGE)

13. You will be prompted for information about your Exchange environment, such as the number of Exchange users, the type of server this will be, and the number of users in your organization. Leave the default selections, along with selecting the Connector/Directory Import option under Type of server. Click Next. The Performance Optimizer program will now execute. The length of execution could be several minutes.

14. When Performance Optimizer has finished analyzing your system, it will present a message stating "Disk analysis has completed." Click Next.

15. Performance Optimizer will then present its recommendations for the location of various Exchange files. You may accept the suggested locations, or leave them at their current locations. For this exercise, we will leave them at their current locations (but you may change it if you like). You could receive a screen that states that Performance Optimizer has determined that it would be more efficient to move some files. A "Move files automatically" checkbox will allow you to have those files moved. For this exercise you can leave the checkbox unchecked. Click Next.

16. A congratulations screen will appear informing you that the installation is complete. Click on the Finish button. A message will appear stating that services will be restarted.

After the initial setup, other components can also be installed using their own setup programs. For example, the Microsoft Exchange Key Management Server, which is the Exchange advanced security system, has its own setup program that could be run after the initial setup of your server (this will be covered in Chapter 10). As mentioned earlier, the Enterprise edition of Exchange Server also includes in the EXCHCONN directory a separate Setup program for the connectors for Notes, X.400, OfficeVision/VM, and SNADS.

Postinstallation Considerations

This section discusses some of the results of the Exchange installation, and two postinstallation actions that the installer could take. During the installation of Exchange, some of the activities of SETUP.EXE include: creating an Exchange directory structure, copying files to that directory structure, creating share points to the directory structure, and adding keys and values to the NT Registry. Knowing the results of these activities is helpful for the Exchange administrator, especially in troubleshooting situations (which will be discussed later in this chapter). We will cover the preceding topics under the following headings:

- Default Directory and File Structure for Exchange

- Share Points and Permissions for Exchange Directories

- Exchange Entries in the NT Registry

As mentioned, we will also discuss two postinstallation actions that the installer could perform:

- Execute the Microsoft Exchange Performance Optimizer program

- Install the Microsoft Exchange Administrator program

Default Directory and File Structure for Exchange

The default root directory for Exchange is EXCHSRVR. The SETUP program creates subdirectories under that root directory and copies Exchange files to those subdirectories. Table 4.1 is a listing of the default Exchange subdirectories under the root and the type of files in those subdirectories.

T A B L E 4.1 Default Exchange Directories and their contents	Folder	Contents
	ADD-INS	The ADD-INS directory contains subdirectories with program files that can be used to give additional functionality to Microsoft Exchange. These types of files are sometimes referred to as *extensions*, meaning they extend the basic functionality of Exchange. These files are implemented as DLL files. The complete installation copies files here that pertain to the use of the Microsoft Mail Connector, the Microsoft Schedule+ Free/Busy Connector and the Internet Mail Service.

	Folder	Contents
T A B L E 4.1 *(cont.)* Default Exchange Directories and their contents	ADDRESS	The ADDRESS directory contains subdirectories with program files (DLLs) that can be used to generate foreign addresses for Exchange recipients. When an Exchange Server uses a connector or gateway to create interoperability with a foreign system, the System Attendant component automatically generates a foreign address for each Exchange recipient. This foreign address, also referred to as a proxy address or simply an e-mail address, is what the users of the foreign mail system see and where they send mail. The program files in the subdirectories can generate these proxy addresses. The complete installation downloads files for the following foreign mail systems: Lotus cc:Mail, Microsoft Mail, Internet mail (SMTP), and X.400 mail.
	BIN	The BIN directory contains many of the files that are the components and services of Microsoft Exchange Server and the Microsoft Exchange Server Administrator program.
	CCMCDATA	Files for cc: Mail Connector.
	CONNECT	The CONNECT directory contains subdirectories that hold the files that are the Microsoft connectors. The complete installation downloads files for the following connectors: the Microsoft Mail Connector, the Internet Mail Service, the Microsoft Schedule+ Free/Busy Connector, and the Microsoft Exchange Connector for Lotus cc:Mail. An additional subdirectory (Trn) contains files for translating messages into other languages.
	DSADATA	The DSADATA directory contains the file (DIR.EDB) that is the Directory Service database. This directory also holds the transaction log files (*.LOG) for the directory database.
	DXADATA	The DXADATA directory contains the file (XDIR.EDB) that is the Directory Synchronization database.
	IMCDATA	The IMCDATA directory contains subdirectories that are used by the Internet Mail Service (IMS) for working files. When the IMS is receiving mail, sending mail, or creating log files, it uses these subdirectories.
	INSDATA	This directory and its subdirectories are used by the Internet News Service to store data related to USENET feeds.

TABLE 4.1 *(cont.)*	Folder	Contents
Default Exchange Directories and their contents	MDBDATA	The MDBDATA directory contains the Information Store database. This database is comprised of the following files: the Private Information Store (PRIV.EDB), which is the server-based storage of mailboxes; the Public Information Store (PUB.EDB), which is the server-based storage of public folder data; and the database transaction log files (*.LOG), which are the files to which data is initially written in order to provide for faster performance and fault tolerance (the log files will be discussed in Chapter 12).
	MTADATA	The MTADATA directory holds the files that make up and relate to the Message Transfer Agent (MTA).
	RES	Holds files that contain message strings used when Exchange logs events to the NT Event Log.
	SAMPAPPS	The SAMPAPPS directory contains subdirectories holding sample Exchange applications and forms. One of the subdirectories, CLIENTS, contains the file SAMPAPPS.PST which provides documentation on creating custom Exchange applications and forms. This information can be copied to a public folder.
	TRACKING.LOG	The TRACKING.LOG directory contains the log files for the messaging tracking feature of the Microsoft Exchange Administrator program.
	WEBDATA	Files for Outlook Web Access.

Share Points and Permissions for Exchange Directories

Table 4.2 lists the Exchange directories that are shared on the network with the specified share names and permissions. (The software requirements mentioned in the *Preinstallation Considerations* section assumes that Exchange was installed on the C: drive.)

TABLE 4.2	Folder	Shared As	Permissions
Microsoft Exchange share points and permissions	C:\EXCHSRVR\ADD-INS	Add-ins	Administrators and Site Service Account: Full Control; Everyone group: Read

T A B L E 4.2 (cont.) Microsoft Exchange share points and permissions	Folder	Shared As	Permissions
	C:\EXCHSRVR\ADDRESS	Address	Administrators and Site Service Account: Full Control; Everyone group: Read
	C:\EXCHSRVR\CONNECT	connect$	Administrators and Site Service Account: Full Control; Everyone group: Read
	C:\EXCHSRVR\CONNECT\ MSMCON\MAILDATA	maildat$	Administrators and Site Service Account: Full Control; Everyone group: Full Control
	C:\EXCHSRVR\SAMPAPPS\CLIENTS	Samples	Administrators and Site Service Account: Full Control; Everyone group: Full Control
	C:\EXCHSRVR\RES	Resources	Administrators and Site Service Account: Full Control; Everyone group: Read
	C:\EXCHSRVR\TRACKING.LOG	tracking.log	Administrators and Site Service Account: Full Control; Everyone group: Read

Exchange Entries in the NT Registry

During installation, SETUP creates entries in the NT Registry. Some of these entries are mentioned here.

Registry information about the presence of the Exchange application on this machine, as well as the directory location of the installation, is found in the following Registry location:

```
HKEY_LOCAL_MACHINE

\SOFTWARE

\Microsoft

\Exchange

\Setup
```

The following Registry location records the settings for the various Event Logs created by the different Exchange components.

```
HKEY_LOCAL_MACHINE

                \SYSTEM

                        \CurrentControlSet

                            \Services

                                \EventLog

                                    \Application

                                        \<Exchange components>
```

The Exchange component settings are stored in the Registry at the following location:

```
\HKEY_LOCAL_MACHINE

                \SYSTEM

                        \CurrentControlSet

                            \Services

                                \<Exchange component>
```

License settings for Exchange are stored in:

```
\HKEY_LOCAL_MACHINE

        \SYSTEM

            \CurrentControlSet

                \Services

                    \LicenseInfo

                        \MSExchangeIS
```

Microsoft Exchange Administrator Program

A powerful feature of Microsoft Exchange is the ability to centrally administer an entire Exchange organization. This is accomplished through the Microsoft Exchange Administrator program. This Windows NT program can run on any NT machine, server or workstation, on the Exchange network. From this single point, an administrator can administer all the Exchange Servers in the organization. This is sometimes referred to as single-seat administration.

The executable program for Microsoft Exchange Administrator is ADMIN.EXE, which is stored in the \EXCHSRVR\BIN directory. While the Exchange setup program can install the Administrator program on the Exchange Server machine, the administrator will probably also want this program on their Windows NT workstation. Installing this program also installs a new version of Windows NT Backup and installs extensions to the User Manager for Domains and Performance Monitor programs. These changes enable those programs to work with Exchange Server.

The Administrator program uses RPCs to communicate with the various Exchange Servers. But some network links, due to slow speeds, do not support RPC connections. If that is the case between the machine running the Administrator program and a particular remote Exchange server, then a copy of the Administrator program must be running on the remote Exchange server's local area network.)

Microsoft
✓ *Exam*
Objective   **Diagnose and resolve server installation problems.**

Troubleshooting an Exchange Installation

If any problems arise during an Exchange installation, you may want to investigate the following areas:

- **The security context of the Site Service Account**   This account must be accessible by all servers in the site.

- **The setup log**   While SETUP is running, it creates a log of what it is attempting. This log file, called Exchange Server Setup.LOG, is stored in the root directory of the drive on which Exchange is installed.

- **Share point permissions**   Make sure the necessary Exchange directories are shared.

- **Observe the Exchange Server boot process**   If there are any problems with the Exchange boot process, alert messages can be sent to the console and/or written to the NT Event Log. The installer may also want to check that all the necessary Exchange services have been started. This can be done by going to Control Panel/Services, or by going to a command prompt and executing NET START. Some Exchange services are dependent on other NT services being started. If the dependent service is not started, the Exchange service will not start.)

Microsoft
✓ ***Exam***
Objective

Identify strategies for migration from previous versions of Exchange Server to Exchange Server 5.5.

Diagnose and resolve upgrade problems.

Upgrading a Server

Before undertaking an upgrade, you should always perform a complete backup of your current installation. If something goes drastically wrong with the upgrade, you could then go back to your previous installation. You should also turn off all server monitor programs running on the computer that you will perform the upgrade on.

An upgrade is started in the same way the initial setup is: by executing SETUP.EXE. SETUP first checks for any existing Exchange Server components on that computer. If it finds some, it goes into maintenance mode and enables the choice of performing an upgrade. There are two upgrade options:

- Standard upgrade

- Fault-tolerant upgrade

The standard upgrade option upgrades your current Exchange databases in their current locations. If the upgrade fails, you would have to restore those databases from your backup media.

The fault-tolerant upgrade option backs up each database to a different, temporary location before it begins the upgrade. If the upgrade fails, the original databases will still be in their original locations. This upgrade option requires at least twice the available disk space as the size of your Information Store, and cannot be a network drive. The fault-tolerant upgrade option is not possible when upgrading from Exchange Server 4.0.

The time required to perform an upgrade will depend on the size of your Information Store. Large Information Stores can take more than a day.

The next two sections will discuss some of the particulars of upgrading to Exchange Server 5.5 from the earlier 4.0 and 5.0 versions.

Upgrading from Microsoft Exchange 4.0 to 5.5

In a single-server site, you may upgrade from version 4.0 to 5.5 in a straight-forward manner. But if you have a multi-server site, you must take into account the Service Pack version of your current Exchange servers. A service pack is a collection of software Microsoft puts together that adds to or amends a particular software product (e.g. bug fixes are many times included in a service pack). Service Pack 2 (SP 2) for Exchange Server 4.0 (also known as Exchange Server 4.0a) instituted some new changes to the Exchange directory schema. A schema is the set rules defining a directory's hierarchy, objects, attributes, etc. The upgrade procedure to Exchange Server 5.5 needs the new schema found in 4.0 SP 2. Therefore, if you have installed SP 2 on all your Exchange servers, you can upgrade those servers to 5.5 in any order. This is the Microsoft recommended procedure.

You can determine the service pack number of Exchange Server by accessing the Help menu and the About Microsoft Exchange Server option in the Exchange Administrator program. If you need to, you can download SP 2 from the Microsoft Web site, or order it on compact disc from the Microsoft Order Desk at (800) 360-7561.

Some situations will have servers that do not have SP 2 and that cannot all be upgraded within the same time frame. That scenario requires you to first upgrade any directory replication bridgehead servers in the site to SP 2 and to

Exchange Server 5.5. A directory replication bridgehead server is a server connected to another site and that exchanges directory information with that site (e.g. mailbox names, public folder names, etc.; Chapter 13 will further discuss this topic).

After you have upgraded all the directory replication bridgehead servers in the site, and after directory replication has taken place within that site, you should restart all the servers running Exchange Server 4.0. This process will place the new directory schema on all the servers in the site. You can then upgrade the remaining servers to Exchange Server 5.5 in any order.

Upgrading from Microsoft Exchange 5.0 to 5.5

Upgrading from Exchange Server 5.0 to 5.5 is very straightforward. The upgrade will automatically back up your Web Connector files, in case they have changed since their initial installation. The backup directory is Web-data\<language>\<5.5>.temp. The language variable will be filled with your language, and the 5.5 variable will be a number that increases each time you perform an upgrade.

Installing Exchange Server on Clustered Servers

As stated earlier in this chapter, the Enterprise edition of Exchange Server 5.5 can work with Microsoft Cluster Server. Cluster Server logically groups servers into an interdependent system, called a cluster, for the purpose of fault tolerance. Servers in a cluster are designated either as an active node or as a secondary node. An active node is the server that normally provides services to users. A secondary node "stands by" to take over for the active node in the event of an active node failure. For example, if two Exchange servers are in a cluster, one would be the active node, meaning that it is the primary messaging server that processes, stores, and routes messages. The other server, the secondary node, would take over those duties in the event of a failure of the active node. The process of a secondary node taking over the duties of the active node is called a *failover*.

When installing Exchange Server into a cluster, it must be installed first on the active node. SETUP will recognize that this computer is the active node of a cluster and will prompt you for the name of the cluster. SETUP will then add the Exchange components as resources to that cluster.

When you install Exchange Server on the secondary node, SETUP will recognize that Exchange is already installed on the active node. By performing the installation on the secondary node, the active node will failover to the secondary node to enable the installation to continue.

After the installation is complete on both nodes, use Cluster Administrator to configure the failover rules for the Exchange operations. For example, a failover rule could state that if the Information Store on the active node goes down, there will be a failover to the secondary node.

Summary

Although installing Microsoft Exchange Server is a straightforward process, you still must understand some important concepts.

One of the most important phases of an installation is preinstallation. Before starting the actual installation, you must make sure the minimum requirements for Exchange are met. You must also create the site service account which is used by the Exchange services for operation. License issues must be addressed to ensure compliance with legal issues. Because Exchange utilizes user accounts from Windows NT Server accounts databases, Exchange sites must interface with NT domains. Finally, you must know whether the planned new Exchange server is going to join an existing site or create a new site. When joining a site, you must know the name of an existing Exchange server in that site. When creating a site, you must know the name of or create a name for the organization, and enter a name for the new site.

There are three types of installation options:

- **Typical**   This option installs all the Exchange Server software, the Administrator program, but none of the connectors or online documentation.

- **Complete/Custom**   This option installs all the Exchange Server software, the Administrator program, connectors, and online documentation.

- **Minimum**   This option installs only the Exchange Server software.

After an Exchange Server installation, you should know the directory structure that SETUP has created. The default directory name for the installation is EXCHSRVR. Share points and modifications to the NT Registry are also made by SETUP.

At the end of the installation procedure, you have the option of running the Performance Optimizer program. This program will analyze the server's hard disk and memory configuration. It will then recommend any changes to the location of Exchange directories and the memory configuration.

Once the installation is complete, the installer should consider installing the Microsoft Exchange Server Administrator program. If the Typical or Complete/Custom options were used during installation, this program is already installed on the Exchange Server machine. But as the administrator of the Exchange system, you will probably want this program on your Windows NT workstation.

Review Questions

1. One of your company's locations contains an Exchange site with 25 users, each using Microsoft Outlook. You have purchased 25 client access licenses. The company hires 10 new employees that will connect to the site remotely. Five of the new users will be using POP3 applications, and five will be using HTTP applications. How many additional client access licenses must you purchase?

    A. 0

    B. 2

    C. 5

    D. 6

    E. 10

    F. 12

2. You have upgraded your Exchange server by adding RAM and a hard disk. What should you do to make sure that Exchange will take maximum advantage of these changes?

   A. Run Microsoft Exchange Performance Optimizer.

   B. Run online maintenance.

   C. Run Microsoft Exchange setup again.

   D. Run the Migration Wizard.

3. You manage two Microsoft Windows NT Server domains. The domains are named Personnel and Resources. The Personnel domain contains all user accounts, while the Resources domain contains all servers. You will be installing Microsoft Exchange Server into the Resources domain. You would like to use the Windows NT user accounts in the Personnel domain with mailboxes on the Exchange server. What type of trust relationship must be established between the two domains?

   A. No trust relationship is needed.

   B. The Personnel domain must trust the Resources domain.

   C. The Resource domain must trust the Personnel domain.

4. The minimum amount of RAM needed by Microsoft Exchange Server is:

   A. 24

   B. 48

   C. 64

   D. 128

5. \The Site Services Account must be configured:

   A. As a regular user account

   B. As a member of the Mail group

   C. After the Exchange installation

   D. As a member of the Domain Administrators global group

6. Which file would be useful in a troubleshooting situation?

  A. Exchange Server Setup.LOG

  B. ERROR.LOG

  C. SETUP.EXE

  D. VIEWLOG

7. The default location of the Exchange directory is:

  A. \EXCHANGE

  B. \MICROSOFT\EXCHANGE

  C. \EXCHSRVR

  D. \\EXCHANGE

8. The Internet Mail Service requires this protocol to be running on the Exchange Server:

  A. NWLink

  B. Ethernet

  C. TCP/IP

  D. SNA

9. This Windows NT-based program analyzes your Exchange Server machine and makes recommendations for better performance:

  A. Administrator program

  B. SETUP.HLP

  C. ANALYZER

  D. Performance Optimizer

10. If there is a problem with the Exchange Server boot process, one action would be to view:

A. The Event Log

B. My Computer

C. Microsoft Explorer

D. Administrator Tools / User Manager for Domains

11. The following is one of the configuration requirements for the operating system that Microsoft Exchange Server uses:

A. Page file size equal to 50 plus the amount of RAM

B. NETBEUI

C. NWLink

D. Ethernet

12. Two sites, siteA and siteB, were both using version 4.0 of Exchange Server. The two sites also had directory replication configured between them. But after upgrading some of the servers in siteA to version 5.5, directory replication between the two sites stops working. Which of the following is a solution?

A. Uninstall version 5.5, and reinstall version 4.0.

B. Directory replication between sites cannot work until all servers have the same version.

C. Internet Mail Service must be used for directory replication.

D. Upgrade all directory bridgehead servers to version 5.5.

13. When adding a Microsoft Exchange Server to an existing site, which two pieces of information do you need to know?

   A. The name of an existing Exchange Server in that site and the password for the site service account in that site

   B. Organization name and site name

   C. Site name and administrator's user account

   D. Organization name and administrator's user account

14. Which of the following is a requirement for Exchange Server 5.5 to work with Microsoft Cluster Server?

   A. The purchase of a 1000-user license

   B. Microsoft Windows NT Server version 5

   C. X.400 Connector

   D. The Enterprise Edition of Exchange Server 5.5

15. Which Microsoft Windows NT Server 4.0 service pack is required to install Exchange Server 5.5?

   A. SP3

   B. SP2

   C. SP4

   D. SP5.5

16. Which Exchange Server 4.0 service pack is needed to perform an upgrade to Exchange Server 5.5?

   A. SP3

   B. SP2

   C. SP4

   D. SP5.5

CHAPTER

5

Recipients in a
Microsoft Exchange Environment

ne of an administrator's most important tasks is to create and configure Exchange *recipients*. A recipient is an object that can receive a message. In this chapter, we will discuss the types of recipients, their creation, and their properties.

Exchange has four main types of recipients:

- **Mailboxes**   A mailbox is a storage location on a Microsoft Exchange server that, along with a client program, allows information to be sent, received, and organized. E-mail messages, forms, and file attachments are some of the typical types of information that can be sent to and stored in a mailbox.

- **Distribution lists (DL)**   A distribution list is a grouping of recipients. A single DL can represent a number of other recipients. Using DLs makes mass mailing easy. A message sent to a DL can be read by all the members of that DL.

- **Custom recipients**   A custom recipient is an e-mail address to a non-Exchange e-mail user. By using custom recipients, Exchange users can see a directory listing of non-Exchange mail users and send them messages. (The necessary connector components and other software must be in place.)

- **Public folders**   A public folder is like a public mailbox. It is a container for information to be shared among a group of people. Public folders can contain e-mail messages, forms, word processing documents, spreadsheet files, and files of many other formats. Public folders can also be configured to send information to other recipients.

The rest of this chapter discusses the creation and properties of these four recipient objects as well as some related management tasks.

Don't Want to Be Distracted by Those Other People

A pastor answered his telephone one Sunday afternoon. The caller wanted to know if the pastor's church would be open for worship on Sunday evenings. "Yes, it is open, but the regular worship service is on Sunday mornings," the pastor replied. He then asked if the caller would like to worship with the rest of the congregation on Sunday mornings. "Oh no!" answered the caller, "I do not want to be distracted by all those other people."

Although distractions are part of any communal enterprise, those other people are essential to the enterprise. The recipients talked about in this chapter represent those other people.

Microsoft ✓ *Exam* *Objective*

Configure Exchange Server for message recipients.

- Configure mailboxes
- Configure custom recipients
- Configure public folders
- Configure distribution lists
- Configure site addressing
- Configure container-level search controls
- Configure Address Book views

Mailbox Objects

As mentioned, a mailbox is a specific storage area on an Exchange server where information can be sent, received, and organized. An Exchange mailbox, along with client software, enables users to perform a wide range of powerful messaging functions. A mailbox and the client software that uses it are analogous to a container box and the person who uses it. The box has certain characteristics, like shape, width, length, depth, etc., that determine what the person can do with the box. But the *person* is the active party who uses the box for some activity. As with all analogies, this one cannot be pushed too far. Exchange mailboxes also have active features, such as AutoAssistants. Now we will examine the creation and configuration of mailbox objects.

Creating a Mailbox

The vast majority, if not all, of your users are going to need a mailbox. Mailboxes must be created before any Exchange client software can be used. The following programs can be used to create and configure a mailbox:

- Microsoft Exchange Administrator program

- Microsoft Windows NT User Manager for Domains program

- Microsoft Exchange extract and import tools

Microsoft ✓ *Exam* *Objective*	**Configure address lists and accounts by using the Administrator program.**

Exchange Administrator Program

One of the functions of the Microsoft Exchange Administrator program (ADMIN.EXE) is creating and configuring mailboxes. To create a mailbox within this program, choose the File menu and then the New Mailbox option. You will then be presented with a number of property pages that can be used to configure the mailbox (these will be discussed shortly).

Part of the process of creating a mailbox is to assign it a primary Windows NT *user account*. The user account can be an existing account, or a new account created while in the Administrator program. The last function is possible because the Microsoft Exchange Administrator program has built-in functionality to create accounts in the NT domain SAM. This allows the Administrator program to create new Windows NT user accounts, at the same time it creates a mailbox. Later in this chapter, Exercise 5.2 will provide the steps to create a mailbox through this program.

Exchange Administrator can be configured to use a specified Windows NT domain as the default domain when presenting existing user accounts for the primary Windows NT user account. This is done through the Tools menu, Options, and the Permissions tab.

Windows NT User Manager for Domains Program

Another program that can be used to create a mailbox is the Microsoft Windows NT User Manager for Domains. When Microsoft Exchange Server is installed, an Exchange module, MAILUMX.DLL, is added to the User Manager for the Domains program. This dynamic link library adds some of the functionality of the Exchange Administrator program to User Manager for Domains. Whenever a Windows NT user account is created in User Manager for Domains, an Exchange mailbox can also be created. This also applies to deleting a mailbox when the NT user account is deleted. Later in this chapter, Exercise 5.3 will provide the steps to create a mailbox through this program.

Exchange Extract and Import Tools

Microsoft Exchange can create Exchange recipients from existing user accounts. Two types of software tools, called *extract tools* and *import tools*, work together to accomplish this. Extract tools collect information about the user accounts. Import tools take that information and use it to create Exchange recipient objects.

 Extract tools and import tools can also be used to create Exchange recipients from user accounts that are on an existing non-Exchange mail system. In this scenario, these tools can be used to not only create an Exchange mailbox, they can also create a Windows NT account, copy the contents of the foreign mailbox, and copy address book and folder information. This process is referred to as a *migration*. Migrations are covered in Chapter 16.

Extract Tools The Microsoft Exchange Administrator program can be used to extract and import user information from Windows NT and NetWare systems. Each is discussed here:

- **Extract Windows NT Account List** The Extract Windows NT Accounts List tool can take data from a trusted Windows NT or LAN Manager domain and prepare that data for the creation of recipient objects on a Microsoft Exchange server. This extraction tool can be executed through the Exchange Administrator program, Tools menu, and the Extract Windows NT Account List option. It can also be executed using the command prompt. The user account executing this program must have administrative privileges and must select a domain controller in the relevant domain. Exercise 5.4, later in this chapter, will provide the steps to perform this type of extraction.

- **Extract NetWare Account List**   This program works like the previous tool, except that it prepares NetWare user accounts as the source data. The NetWare server can be any NetWare 2.x, 3.x, or 4.x running in bindery emulation mode. This tool can be executed through the Exchange Administrator program, Tools menu, and the Extract NetWare Account List option. The user executing this program will be prompted to log on to the NetWare server. They must log on as a user with supervisor rights to that NetWare server.

Additional extraction tools that can be used to migrate non-Exchange mail users will be discussed in Chapter 16.

Import Tools   After the data from the other system is prepared with the relevant extraction tool, the Microsoft Exchange Directory Import tool can be used to create Exchange recipient objects and import other specified data. This program is executed through the Microsoft Exchange Administrator program, using the Tools menu, Directory Import option.

Along with creating recipients, the Directory Import tool can also be used to modify existing recipients. For example, you could use the Import tool to add a large number of existing recipients to a distribution list. Exercise 5.5 shows the steps for performing an import.

Properties of a Mailbox

A mailbox object, like all objects, has properties. Those properties are configured and viewed through property pages and the individual attributes on those property pages. Many of the attributes are straightforward and do not warrant any explanation (e.g., phone number). This section describes each property page and the important individual attributes. Exercise 5.3 will walk you through the creation of a mailbox object.

The terms "properties" and "attributes" are used interchangeably.

Mailbox Property Pages

The property pages of a mailbox, or any recipient object, are accessed in one of two ways. With a mailbox highlighted, you can use the File menu and the Properties option to access the property pages. A quicker way is to simply double-click on the mailbox object; this will also bring up the property pages of that particular mailbox. The property pages of a mailbox object are listed in this section, with some of the individual attributes discussed.

General Page   This page records general information about the mailbox, such as name, title, company, department, and address (see Figure 5.1). The following information is on this page:

- **Display name**   This is the name of the mailbox that will be seen in the Administrator window and the Global Address List. By default, the display name is automatically generated by combining the first and last name values. For example, if a first name is "Sue," and a last name is "Todd," then the display name would be "Sue Todd." This field can also be manually edited.

- **Alias**   This is a name that will be used to generate foreign e-mail addresses for this mailbox. By default, the alias name is automatically generated by using the primary NT account as the mailbox alias. For example, if the NT account name was "STodd," then the alias would be "STodd." This field can also be manually edited.

- **Primary Windows NT Account**   This is the NT user account that is associated with this mailbox, and therefore can use this mailbox.

- **Home server**   This is the Microsoft Exchange server on which this mailbox will physically reside. If a server is not specified by the administrator, the Administrator program assumes the home server is the one to which the Administrator program is currently attached.

The Exchange administrator can determine the default naming convention that will be used to automatically generate the display name and alias. These default naming conventions are configured in the Exchange Administrator program under the Tools menu and Options submenu and the Auto Naming property page. Standard naming conventions that could be used include "first last" (e.g., Sue Todd), "last, first" (e.g,. Todd, Sue), and "first initials last" (e.g., Sue L. Todd). A custom naming convention could also be entered by the administrator. For example, if new display names needed to be last name followed by the initial of the first name, the administrator could enter "%Last 1First" (the percent sign is the symbol for a variable). If a mailbox was created for Sue Todd with this naming convention, her display name would be "ToddS." The display name and alias name generation can have separate naming conventions.

Organization Page   This page contains a field for recording the name of this mailbox user's manager, and another field for recording the people who report to the mailbox user. These people are referred to as *direct reports*. Both of these fields are optional.

Phone/Notes Page   This page contains information on phone numbers, including business, home, fax, mobile, page, and others.

Permissions Page   This page allows you to view and configure the permissions that users and groups have for this mailbox. It should be noted that multiple users could be assigned as the owner of a mailbox. This is useful when you want to create a mailbox that will be used by a group of people, such as a help desk department. A single mailbox could be created and all users of that department could be made an owner of that mailbox.

Distribution Lists Property Page   This page specifies the distribution lists of which this mailbox is a member.

E-mail Addresses Page   Each time an Exchange mailbox is created, a number of non-Exchange mail addresses, also called foreign mail addresses or proxy addresses, are automatically generated for that Exchange mailbox. This allows Exchange mailboxes to be prepared to receive mail from foreign mail systems. Microsoft Exchange automatically generates foreign addresses for the following systems:

- Lotus cc:Mail
- Microsoft Mail
- SMTP
- X.400

If an administrator does not want a particular e-mail address generated for new mailboxes, they can disable that type of address through the Site Addressing properties. This will be covered in Chapter 12.

Delivery Restrictions Page   This page contains information regarding from whom this mailbox will accept or reject messages. The default is to accept messages from everyone (All), and reject messages from nobody (None).

Delivery Options Page   This page can specify a list of users who can send mail "on behalf of" this mailbox user. It also allows mail sent to this mailbox to be rerouted to another mailbox, referred to as an *alternate recipient*. The alternate recipient feature can be configured to receive mail instead of the original mailbox, or along with the original mailbox.

Protocols Page   This page can specify various protocols and character sets that can be used with this mailbox. The protocols include HTTP, IMAP4, LDAP, NNTP, and POP3. By default, each of these are enabled, but this can be overridden at the mailbox or server level. The settings for each of these protocols can also be configured through this page. Encoding methods and character sets are examples of configurable settings. Encoding methods include:

- **MIME** (Multipurpose Internet Mail Extensions)   This is a popular Internet protocol for including multimedia data like graphics, sound, animation, etc. in a mail message.

- **BINHEX** (Binary Hex)   This protocol is popular with Apple computers.

- **UUENCODE** (UNIX-to-UNIX Encode)   This is a popular Internet protocol for encoding binary data in a mail message.

- **Microsoft Exchange Rich-Text Format (RTF)**

Custom Attributes Page   This page permits the viewing of any unique properties that have been defined in the DS Site Configuration object. An administrator can create up to ten custom-made properties. Examples could be employee identification numbers, birthdays, hobbies, bowling averages, or any other information a company might want to store. After the custom attributes have been created, these property fields can be displayed and filled in on every recipient in a site through the Custom Attributes property page.

Limits Page   This new feature of Exchange 5.5 enables mailbox users to retrieve deleted items. But to prevent excessive build-up of deleted items, Exchange allows you to set a retention time for deleted items. That length of time can be configured on this page or at the Information Store (IS) object. The IS default value will be used, but you can configure a mailbox to override that setting by specifying the number of days for deleted item retention. You can also configure a mailbox to keep deleted items (i.e., not permanently deleted) until the mailbox has been backed up.

   Another settable parameter on this page is the storage limits of the mailbox. By default, the IS settings will be used. However, this can be overridden. If it is overridden, you can set values (in kilobytes) for when warnings will be issued, when sending messages will be prohibited, and when sending and receiving messages will be prohibited.

   The last parameter on this page relates to message sizes. By default, a mailbox is configured without any limit on the size of outgoing or incoming messages. But this can be overridden by setting limits (in kilobytes) on either or both types of messages.

Advanced Page   Figure 5.2 depicts the Advanced property page.
   The following attribute fields are found on the Advanced property page:

- **Simple Display Name**   This mailbox name would be used by a non-Exchange mail system that cannot interpret all the characters that could be used in an Exchange mailbox name, such as spaces or characters like *Kanji* (which are icons used in the Japanese language).

FIGURE 5.2

The Advanced property
page of a mailbox

- **Directory Name** This read-only field contains the name used for the mailbox within the Directory Service.

- **Trust level** (0-100) Directory synchronization is a process where directory information is exchanged between Exchange and a non-Exchange mail system, such as Microsoft Mail or Lotus cc:Mail. One factor that synchronization uses to determine what objects to synchronize is the trust level of the object. If the trust level of a mailbox is greater than the level set within the directory synchronization configuration, information about that mailbox will not be replicated during directory synchronization. Directory synchronization will be further discussed in Chapter 15.

- **On-line listings information** Two fields under this label allow you to specify the server name of the Microsoft Internet Locator Service (ILS) and the account name (ILS account) for this mailbox. This is applicable if your network is using Microsoft NetMeeting for online meetings.

- **Home server** The home server is the Exchange server on which this mailbox is physically stored.

- **Hide from address book**   If this property is chosen, this mailbox name will not appear in the Global Address List, similar to an unlisted telephone number. Users can still send mail to this recipient, but they will need to know the mail address to manually enter it.

- **Downgrade high priority X.400 mail**   If selected, this checkbox will disable the mailbox from sending high priority mail to a X.400 mail system. By default, this checkbox is clear. However, if it is checked, all mail marked high priority will be downgraded and sent at a normal priority.

- **Container name**   This read-only field contains the name of the recipient's container where this object resides.

- **Administrative note**   This field can contain any comments the administrator wants to enter.

Mailbox Roles

As mentioned earlier, the Permissions property page allows you to view and configure the permissions that users and groups have for this mailbox (see Figure 5.3). By default, the Permissions property tab is not seen, it is configured through Exchange Administrator to be hidden. To view this tab, you must open the Tools menu, the Options menu, and the Permissions tab. On the screen you will see an option stating "Show Permissions page for all objects." Check the option box if you want to see the Permissions tab for all Exchange objects. Exercise 5.1 outlines these steps in preparation for the following exercises on creating mailboxes.

EXERCISE 5.1

Configuring the Show Permissions Page

1. Start the Microsoft Exchange Administrator program by selecting Start ➤ Programs ➤ Microsoft Exchange ➤ Microsoft Exchange Administrator.

2. In order to view the Permissions page for any Exchange object, open Tools ➤ Options ➤ Permissions. Now check the box next to the option stating "Show Permissions page for all objects." Click OK.

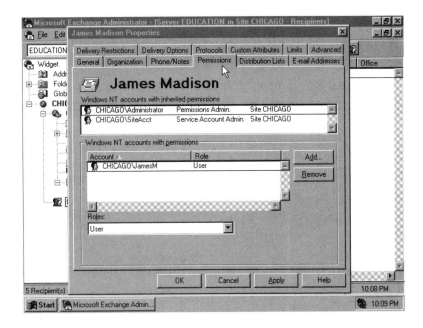

After you have completed Exercise 5.1, you will be able to see the Permissions tab for recipients. The first field on the Permissions page shows the Windows NT accounts with inherited permissions for this mailbox. This information is read-only. The second field on this page shows the Windows NT accounts with permissions, and allows the accounts and permissions to be edited. You assign permissions by giving a user or group a *role* for the mailbox. Roles are sets of permissions that define what activities a user or group can do with regards to this mailbox. Four roles are predefined, and you can create a custom role.

Admin. Role (Administrative)   The Admin. role includes two rights that allow all attributes of a mailbox to be modified. Those rights are:

- Modify User Attributes

- Modify Admin. Attributes

If Outlook Web Access is installed, the Advanced property page will also display a field called "Outlook Web Access Server Name." This is the server name that POP and IMAP users will see when they perform a directory search (LDAP query) for their server.

Permissions Admin. The Permissions Admin. role includes three rights that allow all attributes and the permissions of a mailbox to be modified. Those rights are:

- Modify User Attributes
- Modify Admin. Attributes
- Modify Permissions

Send As The Send As role includes one right that allows another user or group member to send mail addressed from this mailbox.

User The User role, which is the default permission, includes the following three rights:

- Modify User Attributes
- Send As
- Mailbox Owner

The Mailbox Owner right permits a user or group to use this mailbox and receive mail. The user account that is automatically given this right is the primary NT account assigned to this mailbox on the General page.

Now that you know the property pages and attributes of a mailbox, we can proceed with the promised exercises on the different methods of creating a mailbox. Exercise 5.2 outlines the steps in creating and configuring a mailbox through the Microsoft Exchange Administrator program.

Exercise 5.3 will take you through the steps for creating a mailbox through the Windows NT User Manager for Domains program.

Exercise 5.4 shows you the steps to extract all the Windows NT user accounts in the specified domain and prepare that information for the creation of mailboxes for those users. In preparation for this exercise, make sure you have created some users who do not have Exchange mailboxes. If you want to follow our Presidents theme and have the same screen information that this book will have, then create users called JamesM (James Monroe), JohnQA (John Quincy Adams), and AndrewJ (Andrew Jackson). Do not create mailboxes for these users now. You will do that in Exercise 5.5.

Now that the Windows NT user account information has been prepared, it can be imported and used to create Exchange mailboxes for those user accounts. Exercise 5.5 shows those steps.

EXERCISE 5.2

Creating and Configuring a Mailbox through the Exchange Administrator Program

1. Highlight the Recipients container in the left pane.

2. Select File menu ➤ New Mailbox. A Properties window will appear with a number of property tabs relating to a mailbox.

3. On the property tab that is open, the General tab, locate the Name area of the page and enter the name **George** in the First field. In the Last field enter the name **Washington**. Notice that the Display field and the Alias field are automatically completed.

4. You may enter information into the Address fields (such as City: Mount Vernon and State: Virginia) and into the Title field (such as President).

5. Click the Primary Windows NT Account button. A window labeled "Primary Windows NT Account" will appear. Two radio buttons will be on this window. Select the second radio button, labeled "Create a New Windows NT Account." Then click OK. Another dialog box, labeled "Create Windows NT Account," will appear. Select the NT domain in which you want to create this new account. Then, if you like, you may edit the Account Name that has been generated automatically for you (which in this case is GeorgeW). When you are finished, click OK. A dialog box labeled "Microsoft Exchange Administrator" will appear stating "The password for the Windows NT Account you just created was given a blank password. The user will be required to change the password upon first logon." After reading the message, click OK.

6. You may click on the Organization tab and the Phone/Notes tab. Feel free to enter any information you like.

7. Click on the Permissions tab to view the accounts that have permissions to this mailbox. You will see that your site service account has inherited the role of Service Account Admin., and that GeorgeW has the permissions associated with the User role.

8. Click on the E-mail Addresses tab to view the non-Exchange addresses that the System Attendant automatically generates for each Exchange recipient.

EXERCISE 5.2 (CONTINUED FROM PREVIOUS PAGE)

9. You may click on the remaining property tabs. Feel free to add any information you want.

EXERCISE 5.3

Creating and Configuring a Mailbox through the Windows NT User Manager for Domains Program

1. Start the User Manager for Domains program by clicking on Start ➣ Programs ➣ Administrative Tools ➣ User Manager for Domains.

2. While in User Manager for Domains, click on User ➣ New User. The New User dialog box will appear, giving you the ability to input the information you want associated with this new user.

3. The only field that requires information is the Username field. Enter the name **JohnA**. In the Full Name field, enter the name **John Adams**. Enter any other information you would like in any of the other fields.

4. Click Add. The next dialog box you will see will be labeled "JohnA Properties." This is the Exchange properties page for a mailbox for the user JohnA.

5. Enter **John** in the First name field and **Adams** in the Last name field. Notice the Primary Windows NT Account that will be associated with this mailbox, JohnA. Enter any other information you would like in any of the other fields or property tabs.

6. Click OK. You will then be taken back to User Manager for Domains for the creation of any additional user accounts. In preparation for future exercises, create two additional users called Thomas Jefferson and James Madison. Using the same naming conventions (ThomasJ and JamesM), create mailboxes for both users. When you are finished, click Close.

7. Go to the Microsoft Exchange Administrator program and examine the JohnA mailbox.

EXERCISE 5.4

Extracting User Information in Preparation for Creating a Mailbox

1. While in the Microsoft Exchange Administrator program, click on Tools ➢ Extract Windows NT Account List. The Windows NT User Extraction screen will appear.

2. Choose the domain and domain controller from which you want to extract user accounts.

3. Click Browse. In the File name field, you must enter a file name for the information that will be extracted. Choose the file name exercise.csv. Click Save.

4. Click OK. The extraction will now take place. If it is successful, you will see an information dialog box labeled "NT User Extractor Complete" and stating "Extraction of Windows NT user account information to file C:\exchsrvr\bin\exercise.csv is complete. No errors were encountered." Click OK. The next step is the import, which is found in Exercise 5.5.

EXERCISE 5.5

Importing Extracted Windows NT User Accounts and Creating Exchange Mailboxes

1. While in the Microsoft Exchange Administrator program, click on Tools ➢ Directory Import. The Directory Import dialog box will appear.

2. Choose the domain that you chose in Exercise 5.4 and the Exchange server on which you want the mailboxes created.

3. Click Import File. This will enable you to choose the extraction file that has the information you want to import. Choose the exercise.csv file and then click Open.

EXERCISE 5.5 (CONTINUED FROM PREVIOUS PAGE)

4. Click Import to start the import process. If the import is successful, you will see an information dialog box labeled "Directory Import Complete" and stating "The directory import from file C:\exchsrvr\bin\ exercise.csv is complete. No errors were encountered." Click OK.

5. To confirm the import, go to the main screen of the Exchange Administrator program, and locate a user account that did not have a mailbox, for example, AndrewJ. You will see that mailboxes have indeed been created for those accounts. Double-click on one of the names to bring up its property pages. Notice that many of the mailbox attributes are blank. You can input information for those attributes. You also could have used a mailbox template during the import process.

Distribution Lists

A distribution list (DL) is a grouping of recipients. A single DL object can represent a number of other recipients. This allows easy mass mailing. You can send a message to a DL and all the members of that DL will receive a copy of your message. An electronic distribution list is light-years more efficient than the old paper-based distribution list stapled to a memo or report that moved from person to person.

Microsoft ✓ ***Exam*** ***Objective***   **Manage distribution lists.**

Creating and Configuring a Distribution List

Creating and configuring a DL object is very simple. While in the Microsoft Exchange Administrator program, choose the File menu and then the New Distribution List option. You will then be presented with various property pages. Following an explanation of DL properties, Exercise 5.6 will list the steps in creating and configuring a DL.

Properties of a Distribution List

Two property pages connected to distribution lists need to be explained: the General property page and the Advanced property page. We have already discussed the other property pages.

General Property Page

The General property page (see Figure 5.4) contains some of the basic attributes of a distribution list.

FIGURE 5.4

The General properties page of a distribution list

The basic attributes are:

- **Display name**   This is the name that will be seen in the Address Book.

- **Alias name**   This is a shorter name that can be used to refer to the DL and is used to generate some of the non-Exchange addresses for this distribution list.

- **Members**   This is the list of the recipients who are included in this distribution list.

- **Owner** This is the recipient who owns and therefore manages this distribution list. The owner can modify the membership of the distribution list from an Exchange client, without having administrative rights.

- **Expansion server** When a message is sent to a distribution list, a server must *expand* the distribution list into its individual members in order for them to receive the message. Expanding the distribution list entails verifying that members do exist and determining a routing plan to distribute the message. This field lets you specify the server to carry out the functions of the expansion server. The default selection is "Any Server In Site," which means that any server in the site where the DL is homed can execute the expansion server functions. This process can be processor-intensive, so sometimes it is good practice to isolate one server in the site (perhaps with few or no user mailboxes) that will be responsible for all DL expansion in that site.

- **Notes** This field lets you enter additional information, up to 256 characters.

Advanced Property Page

Figure 5.5 illustrates the Advanced property page of a DL.

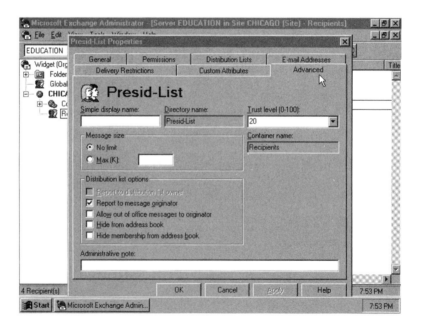

FIGURE 5.5

The Advanced page of a distribution list

The following attribute fields are contained on the Advanced property page of a DL:

- **Simple display name**   This name will appear to non-Exchange clients that cannot read all the Exchange display name characters, such as spaces or Kanji characters.

- **Directory name**   This read-only field contains the name used for the DL within the Directory Service database.

- **Trust level** (0-100)   As we saw with mailboxes, the directory synchronization process exchanges directory information with non-Exchange mail systems. One of the factors this process uses to determine what objects to synchronize is the trust level of the object.

- **Message sizes**   This property can set limits on the maximum size (in kilobytes) of messages sent to this object. The default is No limit.

- **Container name**   This read-only field contains the name of the recipients container where this object resides.

- **Distribution list options**   This section of the Advanced page has options for the following:

  - **Report to distribution list owner**   If checked, this option notifies the distribution list owner when a message sent to the DL has requested a delivery notification or is undeliverable. By default, this is not checked.

  - **Report to message originator**   If checked, this option sends a delivery notification to the message originator for each member of the DL that receives a message requiring a notification. By default, this option is checked. If this is not checked, the message originator will receive a notification from the DL itself, but not from individual members of the DL.

  - **Allow out of office messages to originator**   "Out of Office" is an intelligent agent mechanism. When this option is enabled, senders to the DL will receive "Out of Office" notifications from any users on the DL who have their Out of Office agent enabled. It is not wise to turn this on for large DLs because senders to the DL may get bombarded by Out of Office messages.

  - **Hide from address book**   If this property is chosen, this distribution list will not appear in the Global Address List, in a fashion similar to an unlisted phone number. Users can still send mail to the DL, but they will have to know the DL name and manually enter it.

- **Hide membership from address book**   If this option is checked, the name of this distribution list will appear in the Global Address List, but the individual members of the list will not appear when its properties are viewed.

Exercise 5.6 outlines the steps for creating and configuring a distribution list.

EXERCISE 5.6

Creating and Configuring a Distribution List

1. While in Microsoft Exchange Administrator, select File ➤ New Distribution List. A Properties dialog box will appear with a number of property tabs relating to a distribution list. (If you do not have the Recipients object highlighted in the left pane when you create a new recipient, you will see the message: "Recipients cannot be created in the selected parent container. Do you want to switch to the 'Recipients' container of the site <site name>?" If you click OK, your view in the Exchange Administrator will change to the Recipients container and the Properties pages for the recipient you want to create will appear.)

2. On the General tab, locate the field labeled "Display name" and enter **SalesReps**. Enter the same information in the Alias field.

3. In the Members field, click Modify. In the left list box that contains a listing of Exchange recipients, choose a number of those recipients. One way to do this is to hold down the Control key and click on the recipients you want added as members of this distribution list. After you have selected the recipients, click Add to make them members of the distribution list. As soon as you are finished, click OK.

4. Find the field labeled "Expansion server," and click on the down-arrow to display a list of Exchange servers in the site. You may choose a specific Exchange server to be the expansion server, or leave the default, which is "Any Server In Site."

5. If you have any comments, enter them in the Notes field.

6. When you are finished, click OK.

Custom Recipients

A custom recipient is the address of a non-Exchange mail recipient. The custom recipients are part of the Exchange Global Address List, and therefore permit Exchange clients to send messages to non-Exchange mail users. This also assumes that the necessary connector or gateway is in place between the Exchange system and the foreign system.

Creating and Configuring a Custom Recipient

Custom recipients are created through the Exchange Administrator program, using the File menu and the New Custom Recipient option. You are prompted to select the type of e-mail address to create, and to enter the foreign e-mail address. The standard options for the types of foreign addresses are:

- cc:Mail address

- Microsoft Mail address

- MacMail address (this is Microsoft Mail for AppleTalk)

- Internet address

- X.400 address

- Other address

After an explanation of the properties of a custom recipient, Exercise 5.7 will walk you through the creation and configuration of this type of recipient.

Properties of a Custom Recipient

The properties of a custom recipient are very similar to those of a standard Exchange mailbox. The main difference is that you will be prompted to input the foreign mail address of the custom recipient. This address will be in the format of the foreign mail system (for example, joesmith@widget.com). In this example, joesmith is the username, and widget.com is the domain name.

After inputting the non-Exchange address of the custom recipient, you will be presented with the standard property pages seen with a mailbox recipient. Exercise 5.7 outlines the steps to create and configure a custom recipient.

EXERCISE 5.7

Creating and Configuring a Custom Recipient

1. While in the Exchange Administrator program, select File ➤ New Custom Recipient.

2. The New E-mail Address dialog box appears next. For this exercise, choose the Internet Address option. Then click OK.

3. The next screen to appear will be the Internet Address Properties screen. Type an Internet address, such as:

   joesmith@widget.com.

4. When you are finished, click on the OK button.

5. The Properties dialog box appears next. This dialog box presents the various property pages relating to a custom recipient. On the General page, the only mandatory fields are the Display field, and the Alias field. Feel free to fill in any fields on this page or any of the other property pages for this recipient.

6. When you finish inputting information for this recipient, click OK.

Public Folder Recipients

A public folder is a sharable container of information. It is a recipient object because, in addition to being able to view information in it, users can send information to it. Public folders have four main features:

- **Permissions**   Public folders can have various levels of security attached to them. For example, a particular public folder could allow one group of users to read and add information, while another group is limited to only reading information.

- **Forms**   Electronic forms can be associated with a public folder to provide a format for entering information to the public folder, or to provide a way to view information in the public folder.

- **Views**   In order to better organize and find information, a public folder can be configured by various views, such as by sender, recipient, subject, and time frame.

- **Rules**   A public folder can be configured with rules that pertain to the automatic processing of information sent to it. Actions that could be automatically performed on an incoming message include deleting it, moving it, forwarding it, and replying with a specified message.

Like mailbox objects, public folders are created and stored on a specific home server. But because users on different servers and in different sites could need access to that public folder, public folders can be configured to be copied automatically to other Exchange servers. This is called *replication,* and each copy of the same public folder is called a *replica* (more on this topic in Chapter 9).

While the other recipients are created from the Microsoft Exchange Administrator program, public folders are created through the various Microsoft Exchange client applications, such as the Microsoft Exchange Client and Microsoft Outlook. Many of the properties of a public folder can also be configured through the client software. Because the installation of the Exchange client applications has not yet been covered, the creation and configuration of public folders will be covered in Chapter 9.

Basic Management of Recipient Objects

Even after they have been created, recipient objects still require care from administrators. Some of those basic management activities are:

- Using templates for mailbox creation

- Finding a recipient

- Moving a recipient

- Cleaning a mailbox

- Modifying recipients in a batch process

Each of those activities will be covered briefly in the following discussions.

Microsoft **Manage Users.**
✓ ***Exam***
Objective

Using Templates for Mailbox Creation

A *template* is a pattern that can be used to more efficiently create something, in this case, a mailbox. A template mailbox, or multiple template mailboxes, can be created with the desired default values. These default values can then be used when creating mailboxes through the Duplicate command, Directory Import command, or Migration programs, which all can use a template.

Any mailbox can be used as a template. But no matter what mailbox is used, the first name, last name, display name, alias name, directory name, and e-mail address are not copied to the new mailbox or mailboxes.

A template mailbox is created in exactly the same manner as a user's mailbox, by using the Exchange Administrator program, File menu, New Mailbox option. The properties and values that will be the default are then entered. The template mailboxes should be named something that clearly expresses the nature of the mailbox. They could also be hidden from the GAL so mail is not accidentally sent to them.

Finding a Recipient

The Find Recipients function in the Exchange Administrator program has a function that can search for recipients anywhere in the organization. This function is found in the Tools menu, Find Recipients option. Search criteria can be inputted such as first name, last name, title, department, and others. See Figure 5.6 for an illustration of the Find Recipients window.

Moving a Mailbox

Mailboxes and their contents physically reside on their home server. Mailboxes can be moved to other servers within the same site. This is done through the Administrator program by highlighting the mailbox in the Contents window (the right window pane), selecting the Tools menu, the Move Mailbox option, and choosing the new server to hold the mailbox.

When moving mailboxes to a new home server, the size of the mailbox contents can increase. This is because when a message is sent to multiple recipients homed on the same server, Exchange stores only one copy of the message

FIGURE 5.6

The Find Recipients
window

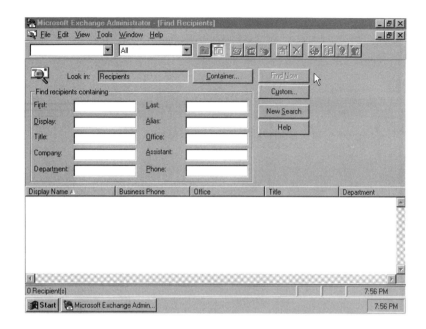

on the server, and gives all the recipients on that server a pointer to that single copy. This is called *single-instance storage*. But when a mailbox is moved to another server, the single-instance storage for that mailbox is lost on the new home server because each message must be copied into that mailbox.

For example, suppose 10 mailboxes take up 55MB of disk space in the Private Information Store. Each mailbox has five messages of 1MB, and a pointer to five single-instance messages of 1MB. If those 10 mailboxes were moved to another server, the single-instance storage would be lost and each mailbox would have 10MB of storage. The Private Information Store on the new server would increase by 100MB.

Mailboxes can also be manually moved to a new home server in a different site. This is done by copying the mailbox contents to a personal folder and then copying that personal folder to the new mailbox in the new site. However, if other recipients try to use the Reply function to a message sent before a mailbox was manually moved, the message will not be delivered because the mailbox that is referenced no longer exists.

Mailboxes might be moved for several reasons:

- To balance the load between servers

- To move mailboxes to a server that is on the same local area network as the mailbox owners

- To take a server down for maintenance reasons and still allow users access to their mailboxes

Because distribution lists and custom recipients are purely logical entities, they do not need to be moved, and therefore cannot be moved.

Cleaning a Mailbox

Cleaning a mailbox refers to deleting certain messages stored in the mailbox. This function is found in the Administrator program, Tools menu, Clean Mailbox option. The administrator can select various criteria and input values to be used in the cleaning process (see Figure 5.7). Some of the criteria are:

- All messages older than (days)

- All messages greater than (K)

- Read items

- Unread items

The administrator also has the option to delete the specified messages immediately, or to have them moved to the Deleted Items Folder.

Modifying Recipients in a Batch Process

There could be instances where many recipients need to be modified. For example, you might need to change the area code of the business telephone attribute for all your recipients. This could be done by manually changing every recipient, but it would be more efficient to use a batch process (i.e., all at once). The latter method uses the Exchange Directory Export and Directory Import utilities, both located on the Tools menu in the Exchange Administrator program.

FIGURE 5.7

The Clean Mailbox
dialog box

The Directory Export utility can be used to copy objects and their properties to a file called an export file. The export file is a text file in a comma-separated value format (CSV). The new properties can be entered in the export file through any application that can read a text file as well as search, replace, and input data (Microsoft Excel is an example). Below is an example of an export file:

```
Obj-Class, Display Name, Alias Name, Home Server, Telephone-
Office1

Mailbox, Mike Andrews, MAndrews, EducationServer, 201-555-6161

Mailbox, Sally Jones, SJones, EducationServer, 201-555-6161
```

The top line in the above example is the header line. It is like the name of the columns in a table. In the example above, the first column name is Obj-Class, which denotes the type of objects in that column, e.g. mailboxes, distribution lists, etc. The remaining headers are self-explanatory. The lines following the header line are the Exchange recipient objects and their properties. In Table 5.1, we placed the export file into a table format.

T A B L E 5.1 An export file in a table	**Obj-Class**	**Display Names**	**Alias name**	**Home Server**	**Telephone-Office1**
	Mailbox	Mike Andrews	MAndrews	EducationServer	201-555-6161
	Mailbox	Sally Jones	SJones	EducationServer	201-555-6161

Before you import this file back into the Exchange Directory, edit the file to reflect the changes you want. First edit the header line to inform the import process how to process the file. This is done by adding the word 'Mode' to the header line; then on each line containing an object (i.e. Mailbox, Mike Andrews, etc.), place the mode that will be used for that line. The options for the Mode field are: create, delete, and modify. The header line for our example would then look like:

```
Obj-Class, Mode, Display Name, Alias Name, Home Server,
Telephone-Office1
```

We would also insert the word 'modify' as a new second field for each object that we want modified. That would look like:

```
Mailbox, modify, Mike Andrews, MAndrews, EducationServer,
201-555-6161
```

The final edit is to use a *search and replace* tool to change the current area code from 201 to the new number, for example, 212. This change, plus our earlier edits, are listed below:

```
Obj-Class, Mode, Display Name, Alias Name, Home Server,
Telephone-Office1
```

```
Mailbox, modify, Mike Andrews, MAndrews, EducationServer,
212-555-6161
```

```
Mailbox, modify, Sally Jones, SJones, EducationServer,
212-555-6161
```

The header line of an import file must include the directory field or alias field, and then each listed object must have a value for that field or fields.

The final step is to use the Directory Import tool to copy our objects and their new properties back into the Exchange Directory.

Summary

Recipients are objects that can receive information. The four main types of recipients are:

- Mailboxes

- Distribution lists

- Custom recipients

- Public folders

A mailbox is a storage location on an Exchange server that allows information to be sent, received, and organized. E-mail messages, forms, and file attachments are some of the typical types of information that can be sent to and stored in a mailbox.

A distribution list is a grouping of recipients. A single distribution list can represent a number of other recipients. This allows easy mass mailing. A message sent to a distribution list can be read by all the members of that distribution list.

A custom recipient is a non-Exchange e-mail address to which Exchange clients can send mail. An Internet user who has a connection to an Exchange server could have an e-mail address defined on the Exchange system. This is an example of a custom recipient and permits Exchange clients to send mail to that Internet user.

A public folder is like a public mailbox. It is an information container that can hold files and forms that multiple users can access.

Review Questions

1. A user named Aaron leaves your company. Management would like a user named Bobbi to assume Aaron's responsibilities. What could you do so that Bobbi can receive Aaron's e-mail messages? (Select the best answer.)

   A. Make Bobbi's mailbox an alternate recipient for Aaron's mailbox.

   B. Disable Aaron's user account and give Bobbi profile permission to access Aaron's mailbox.

   C. Delete Aaron's mailbox and forward all undeliverable messages to Bobbi.

   D. Create a rule in Aaron's mailbox to forward all of Aaron's mail to Bobbi.

2. You want to allow all the personnel in the technical support group to send and receive messages from the same mailbox. What can you do to enable this?

   A. Create a distribution list and designate the mailbox as the owner of the distribution list.

   B. Designate each technical support person as an owner of the mailbox.

   C. Allow each technical support person to send messages on behalf of the mailbox.

   D. Configure each technical support person's account as the primary Windows NT account for the mailbox.

3. The aliases in your organization are formatted as first initial followed by last name. Management would like the format changed to last name followed by first initial. You also want all new aliases to use this new format. What must you do? (Choose all that apply.)

   A. Disable AutoNaming.

   B. Reset One-Off addressing.

   C. Modify all existing aliases.

   D. Modify alias name generation to be %Last%1First.

4. Your company has two domains, Sales and Users. How would you ensure that new Windows NT user accounts that are created when a mailbox is created are placed in the Users domain, rather than the Sales domain?

   A. Use Directory Import to import a list of users from the Users domain.

   B. Add the administrator account in the Users domain to the permissions of the Recipients container.

   C. Create a template mailbox that has an account in the Users domain.

   D. Set the default Windows NT Server domain name to Users in the Microsoft Exchange Administrator program.

5. You have created a distribution list called SalesDL. Whenever someone sends a message to SalesDL that requires a read receipt, the message sender only receives a receipt from the distribution list, not every member of the distribution list. What is the cause of the problem?

   A. The group membership is hidden from the address list.

   B. The distribution list is hidden from the address list.

   C. The distribution list is configured to report to the owner of the distribution list.

   D. The trust level of the distribution list is set higher than the recipients container.

   E. The distribution list is configured to report to the message originator.

6. You have a distribution list with a large number of members. Whenever messages are sent to that distribution list the server experiences high CPU utilization. What could you do to minimize the performance loss on your server?

   A. Remove all unnecessary address spaces from all recipients.

   B. Move all members into their own recipients container.

   C. Specify another server as the expansion server.

   D. Move all recipients to another server.

7. What is one way to transfer mailboxes from one server to another server in the same site?

   A. Designate a new home server for each mailbox.

   B. Back up the Private Information Store on the existing server, and then restore the individual mailboxes on the other server.

   C. Create new mailboxes on the second server that use the same display name as the mailboxes you want to move.

   D. Drag-and-drop the mailboxes on the other server.

8. You need to move 10 mailboxes to another server in the same site. Each mailbox has five unique messages of 1 MB each. Each mailbox also has five single-instance messages of 1 MB each. After you move the mailboxes to the new server, how will the size of the Private Information Store on the new server change?

   A. The Private Information Store will increase by 55 MB.

   B. The Private Information Store will increase by 100 MB.

   C. The size will not increase.

   D. The size will decrease.

9. Two mailboxes have been moved to another server in a different site. After the move, neither user is able to use the Reply feature to successfully reply to messages that were sent by the other user prior to the move. But both users can send messages to other recipients. What is the most likely cause of the problem?

   A. Site affinity is not established between the two sites.

   B. Directory replication is not configured correctly.

   C. The two mailboxes need alternate recipients configured.

   D. The messages that are replied to refer to mailboxes that do not exist.

10. You are using the import utility of Microsoft Exchange Administrator to modify a large number of existing mailboxes. You want to add an area code to the Telephone-Office2 field of each of these mailboxes. The export information of one of these recipients is listed below:

```
Obj-Class,Alias Name,Display Name,Telephone-Office1,
Telephone-Office2

Mailbox,MPeterson,Mary Peterson,801-333-4343,333-5654
```

Which field or fields must you include in your import file in order to add an area code to the Telephone-Office2 field? (Choose all that apply.)

   A. Mode

   B. Obj-Class

   C. Alias name

   D. Display name

   E. Telephone-Office1

   F. Telephone-Office2

11. The following is an example of a mailbox attribute:

   A. Operating system

   B. Groups

   C. Server operating system

   D. Home server

12. Permissions to a mailbox are assigned through:

   A. Roles

   B. UNIX permissions

   C. Custom recipients

   D. DLs

13. The following permits easy mass mailing:

   A. A mailbox with multiple owners

   B. Distribution list

   C. A mailbox with multiple users

   D. A mailbox set to forward messages

14. Within the Exchange environment, a foreign mail user would be this type of Exchange recipient:

   A. Mailbox

   B. A member of the Custom distribution list

   C. Custom recipient

   D. A mailbox with a foreign owner

15. Which of the following does NOT relate to a feature of a public folder?

   A. Views

   B. Rules

   C. Permissions

   D. Expansion Server

16. Copies of the same public folder located on several Exchange servers are called:

   A. Clones

   B. Clone folders

   C. Folder images

   D. Replicas

17. This menu option relates to selectively deleting messages in a mailbox:

 A. Clean Mailbox

 B. Purge Mailbox

 C. Delete Mailbox

 D. Remove Mailbox

18. This feature of a mailbox allows it to store and send messages containing formatting, such as underlining, bolding, and fonts:

 A. Font format

 B. Word format

 C. Rich-text format

 D. Data compression

19. This type of program assists in the creation of mailboxes for NetWare users:

 A. Extract tool

 B. NetWare synchtool

 C. Microsoft-NetWare synchronization tool

 D. Cannot be done

20. The default permission for the primary NT account of a mailbox is:

 A. Admin. role

 B. Send as

 C. Permissions Admin.

 D. User

CHAPTER

6

The Architecture and Installation
of the Microsoft Exchange Clients

nderstanding the architecture and design of a software program will help you better understand the features included in that software and help you choose the correct software to install. In this chapter, you will learn about the architecture and installation of the Microsoft Exchange client programs. Specifically, you will cover:

- Client platforms for Microsoft Exchange

- Additional information on the MAPI architecture

- Microsoft Exchange Client

- Microsoft Schedule+

- Microsoft Outlook

- Installing Microsoft Exchange clients

Client Platforms for Microsoft Exchange

The very first order of business is to define what is meant by *clients* for Microsoft Exchange. The best way to do that is to compare and contrast an Exchange client to an Exchange correspondent (this term is the author's). An Exchange client application has the ability to access an Exchange mailbox as the owner of that mailbox, whereas an Exchange correspondent has only the ability to send and receive mail to and from an Exchange user. If an Exchange mailbox was a physical mailbox at the post office, a client would have the key for accessing their mailbox, while a correspondent would only be able to send mail to that mailbox or receive mail from it. An example of a client application is Microsoft

Outlook, and Lotus cc:Mail is an example of an application that could only correspond with an Exchange mailbox. This latter functionality is enabled through Microsoft Exchange connectors or gateways. Applications that can only correspond with Exchange are also referred to as foreign mail clients. The users of foreign mail applications are defined as custom recipients within Exchange. This allows Exchange users to address mail to the foreign mail users. (Exchange interoperability with foreign systems is covered in Chapters 14 and 15.)

There are two main Exchange client application architectures:

- **MAPI (Messaging Application Programming Interface)** MAPI is the Microsoft API used for messaging functions. Examples of MAPI client applications that ship with Microsoft Exchange Server are:

  - Microsoft Exchange Client for DOS

  - Microsoft Schedule+ 7.5 (this product will be renamed Outlook Calendar)

  - Microsoft Outlook 97 version 8.03 (there are versions of this product for Microsoft Windows 3.x, Windows 95, Windows NT, and Apple Macintosh)

- **Internet protocols** Some Internet applications can also be used as clients to Microsoft Exchange. Examples are:

  - Internet mail applications that support Post Office Protocol 3 (POP3) or Internet Message Access Protocol 4 (IMAP4)

  - Web browsers (e.g., Microsoft Internet Explorer, Netscape Navigator)

The forms design tools, Microsoft Exchange Forms Designer and Microsoft Outlook Forms Designer, are also MAPI clients that ship with Microsoft Exchange Server, but they will be discussed in Chapter 8.

The Internet clients are discussed in Chapter 11. This chapter covers the MAPI client applications. Figure 6.1 illustrates foreign mail users communicating with Exchange, and Figure 6.2 illustrates Exchange clients.

FIGURE 6.1

Foreign mail user
communication with
Exchange

FIGURE 6.1

Foreign mail user
communication with
Exchange

FIGURE 6.2

Exchange clients

FIGURE 6.2

Exchange clients

MAPI Architecture

Many messaging systems are divided into a *client-side* and a *server-side*. The client-side provides an interface to users and permits them to read, save, create, and send mail. The server-side programs carry out the client requests. For example, if a client issues a read request for a certain message, the server responds by transmitting the message to the client. The client software is sometimes referred to as the *front-end* to the server software, which can be referred to as the *back-end*. The front-end programs can be thought of as consumers and the back-end programs as producers.

Historically, messaging systems have been implemented using "closed" application programming interfaces (APIs). An API is a collection of instructions, also called *function calls*. When a user wants to read a message stored on the server, the client program issues the relevant API function call and the server responds accordingly.

The problem with the closed API model is that it is proprietary and each vendor had their own APIs. When someone wrote a client program to be used with one of these proprietary systems, it only worked with that system. With this architecture, multiple client programs were needed to connect to multiple messaging systems (see Figure 6.3).

Microsoft decided to remedy this situation by creating a standard messaging architecture known as MAPI. MAPI provides a way for client messaging applications to communicate with multiple messaging systems (see Figure 6.4). Although MAPI is an abbreviation for Messaging Application Programming Interface, it is much more than an API. It is an architecture that specifies components, how they should act, and how they should interface with each other.

Figure 6.5 illustrates the basic architecture of MAPI. The top layer, the client application layer, includes client applications that enable users to perform messaging activities. These client applications are the front-end programs requesting services from the back-end server programs. Client applications can include different messaging services (such as e-mail, fax, voice mail, and paging), as long as they are written to the MAPI specification. The concept of having messages from multiple sources delivered to one place is referred to as the *universal inbox*.

F I G U R E 6.3

Multiple client programs
for multiple message
systems

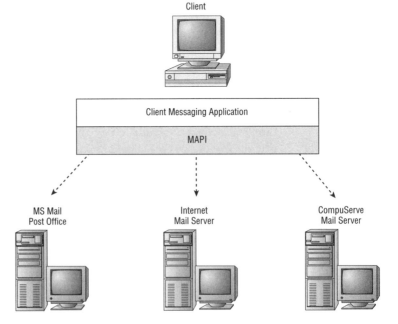

FIGURE 6.5

The Basic MAPI
architecture

Previously, a single client program could not communicate with more than one server program because the server programs all used different APIs. The MAPI architecture solves this limitation by providing a single layer through which the client programs and the server programs can communicate. This is the second layer and is called the MAPI subsystem (see Figure 6.6). The MAPI subsystem is referred to as *middleware* because it acts as a broker between two other layers.

Server programs can still use their own APIs on the back-end. But the vendors of these programs must write a type of client component, called a *service provider*, that will interface their back-end system with the MAPI subsystem. Service providers comprise the third layer in the MAPI architecture (see Figure 6.7). Client software communicates with the MAPI subsystem, which communicates with a service provider, which communicates with the back-end message server. This is how a single client application, using multiple service providers, communicates with multiple back-end message servers.

The next sections will provide additional details on the MAPI architecture.

FIGURE 6.6

The MAPI subsystem

FIGURE 6.7

MAPI service providers

Client Application Layer

Client applications that need to perform messaging functions can have those functions implemented through the usage of MAPI function calls. Examples of these calls are MAPIReadMail, MAPISaveMail, and MAPISendMail. When these instructions are executed in a client application, they initiate an action in the MAPI subsystem, which then interfaces with service providers, which interface with a server messaging system, such as Microsoft Exchange Server or CompuServe Mail.

MAPI encompasses three major API sets:

- **Simple MAPI**   This is a set of 12 straightforward messaging functions, like reading (MAPIReadMail) and sending (MAPISendMail) messages. It is included in *messaging-aware* applications like Microsoft Word.

- **Common Mail Call (CMC)**   This is a set of 10 messaging functions similar to Simple MAPI. CMC is geared for cross-platform, operating system independent development. CMC was developed by the X.400 Applications Programming Interface Association (XAPIA).

- **MAPI 1.x** (also called Extended MAPI)   This is the newer, more powerful MAPI standard. It includes the abilities of Simple MAPI, but adds many other instructions for complex messaging functions, such as custom forms.

See Figure 6.8 for a depiction of these three APIs in the MAPI architecture.

These three API sets allow developers to create client messaging applications that fall into two broad categories:

- **Messaging-aware applications**   These are applications like Microsoft Word that have some messaging functions included, like a send option on the File Menu. Messaging is not essential to these applications. Simple MAPI or CMC is most conveniently used as the messaging API.

- **Messaging-based or messaging-enabled applications**   These are applications like Microsoft Outlook that require messaging functionality. The comprehensive function call set of Extended MAPI is normally required to implement these applications.

FIGURE 6.8

The three MAPI API sets

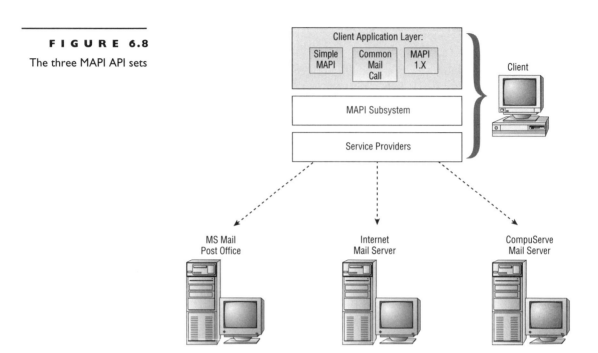

MAPI Subsystem

The second layer of the MAPI architecture is the MAPI subsystem (see Figure 6.9). This component is shared by all applications that require its services and is therefore considered a *subsystem* of the operating system. Microsoft includes the MAPI subsystem with the 32-bit Windows 95 and Windows NT operating systems, and the file MAPI32.DLL is the primary function library for these operating systems. The MAPI subsystem for 16-bit Windows 3.*x* is loaded with the installation of the Exchange client and the file MAPI.DLL is the primary function library.

The MAPI subsystem is also referred to as the *MAPI runtime.*

The MAPI subsystem provides a single interface for client applications. Communication with all MAPI compliant server messaging systems is facilitated by interfacing with the MAPI subsystem. It is the middleware or broker in the messaging environment. The subsystem manages memory, administers profiles, routes client requests to the relevant service provider, and returns results from servers via service providers.

The MAPI subsystem also presents a single, virtual address book and a single, virtual storage area to the user. As you will learn in the next section, multiple service providers can create multiple address books and multiple message stores. The MAPI subsystem presents all of these through a unified interface. Consequently, even though an e-mail program and a fax program are being used, the user can view all addresses in one virtual address book. Because all data can be kept in the same virtual storage area, users can organize information based upon logical categories (e.g., all communication from Jane) rather than by application (e.g., e-mail directory, fax directory, etc.).

MAPI Service Providers

The third layer contains components called service providers. These replaceable components (manifested as DLL files) communicate with the messaging system back-end. There are three main types of service providers:

- Address book providers

- Message store providers

- Message transport providers

The following three sections discuss these service providers.

A *provider* is sometimes called a *driver*.

Address Book Providers

An address book provider is a component that interacts with a database of message recipients. Some of these providers create their own address databases, called personal address books (PAB), others can access address books on a server. Address book providers can be written for many kinds of back-end systems; and because they all interface with the MAPI subsystem, a user can still have a single, virtual address book.

The following are three examples of address book providers:

- **Global Address List (GAL)**   This provider enables a client application to view an Exchange server's Global Address List (GAL). The GAL is a database of all the recipients in an Exchange organization, such as mailboxes, distribution lists, custom recipients, and public folders.

- **Personal Address Book (PAB)**   This provider, also called the Local Address Book, enables the creation of a customized address book. Users can include frequently used e-mail addresses, as well as custom recipients and distribution lists the user creates. Message recipients are not the only type of information that can be stored. Phone and fax numbers, postal addresses, and other information can be stored here. This address book can be stored on the user's machine or on a server. The file extension of this address book is PAB, for Personal Address Book.

- **Offline Address Book (OAB)**   This address book provider permits an Exchange server's GAL to be downloaded to a user's machine. This can be useful when working offline. The file extension of this local database is OAB, for Offline Address Book.

See Figure 6.10 for a depiction of the address book providers in the MAPI architecture.

FIGURE 6.10

Address book providers

Message Store Providers

Message store providers are components that manage a database of messages. This entails client message storage, organization, submission for sending, and retrieval of messages and attachments. Storage is organized in a hierarchical tree of folders. Views can be created to allow the user to see messages based on certain criteria, like subject or date. Searches can also be conducted to retrieve specific information.

Message store providers can use server-based storage or client-based storage. The following are four examples of message store providers (see Figure 6.11):

- **Private folders**   This provider enables client access to an assigned mailbox on an Exchange server (i.e., the home server of the mailbox). *Private folders* is another name for what is more commonly referred to as *mailboxes*. They are called "private" because they are, more often than not, associated with a single user (even though several users can be given permission to use a single mailbox). All private folders are stored on an Exchange server in the Private Information Store which is managed by the Information Store service. The advantages of this type of storage are compression, security, and centralized backup.

- **Public Folders**   Public folders are the groupware component of Exchange Server. This provider allows a client to access the hierarchical tree of public folder storage to which everyone in the Exchange organization has access. Public folders are stored on Exchange servers in the Public Information Store which is managed by the Information Store service.

- **Personal folders (PST, Personal STore)**   A personal folder store is a file-based storage container independent of the Exchange Server back-end. The file that comprises a set of personal folders has the PST extension. A PST file can be stored on the user's local machine or on a shared directory on a network server. As with private folders, a user can create a hierarchical tree of folders within a personal folder store. Up to 16,000 entries and 2GB of data can be placed in a personal folder store. Personal folder stores can be assigned a password for protection. Personal folders can also be designated as the location to where incoming mail messages are moved. Although all mail is always first sent to private folders on an Exchange server, users can configure their private folders to route messages to their personal folders. Because of storage technologies used in the Private Information Store, information moved from that location to a personal folder will take up more space in the personal folder.

Passwords assigned to a personal folder cannot be viewed by the Exchange administrator. Therefore, if a user forgets this password, the information in that folder is inaccessible.

FIGURE 6.11

Message store providers

- **Offline folders (OST, Offline STore)**   If mailbox storage is left in the default location (the Private Information Store) and offline access to that data is also needed, the user can utilize an offline folder. An offline folder is a local copy of the user's private folders from the Private Information Store. The mailbox on the server remains the master copy. Offline folders have the OST file extension.

Message Transport Providers

Message transport providers manage the physical transportation of messages between a MAPI client and a back-end system (see Figure 6.12). They are like gateway components. They take a MAPI message and translate it to the format of the back-end system and send it. They do the reverse for incoming messages. Message transport providers work with any of the Microsoft supported network protocols, such as TCP/IP, IPX/SPX, and NetBEUI.

Examples of back-end systems that have message transport providers are:

- Microsoft Exchange Server

- Microsoft Network online service (MSN)

- Microsoft Fax

- Microsoft Mail

- Internet Mail

- CompuServe Mail

FIGURE 6.12

Message transport
providers

Message Spooler

The message spooler is an independent process that manages the flow of messages between the message store and the transport providers. It is like a queue where incoming and outgoing messages are sent, and from there are routed to the necessary provider. When a message is marked for sending, a message store provider will send it to the message spooler. The message spooler then selects, based on the destination address, a message transport provider that can send the message to the relevant messaging system.

Messaging Profiles

A messaging profile is a collection of configuration parameters for MAPI operations. The first time a user starts a MAPI-based application, the Profile Wizard runs and prompts for various operational parameters relating to messaging. For example, the user is prompted to choose the *information services* to be used, such as Microsoft Exchange Server, Microsoft Fax, Internet Mail, and others. Information services are collections of the various providers described earlier. The user is also prompted to configure his personal address book information service. Other information in the profile relates to message handling, such as saving sent mail or generating a delivery receipt. When the MAPI subsystem starts, it reads this profile to see what services to load and how to operate (see Figure 6.13).

A user can have several profiles for one particular machine. For example, a user's computer might be a laptop that is used both at the office and on the road. When at the office, the user profile connects the user to an Exchange server at the office. When traveling, a different profile connects the laptop to the Internet. (As you will learn in Chapter 10, you can also connect to an Exchange server through the Internet.) Multiple profiles for a particular machine are also useful when several people use the same machine.

Common Features of MAPI-Based Applications

Many common features are found in MAPI-based applications, including the following:

- **Universal inbox**   Information from multiple sources (e.g., Exchange Server, Internet, etc.) and of varying types (e.g., e-mail, faxes, documents, and voice mail) is delivered to a single Inbox folder.

FIGURE 6.13

Messaging profile

 Reads:

Messaging Profile:
Address Book Provider = GAL
Message Store Provider = Private folders
Message Transport Provider = Microsoft Exchange Server
Home Server = ScienceServer
Mailbox name = Bill Nye
Save Sent Mail = Yes
Generate delivery receipt = Yes
(others)

- **Single address book** A standard user interface to the address book is provided. Information from all the address books configured in the current profile is consolidated into one place.

- **Hierarchical storage** Messages and other items can be organized into a user-customizable hierarchical tree of folders. Four special folders are always present in the default store. They are the Inbox, Deleted Items, Sent Items, and Outbox folders.

- **Custom views** Information stored in folders can be sorted and viewed using many types of criteria, such as author, date, keyword, or type of content.

- **Rich-text formatting** Users can create message content that uses the rich-text format, which includes underlining, italic, bolding, bullet points, colors, fonts, different character sizes, and letter strikethrough.

Microsoft Exchange Client

T he Microsoft Exchange Client for DOS is a feature-rich e-mail program designed to run in the 16-bit environment of MS-DOS. As with all client applications that access Microsoft BackOffice server products, a Client Access License (CAL) must be purchased for each client to legally access a server.

Table 6.1 lists some features that Microsoft Exchange Client has in addition to the common MAPI-based features listed earlier.

	Feature	Description
TABLE 6.1 Additional features of Microsoft Exchange Client	Public folders	Public folders are the groupware component of Exchange Server. They allow all users in the Exchange organization to share information.
	Inbox Assistant	When running against an Exchange server back-end, software agents, also called *rules,* can be applied to a mailbox to automatically process messages. Actions that can be taken include automatically placing incoming messages in certain folders, automatically forwarding certain messages to specified users, or automatically generating a reply to a message.
	Search tool	Users can search and retrieve messages in their mailboxes using a variety of search criteria, such as sender, date, and subject.
	Microsoft Word as message editor	Even though the Exchange Client includes a rich-message editor, it can be configured to use Microsoft Word as the message editor instead.
	Compound messages and drag-and-drop editing	The Exchange Client is OLE 2.0 (Object Linking and Embedding) compliant, and therefore allows the creation of compound documents. For example, a user can drag-and-drop a group of cells from a spreadsheet into an e-mail message.
	Secure messages	Exchange Server can provide advanced security through the use of digital signatures and message encryption. These features can be invoked using the Exchange client (more on this in Chapter 10).

T A B L E 6.1 (cont.) Additional features of Microsoft Exchange Client	**Feature**	**Description**
	Remote mail	Because more and more workers spend some of their work time outside of the office, special features relating to remote access have been incorporated. These features allow the remote mail user to more efficiently use online time. For example, a remote user can access a mailbox and selectively download incoming mail to a remote computer. Outgoing mail created at a remote computer can be held and then sent out at one time.
	Delegate access	Some users need to allow other users to access their mailboxes. For example, a manager might want a secretary to read meeting request messages in order to handle the manager's schedule. In many mail systems, this would be accomplished by having the secretary log on as the manager, creating an obvious security hole. The Exchange Client solves this problem by allowing the manager to grant the secretary permission to access the manager's mailbox. This permission can even be applied on a folder-by-folder basis. The secretary can also be granted permission to send messages on behalf of the manager, or even send messages addressed from the manager with no indication that the secretary was involved.
	Send/Receive electronic forms	Users can send and receive electronic forms through the Microsoft Exchange Client application.

A program referred to as "Microsoft Exchange," "Inbox," or "Windows Messaging" is included with Windows 95. Although their names are the same, the program included with Windows 95 and the one included with Microsoft Exchange Server are not the same. The one that comes with Windows 95 cannot be used as a client to Exchange Server, but can be upgraded to the program included with Exchange Server as long as a CAL is purchased.

Due to operating system constraints, the Microsoft Exchange Client for MS-DOS has fewer features and a different interface than the Windows-based clients. The following are the major differences:

- Forms are not supported

- Microsoft Mail messages (MMF files) and personal address books (PAB files) cannot be imported

- Remote features, such as downloading headers only, are not available

- Only one AutoSignature entry is permitted

Microsoft Schedule+

Microsoft Schedule+ version 7.5 is a MAPI program that includes scheduling, contact, and task management functions. All of these functions apply to both individual and group use. Schedule+ 7.5 is included with Exchange Server and can be used as a client to Exchange Server. It is designed to work with the Exchange Client, and is available for 16-bit and 32-bit environments.

As mentioned earlier, Microsoft Schedule+ 7.5 is being renamed Outlook Calendar.

Architectural Design

Four of the major design elements of Microsoft Schedule+ 7.5 are:

- **Integration with Microsoft Exchange Server**   Many of the features of Schedule+ (such as meeting requests and notifications) utilize the messaging functions of Microsoft Exchange Server.

- **Contact list**   Schedule+ includes a type of electronic Rolodex of contacts; including names, addresses, phone and fax numbers, and other types of information.

- **Time management functions**   Users can manage their schedules, events, tasks, and projects. This applies to groups as well as individuals.

- **User permissions**   Because it can function as a groupware application, Schedule+ enables permissions to be assigned to information to control who can access it, and what they can do to the information. For example, you could create a Schedule+ account for a conference room, to view and reserve its use. Most employees will only need to view that schedule, so you grant them the Read permission for the conference room schedule. The managers group, however, will need permissions to Read and Create items in that schedule. Finally, someone will need to manage the conference room schedule. So you give a user named Mary the **Delegate Owner** permission, which grants the ability to read, create, and modify the schedule. This permission also enables Mary to view scheduled items marked private. With this permission, Mary also receives a copy of all meeting requests sent to this schedule.

These major design elements are implemented through the Schedule+ user interface which includes four main tools (see Figure 6.14 for an illustration of the Schedule+ main screen). You will learn more about these tools in the following discussion.

FIGURE 6.14

The Schedule+ main screen

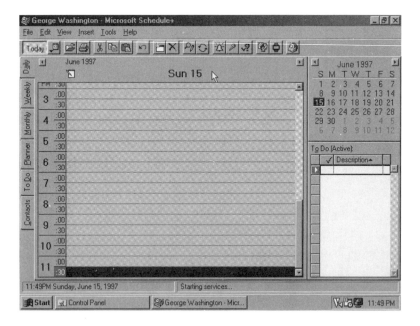

Tabs

The Schedule+ Tabs are found on the left side of the main screen. They are the main navigation feature of Schedule+ because they enable switching between different views of information. Table 6.2 describes the six default tabs.

T A B L E 6.2 The six default tabs of Schedule+	Tab	Description
	Daily	Displays the Daily Calendar in a format similar to most paper-based day schedulers.
	Weekly	Displays a Weekly Calendar with any scheduled events.
	Monthly	Displays a Monthly Calendar with any scheduled events.
	Planner	Displays a calendar (number of days depends on screen size) for the purpose of scheduling meetings. Current meetings are shown with lists of attendees.
	To Do	Displays the To Do List functions that allow a user to enter, organize, and display tasks.
	Contacts	Displays the Contacts List, which is like a paper-based cardfile, but allows much more information.

Daily Calendar

The current day's calendar is displayed in this view, although any day of the year can be displayed. The calendar shows any appointments, meetings, or events scheduled for the day. Users can navigate backward or forward a day by clicking on the Previous or Next buttons at the top of the daily calendar.

Date Navigator

The Date Navigator appears in the top-right of the main screen, and enables users to select any day of the month to view its daily schedule. A different month can be selected by clicking the Previous and Next buttons on the top of the calendar.

To Do List

The To Do List enables the creation, organization, and display of tasks or projects. The display will show what is scheduled for the day chosen in the Daily Calendar and all incomplete tasks that aren't scheduled for any particular day.

Microsoft Schedule+ Features

Table 6.3 summarizes information on the main features of Schedule+.

TABLE 6.3	Features	Description
Features of Microsoft Schedule+	Creating appointments	Users can schedule an activity for a specific time. This can be done while in any of the calendar views by choosing the Insert menu, Appointment option. Appointments can be designated private, tentative, or recurring: • Private means details of the appointment are hidden to all users except those with special access permission. Other users can still see that the time is blocked. • Tentative means the appointment does not show up as a busy time slot. • Recurring appointments occur at regular time intervals, such as 9 AM every Tuesday. Alarms can be set to remind the user of an appointment.
	Inviting attendees	When scheduling a meeting, you can invite other attendees. Schedule+ sends an Exchange message to the people specified and they can either accept, accept tentatively, or reject the meeting.
	Viewing other people's free/busy times and schedule details	By default, users can view free and busy times of all other users, but they are prevented from viewing the details of other people's schedules. Permissions can be set to allow different degrees of access to details of user schedules.

TABLE 6.3 (cont.) Features of Microsoft Schedule+	Features	Description
	Task management	A task is a specific activity that needs to be tracked but does not have to be assigned to a specific time slot. Tasks are displayed in the To Do List. Tasks can be created with a priority setting, the date to be completed, the number of days to completion, and even the percentage of the task completed. Tasks can be made private or public.
	Project management	Tasks are grouped together into projects. This allows for easier viewing and management. Projects can be made private or public.
	Alarms	Alarms are reminders that can be set for appointments, events, or tasks. The alarm is in the form of a pop-up message and optionally plays a sound.

There is no Schedule+ for MS-DOS.

Microsoft Outlook

Microsoft Outlook fits into several application categories. It is a personal information manager (PIM) because it functions as a personal calendar, scheduler, contact management, and task management. It is also a messaging application because it includes a powerful e-mail program and forms program. And finally, it is a groupware application because it can access Exchange Server public folders and enables calendars, schedules, contact information, and task information all to be used in a group context. All of this functionality exists through a single, integrated, desktop environment. Microsoft Outlook is the combination of the functions of Microsoft Exchange Client and Schedule+, along with many new and powerful features.

Microsoft Outlook is included with Microsoft Exchange Server as one of its client applications. It is also part of the Microsoft Office 97 suite of applications, and as such is tightly integrated with the other Office 97 applications. Outlook can also be purchased as a stand-alone product. Outlook is fully MAPI compliant. Microsoft Outlook comes with versions for Microsoft Windows 3.*x*, Windows 95, Windows NT, and Apple Macintosh.

Even though Microsoft Outlook is shipped with Microsoft Exchange Server, it requires a Microsoft Exchange Client Access License (CAL) to legally access an Exchange server. This is the same requirement for all client applications that access Exchange Server.

Architectural Design

Microsoft Outlook is designed to be a desktop information manager. This means it integrates personal and groupware tools, as well as their information, in a unified manner. This goal was achieved by including the following design features:

- **Single application, multiple functionality**   From a single interface, users can execute numerous programs like e-mail, calendar, contact list, and task list.

- **Integrated user interface**   All the tools in Outlook are seamlessly integrated. For example, Outlook includes a feature called the *Outlook Bar*. This is a navigation tool that creates shortcuts to a user's e-mail inbox, calendar, contacts, tasks, and folders. Outlook, as a MAPI program, provides a single address book that can be used for e-mail, phone dialing, faxing, and other functions. The Outlook interface permits users to access both local file folders and Exchange public folders.

- **Custom forms using Office 97**   Outlook is tightly integrated with Microsoft Office 97. One example of this is Outlook's ability to create and send forms that include objects created in any of the Office 97 applications. For instance, an expense report form that includes an Excel spreadsheet can be created. Because of Microsoft object technology (see note), the spreadsheet contained in the form will not be merely rows and columns, but will include the Excel code to execute the functions of the spreadsheet. The form's users can input their numbers, have the spreadsheet calculate them, and then have the form automatically sent to a designated person. Outlook, along with Microsoft Office 97, enables the creation of instant groupware applications.

ActiveX is an object technology developed by Microsoft. It is an extension of the earlier OLE technology. ActiveX allows programs to exchange objects that include both presentation data (i.e., what you see on the screen) and native data (i.e., the executable code to manipulate the presentation data).

Features of Microsoft Outlook

Microsoft Outlook includes some very powerful messaging, groupware, and personal productivity features. Tables 6.4, 6.5, and 6.6 describe many of the those features.

TABLE 6.4 Messaging features of Microsoft Outlook	**Main Function**	**Features**
	E-mail	**AutoNameCheck** Outlook will check the name typed in message headers against the address book as soon as the user tabs out of the entry fields.
		Message recall A user may recall a sent message, assuming the recipient has not already opened it.
		Voting Users can create messages that include voting buttons in the message when received. Recipients can click one of the button choices and submit their choice back to the sender. The sender can automatically track responses to a question or issue.
		Message tracking All the information about delivery, receipt, recall, and voting notifications is tabulated on the original message in the sender's mailbox.
		AutoPreview The first few lines of each message can be displayed without requiring the user to open the message in a separate window. This allows users to quickly view the contents of messages.
		MessageFlags Users can place *flags* (i.e., notices) on messages to aid in sorting and prioritizing messages. Flags include reply, read, "for your information," or any custom text.

TABLE 6.4 (cont.) Messaging features of Microsoft Outlook	Main Function	Features
	E-mail	**Hyperlinks to URLs** If a message includes a Web URL address (Uniform Resource Locator), Outlook will recognize that address. If the user clicks on the address, Outlook will start the user's Web browser and connect to that location. **Retrieve deleted items** Users can retrieve deleted items from their mailboxes through the Recover Deleted Items command in Microsoft Outlook 8.03. Recovered mailbox items are placed in the Deleted Items folder. This functionality is made possible by the Exchange Information Store and is configured through the Private Information Store and individual mailboxes.

TABLE 6.5 Groupware features of Microsoft Outlook	Main Function	Features
	Group scheduling	**Browsing free/busy information** Users can browse other users' free/busy schedule information. **Meeting request processing** If a user sends another user a meeting request, that request is automatically copied from the inbox to the Calendar as a tentative meeting. **Delegate access** Users can grant other users the right to read and modify their schedules.
	Group calendars, contact lists, and task lists	**Public folder use** Calendars, contact lists, and task lists can all be published to public folders to allow group access to that information.
	Group task management	**Task tracking** Users can send tasks to other users and the status of those tasks can be automatically tracked. **Status reports** An automatic status report on a task containing details such as whether the task has been started, the percentage complete, the hours spent working on the task, and the task owner's name can be sent as a mail message.
	Forms and Office 97 objects	**Inclusion of Office 97 objects** Microsoft Office 97 applications can be used to create both presentation material and executable material for Outlook forms. For instance, Microsoft Word can compose the text of a form, and Microsoft Excel can add a spreadsheet to a form.

T A B L E 6.6	**Main Function**	**Features**
PIM features of Microsoft Outlook	Functional integration within Outlook	**Outlook Bar** This navigation tool permits the creation of shortcuts to a user's e-mail inbox, calendar, contacts, tasks, and folders. **AutoCreate** Outlook can automatically convert one Outlook item into another. For example, if an e-mail message represents a task a user needs to complete, the user can drag-and-drop the e-mail message into the Task folder and Outlook will automatically convert it to a task.
	Document browsing and retrieval	**Outlook Journal** This feature maintains a log of users' actions, what they did and when they did it. Users can then search for items based on when they were created, not just on what they are named or where they were saved. **Outlook Views** Outlook comes with dozens of standard views of information, and users can create their own customized views.
	Calendar/Schedule features	**AutoDate** Outlook understands natural language input for dates, and can convert loosely worded dates into discrete calendar dates. For example, if a user types "the third Wednesday of October," Outlook will automatically convert that to " Wednesday 10/15/97 5:00 PM."
	Contact Manager features	**Single address book** The lists of contacts in Contact Manager can be used to address e-mail or a fax, and even jump to a Web site or dial a phone.
	Functions for portable computer users	**Local replication** Information users input into Outlook while on the road with the portable computer can later be easily replicated back to their Exchange server. **Time switching** Outlook can change the system time and time zone as mobile users move from one location to another.
	Microsoft Office 97 integration	**Office 97 interface** Outlook shares many user interface elements with the other Office 97 applications, such as command bars, menus, shortcut menus, tabbed dialog boxes, and toolbars.

T A B L E 6.6 (cont.) PIM features of Microsoft Outlook	**Main Function**	**Features**
	Microsoft Office 97 integration	**Single address book** The other Office 97 applications can use the Outlook Contact Manager address book. **Attachments** Users can attach any Office 97 document to any Outlook item, such as an e-mail, contact, or task. **Mail merge** Users can perform a mail merge between the Outlook Contact Manager and Microsoft Word. **Word 97 and e-mail** Word can be used as the text editor for creating e-mail content. **Drag-and-drop** Users can drag-and-drop information between Office 97 applications and Outlook modules. **Outlook Journal** Office files can be located using Outlook Journal. **Office 97 objects and forms** As stated earlier, objects created in Office 97 applications can be included in Outlook forms.
	Importing and exporting data	**Import and export of data** Microsoft Outlook can import and export data from and to all Microsoft calendar and mail products, as well as many third-party PIM and messaging products.
	Visual Basic for Applications (VBA)	**VBA integration** Outlook includes Microsoft object technology and therefore can be used with Microsoft's Visual Basic for Applications to create compound applications.

Microsoft* ✓ *Exam Objective

Choose Microsoft Exchange Client installation and integration strategies. Elements include:

- Network installation
- Client computer installation
- Scripted client installation
- Forms interoperability
- Schedule+ interoperability
- Calendar interoperability

Interoperability and Upgrading

Microsoft Outlook can interoperate with the other Exchange MAPI-clients such as Microsoft Exchange Client and Schedule+. There are some compatibility issues relating to the use of electronic forms. These issues will be addressed in Chapter 8. Exchange Client and Schedule+ can also be upgraded to Microsoft Outlook.

Installing Microsoft Exchange Clients

In this section, you will review the information necessary to install the Microsoft Exchange client programs. You can work through a hands-on exercise detailing the steps to install Microsoft Outlook. Our main topics of discussion will be:

- Installation requirements

- Two main installation options

- Customizing the client installation

- Troubleshooting a client installation

Microsoft ✓ *Exam* *Objective* | **Install and configure Exchange Server client computers.**

Installation Requirements

The hardware requirements for the different Exchange client programs vary depending on the operating system platform. Table 6.7 lists the hardware requirements for each scenario. The numbers in the table are minimum requirements, not recommendations. The requirements for optimal performance will vary depending on the deployment scenario. Also, the numbers in the table for free disk space are only for the storage of the program files. They do not relate to any local storage needed for data files (e.g., stored messages, large address book, etc.). The chart references minimum and maximum disk space. The difference will depend on the optional modules you load during installation (e.g., how many information services you choose). Microsoft Schedule+ is included in the requirements for the Exchange Client.

	Client Software	Operating System	RAM Required	Disk Space (minimum/ maximum)
T A B L E 6.7 Hardware requirements for the Microsoft Exchange clients	Microsoft Exchange Client	MS-DOS	1MB	2MB/3MB
	Microsoft Outlook	Windows 3.x	8MB	12/24MB
	Microsoft Outlook	Microsoft Windows 95 or NT	8MB Windows 95 16MB NT	26MB/46MB
	Microsoft Outlook	Apple Macintosh	8MB	14MB

All of the table's scenarios, with the exception of the Macintosh client, require the client to have a connection to the Exchange server that will support RPC communication. That means the network connection needs to be at LAN speeds, or a permanent WAN connection of at least 128Kbps (a much higher speed would be recommended). It also means that the client machine needs to use a network protocol that is also being used on the Exchange server. Options are TCP/IP, IPX/SPX, or NetBEUI. Macintosh clients are the exception. These clients use the AppleTalk File Protocol (AFP), and require the Windows NT Services for Macintosh to be run on the Exchange server.

Two Main Installation Options

The installation of the Exchange clients is very similar across the Windows platforms. They all start by executing SETUP.EXE and following the on-screen instructions. If you are installing the client for Microsoft Windows 3.x, you would run setup from the OUTLOOK.W16 directory, while those using Windows 95 or Windows NT would run setup from the OUTLOOK.W32 directory.

There are two main installation options relating to where the client files will be installed, whether all on the local machine, or most of them on a network share point. Those two options are referred to as:

- Local installation
- Shared installation

Local Installation

In a local installation, the client program files are installed on the client's local workstation. This option can be used on all client platforms, assuming the required amount of disk space is available. There are three types of local installations:

- **Typical**   This option installs the components required by the typical user. It is available for Microsoft Exchange Client, Schedule+, and Outlook.

- **Custom**   This option allows the installer to choose the components to install. This option is also available for Microsoft Exchange Client, Schedule+, and Outlook.

- **Laptop**   This option installs only the minimum components necessary. It is only available for Microsoft Exchange Client and Schedule+.

Exercise 6.1 will walk you through a local installation of Microsoft Outlook. The exercise assumes that the computer being used for the installation is running Microsoft Windows 95 or Windows NT, and has a CD drive.

EXERCISE 6.1

A Local Installation of Outlook

1. Log on as administrator to a machine on which you want to install Outlook.

2. Once logged on, click the Start button, and then click Run.

3. In the Open box, type:
   <drive letter of CD disc>:OUTLOOK.W32\SETUP.

   A Microsoft Outlook 97 Setup dialog box will appear.

4. Click Continue.

   The Name and Organization Information dialog box will appear.

5. In the Name box, type **<your name>**.

6. In the Organization box, type **<your organization name>**, and then click OK.

---

7. Click OK to confirm the registration information.

   A dialog box will appear and ask for the CD Key number.

8. Enter the CD Key number that came with your Outlook product, then click OK.

   A dialog box will appear, confirming your CD Key number.

9. Click OK.

   A dialog box will appear, showing the default directory path for the installation of the Outlook files.

10. Click OK.

    A dialog box will appear, displaying installation options.

11. Click Custom.

    The Custom dialog box will appear.

12. Click Continue to accept the default selections.

    Files will now be copied to your local hard drive.

    A message box will appear, indicating that Setup completed successfully.

13. Click OK.

14. The next steps are to run Outlook and configure a profile. We will cover these topics in Chapter 7.

A Network Installation   A local installation does not preclude the source files for the setup from residing on a network drive. An administrator could copy the setup files to a network share point. Users would then connect to that share point from their client computers and execute the SETUP.EXE program. This way, the Exchange client application would still be installed on the user's local computer. This type of installation is called an *over-the-network installation* or a *network installation*. The primary steps for this method are discussed next.

From a network server, an administrator would insert the Outlook CD and navigate to the appropriate language directory (e.g., ENG). The file that will initiate the network installation is UCSETUP.EXE. That file will start a wizard that will present the administrator with various straightforward questions. One of the questions regards which setup you would like to perform, either Complete or Custom. The Complete option will install all the versions of Outlook (MS-DOS, Windows 3.*x*, Windows 95, Windows NT), while the Custom allows the administrator to choose the versions. Another important question relates to the server directory where the setup files will be placed. That directory will later be referred to as the installation point, or client installation point. The wizard will automatically copy the setup files to this point and will share the directory. The default name of the parent directory of the installation point is \CLIENT. The DOS client files would be placed in \CLIENT\ EXCHANGE.DOS. The Windows 3.*x* files would be placed in \CLIENT\ OUTLOOK.W16. The Windows 95 or Windows NT files would be placed in \CLIENT\OUTLOOK.W32.

After an administrator has completed setting up the installation point, they would inform their users of that share point. Users could connect to that location, navigate to the appropriate subdirectory, and execute SETUP.EXE. They would get the source files for the installation from the share point, but the client application would still be installed on the user's local computer.

Shared Installation

A shared installation installs most of the client files on a network shared directory, and some of the files on the user's computer. After the installation, whenever the user executes the Exchange client application, it is loaded from the shared directory, but it runs on the user's computer. This option requires the least amount of disk space on the client computer. To perform a shared installation, the installer must first create a network share point. The procedure is slightly different depending on the operating system of the client computer. We will discuss creating a shared installation for MS-DOS clients and Windows-based clients next.

MS-DOS Clients On the machine that will hold the shared installation, the installer executes the SETUP program for the MS-DOS version of the client program and then chooses the Shared option. The installer will be prompted for the directory path where the shared files are to be copied. This location is called the Install Point For Shared Mail. The SETUP program will then copy all the necessary files for a shared installation to this location.

Windows-Based Clients   On the machine that will hold the shared installation, the installer executes the SETUP /A command. The /A switch tells the SETUP program to perform a shared installation.

This scenario is complicated slightly if the client computers are using a shared copy of their operating system. If this is the case, the installer must also be running that same shared copy of the operating system WHEN the shared installation of the Exchange client software is performed. If there are multiple locations of the shared operating system, the Exchange client installer must do a shared installation of the Exchange client software at every one of those locations. These steps ensure that all of the necessary Exchange client files are copied to the shared operating system locations.

The Microsoft Exchange clients for Macintosh do not support a shared installation.

Performing the Shared Installation   Once the shared installation point has been created, the installation on the client computer is the same as a local installation, with a few exceptions. The installer will be presented with an installation choice called "Workstation." This option should be chosen. A dialog box asking for the location of the shared Microsoft applications, like the spell checker, may also appear.

Postinstallation Issues

The installation of an Exchange client program makes changes to the client computer configuration. These changes depend on the client operating system in use. This information is summarized in Table 6.8.

TABLE 6.8 Client configuration changes from the Exchange installation	Operating System	Configuration Changes
	Microsoft Windows 3.x	The WIN.INI file is modified to include a section called Mail that contains the path and file names of the OLE and MAPI settings. The installation program also creates an EXCHNG.INI file in the Windows directory. This file contains the settings used by some of the client processes, such as the RPC binding order.

TABLE 6.8 (cont.) Client configuration changes from the Exchange installation	**Operating System**	**Configuration Changes**
	Apple Macintosh	The setup program creates an Exchange folder that contains the following items: • **Exchange Settings** Used to manage profiles. • **Inbox Repair Tools** These tools can scan and perform diagnostics on a user's personal storage. • **Microsoft Exchange and Schedule+** Includes the e-mail and scheduling programs. The setup program also creates a folder, called Exchange Temp Items, that contains temporary data the client program might access during a session. The setup program also writes configuration information to the Preferences folder.
	Microsoft Windows 95 and NT	All configuration information is written to the Registry.

Customizing the Client Installation

As you saw earlier, the installation of the Exchange clients can be done by placing the setup files on a shared directory on a server and allowing clients to connect to that directory and execute SETUP.EXE. That method was called an over-the-network installation, or a network installation. Another step that an administrator could take is to predetermine and customize the setup options and messaging profiles that will be used in the client installations. Rather than having the individual users wrestle with various setup options, an administrator can predetermine those options, making the setup easier for the user and creating a standard installation. This type of installation scenario is called a *scripted installation*.

The process for customizing a network installation is different for the 16-bit and 32-bit Outlook versions. Both will be discussed below under their respective headings.

Customizing the Network Installation of Outlook Windows 3.x Client

Whenever you run the setup program for the Windows 3.*x* version of Microsoft Outlook, it looks for two script files containing installation and profile instructions. The two script files are:

- EXCHNG.STF

- DEFAULT.PRF

EXCHNG.STF (SeTup File) contains the installation options for the SETUP.EXE program. These options relate to the client installation directory, such as C:\Exchange, the services that will be installed, such as the Microsoft Exchange Server service, and the network protocols that will be used, such as TCP/IP or IPX. Microsoft has pre-set default options in EXCHNG.STF that can be used. But an administrator can modify those settings by editing the EXCHNG.STF file through a text editor, or by executing a program called *Setup Editor*. Setup Editor is a Windows-based application that enables an administrator to set the options in the EXCHNG.STF file. An administrator who is having their users use the over-the-network installation method could first run Setup Editor to set the installation options that SETUP.EXE would use. Users would then connect to the network directory to execute SETUP.EXE, which would read EXCHNG.STF for its instructions. This scenario would allow the administrator to determine a standard installation of the Outlook client.

DEFAULT.PRF (PRoFile descriptor file) contains the default profile information. This file is created when an administrator runs the Setup Editor program and modifies the configuration of the 'user options.' In this file, the administrator can set many user options, including the name of the home server, whether receipts will be used with outgoing mail, how the spell checker will work, and many other parameters. An administrator can therefore customize a default messaging profile for users. That profile would then be used whenever a user connects to the network directory containing the installation files (also called the client installation point, or the installation share point) and executes SETUP.EXE. The setup program would see the DEFAULT.PRF file, and would then start the *Automatic Profile Generator* (NEWPROF.EXE). That program uses the information in the DEFAULT.PRF file to create a messaging profile for that user. The scenario just described requires the DEFAULT.PRF file to be in the installation share point.

Because of the potential importance of the Setup Editor in your environment, the three main menu options of this program are described below. Setup Editor (STFEDTR.EXE) is found on the Microsoft Exchange client CD, and it could have also been installed into the Microsoft Exchange program group on the server.

Many of these topics, such as messaging profiles, PRF files, and the Automatic Profile Generator, will also be discussed in Chapter 7.

Setup Editor has three main steps:

1. **Select a client installation point**   This is the network directory containing the client installation files, two of which are the script files (DEFAULT.PRF is actually created during the execution of the Setup Editor). Because the Setup Editor will be writing changes to the two script files, the client installation point cannot be a CD-ROM or a directory where the administrator does not have write permission. The client installation files should be copied to a network share point where the script files can be modified and where users can connect to and run the SETUP.EXE program. Users will need to have at least Read permission at this directory.

2. **Modify Setup program options**   These options control how the setup program will function. The options the administrator chooses will be stored in EXCHNG.STF. When a user runs SETUP.EXE from this client installation point, SETUP.EXE will operate based upon the settings in EXCHNG.STF, also located at this client installation point.

3. **Set user options**   These options are written to the DEFAULT.PRF and will be used when each user's message profile is created at installation.

The following scenario illustrates the use of a network installation and the use of customizing the setup script files. A network has hundreds of users. You have just installed Microsoft Exchange Server on five servers. You have also created an installation point on one of those servers. You would like clients to connect to this one server and perform over-the-network installations. But you would also like the clients to have the option during their installations to select any of the five Exchange servers as their home server. How would you do that? You would have to create five different shares, each containing a DEFAULT.PRF that pointed to one of the five home servers. Users would then connect to the share for the home server they need and proceed with the over-the-network and scripted installation.

Customizing the Network Installation of the Outlook 32-Bit Clients

Customizing a network installation for the 32-bit Outlook clients is fairly different than it is for the 16-bit clients. The 32-bit clients have no equivalent to the Setup Editor, yet the principles are the same. The administrator has to customize the script files that clients will use from the installation point. That includes a script file for the setup options and a script file for the messaging profile options. The Outlook 32-bit clients use the file OUTLOOK.STF for their setup options, and the file OUTLOOK.PRF for the message profile options.

An administrator can customize OUTLOOK.STF through the Network Installation Wizard (NIW). This wizard does not ship with Exchange but is available with the Microsoft Office 97 Resource Kit and from the Microsoft Web site. OUTLOOK.STF, like EXCHNG.STF, allows the customizing of such things as the client installation directory, the components that will be installed (e.g., Microsoft Exchange Server, Microsoft Mail, etc.), the services that will be installed (e.g., Personal Address Book, Personal Folders, etc.), and the network protocols and their binding order.

The OUTLOOK.PRF file, which contains the default profile information, can only be modified the old-fashioned manual way: with a text editor. An administrator opens this file with a text editor like Microsoft NotePad and makes the necessary changes. OUTLOOK.PRF, like DEFAULT.PRF, allows the customization of such things as reading mail, sending mail, the spell checker, and many other user options.

When a Windows 95 or Windows NT client connects to the appropriate installation point and executes SETUP.EXE, the setup program will read both of the above files for its instructions. As a way of review, the following paragraphs present a couple scenarios of a scripted installation.

You have just installed Microsoft Exchange Server. You now need to install Microsoft Outlook on a large number of clients. While those clients use both IPX and TCP/IP, you are informed that they are to use only IPX when connecting to the Exchange server. You decide to use the network installation method (i.e., over-the-network) for the client installation. But what file would you have to modify to predefine that all 32-bit Outlook clients use only IPX to connect to their Exchange server? The answer is: OUTLOOK.STF. Network protocols and their binding order are set in an STF file. User options, such as how spell checker will operate, are set in a PRF file.

This next scenario relates to how you would get the Personal Address Book (PAB) service installed during a scripted installation. You have a standard PAB contained in the file MAILBOX.PAB and located at the network share point of G:\APPS\EXCHANGE. You also have a drive letter mapped to G: in your network login script that is used by all users. The Exchange Server service and PAB service are included in the OUTLOOK.PRF at the installation point. The final step in getting the PAB service installed during the scripted installation is to log on as the user before you install Microsoft Outlook.

The Setup Editor is not applicable to the Microsoft Exchange Client for DOS or Microsoft Outlook for Windows 95 or Windows NT.

Troubleshooting a Client Installation

If you encounter problems with a client installation, check the following items first:

- Have the user and server names been entered correctly?

- Is the Directory Service running on the user's intended home server?

- If Windows for Workgroups is installed on the client, is the necessary patch installed as directed by Microsoft Exchange Server Installation Guide?

Other items to verify include the network connection to the server, and the hardware and software requirements for the client software.

Summary

Microsoft Exchange client applications are programs that can access Exchange mailboxes and public folders. These client applications include MAPI-based programs, such as Microsoft Exchange Client for DOS, Schedule+, and Outlook. Some Internet applications can be clients to Microsoft Exchange Server. These include Internet mail applications that support Post Office Protocol 3 (POP3), and Web browsers like Microsoft Internet Explorer.

The MAPI architecture provides a standard architecture for client-server messaging. It includes three architectural layers, the client application layer, the MAPI subsystem layer, and the service provider layer. There are three main types of service providers: address book providers, message store providers, and message transport providers.

The Exchange MAPI client applications share many features, such as a universal inbox, single address book, hierarchical storage, custom views, and rich-text message formatting.

Microsoft Outlook is a client program that can be used with Microsoft Exchange Server. It is tightly integrated with Microsoft Office 97 and includes many very powerful personal, group, and messaging features.

Installing the Microsoft Exchange client applications is a relatively straightforward procedure. For most of the client applications, the installer has the option to perform a local or shared installation.

Review Questions

1. You have created a Microsoft Exchange client network installation point on one of your servers. You want to predetermine the client settings in order to create a standard installation. What do you need to do to predefine the user settings of the Exchange client?

   A. Edit DEFAULT.PRF and copy this file to the installation share point.

   B. Edit DEFAULT.PRF and copy this file to each user's home directory.

   C. Edit TEMPLATE.PRF and copy this file to the installation share point.

   D. Edit TEMPLATE.PRF and copy this file to each user's home directory.

2. Clients on your network use both IPX and TCP/IP. But for your Microsoft Outlook installation for 32-bit clients, you want them to only use IPX. What file would you have to modify?

A. OUTLOOK.PRF

B. DEFAULT.PRF

C. EXCHNG.STF

D. OUTLOOK.STF

3. You have a standard PAB contained in the file MAILBOX.PAB and located at the network share point of G:\APPS\EXCHANGE. You also have a drive letter mapped to G: in your network login script that is used by all users. The Exchange Server service and PAB service are included in the OUTLOOK.STF at the installation point. There is also a DEFAULT.PRF file at the installation point. What is the final step in getting the PAB service installed during a scripted installation?

A. Log on as user before you install MS Outlook

B. Log on as administrator before you install MS Outlook

C. Place an empty mailbox.pab in every user's G:\EXCHANGE folder

D. Log on as site service account before the installation

4. Your network has hundreds of users. You have just installed Microsoft Exchange Server on five servers. You have also created an installation point on one of those servers. You would like clients to connect to this one server and perform an over-the-network installation. But you would like the clients to have the option during their installations to select any of the five Exchange servers. How would you do that?

A. Leave the Exchange server field blank in DEFAULT.PRF

B. Enter "any" in the Exchange server field in DEFAULT.PRF

C. Delete the Exchange server field in DEFAULT.PRF

D. Configure separate shares for each server and set the default in DEFAULT.PRF accordingly

5. The term used to describe the collection of MAPI configuration settings is:

  A. MAPI subsystem

  B. Service provider

  C. API

  D. Profile

6. A PST file is also known as what type of message storage?

  A. Personal folder

  B. Private folder

  C. Offline folder

  D. Macintosh folder

7. An inbox assistant is a:

  A. Secretary

  B. Temporary employee

  C. Permissions set on a mailbox

  D. Software agent that can apply rules to a mailbox

8. Which of the following features enables a Microsoft Outlook user to place notices on messages to help prioritize them?

  A. Message recall

  B. AutoNameCheck

  C. Voting

  D. Message flags

9. Which of the following are two navigational aids in Microsoft Outlook?

    A. Outlook Bar

    B. Tabbed Windows

    C. AutoDate

    D. Message recall

10. The following line would be used to set up a shared installation point for Windows-based clients:

    A. SETUP /A

    B. INSTALL /N

    C. INSTALL /A

    D. SETUP /A /N

11. Microsoft Schedule+ enables the grouping of tasks into a:

    A. Task commune

    B. Task group

    C. Project

    D. Task community

12. If you wanted all new client installations to be configured to use IPX and not use TCP/IP, you would perform which action?

    A. Use Setup Editor to remove TCP/IP from the RPC binding order

    B. Do nothing, that is already the default

    C. This can not be done

    D. Run SETUP.EXE /A

13. You have created a Microsoft Schedule+ account for a conference room. You want to grant Joan permissions to read, create, and modify the schedule for the conference room, including information marked private. You also want all meeting requests for the conference room to be forwarded to Joan. How should you configure the permissions in the Set Access Permissions dialog box?

A. Select Create in the User role box, and check the "User receives meeting requests sent to me" check box.

B. Select Modify in the User role box, and check the "User receives meeting requests sent to me" check box.

C. Select Delegate Owner in the User role box.

D. Select Delegate in the User role box.

CHAPTER

7

Configuring Microsoft Exchange Clients

he Microsoft Exchange MAPI clients include many powerful features, as described in the previous chapter. In this chapter, we will discuss how to configure and take advantage of those features. We will also discuss importing messages and address information when upgrading from other messaging clients. Finally, we will discuss how NetWare clients access a Microsoft Exchange server.

Microsoft* Exam *Objective

Install and Configure Exchange Server Client Computers.

By the end of this chapter, you will be familiar with:

- Messaging profiles

- Configuring the RPC transport

- Remote mail

- Importing messages and address information

- Microsoft Exchange clients in a NetWare environment

Messaging Profiles

As you learned in the previous chapter, a messaging profile is a collection of configuration information used by the MAPI components. In this chapter, you will learn more about:

- Messaging profile information

- Creating messaging profiles

- Editing messaging profiles

- Optional profile settings in Microsoft Outlook

- Profiles and roving users

Messaging Profile Information

The information in a messaging profile relates to much of the operation of a MAPI client application. Information found in a profile includes how to connect to back-end systems, where to store messages, and how to handle messages. Table 7.1 summarizes some of this information and indicates the default configuration. This table gives an overall view of a profile. The details of each item will be discussed after the table.

TABLE 7.1 Some information in a messaging profile	Category	Options
	Information services	• Microsoft Exchange Server (default) • Personal folders (PST) • Personal Address Book (PAB) (default) • Outlook Address Book (default when Outlook is installed) • Microsoft Mail (default) • Internet Mail (default) • Microsoft Network (MSN) • Microsoft Fax • CompuServe Mail
	Information storage	• Where to deliver incoming mail • Offline folders (OST) (if the Microsoft Exchange Server information service is being used) • Message handling settings
	Delegate access	• Additional Exchange Server mailboxes to which to connect
	Remote mail	• Phone book entry to dial • Dial-up schedule • Items to retrieve when using remote mail

Information Services

A profile specifies the information services to be used. Information services are collections of MAPI providers that permit access to back-end messaging systems (see the previous chapter for details on MAPI providers).

When an information service is added to a profile, additional information specific to the information service needs to be provided. For example, when the Microsoft Fax information service is added, the fax telephone number must be specified.

Here are some more details on the information services that are included with the Exchange clients:

- **Microsoft Exchange**   Choose this information service if the user has a mailbox account on an Exchange server. When this information service is included in a profile (it is by default), the user will be prompted to enter the following information:

  - Name of the user's Exchange server (also known as the user's home server)

  - Name of the user's Exchange mailbox (the alias name or display name as configured on the Exchange server can be specified)

- **Personal folders**   Personal folders can be used for storage instead of or in addition to a user's mailbox private folders in the Exchange Server Private Information Store. A profile can be configured to deliver mail to the Inbox folder of a personal folder store. In this case, messages are still delivered to a user's mailbox on the Exchange server first, but will then be automatically downloaded to the user's personal folder store when the user logs on with the Exchange client. Some reasons to use personal folders are:

  - To backup folders and messages

  - To copy a portion of your server-based mailbox to a portable computer for access when not on the network

  - To archive old messages

One has to take care when using both a personal folder on a home computer and a private folder on a server. For example, a user could use Microsoft Outlook on both their office computer and their home computer. If the Microsoft Outlook on the home computer was configured to have mail delivered to a personal folder on that computer, the following scenario could take place. The user, while at home, could connect to their office server and read the mail they received that day. The next day at the office, the user attempts to read the previous day's mail, but it is not in their inbox. That is because that mail was delivered to the PST file on the user's home computer.

- **Microsoft Mail**   Provides access to a mailbox account on a Microsoft Mail post office. This information service is included in new profiles by default.

- **Microsoft Network**   This information service is only loaded with the MSN online service and is only supported on Windows 95.

- **Microsoft Fax**   This information service is included with Windows 95 and is only supported on Windows 95.

- **Internet Mail**   This information service enables a user to send and receive mail over the Internet using the SMTP and POP3 protocols.

- **CompuServe Mail**   This information service is included with Windows 95 and is only supported on Windows 95.

Information Storage

Information storage options in a profile include the following:

- **Where to deliver incoming mail**   As mentioned previously, a personal folder store can be specified as the location to where incoming mail is delivered. When the Microsoft Exchange Server information service is included in a profile, incoming mail is kept in the Exchange Server mailbox by default.

- **Offline folders**   When the Microsoft Exchange Server information service is included in a profile, users may download their mail messages to offline folders on their local machines. These folders are useful for doing work away from a network. When users connect again to their Exchange server, any changes they made offline are synchronized with that server.

Any server-based folder can be specified for offline use. To make an offline folder copy of a public folder, the public folder must first be designated as a Favorite folder by the user (if a user does not see the Synchronization tab among the property pages of a public folder, it is because that public folder has not been designated as a Favorite folder). Offline folders are stored in an OST file.

- **Message handling settings**

  Options for when a new message arrives:

  - Play a sound

  - Briefly change the pointer

  - Display a notification message

  Options for deleting messages:

  - Warn before permanently deleting items

  - Empty the Deleted Items folder upon exiting

  Options after moving or deleting an open message:

  - Open the item above it

  - Open the item below it

  - Return to the main window

Additional options will be covered later in this chapter under "Optional Profile Options in Microsoft Outlook" and in Table 7.2.

Delegate Access

The Exchange MAPI clients enable a user to make another user a delegate for a mailbox or schedule. The delegate can then access the mailbox or schedule and, depending on the level of permissions granted, perform various functions. This feature is useful if a user is going out of town and wants another person to read his or her messages. The mailbox owner could assign a delegate and give the delegate the ability to read mail. Another scenario is when a manager has an assistant who handles scheduling. The assistant would need to access the manager's mailbox, read messages pertaining to scheduling requests, and respond to those requests on behalf of the manager. The manager could accomplish this by making the assistant a delegate and granting the necessary permissions to read and send mail on the manager's behalf.

Mailbox Owner Assigning Delegate Access   One way to make another user a delegate to your mailbox is to give them *permissions* to your mailbox. Individual permissions include create items, read items, create subfolders, edit items, and delete items. Any combination of these permissions can be assigned. Predefined groupings of permissions, called roles, can also be used. For example, if a mailbox owner wanted another user to be able to read items in their inbox, they could assign the Reviewer role to the delegate at both the Mailbox and Inbox objects. The delegate would then have the ability to read, and only read, the items in the mailbox owner's inbox. Exercise 7.1 outlines the steps to assign permissions.

EXERCISE 7.1

Assigning Read Permission

1. For this exercise to be performed, there must be other users with NT accounts and Exchange mailboxes different from your own. You will delegate access to your mailbox to one of these other users.

2. While in Microsoft Outlook, right-click on your Inbox, then click on Properties. The Properties dialog box will appear.

3. Click the Permissions tab.

4. Click Add. The Add Users dialog box will appear.

5. Choose the user to whom you want to delegate access to your mailbox.

6. Click Add, then click OK. The Properties dialog box will now appear.

7. In the Name box, select the delegate's name, then in the Roles list select Reviewer. This role will permit the delegate to view the contents of your Inbox folder.

8. Click OK. The user you chose in Step 5 now has permission to open your Inbox and view messages.

Users can also delegate authority by giving another user the ability to send mail *on behalf of* them, or send mail *as* them. These two permissions are discussed here:

- **Send On Behalf Of**   A delegate who has this permission can send mail on behalf of the delegator. When a recipient gets the message, the header indicates that the message was sent from the delegate *on behalf of* the delegator. This permission can be assigned from either an Exchange MAPI client or from the Exchange Administrator program. Exercise 7.2 covers granting the Send On Behalf Of permission.

EXERCISE 7.2

Assigning Send On Behalf Of Permission

1. In Microsoft Outlook, select Tools ≻ Options. The Options dialog box will appear.

2. Select the Delegates tab. The Delegates box will be empty.

3. Select Add. The Add Users dialog box will appear.

4. Select the user you want to designate as a delegate, then click Add, and then click OK. The Delegate Permissions dialog box will appear.

5. Click OK again. The user you selected now has the ability to send mail on behalf of this mailbox owner.

- **Send As**   This permission allows the delegate to send mail and have it appear as if it were sent by the mailbox owner. When a recipient gets the message, the header indicates that the message was sent from the delegator with no indication of the delegate's name at all. Recipients do not know of the delegate's involvement. This permission can only be assigned from the Exchange Administrator program. Exercise 7.3 outlines the steps for assigning the Send As permission.

Using Delegate Access   To operate as a delegate user of a mailbox, the delegate must add the other mailbox to the active profile. When this is done, the other mailbox will appear in the delegate's folder list. Depending on the permissions given, the delegate can then read, edit, create, and delete messages in folders. Exercise 7.4 shows the steps for opening a mailbox as a delegate user.

EXERCISE 7.3

Assigning Send As Permission

1. On the Exchange server, start the Exchange Administrator program.

2. Choose Tools ➤ Options. Choose the Permissions tab on the Options dialog box. Ensure that the Show Permissions Page for All Objects checkbox is selected. Click OK.

3. Select the Recipients container in the left pane. Then, in the right pane, double-click a recipient whose mailbox is to have a delegate with the Send As permission. The Properties page containing all the tabs for this mailbox will appear.

4. Select the Permissions tab.

5. Click Add. Now select the user you want to give Send As permission. After doing this, click Add and then OK.

6. Click the down-arrow in the Roles box. Select the Send As role.

7. Click OK. The user you chose in Step 2 now has the ability to send mail as if they were the owner of this mailbox.

EXERCISE 7.4

Opening a Mailbox as a Delegate User

1. Log on as the user you chose in Exercise 7.1, Step 5.

2. Start Microsoft Outlook.

3. Choose Tools ➤ Services. The Services dialog box will appear.

4. Select Microsoft Exchange Server and then click Properties. The Microsoft Exchange Server dialog box will appear.

5. Select the Advanced tab.

6. Click Add.

EXERCISE 7.4 (CONTINUED FROM PREVIOUS PAGE)

7. In the Add Mailbox box, type the name of the mailbox to which you have been assigned permissions. Then click OK. Click OK on the Microsoft Exchange Server properties dialog box. The Services dialog box will appear.

8. Click OK. Notice that the other mailbox to which you have been assigned delegate access appears in the folder list (click the Folder List toolbar button to display the folder list if it is not shown).

A delegate who has been granted Send On Behalf Of permission can send a message for the other user by choosing the From field on the View menu of a Compose Message window. In the From field, the user can enter the name of the user they want to Send On Behalf Of

Creating and editing a messaging profile will now be covered in more detail.

Creating Messaging Profiles

There are three primary methods to create a profile:

- Setup program and DEFAULT.PRF or OUTLOOK.PRF

- Setup program and the Profile Wizard

- Control Panel

Setup Program and DEFAULT.PRF or OUTLOOK.PRF

During an Exchange MAPI client installation, the SETUP program will look for a file named DEFAULT.PRF (if Microsoft Exchange Client for MS-DOS) or OUTLOOK.PRF (if Microsoft Outlook). These files contain default information that the SETUP program will use to create a profile during installation. The DEFAULT.PRF file can be created using the Setup Editor program or by using a text editor to modify the DEFAULT.PRF file in the Exchange Client installation point. OUTLOOK.PRF can only be edited by a text editor. Administrators can use these files to eliminate the need for the installer to create profiles and ensure that all clients installed are using a consistent profile.

Setup Program and the Profile Wizard

If the DEFAULT.PRF or OUTLOOK.PRF do not exist, the Setup program will automatically start the Profile Wizard, which prompts the installer for the profile information. The installer may accept or change the defaults the Profile Wizard presents. The defaults are noted by parentheses in Table 7.1.

Control Panel

After an installation, a new profile can be created using the Mail and Fax applet in the Control Panel. After launching the applet, click Show Profiles, and then click Add. The Profile Wizard will start up and guide you through creating a new profile.

Editing Messaging Profiles

Profiles can be edited any time after the client is installed. If you want to edit an existing profile, you can use the Mail and Fax applet in the Control Panel. Also, the profile that is currently in use can be edited from within the Exchange client or Outlook by choosing the Services option on the Tools menu. We will discuss these two scenarios in greater detail next.

Editing an Existing Profile

The Mail and Fax applet in the Control Panel can be used to edit an existing profile. This applet can be used after a messaging product has been installed on a user's computer. Sometimes information needs to be manually added to a profile before a newly installed messaging product is fully configured for use. If there are applications using the MAPI subsystem at the time the profile is edited, they will all need to be stopped and restarted before the changes made to the profile will take effect.

Editing a Current Profile

If a user wants to make profile changes without having to log off and back on again to make those changes effective, the user can edit the current profile through the Services option on the Tools menu. Any changes made to the profile in this way become effective immediately, but some settings cannot be changed while the profile is in use.

Optional Profile Settings in Microsoft Outlook

MAPI applications have the functionality to allow users to set some of their messaging profiles within the application. For example, choosing Options from the Tools menu from within Outlook (see Figure 7.1) will bring up a dialog box containing numerous tabs, also called property pages, that allow users to set various options pertaining to their messaging environment. Table 7.2 provides a description of each property page.

FIGURE 7.1

The Microsoft Outlook
Options screen

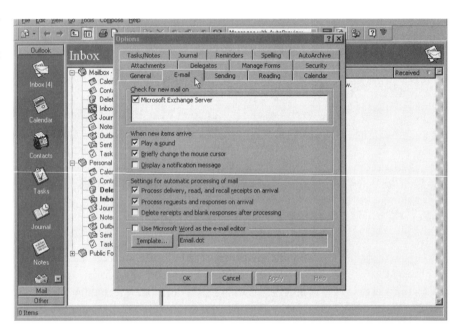

T A B L E 7.2	**Property Page**	**Description**
Microsoft Outlook property pages	General	• When starting Outlook, prompt the user for the profile to use, or always use a designated profile, or start in a particular folder.
		• Deleting message options:
		Warn before permanently deleting
		Empty the Deleted Items folder on exit
		• Dialing options:
		Settings for speed dialing
		Settings for phone number formatting
		Settings for phone number dialing
		• Add-In Manager

T A B L E 7.2 (cont.) Microsoft Outlook property pages	**Property Page**	**Description**

	E-mail	• Where to check for new mail
		• Notification of new mail options:
		    Play a sound
		    Briefly change the mouse cursor
		    Display notification message
		• Settings for automatic processing of mail

	Sending	• Sending mail options:
		    Use a particular font
		    Set importance of mail
		    Set sensitivity of mail

	Reading	• After moving or deleting an open message, options:
		    Open the message above it
		    Open the message below it
		    Return to the Outlook window
		• When replying or forwarding a message, options:
		    Include and indent the original text
		    Close the original message
		    Set the font or color settings

	Calendar	• Define the work week • Define working hours • Appointment defaults • Set Microsoft Schedule+ as the primary calendar
	Tasks/Notes	• Define task working hours • Define task color options • Define task and note defaults
	Journal	• Define items and contacts for journal entries
	Reminders	• Define actions to initiate when a reminder comes due
	Spelling	• Always suggest replacements for misspellings • Always check spelling before sending • Ignore words in uppercase • Ignore words with numbers • Ignore original message text in a reply or forward

TABLE 7.2 *(cont.)* Microsoft Outlook property pages	Property Page	Description
	AutoArchive	• Define settings for when and where to perform automatic archiving
	Attachments	• Provides security options for handling attachments and links in messages
	Delegates	• Define others who may send mail on your behalf
	Manage Forms	• Install and manage forms from the various forms libraries
	Security	• Set up advanced security

A Microsoft Outlook profile can be configured to require a user to input their Windows NT domain password each time Outlook is started. That is configured through Tools | Services | Microsoft Exchange Server | Properties | Advanced tab. On the Advanced tab there is a checkbox labeled "Use network security during logon." If that box is checked (the default), the password the user inputted during normal Windows NT domain logon will be used by Microsoft Outlook. If that box is not checked, the user will have to enter their Windows NT domain password at each startup of Microsoft Outlook.

The Microsoft Outlook Address Book can also be configured in a messaging profile. For example, suppose someone wanted to group users by their building and use those groupings in the Outlook Address Book. That could be done by creating Contacts folders for each building (e.g. Building 4 Contacts, etc.). Then creating contact items for each user and placing those items in the relevant contact folder. Finally, you would access the "Outlook Address Book" property page of each of the Contacts folders and check the box that states "Show this folder as an e-mail Address Book." The procedure described above would enable that Microsoft Outlook user to choose e-mail addresses by building when composing a message.

Profiles and Roving Users

Roving users are people who use multiple computers on the network. Because messaging profiles are stored on users' local workstations, a problem arises when roving users move to different computers but still want to use the same profile. Solutions to this situation vary depending on the operating system used by the client. The following sections discuss these solutions.

MS-DOS Clients

The Exchange Client for MS-DOS normally stores its messaging profile in the user's Exchange directory in a file named EXCHANGE.PRO. For a roving user, the Exchange directory and the EXCHANGE.PRO file can be copied to the user's home directory on a server. Then, regardless of the machine being used, the user accesses his or her home directory on the server and runs the Exchange Client from that directory. The Exchange Client will automatically look for the profile in the same directory.

If a roving user wants to run a local copy of the Exchange Client, the profile in the home directory on the server can still be used. This is done by using the -P switch on the command line when executing the Exchange Client. This switch takes an argument that specifies the path to the profile, for which the roving user can provide his or her home directory on the server.

Windows 3.x Clients

To support roving users on Windows 3.*x,* the file containing the user's profile, EXCHNG.INI, can be placed on a server, and the Exchange Client on each computer the roving user uses can be configured to find the profile on that server. The WIN.INI file must be modified to do this.

Modifying WIN.INI   The Exchange Client looks for the EXCHNG.INI file in a directory path specified in the WIN.INI file. The keyword for the path is found under the MAPI section in WIN.INI as follows:

```
[MAPI]

ProfileDirectory16=<path>
```

The user can specify the path to the network directory where the messaging profile has been placed.

Windows 95 and Windows NT Clients

Windows 95 and Windows NT maintain user configuration information in user environment profiles (not to be confused with the messaging profiles discussed in this chapter). Environment profiles can be stored on a local machine or on a server. Because a messaging profile is included within the environment profile, Windows 95 and Windows NT have built-in support for roving users. The roving user only needs to use a server-based user environment profile to be able to use more than one machine on the network.

Configuring the RPC Transport

The Exchange MAPI-based clients use the RPC protocol to perform client-server interactions. The RPC protocol uses other protocols to establish a connection with the server and to physically move its information. Table 7.3 describes the protocols that RPC can use.

	Network Protocol	Description
TABLE 7.3 Protocols available for RPC use	Local RPC (LPC)	This communication method is used when the client and the server are on the same machine. No network traffic is generated.
	TCP/IP	RPC can use the Windows Sockets interface and TCP/IP to communicate with an Exchange server.
	Sequenced Packet Exchange (SPX)	RPC can use the Windows Sockets interface and the Novell IPX/SPX protocol to communicate with an Exchange server.
	Named Pipes	RPC can use Named Pipes.
	Network Basic Input/ Output System (NetBIOS)	NetBIOS is a protocol that creates a two-way conversation between a client and a server. NetBIOS uses network protocols to physically carry its information. It will work with TCP/IP, IPX/SPX, and NetBEUI. RPC can use NetBIOS to communicate with an Exchange server.
	Vines IP	Vines IP is a network protocol used in Banyan Vines networks. RPC can use this protocol to communicate with an Exchange Server. This protocol is only supported on the Windows 95, Windows NT, and Windows for Workgroups platforms.

Any one of the scenarios in Table 7.3 will allow a MAPI client using RPC to perform client-server interactions with an Exchange Server. RPC will try these different scenarios until it establishes a session with the server. The order that RPC uses to establish a connection depends on the operating system of the client. Table 7.4 shows the protocol order.

TABLE 7.4 Protocol order used by RPC	**Windows 95, Windows NT**	**Windows 3.x**	**MS-DOS**
	Local RPC	Named Pipes	Local RPC
	TCP/IP	SPX	Named Pipes
	SPX	TCP/IP	SPX
	Named Pipes	NetBIOS	TCP/IP
	NetBIOS	Vines IP	NetBIOS
	Vines IP		

Microsoft ✓ *Exam Objective*

Diagnose and resolve problems with client connectivity.

See also the discussion on the RPC Ping utility in the "Troubleshooting" section in Chapter 12.

Although each of the protocols listed are automatically attempted until one succeeds, if a protocol is not supported on the system it may take an extended time for that protocol to time-out before the next protocol is attempted. This can cause an unwanted delay every time a user logs on. Therefore, it may be necessary to reorder the protocols so that those supported by your network are at the top of the list.

The connection orders in Table 7.4 can be modified before a client installation. This can be done using the Setup Editor utility or by manually editing lines in the configuration file (STF or INI) that Setup uses. After an installation, manual editing is the only way to change the order. The following two sections explain how to manually modify the connection order before and after an installation.

The phrases "RPC connection order" and "RPC binding order" are synonymous.

Preinstallation Modification of the RPC Connection Order

As mentioned, the RPC connection order that will be used in an installation can be determined before setup. This can be done by manually editing certain files and certain parameters in those files. That information is presented below and organized by operating system platform.

Windows 95 and Windows NT Clients

The SETUP program reads instructions from the EXCHNG.STF file. To change the RPC connection order, modify the following lines:

```
61 AddRegData   """LOCAL"",

""Software\Microsoft\Exchange\Exchange Provider"",
""Rpc_Binding_Order"",

""ncalrpc,ncacn_ip_tcp,ncacn_spx,ncacn_np,net-
bios,ncacn_vns_spp"""
```

As you can see in the previous line, the default order is LPC, TCP/IP, SPX, Named Pipes, and NetBIOS (this can also be seen in Table 7.4).

Windows 3.x Clients

The file EXCHNG.STF is also the file that SETUP reads for Windows 3.x clients. The following lines can be modified to change the RPC connection order:

```
62 AddIniLine """exchng.ini"", ""Exchange Provider"",
""RPC_Binding_Order""cacn_np,ncacn_spx,ncacn_ip_tcp,net-
bios,ncacn_vns_spp"""
```

MS-DOS Clients

For MS-DOS clients, SETUP reads configuration information from the file MLSETUP.INI. To change the RPC connection order, you must edit the following line in that file:

```
RPC_BINDING_ORDER=ncalrpc,ncacn_np,ncacn_spx,ncacn_ip_tcp,netbios
```

Postinstallation Modification of the RPC Connection Order

After installation is completed, the RPC connection order can only be changed by manually editing the appropriate files or the Registry. The method varies depending on the operating system. The following sections give the details.

Windows 95 and Windows NT Clients

To modify the RPC connection order on Windows 95 or Windows NT, the Rpc_Binding_Order value in the Registry must be modified. This value is found in the following key in the Registry:

```
\HKEY_LOCAL_MACHINE

    \Software

        \Microsoft

            \Exchange

                \Exchange Provider
```

Windows 3.x Clients

The RPC connection order can be modified on Windows 3.*x* clients by editing the Rpc_Binding_Order value in the EXCHNG.INI file.

MS-DOS Clients

When the MS-DOS Exchange client application is installed, the environment variable, RPC_BINDING_ORDER, is set in the AUTOEXEC.BAT file. This variable contains the RPC connection order and can be edited after the installation.

Remote Mail

As discussed previously, remote mail gives a user the ability to access and use his or her mailbox through a remote connection to the Exchange server. Certain technologies at the client and the server make this access possible. Our discussion will divide these technologies into the following four categories:

- Remote connection options
- Protocols supported
- ShivaRemote installation and configuration
- Remote mail features

Remote Connection Options

The remote connection method used to connect Exchange MAPI clients to an Exchange server depends on the operating system the client is using. The three remote connection options that can be used are:

- Microsoft Remote Access Service (RAS)
- Microsoft Dial-Up Networking (DUN)
- ShivaRemote

Microsoft Remote Access Service (RAS)

RAS is a subsystem included with Windows NT that enables dial-up access to a remote computer. By using RAS client software and a supported modem, a user can establish a dial-up connection to a RAS server and through it to an Exchange server, which can either be on the same computer as the RAS server or on its nerwork. This allows a remote user to access his or her mailbox on an Exchange server. RAS client software is also included with Microsoft Windows for Workgroups.

Microsoft Dial-Up Networking (DUN)

DUN is a subsystem included with Windows 95 that enables dial-up access to a remote computer. A remote Exchange client can use DUN to connect to an

Exchange server. Some of the remote access servers that a remote DUN client can connect to are Windows 95 dial-up server, RAS server, Shiva LanRover, and Shiva NetModem.

ShivaRemote

ShivaRemote is dial-up client software from the Shiva Corporation that is included with Exchange Server. It permits dial-up access to remote computers. ShivaRemote can run on MS-DOS, Windows 3.*x,* and Windows for Workgroups clients.

Protocols Supported

RAS, DUN, and ShivaRemote all use the *Point-to-Point Protocol (PPP)* to physically transfer information between the remote client and the server. PPP plays a role similar to a LAN adapter driver. PPP takes *datagrams*, which are chunks of data that are to be transferred, and frames them for network transfer. The remote user's modem takes the place of a LAN adapter.

The datagram protocols, also called network protocols, that can be used with these three remote connection options are TCP/IP, IPX, and NetBEUI. ShivaRemote only supports the Novell IPX implementation, not the Microsoft implementation.

In the next section, we will discuss the installation and configuration of ShivaRemote. RAS and DUN will not be discussed because they are covered in other Microsoft courses and exams.

ShivaRemote Installation and Configuration

Exchange Server ships with two versions of ShivaRemote, one for MS-DOS clients and one for Windows 3.*x* and Windows for Workgroups clients. The installation procedure for each is different.

MS-DOS Clients

During the normal installation of the MS-DOS Exchange client, a check box option is used to specify ShivaRemote installation. The ShivaRemote files are placed in the Exchange client directory. There is no separate installation program for ShivaRemote. If the initial installation of the Exchange client did not include ShivaRemote, but it is desired at a later time, the Setup can be run again to add ShivaRemote.

Each time a user wants to use ShivaRemote, CONNECT.EXE must be run to establish the physical connection to the server. This must be done before the user runs the MS-DOS Exchange client. Note that the MS-DOS clients do not have the capability to download only message headers during a remote connection to an Exchange server.

Windows 3.x and Windows for Workgroups Clients

When the Typical setup option is specified during a Windows 3.*x* Exchange client installation, a setup icon for ShivaRemote is created in the Microsoft Exchange program group. To utilize remote dial-up functionality, the user must run this ShivaRemote setup program. The program will copy all the ShivaRemote files to the specified setup directory, except the files VNB.386 and CTL3D.DLL, which are copied to the <Windir>\SYSTEM directory. The setup program will also add the DIAL.386 driver to the SYSTEM.INI file, add the Shiva directory to the PATH statement in the AUTOEXEC. BAT file, and make some changes to the WIN.INI file. Before the setup program makes these changes it will back up the original files with .000 extensions to the Shiva directory.

The user must manually add the following lines to the CONFIG.SYS file:

```
device=c:\<Windir>\protman.dos /i:c:\<windir>
```

```
device=c:\<Shiva_dir>\dialndis.exe
```

The user must also add the following line, if it is not already present, to the AUTOEXEC.BAT file:

```
net start
```

If Windows for Workgroups is being used, the SYSTEM.INI file must also be modified by including the following line:

```
LoadRMDrivers=Yes
```

If a client is using Protected Mode Networking, the user must install the Shiva dial-in driver using the Network Application program found in the Network program group. In the list of adapters, the user must choose Unlisted and then enter the path to the Shiva files. The user will then have the option to install the protected mode dial-in driver and must configure it for the appropriate protocols. The computer must be restarted for the changes to take effect.

Remote Mail Features

Exchange MAPI clients have an option on the Tools menu named Remote Mail. This option enables a user to view new messages on an Exchange server, select specific messages to download to the offline Inbox, and send messages waiting in the Outbox. Downloading only the new messages is much faster than synchronizing the entire mailbox, as is done when using offline folders. All of these remote client features are only possible when connecting to Exchange Server.

Remote mail can be scheduled to automatically dial in to an Exchange server at specified times. This option can be used to take advantage of off-peak telephone rates.

Another feature of remote mail is the ability to create filters relating to retrieving remote mail. Rather than being forced to retrieve all your remote mail, you can designate conditions (i.e. filters) that must be met for a message to be downloaded. Conditions could include only retrieving messages sent by certain users, or only messages with a certain value in the subject field. There are even advanced filters such as message size and the date the message was received by your server mailbox.

Importing Messages and Address Information

Exchange MAPI clients can import messages and address books from the Microsoft Mail environment. This is useful for former users of Microsoft Mail who have upgraded to Exchange. Microsoft Mail messages are imported to Exchange folders and are not deleted from the original location.

Importing Messages

Microsoft Mail messages are stored in a file with the MMF extension, which can be password protected. A user must know the password to perform the import. MMF files also contain a copy of the user's Personal Address Book (PAB). When importing, the user is given the option to import either the messages, the address entries, or both. The imported messages must be placed in an Exchange personal folder store (PST). This can be an existing folder, or a folder can be created during the import procedure.

Messages can be imported from within an Exchange MAPI client. When the Import option on the File menu is chosen (the option is named Import and Export in Outlook), the user is prompted for the MMF password, what to import, and the folder to import messages to. Imported messages cannot be exported back to the Microsoft Mail environment.

The MS-DOS Exchange Client does not have the Import option.

Importing Address Book Information

Microsoft Mail Personal Address Books (PAB) can also be imported into the Exchange client environment. The imported address entries will be added to the current Exchange Personal Address Book entries. If any conflicts or errors occur during the import, the user will be notified. The address book import process is started the same way as the message import process, by choosing Import from the File menu (Import and Export in Outlook).

Exchange Clients in a NetWare Environment

Exchange Server is an application server—specifically, a messaging server. As such, it can be used in a Novell NetWare environment. NetWare clients can run the Exchange client software and connect to an Exchange server (see Figure 7.2). To accommodate NetWare clients, an Exchange server will require some additional configuration, which could include the following:

- NWLink installed on the Exchange server

- SAP running on the Exchange server

- NetWare clients correctly configured

FIGURE 7.2

NetWare clients acting as
Exchange clients

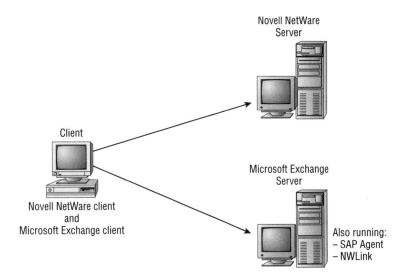

NWLink Installed on the Exchange Server

Most Novell NetWare networks use the Internetwork Packet Exchange (IPX) and Sequenced Packet Exchange (SPX) network protocols. If NetWare clients are to be clients to an Exchange server, then the Exchange server must also use these network protocols. This is enabled by loading and binding the Microsoft NWLink protocol on the Exchange server. NWLink is Microsoft's 32-bit implementation of the IPX/SPX protocols. NWLink supports RPC communication between the NetWare clients and the Exchange server over the IPX/SPX protocols. Running NWLink on the Exchange server does not preclude using other network protocols simultaneously.

If the NetWare clients are not using IPX/SPX, but are instead using TCP/IP, then the Exchange server needs to be running TCP/IP.

Various configuration parameters for NWLink relate to how NetWare clients can communicate with the Exchange server. These parameters are:

- **Frame type** A frame is the information carrying package created by Data Link protocols, such as Ethernet, Token Ring, or FDDI. These protocols can use different formats when creating *frames*. The different formats are called frame types. For communication to take place, both sides need to use the same frame type. Consequently, the Exchange server must use the same frame type as the NetWare clients.

- **Internal network number**   If the Exchange server has multiple network cards or is using multiple frame types, the server's network card and frame type being accessed by the NetWare clients must be assigned the network address of the Novell network. This address is referred to by Microsoft as the *internal network number*. The Exchange administrator can get this number from the NetWare system administrator. The number must have a value other than 0.

SAP Running on the Exchange Server

SAP stands for Service Advertising Protocol, a Novell protocol used by servers to advertise their services to clients and other servers. Information in the advertisement, called an SAP broadcast, consists of the name and location of the server. NetWare clients learn of the presence of servers by listening to the SAP broadcasts sent from servers. After learning of a server, a NetWare client can then access and use its services. Therefore, if an Exchange server wants to service NetWare clients, it too must utilize SAP.

An Exchange server can utilize SAP by having the Microsoft Gateway Service for NetWare (GSNW) component loaded and configured. Once this is done, the Exchange server is what Microsoft refers to as an SAP agent and can advertise its services by sending out SAP broadcasts.

If a *router* exists between the Exchange server and the NetWare/Exchange clients, the router must be configured to pass SAP broadcasts. Exchange Server uses SAP server type 0x640 to identify itself. This is the unique number that identifies the type of server that is advertising.

NetWare Clients Correctly Configured

There are also some steps that need to be done to the NetWare clients to enable them to access an Exchange server. Logging on to an Exchange server involves being authenticated in a Windows NT domain. This poses a challenge because Novell's NetWare client software does not support RPC communication, and therefore does not permit a client to be authenticated in a Windows NT domain (i.e. logon to the NT domain). Microsoft has solved this by providing various client programs. The Microsoft software that implements this depends on the operating system used by the NetWare client.

NetWare clients using Windows 95 and wishing to access an Exchange server would need to run the Client for Microsoft Networks program. If using Windows NT Workstation, a NetWare client would need to use the Windows NT Workstation service, which is included with this operating system. Both of these programs serve as a redirector, redirecting Exchange client requests to a Windows NT domain controller or Exchange server. Obviously, one of the Microsoft Exchange client applications, such as Outlook or the Exchange Client, would also need to be running on the NetWare client.

NetWare clients using Windows 3.*x* or MS-DOS and wishing to access an Exchange server use special RPC components to participate in a Microsoft network. These RPC components are automatically installed when the Exchange client software for Windows 3.*x* or MS-DOS is installed.

Summary

A messaging profile is the collection of configuration information used by a MAPI application, such as Microsoft Exchange Client or Microsoft Outlook. Some of the information contained in a profile indicates the information services to be used, such as Microsoft Exchange Server, Microsoft Fax, or Internet Mail. Other information in the profile relates to information storage, delegate access, and remote mail. Profiles can be created at the time of the client software installation. They can also be created and edited after the installation.

Exchange MAPI applications use the RPC protocol to perform client-server interactions. The RPC protocol uses a network protocol to physically transport its information. The order in which RPC attempts to use network protocols can be configured.

The Exchange MAPI clients support remote mail features that enable users to dial in to an Exchange server and access their mailboxes.

Some users will be upgrading from Microsoft Mail to Exchange. The Exchange MAPI clients permit a user's existing Microsoft Mail messages and address book entries to be imported into Exchange.

Review Questions

1. A user named Jane uses Microsoft Outlook on both her office computer and her home computer. One night at home, Jane connects to her office server in order to read her mail. The next day at the office when Jane attempts to re-read the previous day's mail, there are no messages in her inbox. What is the most likely cause of this situation?

    A. Jane's mail was delivered to an OST file on her home computer.

    B. Jane's home computer is still logged on to the server.

    C. Jane did not synchronize her mailbox with the server.

    D. Jane's mail was delivered to a PST file on her home computer.

2. Patty has a laptop computer that she uses both at the office and when out of office doing work. Her laptop is configured with an OST file. She routinely synchronizes her laptop computer with the office server. Patty has identified a public folder that she would like to designate as an offline folder, but she does not see the Synchronization tab among the property pages of that public folder. What does she have to do to enable synchronization with that public folder?

    A. The administrator must configure that public folder for synchronization.

    B. The owner of the folder must configure it for synchronization.

    C. Patty must designate the public folder as a Favorite folder.

    D. Patty must log off the server, and the folder will synchronize.

3. Lou has a laptop computer for doing work away from the office and a desktop computer at the office. Microsoft Outlook is installed on both computers. Lou would like to see all his messages while using either computer. The laptop computer does not have a continuous connection to the office server, but Lou would like to be able to read and compose messages while using the laptop offline. How should Lou configure his two computers?

A. Configure the laptop computer with an OST file, and the desktop computer to access his private folders in the Information Store.

B. Configure both computers with PST files.

C. Configure both computers to access his private folders in the Information Store.

D. Configure the laptop computer with a PST file, and the desktop computer to access his private folders in the Information Store.

4. You have configured Microsoft Outlook with an OST file. Your server suffers a major hardware failure. You also cannot recover Exchange data from your backup media. You reinstall Microsoft Exchange Server. What can you do to recover as much data as possible to your mailbox in the Private Information Store?

A. Copy the OST file to your server and synchronize your folders.

B. Copy the PST file to your server and synchronize your folders.

C. Rename the OST file with a PST extension and synchronize your folders.

D. While working offline, create a PST file and move the contents of your OST file to that PST file, then copy the contents of that PST file to your mailbox in the Private Information Store and synchronize your folders.

5. How would you group users by buildings from within the Microsoft Outlook Address Book?

A. Create new recipient containers.

B. Use AutoNaming.

C. Create public folders for each building and add a listing of the people in those buildings.

D. Create new Contacts folders for each building, designate those folders as part of the Outlook Address Book.

6. Management has asked you to add another layer of security to the use of Microsoft Outlook. They would like users to have to enter their password at each startup of Microsoft Outlook. How could Outlook be configured to require a password?

   A. Configure each mailbox object to require a password.

   B. Clear the "Use network security during logon" checkbox in each user's profile.

   C. Configure "Required passwords" through Server Manager.

   D. Configure each home server to require a password.

7. You are the administrator of a Microsoft Exchange site. A user named Chet wants to allow another user named Davina to read, and only read, items in his inbox. What should you do so Davina can read items in Chet's inbox?

   A. Designate Davina a delegate to Chet's mailbox.

   B. Instruct Chet to designate Davina the Reviewer role at the Mailbox and Inbox objects.

   C. Instruct Chet to designate Davina the Reviewer role at the Inbox object and the Exchange Server properties page.

   D. Add Davina's network account to Chet's mailbox.

8. You will be using a scripted installation to setup a number of Microsoft Exchange Client applications. You will use Setup Editor to modify EXCHNG.STF. Even though all workstations use both TCP/IP and IPX, you want clients to use only IPX when connecting to their Microsoft Exchange servers. What should you do to accomplish that configuration?

   A. Remove TCP/IP from the RPC binding order in the installation script.

   B. Remove TCP/IP from all workstations.

C. Unbind TCP/IP from workstation network adapters.

D. Unbind TCP/IP from the Microsoft Exchange server network adapter.

9. Your network uses IPX as its only network protocol. Your Microsoft Exchange Server has two network adapters. One adapter is connected to the internal LAN and uses IPX. The other adapter is connected to an outside WAN and uses TCP/IP. Users on the internal LAN use Microsoft Outlook to connect to the Microsoft Exchange Server. When these users attempt to connect to the Microsoft Exchange Server, it takes up to 10 minutes to connect and to send mail. What can be done to reduce the time to connect and send mail?

A. Bind TCP/IP to the network adapter of each client computer.

B. Bind TCP/IP to the internal network adapter of the Microsoft Exchange Server.

C. Change the RPC binding order on the Microsoft Exchange Server.

D. Change the RPC binding order on each client computer.

10. Clients use Dial-Up Networking to access the Microsoft Exchange server. These clients would like to download only those messages that are smaller than 20 KB, and would like to do that without having to examine the size of each message. How could that be done? (Select the best answer.)

A. Create a rule in the Out of Office Assistant that downloads only messages smaller than 20 KB.

B. Create a rule in the Inbox Assistant that downloads only messages smaller than 20 KB.

C. Configure the advanced filter options for remote mail to download only messages smaller than 20 KB.

D. Configure a view based on size, and then download only those messages smaller than 20 KB.

11. You need to install Microsoft Exchange Server on a Novell NetWare network. You would like to use a network installation to setup Microsoft Outlook on all the clients. The network uses IPX as its only network protocol. What must you do to install Microsoft Outlook on each client and to enable them to connect to the Microsoft Exchange server? (Choose all that apply.)

    A. Create a network share point with Read permission for all clients.

    B. Create a network share point with Execute permission for all clients.

    C. Install and configure the SAP Agent on the Microsoft Exchange Server.

    D. Install and configure NWLink IPX/SPX Compatible Transport on the Microsoft Exchange Server.

    E. Install and configure TCP/IP on all client computers.

12. You are installing Microsoft Exchange Server to your Novell NetWare network. All client computers run Windows 95, Novell NetWare32 client, and Microsoft Outlook. What two actions must be done to enable these client computers to communicate with the Microsoft Exchange server? (Choose two.)

    A. Install the Client for Microsoft Networks on each client computer.

    B. Configure IPX Routing on the Microsoft Exchange Server.

    C. Install NWLink IPX/SPX Compatible Transport on each client computer.

    D. Install Gateway Service for NetWare on the Microsoft Exchange Server.

13. Which of the following is NOT a default information service in a messaging profile?

    A. Microsoft Fax

    B. Microsoft Mail

    C. Microsoft Exchange

    D. Both A and B

14. From which programs can the Send On Behalf Of permission be assigned?

   A. Microsoft Exchange Client

   B. Microsoft Outlook

   C. Microsoft Exchange Administrator program

   D. All of the above

15. Which of the following information files does SETUP look for when building a messaging profile?

   A. DEFAULT.PRF

   B. PROFILE.DAT

   C. PROFILE.PRF

   D. DEFAULT.DAT

16. What file contains the profile for an MS-DOS client?

   A. PROFILE.DOS

   B. PROF-MS.DOS

   C. EXCHANGE.PRO

   D. DOS.PRO

17. Which of the following is NOT a feature of remote mail?

   A. PCMCIA cards

   B. Downloading only new messages

   C. Offline folders

   D. Working offline

18. Which of the following relates to remote mail?

A. Offline address book

B. Scheduled connections

C. ShivaRemote

D. All of the above

19. Which of the following file types can be imported by the Exchange Client?

A. MMX

B. GIF

C. MMF

D. Both B and C

20. Exchange clients have which of the following as notification options for new mail?

A. Play a sound

B. Blinking screen

C. Briefly change the pointer

D. Both A and C

21. Which of the following programs can be used to edit a messaging profile?

A. WordPad

B. PaintBrush

C. Server Monitor

D. The Mail and Fax applet in the Control Panel

22. Which of the following is required for a folder to be designated for offline use?

   A. It must have a size limitation

   B. It must have a password

   C. It must not have a size limitation

   D. It must be designated as a Favorite folder

CHAPTER

8

Microsoft Exchange Forms

Most organizations generate mountains of paperwork. There are forms for expense reports, check requests, order entry, vacation requests, customer tracking, surveys, and many, many other purposes. Paper-based forms are bulky, they can be lost, they have to be physically delivered by a person, and they have to be filed. A solution to these problems is to use electronic forms.

Electronic forms are e-mail with built-in fields and, if desired, built-in actions. They can be used instead of paper-based forms to automate and streamline organizational functions. Each of the forms mentioned in the previous paragraph can be implemented as an electronic form (see Figure 8.1 for a typical electronic form). Electronic forms can be easily stored, backed up, transported through e-mail, and even configured for automation. An example of e-form automation is a check request form that is automatically routed to the correct check signature authority based upon the amount of the check request. Electronic forms can be used in place of just about any paper-based form or any process that requires the acquisition of structured data (i.e., the data in the fields of a form). The completely paperless office is not quite a reality today, but electronic forms are a key technology for realizing this goal.

This chapter discusses how to create forms to be used in stand-alone and folder-based applications. The following main steps to create an Exchange form will be covered:

- Creating forms libraries

- Designing forms

- Installing forms

The term "electronic forms" will often be shortened to simply "forms" throughout the rest of this book.

FIGURE 8.1

A typical electronic form

Electronic Forms

Two powerful programs that design and create forms, Microsoft Outlook Forms Designer and Microsoft Exchange Forms Designer (EFD), are included with Exchange Server.

Microsoft Outlook Forms Designer is a 32-bit program that creates 32-bit forms. The forms it creates can only be accessed using the Microsoft Outlook client. Microsoft Exchange Forms Designer (EFD) is a 16-bit program that creates 16-bit forms. Forms created by EFD can be accessed using any of the Windows 16-bit or 32-bit Exchange clients (including Outlook).

These two form design tools and the forms they create will not run on the MS-DOS or Macintosh operating systems.

Both programs provide a visual, nonprogrammatic method to design and create forms. To design a form, users simply drag-and-drop objects (like text entry fields, checkboxes, and drop-down lists) onto a form. Users can also assign properties to these objects, such as font size, color, alignment, and even actions. The form design process is further simplified by the inclusion of numerous premade forms, called sample forms or applications. These sample forms can be used without modification, or they can be easily customized through the drag-and-drop interface.

Both the Outlook Forms Designer and the EFD are front-end programs to a specialized version of Microsoft Visual Basic. While the user is creating a form through the visual nonprogrammatic interface, Visual Basic is running "under the hood." This means the source files of both sample forms and new forms can be loaded into Visual Basic for further customization. Specialized forms that send data to a database, or forms that include multimedia, can be created by modifying forms in Visual Basic. Therefore, Exchange forms are extensible.

Two primary types of applications can be built using Exchange forms:

- Stand-alone applications

- Folder-based applications

Stand-alone form applications are forms that are sent from one person to another (for example, an expense report form that is filled out and sent to the user's manager). When forms are used in this manner, they are referred to as *Send forms*.

Folder-based applications utilize folders that have forms associated with them. Forms provide an easy and effective way to send and view data in a folder. Forms used this way are referred to as *Post forms*. Using folder-based applications can solve some problems that arise when using simple Send forms. For example, if a team of people is working on the same project, they are probably going to send many electronic messages between themselves. Some messages are even going to be sent to several people via carbon copies, forwarded messages, and reply messages. The result is a long list of unstructured information that takes a long time to sift through, and takes up unnecessary space. One solution is to create various forms for submitting, reading, replying, and modifying data. These forms can be associated with a public folder for the members of the team to use. Information becomes centralized and organized. Using forms in a public folder offers increased security and a more efficient use of space.

Creating Forms Libraries

Forms libraries are containers used to store, group, and make forms available to users. Placing a form in a forms library is also referred to as *installing the form* or *publishing the form*. There are three types of forms libraries:

- **Organization Forms Library**   Forms in this library are available to everyone in the Exchange organization. This library makes it easy to distribute forms to a large number of people. The organization forms library is actually a public folder that is stored on an Exchange server, and it can be replicated to multiple Exchange servers in the same way any other public folder can. The Exchange administrator can give the organization library an arbitrary name, or keep the default name, Organization Forms. An Exchange organization may cover multiple locales around the world, so different language translations of the same forms may need to be made available. The Exchange administrator can create individual organization forms libraries for each language that is required. Each of these libraries is maintained as a separate public folder. Forms stored in the organization forms library are usually Send forms.

- **Personal Forms Library**   A personal forms library is stored in a user's mailbox and holds forms used by that user only. Forms stored in a personal forms library are usually Send forms.

- **Folder Forms Library**   Forms can be saved in a public folder, a private folder, or a personal folder. Forms are placed in a public folder for group access. The forms that are usually placed in a folder forms library are Post forms.

The Exchange administrator creates the organization forms library using the Exchange Administrator program. Because this library is actually a public folder, permissions on the library can be assigned to Exchange users (see Chapter 9 for information on public folder permissions). This enables the administrator to decide who can access the library and what they can do with it. A user must have the Folder Owner permission to install a form in a library. Exercise 8.1 walks you through the procedure to create the organization forms library.

EXERCISE 8.1

Creating the Organization Forms Library

1. While in the Exchange Administrator program, choose Tools ➤ Forms Administrator. The Organization Forms Library Administrator dialog box will appear.

2. Click New. The Create New Forms Library dialog box will appear.

3. Keep the default Library folder name, Organization Forms. Next, choose the relevant language, such as English (USA), and click OK. The Organization Forms Library Administrator dialog box will reappear.

4. Click Permissions. The Forms Library Permissions dialog box will appear.

5. Click Add. Highlight the user George Washington and then click Add. Click OK. The Forms Library Permissions page will reappear with George Washington assigned the Reviewer role.

6. Highlight the user George Washington. Click on the down-arrow next to the Roles list box. Choose the role Owner. You can now log on as George Washington and publish the forms you will create later in this chapter. Click OK.

7. Click Close.

Once form libraries have been created, forms can be designed and installed in these libraries. This will be discussed in the next two sections.

Designing Forms

Exchange provides two tools that can be used to design forms, the Outlook Forms Designer and the Exchange Forms Designer. Neither of these tools require programming to create a form, and both come with sample forms that can be used with or without customization. In this section, we will discuss these tools and the interoperability of the forms they create with client applications.

Microsoft Outlook Forms Designer

Sometimes the best way to explain something is to start at the end and work back. We will do this by first discussing the characteristics of an Outlook form, then covering the features that assist in the creation of an Outlook form, and finally outlining the actual steps to design and create a form.

Outlook Form Characteristics

The Outlook Forms Designer creates full-featured, yet small (average size 10K), 32-bit forms that can be quickly loaded and sent. The forms created are not *compiled*, meaning they are not translated into machine code (1s and 0s). Instead the source code is interpreted every time the form is loaded. This is an advantage because it allows forms to be easily modified. Forms can be linked to other Office 97 objects and even to items on the Web. For example, a chart created in Microsoft Excel could be embedded in an Outlook form. Another example is a Web page containing a registration button that is linked to an Outlook form. When a Web user clicks on that button the Outlook form is displayed requesting the user's registration information.

Microsoft Outlook Forms Designer Features

As stated earlier in this chapter, Outlook Forms Designer provides a visual, nonprogrammatic interface for forms creation. A user can simply choose a sample form, and then drag-and-drop the sample objects or new objects around on the form. The user can also assign properties and events to objects by accessing an object's property pages.

Outlook Sample Forms   Users are not relegated to creating forms from scratch. Outlook Forms Designer comes with numerous sample forms that can be used unchanged, or easily modified without any programming. They can also be modified using Visual Basic. Table 8.1 lists and describes these sample forms. More sample Outlook forms can be downloaded from the Microsoft Web site, `http://www.microsoft.com`.

	Sample Form	Description
T A B L E 8.1 Outlook Forms Designer sample forms	Expense Report	Contains fields for various expense report information, such as name, date, expense categories, and subtotals. This form is patterned after a Microsoft Excel spreadsheet.
	Help Desk	Contains fields for making requests to a help desk, such as fixing or ordering equipment. This form also enables status tracking of the help desk request.

	Sample Form	Description
TABLE 8.1 (cont.) Outlook Forms Designer sample forms	Job Candidate	Contains fields for an interviewer to enter various information about a job candidate so this information can be posted in a public folder. Several interviewers can post their comments on a candidate, and then a supervisor can view this information.
	Sales Management	Contains fields relating to contact management (e.g., name, address, phone) and sales processes (e.g., meeting schedules). Permits sales management to store and view structured information.
	User Group	This form is part of an online discussion folder, where users can post, read, and respond to user-generated topics. Topics can be grouped by *discussion thread* to make a discussion easy to follow.
	Vacation Report	Contains fields relating to vacation requests and approvals.
	While You Were Out	Enables someone to take a message for another person, and to send the message to that person's mailbox.

Form Types When designing a form from scratch, a user can choose from various standard types of forms. These form types are described in Table 8.2.

	Form Type	Description
TABLE 8.2 Form types	Mail Message	Used to create Send forms, which can be used to send and receive information between recipients. Use this form type to create stand-alone form applications.
	Post	Used to create Post forms, which can be used to post information to a folder. If posted in a public folder, a group of users can view and respond to the postings. Folder-based applications are created by adding Post forms to a public folder and then customizing the permissions, views, and rules on that folder.

T A B L E 8.2 *(cont.)* Form types	**Form Type**	**Description**
	Office 97 Document	Forms can include Office 97 documents. For example, a Microsoft Excel spreadsheet could be used in a form. The Outlook form, in a sense, wraps around the Office 97 document, allowing the document to be sent to other recipients.
	Contact, Task, and Calendar	Standard forms in Outlook are used to create new contacts, tasks, appointments, and meetings. These standard forms can be modified using Outlook Forms Designer.

Standard Design Features   Table 8.3 summarizes the features that help a user design a form.

T A B L E 8.3 Standard design features	**Feature**	**Description**
	Alignment	Various alignment options assist the user when placing items on a form. Alignment options include left, center, right, top, middle, bottom, and snapping to a grid.
	Adjustable grid size	Enables the accurate positioning of items on a form.
	AutoLayout	Outlook Forms Designer can automatically position items on a form. For example, if a new item is placed below an existing item, AutoLayout will automatically left-align the new item with the existing item.

Figure 8.2 shows a design window in Outlook Forms Designer.

Advanced Design Features   Outlook Forms Designer includes design features that can be used to create advanced forms. Two of these features are described in Table 8.4.

276 Chapter 8 · Microsoft Exchange Forms

A design window in
Outlook Forms Designer

	Feature	Description
TABLE 8.4 Advanced design features	Access Expression Service	A user can design a form that includes formula-based fields or validated or calculated fields. For example, a calculated field might total the number of days requested for vacation or a validated field might enforce a check request amount to be less than a certain ceiling.
	Visual Basic Scripting	Although Outlook Forms Designer is a nonprogrammatic forms-creation tool, the source code of the forms it creates is in Visual Basic format. Consequently, the source code of a form can be modified using Visual Basic or Visual Basic Scripting Edition (VBScript).

Designing and Creating an Outlook Form

You now have the necessary knowledge to proceed with the steps to create an Outlook form. The Outlook Forms Designer is started from within Outlook. Under the File menu, choose the New option, and then choose an Outlook component that will serve as the basic building block of the form. After the form is loaded, choose the Tools menu on the form window, and select the Design Outlook Form option. This option runs the Outlook Forms Designer.

Exercise 8.2 will walk you through the basic steps to create a form with the Outlook Forms Designer. Figures 8.3A and 8.3B depict the form that you will create in this exercise.

EXERCISE 8.2

Creating a Customer Tracking Form with Outlook Forms Designer

1. While in Outlook, choose File ➤ New ➤ Contact. You will see a window titled "Untitled-Contact." This loads the Outlook contact form which will serve as a building block for our form.

2. From the Untitled-Contact window, choose the Tools menu, then choose Design Outlook Form. The window will now be titled "Untitled-Contact (Design)." The Outlook Forms Designer is now running. Maximize the window.

3. Click the tab labeled "(Properties)." In the Form Caption box, enter **Customer Tracking for Widget, Inc**.

4. Click the tab labeled "(P.2)." Under the Form menu, choose Rename Page. The Rename Page dialog box appears. In the Page Name box, enter **More Info**. Click OK. Now we will begin dragging-and-dropping objects onto the new form.

5. In the Field Chooser palette window, click Full Name and drag it to the upper-left corner of the form. A text entry field labeled "Full Name" will be added.

6. Click the down-arrow on the Field Chooser palette, and click Personal fields. From the options that now appear, drag Anniversary, Children, Hobbies, Referred By, and Web Page to the area below the Full Name field.

EXERCISE 8.2 (CONTINUED FROM PREVIOUS PAGE)

7. Click the New button at the bottom of the Field Chooser palette. The New Field dialog box appears. In the Name box, enter **Key Customer**. In the Type list, choose Yes/No. Click OK.

8. Drag the Key Customer field to the area under the Web Page field. You should notice that the Yes/No option is displayed as a check box.

9. On the File menu, choose Save As. The Save As screen will appear. In the File name field, type **cust-track-form**. Select Outlook Template in the Save type field. Click Save. The form will be saved with this name.

10. The form is now created, but it is not available for use. It must be installed in a forms library. The installation is performed in Outlook, but this step will be covered in the section "Installing Forms" and in Exercise 8.4.

FIGURE 8.3A

The form created in Exercise 8.2

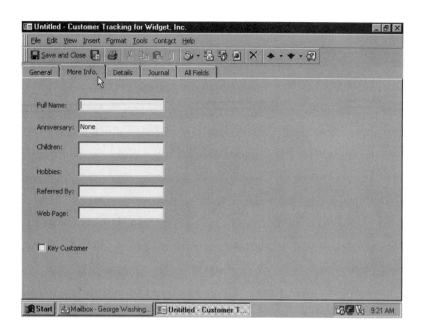

FIGURE 8.3B

The form created in
Exercise 8.2

Now you need to create a Task Form. Exercise 8.3 will help you get
started. Use your creativity to design and finish the form yourself.

EXERCISE 8.3

Creating a Task Form with Outlook Forms Designer

1. In Outlook, choose File ➢ New ➢ Task. You will see a window titled
"Untitled-Task." This loads the Outlook task form which will serve as
a building block for our form.

2. From the Untitled-Task window, choose the Tools menu, then choose
Design Outlook Form. The window will now be titled "Untitled-Task
(Design)." The Outlook Forms Designer is now running. Maximize
the window.

3. Click the tab labeled "(Properties)." In the Form Caption box, enter
Task Form, Accounting Dept.

4. Design the form any way you would like.

EXERCISE 8.3 (CONTINUED FROM PREVIOUS PAGE)

5. When you have finished designing the form, save it by choosing the File menu, and Save As option. Name it **task-form**. Select Outlook Template in the Save as type field.

6. As with the last exercise, this form is created, but is not available for use. The form must be installed in a forms library while in Outlook. You will perform this procedure in Exercise 8.4.

Exchange Forms Designer

We will now discuss the characteristics of an EFD form, the features that assist in the creation of a form using EFD, and the steps to create a form using EFD.

EFD Form Characteristics

Whereas Outlook forms are 32-bit and not compiled, EFD forms are 16-bit and compiled. After an EFD form has been created, it is installed in a forms library. For EFD forms, forms are compiled into executable files at the moment they are installed in a library (there is more on this process in the section Installing Forms).

Exchange Forms Designer Features

Some EFD features are similar to those in Outlook Forms Designer. Both tools enable a drag-and-drop manipulation of objects, like text entry fields and checkboxes, in order to design a form. Both tools include sample forms that can be used immediately or customized. Forms created with both tools can be extended with Visual Basic programming.

Two of the main differences between EFD and Outlook Forms Designer are that EFD builds compiled forms, and EFD cannot use Office 97 objects as part of a form because EFD is a 16-bit application. Also, EFD and Outlook Forms Designer include different sets of sample forms.

Exchange Forms Designer Sample Forms   Exchange Forms Designer comes with many useful sample forms. These forms can simplify record keeping, enhance office communication, and increase staff efficiency. Table 8.5 lists and describes the sample forms that come with Exchange Forms Designer.

	Sample Form	Description
TABLE 8.5 Exchange Forms Designer sample forms	Anonymous Submissions	Enables anonymous information to be posted to a public folder.
	Charity Donation	Includes fields for a charity name and amount to donate.
	Classified Ads	Enables classified ads to be posted to a public folder.
	Chess	A demonstration form showing how Visual Basic, Active Messaging, and Exchange can be used to create a form-based application. Users can play chess via e-mail, complete with a view of the board, using this nifty sample.
	Customer Tracking	Includes fields relating to various customer information. Can be used to track customer contacts and information.
	Discussion and Response	This form is part of an online discussion folder, where users can post, read, and respond to user-generated topics. Topics can be grouped by *discussion thread* to make a discussion easy to follow.
	Help Desk	Includes fields for help desk requests, such as fixing or ordering equipment.
	Hot Topics	Enables moderator approved news items to be submitted.
	Interpersonal Forms	A collection of forms that are appropriate for inclusion in the organization forms library. Includes the following forms: Answer, Bug Report, Charity Donation, Purchase Offer, and Vacation/Sick-Day.
	Schedule Time Away	Includes fields for submitting vacation or sick-day requests.
	Survey	Includes fields that can be customized to create polls or surveys.

Exchange Forms Designer Interface   EFD includes a toolbox palette which permits a user to drag-and-drop text entry fields, drop-down lists, and other elements onto a form. EFD also includes a toolbar that allows easy access to functions such as changing colors, creating tables, and saving forms. The sample forms mentioned earlier can be used as a starting point for creating a custom form. EFD also includes the Forms Design Wizard. The Wizard guides the user through the process of creating a new form. When the Wizard is complete, the user can further customize the new form using the tools in EFD.

Designing and Creating an EFD Form

The Exchange Forms Designer can be launched from within the Exchange Client application. Start EFD by choosing Application Design, Forms Designer from the Tools menu. When EFD starts, it prompts the user to choose the Form Template Wizard, or a sample form from the Template List, or another existing form. After a form has been created, it can be saved by choosing Save from the File menu, or by clicking the Save toolbar button. When an EFD form is saved, it is stored in an Exchange Forms Project (EFP) file. This is a Microsoft Access 2.0 database file containing all the information about the form's structure and functionality. The EFP file is used to generate Visual Basic source code during the installation of the form (see "Installing Forms.")

Interoperability Issues

Outlook users can use forms created by either the Outlook Forms Designer or EFD, but Exchange Client users cannot use forms created by the Outlook Forms Designer. Microsoft Mail and other foreign mail system users cannot use forms created in either the Outlook Forms Designer or EFD. This is an important issue to keep in mind when designing an Exchange organization. If all users will be using Outlook, then the Outlook Forms Designer is the obvious choice for forms creation. But if some users are using Outlook and some are using the Exchange Client, then EFD should be used until all users have been upgraded to Outlook.

Comparing Outlook Forms Designer and EFD

Table 8.6 summarizes and compares the two forms creation programs.

T A B L E 8.6 Comparison of Outlook Forms Designer and EFD	**Outlook Forms Designer**	**Exchange Forms Designer (EFD)**
	32-bit forms	16-bit forms
	Visual, nonprogrammatic design method	Visual, nonprogrammatic design method

TABLE 8.6 (cont.) Comparison of Outlook Forms Designer and EFD	**Outlook Forms Designer**	**Exchange Forms Designer (EFD)**
	Forms not compiled	Forms compiled
	Send and Post forms	Send and Post forms
	Microsoft Office 97 integration	No Microsoft Office 97 integration
	Sample forms included	Sample forms included
	Form code can be extended using Visual Basic	Form code can be extended using Visual Basic
	Can be read by Outlook, but not by the Exchange Client	Can be read by Outlook or the Exchange Client

Installing Forms

After a form is created, it must be installed in a forms library before it can be used. Installation in a library makes a form available to a specific user or a group of users. The installation process puts a form in the necessary format and location for use. Outlook, EFD, and the Exchange Client can each be used to install (or *publish*) a form.

Installing a Form Using Outlook

After a form has been created using the Outlook Forms Designer, the user can install it from within Outlook. Choose Options from the Tools menu and select the Manage Forms property page on the Options dialog box that appears. Click the Manage Forms button to open the Forms Manager. The Forms Manager is used to install forms into libraries and move forms between libraries. Forms can also be installed directly from the form window when they are created. A user installing a form into a folder needs the Folder Owner permission on that folder. Exercise 8.4 outlines the steps for this process.

EXERCISE 8.4

Installing a Form Using Outlook

1. If you still have the task form loaded, you can install it by choosing File ➤ Publish Form As. The Publish Form As dialog box will appear (if this form is not loaded, go to Step 5).

2. Click Publish In. The Set Library To dialog box will appear.

3. In the Forms Library list, click Organization Forms, and then click OK.

4. Click Publish.

5. If the task form is not loaded, go to the Outlook Bar (the icon and options on the far-left side of your Outlook window), and click on the Other option. This will bring up the icons for My Computer, My Documents, and Favorites. Click on My Documents or navigate to the folder in which you saved the task form.

6. In the right content pane, locate and double-click on the TASK-FORM.OFT file. This will bring up the task form. To see the information that you designed, choose Tools ➤ Design Outlook Form.

7. To publish this form, choose File ➤ Publish Form As. The Publish Form As dialog box will appear.

8. Click Publish In. The Set Library To dialog box will appear.

9. In the Forms Library list, click Organization Forms, and then click OK.

10. Click Publish.

11. Choose File ➤ Close.

12. You also need to publish the Customer Tracking for Widget, Inc. form. We saved this form, so use the procedure outlined in Steps 5 – 10 to retrieve it.

Installing a Form Using EFD

Immediately after creating and saving a form in the EFD program, the form can be installed. To do this, choose the Install option from the File menu.

When this option is selected, three processes occur automatically, and a fourth process requires user input. The four processes are listed here:

1. **Generation of source code** The EFD program takes the information in the Exchange Forms Project (EFP) file and generates Visual Basic source code in a file with a VBP extension. The EFP file was created when the form was saved.

2. **Compiling into an executable file** The EFD program compiles the Visual Basic source code into an executable file (EXE).

3. **Creation of a configuration file** The EFD creates a text file containing configuration information about the compiled form. Information includes the form's executable name, message type (i.e., Send or Post form), and a list of fields on the form. The configuration file has a CFG extension and is stored in the <form_name>.vb directory. This file is used in the next step.

4. **Install in a forms library** The user now specifies the forms library where the form is to be installed. After Step 3 is complete, the Set Library To dialog box will appear. The user selects the destination forms library in this dialog box.

Installing a Form Using the Exchange Client

If a form has already been compiled in EFD, it can be installed through the Exchange Client. To do this, choose Options from the Tools menu and select the Exchange Server tab from the Options dialog box that appears. Click the Manage Forms button on this tab to invoke the Forms Manager. The Forms Manager can be used to install new forms and move forms between forms libraries. A user installing a form into a folder needs the Folder Owner permission on that folder.

Summary

Electronic forms can be used instead of most paper-based forms to provide a more efficient method of communication. Send Forms can be used to send information to other users. Post Forms can be used to post information to a personal, private, or public folder. Forms posted in public folders can be used as the foundation for a folder-based application.

Exchange Server ships with two forms design programs, Outlook Forms Designer, and Exchange Forms Designer (EFD). Outlook Forms Designer is a 32-bit program that creates small, fast-loading, uncompiled 32-bit forms. It integrates very tightly with Microsoft Office 97. EFD is a 16-bit program that creates compiled forms. Both programs provide a visual, nonprogrammatic method to create forms. They also both provide sample forms that can be used immediately or customized.

After forms have been created, they are installed, or published, in a forms library. This makes the form available for use to a user or group of users. Security can be applied to a forms library to configure who can install and use forms.

Both forms design programs use a specialized version of Visual Basic. The forms that are created can therefore be further customized or extended by loading the form file into Visual Basic and adding further program code.

Users send and receive forms through their normal Exchange client programs, such as Outlook and the Exchange Client.

Review Questions

1. Various users in your organization need to use electronic forms while offline. To accommodate this scenario, you e-mail the necessary forms to these users while they are online. What else must be done for these users to use these forms while offline?

   A. Install Microsoft Visual Basic on each client computer.

   B. Install the forms into a public folder library.

   C. Install the forms into the organization forms library.

   D. Install the forms into a personal folder on each client computer.

2. A form that is used to directly input information into a public folder is called:

   A. A Send form

   B. An Input form

   C. A Folder form

   D. A Post form

3. The Exchange Client can send and receive Outlook forms.

   A. True

   B. False

4. The following procedure makes forms available for use:

   A. Installing or publishing forms

   B. Customizing in Visual Basic

   C. Saving in the FRM format

   D. Saving to the Access database

5. If a form needed wide availability, it would be installed in this location:

   A. Personal folder

   B. Organization forms library

   C. Administrator's mailbox

   D. A public mailbox

6. Outlook can send and receive forms created in EFD.

   A. True

   B. False

7. Which of the following is NOT a design feature of Outlook Forms Designer?

  A. AutoLayout

  B. Alignment

  C. Visual Basic scripting

  D. Lotus Notes formatting

8. EFD saves form information in this database format:

  A. Microsoft Access

  B. SQL

  C. Paradox

  D. DB2

CHAPTER

9

Public Folders as a Client Resource

P ublic folders are one of the most important objects in an Exchange environment. They are a key element in the creation of folder-based applications, such as bulletin boards, discussion groups, help desks, and many others. Public folders allow multiple users to effectively and efficiently share information. In this chapter, you will learn to:

- Create public folders

- Configure public folders

- Use public folders

- Customizing public folders

The tasks described in this chapter can all be performed by client users. Chapter 12 will cover public folders from the perspective of an Exchange administrator. Topics covered in that chapter will include public folder replication, storage limits, creating dedicated public folder servers, and many others.

Creating Public Folders

P ublic folders are created using Exchange MAPI-based clients. They cannot be created from the Exchange Administrator program. It is a very simple process for users to create new public folders, assuming they have been granted the necessary permissions by the administrator and have a basic understanding of public folder functionality.

Public Folder Hierarchy

Public folders are organized hierarchically, like a directory structure (see Figure 9.1). The root, or highest level, is called the *top-level*. By default, all users may create folders at this level, but the Exchange Administrator program can be used to modify the list of users who have permissions to create top-level folders. It is important to have this administrator control so that users don't clutter up the root of the tree and make it difficult to navigate. Exercise 9.1 outlines the steps to modify the permissions.

FIGURE 9.1

Public folder hierarchy

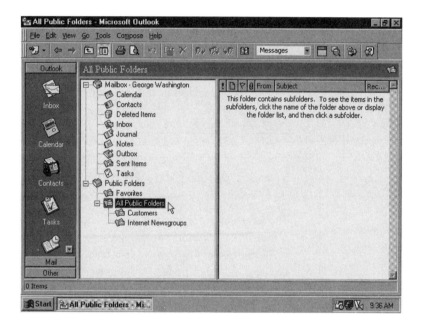

Subfolders can be created within the top-level folders. Subfolders can also have subfolders, and those subfolders can also have subfolders...and so on (see the sidebar). Subfolders are like subdirectories in a directory structure. A folder's owner (who is, by default, the user who created the folder) determines who may create subfolders in a folder by assigning the necessary permissions. Create Subfolders is the name of the permission that must be granted (permissions are discussed in the section "Configuring Public Folders").

EXERCISE 9.1

Modifying the Top-Level Permissions

1. Start the Exchange Administrator program and connect to the Exchange server.

2. In the left pane, click to expand your site object, then click on the Configuration object within it.

3. In the right pane, double-click on the Information Store Site Configuration object. This will bring up the property pages for Information Store Site Configuration.

4. Click on the tab labeled "Top Level Folder Creation." You will see two list box fields that allow you to specify who may or may not create public folders at the top-level of the public folder hierarchy. For our purposes, do not change the default.

Turtles All the Way Down

The following story may not be true, but it is funny. Some years ago, a famous professor of astronomy at an Ivy League college went on a speaking tour of small, out-of-the-way towns. He would speak and show slides of planets, solar systems, and other bodies in the universe. At the end of his presentations, he would answer questions. At one meeting, an old man got up and thanked the professor for coming and talking. But he made it quite clear that he thought everything the professor had said was bunk because the Earth rested on the back of a big turtle. After hearing this, the professor smiled and wanted to know what the turtle rested on. The old man replied that the turtle rested on the back of another bigger turtle. As the professor began to ask what that turtle rested on, the old man interrupted him by saying, "Oh no, you can't trick me. The answer is turtles all the way down!"

Programs and Procedure to Create Public Folders

The Exchange Administrator program can be used to manage public folders, but not create them. Both Outlook and the Exchange Client programs can be used to create public folders. In Outlook, a public folder can be created by choosing Folder, Create Subfolder from the File menu. The Create New Folder dialog box will appear, prompting you for various information. Exercise 9.2 will walk you through these steps.

EXERCISE 9.2

Creating a Public Folder with Outlook

1. Log on to the Windows NT domain as GeorgeW.

2. Start Outlook, click on the File menu, choose Folder ➢ Create Subfolder. The Create New Folder dialog box will appear.

3. In the Name field, enter a name for the public folder you are creating. For this exercise, enter the name **Customers**.

4. In the Make this Folder a Subfolder Of field, expand the Public Folders object, and then select the All Public Folders object within it.

5. Type the following in the Description field: **This folder contains various information relating to customers of Widget, Inc.** Click OK.

6. If the Folder List is not visible, click the Folder List tool button on the toolbar, or choose Folder List from the View menu. The folder hierarchy will be displayed in a new pane. Maximize Outlook, and if necessary, enlarge the Folder List by grabbing its right border and resizing it to a suitable viewing width.

7. Notice the Customers public folder directly under the All Public Folders object. Click on the Customers folder to see that there are no items in it yet.

Configuring Public Folders

$\mathbf{T}$he key configuration elements of public folders are:

- Permissions

- Forms

- Rules

- Views

Public folders have a set of property pages that are used for configuration. There are two ways to display these property pages. One way is to highlight the public folder, click the right mouse button, and choose Properties from the pop-up menu that appears. Another way is to highlight the public folder and then choose Folders, Properties for <public folder name> from the File menu.

Permissions

By assigning permissions, a public folder owner can choose which users have access to the folder, and what actions those users may perform. There are eight individual permissions and nine groupings of permissions, called roles, that can be assigned. Table 9.1 describes the permissions, descending from the permission with the most capabilities to the permission with the fewest capabilities. The word "items," as used in this table, refers to the contents of the public folder, such as e-mail messages, forms, documents, and other files.

T A B L E 9.1

Public folder permissions

Permission	Description
Folder Owner	Can change permissions in a folder and perform administrative tasks, such as adding rules and installing forms on a folder
Create Items	Create new items in a folder
Create Subfolders	Create subfolders within a folder
Edit Items	Edit (modify) items in a folder
Delete Items	Permanently delete items in a folder

	Permission	Description
TABLE 9.1 (cont.) Public folder permissions	Read Items	Open and view items in a folder
	Folder Contact	Receive e-mail notifications relating to a folder. Notifications include replication conflicts, folder design conflicts, and storage limit notifications. (There is more on this in Chapter 12.)
	Folder Visible	Whether the folder is visible to the user in the public folder hierarchy

Table 9.2 lists the predefined groupings of permissions into roles.

TABLE 9.2

Predefined roles and their permissions

Role	Folder Owner	Create Items	Create Subfolder	Edit Items	Delete Items	Read Items	Folder Contact	Folder Visible
Owner	✓	✓	✓	✓ (all)	✓ (all)	✓	✓	✓
Publishing Editor		✓	✓	✓ (all)	✓ (all)	✓		✓
Editor		✓		✓ (all)	✓ (all)	✓		✓
Publishing Author		✓	✓	✓ (own)	✓ (own)	✓		✓
Author		✓		✓ (own)	✓ (own)	✓		✓
Nonediting Author		✓			✓ (own)	✓		✓
Contributor		✓						✓
Reviewer						✓		✓
None								✓

Custom roles consisting of any combination of individual permissions may also be assigned.

When a public folder is created, the following three users are included on the permissions list by default (see Figure 9.2):

- **The user who created the public folder**. This user is automatically assigned the Owner role. The Owner of a folder may also grant other users this role.

FIGURE 9.2

The Permissions property page of a public folder

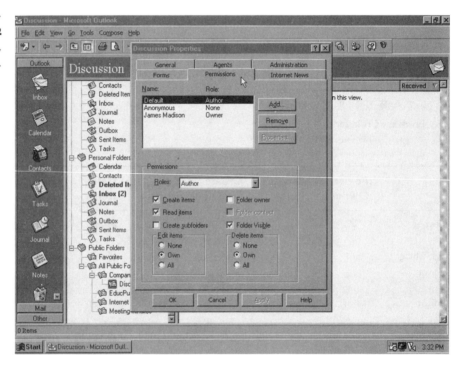

- **A special user called Default**. This user represents all users who have access to the public folder store who aren't explicitly listed in the permissions list. On top-level folders, the Default user is automatically granted the Author role (this can be modified). The Author role enables users to create subfolders under the top-level folder. Below the top-level folders, the Default user automatically inherits the permissions it has at its parent folder.

- **A special user called Anonymous**. The Anonymous user represents all users logged on with anonymous access. For example, an Exchange server could contain public folders holding promotional information for public viewing. People without NT user accounts could use a Web browser or news reader program and the anonymous account to access the Exchange server and read the promotional information. Any permissions assigned to the Anonymous account will be applied to these users.

The three users listed above cannot be removed from the permissions list of a public folder. However, the particular roles and permissions they have can be modified. All other users can be removed from a permissions list.

Exchange administrators can always designate themselves owners of public folders. This is especially important if the recipient that is the owner of a public folder (or all Windows NT accounts that are on the permissions list of that recipient) is deleted.

Exercise 9.3 outlines the steps to configure the permissions on the Customers public folder.

EXERCISE 9.3

Configuring the Permissions on a Public Folder

1. In Outlook, highlight the Customers public folder. Click the right mouse button and choose Properties from the pop-up menu. The Customers Properties dialog box will appear.

2. Click on the Permissions tab. Notice that (because this is a top-level folder) the Default user has the Author role. Notice that the user who created this public folder, GeorgeW, has the Owner role.
   Brian S

3. Highlight the Default user, then click on the down-arrow in the Roles field. Choose the None role from the list.

4. Click Add and highlight the user *Bruce m* Thomas Jefferson. Then click Add and click OK. The user Thomas Jefferson is added to the access list for the public folder with the role of None. This role was automatically assigned because the Default user's role is None. Change Thomas Jefferson's role to Author. Notice that Thomas Jefferson now has the Create items and Read items permissions. This role also allows him to edit and delete his own items.

5. Click OK to save the configuration. These permissions will be tested in the section "Using Public Folders" later in this chapter.

Hiding Public Folders

Public folders can be hidden from the GAL and the public folder hierarchy. Hiding public folders can be part of your security plan. The following bullet points contain information about the different aspects of this topic:

- **Hiding a public folder from the GAL**   By default, each public folder is hidden from the GAL. A public folder can be made visible by clearing the "Hide from address book" checkbox found on its Advanced property page.

- **Hiding a public folder from the public folder hierarchy**   By default, all public folders and their content is visible in the public folder hierarchy to all other recipients. To make the contents of a particular public folder hidden, you must revoke the Read Items permission for the recipient or recipients at that particular folder. If you wanted to hide not merely the contents of a public folder, but also its very listing in the hierarchy you can revoke the Read Items permission at the parent folder of the folder you want hidden. Since a subfolder is considered part of the content of its parent folder, revoking this permission at the parent folder can prevent the viewing of that subfolder in the hierarchy.

Many times an organization will create a top level called Hidden Folders that will contain all the folders they want hidden from the majority of their users. The Default user will be assigned the None role at Hidden Folders, which will prevent them from viewing all subfolders. Even the top-level folder Hidden Folders could be made invisible by revoking the Folder Visible permission from the Default user. To enable the users who do need to access the subfolders under this root, distribution lists would be created and assigned the relevant permissions at this root and any subfolders.

Forms

Forms can be associated with a public folder, allowing users to submit structured data into the folder. The list of forms associated with a public folder is found in the folder's property pages. Exercise 9.4 walks through the steps to associate a form with a public folder.

EXERCISE 9.4

Associating a Form with a Public Folder

1. In Outlook, highlight the Customers public folder in the hierarchy in the Folder List. Choose File ➤ Folders ➤ Properties for "Customers." The Customers Properties dialog box will appear.

2. Click on the Forms tab. Notice that there are currently no forms associated with this public folder, but that the Allow These Forms in This Folder field is set to Any Form. You are going to associate a specific form with this folder and configure it as the only form to be used with this folder.

3. Click Manage. The Forms Manager will appear listing the forms published in the Organization Forms library. In Chapter 8 you created the Customer Tracking for Widget, Inc. form. This form will appear in the list box under the Organization Forms library.

4. Click on the Customer Tracking for Widget, Inc. form, then click Copy. Because this form was already installed, all you have to do now is click Close. Notice that this form is now associated with this public folder.

5. Under the Allow These Forms in This Folder field, choose Only Forms Listed Above. Then click OK. The form installation performed in this exercise will be tested in the section "Using Public Folders."

Rules

Rules consisting of conditions and actions can be configured on public folders. Rules allow a public folder to automate certain procedures. The following is a list of some of the conditions (or *criteria*) that can be used in a rule:

- **From**   Message from specified recipients.

- **Sent To**   Message sent to specified recipients.

- **Subject**   Specified text in the Subject heading of a message.

- **Message Body**   Specified text or phrase in the body of a message.

- **Size**   A specified size of a message, "At least" x size, or "At most" x size.

- **Received**   A specified date range that a message was received within.

The following actions can be triggered if the preceding conditions are met:

- **Delete**   Delete the message.

- **Reply With**   Reply to the message's sender with a specified message template.

- **Forward To**   Forward the message to specified recipients.

A rule could be used, for example, to keep postings separate from replies. If a company had a public folder called Company Events containing information on upcoming company events, users could be given permission to provide feedback on these events by sending replies to this folder. However, the number of replies in this folder could hinder users from finding the original events posting. To resolve this, the owner of this folder could create a subfolder called Discussions. The owner could then create a rule for Company Events that states that all replies to this folder should be forwarded to the Discussion folder. For this example to work, the preceding folders must be visible in the GAL.

Rules are added to public folders by clicking the Folder Assistant button on a folder's Administration property page. Clicking this button displays the Folder Assistant dialog box which enables you to add, edit, delete, and order rules for a public folder. Exercise 9.5 outlines the steps to create a rule on a public folder.

Views

Outlook and the Exchange Client include many powerful features to view items in a folder. Some of the features in Outlook are listed in Table 9.3.

The next section will cover using some of the features discussed earlier in this chapter.

EXERCISE 9.5

Creating a Rule on a Public Folder

1. In Outlook, highlight the Customers public folder. Click the right mouse button and choose Properties from the pop-up menu. The Customers Properties dialog box will appear.

2. Click on the Administration tab.

3. Click Folder Assistant. The Folder Assistant dialog box will appear.

4. Click Add Rule. The Edit Rule dialog box will appear. In the Subject field type **Acme**, and in the Message Body type **Acme** again. This is the condition part of the rule.

5. Now we will set the action part of the rule. Click the Forward check box, and then click To. The Choose Recipient dialog box will appear. In the Show Names from The field, choose Global Address List. Then, choose the user Andrew Jackson and click To. Click OK. Then click OK successively on the next three dialog boxes. The rule is now saved within the properties of the Customers public folder. This rule will be tested in the "Using Public Folders" section.

T A B L E 9.3 Outlook features	Feature	Examples
	Sort	Sort items by who they are from, who they are to, importance, subject text, sensitivity, or other properties.
	Filter	Filter items by words of phrases contained in the subject text or message body, who they are from, who they are to, what time they were sent, or other properties. Only items that pass through the filter are displayed in the contents pane.
	Group By	Group items by when they are due, who they are from, who they are to, importance, subject text, sensitivity, or other properties.

Using Public Folders

T his section and its exercises cover how to add content to a public folder.

Adding Content to a Public Folder

The two primary methods to add content to a public folder are:

- Posting forms
- Mail messages

Posting

If a public folder is configured to accept postings, which is the default, users who have the necessary permissions can post data to the public folder. To post, a user must highlight the public folder and either click the Post tool on the Toolbar, or choose New Post in This Folder from the Compose menu. Posting is an easy and efficient method of adding content to a public folder because the user does not have to address the message as they do when sending a mail message to a public folder. Exercise 9.6 outlines the steps for this procedure.

Another method of adding content to a public folder is to drag-and-drop a Microsoft Office 97 object directly into the folder. This method is equivalent to posting an item to the folder.

Mail Messages

A mail message can be sent to a public folder. As you will remember from Chapter 4, a public folder is a recipient, and can therefore receive and send messages. Exercise 9.7 outlines the steps to send a mail message to a public folder.

EXERCISE 9.6

Posting Information to a Public Folder

1. In Outlook, highlight the Customers public folder.

2. Choose File ➢ New ➢ Choose Form. The New Form dialog box will appear.

3. Highlight the Customer Tracking for Widget, Inc. form. Click OK. The form will appear.

4. Enter the following in the Full Name field: **Dolly Madison**.

5. Enter the following in the Company field: **Acme**.

6. Enter some text in the body.

7. Click on the More Info. tab to view the page you designed. Enter some information.

8. When you are finished entering information, click the Save and Close toolbar button.

9. Notice the new entry in the Customers public folder. If you double-click that entry, you will see the information you just entered.

10. To test our configuration of the forms associated with this public folder, try to use the Task Form, Accounting Dept. form to post information to this public folder. You should not be able to do so because we configured this public folder to use only the Customer Tracking form.

11. To test Thomas Jefferson's permission assignments at this folder, log on as Thomas Jefferson and post some information to the Customer folder. Use the Post button on the Toolbar to enter information into this folder. We gave Thomas Jefferson the Author role, so you should be able to post.

12. Log on as Andrew Jackson. Can you enter information into the Customer folder? Did we give Andrew Jackson any permissions to the folder?

13. Log back on as George Washington to prepare for the next exercise.

EXERCISE 9.7

Sending a Mail Message to a Public Folder

1. In order for someone to send a mail message to a public folder, the public folder must be visible in the address book. By default, public folders are not visible in the address book. To perform this exercise, we must make the Customers public folder visible. While in Exchange Administrator, navigate to and highlight the Customers public folder under the Public Folders container. Click File ➤ Properties. The Customers Properties pages appear. Click the Advanced page. Notice the checkbox labeled "Hide from address book." It is checked. For this exercise, clear this checkbox. Click OK. This public folder will now be visible in the address book.

2. Make sure you are logged on as George Washington. In Outlook, choose Compose ➤ New Message. An untitled mail-message window will appear.

3. Click To. In the Show Names from The field, choose Global Address List. Find the Customers public folder in the Global Address List.

4. Select the Customers public folder and click To. Click OK.

5. In the Subject field, type **Acme Proposal**.

6. In the body of the message enter the following: **I think we can lower our unit price and increase the units shipped in regard to the Acme proposal. What are your thoughts?**

7. Click the Options tab. In the Importance field, choose High. For Tracking options choose Tell Me When this Message Has Been Read.

8. Click the Send tool in the Toolbar.

9. To test the rule we assigned to the Customer folder, log on as Andrew Jackson and see if the Folder Assistant automatically sent Andrew Jackson the information about Acme that was posted to the Customer folder.

Customizing Public Folders

Public folders can be turned into customized applications through the use of the Microsoft Exchange Scripting Agent, Microsoft Exchange Event Service. Each of these elements, plus the topics of security and Microsoft Outlook, will be introduced in the following paragraphs.

Scripts

One of the properties that a public folder can have is a script written in Microsoft VBScript or Microsoft JScript. A script can contain the instructions for carrying out various actions. For example, a script could be created that would read the amount of a purchase request posted to a folder, compare that amount to a database containing the people with approval ability of various amounts, and then forward the posting to the appropriate person.

Microsoft Exchange Event Service

The Microsoft Exchange Event Service is the component that monitors public folders that have scripts. The Event Service watches for a designated event or events to occur in folders and serves as a trigger mechanism for scripts to be executed. The Event Service can monitor such folder events as postings, changes, and deletions. When the Event Service detects the designated trigger mechanism, it automatically starts the Scripting Agent.

Microsoft Exchange Scripting Agent

The Scripting Agent is the component that reads and executes the script attached to the public folder. It can carry out instructions by accessing databases, spreadsheets, gateways, and many other programs and services.

Security

To create, edit, or save a script for a folder, the user must have the Author role set of permissions. This is done in the Exchange Administrator program. In that program under the objects Folders/System Folders is an object called Events Root. The Events Root object contains a folder called EventConfig_ <server name> that allows the administrator to assign the Author role to the users needing to create, edit, or save scripts. When a user has this permission in the EventConfig folder, they will see the Agents tab when viewing the properties of a public folder through their client application.

Microsoft Outlook and Scripts

Microsoft Outlook, version 8.03 or later, enables users to create, edit, or save a script for a public folder. If a user has the necessary permissions, they can access the Agents property page of a folder. There they can create an agent or agents that define the events that will be the trigger mechanism for the script, and create or edit the script (Edit Scripts button). By default, Outlook will use Microsoft Notepad as the editor for the script. But if the user has Microsoft Visual InterDev installed, it also can be used as the editor.

For more information on these topics see the Microsoft Platform Software Development Kit (SDK).

Summary

Public folders are an efficient and effective way to share data among several people. Permissions, forms, rules, and views can be configured on public folders to create folder-based applications. Users can easily create public folders using Outlook or the Exchange Client.

Permissions enable a folder owner to specify who can access a folder, and what users can do in that folder. Associating a form with a public folder assists users in submitting structured information into the folder. Rules on public folders can perform automated actions when the appropriate conditions are met. Public folders can hold a large quantity and variety of information, so views can be leveraged to display the pertinent items in a desired way.

Adding content to public folders is very easy. It can be done by posting directly to a public folder, or by sending the public folder regular e-mail messages.

Review Questions

1. A user named Parry is the owner of a public folder named Research. Parry leaves your company and another administrator deletes Parry's user account. What would you as an administrator have to do to modify the permissions on the Research folder?

   A. Make the site service account the owner of the Research folder.

   B. Restore a backup tape of the server that was created before Parry was deleted.

   C. Designate your account as the owner of the Research folder.

   D. Grant your account the right to log on as a service.

2. You want to create a public folder hierarchy that has both visible and hidden folders. You have created a distribution list called HR that contains the users who do need to view the hidden folders. What would be an efficient way of allowing the users who do need to view the hidden folder hierarchy the ability to do that?

   A. Give the List permission to the HR distribution list at each hidden folder.

   B. Give the Folder contact permission to the HR distribution list at each hidden folder.

   C. Create a root folder that contains all the hidden folders. Revoke all permissions for the Default user. Give Folder Visible permission to the HR distribution list at the root of the hidden folder hierarchy. Ensure that the HR DL has the Read items permission on each of the root's subfolders either explicitly or through the Default entry.

   D. Give the Create subfolders permission to the HR distribution list at each hidden folder.

3. You own a public folder called Company Events. Because of the large number of comments about the events sent as replies, users have a hard time distinguishing the original postings from the replies. You decide to create a subfolder called Discussions that you want to hold the replies to the Company Events postings. What is the most efficient way to ensure all replies to Company Events go to the Discussions folder?

A. Tell users to use the Discussions folder as a Cc recipient whenever they reply to Company Events.

B. Configure a rule for Company Events that forwards everything to the Discussions folder except items from users that need to post company event items to the Company Events folder.

C. Have all users make the Discussions folder a Favorite folder.

D. Configure Company Events to delete everything it receives.

4. What must be done to enable certain users to add scripts to public folders?

A. Check the Enable Scripts box on each folder.

B. Install the Scripting Agent on each user's computer.

C. The Information Store database must be configured for a mirrored striped disk array.

D. Each user must be given the Author role for the EventConfig folder.

E. Each user must be given the Author role for each folder they need to add a script to.

5. Which of the following relate to assigning rules to a public folder?

A. Conditions

B. Actions

C. Folder Assistant

D. All of the above

6. Public folder permissions are grouped into predefined:

   A. Hives

   B. Clone sets

   C. Roles

   D. Sets

7. If the recipient who is the owner of a public folder is deleted, what can be done in order to allow the administrator to grant permissions to other recipients?

   A. Delete the public folder, and re-create it.

   B. Designate the recipient used by the administrator as the owner.

   C. Give the administrator account the "right to logon as a service".

   D. Restore a backup tape that was made before the previous recipient was deleted.

8. What must you do to hide a subfolder from a particular recipient?

   A. Revoke the Read Items permission from that recipient at the parent folder.

   B. Revoke the Read Items permission from that recipient at that subfolder.

   C. Hide the root folder above that subfolder.

   D. A subfolder cannot be hidden, only its contents.

9. By default, all public folders can be seen in the GAL.

   A. True

   B. False

10. By default, all public folders are visible in the public folder hierarchy.

   A. True

   B. False

CHAPTER

10

Advanced Security

As computer networking has become more and more pervasive, the information transported over networks has become more important and valuable. As a result, some unscrupulous people try to steal information and disrupt business affairs. E-mail messages are susceptible to eavesdropping, tampering, and forgery. These and other security threats can be prevented by implementing advanced security measures.

Theft, tampering, and forgery can be countered through *cryptology,* which is the study and implementation of hiding and revealing information. The word cryptology comes from two Greek words, *kryptos*, which means "hidden," and *logos*, which means "word." A cryptological method can take information in standard format, called *plaintext* or *cleartext,* and hide it by scrambling it to make it unintelligible. This is called *encryption.* Encrypted information is sometimes called *ciphertext.* Most methods of hiding information do so by rearranging patterns or substituting characters with other characters (see the sidebar "The Caesar Code"). The procedure used to scramble information is called an *encryption.* The procedure used to unscramble the information back to plaintext, so that it can be read, is called *decryption.* Cryptology provides for confidentiality by preventing stolen data from being read or altered, making it useless to the thief.

Encryption methods are also used to authenticate the identity of the sender of a message. They verify that a message was really sent by the person from whom it indicates it was sent. Authentication discourages forgeries and data tampering.

Advanced security is not enabled by default in Exchange Server or the Exchange client programs. But if a network environment requires this level of security, it can be configured and implemented. This chapter provides a brief background on advanced security methods and standards, and describes how Exchange uses them. In this chapter, we will discuss:

- Encryption methods and standards

- Installation and architecture of Exchange advanced security

- Configuring advanced security

- Operation of advanced security

- Managing advanced security

- Multiple sites and advanced security

- Troubleshooting security problems

The Caesar Code

One early form of cryptology was the Caesar code:

a b c d e f g h i j k l m n o p q r s t u v w x y z

D E F G H I J K L M N O P Q R S T U V W X Y Z A B C

To encrypt a message, its letters are taken one by one and substituted with the letters appearing below them. The message "Send spears" would be encrypted as "VHQG VSHDUV." The substitution method used today is much more complicated.

Encryption Methods and Standards

Modern encryption methods scramble information by running a mathematical algorithm (i.e., a formula) involving a randomly chosen number, on the data to be encrypted. The random number is called a *key*. The key is added to the algorithm by a user or by software. Because the algorithm can remain constant, and may even be published, the keys are what add the variations and secrecy to the encryption. For example, a sender encrypts data using an agreed upon algorithm and a secret key. The recipient, using the same algorithm, must supply the same secret key for the algorithm to decrypt the data.

The length of a key determines the difficulty of breaking the encryption. Each bit in a key can be in one of two states, a one or a zero. A key of 4 bits would have only 16 (2^4) unique combinations. If the algorithm were known, it would be simple to try every possible key with the algorithm and decrypt any message. But a key of 56 bits would have 2^{56} unique combinations, which is 72 quadrillion possible keys. Keys do not make encryption unbreakable, but they make it costly, time consuming, and impractical to break. With the computer hardware available in the 1970s, it would take over 2,000 years to decrypt a message encrypted with a 56-bit key. Recently, a network of computers working together was able to decrypt a message with 56-bit encryption in less than 6 months. Therefore, as computers get more powerful, more bits are needed to keep encryption strong. We will discuss the two basic types of key mechanisms: public/private key pairs and secret keys.

Public/Private Key Pairs

Some encryption methods assign each user a key which is divided into two mathematically related halves, called a *key pair*. One half of the key is made public and is called the *public key*. The other half is known only by one user and is called the *private key*. Some encryption protocols have the sender encrypt a message using the recipient's public key. The only key that can be used to decrypt the message is the other half of the key, the private key, which is known only to the recipient. Because there are two different keys, this method is referred to as being asymmetrical. Figure 10.1 illustrates the use of public/private key pairs. This technique is often called simply *public key encryption*. One of the most frequently used public key protocols is called RSA.

FIGURE 10.1

Public key encryption

Directory of Public Keys

Users	Public Keys
User A	2243
User B	4124

User A

User B

1. User A reads User B's public key

User B's public/private key pair = 4124 7217

Encrypted Message → Decrypted Message

2. Message encrypted using User B's public key

3. Message sent

4. Message decrypted using User B's private key

RSA Public Key Protocol

The RSA protocol was developed in the late 1970s by Ron Rivest, Adi Shamir, and Leonard Adleman. They used the first letters of their last names, RSA, to name the protocol. The RSA protocol is computationally intense and slower than other methods, so it is not usually used to encrypt large amounts of data. However, it *is* used for secure user authentication.

Just as a fingerprint or retinal pattern can be used to uniquely identify a person, a key pair can be used to identify a message sender. When keys are used in this manner they help to create what are called *digital signatures*. A digital signature is added to a message by a sender. When the recipient receives the message, they use the digital signature to authenticate (i.e. prove) the sender's identity. Digital signatures help protect against message forgeries.

The following lists the main procedures and protocols used in the Exchange digital signature mechanism:

1. A sender's security software performs a set mathematical formula on a message, which produces a unique 128-bit value (the message is not affected). This process is called *hashing,* and the value produced by the hashing is called a *message digest,* or simply a *digest* (this is similar in concept to a checksum). The protocol used to perform the hashing is Message Digest 5 (MD5).

2. The message digest is then encrypted by using a 512-bit RSA algorithm and the sender's private signing key. The encrypted message digest is the digital signature.

3. The digital signature, along with a certificate that contains the sender's public key, are sent along with the message (certificates are discussed later in this chapter).

4. The recipient's security software reads the plaintext message to learn the identity of the sender (i.e. the name in the From field).

5. The recipient's security software then uses the sender's public signing key to decrypt the encrypted message digest (i.e. the digital signature). If this operation is successful, it authenticates the identity of the sender, because only the public signing key of the sender could decrypt the encrypted message digest. A forger could place someone's name in the From field, but they would not be able to forge that person's digital signature because the forger does not know that person's private signing

key, because it is secret. When a recipient tries to decrypt an encrypted message digest using the forged sender's public signing key, it will not work. The two key halves will not be mathematically related. The recipient will know the message is not authentic.

6. The recipient's security software, which now knows the message digest that the sender calculated, performs its own hash on the message. If the two values are the same, this proves the message was not tampered with during transit. Conversely, if someone captured a message and modified it before sending it back on its way, the message digest the recipient will arrive at and the one sent by the sender will not be the same. This is because the recipient is performing the hash on a different message than the sender.

Figure 10.2 summarizes the main steps in this process.

FIGURE 10.2

Public key method used for authentication

To implement public key encryption, private keys must be securely assigned, and public keys must be accessible to all users. Keys also should be changed periodically. These management issues can be handled manually when there are only a few users. But when there are numerous users, such manual management can overwhelm an administrator. This problem is solved by an automated server process called a *Certification Authority.*

Certification Authority

A public key protocol relies on a central authority to create, distribute, publish, and validate keys. The server that performs these roles is called the Certification Authority (CA). The CA is a key distribution center that responds to requests for new key assignments by creating new public/private key pairs and delivering them to clients. The CA also publishes public keys in a directory for user access.

A CA also keeps a list of expired keys and revoked keys called the Certificate Revocation List (CRL). When client software attempts to use a public key, it checks the CRL to determine if the public key is still valid. If not, the key cannot be used.

One CA implementation standard, published in 1988, is ITU X.509. The Exchange Key Management (KM) server component conforms to this standard. Figure 10.3 illustrates the roles of the KM server CA.

Secret Keys

Authentication only provides proof of identification and proof of data integrity. It *does not* encrypt the message data. Encryption is normally achieved with *secret keys*. A secret key mechanism uses the same key to both encrypt and decrypt information. When a message is encrypted, the key used by the algorithm is sent along with the message. The recipient uses the single secret key to decrypt the information. To prevent someone from simply reading the secret key appended to the message, the secret key must be securely transferred between the sender and recipient. This is usually done by encrypting the secret key so that the recipient, and only the recipient, can decrypt it. After decrypting the secret key, the recipient uses it to decrypt the message.

Because there is only one key, the secret key scheme is a symmetrical method, and sometimes referred to as the *shared-secret* method. Data Encryption Standard (DES) uses the secret key method.

Data Encryption Standard (DES)

DES was developed by IBM and in 1977 was accepted by the United States government as an official standard. DES is extremely secure and is used by many financial institutions for electronic fund transfers. DES uses a 64-bit key. The only method of cracking a DES-encrypted message is the brute-force approach of attempting every possible key.

Software-based DES encryption can be performed about 100 times faster than RSA encryption. Because of its speed, DES is suited for encrypting and decrypting large amounts of data.

When a message is encrypted in Exchange using DES, the secret key is encrypted with RSA and sent in a *lockbox* with the message. This type of hybrid system leverages the speed advantages of DES, and the strength of 512-bit public key RSA. When the message is received, the recipient's private key is used to decrypt the secret key lockbox, and the secret key is used to decrypt the message. Figure 10.4 illustrates this type of hybrid system.

United States export law allows Exchange's DES implementation to be sold only in the United States and Canada.

CAST

Another protocol that uses a secret key mechanism is the CAST protocol. CAST derives its name from the initials of its developers, Carlisle Adams and Stafford Tavares, who worked at Northern Telecom Research. CAST uses a variable-length key between 40 and 128 bits. Exchange can use CAST 40, which uses a 40-bit key, and CAST 64, which uses a 64-bit key. A 64-bit key is 16 million times more secure than a 40-bit key.

FIGURE 10.4

A hybrid encryption system using both RSA and DES

United States export law allows CAST 64 to only be sold in the United States and Canada. Only the CAST 40 option can be used in the international version of Exchange. In addition, France prohibits the import of any encryption implementations. Table 10.1 provides a summary of the encryption protocols Exchange supports, and the locales where they can be used.

512-bit RSA is legally exported to all international locations because it is used only to digitally sign messages and encrypt lockboxes. Only technology that encrypts message content is prohibited for export.

TABLE 10.1

Summary of encryption protocols

Protocol	Use	Key Length	Locations
RSA	Authentication (digital signatures)	512-bit	All
DES	Data encryption	64-bit	U.S. and Canada
CAST 64	Data encryption	64-bit	U.S. and Canada
CAST 40	Data encryption	40-bit	International, except France

The terms "encryption" and "authentication" are often substituted with the terms "sealing" and "signing" respectively in Exchange Server and its documentation.

Now that you have an adequate understanding of the appropriate security protocols, we can discuss using Exchange Server's advanced security.

Installation and Architecture of Exchange Advanced Security

Various components implement advanced security in an Exchange environment. Some of them run on a Microsoft Exchange server and some run on client workstations.

Installing Advanced Security

This chapter focuses primarily on the KM server installation because client-side security components are automatically installed during a client installation. The following topics will be discussed:

- Key Management server installation

- Starting Key Management server

- Upgrading Key Management server

KM Server Installation

To deploy advanced security in an Exchange organization, one and only one server in the organization must be configured as the Key Management (KM) server. That server computer should:

- Be in the domain you use for centralized administration

- Be backed up regularly and physically secure

- Use Windows NT Server File System (NTFS)

If maximum security is required, the KM server could be installed on a dedicated server and in a separate site. A dedicated server is not needed for performance reasons, but could be used for additional security.

Passwords and KM Installation   Two passwords are involved with installing and configuring the KM component. They are referred to as:

- Key Manager service password

- Advanced security administrator password

When KM is installed the installer will be provided a Key Manager service password. This password will later be used to start the Microsoft Exchange Key Management service. The installer can choose to have this password written to a blank, formatted floppy disk. This option requires two blank, formatted floppy disks, because SETUP will create a backup copy of the disk containing the password. When the disk option is chosen, the Key Management Server service will read the password from the floppy disk each time it is started. The Key Management Server service will not start without the disk. If the disk option is not chosen, the password will be displayed on the screen for the installer to make a note of it. The password will then need to be entered into the startup parameters of the Key Management Server service. This is done through Control Panel and the Services applet. The password is case-sensitive.

The setup of Key Management will create two objects in the Exchange hierarchy, named "CA" and "Encryption," both located in the Configuration container. The advanced security administrator password is used by an administrator to access and configure these objects after the installation. The default password is the word "password." It is strongly recommended that this default password be changed immediately after installation. Because multiple administrators could be handling advanced security operations, Exchange permits each administrator to have a different advanced security administrator password.

KM Server Setup   The KM server is installed by selecting it during the Microsoft Exchange Server setup. If Exchange server is already installed on the computer that will be the KM server, execute the following steps:

1. Insert the Microsoft Exchange Server compact disc into the CD-ROM drive.

2. Run SETUP.EXE for your computer type (e.g., I386).

3. Choose Complete/Custom.

4. Select Microsoft Exchange Server, and then click on Change Option.

5. Choose Key Management Server.

Starting KM Server

After the KM server is installed, it must be manually started. This is done through Control Panel and the Services applet. Use the steps outlined below:

1. While in Control Panel, choose Services, and then double-click on Microsoft Exchange Key Management Server.

2. Select Automatic under Startup Type, then click OK. Insert the disk containing the Key Manager service password. If you did not use the floppy disk option during setup, type the password in the Startup Parameters box.

3. Click on Start.

Once the preceding steps have been taken, the KM server will be started each time that server is started.

Upgrading KM Server

If an earlier version of KM server is already installed, it can be upgraded by simply running the Exchange Server SETUP containing the new version and selecting the KM Server option (this was described under the heading "KM Server Setup").

Before performing an upgrade, you must have:

- The original KM server startup floppy disk, or know the password

- A blank, unformatted floppy disk, which will be used to backup the Key Manager service password

Client Advanced Security Installation

During the Exchange client setup, the necessary advanced security programs are copied to the client workstation. Depending on the client operating system, the main function library will be either:

- ETEXCH.DLL (16-bit Windows – Windows 3.*x* and Windows for Workgoups)

- ETEXCH32.DLL (32-bit Windows – Windows 95 and Windows NT)

Advanced security is available only for Windows-based clients. Other platforms such as MS-DOS are not supported.

Before security can be enabled and used, the KM administrator must configure each user's mailbox for advanced security and create certificates.

Exchange Advanced Security Architecture

When configuring Exchange advanced security, it is helpful to have an understanding of the communications that take place among the integral components. The following components will be discussed:

- **Client Components**   Functions in the client security libraries, ETEXCH.DLL and ETEXCH32.DLL, communicate with the Exchange Server System Attendant service (SA) during the initial configuration of advanced security. Client requests for keys and certificates are directed to the SA. Thereafter, the client security functions communicate with the DS to read public keys. The SA communication is illustrated in Figure 10.5.

- **System Attendant (SA)**   After receiving a client request for advanced security initialization, the SA passes the request message to a function in the KM Security DLL. The SA essentially acts as middleware between the client and the KM server. This is illustrated in Figure 10.6.

- **KM Security DLL**   When the KM Security DLL receives client messages via the SA, it passes the security requests to the Key Manager service for processing. This is illustrated in Figure 10.7.

  - **Key Manager Service**   The Key Manager service creates keys and certificates for the client, and communicates this information to the following three places (see Figure 10.8).

FIGURE 10.5

FIGURE 10.5

Client security communication with the System Attendant

FIGURE 10.6

System Attendant communication with the KM Security DLL

FIGURE 10.7

The KM Security DLL calls
on the Key Manager
service.

Exchange Client

Microsoft Exchange Server
and
Key Management Server

Passing of security requests

DS	IS	MTA	SA	Key Manager Service	KM Security DLL	KM Database

Administrator's
Console

FIGURE 10.8

The Key Manager service
distributes keys and
certificates.

Exchange Client

Microsoft Exchange Server
and
Key Management Server

Publishing of
public keys

Storage
of keys and
certificates

DS	IS	MTA	SA	Key Manager Service	KM Security DLL	KM Database

For delivery of keys and certificates to clients

Administrator's
Console

- **SA**   The System Attendant delivers keys and certificates to clients.

- **KM database**   This database is where keys and certificates are centrally stored.

- **DS**   Public keys used for sealing messages are made publicly available in the DS. The Key Manager service also stores the CRL in the DS.

- **Security Administration DLL**   The Exchange Administrator program uses the security administration DLL for advanced security configuration and management. This DLL communicates directly with the Key Manager service as illustrated in Figure 10.9.

FIGURE 10.9

The Security Administration DLL communicates with the Key Manager service.

Now that you have installed advanced security and understand its architecture, we will discuss its configuration.

Configuring Advanced Security

Advanced security must be configured on both the KM server and the client workstations. This section covers both configurations. The KM server must be configured first.

Microsoft ✓ *Exam Objective*   **Configure Security.**

Configuring the KM Server

A KM administrator uses the Exchange Administrator program to configure advanced security. Organization-wide and individual mailbox configurations must be made.

Organization-Wide Configurations

A KM administrator can configure the preferred encryption algorithm for the organization. This is configured on the Security property page of the Encryption object in the Configuration container. The options for North America are CAST-64 (the default) and DES. Locales outside of North America can only use the CAST-40 algorithm.

Another organization-wide configuration is the selection of users to be KM administrators. This configuration is also performed in the Security property page of the Encryption object. Exercise 10.1 outlines the steps for configuring the organization-wide settings.

This exercise assumes that you have already installed the Key Management server. If not, you may accomplish that by following the steps outlined in the earlier section labeled "KM Server Setup."

EXERCISE 10.1

Organization-Wide Configuration of Advanced Security

1. In the Exchange Administrator program, expand the site object and choose the Configuration container. In the Configuration container, double-click on the Encryption object. The Encryption Properties dialog will appear.

2. Click on the Security tab. The top section of this page, labeled "Preferred encryption algorithm," allows you to configure the message encryption algorithms that will be used when sending to sites in North America and sites in other locales.

3. To modify the list of KM administrator accounts, click the Key Management Server Administrators button.

4. The Key Management Administrator Password dialog box appears. Type **Password** and click OK. The Key Management Server Administrators dialog box will appear. If you would like to add another KM administrator, click Add Administrators. If you would like to change the KM password, click Change Password. If you change the password, do not forget the new one.

Individual Mailbox Configuration

The mailbox object of each user that is to use advanced security must be enabled for advanced security. To enable a mailbox, the KM administrator must click the Enable Advanced Security button on the mailbox's Security property page and provide the mailbox user with the token displayed. When advanced security is enabled, the following actions automatically take place:

1. The Security Administration DLL (SECADMIN.DLL) transfers the mailbox security information to the Key Manager service on the KM server. This information is accompanied with the KM administrator's password in order to access the Key Manager and KM database.

2. The Key Manager service generates a sealing key for this mailbox and writes it to the KM database. This will be used by either the DES or CAST protocol for data encryption.

3. The Key Manager creates a random, 12-character security token. This is a password that the client will show to the KM server in order to receive its mailbox's keys and certificates. This prevents user B from asking and receiving user A's private keys.

4. The Security Administration DLL displays the secret token in the dialog box in the Exchange Administrator program. A KM administrator needs to convey this token to the user.

Exercise 10.2 outlines the steps to configure advanced security on individual mailboxes.

EXERCISE 10.2

Configuring Advanced Security on Individual Mailboxes

1. In the Exchange Administrator program, expand your site object and choose the Recipients container. Double-click on the George Washington mailbox recipient. The George Washington Properties dialog will appear.

2. Click on the Security tab. The Key Management Server Password dialog box will appear. Enter the correct password. If you did not change it in Exercise 10.1, the password is still "password."

3. Click Enable Advanced Security. An information dialog box will appear stating that advanced security has been enabled. At the bottom of this dialog box will be the security token that the user George Washington will need to enter when he configures his client software. Write this value down. Click OK. Then click OK again.

4. Configure advanced security for the Andrew Jackson mailbox. We will use these two mailboxes to send secure messages back and forth later in this chapter.

After the administrator configures a user's mailbox, that user can configure the client security components on his or her local workstation.

Configuring the Client

The user configures the client security components through the Exchange client software, either Exchange Client or Outlook. In both of these programs, configuration is performed by choosing Options from the Tools menu, and selecting the Security property page (see Figure 10.10). The user can choose to encrypt messages and attachments, and to add digital signatures to messages. Also, the name of the file that will hold private keys and signing certificates can be specified (it must have an .EPF extension). Because the information in this file is sensitive, it is encrypted and can only be accessed with a password.

FIGURE 10.10

The Security property page in the client software

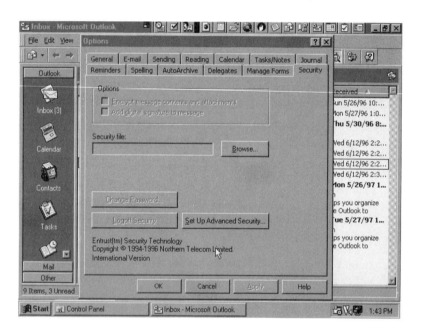

Before a user can configure advanced security, they must request and receive their keys and certificates from the KM server. To do this the user must click the Set Up Advanced Security button and enter the security token they received from the KM administrator. This will prove to the KM server that they have permission to receive the keys and certificates for this mailbox. The following step is performed by the client security DLL:

1. The client security DLL (either ETEXCH.DLL or ETEXCH32.DLL) generates the user's public and private signing keys. The private signing key is stored and encrypted in the user's local .EPF file. The public signing key is encrypted with the user's security token and sent as a mail message to the SA. The SA transfers this message to the SA on the KM server if it is not the local server.

The following steps take place on the KM server.

2. The SA on the KM server passes the user's mail message to the KM Security DLL, which passes it to the Key Manager service. The user is notified of a successful submission.

3. The Key Manager service decrypts the message using the user's security token that was assigned earlier, and then writes the user's public signing key to the KM database. The Key Manager then creates two certificates, one for sealing and one for signing, and sends them to the client.

Step 4 is performed by the user, and Step 5 is performed by the client's security DLL.

4. When the user receives the certificates, he or she must supply the user account password. This verifies that this user is the one who made the advanced security request in Step 1.

5. The client security DLL takes the user's public sealing key and communicates it to the DS on the client's home server. The server will replicate this information in the normal course of DS replication.

When mailboxes and client software has been configured, the KM server does not need to be online for advanced security to function. Private keys and certificates are available from the local .EPF file, and public keys and certificates are available from the DS. The KM server only needs to be running to initialize new advanced security clients

Exercise 10.3 outlines the steps to configure the client security components.

Now that the KM server, mailboxes, and client security components are configured, advanced security operations can commence.

EXERCISE 10.3

Configuring the Client Security Components

1. At the client workstation, log on with the GEORGEW user account. Then run Outlook.

2. In Outlook, choose Tools ➢ Options. The Options dialog will appear. Choose the Security tab.

3. Click Set Up Advanced Security. The Setup Advanced Security dialog will appear.

4. In the Token field, enter the security token that was generated in Exercise 10.2 Step 3.

5. In the Password and Confirm Password fields, type **dollar.** This new password will be used to access the certificates that contain your keys for signing and sealing messages. Click OK. An informational dialog box will appear stating that you will be notified when your security request has been processed by the Key Management server. Click OK. On the Options dialog box, click OK.

6. Check your Inbox, you will soon receive a message from the System Attendant. Notice that the envelope icon for this message has a lock on it.

7. Double-click on the message from the System Attendant. A dialog box will appear prompting you for your password. This is the password you entered in Step 5 (**dollar**). Enter **dollar** and click OK. An informational dialog box will appear stating that you are now security enabled and can sign and encrypt messages. Click OK.

8. Log on with the Andrew Jackson user account and configure the security components. Remember, Andrew Jackson has a different security token than George Washington. Also remember to write down Andrew Jackson's personal security password. Both user accounts need to be configured so we can send and receive secure messages in Exercises 10.4 and 10.5.

Advanced Security Operation

Advanced security is very straightforward to use. Most of the operation is automatic and transparent to the user. This section will discuss the steps involved in signing and verifying a message, and sealing and unsealing a message. Exercises 10.4 and 10.5 will provide an opportunity to use these features. This section will conclude with a description of some advanced security operational scenarios.

Signing/Verifying a Message

As explained earlier in this chapter, the RSA public key method is used for digital signatures. The following two sections outline the procedures for signing a message and verifying a signature on a message.

Signing a Message

The steps for signing an outgoing message are:

1. The client security DLL calculates a message digest from the outgoing message.

2. The user is prompted for the security file password. When the correct password is entered, the client security DLL decrypts the user's private signing key.

3. The private key is used to encrypt the message digest, thereby creating a digital signature.

4. The client software appends the digital signature and the user's signing certificate (which contains his or her public signing key) to the plaintext message. The message is then sent.

Verifying a Message

The steps for verifying a digital signature on a received message are:

1. The client security DLL checks the CRL in the DS for the sender's signing certificate. If it is on the list, the recipient is notified that the sender certificate cannot be trusted. If it is not on the list, the client software uses the sender's public signing key to decrypt the message digest.

2. The recipient's client software calculates the message digest of the message and compares its value with the one decrypted from the message. If they are not the same, the recipient is warned that the message has been altered since it was signed. Otherwise, the message has arrived intact and the sender's identity has been authenticated.

Sealing/Unsealing a Message

Exchange can use either the DES or CAST protocol to seal messages. These mechanisms were discussed earlier in this chapter. The following two sections outline the steps performed by the Exchange software when sealing and unsealing messages.

Sealing a Message

The steps that occur when sealing an Exchange message are:

1. The sender's security DLL generates a random secret key, also called the *bulk encryption key*. This key is used to seal the message with DES or CAST depending on the Exchange server configuration.

2. The sender's security DLL accesses the DS to obtain each recipient's public sealing key.

3. Each recipient's public sealing key is used to encrypt the secret key in lockboxes which will be sent along with the sealed message. One lockbox is attached for each recipient. If the message is being sent to distribution lists (DLs), the DLs are expanded on the client and a lockbox is attached for each DL member. One copy of the actual message content is included (in sealed form).

4. The message containing sealed content and lockboxes is sent to the recipients.

Unsealing a Message

The steps to unseal a message are:

1. The recipient's security DLL retrieves the recipient's private sealing key from the .EPF file and uses this key to unseal the lockbox.

2. The unsealed secret key is then used to unseal the message contents.

Now that you have learned about signing and sealing messages, Exercise 10.4 will walk you through the steps. Exercise 10.5 will take you through the necessary steps to verify and unseal a message.

EXERCISE 10.4

Sending a Signed and Sealed Message

1. Log on as GeorgeW and start Outlook.

2. Click the New Mail Message tool button on the toolbar. A new message window appears.

3. Click To. The Select Names dialog box appears. In the Show Names From The drop-down list, choose Global Address List. Find and select Andrew Jackson in the leftmost listbox. Click To and then click OK.

4. In the Subject field, type **Advanced Security Test**.

5. Type a short message in the body.

6. Click the Seal Message with Encryption toolbar button. This tool button is found on the right side of the toolbar and appears as an envelope with a lock attached.

7. Click the Digitally Sign Message toolbar button directly to the right of the Encryption button.

8. To send the message, click the Send button on the toolbar. The Microsoft Exchange Security Logon dialog box will appear (see Figure 10.11).

9. In the Security password box, type GeorgeW's security password, **dollar**. This will permit your private key to be used to digitally sign the message, and your secret key to be used to seal the message. Click OK. The message is now sent.

FIGURE 10.11

Microsoft Exchange
Security Logon screen

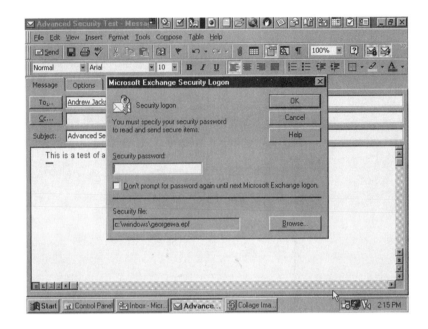

EXERCISE 10.5

Verifying and Unsealing a Message

1. Log on as AndrewJ, and start Outlook.

2. If your Inbox is not already visible, open it. Notice the message from GeorgeW. The envelope icon has a lock on it, signifying that it is sealed (see Figure 10.12).

3. Double-click on the sealed message from GeorgeW. The Microsoft Exchange Security Logon dialog box will appear.

4. In the Security password box, enter AndrewJ's security password. Click OK. The message content will appear.

5. When you are done, close the message.

FIGURE 10.12

The Inbox with a signed
and sealed message

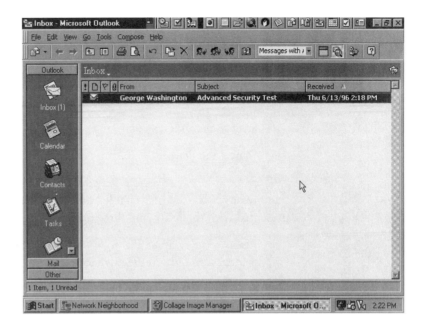

Advanced Security Scenarios

This section describes some scenarios you may encounter with your deployment of advanced security.

Using Different Sealing Protocols

If a user sends a message to multiple recipients that are enabled for different
sealing protocols, the weakest sealing protocol of the lot will be used to seal the
message. For example, if some recipients are enabled for CAST-64 and others
are enabled for CAST-40, Exchange will use CAST-40 to seal the message.

Changing the Preferred Encryption Algorithm

The KM administrator may change the preferred encryption algorithm of a site.
This is done through the Encryption object and the Security property page.
After changing the site configuration, the administrator would then have to
recover the security keys for all security-enabled mailboxes in that site.

Sending Messages to Recipients Not Configured for Advanced Security

If a user attempts to send a sealed message to a recipient that is not advanced security enabled, the message cannot be delivered. The sender will be presented with the following two options:

- Send the message as plaintext

- Cancel the delivery

If a user attempts to send a sealed message to a number of recipients, some that are advanced security enabled and some that are not, the sender will be presented with the following three options:

- Remove the recipients who are not advanced security enabled, and send the message only to the advanced security enabled recipients

- Send the message as plaintext to the entire list of recipients

- Cancel the delivery

Forwarding a Sealed Message

Recipients who can unseal a message can modify the message and forward it to other recipients. It may seem obvious, but users should remember that once sensitive data is received and unsealed, it is up to the recipients to preserve the confidentiality of the information.

Managing Advanced Security

Once advanced security is installed and configured, administrative duties are minimal. KM administrators will primarily perform the following three tasks:

- Key and certificate management

- KM database and server management

- Batch creation of security tokens

Key and Certificate Management

Certain scenarios require key and certificate management. When users leave the organization, their advanced security capabilities need to be disabled. The KM administrator does this by revoking user key and certification information. When a user password is forgotten or an .EPF file is corrupted or lost, the KM administrator can save the day by recovering key and certificate information. Also, keys and certificates expire after a certain amount of time elapses. Client software can request a renewal when the expiration date approaches. Revocation, recovery, and renewal procedures are discussed next.

Revocation

To revoke advanced security keys and certificates from a mailbox, a KM administrator uses the Exchange Administrator program. In the procedure outlined here, the KM administrator performs Step 1 and the remaining steps occur automatically.

1. In the Exchange Administrator program, the KM administrator chooses the mailbox that is to have advanced security revoked, and clicks the Revoke Advanced Security button on the Security property page. After the administrator provides the KM password, the process to revoke the user's security keys and certificates begins.

2. The security DLL locates the KM server and tells it which mailbox is to have its security configuration revoked.

3. The KM server adds the user's signing and sealing keys to its revocation list.

4. The KM server informs the DS to add the user's sealing certificate to the CRL. The user's ability to sign and seal messages is now revoked.

5. A dialog box appears in the Exchange Administrator program indicating the revocation is complete.

The revocation process does not delete keys from the KM database, but rather makes them unusable for future sealing. The revoked keys are still available for a KM administrator to use to unseal any messages still signed and sealed by those keys.

Recovery

Users' private keys are stored on their computers in their .EPF file. The user must provide the correct password to access these keys. If a user forgets this password, or the .EPF file becomes corrupted or gets accidentally deleted, the user will not be able to unseal messages, or send signed or sealed messages. The KM administrator can fix this situation by performing a recovery.

A recovery is similar to enabling advanced security. To do a recovery, the KM administrator clicks the Recover Security Key button on the Security property page of the affected user's mailbox. The KM server then sends the user a history of the keys associated with the mailbox, including the current keys and certificates. The user must then reconfigure advanced security on his or her workstation to create a new .EPF file.

Renewal

New certificates are valid for 18 months. At the end of this period, the certificate must be renewed, or "rolled over." When certificates near expiration, the Exchange client software sends a request for renewal.

KM Database and Server Management

Because the KM database contains the master copy of all private sealing keys and all public signing keys, its maintenance is important. Two management activities will be discussed in this section:

- Creating additional KM administrators
- Batch creation of security tokens

Creating Additional KM Administrators

The user account that performs the installation of a KM server, is by default the initial KM administrator. The default password that this user must initially use to perform KM functions is "password." This password should be changed as soon as possible. Additional users can be assigned KM administrator rights through the Encryption object in the Configuration container. Each additional KM administrator should have his or her own password.

Batch Creation of Security Tokens

It is often inconvenient to configure advanced security one mailbox at a time. If a large batch of users need advanced security configured, the Security Import utility (SIMPORT.EXE) can be used.

The Security Import utility can create security tokens for multiple users in a batch process (i.e., processing a group of mailboxes at one time). This process must be performed one server at a time. When the Security Import utility is run, it will prompt the administrator for the following information:

- Site name

- Home server

- KM administrator password

- KM server name

The program will create the user keys and certificates and write each user's security token information to a file called SRESULTS.TXT. Here is an example of the format of this file:

```
/o=widget/ou=chicago/cn=recipients/cn=jwilson, ISLIWXIWLELE
```

```
/o=widget/ou=chicago/cn=recipients/cn=gwashington, RRXOWQMTPCJF
```

The KM administrator reads the security token at the end of each line and securely passes it to the corresponding user.

Multiple Sites and Advanced Security

While there is only one KM server for an organization, each site must have an object in the DS that points to the KM server. To create this object, run the KM server Setup program on one Exchange server in each site. KM Setup will detect an existing KM server in the organization and just install the appropriate object in the local site instead of installing an additional KM server. To determine if a KM server already exists in the organization, KM Setup reads the DS on the local server, so be sure DS replication to this server is complete before running KM Setup.

The DS object pointing to the KM server enables each Exchange server in the organization to receive security requests from clients and forward them to the KM server.

If a KM server has been installed in another site, but DS replication to the local site has not yet been completed, KM server Setup will create a KM server in the local site.

Troubleshooting Security Problems

The common security problems involve the startup password for the KM Server service and issues relating to enabling clients for advanced security. These problems and their solutions will be covered next.

Microsoft
✓ *Exam*
Objective

Diagnose organization security problems.

Table 10.2 provides a list of common advanced security problems and their solutions.

T A B L E 10.2	Security Problem	Solution
Common security problems and their solutions	KM Server service will not start.	Either the startup floppy disk is not inserted, or the password value is not entered, or entered incorrectly, in the startup parameters for the Key Management Server service. The latter situation can be checked through Control Panel and the Services applet. Also note that the password is case sensitive.

TABLE 10.2 (cont.) Common security problems and their solutions	Security Problem	Solution
	The KM server is not running immediately after its installation.	Manually start the KM Server service from Control Panel and the Services applet.
	A user cannot use advanced security.	Enable advanced security for the user's mailbox. Inform the user of their security token. Instruct the user how to enable advanced security in their Exchange client application.
	A user forgets their password for access to their private security keys.	KM administrator must perform a recovery of that user's security keys. That is done through the Exchange Administrator program and the Security property page of that mailbox.
	A user's security keys expire and they cannot use advanced security.	KM administrator must perform a renewal of that user's security keys. That is done through the Exchange Administrator program and the Security property page of that mailbox.

Summary

Advanced security facilitates the authentication of a message sender's identity and the privacy of message data. Authentication is accomplished using digital signatures and message privacy is maintained using encryption. In Exchange terminology, "signing" refers to authentication and "sealing" refers to encryption.

The RSA protocol is used by Exchange to implement digital signatures. RSA uses a key pair that includes a public key that can be accessed by anyone, and a private key that is only known by one user. While these two keys are different, they are mathematically related and information is unlocked with the other half of the key that was used to lock it.

The protocols that Exchange uses for sealing data are DES and CAST. These protocols utilize a single secret key that is used to both seal and unseal message content. This secret key is itself sealed using RSA and sent along with the message.

The components that make up the advanced security subsystem in Exchange include the Key Manager service, the KM Security DLL, the System Attendant, and the Security Administration DLL. There is also a KM database, which contains a master copy of all users' keys and certificates.

One Exchange server in the organization acts as the KM server. Other Exchange servers have a DS object pointing to the single KM server.

Only the Outlook client supports advanced security. The 16-bit client security library is named ETEXCH.DLL and the 32-bit version is named ETEXCH32.DLL.

KM server management duties include key and certificate revocation and client security information recovery and renewal. The KM database can be backed up, restored, or moved across servers. The KM server can be configured to support multiple administrators. The Security Import utility allows you to configure batches of users for advanced security at one time.

Review Questions

1. You have just installed the Exchange Key Management server. During the setup, you chose not to use the floppy disk option for the KM service password. A few days later that server is shut down and restarted, but the Key Management server does not start. What is the likely cause of the problem?

   A. The Microsoft Exchange Key Management service was started without the password as a startup parameter.

   B. The Private Information Store is not started.

   C. The SA was started without the password as a startup parameter.

   D. The floppy startup disk was not inserted into the drive.

2. As administrator of a KM server, you receive a request to enable advanced security from a user named Alex. What must you do to accomplish that? (Choose all that apply.)

   A. Instruct Alex on how to use Windows NT domain logons.

   B. Enable advanced security as a property of Alex's mailbox.

   C. Instruct Alex how to perform person-to-person key exchange.

   D. Instruct Alex to configure his workstation as a certificate authority.

   E. Provide a security token to Alex and have him enter it in his Microsoft Outlook application.

3. Your KM server is configured to use CAST-40 encryption. You now want to change the encryption protocol to CAST-64. What must you do to change and enable clients to use the new protocol? (Choose all that apply.)

   A. Reinstall KM server.

   B. Stop and restart the System Attendant.

   C. Configure each Exchange client application to use the new protocol.

   D. Change the preferred encryption protocol in the properties of the Encryption object.

   E. Recover the client encryption keys from all of the Exchange recipients.

4. There can be only one KM administrator.

   A. True

   B. False

5. Client software must be configured before a user's mailbox can be configured.

   A. True

   B. False

6. Which program can create security tokens in a batch manner?

   A. SIMPORT.EXE

   B. BATCH.BAT

   C. BATCH.EXE

   D. SECADMIN.DLL

7. What program is used to revoke a user's keys and certificates?

   A. Exchange Administrator

   B. SIMPORT.EXE

   C. KM database

   D. REVOKE.EXE

8. The MS-DOS-based Exchange client, although slow, can perform signing and sealing operations.

   A. True

   B. False

9. CAST-64 cannot be used in the United States.

   A. True

   B. False

10. What core Exchange component is involved in the initialization of advanced security for a client?

   A. MTA

   B. IMS

   C. POP3

   D. System Attendant

11. What is the extension of the client-side file that stores a user's security information?

    A. .EPF

    B. .EFP

    C. .KMS

    D. .KM

12. Which of the following must an administrator do to enable advanced security for a user?

    A. Enabled advanced security on the Security property page of that user's mailbox

    B. Have the user first install and configure advanced security on their computer, then have the user inform the administrator of their configuration

    C. Inform the user of their security token which will be used to configure their client software

    D. Both A and C

CHAPTER

11

Internet-Based Exchange Clients

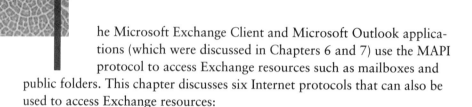

he Microsoft Exchange Client and Microsoft Outlook applications (which were discussed in Chapters 6 and 7) use the MAPI protocol to access Exchange resources such as mailboxes and public folders. This chapter discusses six Internet protocols that can also be used to access Exchange resources:

- **Post Office Protocol (POP3)**   Retrieves mail from the Inbox folder of a mailbox on a remote server mailbox.

- **Internet Message Access Protocol (IMAP4)**   Retrieves mail from a mailbox on a remote server, access includes personal and public folders as well as the Inbox folder.

- **HyperText Transfer Protocol (HTTP)**   Handles data transfer between World Wide Web servers and browsers.

- **Lightweight Directory Access Protocol (LDAP)**   Provides access to directory information.

- **Network News Transfer Protocol (NNTP)**   Transfers data between newsgroup servers, and newsgroup servers and newsgroup reader programs.

- **Internet Relay Chat (IRC)**   Enables online, real-time chat sessions.

Exchange Server's support for these four protocols permits a large number of Internet client applications to act as Exchange clients. This chapter provides a brief background on each protocol and then discusses how to implement each protocol within Exchange Server and on the clients. All of these protocols are configured in a common manner in Exchange Server, so we begin with an overview of Internet protocol configuration. The last section of this chapter will discuss firewalls and their relevance to the protocols in this chapter.

Microsoft
✓ Exam
Objective

Configure Internet protocols and services. Protocols and services include:

- POP3 and IMAP4
- Active Server and HTTP
- NNTP
- LDAP

Protocol Configuration Overview

POP3, IMAP, LDAP, and NNTP are built into the core components of Exchange Server. POP3, IMAP, and NNTP are part of the Information Store, and LDAP is part of the Directory Service. But while they are built in to Exchange Server, they can also be disabled. HTTP is not built in to the core components, and is only present if Outlook Web Access is installed during the Exchange setup.

Each protocol is configured using the Exchange Administrator program. Some of the settings for HTTP must be configured on the Microsoft Internet Information Server (IIS). This is because the Outlook Web Access that Exchange uses are installed on an IIS computer.

This section will provide an overview of topics that relate to configuring any of the Internet protocols mentioned above. Following this overview, the properties and configuration of each individual protocol will be discussed.

Protocols Container

Each site and server object in the Exchange hierarchy contains a Protocols container. An administrator can set protocol defaults and configure related functions by configuring the container's four property pages (to access these pages, highlight the Protocols container and click on the Properties option under the File menu).

General Property Page

The General property page is used to change the display name of the container and enter an administrative note. This page also shows the directory name of the container in a read-only field.

Permissions Property Page

This page is visible only if the Exchange Administrator program has been configured to display permission pages for objects (see Step 2 of Exercise 7.3 in Chapter 7). Permissions determine which users or groups have management access to the protocol objects in this container, and what type of access they have. Roles or individual rights can be assigned to users or groups.

Connections Property Page

The Connections property page enables an administrator to accept or reject POP3, LDAP, and NNTP connections to Exchange servers based on client IP addresses. By default, any client can connect. HTTP connections are not affected by this property page, but they can be restricted using the Microsoft IIS Internet Service Manager program.

MIME Types Property Page

MIME (Multipurpose Internet Mail Extensions) is a standard that allows non-textual content types to be included in an SMTP message. MIME content types include audio, image, HTML (HyperText Markup Language), and video. An administrator can use the MIME Types property page to associate MIME attachment content types to file name extensions. For example, the text/html MIME content type is by default associated with the .HTML file extension. This identification allows the client's operating system to select the appropriate application to access an attachment.

Protocols and the Exchange Hierarchy

The POP3, IMAP4, LDAP, and NNTP protocols can be configured at the site and server levels of the Exchange hierarchy. The HTTP protocol can be configured at the site level. In addition, each of the four protocols can also be configured on an individual mailbox. Custom recipients can be individually configured for IMAP, HTTP, LDAP, and NNTP. Therefore, an Exchange administrator has great flexibility in configuring the Internet protocols.

By default, each protocol is enabled at every hierarchical level. An administrator can enable or disable protocols at various levels to provide users with the necessary functionality. The following are some example configurations:

- A protocol can be enabled at the site level, but disabled on some servers in the site. To do this, the administrator would enable the protocol at the site level and selectively disable the protocol at individual servers. Then, clients using the protocol can only connect to those servers that have not had the protocol disabled.

- A protocol can be disabled at the site level, yet enabled at specific servers in the site. Clients using the protocol can only connect to those servers that have the protocol enabled.

- A protocol can be enabled at both the site and server level, but disabled at certain mailboxes. Clients that have not had the protocol disabled at their mailboxes can connect to the server using the protocol.

If a protocol is disabled at the server level, the settings on the mailboxes and custom recipients on that server are irrelevant. Users on that server will not be able to connect using the protocol.

Post Office Protocol (POP3)

The Post Office Protocol version 3 (POP3) enables a client to retrieve mail from a remote server mailbox. A user who is not always attached to their network can have their mailbox on a server that is permanently attached to the network. Mail sent to that user would be delivered to the server-based mailbox. The server acts as a sort of mail-drop. Clients can remotely connect to the server and download their mail to their computer. The protocol used to both store the mail on the server and to download the mail to the client is POP3. In this capacity, the server is referred to as a POP server, and the client as a POP client. POP3 cannot be used to send mail, it is only a retrieval protocol. Simple Mail Transfer Protocol (SMTP) is still used to transfer mail between mailboxes.

The remainder of this section covers these POP-related topics:

- POP3 architecture

- Exchange Server POP3 Overview

- Configuring a POP3 client

- Troubleshooting POP3

POP3 Architecture

POP works through a simple request-response mechanism. A POP client sends request commands, and a POP server sends responses back to the POP client. These client-server interactions can be divided into three main states:

- Authorization

- Transaction

- Update

Authorization, also called *greeting*, is the client logon to the POP server. The POP username and password are sent to the POP server. After a successful authorization, transactions can take place between the POP client and server. The POP client can request the number and size of messages in its mailbox, and messages can be downloaded and deleted. After the POP server has responded and the POP client is finished, the POP client issues a QUIT command. This ends the POP session and causes the POP server to enter the update state for the user's mailbox. Messages may be deleted during the update state.

POP uses TCP/IP as its transport protocol. The session, or *conversation*, between the POP client and server takes place on TCP port 110. A *port* is a numeric identifier assigned to an application or protocol and is used to route incoming packets to the correct application. Just because a packet has arrived at the correct computer, it still has to be delivered to the correct application on that computer. POP clients address the requests to port 110 on the POP server. The POP server listens to port 110 for those requests (this same principle is applicable to LDAP, HTTP, and other Internet protocols). The third revision of the POP standard, POP3, is documented in RFC 1939.

 You may be familiar with Ethernet or Token Ring addresses, which are used to deliver a frame to a specific computer. You may even be familiar with network addresses, such as IP addresses, which are used to route packets to the correct networks and computers. Ports are yet another type of address that are used to route packets to the correct applications on a machine.

Exchange Server POP3 Overview

POP3 is integrated into the Information Store (IS) component of Exchange Server. Although it is not a separate service, the POP3 functionality is sometimes referred to as the Exchange POP3 Service. It permits any POP3-enabled e-mail program to connect to an Exchange server and retrieve mail (see Figure 11.1). Only messages in the Inbox folder of a mailbox can be accessed. Messages in other folders are not accessible. The POP3 Service does not permit access to encrypted messages.

FIGURE II.I

Exchange and POP3

As mentioned previously, POP3 retrieves mail, but does not send it. The Simple Mail Transfer Protocol (SMTP) is used to send mail. SMTP functionality can be added to an Exchange server by using the Exchange Internet Mail Service (IMS). The IMS enables an Exchange server to send and receive SMTP messages through port 25. When POP3 and the IMS are running, a remote client can connect to the Exchange server, retrieve mail using POP3 on port 110, and send mail using SMTP on port 25. The IMS passes incoming SMTP messages to the IS for delivery. Chapter 14 covers the IMS in detail.

POP3 Site and Server Configuration

The site and server level POP3 objects have four property pages in common (five if the Permissions page is displayed). Table 11.1 lists and describes these property pages.

T A B L E 11.1	Property Page	Description
Property pages on the site and server POP3 objects	General	This page contains a checkbox to enable or disable the POP3 protocol. The default is enabled. You can also set the display name of the POP3 object and view its directory name in a read-only field. An administrative note field is also available. At the server level, this page contains a checkbox to specify whether the site level settings should be used for the server. The default is to use the settings from the site object.
	Authentication	This page is used to select the authentication protocols that POP3 clients must use to log on to the Exchange server with the POP protocol. The options are: • Basic (Cleartext). Authentication through an unencrypted user name and password. • Basic (Cleartext) using SSL. Secure Sockets Layer protocol is used to encrypt user name and password. • Windows NT Challenge/Response. Authentication uses Windows NT network security and an encrypted password. This method is supported by Microsoft Mail and News version 3.0 or later, and Microsoft Outlook Express. • Windows NT Challenge/Response using SSL. Authentication uses Windows NT network security through a SSL-encrypted channel. This method is supported by Microsoft Outlook Express. • MCIS Membership System. Authentication uses Windows NT network security through a MCIS Membership System and over a SSL connection. MCIS stands for Microsoft Commercial Internet Server. • MCIS Membership System using SSL By default, an Exchange server will allow a POP3 or IMAP4 client to be authenticated with any of the above authentication protocols, with the exception of the MCIS options. But an administrator could also select those options.

	Property Page	Description
T A B L E II.I *(cont.)* Property pages on the site and server POP3 objects	Message Format	This page is used to set the encoding method and character set used when converting Exchange messages for retrieval by POP3 clients. ▪ MIME ▪ UUENCODE. (includes option to use Binhex with Macintosh clients) Many international character sets are available. The default is US-ASCII. You can also specify whether Microsoft Exchange rich-text format can be used in POP3 messages.
	Idle Time-out	This page is used to configure how long an idle POP3 connection will be held open before automatically closing. Options include: ▪ Do not close idle connections ▪ Close idle connections after a specified number of minutes The default is to close idle connections after 10 minutes.

The server level POP3 object also contains a Diagnostics Logging property page that can be used to specify the type and amount of information the POP service logs to the Windows NT application event log. Exercise 11.1 outlines the steps for accessing the POP3 property pages and attributes.

POP3 Mailbox Configuration

An administrator can override server level settings at the mailbox level using the Protocols page of a mailbox object. A mailbox can independently have POP3 enabled or disabled or have unique POP3 settings. As mentioned earlier, if a protocol is disabled at the server level, the settings at the mailbox level have no effect.

Internet Mail Service (IMS) Configuration

POP3 only enables clients to retrieve mail. If a client needs to send mail, the Exchange server must have an Internet Mail Service (IMS) providing SMTP support. The POP3 client does not have to actually forward messages to the Internet but can instead rely on the IMS for the delivery of submitted messages. Chapter 14 discusses the role of an IMS within an SMTP mail system.

EXERCISE 11.1

Configuring POP3 at the Site Object

1. In Exchange Administrator, navigate to the Protocols container by expanding the site object and its Configuration container. Click on the Protocols container in the left pane to display the individual protocol objects in the right pane.

2. Double-click on the POP3 (Mail) Site Defaults object. The property pages for this object will appear. A checkbox on the General page allows you to enable or disable POP3 for the site.

3. Select the Message Format page. Examine the options on the drop-down menu. Click the Help button for information on the message encoding formats.

4. Feel free to examine any of the other property pages. When you are finished, click OK to save any changes you made, or click Cancel to discard them.

Users of TCP/IP-based applications like POP3 and SMTP normally use friendly computer names when performing actions (e.g., SEND joesmith@widget.com) rather than IP addresses (e.g., SEND joesmith@131.54.23.48). A database that maps friendly names to IP addresses must exist so that information can be routed to the correct computer over the network. A Domain Name System (DNS) server is the database that fills this role. In most configurations, the IMS requires that a DNS server be designated. The DNS server's location is specified using the Network Control Panel applet to configure the DNS property page of the TCP/IP protocol.

Configuring a POP3 Client

The following information must be configured on a POP3 client in order to connect to a POP3 server (in this case, the POP3 server is an Exchange server with the Exchange POP3 Service enabled):

- **POP3 server name**   The computer name of the home server of the Exchange mailbox.

- **SMTP server name**   The computer name of the Exchange server that is supporting SMTP by running the IMS.

- **POP3 account name**   The name the POP3 client must use when being authorized by a POP3 server. The Exchange POP3 Service requires a Windows NT domain and user account that has read permissions on the Exchange mailbox, followed by the alias name of the mailbox in the format *domain\account\alias*. If the account name and alias are the same, the alias name can be left off.

- **POP3 account password**   The Exchange POP3 Service requires the password of the Windows NT user account that is specified in the POP3 account name field.

- **POP3 client e-mail address**   The SMTP address of the POP3 client. For an Exchange mailbox, this is the SMTP address found on the E-mail Addresses property page of the mailbox.

Table 11.2 provides sample information and shows how that information can be used to configure a POP3 client.

	Sample Information	POP3 Client Configuration
T A B L E 11.2 An example of a POP3 client configuration	Computer name running the Exchange POP3 Service= Education	POP3 server name=Education
	Computer name running the Exchange IMS= Education	SMTP server name=Education
	Window NT account with read permission on the mailbox=NTDomain\GeorgeW Alias name of mailbox= GeorgeW	POP3 account name=NTDomain\GeorgeW\GeorgeW or simply NTDomain\GeorgeW
	Password of GeorgeW=woodenteeth	POP3 account password=woodenteeth
	Domain name=Chicago.com Alias name of mailbox=GeorgeW	POP3 client e-mail address=GeorgeW@Chicago.com

Troubleshooting POP3

When a POP3 client connects to a POP3 server but encounters problems during the session, protocol logging can be turned on to help troubleshoot. Protocol logging records the entire conversation between the POP3 client and server by writing that information to a log file.

By default, protocol logging is turned off. It can be enabled and configured in the Registry of the Exchange POP3 server. Two settings, both under HKEY_LOCAL_MACHINE\System\CurrentControlSet\Services\MSExchangeIS\ ParametersSystem, are used to control logging. This one is used to enable logging:

```
POP3_Protocol_Logging_Level= <numeric value of 0, 1, or 4>
```

A value of 0 configures no logging. A value of 1 configures minimum logging, and 4 maximum logging.

This setting specifies the directory and file name that will contain the logging information:

```
POP3_Protocol_LogPath= <directory_path>
```

A potential problem involves upgrading Exchange Server and its effect on POP3. If you upgrade an Exchange server from version 4.0 to 5.0 and then enable POP3, users will not be able to use POP3 to access their mailboxes. This is because the Exchange POP3 service needs to use the site service account to log on to the Exchange Server on behalf of the POP3 client. The POP3 service can then retrieve mail messages for the POP3 client. For this operation to work, the site service account must have the Windows NT right of "Act as part of the operating system." When upgrading Exchange Server from version 4.0 to 5.0, this right must be manually granted the site service account. After this is done, the POP3 clients will be able to access their mailboxes.

Internet Message Access Protocol

The Internet Message Access Protocol version 4 (IMAP4) is one of the added features of Microsoft Exchange Server 5.5. As with POP3, IMAP4 is built into the Exchange Information Store. This enables Internet e-mail applications using IMAP4 to retrieve data from an Exchange server. As with POP3, IMAP4 can only retrieve data and must use the SMTP functions of the Exchange Internet Mail Service (IMS) to send data.

Microsoft Outlook Express is an example of an IMAP4 client application.

One of the main differences between IMAP4 and POP3 is the Exchange folders they can access. POP3, as mentioned earlier, can only access the Inbox folder of a mailbox. IMAP4, however, can also access personal and public folders. IMAP4 also includes other advanced features (and non-POP3 features) such as search capabilities and selective download of messages or even only the attachment of a message.

Microsoft ✓ *Exam* *Objective*	**Develop a long-term coexistence strategy. Protocols include:** • IMAP • LDAP

Exchange Server IMAP4 Overview

IMAP4 has many of the same properties as POP3, such as authentication, message format, and idle time-out. Some of these pages have additional attributes not present with POP3. IMAP4 also allows anonymous user access, meaning that an IMAP4 user without a Windows NT user account could access the server. Table 11.3 lists and describes the property pages and attributes of the IMAP4 object.

T A B L E 11.3 Property pages of the IMAP4 object	**Property Page**	**Description**
	General	**Display name**. This is the name that will appear in the Exchange Administrator window. This name can be edited. **Directory name**. This is the name defined during installation. This is a read-only field. **Enable protocol**. As with the other Internet protocols, IMAP4 can be enabled or disabled at both the site and server levels. The default is enabled. **Include all public folders when a folder list is requested**. This option, which is enabled by default, permits a complete listing of public folders to be sent to an IMAP4 client in response to the IMAP List command. Some IMAP4 client applications, however, encounter poor performance when downloading a large list of public folders. If that is the case, this field can be cleared (i.e., unchecked). **Enable fast message retrieval**. This option, which is enabled by default, permits an Exchange server to approximate the sizes of messages when reporting to an IMAP4 client application. Approximating message sizes increases the speed of message retrieval. Some IMAP4 client applications, however, require a server to report the exact message size. If that is the case, this field can be cleared (i.e., unchecked).

TABLE 11.3 *(cont.)* Property pages of the IMAP4 object	**Property Page**	**Description**
	Authentication	An Exchange server can allow IMAP4 clients to be authenticated with the same protocols that were options with POP3. While the options are the same for both IMAP4 and POP3, each can be configured with a different set of authentication protocols. This is true for any of the other attributes IMAP4 and POP3 have in common.
	Anonymous	This page enables an Exchange server to allow IMAP4 users without Windows NT user accounts to access it. If this option is selected, the administrator can also choose the Windows NT user account that will be used by the anonymous IMAP4 client. By default, this option is disabled. Anonymous access was not a feature available with POP3.
	Message Format	This page is used to set the encoding method and character set used when converting Exchange messages for retrieval by IMAP4 clients. The encoding options are: • **MIME**. Both the message body and attachments will be encoding with MIME. • **Provide message body as plain text**. The message body will be placed in plain text and any attachments in MIME. • **Provide message body as HTML**. The message body will be placed in HTML format and any attachments in MIME. If both this option and the immediate preceeding option are selected, Exchange will generate both a plain text and HTML for the message body.
	Idle Time-out	As with POP3, IMAP4 on an Exchange server can be configured to either not close idle connections from IMAP4 clients, or to close those connections after a specified period of time. If the latter option is chosen, the default time period is 30 minutes.

Because of Exchange Server's support of IMAP4 and POP3, many Internet mail programs can be used as clients to Exchange Server.

HyperText Transfer Protocol (HTTP)

The World Wide Web (WWW) has become one of the most pervasive networks in the world. Servers all over the world are added to the Web daily, and the number of Web users is skyrocketing. Two standards used in the implementation of the WWW are HyperText Markup Language (HTML) and HyperText Transfer Protocol (HTTP). HTML is used to create hypertext and multimedia documents on the WWW. Hypertext is used to link one WWW object to another. For example, a word in a Web document can have a link to a Web document on another server. The other server could be anywhere else on the Web. Clicking on that word transfers the user to the linked document. Words, phrases, buttons, pictures, and other objects can have links. Multimedia (sound, video, and animation) can also be included in an HTML document. HTTP is the protocol used to connect a Web client program, called a Web browser, to a Web server. HTTP handles application-to-application communication.

Microsoft has developed technology that enables Web clients to access Microsoft BackOffice applications, like Exchange Server. The term Active Platform describes the collection of technologies that makes this possible. Simply put, Active Platform technology turns a Microsoft Internet Information server (IIS) into a Web gateway to BackOffice applications. This makes it possible for a Web client using a standard Web browser to access Exchange resources like the DS, mailboxes, public folders, and schedules. Active Platform technologies translate between HTML and the various BackOffice application formats such as MAPI. Figure 11.2 depicts the Active Platform architecture.

The remainder of this section discusses:

- The Active Platform

- Microsoft Outlook Web Access

The Active Platform

Active Platform refers to the collection of technologies that enable Web clients to access BackOffice applications. In this context, the term "platform" is synonymous with the term "architecture." The best way to explain this architecture is to start at the client-side and work through to the server-side.

The two main technologies that comprise the Active Platform are:

- ActiveX

- Active Server

ActiveX

All of the Active Platform technologies are based on *ActiveX*. ActiveX is a
Microsoft specification for software objects. The term *control* refers to an
object. A control is a self-contained software component that has properties
(e.g., size, color, content) and methods (e.g., the code to print or edit content).
An example of an ActiveX control might be a graphic control. A program
could send an ActiveX control containing a graphic to another program on a different computer. The second program would have all the necessary information

to access and manipulate the graphic. A control or object is like a container, containing both content and programming code. ActiveX is part of the Microsoft programming architecture called the Component Object Model (COM).

Active Server

Active Server is a set of components running on a Microsoft Internet Information Server 3.0 (IIS) that enable Web clients to access Microsoft BackOffice applications, such as Microsoft Exchange Server (see Figure 11.3). The main components that implement Active Server are:

- **Collaboration Data Objects (CDO)**   The libraries of functions providing basic messaging functions to Active Server Pages.

- **Active Server Pages (ASP)**   Programs, written to the ActiveX standard and running on an Active Server, that provide access to a specific Microsoft BackOffice application, such as Microsoft Exchange Server.

FIGURE 11.3

The role of ActiveX in the Active Platform

Collaboration Data Objects (CDO)   Collaboration Data Objects (CDO) are two libraries of messaging functions that can be used by server applications running on the Active Server (see Figure 11.4). The CDO libraries are:

- **CDO Object Library**   The CDO Object Library provides basic access functions to Microsoft BackOffice applications. When used to access Microsoft Exchange, this includes logon services, access to Inboxes and public folders, and access to the Exchange Directory. Developers can create Active Server applications that include instructions to the CDO Object Library to carry out these functions.

FIGURE 11.4

The Active Server components of Exchange Server

- **CDO Rendering Library**   The CDO Rendering Library contains the functions to convert data from the various Microsoft formats (e.g. Rich-Text Format) to the standard Web format of HTML. For example, when a Web client retrieves data from the Exchange Information Store, it is the CDO Rendering Library that converts that data into an HTML page. Developers can place in their application the instructions for this functionality, and it is implemented through the CDO Rendering Library.

Collaboration Data Objects was formerly called Active Messaging, which itself, was formerly called OLE Messaging.

Active Server Pages   While the CDO components provide basic messaging services, other server applications must be present to enable access to specific Microsoft BackOffice applications. The server applications that fit this role are called Active Server Pages (ASP). ASP are programs written to the ActiveX standard and running on an Active Server that provide access to a specific Microsoft BackOffice application (see Figure 11.5). While developers can create their own customized ASPs, Microsoft has created various ASP applications, one of which is Microsoft Outlook Web Access (OWA).

Microsoft Outlook Web Access (OWA)

One of the components that ships with Microsoft Exchange Server is Microsoft Outlook Web Access (OWA). Outlook Web Access is an ASP that is installed on an Active Server and enables Web clients to access a Microsoft Exchange server (see Figure 11.6). Users of Web browsers, regardless of their operating system, can be clients to Exchange Server through this capability. A Web browser could be used to access an individual mailbox for reading or sending messages, public folders for reading or posting, a Global Address List (GAL), and calendars. Microsoft Exchange can even be configured to allow access from anonymous Web users (i.e., users who do not have Windows NT user accounts).

Microsoft Outlook Web Access was formerly called Exchange Web Client.

FIGURE 11.5

Active Messaging in the
Active Platform

Microsoft Outlook Web Access and Active Server serve as a gateway or
translator between the protocols used in a Web environment and those used in
the Microsoft environment. For example, when a Web user attempts to read a
message in their Exchange Inbox, their Web browser creates and sends that
read instruction using the HTTP protocol. The Active Server running OWA
receives that HTTP read instruction and translates it into a MAPI read instruction. The Active Server then establishes a RPC connection to the relevant
Exchange server and passes the MAPI instruction to that server. The reverse
process takes place when the Exchange server sends the message to the Web user.
Content is also translated on the Active Server. When Exchange data is sent to
a Web user, the Active Server translates that data into the HTML format for
reading in a Web browser. The reverse process takes place when Web data is
sent to an Exchange server.

FIGURE 11.6

Active Server Pages in the
Active Platform
architecture

The remainder of this section will cover the following topics:

- Installing Microsoft Outlook Web Access

- Configuring HTTP on the Active Server

- Configuring HTTP on an Exchange server

- Web clients and Microsoft Outlook Web Access

Installing Microsoft Outlook Web Access

A requirement for installing OWA is the presence on your network of a Microsoft Internet Information Server 3.0 with Active Server Pages. The use of the phrase "Active Server Pages" in the last sentence refers to the components on IIS that processes .asp files. The phrase is used for both the components that process .asp files and the .asp files themselves.

HTTP is not built-in to the core components of Exchange, as are the other protocols discussed in this chapter. It is an installation option during the setup of Exchange Server (a default option), and is referenced on the setup screen as the "Outlook Web Access." If chosen, this option will install OWA on your IIS.

If the Exchange server and the IIS are on the same computer, no input is required from the installer. If they are on different computers, the installer will be prompted for the NetBIOS computer names of the IIS computer and the Exchange server.

Once the setup is complete, the Exchange hierarchy will have an object in the site Protocols container labeled "HTTP (Web) Site Settings." That object can be used to configure HTTP for the site. HTTP can also be enabled or disabled at the mailbox level. Since it is physically installed on an Active Server/IIS, HTTP has some of its properties configured on an Active Server. The topic of configuration is next.

Configuring HTTP on the Active Server

Some of the configuration of HTTP is done on an Exchange server and some on the Active Server. The main things configured on the Active Server are:

- Authentication

- Encryption

- Rejecting IP addresses

Authentication   Authentication protocols can be set for the Active Server through the use the IIS management program Internet Service Manager. The supported protocols are Basic (Clear Text) and Windows NT Challenge/Response. An administrator can enable either or both of these protocols.

Encryption   The data passed between an Active Server and a Web client can be encrypted. The Internet Service Manager is used to enable that scenario. The encryption protocol used by an Active Server is the Secure Sockets Layer (SSL). SSL can be used with both the Basic (Clear Text) and Windows NT Challenge Response authentication protocols. Normally, Web browsers use port 80 to communicate with a Web server (in our case, the Active Server). But when a Web browser and a Web server communicate using SSL, port 995 is used.

Rejecting IP Addresses   Administrators can use the Internet Service Manager to reject designated IP addresses or ranges of addresses of Web clients. The Microsoft Exchange Administrator program can be used to reject IP addresses for clients using POP3, IMAP4, NNTP, and LDAP, but not for HTTP, which is used by Web browsers. As stated, that must be done on the Active Server through the Internet Service Manager.

Configuring HTTP on an Exchange Server

Even though HTTP is running on an Active Server, it is represented by the HTTP object at the site level of the Exchange hierarchy. It is also represented on the Protocols property page of a user's mailbox. When an Active Server attempts to establish a connection to a mailbox on an Exchange server, the Active Server first determines the enable/disable status of the HTTP object at the site level. If that is enabled (which is the default), then it determines that status at the particular mailbox. If HTTP is enabled at the site level but not at a particular mailbox, the Web user will receive an error message stating that the server is down or that HTTP access is disabled.

The HTTP object at the site level contains three property pages (not counting the Permission page). Each page is briefly described in Table 11.4.

	Property Page	Description
T A B L E 11.4 Property pages of the HTTP object	General	HTTP can be enabled or disabled at the site level. Anonymous access can be enabled or disabled for accessing anonymous public folders and for browsing the Global Address List.
	Folder Shortcuts	Contains the list of pubic folders that will be available to anonymous Web users. For these folders to be seen, the General page must also have enabled anonymous access to anonymous public folders.
	Advanced	Enables the setting of the maximum number of Address Book (i.e. GAL) entries that will be returned to an authorized Web client. The default amount is 50. No limit can also be configured. If no limit is selected, then the entire Address Book is sent to the client. That can be bad for performance when large directories are involved.

A couple additional comments about anonymous access to public folders is warranted. If a public folder is listed on the Folder Shortcuts page, but the "Allow anonymous user access to anonymous public folders" is disabled, the Web client will receive the following message:

```
The page has been disabled, please see your administrator
```

Any public folders that need to be accessed by anonymous Web clients need to be explicitly listed in the Folder Shortcuts page. Subfolders will not be seen unless explicitly listed on the Folder Shortcuts page.

The final requirement for an anonymous Web client to view a public folder is for that folder to have at least the Reviewer role (Read and Folder Visible permissions) given to the Anonymous user account. That can be done through an Exchange client application, such as Microsoft Outlook, and the folder's Permissions property page. It can also be done through the Exchange Administrator program and the Client Permissions button on the General property page of a folder.

Web Clients and Microsoft Outlook Web Access

Any Web browser that supports Frames and JavaScript can be a client to Microsoft Exchange Server. That fact extends the number of client operating systems that can be used with Exchange.

A Web client initiates access to their mailbox by entering a Uniform Resource Locator (URL) in the following format:

```
http://<IIS_server_name>/exchange
```

The next step is for a logon script (logon.asp) to be executed on the Active Server that will lead the Web client through the authentication process. If the Web client is using the Basic (Clear Text) authentication protocol, they will be prompted for a logon name. They must enter that name in the format of domain\ *NT_account*. Once logged on and depending on permissions, a Web client can access their mailbox, calendar, and public folders.

If anonymous access is enabled (the default), a Web client may use the word "anonymous" to log on to the Exchange server. An organization could use this functionality to give the general public access to product, sales, or support information placed in public folders.

Lightweight Directory Access Protocol (LDAP)

The Lightweight Directory Access Protocol (LDAP) provides client access to a directory service. An LDAP conversation can take place between an LDAP-enabled client and a server that responds to LDAP requests. LDAP supports actions such as querying, reading, sorting, and deleting directory objects. For example, an LDAP client could send a query to an LDAP server requesting the telephone number of a user named Pat Nixon. The LDAP server would search the directory and send back the answer to the LDAP client. LDAP requires TCP/IP on both the client and the server.

Exchange Server integrates LDAP directly in the DS component, and LDAP support is enabled by default. An administrator can disable this protocol at the site and server levels. Even though it is part of the DS component, LDAP is configured using objects in the site and server Protocols containers.

The LDAP object under the Protocols container has five property pages (the standard Permissions page is also shown if Exchange Administrator is configured to display it on all objects). They are explained in Table 11.5.

Microsoft ✓ *Exam Objective*

Develop a long-term coexistence strategy. Protocols include:

- IMAP
- LDAP

	Property Page	Description
TABLE 11.5 The property pages of the LDAP object	General	This page shows the display name (which can be modified) and the directory name (which is only informational) of this object. The most important attribute of this page is the ability to enable or disable LDAP. This page also provides an administrative note field.

	Property Page	Description
T A B L E 11.5 *(cont.)* The property pages of the LDAP object	Authentication	This page is used to set the authentication protocol that must be used by an LDAP client when accessing an Exchange server. The options are Basic (Clear Text) with and without SSL, Windows NT Challenge/Response with and without SSL, and MCIS Membership System with and without SSL. The default is for all options except MCIS to be selected
	Anonymous	This page is used to enable or disable anonymous user LDAP access to Exchange. The default is enabled. If disabled, all LDAP clients need to log on with a valid Windows NT user account and password.
	Search	This page is used to configure how substring directory searches are handled and the maximum number of search results to return (default is 100).
	Referrals	Exchange LDAP can use LDAP servers outside its Organization to which LDAP client searches can be forwarded. The LDAP servers outside the Organization are referred to as "referrals."
	Idle Time-out	This page is used to configure how long an idle LDAP connection will be held open before automatically closing. Options include: • Do not close idle connections • Close idle connections after a specified number of minutes The default is to close idle connections after 10 minutes.

Exercise 11.2 outlines some of the steps to configure the LDAP protocol at the site object.

Two additional comments about anonymous access and referrals. An organization must be careful about allowing anonymous access. People not in your organization could use anonymous access to view sensitive information about your organization. Disabling anonymous access would help prevent that situation. If you do need anonymous access, you could restrict the directory attributes that anonymous LDAP clients can view. That procedure is accomplished through the DS Site Configuration object and its Attributes property page. That page can be used to determine what attributes are viewed by anonymous LDAP clients. For example, an Exchange administrator might want telephone numbers to be invisible to anonymous LDAP clients. The administrator would clear the checkbox for the Telephone-Number attribute for anonymous requests.

As stated in Table 11.4, referrals relate to LDAP servers that can be forwarded client requests. For example, LDAP clients that connect to organization A could also periodically need to view directory information from organization B. One way to accomplish this is to configure LDAP on organization A to use as a referral a LDAP server in organization B.

EXERCISE 11.2

Configuring the LDAP Protocol at the Site Object

1. In Exchange Administrator, navigate to the site object. Choose the Protocols container within the site Configuration container. Double-click on the LDAP (Directory) Site Defaults object in the right pane. The properties pages for this object will appear.

2. The General page is where you enable or disable the LDAP protocol.

3. Select the Anonymous page. This page is where you enable or disable anonymous LDAP client access.

4. Feel free to investigate other properties of this object. When you are finished, click OK or Cancel.

Network News Transfer Protocol (NNTP)

USENET is a network within the Internet that is comprised of numerous servers containing information on a variety of topics. Each organized topic is called a *newsgroup*. A newsgroup can be thought of as a discussion group or a bulletin board. The USENET servers are also referred to as newsgroup servers. Users access these newsgroups to post information or to read other people's postings. Users interact with newsgroups through client applications referred to as newsgroup readers.

Clients and servers use the Network News Transfer Protocol (NNTP) to transfer information across USENET. When a client reads or posts information to a newsgroup server, NNTP is used for this exchange.

NNTP is also used to transfer newsgroup content between servers. This function is referred to as a *newsfeed*. A newsgroup server can be configured to send all or some of its newsgroups to other servers. When one server actively sends information to another server, it is referred to as a *push feed* (it is also referred to as *publishing*). A server also can be configured to request that information be sent to it from another server. This is referred to as a *pull feed*. Push feeds are usually used with large newsfeeds. A pull feed allows a local administrator to specify which and when newsgroups are received.

NNTP is included with Microsoft Exchange Server by being incorporated in the Information Store. Even though it is a part of the IS, NNTP has its own object in the Exchange hierarchy, under the Protocols container at both the site and server levels. While NNTP does not have its own installation, the newsfeeds between an Exchange server and the USENET do need to be setup. This is done through the Newsfeed Configuration Wizard. The Wizard prompts the installer for such information as the name of the USENET host, the host's IP address, the type of newsfeed, such as inbound (i.e., receiving data), outbound (i.e., publishing data), or inbound and outbound. When a newsfeed is configured between an Exchange server and the USENET, this functionality is referred to as the Internet News Service (INS). INS enables an Exchange server to function as a newsgroup server. It can publish public folder content as newsfeeds to other USENET servers. It also can receive newsfeeds from the USENET and place newsgroups in public folders. To receive newsfeeds, INS can either pull a newsfeed or receive a push. See Figure 11.7 for an illustration of INS.

Once a newsfeed is configured, it is represented in the Connections container of a site as an object. The property pages of a newsfeed object can be used to configure the newsfeed after its creation. Much of the information that was inputted to the Wizard can be later viewed and modified through the newsfeed object. For example, if the IP address of the USENET host changes, the new address can be inputted to the properties of that newsfeed, rather than creating a new newsfeed with the Wizard.

Another element of the INS environment that can be configured is the NNTP communication between an Exchange server and USENET hosts. That is done on an Exchange server through the NNTP object under the Protocols container of a site or server. One of the properties that can be configured with the NNTP object is anonymous access. An Exchange server can enable or disable anonymous NNTP clients from accessing its published newsgroups.

FIGURE 11.7

Internet News Service (INS) and the USENET

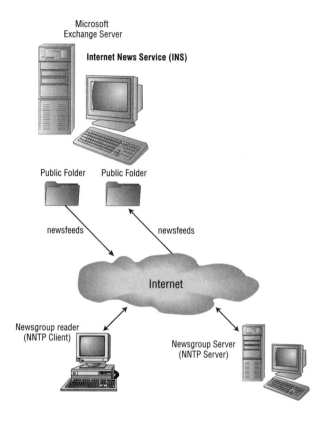

The remainder of this section will cover the above topics in more detail and will be organized into the following headings:

- Newsfeed Configuration Wizard

- Newsfeed property pages

- NNTP property pages

- Publishing a public folder as a newsgroup

- Receiving a newsgroup

Newsfeed Configuration Wizard

Microsoft Exchange Server includes a Newsfeed Configuration Wizard for the creation of newsfeeds. The Wizard is accessed through the Microsoft Exchange Administrator program, and the File menu, New Other, and Newsfeed command. The Wizard can be run more than once to create as many newsfeeds as are required. For example, a newsfeed could be created for publishing information to one particular newsgroup server, and another newsfeed created for receiving information from a different newsgroup server. It is also possible to have one newsfeed that both publishes and receives information.

The Newsfeed Configuration Wizard works by presenting a series of questions and placing the input to those questions into a new newsfeed object. That object will be placed in the Connections container of the site. Some of the configuration information requested by the Wizard is found in Table 11.6. Figure 11.8 shows the startup page of the Newsfeed Configuration Wizard.

FIGURE 11.8

Startup page of the
Newsfeed Configuration
Wizard

T A B L E 11.6	**Wizard Dialog Box**	**Description**
Newsfeed Configuration Wizard	Installed Server	This is the name of the Exchange server that will receive the newsfeed. The default is the server on which the administrator is currently logged.

TABLE 11.6 *(cont.)* Newsfeed Configuration Wizard	**Wizard Dialog Box**	**Description**
	Type of Newsfeed	Specifies the type of newsfeed. Options include inbound and outbound, inbound only, and outbound only. If an inbound newsfeed is chosen, the type of newsfeed must also be configured as either push or pull. See Figure 11.9 for a graphic of this page.
	Connection Type	Specifies the type of network connection to be used for connection to the USENET. The options include LAN and Dial-Up Networking (DUN). Figure 11.10 shows the Connection Type page.
	Schedule	Permits the administrator to configure the connection frequency to another newsgroup server (this can't be set on push newsfeeds). Once setup is complete, the administrator can create a custom schedule through the Schedule property page on the newsfeed object the Wizard creates.
	Host Computer	Specifies the computer that sends newsfeeds to this Exchange server. Identified by either a host name or an IP address.
	Security	Provides for the following security configurations: • How the Exchange server logs on to another newsgroup server (pull feed). • How another newsgroup server logs on to the Exchange server (push feed).
	Administrator	Selects the newsgroup administrator that will receive any Exchange newsgroup management messages. This account also becomes the owner of all public folders configured for INS.
	Active File	Allows the importing or downloading of the active file. This file contains the list of all available newsgroups on the USENET host. This file is provided by your provider of the USENET host, such as your Internet Service Provider (ISP). If you have already secured the file, such as through e-mail or an FTP download, the Wizard allows you to import the file into the newsfeed configuration. If you have not already secured the file, the Wizard has the option to download the file now. A third option is to add the active file later. That is done on the Inbound property page of that particular newsfeed, and through the New Active List button on that page.

Additional comments are warranted about the topic of types of newsfeeds.

FIGURE 11.9

Setting the type of
newsfeed

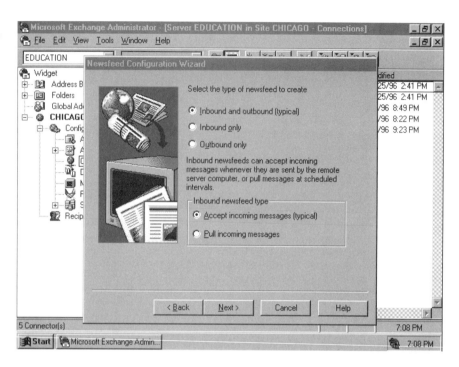

FIGURE 11.10

Setting the connection
type of a newsfeed

Types of Newsfeeds

Newsfeeds come in two types, inbound and outbound. As their names denote, an inbound newsfeed is newsgroup information coming into an Exchange server from a USENET host, while an outbound newsfeed is newsgroup messages being sent out from an Exchange server to another USENET host. A newsfeed can also be configured to use both inbound and outbound. Both types of newsfeeds are discussed further below.

Inbound Newsfeeds   An inbound newsfeed is where newsgroups are sent by a USENET host to an Exchange server running INS. The inbound newsgroups are placed in designated public folders where Exchange clients can access them. Inbound feeds can be configured as either a push ("Accept incoming messages" in Figure 11.9) or a pull ("Pull incoming messages" in Figure 11.9).

- **Push feed**   A push feed is where the USENET host initiates the newsfeed to an Exchange server on its schedule. The USENET host sends 'control messages' along with the newsfeed content. These control messages are like 'header' information stating what is in the newsfeed. The control messages and newsfeed content are queued up on the Exchange server until the INS administrator accepts or rejects the newsfeed. Control messages are further discussed under the section "NNTP Properties Pages." Push feeds are usually used with large newsfeeds and where there is a high speed network in place between the servers.

- **Pull feed**   A pull feed is where the Exchange server requests particular newsgroups from a USENET host. Pull feeds give the INS administrator more control over the schedule and content of the newsfeeds, and work best when a smaller number of newsgroups are needed over a slower network connection, such as a dial-up connection. If your Internet Service Provider (ISP) provides newsgroup access but does not configure newsgroup selection on a customer-by-customer basis, then you would have to configure an inbound pull feed if you did not want their entire newsgroup collection.

Outbound Newsfeeds   Outbound newsfeeds allow an Exchange server to publish newsgroup messages to the USENET. If an outbound feed was selected, the Wizard will present the installer with the opportunity to select the Exchange public folders that will be part of the outbound feed (i.e., published as newsgroups to the USENET). Prior to that step, the installer must have designated the relevant public folders for inclusion in a newsfeed. That is done through the Tools menu and Newsgroup Hierarchies option of Exchange Administrator. If, after the newsfeed is created, additional public folders need to be added to the newsfeed, that can be done through the Tools/Newsgroup Hierarchies, and then the Outbound property page of the newsfeed object. Those procedures will be discussed further under the sections "Newsfeed Property Pages" and "Publishing a Public Folder as a Newsgroup."

As mentioned, after a particular newsfeed is created, it is represented as a newsfeed object in the Exchange hierarchy. The following section discusses newsfeed objects and their properties.

Newsfeed Property Pages

Each newsfeed is represented as an object under the Connection container of a site. The name given a newsfeed is made up in part of the name of the USENET host that was entered in the Newsfeed Configuration Wizard, and the Exchange server name the newsfeed is created on. For example, if the Exchange server name is EDUCATION, and the USENET host name was XMissionNet, then the newsfeed will be called "Newsfeed XMissionNet (EDUCATION)." Much of the configuration entered into the Wizard can be viewed and modified through the properties of a newsfeed object. Those properties are discussed in Table 11.7.

T A B L E   11.7

Newsfeed property pages

Property Page	Description
General	Provides fields for the newsfeed name and administrator mailbox. This is where you enable or disable the newsfeed.
Messages	Controls the inbound and outbound message sizes.
Hosts	Specifies the names of the remote newsgroup servers being sent newsfeeds. Specifies the hosts sending newsfeeds to this Exchange server.
Connection	Controls the type of connection used to connect to remote hosts. The options are LAN and DUN.
Security	Provides the selection of the outbound user name and password and the inbound user name.

TABLE 11.7 (cont.) Newsfeed property pages	**Property Page**	**Description**
	Schedule	Controls the frequency of inbound pull feeds and outbound feeds.
	Advanced	Used to mark all newsgroup messages as being delivered. This is normally used to cancel processing of queued messages when a backlog occurs.
	Outbound	Shows the public folders that are in the Newsgroup Hierarchy (set through the Tools/Newsgroup Hierarchies in Exchange Administrator) and allows the selection of those folders that will be included or excluded from this outbound newsfeed. Figure 11.11 shows this page.
	Inbound	Specifies the newsgroups to publish to this Exchange server. The list of newgroups to choose from is determined by the active file.

FIGURE 11.11

Outbound property page

The following are two short examples of how the Outbound page and the Inbound page could be used. Suppose you were an administrator of an Exchange server that provided newsfeeds to a subsidiary that retrieved newsgroups from your server. You would have to include at least one public folder newsgroup in the Outbound page in order for your server to process the requests from the subsidiary.

Another scenario could have your server receiving an inbound/push feed from an Internet Service Provider (ISP). As an administrator, you could notice a newsgroup in the public folder hierarchy that you do not want to receive. To permanently remove this folder from the newsfeed and public folder hierarchy, you would have to reject the newsgroup on the Inbound property page and delete the folder from the public folder hierarchy.

NNTP Property Pages

The NNTP object, found under the Protocols container at both the site and server levels, allows the configuration of the NNTP communication between Exchange servers and USENET hosts and clients. Table 11.8 will provide an overview of the property pages of this object.

T A B L E 11.8 NNTP property pages	**Property Page**	**Description**
	General	Contains display name and Directory name fields, as well as the ability to enable/disable NNTP and enable/disable client access through this protocol. If these configurations are done at the site level, they will apply to all servers in that site unless overridden at a particular server. If the "Enable client access" is disabled, NNTP clients will not be able to access Exchange public folders published as newsgroups. This page also contains an administrative note field.
	Newsfeeds	Contains a listing of all newsfeeds. The properties of a newsfeed can be accessed through the Properties button on this page. The same property pages are accessed as through a newsfeed object under the Connections container.

	Property Page	Description
TABLE 11.8 (cont.) NNTP property pages	Control Messages	This page displays the Control Message Queue. A control message is a type of notification that someone is attempting to send a new or deleted newsgroup in a newsfeed, or when someone attempts to delete a single message in a newsgroup. An administrator has the option to accept or delete these actions by accepting or deleting their respective control messages. By queuing up these actions and using control messages, an administrator has control over inbound newsfeeds.
	Authentication	The Exchange NNTP server can require various methods of authentication from other NNTP servers and clients. Authentication methods include: Basic (Clear Text) with or without SSL; Windows NT Challenge/Response with or without SSL; MCIS Membership System with or without SSL.
	Message Format	Message encoding, such as MIME or UUENCODE, can be set on this page, as well as support for NNTP clients that can read S/MIME signatures (i.e., Secure/MIME).
	Idle-Time-out	Idle NNTP connections can be set to not time-out, or to time-out after "x" minutes, the default is 10 minutes.
	Anonymous	Exchange NNTP can enable or disable anonymous NNTP client access. The default is disabled.

The use of the Control Messages page is seen in the following scenario. A Microsoft Exchange user reports that several recently created newsgroups are not listed in your company's newsgroup hierarchy of public folders. You check the Control Messages page and notice that those newsgroups have been received and are queued up, waiting to be accepted or deleted. You accept the queued control messages to allow the new newsgroups into your newsgroup hierarchy.

As a way to tie together the preceding material on NNTP, the next two sections provide a brief overview of the steps involved in publishing and receiving a newsgroup. The following server-side procedures are a review of material already covered, while new material will be presented on the client-side procedures.

Publishing a Public Folder as a Newsgroup

The major steps in publishing a public folder as a newsgroup are as follows:

1. Select the public folders that are to be published to the USENET. This is accomplished through Exchange Administrator and the Tools menu, Newsgroup Hierarchies option.

2. Install Internet News Service (INS). You do this by executing the Newsfeed Configuration Wizard, which is started through the Exchange Administrator program, and its File menu, New Other, and Newsfeed option. The type of newsfeed for publishing information must be Outbound, or Inbound/Outbound. The Wizard will allow the selection of the public folders in the newsgroup hierarchy that will be published in this newsfeed. That procedure can also be done later through the Outbound property page of the newsfeed object.

3. Configure the NNTP communication parameters through the NNTP object (optional).

4. The owners of folders in the newsgroup hierarchy can exercise control over their folders. Control includes whether a folder can be accessed by NNTP newsreaders (done through the Internet News tab), who can access the folder, whether there is anonymous access, and the particular permissions users will have at the folder. These actions are accomplished through the Exchange or Outlook client applications and the property pages of a folder.

Receiving a Newsgroup

The major steps in receiving a newsgroup in a newsfeed from a USENET host are outlined below.

1. Install Internet News Service (INS). Execute the Newsfeed Configuration Wizard, which is started through the Exchange Administrator program, and its File menu, New Other, and Newsfeed option. The type of newsfeed for receiving newsgroups must be Inbound, or Inbound/Outbound. The installer must also choose between a push feed or a pull feed. Also, an active file containing a listing of the newsgroups in the newsfeed must be imported into the configuration.

2. The administrator must periodically check the Control Message Queue, accessed through the Control Messages property page of the NNTP object, to accept or delete changes sent from the host.

Internet Relay Chat (IRC)

The Internet Relay Chat (IRC) protocol enables users to communicate with each other through text-based, real-time conversations, also simply called 'chats.' A chat takes place over what is called a channel, also sometimes called a discussion group or a conference. For instance, an administrator could set up a channel for product brainstorming. Users could join that channel and communicate in the chats on that channel. IRC has been a part of the TCP/IP protocol suite for a long time and is used in many private and public networks.

IRC is a client/server protocol. IRC client applications provide the user interface for joining a channel, listing who is online, and entering and reading chat information, among other functions. IRC clients communicate with other IRC clients through an IRC server, or servers. An IRC server acts as a type of conversation router. A server creates a channel that enables clients to chat with each other through the server. The commands and data sent from one client to another client actually first go to the IRC server, which then processes them and routes them to the relevant client or clients.

Microsoft Exchange 5.5 provides IRC functionality, along with extended functions, through the Microsoft Exchange Chat Service and Internet Locator Service (ILS). The Chat Service enables live conferencing over the Internet or an intranet. Online text-based chat sessions, groupware applications, and gaming applications are all supported through this platform. The Chat Service can be run in a standalone scenario (i.e., a single Chat server), or on a number of servers creating a large chat network. The Microsoft Exchange Chat Service extends the functions of IRC by adding better performance (e.g., smaller packets are used), security features (e.g., authentication and access control), and the transmission of data as well as text. These additional features are the result of Microsoft using the Microsoft Internet Chat (MIC) protocol, which uses IRC as a base of functions, and then adds to them. A large number of IRC and MIC client applications can be used with this service, one of which is Microsoft NetMeeting, which includes the MIC protocol and can communicate both text and data.

The Internet Locator Service tracks online participants and enables users to locate another user or particular conversation. Because the ILS and the Chat Service are included with Microsoft Exchange, chat clients can use the Exchange directory, select a name, and initiate a chat. If participants are using Microsoft NetMeeting, the communication can also entail collaborating on a document, whiteboarding, or video conferencing.

The following material is not an exhaustive examination of the Chat Service and ILS, but simply an introduction and the necessary information for the Microsoft Exchange exam. The following topics will be introduced: Requirements, Installation, Configuration, and Management.

Requirements

The Microsoft Exchange Chat Service and Internet Locator Service run on a Microsoft Internet Information Server 3.0. Because these products are based on the Internet protocol IRC, the TCP/IP protocol is also required as the network protocol. While not a requirement, the Domain Name System (DNS) can also be used in this environment.

The only client requirements are the obvious ones, a user must have an IRC or MIC client application, like Microsoft NetMeeting, and be using TCP/IP.

Installation

The Microsoft Exchange Server CD contains the setup for both the Chat Service and the ILS. Each setup is represented by a menu option on the Microsoft Exchange Server Setup menu that automatically runs when the CD is inserted. Another option is to manually access the CD and the \chat\setup\ <platform> directory and execute the Chat setup.

Configuration

Because both the Chat Service and the ILS are running on an IIS 3.0 server, it makes sense that both can be configured through the Microsoft IIS Internet Service Manager (ISM). The ISM can be used for such actions as creating and configuring channels, restricting user access from the server or from a channel or channels, enabling anonymous access, and granting access rights. Additional information on access rights and configuring an Exchange recipient will be discussed in the next two sections.

Access Rights

Users can be given access rights to control their access to a channel, and what they can do on that channel. Some of the access rights are:

- Channel host (called Full_Access in the Registry). Has all privileges on a channel including the ability to eject participants off the channel.

- Channel spectator (called Read_Only in the Registry). Can observe a chat on a channel, but cannot contribute.

- Channel participant (called Set_Value in the Registry). Can observe and contribute to a chat on a channel.

- None. Disallows access to a channel unless anonymous clients are permitted.

If an administrator wanted to prevent a user from using a channel, the administrator would add that user's name to the channel and give them the None permission on that channel. Note that even if a user has been given the None access right to a particular channel, and anonymous access is permitted, that user could access that channel through anonymous access and would have the access rights set on the Everyone object (the default is Channel Spectator, i.e., Read).

Configuring an Exchange Recipient

Microsoft Exchange recipients can be configured to receive chat calls. For example, if an Exchange custom recipient needed to receive Microsoft Net-Meeting calls, an administrator would configure the ILS server and account name for that custom recipient, and would configure the custom recipient with the ILS server name and account name (accomplished through the Advanced property page).

Management

The Internet Service Manager (ISM) can be used to manage and troubleshoot the Chat Service and ILS. ISM could be used in the following two situations.

From time-to-time, an administrator could need to shutdown one of a collection of chat servers without chat users noticing the shutdown. That could be accomplished by performing what is called a "smart-bleed" of a chat server. The steps to smart-bleed a chat server follow:

1. Disable new connections using the Chatcmd.exe command line utility by typing

   chatcmd *server_name* /setmodes=disablenew

2. Open Performance Monitor. (Click Start, Programs, Administrative Tools, and click Performance Monitor.)

3. Click Edit and then click Add to Chart and select Chat Service in the Object box. Then click Current Users in the Counter box to monitor the number of users currently logged onto the chat server.

4. When the number for Current Users reaches zero, it is safe to shut down the server.

Another management situation relates to preserving a chat network configuration. For example, imagine a chat network with five chat servers. It would make sense to preserve the configuration of this network if a disaster required the re-creation of the network. Preserving a configuration can be done by backing up all the servers and saving the .rsp file.

Firewalls

A firewall is a set of mechanisms that separates and protects your internal network from unauthorized external users and networks. Firewalls can restrict inbound and outbound traffic, as well as analyze all traffic between your network and the outside. Different criteria can be used by a firewall to analyze traffic, such as IP addresses and TCP/IP port numbers. The remainder of this section will cover port numbers and example security scenarios that use a firewall.

Port Numbers

A port number is a numeric identifier assigned an application and that is used to route packets to the correct application on a computer. Just as Media Access Control (MAC) addresses are used to deliver frames to the correct physical computer (actually to the network adapter), and IP addresses are used to route packets to the correct logical computer (e.g., 147.4.56.76), port numbers are used to route a packet to the correct application after the packet has arrived at its destination computer. Multiple applications could, and probably are, running on a server. When a packet arrives at that server, it cannot be delivered to just any application. POP3 client requests are not going to be understood by an LDAP server application.

The many protocols have assigned port numbers, referred to as *"well-known"* port numbers. Table 11.9 lists some of the protocols discussed in this book and their well-known port numbers.

T A B L E 11.9 Some well-known port numbers	Protocol	Port Number
	DNS	53
	HTTP	80
	HTTP/S (HTTP with SSL)	443
	IMAP4	143
	IMAP/S (IMAP with SSL)	993
	IRC	194
	LDAP	389
	NetBIOS name service	137
	NNTP	119
	POP3	110
	RPC	135
	SMTP	25

One way a firewall can work is by prohibiting certain port numbers or allowing only designated port numbers to pass through the firewall. This functionality can be used to restrict the applications that can be used to access your network. For example, if a firewall was configured to prohibit port 80,

HTTP clients would not be able to pass through the firewall and communicate with any internal servers. An especially important topic relating to Exchange is firewalls and RPC. That will be discussed under the next heading.

Firewalls and RPC Communication

By default, Exchange MAPI clients always connect to port 135 on an Exchange server. That port is used by the Windows NT RPC End-Point Mapper service. This mapper service dynamically assigns port numbers to the Directory Service and the Information Store for client/server RPC communication. The service then tells clients what dynamically assigned port numbers to use to access the Exchange DS and IS.

A potential problem can arise if your firewall is configured to allow only certain port numbers. The firewall in that scenario would not accommodate dynamically assigned numbers. The solution is to force Exchange to use fixed port numbers for DS and IS communication. That is done through the Windows NT Registry and the following keys:

```
HKEY_LOCAL_MACHINE\SYSTEM\CurrentControlSet\Services\
MSExchangeDS\Parameters\TCP/IP port

HKEY_LOCAL_MACHINE\SYSTEM\CurrentControlSet\Services\
MSExchangeIS\ParametersSystem\TCP/IP port
```

The port numbers you configure in the Registry, along with port 135 for the Mapper service, would then have to be configured as open on the firewall.

Security Scenarios Using a Firewall

Firewalls are useful in a number of ways. Some of those ways are illustrated in the following scenarios.

Scenario 1

You have just configured your Exchange server for IMAP4 client access. IMAP4 clients can be authenticated with either Basic (Clear Text), Windows NT Challenge/Response, or Windows NT Challenge/Response with SSL. The administrator of your firewall tells you that the firewall will allow traffic from SMTP (port 25), IMAP4 (port 143), and HTTP (port 80). What additional traffic must the firewall be configured to allow for your Exchange server IMAP4 configuration to be used? Because the Exchange server is using SSL as one of its authentication methods, IMAPS (993) would also need to be opened on the firewall.

Scenario 2

A new Exchange server has been installed and configured for LDAP, HTTP, and POP3. The network project plan calls for allowing the following clients to access this server: LDAP, Web software using Windows NT authentication, POP3, and Microsoft Outlook using secure passwords. You refer to the current firewall configuration and see that it is open to DNS, HTTP, SMTP, and ports higher than 1023. What, if anything, must you do to enable the desired Exchange clients to pass through the firewall? The answer is: open LDAP (port 389), POP3 (port 110), and the RPC End-point Mapper Service (port 135). Without these changes, the firewall would not allow traffic from LDAP, POP3, or Exchange MAPI clients (which Outlook is).

Scenario 3

In each of the next three scenarios (including this one), you will see the same starting situation. But each scenario will require different mandatory and optional results, as well as presenting different possible courses of action.

Current Situation   Your Exchange server is using TCP/IP and is configured with LDAP, HTTP, and POP3. A firewall sits between your network and the Internet. Your Exchange server has its name and IP address entered into a public DNS server on the Internet.

Your network's firewall prohibits traffic on all ports that are not explicitly allowed. The ports that are open are port 25 (SMTP), port 53 (DNS), port 80 (HTTP), and all ports greater than port 1023.

Required Results   Management would like users to be able to connect over the Internet to your Exchange server using Microsoft Outlook and LDAP applications. Policy dictates that passwords be transmitted in a secure manner.

Optional Results   While not required, management would like Web clients that do not support Windows NT Challenge/Response authentication to be able to connect to your Exchange server. Another preference is for POP3 clients to connect to the Exchange server and download their messages.

Proposed Course of Action One proposed course of action is to do the following:

- Assign port numbers to the Exchange Directory Service and Information Store. Then allow those ports through the firewall.

- Configure LDAP on the Exchange server to allow anonymous access.

- Configure the Exchange protocols to use SSL as an authentication method.

- Allow SSL traffic through the firewall.

- Allow LDAP traffic (port 389) through the firewall.

- Allow RPC traffic (port 135) through the firewall.

- Allow POP3 traffic (port 110) through the firewall.

See Figure 11.12 for a depiction of this scenario.

FIGURE 11.12

Scenario 3 illustrated

Microsoft Exchange Server

Current Situation

Configured:
- LDAP
- HTTP
- POP3

Opened Ports:
- SMTP (25)
- DNS (53)
- HTTP (80)
- Greater than 1023

Firewall

Proposed Actions
- Assign port numbers to DS and IS
- Enable LDAP anonymous access
- Enable SSL authentication
- Open DS and IS port numbers
- Open LDAP
- Open POP3
- Open SSL
- Open RPC

Internet

Microsoft Outlook   LDAP Client   POP3 Client

Required
- Microsoft Outlook and LDAP clients to access server
- Secure password transmission

Optional
- Web clients without NT challenge/ Response to access server
- POP3 clients to access server

Results of the Proposed Actions   This course of action would meet both required results, and both optional results. The key actions were forcing Exchange to use fixed port numbers for the DS and IS, configuring of SSL on the Exchange server, and enabling the firewall to allow LDAP, POP3, SSL ports, RPC, and the fixed port numbers for the DS and IS.

Scenario 4

As mentioned earlier, the following current situation, required results, and optional results are the same as above. The difference in this scenario is the proposed actions and, possibly, the results of those actions.

Current Situation   Your Exchange server is using TCP/IP and is configured with LDAP, HTTP, and POP3. A firewall sits between your network and the Internet. Your Exchange server has its name and IP address entered into a public DNS server on the Internet.

Your network's firewall prohibits traffic on all ports that are not explicitly allowed. The ports that are open are port 25 (SMTP), port 53 (DNS), port 80 (HTTP), and all ports greater than port 1023.

Required Results   Management would like users to be able to connect over the Internet to your Exchange server using Microsoft Outlook and LDAP applications. Policy dictates that passwords be transmitted in a secure manner.

Optional Results   While not required, management would like Web clients that do not support Windows NT Challenge/Response authentication to be able to connect to your Exchange server. Another preference is for POP3 clients to connect to the Exchange server and download their messages.

Proposed Course of Action   One proposed course of action is to do the following:

- Assign port numbers to the Exchange Directory Service and Information Store. Then allow those ports through the firewall.

- Configure LDAP on the Exchange server to allow anonymous access.

- Allow LDAP traffic (port 389) through the firewall.

Results of the Proposed Actions This course of action would not meet the required results because port 135, used by the Mapper service, is not open on the firewall, and there is no capability to use secure passwords. Only one of the optional results is met, namely Web access to your server (that ability was already inherent in the current situation). The POP3 optional result is not met because POP3 is not allowed through the firewall.

Scenario 5

The final scenario presents the same situation as the previous scenario, but proposes a different course of action.

Current Situation Your Exchange server is using TCP/IP and is configured with LDAP, HTTP, and POP3. A firewall sits between your network and the Internet. Your Exchange server has its name and IP address entered into a public DNS server on the Internet.

Your network's firewall prohibits traffic on all ports that are not explicitly allowed. The ports that are open are port 25 (SMTP), port 53 (DNS), port 80 (HTTP), and all ports greater than port 1023.

Required Results Management would like users to be able to connect over the Internet to your Exchange server using Microsoft Outlook and LDAP applications. Policy dictates that passwords be transmitted in a secure manner.

Optional Results While not required, management would like Web clients that do not support Windows NT Challenge/Response authentication to be able to connect to your Exchange server. Another preference is for POP3 clients to connect to the Exchange server and download their messages.

Proposed Course of Action One course of action would be to do the following:

- Assign port numbers to the Exchange Directory Service and Information Store. Then allow those ports through the firewall.

- Configure LDAP on the Exchange server to allow anonymous access.

- Allow LDAP traffic (port 389) through the firewall.

- Allow RPC traffic (port 135) through the firewall.

Results of the Proposed Actions   This course of action would meet one of the required results, namely, allowing Microsoft Outlook and LDAP clients to access the Exchange server. The second required result, secure passwords, is not met because there is no use of an authentication method using SSL. Only one of the optional results is met, namely, Web access to the server. The other optional result, POP3 client access, is not met because the firewall does not allow POP3.

Summary

Exchange Server support for the IMAP4, POP3, HTTP, LDAP, NNTP, and IRC Internet protocols expands the number of client applications that can access Exchange.

IMAP4 and POP3 enable an e-mail program to retrieve messages from a remote server mailbox. Internet users who have Exchange mailboxes can use these protocols to retrieve mail.

HTTP is the primary protocol used for client-server interactions on the World Wide Web. Exchange Server supports HTTP using the Microsoft Active Platform architecture, and thereby allows Web users to access Exchange resources such as mailboxes, public folders, and calendars using a standard Web browser.

LDAP is used to give client applications access to directory information. LDAP support is integrated in the Exchange DS, allowing Internet client programs using LDAP to access the Exchange DS.

Exchange Server supports NNTP, and can therefore operate as part of the USENET. Exchange can both publish public folders to the USENET, and receive newsfeeds from the USENET. Newsgroups received from newsfeeds are published in public folders.

The Internet Relay Chat (IRC) protocol can be used in an Exchange environment to provide online, real-time chat sessions between users.

Review Questions

1. An IMAP4 client connects to your Exchange server and receives an error message stating that the message size is unknown. Which of the following should you do to fix this problem?

   A. Enable MCIS.

   B. Increase the Idle-Timeout.

   C. Use Plain-Text authentication.

   D. Clear the "Enable fast message retrieval" check box.

2. What are the requirements to allow an Exchange server to permit Web client access? (Choose four.)

   A. LDAP

   B. HTTP at the site

   C. HTTP at the server

   D. HTTP at the organization

   E. HTTP at the mailbox

   F. Active Server

3. How would you enable Web clients to access an Exchange server using the Windows NT Challenge/Response authentication method?

   A. Internet Service Manager

   B. HTTP properties

   C. INS properties

   D. POP3 properties

4. Your network includes an Active Server with Microsoft Exchange Outlook Web Access. The Webdata folder is a virtual directory on the IIS server with an alias of /Exchange. Your Exchange server has HTTP enabled. A Web client reports that when they attempt to connect to the Exchange server they receive an error stating "server is down or HTTP access is disabled." You check the OWA service and it is running. What is the problem?

   A. HTTP is disabled at the organization

   B. HTTP is disabled at the mailbox

   C. The MTA is stopped

   D. HTTP should be disabled on the Exchange server, and only enabled on the Active Server

5. Your organization contains two interconnected networks and corresponding Exchange sites named Accounting and Research. Both networks use IPX and TCP/IP. The X.400 Connector is used to connect the two sites. No directory replication is configured between the sites. Your Exchange servers have LDAP enabled. The users in the Accounting site report that they cannot access the LDAP directory. You find out that all the users in the Accounting network use only IPX. What can be done to allow the Accounting users to access the LDAP directory?

   A. Configure directory replication

   B. Configure the Site Connector

   C. Install TCP/IP on all the Exchange servers in the Accounting site

   D. Install TCP/IP on all the client computers in the Accounting site

6. How can you restrict anonymous LDAP access to directory properties of recipients, but still allow Web clients with authenticated names to access those properties?

   A. Disable HTTP at the site

   B. Disable anonymous access through the LDAP object

   C. Define the Guest account as the anonymous account

   D. Temporarily disable LDAP

7. You have enabled LDAP and allowed anonymous access. But you realize later that there are certain directory object attributes that you do not want to be viewed through anonymous access. What can be done to hide those attributes?

    A. Set LDAP to allow only initial substring searches

    B. Remove those attributes from each object

    C. Configure the trust levels of the containers

    D. Clear the fields of those attributes in the DS Site Configuration object

8. Two organizations, Organization A and Organization B, need a long-term coexistence strategy. How could you allow LDAP clients to connect to Organization A and see the directories of both Organization A and Organization B?

    A. Directory replication

    B. Anonymous access

    C. Select Organization B as the default LDAP referral for Organization A

    D. Select Organization A as the default LDAP referral for Organization B

9. A Microsoft Exchange user reports that several recently created newsgroups are not listed in your company's newsgroup hierarchy of public folders. What must you do so that those newsgroups will be listed?

    A. Accept the queued control messages

    B. Download the newscr file from your ISP

    C. Configure the newsfeed as a pull feed

    D. Configure the newsfeed type as Outbound

10. Your company receives newsfeeds from your Internet Service Provider (ISP). You notice a folder within the newsgroup hierarchy that you do not want to receive. What must you do to permanently remove this folder from the hierarchy?

    A. Rename the folder

    B. Exclude the folder from the newsfeed

    C. Clear the folder's Folder Visible attribute

    D. Delete the folder through Microsoft Outlook

11. Management has decided to allow company access to various newsgroups. Your Internet Service Provider can provide full newsgroup access, but they do not configure newsfeeds on a customer-by-customer basis. How would you configure the transfer of the newsfeeds?

    A. No transfer type is necessary

    B. Configure it for both push and pull

    C. Configure it for a push transfer only

    D. Configure it for a pull transfer only

12. Your company provides newsfeeds to a subsidiary that retrieves news updates from your server. What would you have to do to enable your server to process those requests?

    A. Configure a pull transfer

    B. Configure a push transfer

    C. Include the relevant newsgroups in the Outbound property page

    D. Enable newsreader support

13. You have assigned the chat account the access right of None. You have also permitted anonymous accounts to access your chat network. What type of access does the chat account have in this scenario?

   A. Channel host

   B. Channel spectator

   C. Channel participant

   D. None

14. How would you prevent a certain user from accessing a particular channel on your chat network?

   A. Assign the user the None access right for that channel.

   B. Disable anonymous access.

   C. Delete that user on the ILS.

   D. Delete the chat service custom attribute for that user.

15. How would you configure a custom recipient to receive Microsoft Net-Meeting calls?

   A. Configure a new e-mail address type with the host name of the ILS server.

   B. Configure the LDAP properties with the IP address of the chat server.

   C. Configure a custom attribute with the IP address of the directory server.

   D. Configure the ILS server with an account name for the custom recipient and configure the custom recipient with the ILS server name and account name.

16. How would you shut down one of five chat servers on your network without being noticed by users?

A. You cannot do it.

B. Smart-bleed the chat server

C. Execute StealthDown

D. Execute GracefulShutdown

17. Your network contains five chat servers. You would like to preserve the configuration of the chat network in the case of a disaster. What two things would you have to do? (Choose two.)

A. Back up all servers.

B. Export the Registry.

C. Save the .rsp file.

D. Use the ListConfig utility.

18. You have just configured your Exchange server for IMAP4 client access. IMAP4 clients can be authenticated with either Basic (Clear Text), Windows NT Challenge/Response, or Windows NT Challenge/Response with SSL. You are informed by the administrator of your firewall that the firewall will allow traffic from SMTP (port 25), IMAP4 (port 143), and HTTP (port 80). What additional traffic must the firewall be configured to allow for your Exchange server IMAP4 configuration to be used?

A. IMAPS (993)

B. HTTPS (443)

C. NetBIOS (137)

D. RPC Endmapper (135)

19. A new Exchange server has been installed and configured for LDAP, HTTP, and POP3. The network project plan calls for allowing the following clients to access this server: LDAP, Web software using Windows NT authentication, POP3, and Microsoft Outlook using secure passwords. You refer to the current firewall configuration and see that it is open to DNS, HTTP, SMTP, and ports higher than 1023. What, if anything, must you do to enable the desired Exchange clients to pass through the firewall?

   A. Open LDAP (389)

   B. Open POP3 (110)

   C. Open SSL

   D. Open port 135 for the RPC Endmapper service

   E. All of the above

20. Your Exchange server is using TCP/IP and is configured with LDAP, HTTP, and POP3. A firewall sits between your network and the Internet. Your Exchange server has its name and IP address entered into a public DNS server on the Internet.

Your network's firewall prohibits traffic on all ports that are not explicitly allowed. The ports that are open are port 25 (SMTP), port 53 (DNS), port 80 (HTTP), and all ports greater than port 1023.

Management would like users to be able to connect over the Internet to your Exchange server using Microsoft Outlook and LDAP applications. Policy dictates that passwords be transmitted in a secure manner.

Optional Results

While not required, management would like Web clients that do not support Windows NT Challenge/Response authentication to be able to connect to your Exchange server. Another wish is that POP3 clients could connect to the Exchange server and download their messages.

Proposed Course of Action

1. Assign port numbers to the Exchange Directory Service and Information Store. Then allow those ports through the firewall.

2. Configure LDAP on the Exchange server to allow anonymous access.

3. Configure the Exchange protocols to use SSL as an authentication method.

4. Allow SSL traffic through the firewall.

5. Allow LDAP traffic (port 389) through the firewall.

6. Allow RPC traffic (port 135) through the firewall.

7. Allow POP3 traffic (port 110) through the firewall.

What results does the proposed solution produce?

A. The proposed solution produces the required results and the optional results.

B. The proposed solution produces the required results and produces only one of the optional results.

C. The proposed solution produces the required results but does not produce either of the optional results.

D. The proposed solution does not produce the required results.

21. Your Exchange server is using TCP/IP and is configured with LDAP, HTTP, and POP3. A firewall sits between your network and the Internet. Your Exchange server has its name and IP address entered into a public DNS server on the Internet.

Your network's firewall prohibits traffic on all ports that are not explicitly allowed. The ports that are open are port 25 (SMTP), port 53 (DNS), port 80 (HTTP), and all ports greater than port 1023.

Management would like users to be able to connect over the Internet to your Exchange server using Microsoft Outlook and LDAP applications. Policy dictates that passwords be transmitted in a secure manner.

Optional Results

While not required, management would like Web clients that do not support Windows NT Challenge/Response authentication to be able to connect to your Exchange server. Another preference is for POP3 clients to connect to the Exchange server and download their messages.

Proposed Course of Action

1. Assign port numbers to the Exchange Directory Service and Information Store. Then allow those ports through the firewall.

2. Configure LDAP on the Exchange server to allow anonymous access.

3. Allow LDAP traffic (port 389) through the firewall.

4. Allow RPC traffic (port 135) through the firewall.

What results does the proposed solution produce?

A. The proposed solution produces the required results and the optional results.

B. The proposed solution produces the required results and produces only one of the optional results.

C. The proposed solution produces the required results but does not produce either of the optional results.

D. The proposed solution does not produce the required results.

22. Your Exchange server is configured for anonymous LDAP clients, but those clients that are outside your firewall report that they cannot access the directory. What is the problem?

A. The DS needs to be stopped and restarted.

B. Windows NT Challenge/Response needs to be enabled.

C. The LDAP port is not open on the firewall.

D. Clear Text authentication is needed.

23. If you wanted to prevent anonymous users using LDAP from seeing a particular Exchange attribute, like telephone numbers, where in the Exchange hierarchy would you have to go to prevent this?

    A. Information Store Site Configuration

    B. Encryption object

    C. Directory Replication object

    D. DS Site Configuration

24. If you wanted to reject certain IP addresses of Web clients from accessing your Exchange server, what program would you use?

    A. Microsoft Exchange Administrator

    B. Network applet in Control Panel

    C. Internet Service Manager

    D. Link Monitor

25. Which of the following is a reason why POP3 clients could not see e-mail messages in subfolders of their Inbox?

    A. POP3 can only access messages in the Inbox, not subfolders of the Inbox.

    B. LDAP is not enabled at the mailbox object.

    C. NNTP is not enabled at the mailbox object.

    D. The IIS computer is down.

26. Which of the following would have to be configured for an anonymous Web client to be able to read a public folder?

   A. The Web client would have to log on using a Windows NT account.

   B. The public folder would have to be listed in the Folders Shortcuts.

   C. The folder owner would have to grant the Read permission to the anonymous user type.

   D. Both B and C

27. For POP3 clients to be able to send Internet mail from their mailbox, what other component must be operational on the Exchange server?

   A. LDAP

   B. NNTP

   C. Active Server Components

   D. Internet Mail Service (IMS)

CHAPTER

12

Managing an Exchange Environment

Even after an Exchange Server environment is operational, it still requires "care and feeding." Databases must be maintained and backed up. Storage limits might need to be set. Message transfer parameters might need to be modified. These are just some of the management tasks in an Exchange environment. One nice thing is that most of these tasks are automatically performed while a server is online. However, administrators still have the ability to control some of the settings of those automatic tasks and, if the situation warrants it, to perform various manual and offline management tasks.

This chapter covers these and other management tasks and the programs and procedures used to accomplish them. In this chapter, you will learn about:

- Windows NT Server tools

- Exchange Administrator program

- Managing public folders

- Managing user storage

- Managing Exchange databases

- Managing message delivery

- Troubleshooting

Windows NT Server Tools

Exchange Server is tightly integrated into Windows NT Server and leverages the management tools built into the operating system. In this section, we will discuss these tools:

- Control Panel/Services

- Event Viewer

- Performance Monitor
- Registry Editor
- Server Manager
- Task Manager

Control Panel/Services

Control Panel/Services can be used to check the status of the Exchange Server services. It can be used to start, stop, and pause a service. It can also be used to configure the startup parameters of a service.

Event Viewer

All Exchange services write event information to the NT Event Log. Administrators should regularly (daily is recommended) view the event log for management and troubleshooting purposes using the Event Viewer application. Exchange services can be configured to log different amounts and types of events for diagnostic logging (this will be discussed further in the "Server Management" section). The vast majority of Exchange information is written to the Application Event Log. The administrator may want to increase the maximum size of this log (the default is 512KB) if logging levels are turned up for troubleshooting or just to maintain the events that have occurred over a longer period. Event Viewer can also be used to view the event logs of a remote server.

Microsoft ✓ *Exam* *Objective*   **Diagnose and resolve server resource problems.**

Performance Monitor

The Exchange Server SETUP program adds Exchange-related counters to Performance Monitor, making it possible to view the performance of various Exchange activities. Setup also adds a number of preconfigured Performance Monitor counter configurations to the Microsoft Exchange program group. For example, the configuration "Microsoft Exchange Server Load" tracks items such as messages submitted and delivered, and the number of times the Directory is read.

The following is a case study of using Performance Monitor to manage Exchange Server. An administrator is receiving reports from users that the Exchange server response time is slow. A quick examination shows that the server's disk is almost constantly active. The administrator decides to take a deeper look and, using Performance Monitor, collects the following information about that particular Exchange server:

%Processor time=70

%Disk free space=60

Pages/sec=40

Avg. Disk sec/Transfer= 0.02

The administrator then compares these statistics to the "rule of thumb" thresholds that their organization has determined. The following are those thresholds, which when exceeded, have been associated with performance problems:

%Processor time >80%

%Disk free space <10%

Pages/sec >5

Avg. Disk sec/Transfer >.3

Comparing the current statistics with the thresholds, the administrator sees that the Pages/sec number is over the threshold. This suggests that there is not enough memory to cache information, therefore leading the system to page data to the disk. The administrator decides to add memory to this server and continue to monitor the situation.

Microsoft Performance Monitor can also be used to warn you of a situation and therefore help you prevent a particular problem. For example, if all available disk space is used, your IS will stop. You could configure Performance Monitor to send you an e-mail message when the available disk space reaches a specified low level. You could then take steps to prevent all disk space from being used and therefore prevent the IS from being stopped.

Registry Editor

Like all Windows 95 and NT applications, Exchange Server stores some configuration information in the registry. This information can be read and modified using the Registry Editor application (regedit.exe). All the registry settings for Exchange Server are stored under the keys HKEY_LOCAL_MACHINE\ SOFTWARE and HKEY_LOCAL_MACHINE\SYSTEM. You normally will not need to edit the registry directly. Most configurations are made through the Exchange Administrator program and are automatically written to the registry.

Server Manager

Server Manager can be used to view and manage the services of a server, and to send messages to connected users. These functions can be performed for any server, local or remote.

Task Manager

Task Manager displays the programs and processes running on a computer. It also displays various performance information, such as CPU and memory usage. An Exchange administrator can use this tool to view the overall health of a server. Task Manager is accessed by right-clicking on the Task bar and choosing the Task Manager menu option.

Exchange Administrator Program

The Exchange Administrator program (ADMIN.EXE) is the primary tool for managing an Exchange environment. We have already seen, in Chapter 5, how it is used to create and manage recipients. This section discusses how it can be used to manage other Exchange activities relating to site and server management. In this section, you will learn about:

- Installation and implementation

- General features

- Address book views

- Permissions in Exchange Administrator

- Site management

- Server management

- Running Exchange Administrator in raw mode

Installation and Implementation

Exchange Administrator runs on Windows NT and can be installed on the Exchange Server computer or an administrator's computer (assuming it is running Windows NT). To install it, run the Exchange Server SETUP program, select the Custom installation option, and then select Microsoft Exchange Administrator. Exchange Administrator is also installed when the Typical installation option is selected. Connections are made to other servers through the File menu and "Connect to server" option. The dialog box that appears allows you to browse the network and choose the server to connect to, or you may type the server's computer name (i.e., the NetBIOS name) or IP address.

If an organization's network infrastructure supports RPC connections between sites, Exchange Administrator can perform *single-seat administration*. This means an administrator can connect and manage every Exchange server in an organization from one workstation.

General Features

Before we discuss the specific uses and details of Exchange Administrator, we need to examine some of the general features of the program—features relating to the interface, who can use the program, and what functions they can perform.

Administration Window

The Administration window displays a graphical representation of the Exchange hierarchy. The display is divided into two parts:

- **Container pane**   The left pane displays all the container objects in the Exchange hierarchy.

- **Contents pane**   The right pane displays all the objects in the container selected in the container pane. The contents pane can display both container and leaf objects. Both of these are discussed next.

Types of Objects

As you learned in Chapter 2, Exchange entities like sites, servers, and mailboxes are represented as objects. There are two types of objects:

- **Container objects**   A container object contains or groups other objects. The recipients object, which contains mailboxes, DLs, custom recipients, and public folders is an example of a container object.

- **Leaf objects** A leaf object does not contain any other objects. A mailbox is a leaf object.

Figure 12.1 shows the two panes and two types of objects displayed in Exchange Administrator.

Customizing Exchange Administrator

Exchange Administrator can be customized to meet the needs of a particular administrator or organization. Some of the ways in which it can be customized are listed in Table 12.1. The first two options in Table 12.1 are settings that are saved for the particular administrator who sets them. The remaining options are in effect for all administrators who run Exchange Administrator from the same workstation.

T A B L E 12.1	**Custom Option**	**Purpose**
Exchange Administrator custom options	Views	The View menu contains a Sort by option that can be used to sort recipients either by Display Name (the default) or by Last Modified Date.
	Columns	The View menu also contains a Columns option that can be used to choose which columns to display in the contents pane and the order in which to display them.
	Auto naming	An administrator can determine how the display name and alias name attributes of a new recipient will be defaulted. Preset or custom naming options can be selected for display name and alias name independently. The default setting for display names is *FirstName LastName*. The default setting for alias names is *FirstNameLastInitial* (no space between them). These settings are accessed by selecting Options from the Tools menu and configuring the Auto Naming property page.
	Permission settings	An administrator can configure whether the Permissions property page is displayed for all objects and whether the specific rights that make up security roles are displayed. These settings are accessed by selecting Options from the Tools menu and configuring the Permissions property page.
	Windows NT domain settings	An administrator can set which Windows NT domain will be used when Windows NT account information is displayed. The administrator can also configure whether or not the primary Windows NT account associated with a mailbox is deleted when the mailbox is deleted. This domain is also used to search for the default primary Windows NT account when a mailbox is created. These settings are accessed by selecting Options from the Tools menu and configuring the Permissions property page.

Microsoft
✓ *Exam*
Objective

Configure Exchange Server for message recipients.

- Configure mailboxes
- Configure custom recipients
- Configure public folders
- Configure distribution lists
- Configure site addressing
- Configure container-level search controls
- Configure Address Book views

Address Book Views

One of the new features of Exchange Server 5.0 is "Address Book View" containers. This feature permits the organizing of addresses from the GAL into groups. Rather then the flat structure of the normal GAL (i.e., a long list containing everybody), this new feature can be used to create address containers based upon such attributes as title, department, city, and state. For example, if your Exchange organization contained 5000 recipients in 20 different cities, you could create an address book view that groups recipients based upon their city. These views can also be made available to Exchange clients. The only way to accomplish this type of organization had been to create separate Recipient containers and create recipients in the correct container.

To create an address book view, click the Address Book View container found in the Organization container. From the File menu in Exchange Administrator, click New Other and then the Address Book View option. A dialog box will appear enabling you to create address book views.

Permissions in Exchange Administrator

Administrative access to Exchange objects can be configured. An administrator can assign permissions to specific users or groups at different levels of the Exchange hierarchy in order to determine who has what type of access to what information. To understand how permissions are assigned, you must understand context levels and roles.

Context Levels The three main tiers of the Exchange hierarchy are the organization, sites, and servers. But for the purpose of assigning administrative permissions, the hierarchy is divided into three levels:

- Organization

- Sites

- Configuration

The organization object is at the top of the hierarchy and contains public folders, the Global Address List, and the site objects. The next level, the site object, contains recipient containers and the configuration object. The last level, the configuration object, contains other containers and objects that facilitate configurations specific to the site. Objects in this level include addressing, MTA site configuration, protocols (e.g., LDAP, NNTP, and POP3), and several others.

These three levels are called *context levels*, or simply *contexts*. Administrative permissions assigned to an object are inherited by all of its child objects within its context. However, permissions are not inherited across context boundaries. Therefore, contexts are self-contained areas that require independently assigned permissions.

Permissions can also be granted at a particular obect within a context. For example, you could assign the Administrator permission to a particular administrator at the Recipients container, and only at that container. That administrator could manage recipients in that container, but could not make changes to the site level or to server level objects, with the exception of recipients on a server. For the above scenario to work, the administrator would also have to be assigned the View Only Admin. role at the site object in order to use Microsoft Exchange Administrator and log on to an Exchange server in the site.

Roles Permissions are granted to users or groups by giving them a group of rights, called a *role*. There are two types of roles: *predefined roles* that consist of a fixed set of rights, and *custom roles* that consist of any combination of individual rights that the administrator desires.

The rights that are used in these roles are listed in Table 12.2.

TABLE 12.2 Exchange rights	Right	Function
	Add Child	Creates child objects, like a mailbox within a recipients container.
	Modify User Attributes	Modifies user-level attributes, like the membership of a DL.
	Modify Admin. Attributes	Modifies administrator-level attributes, like the display name of a mailbox.
	Delete	Deletes objects.
	Logon Rights	Allows access to the Directory. A user must have this right in order to use Exchange Administrator.
	Modify Permission	Modifies permissions on an object.
	Replication	Replicates directory information with other servers. The site service account uses this right to carry out replication with other servers.
	Mailbox Owner	Logs on, reads, creates, and deletes messages in a mailbox. This right is also given to the site service account at the site and configuration objects so service processes can send messages to each other.
	Send As	Sends messages with the recipient object's display name as the return address. This right is also given to the site service account at the site and configuration objects so service processes can send messages to each other.

Not all roles and rights are available on all types of objects.

The predefined roles and their associated rights are listed in Table 12.3.

T A B L E 12.3

Exchange roles and associated rights

	Roles					
Rights	**Admin.**	**Permissions Admin.**	**Service Account Admin.**	**View Only Admin.**	**User**	**Send As**
Add Child	✓	✓	✓			
Modify User Attributes	✓	✓	✓		✓	
Modify Admin. Attributes	✓	✓	✓			
Delete	✓	✓	✓			
Logon Rights	✓	✓	✓	✓		
Modify Permissions		✓	✓			
Replication			✓			
Mailbox Owner			✓		✓	
Send As			✓		✓	✓

If you need to assign rights to multiple administrators who reside in more than one domain, you could use Windows NT global groups. A global group could be created with the multiple administrators as members. That global group could then be assigned a role on the Permissions page of an Exchange object. A global group would be used in this scenario because local groups can only be used in the domain where they are created.

Site Management

Site-wide parameters are inherited by all servers in a site (some of these parameters can be overridden at the server level). To manage a site, objects are configured under the Configuration and Recipients containers. Chapter 5 covered recipient objects, so this discussion focuses on the Configuration container and its objects.

The Configuration container has at least two property pages, the General page and the Service Account Password page (there are three pages if the Permissions page is present). These property pages are accessed by highlighting the Configuration container, then using the File menu, Properties option. The Service Account Password page is used to change the password used by the site service account. For example, suppose someone used User Manager for Domains to change the password of the site service account. The next time the Exchange server is stopped and restarted, none of the Exchange services will start because they will be using the old password. The most efficient way to solve this problem is to use the Service Account Password page to configure the Exchange services with the new password of the site service account. To perform that procedure, you must be able to run the Microsoft Exchange Administrator program, and to run that program the System Attendant and Directory Service must be running. That would be accomplished by manually starting those two services through Control Panel/Services and using the new password in the Startup parameters. Then the Exchange Administrator program can be run and the Service Account Password page accessed in order to change the password for the remaining Exchange services. The rest of the Site Management section will cover the objects under the Configuration container (see Figure 12.2). Table 12.4 summarizes these objects. Additional details on some of these objects are provided in the discussion of management tasks later in this chapter.

F I G U R E 12.2

Configuration container objects

TABLE 12.4	Object	Contents
Configuration objects summary	Add-Ins	Contains add-ins that offer additional administrative user interfaces.
	Addressing	Holds containers containing programs for generating e-mail addresses and information used to customize the fields and controls viewed in client programs. More information on this container follows this table.
	Connections	Holds the connector objects used to connect a site to other sites and non-Exchange mail systems. (See Chapter 13.)
	Directory Replication	Contains configuration information used for directory replication to other sites. (See Chapter 13.)
	Monitors	Contains configuration information used by Link Monitors and Server Monitors. These features are covered later in this chapter.
	Protocols	Contains Protocol objects such as HTTP, IMAP4, LDAP, NNTP, and POP3.
	Servers	Contains all the server objects for the site.
	DS Site Configuration	Contains properties used by the Directory Service in managing the Directory.
	Information Store Site Configuration	Contains properties for the private and public information stores in the site, such as the list of users who can create top-level public folders.
	MTA Site Configuration	Contains properties used by the MTA for message delivery. This is covered in more detail later in this section.
	Site Addressing	Contains properties related to site-wide addressing, such as the format of a site's Internet address, and properties used for message routing, such as route costs. Administrators can also use this object to enable or disable the foreign addresses that are created for each Exchange recipient. For example, if an organization did not want Microsoft Mail addresses automatically created for their Exchange recipients, the administrator would access this object and disable the "MS" address space entry.

TABLE 12.4 (cont.) Configuration objects summary	Object	Contents
	CA	Contains general information and permissions to the Certification Authority. This object is part of advanced security (see Chapter 10).
	Encryption	Contains general information, permissions, encryption algorithm preferences, and key manager administrator permissions properties. This object is part of advanced security (see Chapter 10).

The DS Site Configuration object warrants a brief summary of its properties.

DS Site Configuration Object

The DS Site Configuration object contains configuration information for operating the Directory Service databases in a site. The five property pages for this object are described in Table 12.5 (the standard Permissions page is also shown if Exchange Administrator is configured to display it on all objects).

TABLE 12.5 DS Site Configuration property pages	Property	Description
	General	Two properties on this page relate to how the DS components in a site handle deleted directory objects, such as a deleted mailbox or public folder. The two properties are: • **Tombstone lifetime** Whenever an object is deleted in a Directory, that fact is noted in a piece of information called a Tombstone. Tombstones are replicated to the other servers in a site to notify them to also delete these objects. The Tombstone Lifetime property sets the life span of a tombstone. • **Garbage collection interval** The number of hours between the removal of expired tombstones (garbage).
	Offline Address Book	The Offline Address Book (OAB) is a list of recipient addresses that can be downloaded to a client computer. This page lets you specify which recipients are in the OAB, generate the OAB, and specify which server will store the OAB.

T A B L E 12.5 (cont.) DS Site Configuration property pages	**Property**	**Description**
	Offline Address Book Schedule	Because recipients may be added, deleted, or modified, the OAB needs to be regenerated periodically. This page lets you schedule when to perform the regeneration.
	Custom Attributes	This page permits the creation of custom attributes that are associated with recipient objects. An administrator can add attributes for Social Security numbers or employee numbers, for example. Up to 10 custom attributes can be created.
	Attributes	This page contains properties relating to what attributes will be replicated to other sites, and what attributes can be accessed by anonymous and authenticated LDAP client access.

Exercise 12.1 walks through the steps in managing site-level objects and properties.

EXERCISE 12.1

Managing Site-Level Objects

1. In Exchange Administrator, expand the site object, and then click the Configuration container object. You will see seven container objects directly under the Configuration object in the left pane (the container pane) and the same seven objects along with six additional leaf objects in the right pane (the contents pane).

2. In the contents pane, double-click on the DS Site Configuration object. This will bring up the property pages of this object.

3. Click on the Custom Attributes page. In the Custom Attribute 1 dialog box, type **Employee Number**. In the Custom Attribute 2 dialog box, type **Job Class Level**. Click OK.

4. View the Custom Attributes page of George Washington's mailbox. You will see the two custom attributes you just created. Click OK or Cancel.

Develop the configuration of an Exchange Server computer.

Server Management

Exchange servers can be individually configured with server specific settings. To do this, configure the properties of a particular server container and configure the objects within that server container.

The server configuration objects are described in Table 12.6. The first seven objects in Table 12.6 will appear in every server. The last two will appear only if certain components are installed on that server (those components are noted in Table 12.6). Figure 12.3 shows the objects within the EDUCATION server object.

FIGURE 12.3

Server configuration objects

TABLE 12.6	Object	Description
Server configuration objects	Private Information Store	Use to configure deleted item recovery, set storage limits for mailboxes, view resources such as Windows NT accounts accessing mailboxes, and configure diagnostic logging for the Information Store such as storage limit information. This object is discussed in more detail in the Managing User Storage section later in this chapter.
	Protocols	Contains protocol objects, such as IMAP4, LDAP, NNTP, and POP3.
	Public Information Store	Use to configure deleted item recovery, storage limits for public folders, age limits for items in public folders, replica locations, the replication schedule, and diagnostic logging. This object is discussed in more detail in the Managing User Storage section later in this chapter.
	Server Recipients	Contains the recipients homed on this particular server.
	Directory Service	Use to manually initiate DS functions, such as directory replication with other servers in a site. Diagnostic logging for the DS can be configured using this object.
	Message Transfer Agent	Contains MTA message size limits. Can be used to manually recalculate the routing table. Use to view and change priorities of queued messages. Diagnostic logging for the MTA can be configured using this object.
	System Attendant	Use to configure automatic deletion of message tracking log files after a specified number of days.
	Directory Synchronization	This object will only be present if the Microsoft Mail Connector is installed. Contains the properties of the Directory Synchronization service. Chapter 15 discusses this object in more detail.
	MTA Transport Stack	This only appears if an MTA Transport Stack was installed. This is transport protocol information used by intersite connectors. Stacks are installed by choosing File, New Other, MTA Transport Stack. For example, the TP/4 protocol stack could be installed and then used by the X.400 Connector for intersite communication. More on this is found in Chapter 13.

A server object itself has property pages that are accessed by selecting the server object and choosing Properties from the File menu (see Figure 12.4). Table 12.7 describes these property pages.

FIGURE 12.4

The Diagnostic Logging property page

TABLE 12.7	**Property Page**	**Description**
Property pages on the server object	Services	Displays installed services on this server, and the services to be monitored by server monitors.
	Database Paths	Displays and allows modification to the directory locations for the Exchange database files, such as the DS, the Private Information Store, the Public Information Store, and the various transaction log files. Transaction log files will be discussed later in this chapter.
	IS Maintenance	Contains the schedule for online maintenance of the IS, which includes the defragmenting of the Public and Private Information Stores. (See the "Managing Exchange Databases" section.)

T A B L E 12.7 (cont.) Property pages on the server object	**Property Page**	**Description**
	Advanced	Contains settings related to consistency between the DS and IS, and the Exchange transaction logs. (See the "Managing Exchange Databases" section.)
	Diagnostic Logging	Used to configure the collection of log information for Exchange components. The log information is written to the Windows NT Event Log. For example, information regarding the modification of the MTA service can be logged. If any administrator reconfigures the MTA service, an event will be logged. See Figure 12.4 to view the Diagnostics Logging property page.

Exercise 12.2 reviews managing a server object with Exchange Administrator.

EXERCISE 12.2

Managing a Server Object

1. In Exchange Administrator, double-click on the Servers container object. An object with your server name will appear under this container.

2. Double-click on your server object. Four container objects will appear in the left pane. Those four objects and three or more additional leaf objects will appear in the contents pane.

3. With your server object selected in the container pane, choose File ➢ Properties. This brings up the eight property pages for this server.

4. Click on the Database Paths page. You will see the directory paths where the database and transaction log files are stored.

5. When you are done looking, click OK or Cancel.

Running Exchange Administrator in Raw Mode

The Microsoft Exchange Administrator program can be started in such a way to allow access to every property of an object. When you start this program in this way you are in "raw mode." One way to start Exchange Administrator in raw mode is to access a DOS command prompt, change to the drive where you installed Exchange Server, move to the directory \exchsrvr\bin, and type admin /raw.

One of the uses of raw mode is to delete an object that still appears in the Exchange hierarchy even after it has been deleted. For example, you had created a dirsync server object to assist in the migration of a Microsoft Mail system to your Exchange environment (migrations will be covered in chapter 16). After the migration is completed, you attempt to delete the dirsync server object. But that object remains visible in the hierarchy. When you attempt to delete it again, you receive a message saying that the object does not exist. To remove the object from appearing in the hierarchy, you could run Exchange Administrator in raw mode and then delete the object.

Microsoft ✓ *Exam* *Objective*

Manage public information stores. Elements include:

- Server locations
- Rehoming of public folders

Managing Public Folders

While public folders can be one of the most important resources in an Exchange environment, they must be properly managed to be effective. This section will examine some of the more important issues of public folder management. These issues will be covered under the following headings:

- Creating dedicated public folder servers
- Public folder replicas

Creating Dedicated Public Folder Servers

A dedicated public folder server is an Exchange server that is used to store public folders and has no mailboxes. Dedicating a server for this purpose can increase client access to public folder data and can make for a more central backup strategy.

Implementing a dedicated public folder server involves the following steps:

1. Move public folders to the designated server. This can be done through the Replicas property page of a public folder object, or through the Instances property page of the target Public Information Store.

2. If there are any mailboxes on the designated public folder server, move them to another server. One way to do this is through the Advanced property page of a mailbox object.

3. Configure the servers that will contain only mailboxes, sometimes called private servers, to use the designated server as the location for future public folder creation. This is done on the General property page of the Private Information Store object.

4. Remove the Private Information Store from the dedicated public folder server, and the Public Information Store from the private servers. This is done through the Exchange Administrator program and by deleting the Private Information Store object and Public Information Store object on their respective servers.

Dedicated public folder servers can be an appropriate part of an Exchange environment when there are large amounts of public folder data, a need to off-load processing and disperse the workload, and for a more central backup strategy.

Along with using dedicated public folder servers, you may also restrict public folders to certain servers. That is done by preventing a public folder from being rehomed (i.e., moved to another Exchange server). The General page of a public folder has a checkbox called "Limit administrative access to home site." If that is checked, only users with administrative permissions in the public folder's home site and who are connected to that site can rehome that public folder and create replicas (replicas are discussed next).

Public Folder Replicas

Public folders can be replicated to other Exchange servers. Each copy of a public folder is called a replica. Each replica contains the same information as the original public folder, but resides on a different Exchange server. Replicas can reside in the same site as the home server of the original public folder, and they can reside on servers in different sites.

Reasons for using public folder replicas include:

- **Load balancing** If a large number of users access a particular public folder, access times could be slow. A solution is to create public folder replicas and disperse user access to the various replicas.

- **Fault tolerance** Having a public folder replicated eliminates a single point of failure.

- **Easier access for remote users** If sites are geographically separated and users are accessing public folders in a remote site, it can make sense to distribute those public folders to the other sites through the use of replicas. This can be especially useful when users in one site are accessing public folders in another site over an unreliable network connection. Creating replicas in each remote site would allow users to access the public folders on their own local networks.

The following is a scenario that could warrant the use of public folder replicas. Suppose your organization has four sites, each site consisting of two Exchange servers and 500 users. The four sites are connected with a 256K wide area network (WAN). The available bandwidth during the workday is less than 64K. While at night the available bandwidth is 128K or more. You have created a public folder that contains 600MB of data that is not time critical. Users only access that folder approximately every fifteen minutes, and the folder data is only updated twice a week. A good strategy would be to create a replica of that public folder on every Exchange bridgehead server in the four sites.

Creating Replicas

An Exchange administrator creates replicas through the Replicas property page of a public folder object. A server, or servers, are chosen to house a copy of that particular public folder. When an Information Store detects that it has been chosen to hold a replica, the IS sends a request for the contents of that public folder to a server containing that folder. The request is called a *backfill request,* and the process is called *backfilling* (for more on backfilling see the section "Synchronizing Replicas").

Configuring Replicas

Two important properties of a replica are its replication schedule and affinity number. Both are discussed below.

Replication Schedule   Configuring the times at which a public folder will replicate its content is the primary configuration task. Two important criteria for choosing a schedule are the available bandwidth and the time-sensitiveness of the data. For example, if a replica is located over a slow WAN and contains data that is only periodically changed, or is not time critical, the replication schedule could be set for once a day and late at night.

Two methods can be used to set a replication schedule. Each public folder object has a Replication Schedule property page that can be used to set a schedule. To set one replication schedule that would be inherited by all public folders on a server, you would use the Replication Schedule property page of the Public Information Store object. If an individual public folder has its own replication schedule, the server-level configuration would be overridden.

Exchange servers replicate public folders by taking new, modified, or deleted content, and sending it to all the other servers on the replica list. These updates are sent in the form of messages.

If a replica detects that it is not synchronized with the other replicas, it will initiate the backfill process. This entails sending a request for the missing data to another server containing an updated replica. Three circumstances can cause the backfill process to be initiated:

- A new replica is created and needs to receive the public folder content.

- A message containing updated data was lost in transit.

- A server was restored from backup.

Backfilling helps ensure the integrity of a replica.

A public folder can also be configured to not allow replication to another server. That is configured on the Replication Schedule property page by setting the replication schedule to "Never."

Affinity Number   When a client selects a public folder to view its contents, the IS must decide where that folder resides. If there are replicas of that folder, the IS uses a series of criteria to choose the folder to connect the client with. These criteria are listed below:

I. If the public folder resides on the client's public folder hierarchy server, that server is connected to.

2. If the above criterion is not applicable and there are multiple replicas in the site, the IS uses an algorithm to generate a random number that is used to choose the replica to connect to. This mechanism distributes connections among a number of replicas and produces load balancing.

3. If the IS cannot connect to the random number server, the remaining replicas in the site are tried. Servers that the IS server already has RPC connections with are tried first.

4. If replicas in the local site cannot be connected, the IS will attempt to connect the client to a replica in another site. To help the IS choose the site to connect to, sites can be assigned a public folder affinity number. This is similar to a cost value. The IS uses affinity numbers to determine the order in which different sites are attempted. The site with a remote replica and with the lowest affinity number is attempted first. If two sites have the same affinity number, the IS views them as one logical site and attempts connection to a random replica. Sites without affinity numbers are not attempted.

After a site is connected, the replicas within that site are tried in a random order.

Affinity numbers are applied at the site-level through the Information Store Site Configuration object, and the Public Folder Affinity property page.

Configuring Location Values

Another topic related to replicas is "location values." A location value is a property of a server that helps determine what replicas are used by recipients homed on that server. Location values create, in a sense, subsites of replicas. For example, suppose an organization is made up of a single Exchange site, encompassing both London and Tokyo. Three servers are in London, and two are in Tokyo. You could configure location values on each server so that users in London always access public folders in London before accessing replicas in Tokyo. Likewise, servers in Tokyo could be configured so that users in Tokyo always access public folders in Tokyo before accessing replicas in London. The location value property is found on the General property page of a server object.

Microsoft
✓ *Exam*
Objective

Develop long-term administration strategies.

• Plan a backup strategy.

• Plan a disaster recovery strategy.

• Plan information store maintenance.

• Plan remote administration.

• Plan information retrieval strategies.

Managing User Storage

Anyone who has ever had a personal computer knows how fast a hard drive fills up. No matter how much storage you have, it is not enough. This is even more true for a server, because of its "one to many" relationship with clients. Exchange administrators can maximize the space available by managing mailbox storage and public folder storage.

Managing Mailbox Storage

User mailboxes are stored in the Private Information Store (PRIV.EDB) database on their home Exchange server. Server-based mail storage has the advantages of central administration and central backup. All Exchange storage functions are managed by the IS service. An administrator can manage and monitor mailbox storage by configuring and viewing the Private Information Store object. Exchange Administrator also contains a utility that can delete messages in mailboxes to recover storage space. These topics, along with single-instance storage, are discussed under the following headings:

- Setting mailbox storage limits

- Monitoring mailbox storage

- Cleaning mailboxes

- Diagnostic logging and mailbox storage

- Single-instance message storage

Setting Mailbox Storage Limits

Storage limits for mailboxes can be configured by setting a general default that applies to all mailboxes, or by setting limits on a per-mailbox basis.

Default Storage Limit   The Private Information Store object contains the storage limit attribute. This attribute configures the storage limit default for all mailboxes on the server. The storage limit attribute has two features. One, called "Issue warning," allows you to set a limit for the amount of data allowed in a mailbox before the system sends the user a warning message. The warnings are sent at the times specified on the Storage Warnings page of the Information Store Site Configuration object. The other feature, called "Prohibit send," allows you to set a limit for the amount of data allowed in a mailbox before a user is prohibited from sending mail. The mailbox can still receive mail, but the mailbox user cannot send mail until items are deleted from the mailbox.

Per-Mailbox Storage Limits   An administrator can also set mailbox storage limits on an individual mailbox. This setting overrides the default setting at the Private Information Store object. This configuration is made on the Advanced property page of a mailbox.

Monitoring Mailbox Storage

An administrator can monitor mailbox storage using the Mailbox Resources object under the Private Information Store object. This object displays various information about a mailbox including the total space it uses, and the total number of items it contains.

Cleaning Mailboxes

"Cleaning" in this context refers to deleting data. Exchange Administrator has a cleaning utility that is invoked by choosing Clean Mailbox from the Tools menu. Criteria is selected to determine which messages will be deleted. An administrator can highlight one or more mailboxes and then use this utility to delete messages in those mailboxes.

Diagnostic Logging and Mailbox Storage

The Private Information Store has a Diagnostic Logging property page where the administrator can activate and configure event logging. One of the categories that can be logged is storage limits. Event logs can be viewed using the Windows NT Event Viewer.

Single-Instance Message Storage

The single-instance storage of the IS contributes greatly to keeping storage levels lower than they would be otherwise. If a 10 MB message is sent to a distribution list of 10 users, all on the same server, the IS only stores a single instance of the message and gives each of the 10 members a pointer to the message. Rather than 100 MB of storage being used, only 10 MB is used. If some of the members of a DL are on another server, a copy of the message is sent to that server and recipients. The single instance storage would also apply to that server.

The following is another example of the use of single-instance message storage. You want to estimate the number of messages that will be placed in the Private Information Store. You ask ten users to track the type of messages they receive in one day. The users report back that they each received ten messages. Five of those messages were sent using a local distribution list (i.e., the distribution list was an object on the same server as the message recipients). Two messages were sent to the ten users by using a distribution list from another company that also uses Microsoft Exchange. Three messages were sent to the ten users by using a distribution list from a company that does not use Microsoft Exchange. Before we tell you the answer, try to determine the number of copies of messages in the Private Information Store for the above scenario. What is your guess? The answer is arrived at through the following math: five messages sent to ten users who are part of a local DL=5 (because of single-instance storage); two messages sent to ten users who are a part of a remote DL=2 (because of single-instance storage); three messages sent to ten users who are a part of a foreign DL=3 (because of single-instance storage). The new messages in the Private Information Store would be 10. Even though messages are sent to Exchange recipients from a foreign system, single-instance storage is still relevant within the Exchange environment.

Item Recovery

Microsoft Exchange Server 5.5 has included a new feature whereby deleted items in a mailbox or public folder can be held for a specified period of time before they are permanently deleted. When an item is initially deleted, for example, from a client's Deleted Items folder, it can be held by the server for future recovery. This is sometimes referred to as a "soft delete." An Exchange server holds these soft deleted items in hidden folders in the IS database (PRIV .EDB has a hidden folder and likewise PUB.EDB). While in that state, Exchange clients can recover their deleted items by using such utilities as the "Recover Deleted Items" option on the Tools menu of Microsoft Outlook.

An Exchange administrator can set the number of days soft deleted items will be retained. This property is called "Deleted item retention time," and the value is specified in days. You may also configure an IS database so it won't permanently delete items until it has been backed up. Both of these properties are found on the General property pages of the Private Information Store and Public Information Store objects. As with many properties, an individual recipient, like a mailbox, can be individually configured for "deleted item retention time," or can use the IS defaults (which is the default configuration).

Because soft deleted items are stored in a hidden folder in the IS databases, they take up space in those databases. But soft deleted items do not count against a mailbox storage limit. For example, suppose you had 300 clients, each with a 100 MB storage limit, and each message averaged 10 MB. Even if deleted item retention time was set to seven days, and there was no single-instance messages, mailbox owners would still have a mailbox storage limit of 100 MB. That also means that the Private Information Store would have to have at least 30 GB of space for the maximum storage limit for all the clients. The storage needed above that number would be determined by the number and size of soft deleted items in the PRIV.EDB.

When an item in a public folder reaches its age limit and expires, it cannot be retrieved through the "Recover Deleted Items" feature. But if an item is deleted before its expiration date, then it can be retrieved up to its retention time. For example, suppose a public folder has an age limit for messages of 90 days. The "Deleted item retention time" is set to seven days. A particular item has been in this public folder for 87 days when a user deletes that item. Five days later, a user wants to recover that item. Can they? The answer is yes. Once the item was deleted there was seven days to recover it, and the age limit property was not relevant because the item had been deleted.

When a MAPI-based application, like Microsoft Outlook, is used to delete an item, the item is moved to a hidden folder. The Microsoft Outlook user could recover that item using the "Recover Deleted Items" option on the Tools menu. But if a non-MAPI application, such as an IMAP4 client, deletes an item, the item is marked as deleted and remains in its original folder. To recover this deleted item, the user must use their IMAP4 application. The above facts must be understood when someone uses both MAPI and non-MAPI applications to access their mailbox. For example, a user might use an IMAP4 client while away from the office, and Microsoft Outlook while in the office. While using their IMAP4 client, the user deletes an item in their Inbox. When they get back to the office, the user realizes they need the item they deleted while away. The user would not be able to use Microsoft Outlook to recover that item, but they could recover it with their IMAP4 application.

Managing Public Folder Storage

Public folders are the repository for shared information in an Exchange organization and they can grow to be quite large. Exchange includes many features to help manage public folder storage. These features are exhibited in the following management procedures:

- Setting public folder storage limits
- Setting age limits for data
- Monitoring public folder storage
- Diagnostic logging and public folder storage

Setting Public Folder Storage Limits

Storage limits can be set on public folders at the server level and on individual public folders. Limits on public folder storage can assist in keeping the Public Information Store database from growing too large.

Default Storage Limit   The Public Information Store object can be configured with a storage limit that applies to all public folders on the server. If the limit is reached, warning messages are sent to public folder contacts. The warnings are sent at the times specified on the Storage Warnings page of the Information Store Site Configuration object.

Per-Folder Storage Limits   As with individual mailboxes, you can configure a particular public folder with its own storage limit. This is set on the Advanced property page of the public folder. If the storage limit is reached, a warning message will be sent to the folder contacts.

Setting Age Limits For Data

Another method that can help control public folder storage is to set a maximum length of time an item can be in a folder. This is called an *age limit*. Age limits can be set for all public folders in an IS, or on a per-folder basis. The replicas of a public folder can also be separately configured. Age limits can keep a public folder from growing out of control.

Monitoring Public Folder Storage

Periodically, an administrator will want to check the storage level of public folders. This can be done using the Public Folder Resources object found under the Public Information Store. Clicking on the Public Folder Resources object displays all the folders on the server in the contents pane. Information including the total space used and the number of items in a folder will be displayed. This information can also be accessed through the Public Folder Resources property page of the Public Information Store.

Diagnostic Logging and Public Folder Storage

The Public Information Store can be configured for different levels of event logging. Various categories can be logged, including storage limits.

Managing Exchange Databases

All Exchange data, such as messages and directory information, is stored in various database files. Because of the extreme importance of the files, Exchange has many automatic and online maintenance processes. There are also various offline programs that can manually be run by an administrator to manage these files. Before we cover these programs and processes, we will explore the database technology that Exchange uses. This will serve as a background to the managing of the databases. This section will cover:

- Database technology and files

- Managing the Directory database

- Managing the Information Store databases

- Backing up the databases

Database Technology and Files

There are three primary Exchange database files. The IS component manages PRIV.EDB for the Private Information Store and PUB.EDB for the Public Information Store. The DS component manages DIR.EDB which holds all directory information. Each database also has its own transaction log files, which have a .LOG extension. Some additional files that pertain to the databases will be discussed in the following section. Table 12.8 summarizes this information.

TABLE 12.8	Exchange Component	Default Directory Path and Filename	Transaction Log File
The main Exchange database and transaction log files	Directory Service	\EXCHSRVR\DSADATA\DIR.EDB	EDB.LOG
	Information Store	\EXCHSRVR\MDBDATA\PRIV.EDB	EDB.LOG
		\EXCHSRVR\MDBDATA\PUB.EDB	EDB.LOG

The location of these database files can be modified using the Database Paths property page of a server object (also see Table 12.7). If a server has multiple drives, database files can be located on different drives to improve performance.

The Exchange databases are based on a 32-bit, multithreaded, transaction-based database engine. The engine is specially tailored for Exchange to be fast, compact, and optimized for message databases that experience constant record creation and deletion. One of the reasons the engine is fast is because it uses transaction log files.

Transaction Log Files

When data is to be written to one of the Exchange databases, the database engine does not write the data directly to the database file. The data is first written to a transaction log file, and then later written (or *committed*) to the database through a background process. This method has two advantages. One advantage is performance. When data is written to a transaction log file, it is entered sequentially, always at the end of the file. This can be done very fast. When data is committed to a database file, however, the database engine must search for the appropriate location to place the data. This is much slower than the simple sequential method. The second advantage is fault tolerance. If a database file becomes corrupt, a transaction log file can be used to recreate the database file.

As transactions in transaction log files are committed to the database files, a *checkpoint file* (EDB.CHK) is updated. The checkpoint file keeps track of which transactions in the sequential list still need to be committed to a database by maintaining a pointer to the last information that was committed. This tells the engine that everything after that point still needs to be committed to a database. If a server shuts down abnormally, Exchange can read the checkpoint file to learn where in the transaction logs it needs to start recovering data. The checkpoint file therefore assists in the fault tolerance of Exchange.

Transaction log files can contain up to 5MB of transactions. However, the log files are always 5MB in size no matter how many transactions they contain because the engine creates them as 5MB files and then proceeds to fill them with transactions. The current log file being written to is named EDB.LOG. When it is filled with 5MB of transactions, it is renamed to EDB*nnnnn*.LOG where *nnnnn* is a hexadecimal number, and a new, empty EDB.LOG file is created. The log files will, therefore, accumulate on the hard disk. A way to minimize this is to perform regular full or incremental backups of the databases. During a full or incremental backup, fully committed log files are automatically deleted because the data in them is backed up. This prevents the number of log files from growing until they take up the entire disk.

Transaction log files can also be configured to recycle themselves to prevent constant accumulation on the hard disk. This process is called *circular logging*. Instead of continually creating new log files and storing the old ones, the database engine "circles back" to the oldest log file that has been fully committed and overwrites that file. Circular logging minimizes the number of transaction log files on the disk at any given time. The downside is that these logs cannot be used to re-create a database because the logs do not have a complete set of data. They only have the data not yet committed. Another disadvantage of circular logging is that it does not permit a differential or incremental backup of the databases. Circular logging is the default setting and can be enabled or disabled on the Advanced property page of a server object (see Table 12.7).

A summary and comparison of circular logging enabled and disabled is found below:

Circular Logging Enabled (default)	Circular Logging Disabled
Transaction log files recycled	Old transaction log files stored
Does not permit the recreation of a database	Does permit the recreation of a database
Does not permit differential or incremental backups	Does permit differential and incremental backups
	A full or incremental backup automatically deletes old transaction log files

One other feature of the transaction-based databases is the use of reserve log files. Exchange creates two reserve log files (RES1.LOG and RES2.LOG) for each database. They are used if the system runs out of disk space. If that happens, Exchange shuts down the database service, logs an event to the event log, and writes any outstanding transaction information into these reserve log files. These two files reserve an area of disk space that can be used after the rest of the disk space is used.

Microsoft Exam Objective

Diagnose and resolve server directory problems.

Manage the directory.

Managing the Directory Database

Some maintenance of the Directory database occurs online while the DS service is started, and other maintenance is performed offline while it is stopped.

Online Maintenance of the Directory Database

Whenever a directory object is deleted, the deletion needs to be replicated to the other servers in the site (remember, there is only one logical directory for a site). The unit of information that says an object has been deleted is called a *tombstone*. Tombstones are replicated to other servers. By default, Exchange lets tombstones live for 30 days to ensure that this information is replicated. The 30-day setting can be modified through the General property page of the DS Site Configuration object (see Table 12.5).

A related setting is the Garbage collection interval. This is the time interval at which the expired tombstones are permanently deleted and the space they take is reclaimed. Exchange automatically collects garbage when the system is online. The Garbage collection interval defaults to 12 hours. (You should not change the default under normal circumstances.) This configuration is also found on the General property page of the DS Site Configuration object.

Another online procedure relates to both the DS and IS databases and is called the DS/IS consistency adjustment. As its name implies, this online procedure ensures that the DS and IS databases are synchronized. An example of these databases not being synchronized is a mailbox or public folder existing in the IS but not having an entry in the DS. Most inconsistencies like this are automatically cleaned up through directory replication. But if an inconsistency is not fixed through that process, the DS/IS consistency adjustment should fix it. It does that by monitoring the two databases and, when it finds an inconsistency, time stamping that object. Each time the adjustment is run, if it sees an inconsistent object that has a time stamp older than a day, it cleans up that inconsistency. The one day time filter can be configured by the administrator and an adjustment can be ran for all inconsistencies regardless of timestamps. Initiating and configuring the DS/IS consistency adjustment is done on the Advanced property page of an individual server object.

An example of a scenario when an administrator would manually initiate DS/IS consistency adjustment is after the permanent disconnection of two sites. When two sites are connected and are using the Microsoft Exchange Directory Replication Connector (more on this in chapter 13), directory information is exchanged between the two sites. But if the two sites are permanently disconnected, all the directory information in one site pertaining to the other site must be removed. That can be done by running the DS/IS consistency adjustment.

Offline Maintenance of the Directory Database

Offline maintenance of the Exchange Directory (or Information Store) can be performed by one of two utilities. EDBUTIL.EXE (Exchange Database Utility) can be used on Exchange 5.0 databases, and ESEUTIL.EXE (Exchange Server Database Utility) on Exchange 5.5 databases. To use these utilities, the database service (DS or IS) must be stopped. Some of the functions these utilities perform are listed below:

- **Defragments a database**   Over time, databases can become *fragmented*, which means that the data stored on the disk is noncontiguous. This can be caused by retaining deleted items. A data item may be logically marked as deleted, but physically kept on the disk for possible recovery. When a file is updated, the new data is stored in available free space, which may not be contiguous. Accessing a noncontiguous file causes extra head movement and therefore slower disk access. EDBUTIL can be used to defragment a database and decrease the database file size.

- **Consistency check**   Compares related information in a database to make sure it agrees. For example, pointers in the database that reference other pages of data can become *orphaned* and actually point off to nowhere. If these pointers are ever accessed, erratic behavior may occur. A Consistency check will fix this problem.

- **Recover a database** In a rare case when a database becomes badly damaged and cannot be repaired through the database consistency process, EDBUTIL can attempt to recover the database by reconstructing each entry in the database.

Microsoft ✓ *Exam* *Objective*

Manage the private information stores.

Diagnose and resolve information store problems.

Managing the Information Store Databases

Some maintenance of the Information Store database occurs online while the IS service is started, and other maintenance is performed offline while it is stopped.

Online Maintenance of the Information Store Databases

Exchange Server automatically performs the following maintenance functions on the IS databases:

- Defragments the Private and Public Information Stores

- Removes expired messages based on configured age limits

- Deletes indices created to cache folder views

The defragmenting of the IS can recover a fair amount of disk space. In situations that are approaching the limit of available disk space and that require a quick fix, performing an online IS maintenance can be the answer. The settings for this procedure are accessed through the IS Maintenance property page of a particular server object. If an administrator wanted to initiate this process, they would set this procedure's schedule to "Always." This procedure could be useful if you notice that the size of your Private Information Store is growing fast and approaching the limit of your available disk space. If routine offline maintenance is not scheduled until later, and you do not have additional hard disk space, an interim solution to slow the rate of growth would be to perform online maintenance of the Private Information Store.

As mentioned, you can schedule when these maintenance functions are performed by configuring the IS Maintenance property page of a server. Nonpeak hours are the best time to schedule this because server performance may degrade during maintenance. For example, suppose your Exchange servers are backed up every evening at 1:00 A.M. The backup takes between three and four hours to complete. While you want IS maintenance to take place, you do not want it to conflict with the backups, and you do not want it to impact server response time during regular business hours. The solution is to schedule IS maintenance to occur immediately before the backup.

Offline Maintenance of the Information Store Databases

ISINTEG (Information Store Integrity) is an offline utility that can be used to repair the IS database. To execute it, the IS service must be stopped. If an IS database encounters enough errors to prevent it from starting or to prevent users from logging on to it, ISINTEG can be run to find and eliminate these errors. This utility is found in the \EXCHSRVR\BIN directory.

One scenario that requires the use of ISINTEG is after an offline backup and restore of Exchange. An offline backup is a file-level backup of the IS while Exchange Server is offline (the two files that would be backed up are PRIV.EDB and PUB.EDB). An offline restore is a file-level restore of the IS while Exchange Server is offline.

After the offline restore of the IS, you must execute ISINTEG to patch the IS before it can be used. This is done by executing the following command line:

```
ISINTEG -PATCH
```

Other scenarios that could require the use of ISINTEG is a server's disk becoming full and stopping the IS service, or a power failure shutting down the server and after the restart the IS service will not work. In both of these scenarios, Exchange should automatically roll back to the last checkpoint and be operational. But if that does not occur, you would need to execute ISINTEG with the following parameter:

```
ISINTEG -FIX
```

The EDBUTIL and ESEUTIL programs discussed earlier also can perform offline maintenance of the IS. While ISINTEG only works on the IS databases, these other two utilities operate on both the DS database and the IS databases.

Because IS database maintenance is automatic, manually using ISINTEG or EDBUTIL, or ESEUTIL is not regularly required.

Microsoft ✓ *Exam* *Objective*

Backup and restore the Exchange Server organization.

Backing Up the Databases

Because of the importance of the Exchange databases and transaction logs, backup is essential. When Exchange Server is installed, a new version of Windows NT Backup, one that is Exchange-aware, replaces the existing version. This program can be used to back up Exchange data.

Although there are many backup strategies, three basic strategies will serve as an introduction to this topic. Table 12.9 describes these three basic strategies, along with some of their advantages and disadvantages (a five day work week is assumed).

TABLE 12.9

Three basic backup strategies

Backup Strategy	Description	Advantages	Disadvantages
Full Daily (also called Normal)	A full (i.e., complete) backup is performed every day.	Only one tape is needed to perform a restoration.	Longest amount of time needed to perform the backup.
One full, and four incremental	A full backup is done on day 1. An incremental backup (using a new tape every day) is performed every day for the next four days. This procedure only backs up the new and changed data since the last full or incremental backup (whichever is more recent).	Takes the least amount of time to back up.	Could require up to five tapes to perform a restoration.
One full, and four differential	A full backup is done on day 1. A differential backup (using a single new tape) is performed every day for the next four days. This procedure only backs up the new and changed data since the last full backup.	No more than two tapes, the full and the last differential, are required to perform a restoration.	This strategy takes progressively longer each day.

The Exchange databases and transaction logs can be backed up while an Exchange server is online. If the full backup strategy is used, the following Exchange files are backed up:

PRIV.EDB

PUB.EDB

Transaction log files

Checkpoint file (EDB.CHK)

If a differential or incremental backup is performed, the *.EDB files are not backed up, and only these files are backed up:

Transaction log files

Checkpoint file (EDB.CHK)

For a differential or incremental backup to be performed, circular logging must be turned off.

The next six paragraphs (including this one), will describe some backup scenarios that you should be aware of. In a perfect world, you would perform a full backup of Exchange every night. But if your databases are large, you might not have enough time in one night to do a full backup. One solution to this scenario is to combine backup strategies. For example, a Full (i.e., Normal) backup can be performed every weekend, and a Differential backup every weekday evening. This strategy would have the benefit of minimizing the time to restore. There would be only two tapes to use in the restore, one tape for the Full (i.e., Normal) backup, and one tape with the Differential backup.

A strategy for maximum data recovery could include making sure your Exchange server is not on a domain controller and turning off circular logging. By turning off circular logging you ensure that changes to the Exchange databases are written to log files and kept until the next full or incremental backup. These log files could be used to recover data in the case of a major failure of the databases.

The following scenario also illustrates the role of circular logging in a backup strategy. An organization has an Exchange server with two disk controller/hard drive sets. One hard drive contains the IS databases, the other hard drive the transaction log files. Circular logging is disabled. One day one of the disk controllers malfunctions and corrupts the IS databases. You made a Full backup four days ago, and have done three incremental backups since then. The hardware failure took place 12 hours after the last incremental backup. What information can be restored? The answer is simple: all information stored prior to the last time at which logs were written. The last incremental backup would automatically delete the old log files, because that information is now backed up. All information written to the databases since the last incremental backup (12 hours ago) would also be written to the latest log files. Consequently, all information could be restored, both information on the backup media and information written to the log files since the last backup.

It makes sense, from both a fault tolerance and a performance standpoint, to put the transaction log files on one disk drive and the database files on a different drive. This allows the best recovery of data if the drive containing the database files is corrupted. Performance is increased because the transaction log drive can be dedicated to the sequential writes used with transaction log files and will not be interrupted with the random access read and writes required of the database drives.

This next scenario is similar to some of the previous cases, but with a few new wrinkles. You have an Exchange server that has two drives of the same capacity, but one is faster than the other. Management has mandated that all information be backed up nightly. They also would prefer that the most recent transactions be recoverable, and that there be minimum server response time for users. To meet the required mandate, you configure Microsoft Windows NT Backup to perform a nightly backup. To meet the first optional result, you disable circular logging. The second optional result is met by placing the transaction log files on the faster drive, and the database files on the other drive.

An additional backup strategy is to perform a file copy of the Exchange database files to a disk or removeable media. The three files you would have to backup are PRIV.EDB, PUB.EDB, and DIR.EDB. Those files can only be backed up while Exchange Server is offline and after the services were cleanly shut down.

Restoring the Contents of a Deleted Mailbox

To restore the contents of a deleted mailbox, you need to restore a backup of the entire Private Information Store (PRIV.EDB) that contains that mailbox. Because that backup media will probably not contain the most recent server data, and you would not want to replace your current online data, the restoration must be done to an alternate server. The alternate server must mirror many of the parameters of the mailbox's home server. It must run the same version of Exchange Server, and have the same service pack, the same organization and site name, and sufficient disk space for the PRIV.EDB file. The alternate server, while needing the same organization and site names as the original server, must not be replicated into the same site. After the PRIV.EDB file is restored to the alternate server, the administrator can logon to that server as the owner of the mailbox and copy all the data in the mailbox to a PST file. That PST file can then be given to the user for insertion to their current mailbox.

Standby Servers

Part of a backup and restore strategy could involve using standby servers, also called recovery servers. These are computers that you have prepared to take the place of your Exchange server should it have a catastrophic failure. A standby server would have installed Windows NT Server and Exchange Server and have the same organization and site names as the primary server. Since you want this server to be operational as soon as possible after the failure of your primary server, you need to have the Exchange database files loaded on the standby server, or on media that would facilitate loading on that server. Some organizations create a batch file that stops the Exchange services on the primary server and copies the relevant files to the standby server. Those files are the directory file and the Private and Public Information Store files. These files could also be copied to removable media and then uploaded to the standby server when needed.

It is not recommended that you install Exchange Server on a primary domain controller (PDC) in a domain with no backup domain controllers (BDCs). Exchange clients need to be authenticated by a domain controller in order to access Exchange resources. If a computer serving as both the Exchange server and the PDC has a major failure, the standby server will not do you much good. Even though all the Exchange files are still present, the Exchange clients would not be able to be authenticated.

Troubleshooting Backups and Restores

Problems can occur when you back up or restore servers. Table 12.10 lists some problems (and possible causes) that you may encounter when you perform two common procedures.

Microsoft ✓ *Exam* *Objective*

Diagnose and resolve backup problems and restore problems.

TABLE 12.10	Situation	Problem	Cause/Solution
Backup and restore problems and causes	IS will not start after restoring from an offline backup.	The IS needs to be patched before it can be operational.	The solution is to execute the following command line: ISINTEG –PATCH.
	Restored the Information Store to a different server.	After the restore, users cannot access the Information Store.	The restore was performed on a server in a different Windows NT domain than the original server.
	Backed up an Exchange server that was running on a primary domain controller. Restored the Information Store to a different server.	After the restore, users cannot access the Information Store.	The organization and site names on the new server are not the same as the original server.

You can also use the backup log file, BACKUP.LOG, that resides in your Windows NT directory (e.g., \WINNT) as a diagnostic tool when you troubleshoot.

Microsoft ✓ *Exam* *Objective*

Configure the message transfer agent within a site.

Diagnose and resolve message delivery problems.

Managing Message Delivery

Ensuring the efficient delivery of messages is central to an administrator's job. To accomplish this job, an administrator needs to understand the role of the MTA and its properties. As you learned in Chapters 2 and 3, the role of the MTA is to manage the transfer of data. The transfer can be between servers in the same site, or even between servers in different sites. This chapter covers the former scenario, and Chapter 13 covers the latter. In this section, you will learn about:

- Message tracking

- MTA messaging settings

- The MTACHECK utility

Microsoft
Exam
Objective

Configure message tracking.

Message Tracking

MTA properties are accessed through the MTA Site Configuration object in the Configuration container. One of these properties is message tracking, which can be enabled or disabled. The MTA component manages the delivery of messages to remote servers. If you enable message tracking, the System Attendant will keep a log of routing information for every message the MTA processes. The log file is an ASCII text file that is stored in the directory EXCHSRVR\ TRACKING.LOG. The file naming convention is YYYYMMDD.LOG, where YYYY is the year, MM is the month, and DD is the day. For example, a log file created on February 1, 1997 is called 19970201.LOG.

To use tracking logs, choose Track Message from the Tools menu in Exchange Administrator. You will be able to search for and select the message you want to track.

Microsoft
Exam
Objective

Monitor and optimize the message environment.

MTA Messaging Settings

Other properties of the MTA Site Configuration object relate to the defaults used when sending messages. These properties are found on the Messaging Defaults property page (see Figure 12.5). Four categories of properties are found on this page. Each will be described along with its individual attributes.

FIGURE 12.5

Messaging Defaults
property page

RTS (Reliable Transfer Service) values are properties that indicate how often you want to verify information being sent, how long you want to wait after an error has occurred to resend a message, and how often you want verification from another server that it has received a message. The specific attributes that relate to these settings are described in Table 12.11.

Attribute	**Description**
Checkpoint size (K)	The amount of data to be sent before a *checkpoint* is inserted. A checkpoint is like a bookmark placed in the stream of data being sent. If there is an error in the transfer of a message, the MTA will go back to the last checkpoint and resend data from that point. Using checkpoints causes message transfers to be slightly slower. If a connection is considered unreliable, the checkpoint size should be decreased.
Recovery timeout (sec)	The length of time the MTA waits for a reconnection after an error has occurred. When this time is reached, the MTA will delete the checkpointed information and restart the data transfer from the beginning. If a reconnection is made before this time period is reached, the MTA resends only from the checkpoint forward.
Window size	The window size indicates the number of checkpoints that can be sent before an acknowledgment must be received from the destination. If the window size is reached with no acknowledgment, the data transfer is suspended. The greater the window size, the faster the transfer rate.

T A B L E 12.11
RTS values attributes

Another set of attributes is grouped under the heading "Connection retry values." These values determine how many times you want to try to open a connection, how many times to try to send a message, how long to wait after an error to reopen a connection, and how long to wait to resend a message after an error. The specific attributes that relate to these settings are described in Table 12.12.

T A B L E 12.12
Connection retry value attributes

Attribute	**Description**
Max open retries	The maximum number of times the MTA tries to open a connection before it sends an NDR (Non-Delivery Report) to the sender.
Max transfer retries	The maximum number of times the MTA tries to transfer a message over an open connection.

T A B L E 12.12 *(cont.)* Connection retry value attributes	**Attribute**	**Description**
	Open interval (sec)	The length of time the MTA waits after an error has occurred before it attempts to reopen a connection.
	Transfer interval (sec)	The length of time the MTA waits after a failed transfer before it tries to resend a message over an open connection.

Three attributes are grouped under the heading "Association parameters." An *association* is an open pathway to another system. An association is a subset of a connection. While there may be only a single connection between two systems, there can be multiple associations in that single connection. Association parameters relate to how long to keep an association open, how long to wait for a response before closing the association, and the number of queued messages that will trigger an additional association. The specific attributes that relate to these settings are described in Table 12.13.

T A B L E 12.13 Association parameters	**Attribute**	**Description**
	Lifetime (sec)	The length of time the MTA keeps an association open after it has finished sending messages.
	Disconnect (sec)	The length of time the MTA waits after it sends a disconnect request before it will close the connection.
	Threshold (msgs)	The maximum number of queued messages before the MTA opens another association.

The final group of message defaults is called Transfer timeouts. These attributes specify how long to wait after a transfer failure before sending a Non-Delivery Report (NDR) to the sender. Different transfer timeouts can be assigned for each message priority.

The MTACHECK Utility

The MTA Check utility (MTACHECK) scans a MTA queue looking for corrupted messages that could prevent the MTA from sending messages. MTACHECK will attempt to remedy that situation by rebuilding the MTA queue. This program can run only when the MTA service is stopped. MTACHECK is found in the \EXCHSRVR\BIN directory and can be run from a command prompt.

Troubleshooting

An administrator has many tools and resources to help troubleshoot an Exchange environment. This section discusses some of these, including:

- Client troubleshooting tools

- Diagnostic logs

- Monitors

Client Troubleshooting Tools

Two tools are used to troubleshoot an Exchange client. One repairs personal folder storage, and the other tests connections to a server.

- **Inbox Repair Tool**   SCANPST.EXE tests and repairs a personal folder store (*.PST). It scans for bad blocks and attempts to rebuild them. If a .PST file is corrupted beyond repair, this program will try to evacuate the good blocks of data and remove the corrupted blocks. This program does not need to be run unless there are operational problems with personal folders. On rare occasions, if an Exchange client application is abnormally terminated, a personal folder can become corrupted. You will be notified of the corruption on the next startup of the client application. The Inbox Repair Tool is found in the Exchange client program group. You can also use this utility on OST files. For example, you could receive a message stating that your OST file is damaged. Running SCANPST on the OST file will allow you to access those messages without losing the unsynchronized changes in that file.

- **RPC Ping**   The RPC Ping utility is used to test RPC connections between two computers. It can be used to test the RPC connection between a client and a server. The RPC Ping Server component (RPINGS.EXE for the Intel platform) is run first on the Exchange server. The RPC Ping Client component (e.g., RPINGC32.EXE for 32-bit clients) is then run on the client computer and sends a request to the server. This procedure tests the existence and quality of that connection. There are RPC Ping client versions for Windows 3.*x*, Windows 95, Windows NT, and MS-DOS. Both the client and server side programs are on the Exchange Server compact disc in the SUPPORT\RPCPING directory.

Diagnostic Logs

Many Exchange objects have a Diagnostics Logging property page. This page is used to configure the types and levels of events logged to the Windows NT Event Log. The logs are viewed with the Event Viewer application. This topic was already discussed earlier in this chapter, but because of its use in troubleshooting it is also mentioned here.

Microsoft ✓ *Exam* *Objective*   **Configure a link monitor and a server monitor.**

Monitors

Exchange Server includes two monitoring features that can be used in the management of an Exchange environment. These features are:

- **Server Monitor**   Can be used to monitor the Exchange services running on a server.

- **Link Monitor**   Can be used to test the message link (i.e., connection) between two Exchange servers. A link is tested by sending a message to a designated remote server, or a designated recipient on a remote server.

Multiple monitors can be configured to provide different views, and each monitor can also track multiple servers. The remainder of this section covers the two types of monitors in more detail.

Server Monitor

Server Monitors are a straightforward, yet powerful feature. In addition to monitoring the services running on an Exchange server, server monitors can automatically send notifications and perform specified actions.

A Server Monitor is created by choosing File, New Other, Server Monitor in Exchange Administrator. This brings up the property pages of a new Server Monitor. The five main property pages and their primary attributes are found in Table 12.14 (the standard Permissions page is also shown if Exchange Administrator is configured to display it on all objects).

T A B L E 12.14 Server Monitor property pages	**Property Page**	**Primary Attributes**
	General	• Directory name • Display name • Log file • Polling interval
	Servers	Monitored servers Services to monitor
	Notification	**When** Indicates the time delay after a server goes into an alert or warning state before the notification occurs. **How** Specifies the type of notification event. Options include launch a process, mail message, and Windows NT Alert. **Who** States where the notification will be sent. It is possible to have a series of escalation steps.
	Actions	Attributes include the actions to perform when a service has stopped. Options include take no action, restart the service, and restart the computer. Actions can also be configured separately for the first, second, and subsequent attempts.
	Clock	Attributes include issuing warnings and alerts if the system clocks of the server running the Server Monitor and the server being monitored are not synchronized within a specified range. Clocks can also be automatically synchronized.

As mentioned in Table 12.14, a Server Monitor can be used to synchronize the clocks of various Exchange servers. The clock on the server that runs the server monitor is used for the synchronization.

Server Monitor can be used to pause, stop, and start services on an Exchange server. If you would like to stop the Exchange services on a server without generating an error, you would have to start Microsoft Exchange Administrator with the /t n command line switches (i.e., ADMIN.EXE /t n). "T" stands for temporarily and "n" stands for no error.

Link Monitor

A Link Monitor can be used as an early warning system for problems with links between servers. A Link Monitor is created by choosing File, New Other, Link Monitor in Exchange Administrator. This brings up the property pages of a new Link Monitor.

A Link Monitor has many of the same attributes as a Server Monitor, such as polling interval, notifications, and servers to monitor. One unique attribute of a Link Monitor is *bounce*. Bounce is the longest acceptable round-trip time for a test message to travel between the monitor's home server and the target server. An administrator can set the bounce warning and alert time thresholds.

Starting and Stopping Monitors

After a monitor has been created and configured, administrators are responsible for starting and stopping it. These two actions are discussed in the following text.

Starting Monitors   Monitors can be started two ways:

- Exchange Administrator

- Command prompt

Exchange Administrator can be used to start a monitor. To do so, highlight the particular monitor you want started and choose Start Monitor from the Tools menu. Next, select the server on which to run the monitor. The monitor then starts and the Server or Link Monitor window is displayed.

Monitors can also be started automatically when Exchange Administrator is started. To configure this, leave a monitor started when you exit Exchange Administrator. The monitor will be started automatically the next time Exchange Administrator is launched.

An administrator can also run Exchange Administrator from a command prompt with certain parameters to start a monitor. This is done by accessing a command prompt and changing to the \EXCHSRVR\BIN directory, which contains ADMIN.EXE. The following line is an example of the command line format to use to start a monitor. In this example, *serverA* is the server to which Exchange Administrator will connect and *serverB* is the server on which the monitor *monitor_name* will be run.

```
admin /s serverA /m monitor_name/serverB
```

Stopping Monitors   Stopping a monitor using Exchange Administrator is as simple as clicking on the Close button of the monitor window. Monitors can also be temporarily stopped at a command prompt using the command:

```
admin /t
```

Exercise 12.3 will walks through the steps to create, configure, start, and test a Server Monitor.

Server Monitor

1. Highlight the Monitors object in the Configuration container. Choose File ➢ New Other ➢ Server Monitor. This will bring up the property pages of a new Server Monitor.

2. Go to the General page. In the Directory name and Display name fields, type **ServerMonitor1**.

3. In the Polling interval for Normal, enter 1 minute.

4. Choose the Notification page. Click New. This will bring up the New Notification dialog box.

5. Choose the Notification type of Windows NT Alert and click OK. The Escalation Editor dialog box will appear.

6. Enter the number 1 in the Time delay box. In the "Computer to alert" field, enter the name of your Exchange server. Click OK. Click OK on the alert concerning notifications.

EXERCISE 12.3 (CONTINUED FROM PREVIOUS PAGE)

7. Choose the Servers page. Highlight your Exchange server name in the left listbox and click Add.

8. Click the Services button. In the Installed services list box, highlight the Microsoft Exchange Key Manager. Then click Add and click OK.

9. Click OK to save and exit from the Server Monitor you just created.

10. Before you start your Server Monitor, access Control Panel/Services, and make sure the Microsoft Exchange Key Manager service is running. If it is not, start it (you will need to supply the KM password or a floppy disk with the password on it—see Chapter 10 for details).

11. Back in Exchange Administrator, highlight the Server Monitor you just created and choose Tools ➢ Start Monitor. The Connect to server dialog box will appear.

12. Make sure your Exchange server name is in the dialog box, then click OK. The Server Monitor window will now appear.

13. Use Control Panel/Services to stop the Microsoft Exchange Key Manager service.

14. After a moment, your Server Monitor will generate a Windows NT Alert stating "The service MSExchangeKMS is not available. Its status is Stopped." Click OK. You will also see this information written to the Server Monitor window.

15. To stop the Server Monitor, click the Close box on the Server Monitor window.

Microsoft
✔ *Exam*
Objective

Monitor server performance by using SNMP and MADMAN MIB.

Microsoft Exchange Server 5.5 supports the MADMAN MIB (RFC 1566). This enables third-party SNMP management programs to access the various management statistics of an Exchange server (version 5.5). MIB stands for Management Information Base, and defines a database structure for management statistics. SNMP stands for Simple Network Management Protocol, and defines a set of management objects and procedures for managing enterprise-wide environments.

Summary

Many tools are included with Exchange Server to help manage an Exchange organization. Various Windows NT Server tools, like Event Viewer, can be used by an Exchange administrator. The main tool in an administrator's arsenal is the Exchange Administrator program, which manages objects at the organization, site, and server levels of the Exchange hierarchy.

Exchange Server stores messages and configuration data in various database files. To increase system performance and to facilitate fault tolerance, Exchange Server first writes data to transaction log files. The data is then later committed to the relevant database during a background process.

Server and Link Monitors provide an early warning system for service status and links between servers.

Review Questions

1. You have installed Microsoft Exchange Server on a server that is heavily utilized. After installation, you notice that response times are slow and that the hard disk is constantly active. You use Windows NT Performance Monitor to collect the following statistics:

    % Processor time = 70

    % Disk free space = 60

    Pages/sec = 40

    Avg. Disk sec/Transfer = 0.02

What should you do to reduce disk activity and improve server response time?

A. Install more RAM.

B. Install a faster CPU.

C. Create additional swap files.

D. Install an additional hard disk.

E. Replace the hard disk with a faster hard disk.

2. Your organization had two sites that used the Microsoft Mail Connector for interconnection. Those two sites no longer need to be connected. You consequently try to delete the dirsync server on your server, but it remains visible in the hierarchy. When you attempt to delete it again, you receive a message stating that the object does not exist. How should you delete that object from the directory view?

A. Run Microsoft Exchange Setup with the Recovery option.

B. Perform a DS/IS consistency adjustment.

C. Run Setup to reinstall Exchange Server, and preserve existing settings.

D. Run Exchange Administrator in raw mode and delete the object.

3. Your organization has a single-master domain and a resource domain. The Exchange site service account is in the master domain, while your Exchange servers are in the resource domain. How can you simplify the procedure of assigning Exchange directory permissions to all Exchange administrators?

A. Create a recipients container for all administrators.

B. Create a distribution list that contains all administrators.

C. Create a Windows NT local group that contains all administrators.

D. Create a Windows NT global group that contains all administrators.

4. A site has two Exchange servers, Server A and Server B. All users in the finance department connect to Server A. All users in the marketing department connect to Server B. Each department has its own Exchange administrator. The site has only one recipients container. How would you allow the marketing administrator to manage recipients on both servers, but not manage any other objects in the hierarchy?

   A. Assign permissions to the marketing administrator at the site object.

   B. Assign permissions to the marketing administrator at the organization object.

   C. Add the marketing administrator to the Domain Admins. group.

   D. Assign the administrator role to the marketing administrator at the recipients object.

5. The password of the site service account gets changed in User Manager for Domains. When Exchange Server is shut down and restarted the Exchange services will not start. What can you do to prevent that situation?

   A. Enter the account name and new password in the Services file in the ETC directory.

   B. Run Microsoft Exchange Administrator in raw mode and designate the site service account again.

   C. Assign the site service account the right to log on locally, then restart the computer.

   D. Designate the new password in the site configuration properties.

6. You are running Microsoft Exchange Administrator from your Windows NT Workstation computer. Your computer is using both IPX and TCP/IP. Which naming convention can you use to connect to an Exchange server? (Choose all that apply.)

   A. IP address

   B. NetBIOS name

    C. DNS host name

    D. IPX network number

    E. Media access control (MAC) address

7. Your Exchange recipients do not need a Microsoft Mail proxy address. How can you as the administrator disable the future creation of these addresses?

    A. Delete the Microsoft Mail Connector.

    B. Export the directory, remove the Microsoft Mail address space, then import the directory.

    C. Disable the Microsoft Mail address space in the Site Addressing properties.

    D. Create a blank entry in the address space for the Microsoft Mail Connector.

8. You have been asked as the Exchange administrator to set the default display names to LastName FirstName, such as Smith John. Where do you configure that setting?

    A. The properties of each object

    B. Only on the properties of individual mailboxes

    C. Organization properties

    D. Auto Naming property page of the Exchange Administrator program

9. A single site encompasses London and Tokyo. Three servers are in London, and two are in Tokyo. What can you do to ensure that users in London always access public folders in London before accessing replicas in Tokyo?

    A. Configure site affinity between London and Tokyo.

    B. Configure local address spaces for each public folder.

    C. Set directory replication to use the Site Connector.

    D. Set the location value so that servers in both cities are associated with each other.

10. You have a public folder that you do not want to be replicated or rehomed. How can you accomplish that?

A. Use the X.400 Connector between sites.

B. Set the site affinity number to 100.

C. Set the Replication Schedule property to "Never".

D. Disable the public folder.

11. Your organization has multiple Exchange servers. Currently, when users create public folders they are placed on Server A. After monitoring that server, you notice that its hard disk is almost full. You move all those public folders to Server B. How can you ensure that all future public folders will be created on Server B?

A. Delete all new replicas on Server A.

B. Configure Server B as the public folder server for all recipients on Server A.

C. Use Microsoft Exchange Performance Optimizer to configure Server A as only a private information store server.

D. Restrict top-level folder creation on Server A.

12. Your organization has four sites, each site consisting of two Exchange servers and 500 users. The four sites are connected with a 256K wide area network (WAN). The available bandwidth during the workday is less than 64K. While at night, the available bandwidth is 128K or more. You have created a public folder that contains 600MB of data that is not time critical. Users only access that folder approximately every fifteen minutes, and the folder data is only updated twice a week. On what servers should replicas be placed?

A. On every server

B. On each bridgehead server

C. Only on the server where the public folder was originally created

D. Only on domain controllers

13. Two servers, Server A and Server B, share public folder information across an unreliable WAN network. What can you do so that public folder information is synchronized on both servers?

    A. Create public folders on both servers. Use a distribution list to transfer information between the servers.

    B. Create public folders on both servers. Use a folder rule to transfer information between the servers.

    C. Create a public folder on Server A. Designate Server B as an expansion server.

    D. Create replicas of public folders on both servers.

14. You want to calculate the size necessary for your Private Information Store. You ascertain that the average size of each e-mail message on your server is 10 MB. You ask 10 users to track the type of messages they receive in one day. The users report back that they each received 10 messages. Five of those messages were sent using a local distribution list (i.e., the distribution list was an object on the same server as the message recipients). Two messages were sent to the 10 users by using a distribution list from another company that also uses Microsoft Exchange. Three messages were sent to the 10 users by using a distribution list from a company that does not use Microsoft Exchange. How many copies from the above scenario will be in the Private Information Store?

    A. 10

    B. 37

    C. 55

    D. 100

15. Your Exchange server is backed up every night. Deleted item retention is set to 4 days. If you needed to enable users to restore all their messages what else would you need to do?

    A. Disable circular logging.

    B. Configure client profiles to not delete deleted items on exit.

    C. Configure Deleted item retention to not delete items until after the IS is backed up.

    D. Disable PST files on the local computers.

16. Your network has 300 clients, each with a 100 MB storage limit, and with each message averaging 10 MB. If deleted item retention time was set to 7 days, and there were no single-instance messages, what would be the amount of disk space needed for the maximum storage limit of all mailboxes in the Private Information Store?

    A. 16 GB

    B. 27 GB

    C. 30 GB

    D. 33 GB

17. A public folder has an "age limit" for messages of 90 days. The "Deleted item retention time" is set to 7 days. A particular item has been in this public folder for 87 days when a user deletes that item. Five days later, a user wants to recover that item. What can be done to recover that item?

    A. Nothing can be done.

    B. Run DS/IS consistency adjustment.

    C. Run Exchange Administrator in raw mode, and recover the item.

    D. Instruct the user to use the Microsoft Outlook Recover Deleted Item feature.

18. A client uses an IMAP4 client while away from the office, and Microsoft Outlook while in the office. While using the IMAP4 client, the user deletes an item in their Inbox. On returning to the office, the user realizes the deleted item is still needed. How can the item be recovered?

    A. Use the Recover Deleted Items feature of Microsoft Outlook.

    B. It cannot be done.

    C. Execute ISINTEG –FIX.

    D. Log back in with the IMAP4 client and recover.

19. Deleted Item Retention is enabled on a mailbox. What happens to items when they are deleted?

    A. They become hidden objects in the IS.

    B. They are placed in TEMP.EDB.

    C. They go to the Recycle bin on the local computer.

    D. They are placed in a Personal folder on the local computer.

20. You have your Exchange server backed up using an offline backup procedure. After a hardware failure of that server, you restore the server using the offline backup tapes. But after the restore is complete, the IS will not start. What do you need to do?

    A. Run EDBUTIL.

    B. Run EDBUTIL with the consistency option.

    C. Run SCANPST on each user's OST file.

    D. Run ISINTEG –Patch.

21. A disk containing the IS databases reaches its storage capacity causing the IS to stop. What must you do before you can restart the IS?

    A. Run ISINTEG with the fix option.

    B. Run Setup with the recovery option.

    C. Initiate online maintenance.

    D. Run ISINTEG with the defragmentation option.

22. Your Exchange servers are scheduled for backup every evening at 1:00 A.M. The backup takes between three and four hours to complete. While you want IS maintenance to take place, you do not want it to conflict with the backups and you do not want it to impact server response time during regular business hours. How should you configure IS maintenance?

    A. Schedule IS maintenance every 20 minutes.

    B. Schedule IS maintenance to occur immediately before the backup.

C. Manually start and stop IS maintenance.

D. Run IS maintenance all day on weekends.

23. The Private Information Store on your server is approaching the capacity of its disk. Offline maintenance is not scheduled for another week. You do not want to impose space restrictions on users, but you do need to do something to slow the rate of growth of the Private Information Store. What can you do?

A. Run Microsoft Exchange Performance Optimizer on the Private Information Store.

B. Run MTACHECK.

C. Run the DS/IS Consistency Adjustment.

D. Perform online maintenance of the Private Information Store.

24. The connections between a Site A and Site B have been permanently removed. You notice that public folder replicas from Site A are still showing up in Site B. How can you remove those instances in the directory of Site B?

A. Run EDBUTIL with the recovery option.

B. Manually delete each replica in Site B.

C. Perform a DS/IS Consistency Adjustment.

D. Reinstall the site connectors, and then delete the replicas in Site B.

25. You need to restore a mailbox that was accidentally deleted. The size of the mailbox was limited to 25 MB. The size of the Private Information Store is 500 MB. The size of the entire IS database is 1000 MB. In addition to the space needed for Microsoft Windows NT and Microsoft Exchange Server, how much space will be needed on the standby server in order to restore this deleted mailbox?

A. 25 MB

B. 500 MB

C. 525 MB

D. 1025 MB

26. If you wanted to back up the Exchange database files to a disk, what files would you have to copy?

    A. PRIV.EDB

    B. PUB.EDB

    C. DIR.EDB

    D. EDB.CHK

    E. Transaction log files

27. Your organization has an Exchange server with two disk controllers and hard drives. One hard drive contains the IS databases, the other hard drive has the transaction log files. Circular logging is disabled. One day one of the disk controllers malfunctions and corrupts the IS databases. You made a Full backup four days ago, and did three incremental backups since then. The hardware failure took place 12 hours after the last incremental backup. What information can be restored?

    A. Only the information stored after the last full backup but prior to the last incremental backup.

    B. All information stored prior to the last time the logs were updated.

    C. Only the information stored prior to the last full backup.

    D. Only the information stored after the last incremental backup.

28. You are asked to create a backup strategy that will recover the most data in the event of a major hardware failure. Which of the following would be part of your strategy? (Select the best answer.)

    A. Install Micrsoft Exchange Server on a computer that is not a domain controller. Turn off circular logging.

    B. Install Microsoft Exchange Server on a computer that is not a domain controller. Turn on circular logging.

    C. Install Microsoft Exchange on a primary domain controller. Turn off circular logging.

    D. Install Microsoft Exchange on a primary domain controller. Turn on circular logging.

29. Your organization performs a complete backup every weekend. You have been asked to add a plan to also backup the system every weekday evening with all the changes made since the weekend backup. You also want to minimize the time it takes to restore a system from the backups. How would you configure Microsoft Windows NT Backup?

    A. Set the weekend backup type to Normal. Set each weekday backup type to Incremental.

    B. Set the weekend backup type to Normal. Set each weekday backup type to Differential.

    C. Set the weekend backup type to Copy. Set each weekday backup type to Incremental.

    D. Set the weekend backup type to Copy. Set each weekday backup type to Differential.

30. You are formulating a backup strategy for your company. The computer that will be your Exchange server has two hard drives of equal capacity, with one of the drives significantly faster than the other.

    Required result: A requirement of the backup strategy is to perform a complete backup every night.

    Optional Result 1: One optional result of the strategy is that the most recent database transactions can be recovered in the event of a hardware failure of the drive, or drives, housing the Exchange database files.

    Optional Result 2: Another optional result of the strategy is to minimize server response time for users.

    Proposed Solution: One proposed strategy includes: placing the IS transaction log files and the DS transaction log files on the faster hard disk, and the IS and DS database files on the slower hard disk; enabling circular logging; and performing a nightly backup.

What results does this proposed strategy produce?

A. The required result and both optional results

B. The required result and only one of the optional results

C. The required result and neither of the optional results

D. Does not produce the required result

31. You are formulating a backup strategy for your company. The computer that will be your Exchange server has two hard drives of equal capacity, with one of the drives significantly faster than the other.

    Required Result: A requirement of the backup strategy is to perform a complete backup every night.

    Optional Result 1: One optional result of the strategy is that the most recent database transactions can be recovered in the event of a hardware failure of the drive, or drives, housing the Exchange database files.

    Optional Result 2: Another optional result of the strategy is to minimize server response time for users.

    Proposed Solution: One proposed strategy includes: placing the IS transaction log files and the DS transaction log files on the faster hard disk, and the IS and DS database files on the slower hard disk; disabling circular logging; and performing a nightly backup.

    What results does this proposed strategy produce?

    A. The required result and both optional results

    B. The required result and only one of the optional results

    C. The required result and neither of the optional results

    D. Does not produce the required result

32. You are formulating a backup strategy for your company. The computer that will be your Exchange server has two hard drives of equal capacity, with one of the drives significantly faster than the other.

> **Required Result:** A requirement of the backup strategy is to perform a complete backup every night.

> **Optional Result 1:** One optional result of the strategy is that the most recent database transactions can be recovered in the event of a hardware failure of the drive, or drives, housing the Exchange database files.

> **Optional Result 2:** Another optional result of the strategy is to minimize server response time for users.

> **Proposed Solution:** One proposed strategy includes: placing the IS database file and the IS transaction log files on the faster hard disk, and the DS database file and the DS transaction log files on the slower hard disk; enabling circular logging; and performing a nightly backup.

What results does this proposed strategy produce?

A. The required result, and both optional results

B. The required result, and only one of the optional results

C. The required result, and neither of the optional results

D. Does not produce the required result

33. You have created a standby Exchange server. You want to create a batch file that stops the primary Exchange server and copies all the necessary Exchange files to the standby server. Which of the following files would you include in the batch file copy process? (Select all that apply.)

A. Directory file

B. Checkpoint file

C. Transaction log files

D. PUB.EDB

E. PRIV.EDB

F. Personal Information Store

34. You need to configure a recovery server for your Exchange site. How should you configure the recovery server?

   A. Use the same NetBIOS name as the primary server. Join the existing site.

   B. Use the same organization name as the existing configuration. Use a new site name. Connect the new site to the existing site.

   C. Use the same organization name and site name as your existing configuration. Do not join the site.

   D. Use the same organization name and site name as your existing configuration. Join the existing site.

35. A user receives a message stating that their OST file is damaged. What should you tell them so they can access their messages without losing the unsynchronized changes in that file?

   A. Move the OST file to the server and run ISINTEG.

   B. Use the Migration tool to import the OST into a new mailbox.

   C. Rename the OST file with a PST extension and run SCANPST on the PST file.

   D. Run SCANPST on the OST file.

36. You want to take one of your Exchange servers offline, but you do not want that procedure to generate an error to Server Monitor. What can you do to prevent an error message?

   A. Pause Server Monitor.

   B. Stop Server Monitor.

   C. Use ADMIN /t n.

   D. Use the SHUTDOWN –NoError command.

37. You are running Microsoft Exchange Administrator from your workstation. You will be using Server Monitor to synchronize the clocks on ten Exchange servers. Whose clock will those servers be synchronized with?

   A. The server that is also a PDC

   B. The administrator's home server

   C. The administrator's workstation

   D. Any one of the ten servers

38. Because you have Web clients accessing your Exchange network, you feel the need to monitor the WWW Exchange service. What utility would best answer that need?

   A. Microsoft Exchange Link Monitor

   B. Microsoft Exchange Server Monitor

   C. Microsoft Exchange NT Event Viewer

   D. Microsoft Windows NT Performance Monitor

39. Your company has had problems with Exchange disk drives becoming full and stopping the IS service. What could you do to receive a warning before the IS reaches its limit again?

   A. Configure Microsoft Windows NT Performance Monitor to send you an email message when the Push Notification Cache Size has reached 100 percent.

   B. Configure Microsoft Windows NT Performance Monitor to send you an email message when the available disk space gets low.

   C. Configure Microsoft Exchange Server Monitor to send you a Microsoft Windows NT alert before the IS service stops.

   D. Configure Microsoft Exchange Server Monitor to send you an email message before the IS service stops.

40. Which of the following is NOT true for a differential backup of a database?

A. Backs up new data since the last full backup

B. Backs up modified data since the last full backup

C. Takes progressively longer each day

D. Takes less time than the incremental strategy

41. The diagnostic logging performed by Exchange services is written to this location:

A. Windows NT Event Log

B. \BIN

C. \exchsrvr\bin

D. \logging

42. Which of the following relates to information about a deleted Directory object?

A. RTS values

B. Retry timeouts

C. Bounce

D. Tombstone

43. Which of the following is required for single-seat administration of multiple Exchange sites?

A. RPC connections between sites

B. NNTP

C. POP3

D. X.400

44. Which of the following procedures could help recover significant disk space on an Exchange server?

    A. MTACheck

    B. Server Monitor

    C. Online IS Maintenance

    D. Performance Monitor

45. How would you use Exchange Administrator to group Exchange recipients by city?

    A. Create an address book view container

    B. Autonaming

    C. You cannot group recipients

    D. Delete the GAL and create Personal Address Books

CHAPTER

13

Connecting Exchange Sites

An organization can have more than one Exchange site for various reasons, including geographical layout, administrative needs, and network infrastructure. Sites must be linked with connectors to facilitate message transfer from one site to another. Communication between sites (*intersite* communication) is somewhat different than communication within a site (*intrasite* communication).

For intrasite communication, servers communicate directly with each other using either the MTA or DS. Messages are delivered through MTA-to-MTA communication, and directory information is exchanged through DS-to-DS communication. Both types of communication use the RPC protocol for component interaction. Manual configuration is not necessary for intrasite communication. All the servers on a site "know" each other through directory replication. They can communicate directly with each other because of the availability and speed of network connections required within a site.

Intersite communication requires configuration, but high-speed connections between sites are not mandatory. A software component, called a *connector,* must be installed at each site in order for messages to be passed between sites. When the connector software is in place, the MTAs of each site can send messages to the other sites. The MTAs handle the packaging and routing tasks, while the connector software manages the transportation of the messages to the other sites. Figure 13.1 illustrates intrasite and intersite communication.

There are two types of connectors: messaging connectors and the directory replication connector. Messaging connectors, as you may have guessed, manage the transport of messages. There are four messaging connectors:

- Site Connector

- X.400 Connector

- Dynamic RAS Connector

- Internet Mail Service (IMS)

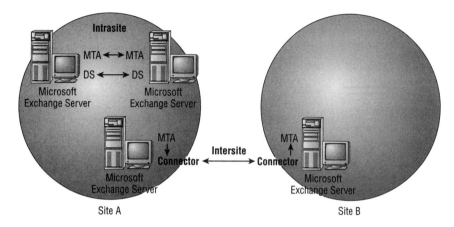

FIGURE 13.1

Intrasite and intersite
communication

The directory replication connector manages the transfer of directory information between sites. This connector can use any of the messaging connectors to transport its directory information to another site.

Some connectors can be used to provide interoperability between Exchange and non-Exchange systems (i.e., foreign systems). Examples of these connectors are the X.400 Connector and the Internet Mail Service (IMS). In this role, a connector can take an Exchange message and translate it into a foreign-system format for delivery to a foreign client. If a message is from a foreign system, these connectors can translate it into the Exchange format (see Figure 13.2). Chapters 14 and 15 will focus on connectors used in this role.

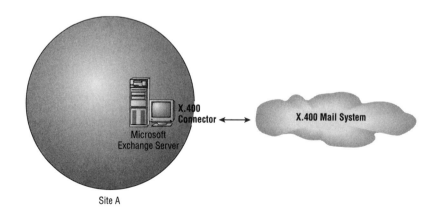

FIGURE 13.2

Connectors used for
interoperability with non-
Exchange systems

When an X.400 or an IMS connector is used to connect two Exchange sites, messages are still translated into the foreign format, but only for passage through the foreign system and for ultimate delivery to the other Exchange site. This temporary translation is illustrated in Figure 13.3.

This chapter will begin by discussing some of the common properties of connectors. We will then cover each of the messaging connectors, along with message routing and tracking. Finally, the Directory Replication Connector and design scenarios will be covered. The headings for these topics are:

- Common connector properties

- Site Connector

- X.400 Connector

- Dynamic RAS Connector

- Internet Mail Service (IMS)

- Message routing

- Connectors and message tracking

- Directory Replication Connector

- Design scenarios

Common Connector Properties

This section examines two connector properties:

- Address space

- Connector cost

Address Space

Each connector has a property called an *address space*. The address space is the set of addresses to remote mail systems or remote recipients to which the connector can send messages. Simply put, these addresses are the remote addresses that can be reached through the connector. A connector must have at least one entry in its address space. An address space entry is in the format of the remote messaging system. For example, if an Internet Mail Service connector is attached to a remote site named Detroit, which is a subdomain of Sales.com, the address space would include the entry:

Type	Address
SMTP	*@Detroit.Sales.com

The asterisk (*) before the @ sign denotes "all" recipients at this site; in the above example, all recipients at Detroit.Sales.com. If an MTA received a message addressed to a user at Detroit.Sales.com, the MTA would examine the routing table to see if there were any connectors with an address space to Detroit.Sales.com. If it found a connector with that address space, it would pass the message to it for delivery (note: routing will be covered later in this chapter).

A connector can also have address space entries to messaging systems of different types from the one used by the connector. For example, the IMS connector used in the previous example, can also be used to send messages to a remote X.400 mail system. In this scenario, the address space would look like:

Type	Address
SMTP	*@Detroit.Sales.com
X400	c=us; a= ; p=AcmeNet; o=Acme

The two address spaces in the example above, suggest that the IMS can deliver messages to the SMTP network Detroit.Sales.com, and can deliver messages to a X.400 network that must be on the other side of at least one other SMTP network, possibly Detroit.Sales.com. That last point is made because the IMS cannot directly connect to an X.400 network. If it could, there would be no need to create the X.400 Connector. But the IMS could be the next step, of possibly many, in the route to a X.400 network.

Address Space Scoping

A new feature in the 5.5 version of Microsoft Exchange Server is address space scoping. Scoping is the ability to limit the use of an address space to a certain scope, such as the entire organization, the site, a group of servers, or even a single server location. This feature gives administrators the ability to better manage routing.

Connector Cost

Two sites can have multiple connectors configured between them (see Figure 13.4). The connectors can be the same type (e.g., all Site Connectors) or different types (e.g., a Site Connector and a Dynamic RAS Connector). Multiple connectors between two sites can use the same network connection (e.g., a Token Ring network), or different connections (e.g., one connector can use a Token Ring network while another connector uses a RAS connection).

Multiple connectors can be used to increase fault tolerance and balance the load. When two or more connectors are configured between sites, messages can be delivered as long as any one of the connectors is available.

When the physical network is not a bottleneck, but message queues are backing up, multiple connectors on the same network can alleviate the traffic jam. Site-to-site traffic can be divided to balance the load among the connectors. When multiple connectors are used to balance the load, all of the connectors must have the same *cost*.

Cost is a property of a connector that denotes the connector's priority of use. The MTA uses costs as one of its criteria for selecting among a number of connectors. A connector can have a cost value of 1–100. The lower the cost, the more frequently the MTA will select it for message transfer (see Figure 13.5).

In this chapter, *local site* refers to your own site, and *remote site* refers to the site to which you are connecting.

Multiple connectors
between two sites

Connector costs

The MTA uses cost values of different
connectors as a factor in making routing decisions.

Site Connector

The Site Connector is the most unique of the four site connectors. The Site Connector is essentially a set of parameters that tell the MTA component how to transfer messages to another site. The Site Connector adds another role to the MTA. With a Site Connector installed, an MTA can perform inter-site communication in addition to intrasite communication.

Requirements

There are two primary requirements if the Site Connector is to be used:

- There must be a permanent, LAN-grade network connection between the two sites. No dial-up connections can be used with the Site Connector.

- The bridgehead server of the local site must be able to authenticate the bridgehead server of the remote site. A bridgehead server is a site server designated as the 'forwarding center' to a remote site (bridgehead servers are discussed shortly).

These requirements are discussed in the following sections.

Network Connection between Sites

Because the Site Connector uses RPC for intersite communication, it requires a permanent, LAN-grade network connection between sites.

This is the same mechanism used within a site. The Site Connector can also use any network protocol that supports RPC, including TCP/IP, IPX/SPX, and NetBEUI.

Service Account

When a Site Connector is used to transport information between two sites, an MTA in the local site must bind to an MTA in the remote site. To do this, the local MTA must use an account that is authenticated by the remote site server (in effect, the local MTA logs on to the remote site server). The account used for this procedure will depend on the cross-site authentication abilities of the two sites. Some common configurations are explained here.

Single Account / Same Windows NT Domain or Two Windows NT Domains with a Two-Way Trust Relationship

If both sites are in the same Windows NT domain, both sites can use the same Exchange site service account for intersite communication. If the sites are in different domains, the same account can be used if the domains have a two-way trust relationship.

Single Account / Two Windows NT Domains with a One-Way Trust Relationship

If two sites are in different Windows NT domains, a remote account can be granted the Service Account permission at the local site's Organization, Site, and Configuration objects. The local site's Windows NT domain must "trust" the remote site's Windows NT domain.

If two sites in two domains are using the same site service account and password, then the only action to configure the Site Connector is inputting the name of the remote server. (If the exam was to ask you for two actions to configure the Site Connector, the other action could be inputting the account and password to use when connecting to the remote sire.)

Designated Remote Account / Different Windows NT Domains

If an administrator does not want to use the same account or does not want to set up trust relationships, he or she can configure the Site Connector to use a designated remote account when connecting to the remote site. The designated remote account is specified on the Override property page of a Site Connector.

Messaging Bridgehead Servers

Certain servers in the local site can be defined as the servers that deliver messages to the remote site. These servers are called *messaging bridgehead servers* (see Figure 13.6). By default, all local site servers are bridgehead servers, which means they will all connect directly to the remote site. But the Site Connector can be configured to use specific servers as bridgehead servers. Use this configuration when not all local site servers have a network connection to the remote site. Non-bridgehead servers route messages destined for the remote site to the bridgehead servers in the local site. A bridgehead server takes responsibility for intersite routing so the non-bridgehead servers do not have to.

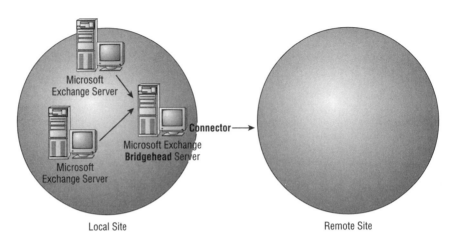

Target Server

A Site Connector will only connect to designated servers in the remote site, called *target servers*. By default, one server in the remote site is designated as a target server, but the target server list can be configured to have any combination of the servers in the remote site act as target servers (see Figure 13.7).

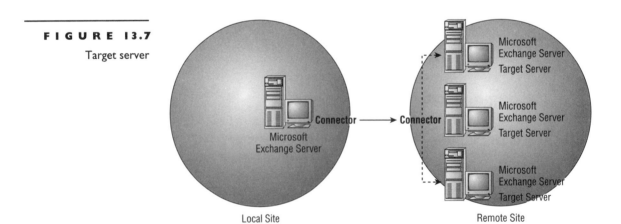

Because there can be several target servers in a remote site, you can set preferences for which server will be selected. Target servers are assigned costs between 0 and 100. The value 0 means that the target server is always to be used if it is available, and 100 means that the target server is to be used only if no other target servers are available. The remaining numbers, 1–99, provide a weighted average that the MTA uses when selecting a target server. For example, if one target server has a cost of 1, and another target server has a cost of 2, the first target server will be used approximately twice as much as the second one. Figure 13.8 illustrates the use of target server costs.

FIGURE 13.8

Target server costs

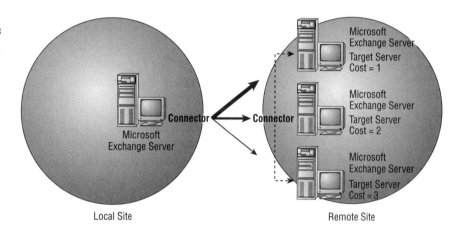

Do not confuse *connector cost* with *target server cost.* The MTA uses connector costs to choose between multiple connectors between two sites. Once a connector is chosen, the MTA can use the target server costs to determine to which particular remote server to send messages.

Site Connector Advantages

Two advantages of the Site Connector are its efficiency and its performance. High-speed network connections and the use of RPC permit information to be sent to another site without being converted to a different message format. Data can be sent directly to an MTA on the other site (just like it would be for intrasite communication). This is approximately 20% faster than the X.400 Connector, which must convert messages into a different format for transportation. The IMS also must convert information from the Exchange format (to SMTP format) to transfer data. Also, with the X.400 connector and the IMS, the connector at the other end must convert messages back to the Exchange format. Because both ends of a Site Connector connection use the Exchange format, no conversion is necessary, so performance is optimal.

The Site Connector is also the easiest connector to configure. Most of its configuration is automatic. It automatically uses the currently configured network protocol for message transportation. If both sites use TCP/IP, the Site Connector automatically uses TCP/IP to move messages. Other connectors (like the X.400 Connector) require a manual configuration of this setting. Another nice advantage of the Site Connector is that both sides of the connection can be configured at once. You do not have to go to the other site and manually configure it before site-to-site communication can take place.

Site Connector Disadvantages

The Site Connector does have disadvantages. It does not allow some of the configuration options that other connectors do. The Site Connector cannot be configured to make scheduled connections to another site, to restrict message size, or to prohibit specific users from using its connection.

Site Connector Summary

Table 13.1 summarizes the properties and requirements of the Site Connector.

T A B L E 13.1 Site Connector summary	Category	Site Connector
	Network connection required	High bandwidth (above 128 Kbps; LAN-grade connection, such as Ethernet or Token Ring)
		Permanent connection
	Data delivery method	RPC
	Transport protocols supported	Any protocol that supports RPC. Examples are TCP/IP, IPX/SPX, and NetBEUI.

	Category	Site Connector
T A B L E 13.1 (cont.) Site Connector summary	Message format	Exchange format
	Amount of configuration required	Minimal
	Cost associated with a connector (1–100)	Yes
	Messaging bridgehead servers	Yes (optional)
	Target servers	Yes (optional)
	Cost associated with a target server (0–100; 0=always use if available; 100=never use, unless no others available)	Yes
	Connection scheduling	No
	Delivery restriction/Control of user access	No
	Delivery restriction/Maximum message size	No
	Override of account used for connector authentication in remote site	Yes (default is site service account)
	Automatic configuration of remote site	Yes (optional)

Trip Analogy

Another way to explain the properties of a connector is to compare it to a trip. A trip takes you where you want to go, and a connector gets your information where you want it to go. This comparison will help you understand how to configure a connector. Table 13.2 compares a site connector to some of the aspects of a trip. The table also lists connector attributes and the property pages on which they are found.

	Trip Analogy	**Connector Equivalent**	**Connector Attribute**	**Property Page**
TABLE 13.2 Site Connector and the trip analogy	Name of this particular trip	Name of this instance of the connector	Display name; Directory name	General
	Destination of the trip	Name of the remote site	Target site	General
		Address of the remote site	Type; Address	Address Space
	Trip starting point	Name of the local bridgehead server	Messaging bridgehead in the local site	General
	Trip chaperon	User account used by connector to be authenticated by the remote site	The default is to use the Site Service Account	Override
	Cost of the trip	Cost of this connector	Cost	General
	Trip restrictions	(not applicable)	N/A	N/A
	Vehicle used for trip	Transport stack	The network protocol currently being used.	(Not applicable)

Exercise 13.1 walks through the steps for configuring a Site Connector. To perform these steps, you need another site to which you can connect.

EXERCISE 13.1

Configuring a Site Connector

1. In Exchange Administrator, navigate to and select the Connections container under the Configuration container.

2. Choose File ➤ New Other ➤ Site Connector. The New Site Connector dialog box will appear.

3. Enter the name of a server in the remote site. Click OK. Exchange Server will use that server to obtain information necessary to configure the Site Connector. When the connection is complete, all servers in the remote site will be target servers by default. You can later reconfigure any subset of the remote servers to be target servers. The Site Connector Properties dialog box will appear, displaying information about the remote site.

4. Click OK. A message box will appear asking if you want to create the Site Connector at the remote site. Click Yes. If you click No, you will have to connect to that site and configure that end of the connection.

X.400 Connector

The X.400 Connector is based on the CCITT X.400 standard. It includes many of the features the Site Connector has, such as the use of:

- Address space

- Connector cost

- Option to override the account used to make the connection

Each end of an X.400 connection must be configured with the name of one remote MTA to which it will connect. The local MTA name is assigned when an MTA transport stack is installed. Typically, the local MTA name is the same as the server name.

Microsoft
✓ *Exam*
Objective

**Configure connectivity to a mail system other than Exchange Server.
Connector types include:**

- X.400
- Microsoft Exchange Connector for Lotus cc:Mail
- Microsoft Mail Connector

(Note: the following section covers the first bulleted point above.)

X.400 and Site Connector Differences

The X.400 Connector has several differences from the Site Connector:

- **Network bandwidth required** The X.400 Connector requires only a low to medium network bandwidth.

- **Can utilize dial-up connections**

- **All data is transferred through messages** The Site Connector uses RPC to transfer data directly between servers. The X.400 Connector (because it was designed for use in large, multirouted network environments) always puts data into a message format for transportation.

- **Different transport stacks used** In addition to supporting the TCP/IP protocol, the X.400 Connector supports two other transport stacks: TP0/X.25 and TP4/CLNP. Each must be installed and configured through Control Panel/Network, and defined as an MTA transport stack in Exchange. Stacks are created using Exchange Administrator by choosing File, New Other, MTA Transport Stack. After a stack is created, an X.400 Connector can be installed and configured.

- **Remote site configuration is not automatic** Unlike the Site Connector, both sides of an X.400 Connector link must be manually installed and configured.

- **Must use messaging bridgehead server**

Additional Features of the X.400 Connector

The X.400 Connector has two main features that are not present in the Site Connector:

- Connection scheduling

- Delivery restrictions

Connection Scheduling

The X.400 Connector and the Dynamic RAS Connector allow connections to the remote site to be scheduled. This feature has four options:

- **Remote Initiated**   This option prevents the local connector from initiating a connection to the remote connector, but instead waits for the remote connector to initiate the connection. After the remote connector has finished sending messages to the local site, the local connector can send all queued (stored) messages to the remote site.

- **Never**   This option disables the connector.

- **Always**   Approximately every 15 minutes, the local connector initiates a connection to the remote connector and sends all queued messages.

- **Selected times**   The connector operates according to the schedule on the Schedule property page. Time intervals can be either 1 hour or 15 minutes.

Delivery Restrictions

The X.400 Connector has two delivery-restriction properties that give an administrator additional control over the connector's use:

- **Which users can use the connector**   The Delivery Restrictions property page allows an administrator to specify which users can use the connector and which users cannot use the connector. The defaults are:

  - "Accept messages from" all

  - "Reject messages from" none

- **Maximum message size allowed over the connector**   The maximum size of messages that can be sent through the connector can be set on the Advanced property page. The default is:

  - No limit

Figure 13.9 provides a graphical summary of the X.400 Connector.

FIGURE 13.9

X.400 Connector
properties

X.400 Connector Advantages

Advantages to using the X.400 Connector include its additional configuration options and its ability to connect to large multirouted networks. An organization can use a public X.400 network, as its messaging backbone. Figure 13.10 illustrates this scenario.

FIGURE 13.10

Using the X.400
Connector as a
messaging backbone

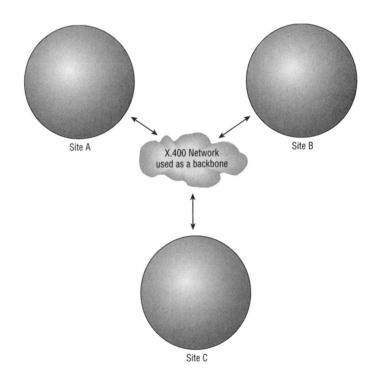

X.400 Connector Disadvantages

One of the X.400 Connector's disadvantages is the increased amount of configuration you may have to do. This is a "good news, bad news" situation. "Good" in the sense that you have a lot of options, "bad" in the sense that you must figure out how to configure them. Another disadvantage is the possibility of a message bottleneck at the bridgehead server. Because the X.400 connector must have a single, messaging bridgehead server at each site, bridgeheads can become bottlenecks if message traffic is heavy.

Creating and Configuring an X.400 Connector

Creating an X.400 Connector is done through the File menu, New Other submenu, and X.400 Connector option. Configuring this connector, like all objects, is done through its property pages. Many of this connector's properties have been mentioned, such as schedule and delivery restrictions. Those properties and many others are very straightforward to configure. But there are some properties that could require a discussion. The next couple of paragraphs cover those topics.

The name an X.400 Connector uses to identify itself to an X.400 network is the computer name the connector is running on. Having a long computer name could be a problem in some situations. If your X.400 network provider does not accept names as long as your server name, then your connector would not be able to connect. You could solve this problem by modifying the name used by the X.400 Connector. That is done through the Override property page and "Local MTA name" field. You would enter in this field a shorter name that would be used to connect to the X.400 network.

Another important parameter is the address designation of a remote host. As mentioned, the X.400 Connector can use a variety of protocol stacks (i.e., network protocols), such as TCP/IP, X.25, and TP4 (Transport Protocol 4; this is an Open Systems Interconnection, OSI, protocol). The address of a remote host must be entered into the X.400 Connector properties in the format used by the protocol stack. For example, if a X.400 Connector is using the TCP/IP stack, then the remote host address could be specified using any of the following naming conventions:

- **Fully qualified domain name (FQDN).** This naming convention would be used when a Domain Name System (DNS) is present.

- **NetBIOS name**. This naming convention would be used when the Windows Internet Name Service (WINS) is used.

- **IP address**. A dotted decimal IP address could be used for the remote host, an example being 130.20.1.101.

The address of a remote host is entered on the Stack property page of an X.400 Connector object.

An organization can use the X.400 Connector along with non-Exchange X.400 MTAs. This could be done for a variety of reasons, such as an X.400 mail system coexisting with or migrating to Microsoft Exchange Server. When this scenario is implemented, it might be necessary for both systems to use the same address space. That would make it possible for external mail to be routed to this organization through either the Exchange X.400 Connector or the non-Exchange X.400 MTAs. Because some of the external mail that will be received by the X.400 Connector could be for non-Exchange recipients, there needs to be a way to inform the Exchange environment that it is sharing the same address space with another system. That is done through the Site Addressing object, General page, and "Share address space with other X.400 systems" checkbox. Using this property allows Exchange to forward the X.400 mail not intended for Exchange recipients to the other X.400 systems in its organization. It also eliminates the Exchange server from generating unnecessary non-delivery reports (NDRs).

Summary and Comparison

Table 13.3 summarizes and compares the X.400 Connector and the Site Connector.

	Category	Site Connector	X.400 Connector
TABLE 13.3 X.400 Connector summary and comparison	Network connection required	High bandwidth (above 128 Kbps; LAN-grade connection, such as Ethernet or Token Ring)	Low to medium (64 Kbps to 2 Mbps)
		Permanent connection	Does not require permanent connection
	Data delivery method	RPC	Messages

	Category	Site Connector	X.400 Connector
T A B L E I 3.3 *(cont.)* X.400 Connector summary and comparison	Transport protocols supported	Any protocol that supports RPC. Examples are TCP/IP, IPX/SPX, and NetBEUI.	TCP/IP TP0/X.25 TP4/CLNP
	Message format	Exchange format	X.400 format
	Amount of configuration required	Minimal	Medium to high
	Cost associated with a connector (1–100)	Yes	Yes
	Messaging bridgehead servers	Yes (optional)	Yes (required)
	Target servers	Yes (optional)	Yes (defines remote connector)
	Cost associated with a target server (0–100; 0=always use if available; 100=never use, unless no others available)	Yes	Not applicable
	Schedules connections	No	Yes
	Delivery restriction/ Control of user access	No	Yes
	Delivery restriction/ Maximum message size	No	Yes
	Override account used for connector authen-tication in remote site	Yes (default is site service account)	Yes
	Automatic configuration of remote site	Yes (optional)	No

Dynamic RAS Connector

The Dynamic RAS Connector utilizes Microsoft's Remote Access Service (RAS) to connect sites. RAS is software that, along with the necessary hardware, enables dial-up network connections. The dial-up connections include modem connections over the normal telephone system, or Integrated Services Digital Network (ISDN), or X.25. The Dynamic RAS Connector can be used to connect two sites that both have RAS servers (see Figure 13.11).

FIGURE 13.11

Dynamic RAS Connector

Site A   Site B

In Figure 13.11, the RAS server is running on the same computer as the Exchange server and the Dynamic RAS Connector. A computer other than the Exchange server can be used to create a dedicated RAS server that processes calls from the remote site.

The Dynamic RAS Connector has many of the same features as the Site Connector and X.400 connectors, including:

- Address space

- Connector cost

- Option to override the account used to make the connection

The Dynamic RAS Connector has many features in common with the X.400 Connector. It can use temporary, scheduled connections between sites. It supports restrictions, such as which users have access to a connection. The Dynamic RAS Connector must be manually configured at both sites it is connecting.

Another feature that the Dynamic RAS Connector shares with some of the other connectors is the ability to override the Exchange MTA settings. It accomplishes this through the MTA Override property page of a Dynamic RAS Connector object. This page is especially important because this connector could be using an expensive dial-up connection. Modifying the MTA settings could help performance and lower costs. For example, a costly dial-up connection could experience frequent line errors, thereby causing long delays between connection retries and increasing connection costs. An Exchange administrator could reduce the delay between connection retries by increasing the "Open interval" of the "Connection retry values." The "Open interval" value is the length of time the MTA waits after an error before attempting another connection. Configuring this could be done on the MTA Override property page of the Dynamic RAS Connector object.

Unique Aspects

The RAS Connector uses a unique security feature called "MTA Callback." If MTA Callback is enabled, the local server initiates a call to the remote server. After the remote server answers the call, the local server terminates the connection. The local server then waits for the remote server to call back the telephone number defined in the MTA callback number field. For this connector feature to be used, RAS callback security must be enabled on the RAS server.

Another unique aspect of the Dynamic RAS Connector is its use of low-bandwidth network connections. Although performance will be compromised, this connector can work with a modem connection running at 64Kbps or less.

RAS Connector Advantages

The RAS Connector's main advantages are its use of temporary and low-bandwidth network connections and its additional configuration options (like scheduled connections and delivery restrictions). You probably will not use it for your main intersite connections. However, you can use it as a backup connection to provide fault tolerance.

RAS Connector Disadvantages

The RAS Connector's main disadvantage is that message transfer will be slow because it uses a low-bandwidth network connection.

Other disadvantages are that it needs a lot of configuration, and that both sides of a connection must be manually configured.

Summary and Comparison

Table 13.4 summarizes and compares the Dynamic RAS Connector to the Site Connector and X.400 Connector.

TABLE 13.4

Dynamic RAS Connector summary and comparison

Category	Site Connector	X.400 Connector	Dynamic RAS Connector
Network connection required	High bandwidth (above 128 Kbps; LAN-grade connection, such as Ethernet or Token Ring)	Low to medium (64 Kbps to 2 Mbps)	Low (less than 64 Kbps for a modem connection; also can use ISDN and X.25 connections)
	Permanent connection	Does not require permanent connection	Does not require permanent connection
Data delivery method	RPC	Messages	Messages
Transport protocols supported	Any protocol that supports RPC. Examples are TCP/IP, IPX/SPX, and NetBEUI.	TCP/IP TP0/X.25 TP4/CLNP	RAS supported protocols, such as TCP/IP, IPX/SPX, and NetBEUI.
Message format	Exchange format	X.400 format	X.400 format
Amount of configuration required	Minimal	Medium to high	Medium to high
Cost associated with a connector (1–100)	Yes	Yes	Yes
Messaging bridgehead servers	Yes (optional)	Yes (required)	Yes (this is inherent, because of the point-to-point topology of RAS)

	Category	Site Connector	X.400 Connector	Dynamic RAS Connector
TABLE 13.4 *(cont.)* Dynamic RAS Connector summary and comparison	Target servers	Yes (optional)	Yes (defines remote connector; called Remote MTA Name)	Yes (because of point-to-point topology of RAS)
	Cost associated with a target server (0–100; 0=always use if available; 100=never use, unless no others available)	Yes	Not applicable	Not applicable
	Connection Scheduling	No	Yes	Yes
	Delivery restriction/ Control of user access	No	Yes	Yes
	Delivery restriction/ Maximum message size	No	Yes	Yes
	Override account used for connector authentication in remote site	Yes (default is site service account)	Yes	Yes
	Automatic configuration of remote site	Yes (optional)	No	No

Internet Mail Service (IMS)

The Internet Mail Service (IMS) can be used for intersite communication. If there is an SMTP mail system between two or more Exchange sites, each site can use IMS to connect through that SMTP system to the other Exchange sites (as illustrated in Figure 13.12). The IMSs in two sites can also connect directly to each other.

FIGURE 13.12

Using IMS to connect
Exchange sites

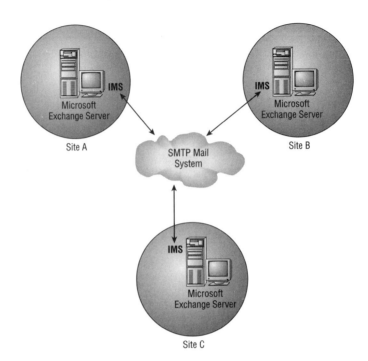

The IMS has many of the same properties seen in the other connectors, such as address space entries, connector costs, delivery restrictions, and configurable security for the remote-site authentication account.

Both ends of a connection must use TCP/IP. Using TCP/IP and an SMTP mail system is advantageous because these protocols are standards-based.

Using IMS to connect Exchange sites also has disadvantages. Data must be converted from the Exchange message format to the SMTP format to be transported over the SMTP mail system, and then reconverted back at the remote Exchange server. These conversions negatively affect performance. Another disadvantage is that the IMS does not allow the scheduling of connections unless a dial-up connection is being used.

Installation and configuration of the IMS is covered in Chapter 14.

Summary and Comparison

Table 13.5 summarizes and compares the IMS to the Site Connector and the X.400 Connector.

T A B L E 13.5 Internet Mail Service summary and comparison	**Category**	**Site Connector**	**X.400 Connector**	**Internet Mail Service**
	Network connection required	High bandwidth (above 128 Kbps; LAN- grade connection, such as Ethernet or Token Ring) Permanent connection	Low to medium (64 Kbps to 2 Mbps) Does not require permanent connection	Low to medium (64 Kbps to 2 Mbps)
	Data delivery method	RPC	Messages	Messages (SMTP)
	Transport protocols supported	Any protocol that supports RPC. Examples are TCP/IP, IPX/SPX, and NetBEUI.	TCP/IP TP0/X.25 TP4/CLNP	TCP/IP
	Message format	Exchange format	X.400 format	SMTP
	Amount of configuration required	Minimal	Medium to high	Medium to high
	Cost associated with a connector (1–100)	Yes	Yes	Yes
	Messaging bridgehead servers	Yes (optional)	Yes (required)	Yes
	Target servers	Yes (optional)	Yes (defines remote connector; called Remote MTA Name)	Not applicable
	Cost associated with a target server (0–100; 0=always use if available; 100=never use, unless no others available)	Yes	Not applicable	Not applicable

	Category	Site Connector	X.400 Connector	Internet Mail Service
TABLE 13.5 (cont.) Internet Mail Service summary and comparison	Connection scheduling	No	Yes	No, except for dial-up connections
	Delivery restriction/ Control of user access	No	Yes	Yes
	Delivery restriction/ Maximum message size	No	Yes	Yes
	Override account used for connector authentication in remote site	Yes (default is site service account)	Yes	Yes, optional security allows an NT account in the remote site to be specified
	Automatic configuration of remote site	Yes (optional)	No	No

Message Routing

The MTA is responsible for delivery of all messages that are destined for a server other than the one upon which they originated. The IS is responsible for local server delivery. Remote message delivery can be intrasite or intersite. For intersite delivery, the MTA will choose a message connector to transport the message.

If there is only one connector between the local site and the remote site, routing is obviously simple. If however, there are several connectors, the MTA will go through a selection process to choose a connector through which to send messages. During the selection process, the MTA reads a routing table called the *Gateway Address Routing Table* (*GWART*).

Gateway Address Routing Table (GWART)

Every connector installed on an Exchange server has an address space, which is the set of addresses that can be reached through the connector. The System Attendant (SA) on each server collects the address space entries for all the connectors on the server and places them in a routing table, called the Gateway Address Routing Table (GWART). Each server in the site exchanges its local GWART information with the other servers in the site, to compile one big site-wide GWART. This means that each site server, even if it does not have a connector homed on it, knows about the connectors it can use in the site.

The GWART can be viewed on the Routing property page of the Site Addressing object which is found in the site Configuration container. The Routing property page also contains a Recalculate Routing button that triggers a GWART rebuild. However, the routing table is automatically rebuilt whenever a change is made to a connector, so you should not need to use the Recalculate Routing function very often.

Each entry in the GWART displays the type of messaging system used at the remote destination, the address of the remote destination, and the cost to reach that destination. Some examples of GWART entries are listed here:

Type	Value	Cost
EX	/o=Widget/ou=Cleveland	2
SMTP	*@Detroit.Widget.com	1
X400	c=us;a= ; p=Widget; o=Miami	2

The EX type is the native Exchange Server address format which uses Distinguished Names (DNs). (Refer back to Chapter 2 for the discussion of DN addresses.) An SMTP or Microsoft Mail destination will have an address using the format of those foreign systems. An X.400 destination will have an Originator/Recipient (O/R) address (see Chapter 2 for a discussion of O/R addresses).

The GWART text file is stored in the \EXCHSRVR\MTADATA directory. The second most recent GWART is always available in a file named GWART1.MTA. If GWART0.MTA gets corrupted, GWART1.MTA can be used for a recovery.

Route Selection Process

The basic steps of the route selection process are outlined here:

1. A local MTA component receives a message for delivery to another site. The MTA temporarily stores the message in a queue while it determines a route for the message.

2. The MTA reads the destination address of the message and queries the GWART for an entry to that destination. If there is only one connector for that destination, the MTA passes the message to the MTA on that connector's server. If there are several entries, the MTA goes through a selection process. Although there are several criteria involved in this process (see note), a key factor is the cost of the route via each connector.

Various criteria may be used to select the route, including the precision of the address space match, delivery restrictions, and message size restrictions on eligible connectors. Also, if the MTA service of a connector's server is stopped, that connector will be bypassed during route selection.

3. After the MTA passes the message to the relevant connector and it is successfully sent, the MTA deletes the message from its queue and notifies the SA component of the successful delivery. The SA writes that information to the tracking log file.

   If the message is passed to a Site Connector and there are multiple target servers in the remote site, the Site Connector uses target server cost (a value used to weigh the frequency of target server use) to choose to which target server should receive the message.

4. If the message cannot be delivered, the local MTA sends the message back to the sending object with a Non-Delivery Report (NDR).

As you know, the MTA and connectors work together to move data between sites. Therefore it is not only the connector and its properties that must be taken into account when designing intersite communication, but also the properties of the MTA. Please see Chapter 12 for some of the properties of the MTA that relate to intersite design.

Microsoft
✓ **Exam**
Objective

Manage connectivity.

Connectors and Message Tracking

Chapter 12 discussed message tracking in an intrasite environment. Message tracking in an intersite environment is very similar from the viewpoint of an administrator. For intrasite message tracking, the MTA Site Configuration object must have message tracking enabled to allow administrators to use the Message Tracking Center to view the routes of messages (the Information Store Site Configuration object can also have message tracking enabled to track local server deliveries). For intersite message tracking, the connectors used to deliver messages must have message tracking enabled. An administrator can then use the Message Tracking Center to track message routing. The tracking utility is accessed through Exchange Administrator, by choosing Track Message from the Tools menu. After selecting a message to track, the Message Tracking Center will display the message's path from its origin to destination, as well as detailed information such as the message size and the time of day it reached each stop along the way.

Microsoft
✓ **Exam**
Objective

Configure directory replication.

Directory Replication Connector

In order for users to view the resources of a remote site (like mailboxes and public folders), directory information must be exchanged between sites. Unlike intrasite directory replication which is automatic and performed by direct DS-to-DS communication, intersite directory replication is performed by the Directory Replication Connector and must be manually configured.

The Directory Replication Connector uses an existing messaging connector to send directory information to a remote site.

The four primary steps to setting up directory replication between sites are listed here and then described in more detail in the following text.

1. Configure the messaging connector to be used for intersite directory replication.

2. Install a Directory Replication Connector for both sites.

3. Identify the directory replication bridgehead at each site that will be responsible for transferring directory updates.

4. Configure a replication schedule to determine how often directory updates will occur.

Message Connector Configuration

If the messaging connector to be used for intersite directory replication is the X.400 Connector, Dynamic RAS Connector, or IMS, the messaging connector must be configured for intersite directory replication. Specifically, it must be "informed" that the remote site it is connecting to is an Exchange Server site. If this is not done with these messaging connectors, the directory replication connection will not be able to use that connector for intersite directory replication. This information is specified on the Connected Sites property page of the messaging connector. Only the site directly at the remote end of a connection needs to be defined. The Site Connector does not need this particular information because it is only used to connect two Exchange sites (so you do not have to tell it that it is connected to another Exchange site).

Directory Replication Connector Installation

The Directory Replication Connector is installed using Exchange Administrator by choosing File, New Other, Directory Replication Connector. The instance of the connector that you have created will be stored in the Directory Replication container within the site Configuration container.

If the Directory Replication Connector will use the X.400 Connector, Dynamic RAS Connector, or IMS for its messaging connector, both sites must have their Directory Replication Connector manually configured. The information that will need to be supplied includes:

- Local bridgehead server

- Remote site name

- Remote bridgehead server

- E-mail address of the remote bridgehead server

When configuring directory replication between two sites on the same network that are connected with a Site Connector, the only information required is the name of the remote site. This option also allows you to automatically configure the remote site for intersite directory replication.

Directory Replication Bridgeheads

When you configure directory replication between two sites, you must choose one server in each site to be the *directory-replication bridgehead server*. All the servers in a site send their directory changes to their local bridgehead server. The local bridgehead server sends the directory information to the remote directory-replication bridgehead server. Only one server in a site can be assigned the duty to replicate with a given remote site. Several servers in one site may be responsible for directory replication with other sites, but no two can replicate with the same remote site. One server can, however, perform directory replication to more than one remote site. These scenarios are illustrated in Figure 13.13.

Intersite Directory Replication

Bridgehead servers must request directory replication information from remote bridgehead servers. Directory information is never automatically pushed to a remote site. The remote bridgehead responds to the request by sending the directory changes. This is in contrast to intrasite directory replication, where servers send a notification of new directory information to the other servers of their site. Those servers then request the new information.

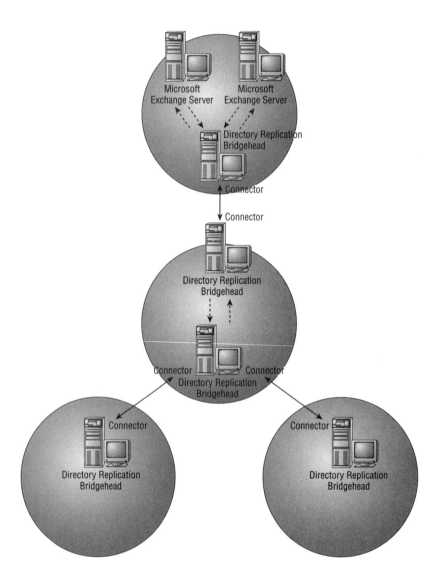

Scheduling Intersite Directory Replication

By default, intersite directory replication occurs every three hours. You can modify the frequency on the Schedule property page of the Directory Replication Connector object. This page allows you to configure the schedule that will be used to request directory updates from the remote bridgehead server.

The requests can be sent Never (disabling the Directory Replication Connector), Always, or at Selected times. Because the Directory Replication Connector uses a messaging connector to transport directory information in the form of a mail message, it is important to take into account the schedule configured on the messaging connector.

Transitive Connections

Directory information can be passed between two sites that do not have a direct connection, if those two sites have a third site in common. In Figure 13.14, Site A and Site C do not have a direct connection between them. But because they each share directory information with Site B, which shares its directory information with both Site A and Site C, all three sites will share the same directory information.

FIGURE 13.14

Transitive connections

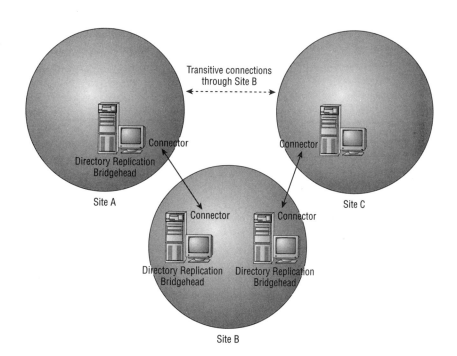

Forcing Directory Replication

Directory replication between sites takes place every three hours or during the configured schedule. When new directory information is created, you may need to force the update of the other directories. Use the Sites property page of a configured directory replication connector. All of the remote sites that this local site receives updates from are listed in the Inbound site listbox on this page. The Outbound sites listbox lists the remote sites that receive updates from the local site. To force a remote site to send its new directory information, highlight the remote site in the Inbound sites listbox and click the Request Now button.

Limiting Intersite Directory Information

Microsoft Exchange enables an administrator to determine what directory information will be passed to other sites. For example, an organization could use custom attributes on a per-site basis. If those custom attributes did not need to be seen in other sites, they could be excluded in intersite directory replication. Use the DS Site Configuration object and the Attributes page to deselect the attributes for intersite replication.

Microsoft ✔ *Exam* *Objective*

Configure the message transfer agent among sites.

Manage connectivity.

Diagnose and resolve connectivity problems. Elements include:

- Foreign connectivity
- Site-to-site connectivity
- Internet connectivity
- Connectivity within a site

Optimize foreign connections and site-to-site connections.

Design Scenarios

After gaining an understanding of connectors (and all the other earlier topics in this book), you now have much of the knowledge necessary to design intersite solutions. This section will describe some sample organizational scenarios and then present a viable intersite design for that scenario.

Scenario 1

Your company has ask you to design an Exchange environment. The company is in two buildings connected by a 33.6 Kbps dial-up connection. There are 20 users in one building, and 25 users in the other building. You find out that the vast majority of messaging will take place among users in their own buildings. What design would you use?

Option A: Single-site, one server

Option B: Single-site, a server in each building

Option C: Two sites, one server in each site

Since intrasite communication requires high-speed connections for RPC communication, Options A and B are out. Option C would work because of the localized traffic patterns and that the Directory Replication Connector can use a slower link.

Scenario 2

Your company has already implemented a multisite Exchange environment. You find out from the network administrator that Exchange is using an excessive amount of the network bandwidth between the two Exchange sites. That administrator also tells you they have noticed fairly large messages being sent between the sites. What could you configure to help solve this problem?

Option A: Limit message size for the MTA.

Option B: Limit outgoing message size for each mailbox.

Option C: Limit incoming message size for the IS.

Options B and C would have an affect on local delivery of messages, which is not the problem. Option A, however, would directly affect the intersite communication.

Scenario 3

Your Exchange environment consists of multiple remote sites. These sites are connected by an unreliable WAN that experiences a high packet loss. You want to configure Exchange to adjust to this reality. One possible adjustment is to decrease the amount of redundant data that is transferred because of a failed or interrupted WAN connection. You access the MTA Site Configuration object and its Messaging Defaults property page. You set a low checkpoint size that is greater than zero, and you set a high recovery timeout (see Chapter 12 and the MTA Messaging Settings).

Scenario 4

You manage a multisite Exchange environment. The sites are connected over a high-cost third-party WAN that charges you for connection time. Even though it is high-cost, there are a lot of line errors that result in transfer delays. The long delays hurt performance and increase connection costs. Until you can find a new WAN vendor, you decide to adjust the amount of time Exchange waits after a line error before it attempts to reopen a connection. You accomplish that by accessing either the MTA Site Configuration object or the Override page of the relevant connector and by increasing the value in the "Open interval" field.

Scenario 5

Your company has just installed 20 new Exchange sites. All of the sites are geographically dispersed but attached to a permanent WAN TCP/IP network. The physical infrastructure of the network is not reliable. Because bandwidth is at a premium, you decide you will schedule the intersite transfer of data at off-peak periods of network traffic. What connector type would you choose?

Option A: Internet Mail Service

Option B: X.400

Option C: Site Connector

Most people will probably choose Internet Mail Service. But that would not meet the design criteria because IMS cannot use scheduled connections (except for dial-up connections). The Site Connector also cannot use scheduled connections. X.400 would meet all the above design criteria. It can use TCP/IP as a transport stack. It can use scheduled connections. And it was designed to operate in a large network.

Scenario 6

Your organization has two Exchange sites connected by a 1.54 Mbps leased line and backed up by a X.25 connection. An X.400 Connector called X400-A uses the 1.54 Mbps line, and another X.400 Connector called X400-B uses the X.25 line. What could you do to ensure that X400-B is used only if X400-A is not available? The answer is: assign a connector cost of 1 to X400-A, and a cost of 100 to X400-B.

Scenario 7

Your organization is made up of five Exchange sites. The five sites are connected using a mesh topology (i.e., each site is connected to each of the other sites). X.400 Connectors are used to connect the sites. Each site also has an Internet Mail Service running. You want to make sure that all outgoing SMTP messages are only sent out of their sites through the IMS server, and not the X.400 Connector. How would you configure the connectors to accomplish that? The answer is: create an SMTP address space on each X.400 Connector, and assign it a cost of 100. An X.400 Connector can deliver SMTP mail. Because you don't want that in this scenario, you have to set a high cost for that to happen. When an MTA sees the two connectors that could deliver the message, it will choose the one with the lower cost. In this scenario, that would be the IMS.

Scenario 8

A company has brought you in as a network design consultant. The company currently has a host-based mail system with five remote locations. All locations are connected with a 56 Kbps network. This company will be migrating to Microsoft Exchange and wants you to recommend a design that will minimize network traffic during peak hours and yet optimize response time for users. Which of the following would you recommend?

Option A: Install a Microsoft Exchange Server at each location. All servers replicate directory information with all other servers and use X.400 Connectors for message transfer.

Option B: Install a Microsoft Exchange Server at each location. All servers replicate directory information with the main office and use X.400 Connectors for message transfer.

Option C: Install a Microsoft Exchange Server at each location. All servers replicate directory information with the main office and use Site Connectors for message transfer.

Option D: Install a single Microsoft Exchange Server at the main office. Clients connect by using remote mail or Web browsers.

The answer is: Option B. Placing servers at each location will dramatically increase user response time, as opposed to connecting over the 56 Kbps link. The X.400 Connector is used because it can be used with slower speed connections, it can also be scheduled to send data during off-peak hours. Configuring directory replication with only the main office lowers the intersite traffic.

Scenario 9

You will be installing two Exchange sites that will be connected with the X.400 Connector. You do not want administrators from one site to be able to administer the other site. What type of trust relationship, if any, would have to be established and what amount of account information would have to be exchanged between the two sites? The answer is: no trust relationship has to be established and no account information has to be exchanged. Each site has only to specify the Remote MTA name, which is the computer name of the other site's server running the X.400 Connector, and the Remote MTA password, which defaults to no password. Only if the remote site has entered an MTA password is there any need for information exchange between the two sites.

Scenario 10

Two of your Exchange sites are connected over a low-speed wide area network (WAN) that also experiences a high latency (i.e., long time for data to reach its destination) and packet loss. What two actions could you take to optimize performance given this scenario? The options put forth by other members of the network team are:

- Reduce the MTA checkpoint size.

- Increase the MTA message threshold.

- Use the Site Connector.

- Use the X.400 Connector.

One action would be to reduce the MTA checkpoint size. The checkpoint size is the amount of data transferred before a checkpoint is inserted in the data stream. A checkpoint is like a bookmark. If an error occurs that causes the message to be resent, the resend can start from the last checkpoint. Reducing the checkpoint size would have the effect of improving performance.

The other action would be to use the X.400 Connector because it is better at using a slower speed and unreliable connection.

Scenario 11

Two Exchange sites are connected over a WAN that charges for total bandwidth used and amount of time connected. How could you modify the MTA Messaging defaults to minimize your costs? Other network administrators suggest the following options:

- Reduce the checkpoint size (K)

- Reduce the recovery timeout interval (sec)

- Set the window size to zero

- Increase the message threshold

If you could do only one thing, which of the above would it be? The best answer would be to reduce the recovery timeout interval. That parameter sets the length of time after an error that the MTA holds the connection open before deleting the checkpointed data and resending from the beginning.

Summary

Connectors are software that can be used to connect Exchange sites. There are two main types of connectors: messaging connectors, and the directory replication connector. Messaging connectors include the Site Connector, X.400 Connector, Dynamic RAS Connector, and the Internet Mail Service.

Each connector contains a property called an address space, which is the set of addresses of remote systems that can be reached through that connector. Some of the other properties that a connector can have are cost, messaging bridgehead servers, target servers, and target server costs.

The connectors installed in a site are part of the site-level configuration and therefore can be used by all the servers in the site. When an MTA on a server receives a message for remote delivery outside the site, it references the Gateway Address Routing Table (GWART) to locate a connector that can be used to deliver the message.

The Directory Replication Connector is used to share directory information between sites. It uses a messaging connector for the actual information transfer.

Review Questions

1. Two Exchange sites are connected through the Dynamic RAS Connector. Even though your WAN connection is expensive, it has frequent line errors causing long delays between connection retries. You want to reduce the delay between connection retries. What option would you modify in the properties of the Dynamic RAS Connector?

   A. Checkpoint size (K)

   B. Disconnect (sec)

   C. Open interval (sec)

   D. Max open retries

2. If two sites in two domains are using the same site service account and password, then what are the only two actions that have to be performed to configure the Site Connector? (Select two.)

    A. Remote server name

    B. Local server name

    C. Account and password used to connect to remote site

    D. Local site service account

3. You want to use an X.400 Connector to send messages to a foreign mail system (i.e., a mail system not part of your organization). The computer name of your X.400 Connector bridgehead is 16 characters in length. But the foreign mail will only accept names up to 8 characters in length. What can you do to remedy this situation on your server?

    A. There is nothing you can do.

    B. Specify a window size of 8.

    C. Add a custom recipient to the X.400 Connector.

    D. Enter an 8 character name in the Local MTA field on the Override page.

4. When configuring the X.400 Connector, what format could a remote host name be in if your network was using the Windows Internet Name Service (WINS)?

    A. Fully qualified domain name (FQDN)

    B. NetBIOS name

    C. IP address

    D. Media Access Control (MAC) address

5. Two of your Exchange sites are connected over a low-speed wide area network (WAN) that experiences high latency (i.e., a long time for data to reach its destination) and packet loss. What two actions could you take to optimize performance given this scenario? (Select two.)

   A. Reduce the MTA checkpoint size.

   B. Increase the MTA message threshold.

   C. Use the Site Connector.

   D. Use the X.400 Connector.

6. Two Exchange sites are connected over a WAN that charges for total bandwidth used and amount of time connected. How could you modify the MTA Messaging defaults to minimize your costs? (Select the best answer.)

   A. Reduce the checkpoint size (K).

   B. Reduce the recovery timeout interval (sec).

   C. Set the window size to zero.

   D. Increase the message threshold.

7. The organization you work for has multiple Exchange sites. The site that you manage, named Research, engages in classified work. MIS management has asked you if there is a way to prevent other sites from seeing the directory information about the recipients in the Research site. But they also want the Research recipients to be able to view directory information from the other sites and be able to send and receive messages from those sites. Can you meet this requirement, and if yes, how?

   A. It cannot be done.

   B. Clear all directory replication attributes in the DS Site Configuration object.

   C. Use the X.400 Connector and set directory attributes to hidden.

   D. Configure the trust levels of all recipients in Research to a higher value than the other recipient containers in the other sites.

8. You need to configure directory replication between two sites. Those two sites do have LAN connectivity. What would you have to do?

   A. Configure directory export and directory import.

   B. Install a dirsync server and dirsync requestor.

   C. Install LDAP support on one server in each site.

   D. Define export containers and import containers on each site.

   E. Configure message transfer between both sites.

9. Your company has asked you to design an Exchange environment. The company is in two buildings connected by a 33.6 Kbps dial-up connection. Building A has 100 users. Building B has 125 users. You find out that the vast majority of messaging will take place between users in their own building. You would also like to minimize directory replication traffic. What design would you use?

   A. A dual-site design, with one Exchange server in each building.

   B. A single-site design, with one Exchange server in Building A.

   C. A single-site design, with two Exchange servers in Building B.

   D. A single-site design, with one Exchange server in each building.

10. Your Exchange site uses custom attributes that should not be replicated to other sites. How would you configure your site to accomplish that?

    A. Specify only the custom attributes in the DS Site Configuration object.

    B. Configure the trust level of your recipients container to be higher than the recipient containers in the other sites.

    C. Configure the permissions on the Directory Replication Connector to be only for the Domain Admins group.

    D. Specify all attributes except the custom attributes in the DS Site Configuration object.

11. You will be installing two Exchange sites that will be connected with the X.400 Connector. You do not want administrators from one site to be able to administer the other site. What type of trust relationship, if any, would have to be established and what amount of account information exchanged between the two sites?

    A. Establish a two-way trust relationship. No account information needs to be exchanged.

    B. Establish a one-way trust relationship in either direction. Both accounts must have the same name and password.

    C. No trust relationship is needed. No account information needs to be exchanged.

    D. No trust relationship is needed. Account and password information must be exchanged.

12. A company has brought you in as a network design consultant. The company currently has a host-based mail system with five remote locations. All locations are connected with a 56 Kbps network. This company will be migrating to Microsoft Exchange and wants you to recommend a design that will minimize network traffic during peak hours and yet optimize response time for users. Which of the following would you recommend?

    A. Install a Microsoft Exchange Server at each location. All servers replicate directory information with all other servers and use X.400 Connectors for message transfer.

    B. Install a Microsoft Exchange Server at each location. All servers replicate directory information with the main office and use X.400 Connectors for message transfer.

    C. Install a Microsoft Exchange Server at each location. All servers replicate directory information with the main office and use Site Connectors for message transfer.

    D. Install a single Microsoft Exchange Server at the main office. Clients connect by using remote mail or Web browsers.

13. Your organization has 20 Exchange sites. They are connected by a wireless WAN that experiences high packet loss. You want to reduce the amount of redundant data that is sent over the WAN due to failed or interrupted connections. What two actions must you take with the MTA properties? (Choose two.)

    A. Set a high recovery timeout.

    B. Set a low recovery timeout.

    C. Set a high checkpoint size.

    D. Set a checkpoint value of zero.

    E. Set a low checkpoint size that is greater than zero.

14. You have three remote Exchange sites. Those sites are connected by an unreliable network. The network protocol used is TCP/IP. You would like to schedule message transfer between the sites during off-peak hours. What connector would you use?

    A. Site Connector

    B. Microsoft Mail Connector

    C. Internet Mail Service

    D. X.400 Connector

15. Your organization is made up of five Exchange sites. The five sites are connected using a mesh topology. X.400 Connectors are used to connect the sites. Each site also has an Internet Mail Service running. You want to make sure that all outgoing SMTP messages are only sent out of their sites through the IMS server, and not the X.400 Connector. Which of the following would accomplish this?

    A. Create an SMTP address space on each X.400 Connector. Assign a cost of 100 to each SMTP address space.

    B. Create an X.400 address space on each Internet Mail Service. Assign a cost of 1 to each X.400 address space.

c. Create an X.400 address space on each Internet Mail Service. Assign a cost of 100 to each X.400 address space.

D. Replace the existing address space on each Internet Mail Service with SMTP address space. Assign a cost of 100 to each SMTP address space.

16. Your organization has two Exchange sites connected by a 1.54 Mbps leased line and backed up by a X.25 connection. An X.400 Connector called Connector A uses the 1.54 Mbps line, and another X.400 Connector called Connector B uses the X.25 line. What could you do to ensure that Connector B is used only if Connector A is not available?

A. Assign an override value for the time-out of Connector A.

B. Assign a cost of 100 to Connector A. Assign a cost of 1 to Connector B.

c. Assign a cost of 1 to Connector A. Assign a cost of 100 to Connector B.

D. Assign routing costs to all target servers.

17. Which of the following statements is NOT true for the X.400 Connector?

A. Requires a high-speed network connection

B. Can use TCP/IP

c. Can be assigned costs

D. Can connect through a public backbone

18. Which of the following is true for the Site Connector?

A. Sends information between sites in a message format

B. Can schedule connections

c. Permits delivery restrictions

D. Uses RPC

19. Using multiple messaging connectors between two sites can provide:

A. Fault tolerance

B. Load balancing

C. A foundation for multiple directory replication connectors between the two sites

D. Both A and B

CHAPTER

14

Internet Mail Service (IMS)

$\mathcal{S}$imple Mail Transfer Protocol (SMTP) is an important part of the Internet protocol suite. Many mail systems, including the Internet, are based on the SMTP standard, which defines message formats and determines transfer methods.

The Internet Mail Service (IMS) is a component that enables an Exchange server to also function as an SMTP server. An Exchange server with an IMS can send and receive SMTP messages just like any other SMTP server. The IMS converts and transfers messages between the Exchange and SMTP environments. To participate in an SMTP environment, the IMS must also work with other Internet protocols such as TCP/IP and Domain Name System (DNS). Figure 14.1 illustrates some of the protocols that are involved with the IMS.

The terms *server*, *computer*, and *host* are equivalent.

FIGURE 14.1

IMS and Internet protocols

In this chapter, you will learn about:

- Domain Name System

- Simple Mail Transfer Protocol

- How the IMS works

- Deploying the IMS

- Troubleshooting IMS

Domain Name System

In a TCP/IP environment, every computer is uniquely identified by a numeric identifier called an IP (Internet Protocol) address. To address a computer, a user needs to know that particular computer's IP address (e.g., 196.112.20.9). Remembering IP addresses is fairly easy in a small network, but it can be very difficult in a large network. Another way to identify computers (and one that is easier for humans) is to give them symbolic names, like SALES-HOST or ACCT-Server. A computer's symbolic name is also referred to as the *host name* or *domain name*.

Although it is easier for humans to work with domain names, the network still requires IP addresses to package and route data. DNS is used to bridge these two addressing schemes. DNS defines a database of domain names and information about those domain names, such as their IP addresses. The computers that hold this database are called DNS server. Programs, like client applications, can have the DNS protocol written into them to allow them to query a DNS server. Programs that query a DNS server are called DNS clients. For example, a user could use a domain name in an address, such as `widget.com`. This is convenient for the user, but the networking software on the client's computer needs an IP address for `widget.com`. Not to worry. The DNS client software will automatically query its designated DNS server for the IP address of `widget.com`. When the DNS client has received that information, the client's networking software can package and send the data.

The next three sections discuss the DNS hierarchy, distribution, and name resolution.

DNS Database Hierarchy

DNS uses a hierarchical structure to organize domain names, which makes it easy to locate and distribute database items. The top-level domains are high-level categories (not specific computers) used to organize the database. Examples of top-level domains are:

GOV   A government body

EDU   An educational institution

COM   A commercial enterprise

The subdomains (under the top-level domains) can be specific hosts (like ACME.COM). You can use another domain name to categorize and group several subdomain names. Using `Chicago.Widget.com` and `Detroit.Widget.com` as examples, COM is the top-level domain and Widget is a subdomain which contains the specific domain names of the computers in that organization (Chicago and Detroit). All three examples are illustrated in Figure 14.2. The DNS naming convention uses a bottom-up hierarchy, meaning that the most specific portion of a name (i.e., the lowest name in a hierarchy) is given first, the next most specific is given second, and so on, finally ending with the top-level domain name (also called a *DNS root)*. Each name in the path is separated by a period. The full domain path (bottom to top) to a specific host is called a *fully qualified domain name (FQDN)*.

FIGURE 14.2

Examples of domain names

In the DNS hierarchy, a domain name that is directly under another domain is called a *subdomain*.

Each entry in a DNS database has information associated with it. Most entries contain the IP address of that domain name. An entry may state the role of that particular host, such as DNS server, DNS client, or *mail exchanger* (MX). A mail exchanger is another name for an SMTP mail server. An MX record can have a weight value. Because a single domain can have several mail exchangers, DNS clients use the MX weight number to choose which MX to use for mail delivery. If there are multiple MXs, a DNS client will choose the MX with the lowest weight value. If that MX is unavailable, the DNS client will choose the MX with the next lowest weight value.

The Exchange server running the IMS will be configured in the DNS database as an MX entry. The IMS can receive SMTP messages sent to Exchange recipients; therefore, it is a mail exchanger.

The DNS hierarchy of domain names is referred to as the *domain name space*.

DNS Database Distribution

In a large environment like the Internet, storage restraints, administrative costs, and performance requirements make it impractical to store the entire global DNS database on a single machine. Various organizations store and administer different parts of the DNS hierarchy. Many DNS servers store parts of the DNS hierarchy, but do not perform administrative tasks.

Each DNS server has a list of other DNS servers it can query. Because an individual DNS server does not have the entire DNS hierarchy, it may receive client queries that it cannot resolve. When that happens, the DNS server queries other DNS servers until it obtains the required information. This procedure is called DNS *name resolution*.

DNS Name Resolution

When DNS client software is installed, it is configured with the location of a DNS server. The DNS client software uses this DNS server whenever a TCP/IP-based application addresses a remote computer using its domain name and in order to map the domain name to its IP address. This process is called *name resolution*. The basic process is outlined in the following steps:

1. A TCP/IP-based application addresses a remote computer using its host name.

2. The DNS client software (also called a *resolver program*) queries its DNS server for the IP address of that domain name.

3. If that DNS server does not contain the needed information, it will query another DNS server on behalf of the DNS client.

The IMS functions as a DNS client by querying a DNS server on behalf of Exchange clients sending messages to SMTP recipients. The presence of the IMS is established on the Internet or intranet because the Exchange server will have a DNS entry registered on DNS servers. This allows SMTP users to locate the Exchange server so messages can be sent to its recipients. Figure 14.3 illustrates using DNS in an Exchange environment with IMS.

FIGURE 14.3

IMS and DNS

SMTP Process

The SMTP process involves a TCP connection, a series of client-server commands and replies, and the use of spooling. We will discuss each of these in the following sections.

TCP Connection

When an SMTP client application sends mail to an SMTP server, it uses TCP to establish a connection with port 25 on the SMTP server. Port 25 is the application doorway on the SMTP server for mail activity. Once that connection is established, a series of commands and replies are exchanged between the client and the server. The connection is similar to a telephone connection, and the commands and responses are similar to verbal communication over a telephone connection.

SMTP Commands and Replies

Now we will examine the steps in the SMTP process (including the TCP connection). In this example, we will send a message. You do not need to remember the reply code numbers. They are included here merely to provide a complete picture.

1. A client establishes a connection with the server at port 25.

2. The server confirms the connection by replying with a 220 reply code, which means "ready for mail."

3. The client computer identifies itself to the server by sending the HELO command with the computer's identity (for example, HELO server1.acme.com).

4. The server confirms the HELO by responding with the 250 reply code (which means "all is well") and its identity. The server may also require a password or some other form of authentication.

5. The client sends the MAIL FROM command that contains the identification of the sender.

6. The server responds with the 250 reply code ("all is well").

7. The sender then sends the RCPT TO command (Recipient To) with the identity of a recipient of the mail message.

8. The server responds with either a 250 reply code or a 550 reply code (which means "no such user here").

9. After all the RCPT TO commands are sent (one command is sent per recipient), the client sends the DATA command indicating that it is ready to send the actual mail message.

10. The server responds with a 354 reply code (which means "start mail input").

11. The client, upon receiving the 354 reply, sends its outgoing mail messages line by line. The data must be in 7-bit ASCII format. If the data is in 8-bit format, it must be translated into 7-bit format using either Multipurpose Internet Mail Extensions (MIME) or UUencode (UNIX-to-UNIX encode).

12. After the data has been sent, the sender sends a special sequence of control characters (e.g., CRLF.CRLF) to signal the end of the transfer.

13. The client sends a QUIT command to end the session.

14. The server responds with the 221 reply code (which means that it "agrees with the termination"). Both sides of the communication close the TCP connection.

When you first read this process, it may seem complicated. However, after you review it, you will begin to see why it is called the "Simple" Mail Transfer Protocol.

SMTP and Spooling

The word "spooling" in this context means "storing." SMTP uses spooling to delay message delivery. For example, when a client sends a message addressed to another user, that message is spooled on the sender's SMTP server. The SMTP server will periodically check its spooled messages and try to deliver them to the relevant users. If it cannot deliver a message, the SMTP server will keep the message spooled and try to deliver it at a later time. When the recipient's server comes online, the SMTP server can deliver the message. If a message cannot be delivered within a time period set by the administrator, the spooled message is returned to the sender with a non-delivery message.

The advantage of the spool mechanism is that the message sender does not have to establish a connection with a recipient's computer in order to send a message. After sending a message, the sender can proceed with other computing activities because he or she does not need to wait online for the message to reach the recipient. The recipient also does not have to be online in order for mail to be sent to him or her.

IMS and SMTP

The IMS uses SMTP to send and receive mail from SMTP servers and clients. For example, an Exchange user, using Outlook, addresses a mail message to an Internet user (that Internet user might be represented in the Exchange address book as a custom recipient). The message leaves the Exchange client in the Exchange format. The IMS on the Exchange server uses the DNS protocol to resolve the recipient's domain name to its IP address. IMS translates the message to the SMTP format, and using SMTP, sends the message to the relevant SMTP server for spooling and delivery to the recipient. In this case, the IMS assumes the role of an SMTP client.

If an SMTP host sends mail to the IMS for delivery to an Exchange recipient, the IMS assumes the role of an SMTP server. After receiving the SMTP message, the IMS resolves the recipient address to the relevant Exchange address, translates the message to Exchange format, and hands off the message to the IS for delivery to the recipient. Both IMS roles are illustrated in Figure 14.4.

F I G U R E 14.4

IMS and SMTP

We have discussed how the IMS uses DNS and SMTP to participate in a TCP/IP-based mail system. We have seen how the IMS enables an Exchange server to perform as a DNS client, an SMTP client, and an SMTP server. We have also seen how the IMS acts as a gateway between Exchange and an SMTP system. In that role, it can translate messages sent from one system to another. In the next section, we will see how the IMS integrates with the other Exchange components.

How the Internet Mail Service Works

In this section, you will learn how the IMS interacts with other Exchange components so that Exchange recipients and SMTP users can exchange messages. Then you will learn about *address encapsulation,* which is the process of creating an SMTP return address for an Exchange sender who does not have one.

Sending Exchange Messages to SMTP Users

In order for an Exchange message to be sent to an SMTP user, the IMS and the other Exchange components complete the following process:

1. An Exchange user creates, addresses, and sends a message to an SMTP user. The user might address the message to an SMTP custom recipient in the GAL, or use a *one-off* address by typing the SMTP address directly into the message window before sending.

2. The Information Store (IS) on the Exchange server receives the message. The IS reads the DS and determines that the recipient is not local to that server. The IS then passes the message to the MTA for routing purposes.

3. The MTA compares the recipient's address with the Gateway Address Routing Table (GWART) and determines that the message must be delivered by the IMS component in that site.

4. If the IMS is local to the MTA, the MTA places the message in a folder in the IS specially designated for the IMS. If the IMS is on a different server than the MTA, the MTA sends the message to the remote MTA on the IMS server. The remote MTA then delivers the message to the IMS folder in the local IS.

5. The IMS picks up the message from the IS, and translates the message and any attachments from Exchange format to SMTP format. During the translation, the IMS references the DS to obtain the SMTP address of the Exchange sender. It uses the address in the FROM field in the header of the outbound message (this field is used by a receiving SMTP server to send back a message receipt or error message). The Exchange sender's SMTP address must be used because the native Exchange address, which is in the form of a Distinguished Name (DN), is not understood by SMTP software. If no SMTP address is available for the sender, the IMS will use a process called address encapsulation (which is explained in the next section).When the translation is completed, the IMS places the message in a subdirectory of the EXCHSRVR/IMCDATA directory, which serves as a temporary holding area for all outbound messages.

6. The IMS now acts as a DNS client, mapping the destination domain name to its IP address. It also acts as an SMTP client by establishing a TCP connection to the relevant SMTP server and participating in the SMTP mail exchange process by using SMTP commands and replies.

When an Exchange recipient is created, a number of foreign addresses (including an SMTP address) are automatically generated for that recipient. To refresh your memory, refer to Chapter 5.

Address Encapsulation

Along with the Exchange Client and Outlook, there are foreign clients that could use the IMS to send and receive messages from SMTP users. An example is a Microsoft Mail user connecting to an Exchange server through the Microsoft Mail Connector. If there is an IMS in the Exchange organization the MS Mail user is connecting to, this user could use the IMS to send messages to SMTP users.

Because the Microsoft Mail user does not have an associated SMTP address (assuming directory synchronization with Microsoft Mail is not being used, so there is no custom recipient representing the user), there is no SMTP return address for this user. The client's native address cannot be used in the FROM field of the message because the SMTP system would not understand that address format. To work around this problem, the IMS uses a process called *address encapsulation.*

The IMS takes a sender's native address and encapsulates it inside a valid SMTP address. The encapsulated address is placed in the FROM field of the message. If a reply or report message is returned from the SMTP system, the IMS can strip the original native address from the encapsulated address and deliver the reply or report message to the sender. The following is an example of a native Microsoft Mail address and how it would be encapsulated by the IMS:

Native Microsoft Mail address:

`MS:SPROCKETS/SERVER1/LJONES`

MS=address type of Microsoft Mail for PC

SPROCKETS=network name

SERVER1=post office name

LJONES=mailbox name

Encapsulated address:

`IMCEAMS-SPROCKETS_SERVER1_LJONES@CHICAGO.WIDGET.COM`

IMC=address type of Internet Mail Connector

EA=Encapsulated address

MS=address type of Microsoft Mail for PC

SPROCKETS_SERVER1_LJONES=encapsulated username

CHICAGO.WIDGET.COM=SMTP address of IMS server

If directory synchronization is enabled between the Microsoft Mail system and the Exchange system, Microsoft Mail users will be defined in the Exchange GAL and will automatically have SMTP addresses (making address encapsulation unnecessary).

Now that you understand the DNS and SMTP protocols and understand how the IMS works, we can deploy an IMS.

Deploying the Internet Mail Service

Once you understand the various protocols and processes, deploying an IMS is relatively simple. An IMS deployment can be divided into three stages:

- IMS preinstallation

- IMS installation

- IMS customization

Each of these stages will be explained in the following sections.

IMS Preinstallation

Before you install an IMS, you need to make some decisions, collect some information, and install and configure the TCP/IP protocol on the IMS server. You need to decide how many IMSs to install and which Exchange servers to install them on. You also need to decide what security to implement. You need to collect information about the SMTP network and the advertisement of the IMS server in DNS. Each of these topics will be covered in the following discussion:

- Using multiple IMS servers

- IMS security

- Connections to an SMTP network

- DNS information to be registered and collected

- TCP/IP protocol

Using Multiple IMS Servers

Although an IMS server can send and receive a large number of messages, some situations may require more than one IMS server in a site. You may need to balance the load or increase fault tolerance.

Load balancing can be accomplished by having one IMS handle all the outgoing messages, while another IMS handles the incoming messages. You may decide to have one IMS handle messages to and from a particular SMTP network, while another IMS handles messages to and from a different SMTP network.

Fault tolerance can be implemented by having two IMSs handle all message traffic to and from an SMTP network. If one IMS is taken offline for maintenance, the other continues messaging services.

IMS can be used as a site connector to connect Exchange sites over an intranet or even the Internet. Each site would have to have an IMS installed and configured with a connection to the other site or sites. This is discussed again under the section "Customizing the IMS" and the Connected Sites property page.

Once the number and purpose of the IMSs in a site is determined, you can decide on which specific Exchange servers to install an IMS.

IMS Security

Four main areas of security can be configured on the IMS:

- **Accepting and rejecting SMTP connections**   By default, an IMS accepts incoming SMTP messages from any IP address. However, if the IMS only needs to accept messages from particular SMTP servers, those server IP addresses can be entered into the IMS configuration and all other connection attempts will be rejected. (See Table 14.2 and the Connections property page.)

- **Limiting message size**   The IMS allows message size limits to be set for both incoming and outgoing messages. If an incoming message exceeds the message size limit, the IMS will not accept it. This prevents large messages from filling up the disk on the IMS server and helps prevent a "*denial-of-service*" attack. A denial-of-service attack occurs when someone sends so many service requests or so much data to your server that your server is overwhelmed and effectively shuts down. Another action you can take to prevent denial-of-service attacks is to configure IMS to reject connection attempts from unknown IP addresses (see first bullet point above).

- **Disable delivery of automatic replies**   Many client applications can generate automatic replies to messages (for example, an out-of-office message). If you do not want this type of message to be sent outbound over the IMS, you can block them on a per-outbound-domain or global basis. (See Table 14.2 and the Internet Mail property page and the Advanced options button.)

- **Restricting user access**   You can specify which Exchange users can and cannot send outbound messages through an IMS. (See Table 14.2 and the Delivery Restrictions property page.)

SMTP Network Connections

An IMS can connect directly to an SMTP server on an intranet or the Internet, or it can connect to an SMTP relay host that forwards mail to and from an intranet or the Internet. The connections between an IMS server and an SMTP network can be permanent TCP/IP connections, such as through a LAN. The connection can also be dial-up using the *Point-to-Point Protocol* (*PPP*) to encapsulate TCP/IP packets for transmission over a WAN. A dial-up connection can be made directly to an SMTP server, or it can be made through an *Internet Service Provider* (*ISP*) and then routed to the destination SMTP server. Dial-up connections may require additional hardware, such as ISDN equipment, and additional software, such as the Microsoft Remote Access Service (RAS). Some of the different connection options are illustrated in Figure 14.5.

DNS Registration

If your network is using DNS, then your IMS server will need a domain name and need that name registered with its DNS server. A domain name can be assigned from either your intranet DNS authority or, if connecting to the Internet, the InterNIC. The InterNIC is an agency that registers domain names on the Internet (the InterNIC actually delegates this task out to a private company).

F I G U R E   1 4 . 5

IMS connection options

1) Dial-up connection using PPP
   to encapsulate TCP/IP
2) Dial-up
3) Permanent LAN connection using TCP/IP

   Once your IMS server is assigned a domain name, that name, along with
the IMS computer's IP address, must be registered with your DNS server.
Your IMS server will also need to be designated within DNS as an MX (Mail
Exchanger). MX designates your IMS as an SMTP server. The insertion of all
this information ensures that SMTP clients and servers can locate and address
your IMS server and recipients. A common IMS scenario is one where Exchange
recipients can send mail through IMS to SMTP users, but SMTP users cannot
send mail to the Exchange recipients. The cause of this problem is usually the
lack of an entry in DNS for the IMS server, or incorrect information in the
DNS server, such as the absence of the MX designation for the IMS server.
   Your IMS server will also need to know the name of the DNS server it is to
use. The name and IP address of that DNS server must be entered using the
Network applet in the Control Panel of the IMS computer. This will allow
your IMS server to locate and address other SMTP clients and servers. If

Exchange recipients are not able to send SMTP mail addressed to host names (i.e., domain names), but can when using an IP address, then your IMS server is probably not configured to use DNS.

The following is another troubleshooting situation that relates to DNS. An Exchange user, Ann, sends a message through the Internet to another Exchange user named Bill at Bill@sprockets.com. Ann receives a non-delivery report (NDR) stating "Recipient Not Found: SPROCKETS.COM." You confirm that Bill's mailbox is configured with the e-mail address SMTP:Bill@sprockets .com. The likely problem in this situation is that sprockets.com is not registered in DNS.

As mentioned earlier, the above DNS procedures are only relevant if DNS is used in your network environment. If WINS or HOSTS files are used instead of DNS, these steps would be irrelevant.

The default domain naming convention that Exchange uses for a site is:

`site.organization.com`

For example, if a site name was Chicago, and the organization name was Widget, then the domain name of the site would be Chicago.Widget.com. An Exchange recipient on that network with the alias of JamesM would have an SMTP address of JamesM@Chicago.Widget.com. This SMTP address would be the return address in any outgoing SMTP mail sent from this Exchange recipient.

The default domain name of a site can also be modified through the Site Addressing object. For example, if the aforementioned address format needed to be changed from @Chicago.Widget.com to @Widget.com, the administrator would enter `@Widget.com` into the SMTP address type in the Site Addressing object. The administrator would even be given the option to have this new address format take effect for all current recipients or for only new recipients. If the former option was chosen, the return SMTP address for the above example would be JamesM@Widget.com.

The format of the SMTP user names can also be modified. For example, the example above, JamesM, was determined because that is the alias of our user James Madison. If all future recipients needed to have a return SMTP address of <first name><last name>, such as JamesMadison@Widget.com, then the Auto Naming feature of Exchange Administrator (Tools/Options) could be used to set alias name generation to %first%last. Modifying Auto Naming does not modify the current recipients' names, only newly created ones. The current recipients would have to have their SMTP e-mail addresses manually changed through their own E-mail Addresses property page.

TCP/IP Protocol

Because SMTP and DNS are part of the TCP/IP protocol suite, they must use the TCP/IP transport stack to transmit and route data. A TCP/IP transport stack must be loaded and configured on the server on which the IMS will be installed (normally, the stack included with Windows NT is used). As part of the installation process of this stack, the IP address, host name, and domain name of that server (the Exchange server) will be defined. The DNS server (or servers) that will be used is also specified. The IP address of the IMS server can be obtained from an organization's intranet authority, from an ISP, or from the Internet authority, the InterNIC.

After you have made the necessary decisions and all your information is collected, you can install the IMS.

Installing an IMS

An IMS is installed using the Internet Mail Wizard. Once installed, an IMS can be stopped and started using Control Panel/Services.

The Internet Mail Wizard provides an easy way to install and configure the IMS. Access the Wizard in Exchange Administrator by choosing File, New Other, Internet Mail Service. The Wizard presents a series of dialog boxes containing questions, options, and input fields. When the Wizard is finished, the IMS will be installed and configured. Table 14.1 describes the dialog boxes that the Wizard presents (pages are referenced according to the information they contain).

T A B L E 14.1 Internet Mail Wizard pages	**Wizard Dialog Box**	**Description**
	Welcome page	This page describes what the Wizard will do.
	Information page	This page states that TCP/IP must be installed, tells what to do if the IMS will be using DNS, and gives information about using a dial-up connection. See Figure 14.6.
	Select the Exchange server	This page lets you specify the Exchange server on which to install the IMS. This page is also where you specify that Internet mail is to be sent through a dial-up connection.
	Dial-up	This page is only displayed if the dial-up connection option was chosen on the preceding page. The Remote Access Service must also be configured on the server that will be running the IMS. An RAS phone book entry for the connection to the remote SMTP server or ISP will need to be configured. The phone book entry must be enabled for TCP/IP.
	How IMS will send mail	There are two options for sending mail: • Use DNS to resolve recipient domain names to their IP addresses. • Use a single SMTP host, called a *relay host,* to send all outbound SMTP messages. The relay host resolves addresses and delivers messages. Figure 14.7 shows this page and Figure 14.8 illustrates the use of a relay host.
	Restrict connections to specified addresses	By default, the IMS will send messages to any SMTP addresses. But it can be configured to send messages to only selected SMTP addresses.
	Addressing for Exchange clients	Use this page to configure the SMTP naming convention that will be used for Exchange recipients. For example, the SMTP address for an Exchange recipient with the alias name Lisa, in an Exchange site named Chicago, in an organization named Widget, would be Lisa@Chicago.Widget.com. This address would be placed in the FROM address field in an outgoing SMTP message header.

TABLE 14.1 (cont.)	**Wizard Dialog Box**	**Description**
Internet Mail Wizard pages	Administrator mailbox	Notifications of SMTP Non-Delivery Reports will be sent to this mailbox. Note that a DL or public folder could be specified here instead of a mailbox.
	Site service account password	The password of the site service account.
	Install page	When the Finish button is selected on this page, the Internet Mail Wizard will install the IMS. The IMS Wizard will: <ul><li>Create an IMS directory object in the site where the IMS is installed.</li><li>Trigger a recalculation of the routing tables in the site where the IMS is installed.</li><li>Configure the IMS to start automatically and start the service.</li></ul>

FIGURE 14.6

Information page of the Internet Mail Wizard

FIGURE 14.7

How IMS Will Send Mail
page

FIGURE 14.8

IMS using a relay host

1) All outbound messages are sent to a relay host.
2) The relay host submits the messages to the
   appropriate recipient hosts.

Exercise 14.1 outlines the steps necessary to start the Internet Mail Wizard
and proceed through its pages. If your Exchange server does not have TCP/IP
installed or does not have a DNS server designated, you will not be able to
perform the final step of the Wizard (the actual IMS installation).

EXERCISE 14.1

Executing the Internet Mail Wizard

1. In Exchange Administrator, choose File ➤ New Other ➤ Internet Mail Service. If the focus is not on the Connections container, an information dialog will appear asking if you would like to switch to the Connections container. If you see this dialog, click OK.

2. Read the Welcome page and click Next.

3. Read the next page, which provides information and describes preinstallation steps you may need to do. When you are done, click Next.

4. The next page lets you choose the Exchange server on which the IMS will be installed. Choose your server if it is not already selected. Click Next.

5. The next page asks you to designate how the IMS will deliver messages. For this exercise, leave the default (which is to use the domain name system (DNS) to send mail). Click Next.

6. Use the next page to restrict the SMTP addresses to which the IMS will send outbound messages. The default is to accept all outbound Internet mail. Leave the default setting, and click Next.

7. The next page lets you specify the domain name to be used in Exchange recipient SMTP addresses. Leave the default, and click Next.

8. The Internet Mail Wizard next prompts you for the Exchange mailbox to which the IMS will send notifications of Non-Delivery Reports. Choose the Select a mailbox or distribution list option. Then click Select. Choose one of the mailboxes you previously created, such as George Washington. Click OK, then click Next.

9. The next page will prompt you to enter the password for the Exchange site service account. If you used the password in Chapter 4, enter 12*12. If you used a different password, enter that password. Then click Next.

10. The final page will inform you that the Wizard is finished gathering information and is now ready to install the Internet Mail Service. Click Finish. If some of the necessary components were not installed or configured (like TCP/IP or a DNS server), an error message will appear.

Customizing the IMS

The Internet Mail Service is represented as an object in the Exchange hierarchy under the Connections container. It can be customized using the properties of this object. Table 14.2 lists the property pages of the IMS object and describes some of the attributes that can be customized on those pages.

TABLE 14.2 Property pages of the IMS object	Property Page	Attributes
	General	Specifies the maximum message size of messages that can pass through this IMS.
	Connected Sites	Displays the other Exchange sites that can receive SMTP mail from this IMS. If two sites are to be directly connected using IMS, the remote Exchange site must be entered into this page in order for directory replication to take place. Indirectly connected sites are automatically listed through the directory replication process.
	Address Space	Lists the remote addresses (the address space) to which this IMS component can send messages. By default, IMS will deliver SMTP mail to all SMTP addresses. But this page could be used to restrict outgoing mail delivery. For example, you could restrict IMS to only deliver outgoing SMTP mail that is addressed to users in the domain Acme.com. To do that, you would enter *@Acme.com into the Address Space property page and have that as the only entry. You could also restrict SMTP mail delivery to a single user, such as bob@Acme.com. In that scenario, IMS would only deliver SMTP mail if it was addressed to bob@Acme.com.
	Dial-up Connections	Contains the attributes for connection and schedule information when using RAS to connect the IMS to a remote SMTP server or an Internet Service Provider (ISP). The default IMS dial-up schedule is every four hours, but that can be modified. If a permanent dial-up connection is needed, the schedule can be set to "All day." This page also allows the use of the ETRN protocol. The IMS server can use an ETRN command to inform the remote SMTP server to start sending messages queued up for delivery to the IMS. If connecting to an Internet Service Provider (ISP) that requires ETRN, ETRN must be used with IMS. If however, ETRN is not supported on your ISP, you must use a different means to dequeue mail.

T A B L E 14.2 (cont.) Property pages of the IMS object	**Property Page**	**Attributes**
	Connections	Lists the attributes used to send and receive messages, such as transfer mode, message delivery method, connections to accept, retry intervals, and message time-out options. This page also allows you to configure IMS to send all outgoing SMTP mail to a designated relay host. That option was present during the Internet Mail Wizard, but can also be configured later through this page.
	Queues	Displays the queues that hold inbound and outbound SMTP messages. Used to monitor and troubleshoot SMTP messages.
	Routing	Contains the options "Do not reroute incoming SMTP mail," and "Reroute incoming SMTP mail (required for POP3/IMAP4 support)." Also contains a configurable routing table that specifies routing locations for designated addresses.
	Security	IMS connections to other SMTP servers can be configured to use SASL, SSL encryption, or Windows NT Challenge/ Response authentication and encryption. SASL stands for Simple Authentication Security Layer. SASL is a standard authentication method used between SMTP clients and servers. This page allows it to be used as a security mechanism between IMS and other SMTP servers.
	Delivery Restrictions	IMS can be configured to restrict the recipients who can send SMTP mail through this IMS. The default is to allow any user in the organization to send mail out through the IMS.
	Advanced	Allows the administrator to handle messages in the IMS outbound queue, such as number and length of time for queued but unsent messages, transfer timeouts, and the total allowable size of queued messages in the outbound queue.
	Diagnostic Logging	Sets which IMS events will be written to the Windows NT Event Log.

T A B L E 14.2 (cont.)	**Property Page**	**Attributes**

Property pages of the IMS object	Internet Mail	Includes the following attributes:
		• **Administrator's mailbox** Lists the mailbox or DL to be used as the IMS administrator's mailbox. Delivery status messages will be sent to this mailbox. The mailbox designated for this function was inputted in the Internet Mail Wizard, but can be changed on this page.
		• **Notification** Enables the configuring of notification messages when a non-delivery report (NDR) is generated.
		• **Message Content** (of outbound attachments) Options include MIME, with plain text or HTML, and UUENCODE, with or without Binhex.
		• **Character Sets** (for MIME and non-MIME)
		• **Clients support S/MIME signatures.** Can be enabled or disabled.
		• **Convert inbound messages to fixed-width font.** Can be enabled or disabled.
		• **Enable message tracking.**
		• **Advanced options** Options include:
		   • Send Microsoft Exchange rich text formatting. Options are: Always; User (which means rich text formatting will only be sent for the recipients the sender has specified); and Never.
		   • Disable Out Of Office responses to the Internet
		   • Disable Automatic Replies to the Internet
		   • Disable sending Display names to the Internet
		• **E-Mail Domain** This button allows you to make different configuration settings for specific domains. Settings like the maximum message size and encoding method can be set for a specific domain.

After any change is made to the IMS configuration, the IMS service must be stopped and restarted for the changes to take effect. In Exercise 14.2, you will use some of the property pages of the IMS object.

EXERCISE 14.2

Using the Property Pages of the IMS Object

1. In Exchange Administrator, highlight the Connections container. In the contents pane, you will see the IMS object you created in Exercise 14.1. Double-click on the IMS object. The property pages of the object will appear.

2. On the General page, set a maximum message size for messages traveling through the IMS.

3. Click on the Delivery Restrictions page, then restrict Andrew Jackson from using the IMS.

4. Click on the Internet Mail page, then change the administrator's mailbox from George Washington to James Madison.

5. Explore the other property pages. When you are finished, click OK to save and exit, or click Cancel to exit without saving.

Troubleshooting IMS

If problems occur when messages are sent or received through the IMS, one of the first troubleshooting steps you can take is to view the IMS queues. Information about a message can help you determine why it is not being properly sent or received. The IMS queues, details about messages in those queues, deleting a message, message tracking, and forcing a retry will be covered in the following sections.

IMS Queues

The Queues property page of the IMS object permits you to access the three IMS queues:

- **MTS Out queue**   This queue receives messages from the MTA on the Exchange server that is running the IMS. These messages are being sent from Exchange users to SMTP recipients.

- **OUT queue**   Messages are sent from this queue to SMTP recipients.

- **IN queue**   This queue receives messages from an SMTP system. These messages are converted to the Exchange format and passed to the Information Store. The MTA retrieves them from the IS and delivers them to the intended Exchange recipient.

After you have selected a queue, you can view details on any message in that queue.

Message Details

If you highlight a message, you can choose the Details button to view the following information about that message:

- Originator

- MTS-ID (Identifies the component that sent the message; it is only available in the MTS queue.)

- Destination host

- Submit time

- Size (in kilobytes)

- Next retry time (Appears only when an attempt to send the message has failed.)

- Retries (Number of times the IMS has attempted to send the message.)

- Expiration (When retries will stop.)

- Recipients (Includes the status of message delivery attempts.)

Detailed information about a queued message can help you track down the reason why it is not being delivered correctly.

Deleting a Message

If a message is hindering the operation of a queue, that message can be deleted. Highlight the message and click Delete. A Non-Delivery Report (NDR) will be sent to the sender of the message.

Message Tracking

As stated in Table 14.2, message tracking can be enabled for the IMS through its Internet Mail property page. Because the IMS works with other Exchange components, tracking an outgoing message sent to an SMTP user can entail other components, such as the Information Store and the Message Transfer

Agent. When an Exchange recipient sends a message destined for an SMTP user, that message is first delivered to the IS. The IS will recognize that the message is for remote delivery and will pass it to the MTA for routing and connector selection. Consequently, to track a message sent to an SMTP network, the IS, MTA, as well as the IMS must be enabled for message tracking.

Forcing a Retry

An administrator can manually force the IMS to retry delivery of a message. To do so, highlight the message and click Retry Now.

Summary

The Domain Name System (DNS) protocol creates a hierarchical, distributed database of domain names and information. These distributed databases reside on computers called DNS servers. When addressing computers on a TCP/IP-based network, you can use domain names instead of IP addresses. DNS client software, also called a resolver program, can query the DNS server for the IP address of a particular domain name. The client's TCP/IP stack can then use the IP address to address and route data. The Exchange Internet Mail Service (IMS) can use DNS to resolve names in outbound SMTP messages and deliver them to the correct SMTP server.

Simple Mail Transfer Protocol (SMTP) defines the mechanism for applications to exchange mail messages. Part of the SMTP mechanism is a series of commands and replies between an SMTP client and an SMTP server. The IMS enables an Exchange server to be both an SMTP client when it sends messages to an SMTP network and an SMTP server when it receives SMTP messages for delivery to Exchange recipients.

The IMS works with the other Exchange components to process Exchange messages that are sent to SMTP users. These components also process messages sent from SMTP users to Exchange users. Translating message formats from one system to another is an important part of this process.

If a client sending through Exchange does not have an SMTP address that can be used in the FROM field of an outgoing message, the IMS will encapsulate the client's address into an SMTP address.

Implementing IMS involves three main stages:

- **Preinstallation**   In this stage, you gather information (such as the IP address of the DNS server that the IMS will use).

- **Installation**   In this stage, you execute the Internet Mail Wizard to install and configure the IMS.

- **Customization**   In this stage, you can modify IMS settings and set advanced options.

Review Questions

1. An IMS server sends mail to a Domain-A and a Domain-B. As IMS administrator, you begin to receive reports that Exchange e-mail attachments sent to Domain-B have been arriving as unreadable text. You investigate and find out that the problem does not exist with attachments sent to Domain-A. You also find out that Domain-A uses MIME while Domain-B uses UUENCODE. How would you fix this problem?

   A. Use the Internet Mail property page and designate UUENCODE as the encoding method for Domain-B.

   B. Use the Internet Mail property page and designate MIME as the encoding method for Domain-A.

   C. Configure Domain-B for SSL.

   D. Configure IMS for SASL.

2. The Internet Mail Service is installed and configured on your network. Exchange recipients can send mail through IMS to SMTP users, but SMTP users cannot send mail to the Exchange recipients. You verify that your IMS server is accessible from the Internet. What is the most likely cause of the problem?

   A. Your firewall is not open to port 110 (POP3).

   B. Your firewall is not open to port 25 (SMTP).

   C. Your client computers are not configured with TCP/IP.

   D. Your client computers are not directly connected to the Internet.

   E. Your domain has no MX record in DNS.

3. You want to restrict delivery of mail from your Internet Mail Service. You want only the recipient terry@retail.com to receive mail from your IMS. What address space would you add to the Internet Mail Service?

   A. *

   B. SMTP*@retail.com

   C. SMTP *@retail.com

   D. SMTP:terry@retail.com

4. You want to change the SMTP addresses of your Exchange recipients from <first name><last initial>@server1.com, to <first name><last name> @server1.com. How would you do that?

   A. Address Space property page

   B. Routing property page

   C. Tools/Options and Auto Naming

   D. One-Off addressing

5. The current fully qualified domain name (FQDN) of your site is server1.highfinance.com. The default Internet mail address for recipients is <alias>@server1.highfinance.com. You need to change the default address to <alias>@highfinance.com. How would you do that?

   A. Use Directory Import.

   B. Modify the Site Addressing properties.

   C. Modify the One-Off Internet addressing template.

   D. Configure default alias name generation.

6. Your Exchange environment uses IMS to send and receive SMTP mail with a company named Sockets & Wrenches. Sockets & Wrenches uses a host-based SMTP mail system. When users on your system send mail to the name of the host at Sockets & Wrenches, it is not delivered. But if those users use an IP address for addressing, the mail is delivered. You are informed that other systems can send mail to Sockets & Wrenches using a host name in the addressing. What should you do to enable your users to be able to send mail to Sockets & Wrenches using a host name in the addressing? (Select the best answer.)

   A. Configure a DNS server in the TCP/IP network configuration on your server.

   B. Configure a HOSTS file on each client.

   C. Configure an LMHOSTS file on each client.

   D. Configure IMS to forward all mail to Sockets & Wrenches.

7. As administrator of an Exchange site with Internet Mail Service, you have been asked to have all outgoing SMTP mail sent to a single SMTP relay host. How should you configure the Internet Mail Service?

   A. Enter the SMTP relay host as an MX record in the DNS.

   B. Enter the SMTP relay host as a CN record in the DNS.

   C. Enter the SMTP relay host in the Internet Mail Service properties.

   D. Make the SMTP relay host the default gateway in the TCP/IP settings of your IMS computer.

8. Your Internet Mail Service uses a dial-up connection to a remote SMTP server. How would you configure the dial-up connection so it could send messages at all times?

   A. Use the Internet Mail Service to configure the dial-up connection page and set the schedule to All Day.

   B. Use the RAS server with a schedule of Always.

   C. Use the Dynamic RAS Connector with a schedule of Always.

   D. Use the RASDial utility to have the connection open at startup.

9. You need the Internet Mail Service to connect two Microsoft Exchange sites over the Internet. These two sites also exchange mail with other SMTP servers on the Internet. How would you configure the connection between these two sites?

   A. In the Internet Mail Service, configure the sites as connected sites.

   B. Have both servers use the same relay host.

   C. Configure the Internet Mail Service to secure all outbound connections.

   D. Configure a Point-to-Point Tunneling protocol (PPTP) connection between the two sites.

10. Your site uses the Internet Mail Service to exchange messages with the Internet. After researching the topic of security, you decide you should take measures to prevent denial-of-service attacks. What two actions should you take?

    A. Use a relay host rather than DNS.

    B. Disable AutoReply to the Internet.

    C. Set size limits for all incoming messages.

    D. Restrict the users who can send outgoing messages.

    E. Configure your firewall to prevent all port 25 (SMTP) traffic.

    F. Reject connection attempts from unknown IP addresses.

11. You are the administrator of an Internet Mail Service. Some of your users report that their e-mail attachments sent to lawfirm.com arrive unreadable. Mail sent to other domains arrives intact and readable. You investigate and learn that the other domains are using MIME, and that lawfirm.com is using only UUENCODE. What can you do so that e-mail attachments sent to both lawfirm.com and other domains are readable?

    A. Use the E-Mail Domain option in Internet Mail Service to use MIME for all domains except lawfirm.com.

    B. Use the E-Mail Domain option in Internet Mail Service to use UUEN-CODE for lawfirm.com.

    C. All users who send attachments to lawfirm.com must add their destination addresses in their Personal Address Books and specify that only MIME is to be used.

    D. All users who send attachments to lawfirm.com must add their destination addresses in their Personal Address Books and specify that only UUENCODE is to be used.

12. Your company, U.S. Water, has just replaced a UNIX-based POP3 and SMTP server with Microsoft Exchange Server and Internet Mail Service. The new server has the same IP address, domain name, and entry in DNS. POP3 clients can access their inboxes and retrieve mail. But when they try to also send mail, they get an error message. What is the most likely cause of the problem?

    A. The POP3 clients do not support Windows NT Challenge/Response.

    B. The POP3 clients do not support SSL.

    C. The Internet Mail Service uses a different address space than the POP3 clients.

    D. The Internet Mail Service is configured to not reroute incoming SMTP traffic.

13. You are the administrator of an Internet Mail Service computer. Users are reporting that messages they send to the Internet are not arriving. You decide to track some of these messages as a troubleshooting step. What Exchange components will you need to configure for message tracking? (Choose three.)

    A. Information Store

    B. Internet Mail Service

    C. Microsoft Exchange Connector for Lotus cc:Mail

    D. Microsoft Mail Connector

    E. Message Transfer Agent

14. An Exchange user, Anita, sends a message through the Internet to another Exchange user named Brooks at Brooks@sprockets.com. Anita receives a non-delivery report (NDR) stating "Recipient Not Found: SPROCKETS.COM." You confirm that Brook's mailbox is configured with the e-mail address SMTP: Brooks@sprockets.com. What is the likely problem?

A. Anita's mailbox is not configured for TCP/IP.

B. Anita has exceeded her mailbox size.

C. Anita's Internet Mail Service has exceeded its licenses.

D. The host sprockets.com is not entered in DNS.

15. Which of the following is NOT a role of the IMS?

A. Automatically generate SMTP addresses for new Exchange recipients

B. Act as a DNS client

C. Act as an SMTP server

D. Act as a mail exchanger (MX)

16. The fully qualified domain name (FQDN) SALES.ACME.COM is in what root domain?

A. COM

B. SALES

C. There is no way to tell.

D. ACME

17. The IMS relies on which component to resolve addresses of Exchange recipients on inbound messages?

A. DNS

B. SMTP

C. Resolver program

D. DS

18. After a change is made to the IMS configuration, the following should be done:

    A. The IMS should be paused and restarted.

    B. The IMS should be reinstalled.

    C. The IMS should be stopped and restarted.

    D. The DNS server should be rebooted.

19. Which of these connections to an SMTP server or ISP does the IMS support?

    A. Permanent connection using TCP/IP

    B. A dial-up connection using PPP

    C. A dial-up connection using POP3

    D. Both A and B

20. Which of the following must be true for the IMS to use RAS for a dial-up connection?

    A. A SAP agent must be configured.

    B. RAS must be installed.

    C. An RAS phone book entry must be created for the remote SMTP server or ISP.

    D. Both B and C

21. Which of the following is the default Exchange naming convention for the domain name of a site?

    A. site.organization.com

    B. organization.site.com

    C. com.organization.site

    D. mailbox_name.site.organization

22. Which process maps domain names to IP addresses?

   A. Address encapsulation

   B. Name resolution

   C. IP wrapping

   D. Address spaces

CHAPTER

15

Connecting to
Microsoft Mail and Lotus cc:Mail

To provide interoperability and a path for migration, Exchange Server includes connectors for systems such as Microsoft Mail (MS Mail) and Lotus cc:Mail. The connectors allow mail transfer and directory synchronization between Exchange and these foreign systems. Organizations can install Exchange and keep their current investment in MS Mail or Lotus cc:Mail, or they can use these connectors while migrating to Exchange. (Migration is the topic of Chapter 16.)

In this chapter, you will learn about:

- MS Mail

- Exchange and MS Mail interoperability

- Lotus cc:Mail Connector

Microsoft
✓ **Exam**
Objective

Configure connectivity to a mail system other than Exchange Server. Connector types include:

- X.400 Connector
- Microsoft Exchange Connector for Lotus cc:Mail
- Microsoft Mail Connector

MS Mail Overview

To understand the MS Mail Connector, you need to have a basic understanding of MS Mail. We will examine four elements of the MS Mail architecture:

- Postoffices

- MS Mail MTA

- Directory synchronization across postoffices

- Gateways from MS Mail to non-MS Mail systems

Postoffices

MS Mail is a *shared-file* mail system. The mail messages are stored as files in a shared directory on a designated computer, called a *postoffice*. An MS Mail system can have more than one postoffice.

MS Mail MTA

If an organization has several postoffices, the MS Mail MTA component routes messages between those postoffices. The MTA is implemented by either the External MTA or the Multitasking MTA.

Directory Synchronization across Postoffices

MS Mail postoffices exchange directory information through the MS Mail *Directory Synchronization Protocol*. A single postoffice is designated as a directory synchronization server (*dirsync server*). DISPATCH.EXE is the MS Mail program that executes the functions of a dirsync server. The dirsync server stores the master copy of a network's directory information (the Global Address List) and sends that list to the other postoffices. These other postoffices are designated as directory requestors (*dirsync requestors*). They send new, locally created directory information to the dirsync server, and they receive the Global Address List from the dirsync server.

Three primary events occur during synchronization: a requestor sends directory information to the server, the server compiles the Global Address List and sends it to requestors, and a requestor rebuilds its Global Address List. Each of these events is initiated at a certain timed interval configured through the following parameters:

- **T1**   The interval used by dirsync requestors to send their postoffice address list to the dirsync server.

- **T2**   The interval used by the dirsync server to compile a new Global Address List and to send that list to the dirsync requestors.

- **T3**   The interval used by the dirsync requestors to rebuild their postoffice address lists.

The default setting for each of these events is once every 24 hours. Each event can also be manually initiated.

Gateways from MS Mail to Non-MS Mail Systems

MS Mail includes optional software that allows it to exchange messages with non-MS Mail systems. Gateways to the following foreign mail systems exist:

- AT&T EasyLink

- IBM PROFS, OfficeVision, and SNADS

- Novell Message Handling System (MHS)

- MCI Mail

- SMTP mail systems

In a typical MS Mail gateway configuration, a dedicated computer runs the gateway software and connects to the foreign mail system. Another postoffice (the *Gateway Postoffice*) is configured to receive all the messages destined for the foreign mail system. The rest of the postoffices send their foreign addressed messages to the Gateway Postoffice, which then sends them to the gateway computer. To send foreign addressed messages to the Gateway Postoffice, a postoffice must have a special software program (the MS Mail 3.*x Gateway Access Component*) installed. (See Figure 15.1 for an illustration.)

FIGURE 15.1

MS Mail gateway configuration

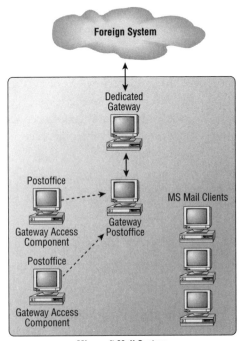

Figure 15.2 illustrates and summarizes the following four architectural elements of MS Mail:

- Postoffice

- MTA

- Directory synchronization

- Gateways

FIGURE 15.2

MS Mail

Exchange and MS Mail Interoperability

For an Exchange and MS Mail system to interoperate, they must be able to exchange messages, directory information, and client schedule information. Three Exchange components enable these operations: the MS Mail Connector, the

Directory Synchronization Agent (DXA), and the Schedule+ Free/Busy Connector. This section provides an overview of these components and their processes. You will learn about:

- MS Mail Connector architecture

- MS Mail Connector roles

- Directory Synchronization Agent (DXA)

- Schedule+ Free/Busy Connector

MS Mail Connector Architecture

The MS Mail Connector enables an Exchange server to function like an MS Mail postoffice. The MS Mail Connector translates Exchange messages addressed to MS Mail users into an MS Mail message format and sends those messages to MS Mail postoffices. It can also receive MS Mail messages addressed to Exchange recipients and translate them into the Exchange message format.

To understand how the MS Mail Connector functions, you need to understand its architecture. This section provides information on the following topics:

- MS Mail Connector Postoffice

- MS Mail Connector Components

- Message flow

- Physical connections

- Using multiple MS Mail Connectors

MS Mail Connector Postoffice

The MS Mail Connector Postoffice is an area on an Exchange server used to store MS Mail messages. This postoffice serves a slightly different purpose than an actual MS Mail postoffice. Rather than sending, receiving, and permanently storing MS Mail messages, this postoffice is only used to send and receive MS Mail messages. When an MS Mail message is received by the MS Mail Connector, it is temporarily stored before it is translated to the Exchange format and sent to the relevant Exchange recipients. When an Exchange message is to be sent to an MS Mail user, it is translated into the MS Mail format and temporarily stored before being transferred to the relevant postoffice. Because it is dedicated to message delivery and has no local mailboxes, this storage is sometimes referred to as a *shadow postoffice*, or as a *gateway postoffice*. Figure 15.3 illustrates the role of the MS Mail Connector Postoffice.

*Temporary storage of incoming and outgoing messages.

The component that submits and retrieves messages from the MS Mail Connector Postoffice and the component that sends and receives MS Mail messages will be discussed next.

MS Mail Connector Components

The MS Mail Connector is made up of two components:

- MS Mail Connector Interchange
- MS Mail Connector (PC) MTA

Both of these are Windows NT services. Both of them use the MS Mail Connector Postoffice to temporarily store MS Mail messages.

MS Mail Connector Interchange The MS Mail Connector Interchange translates messages from the Exchange format to the MS Mail format, and vice versa. When an Exchange user sends a message to an MS Mail user, the

Interchange receives the outgoing message, translates it to the MS Mail format, and submits it to the MS Mail Connector Postoffice. From there it will be sent to the MS Mail system.

If an MS Mail message that is addressed to an Exchange recipient is in the MS Mail Connector Postoffice, the Interchange reads the message, translates it to the Exchange format, and passes it to the other Exchange components for delivery to the Exchange recipients. Figure 15.4 illustrates both of these processes.

FIGURE 15.4

MS Mail Connector Interchange

1) Exchange message
2) MS Mail message
3) MS Mail message
4) Exchange message

MS Mail Connector (PC) MTA   The MS Mail Connector (PC) MTA transfers MS Mail messages between an Exchange server and MS Mail postoffices. The MS Mail Connector (PC) MTA is similar to the Exchange MTA in that it routes and transfers messages.

While an Exchange server can have only one instance of the MS Mail Connector installed, the MS Mail Connector (PC) MTA can be configured with up to 10 instances, allowing a single MS Mail Connector to connect to more than one postoffice. Figure 15.5 illustrates the role of this component.

FIGURE 15.5

MS Mail Connector
(PC) MTA

*Sends and receives MS Mail messages.

The MS Mail Connector (PC) MTA can be configured to make direct or indirect connections to MS Mail postoffices. Both of these options are explained here:

- **Direct Connection to a Postoffice**   When an MS Mail Connector (PC) MTA is configured to send messages directly to a postoffice, the connection is referred to as a *direct connection* to an external postoffice. Mail sent over a direct connection does not go through any other postoffices, and it is sent directly to the destination postoffice. Figure 15.6 illustrates a direct connection to an external postoffice.

FIGURE 15.6

Direct connection to a
postoffice

- **Indirect Connection to a Postoffice** When an MS Mail Connector (PC) MTA has a direct connection to a postoffice that has connections to other postoffices, the MS Mail Connector can use its directly connected postoffice to forward messages to other postoffices. The connection to these "downstream" postoffices is referred to as an *indirect connection*. Figure 15.7 illustrates indirect connections.

FIGURE 15.7

Indirect connections to external postoffices

The next section explains how an Exchange server, with the MS Mail Connector, processes incoming and outgoing MS Mail messages.

Message Flow

This section describes the flow of a message through an Exchange server when the MS Mail Connector is used.

Receiving an MS Mail Message After an MS Mail user has created and sent a message addressed to an Exchange recipient, and after that user's postoffice has transferred the message to the Exchange server, the following processes occur:

1. The MS Mail Connector (PC) MTA receives the message and places it in the MS Mail Connector Postoffice.

2. The MS Mail Connector Postoffice temporarily stores the message until the MS Mail Connector Interchange processes it.

3. The Interchange reads the queued message, translates it to the Exchange format, passes it to the Exchange MTA for delivery, and then deletes the message that was temporarily stored in the MS Mail Connector Postoffice.

4. The Exchange MTA compares the message destination with the Exchange Directory. If the message recipient is on that server, the message is passed to the Information Store (IS) for local delivery. If the recipient is on a remote Exchange server, the MTA transfers the message to that remote server.

Figure 15.8 illustrates these steps.

FIGURE 15.8

An Exchange server receiving an MS Mail message

1) Mail message
2) Temporary storage, MS Mail message
3) Translates, Exchange message
4) Exchange MTA, Exchange message

Sending a Message to an MS Mail Postoffice   After an Exchange user has created and sent a message addressed to an MS Mail recipient, the following processes occur on the Exchange server with the MS Mail Connector:

1. The IS compares the destination address to the Exchange Directory and determines that this message is for remote delivery. Therefore, the IS passes the message to the Exchange MTA.

2. The Exchange MTA temporarily queues the message and then compares the destination address with the Exchange Directory. (This is to determine how the message is to be delivered.) In this case, the Exchange MTA determines that it must use an MS Mail Connector. It then passes the message to the MS Mail Connector Interchange.

3. The Interchange translates the message content from the Exchange format to the MS Mail format. It then passes the message to the MS Mail Connector Postoffice.

4. The MS Mail Connector (PC) MTA scans the MS Mail Connector Postoffice for outgoing messages. When it detects one, it sends the message to the MS Mail postoffice to which it is connected. After sending the message, the MS Mail Connector (PC) MTA deletes the message from the MS Mail Connector Postoffice.

Physical Connections

The MS Mail Connector can use any of three physical connection types to send and receive messages from an MS Mail postoffice. These three connection types are:

- LAN

- Asynchronous modem

- X.25

LAN   The default and preferred connection option between an MS Mail Connector and an MS Mail postoffice is a LAN connection. This connection is the easiest to configure and performs the best. You must configure the network path to the shared directory that serves as the postoffice on the MS Mail server. After you enter that primary piece of information, the MS Mail Connector automatically configures almost everything else.

An advantage of using a LAN connection is that it enables automatic uploading of information about downstream postoffices. You will need to manually enter downstream postoffices when using asynchronous modem and X.25 connections.

Asynchronous Modem   Asynchronous modems can be used to connect an MS Mail Connector and its external postoffice when they are not connected by a LAN. This connection option will normally be slower than a LAN connection, and it will require more configuration and administration on both sides of the connection. The remote network name, postoffice name, telephone number, and other information must be manually entered when configuring the MS Mail Connector.

The remote network containing the MS Mail postoffice must have a computer running either the MS Mail 3.*x* External MTA or Multitasking MTA. Use the External MTA on a computer running MS-DOS. Use the Multitasking MTA if the computer is running Windows NT. The MS Mail Connector will connect to the MS Mail MTA computer in order to deliver messages to the remote postoffice.

X.25 An X.25 connection is another WAN connection that can be used between an MS Mail Connector and an MS Mail environment. This connection can be slower than the LAN option and will require more configuration and administration. The LAN, asynchronous modem, and X.25 connections are illustrated in Figure 15.9.

FIGURE 15.9

Connection options between an MS Mail Connector and MS Mail

Using Multiple MS Mail Connectors

If your organization has a large number of MS Mail postoffices and a large number of messages passed between them and your Exchange system, you might need to configure multiple MS Mail Connectors to handle the load. Although an individual Exchange server can have only one instance of the MS Mail Connector, more than one Exchange server can be configured with an

MS Mail Connector. Because all of the MS Mail Connectors in an Exchange site use the same address space, the site appears to the MS Mail environment as one big postoffice. Using multiple MS Mail Connectors is illustrated in Figure 15.10.

FIGURE 15.10

Using multiple MS Mail Connectors

Utilizing the MS Mail Connector

Network administrators and designers have several ways to utilize the MS Mail Connector in an organization. In addition to enabling message exchange between a single Exchange site and a single MS Mail postoffice, the MS Mail Connector can be used for:

- Backboning MS Mail through Exchange

- Accessing MS Mail gateways from Exchange

- Accessing Exchange connectors from MS Mail

Backboning MS Mail through Exchange

An Exchange site configured with the MS Mail Connector can be used as a messaging backbone for multiple MS Mail postoffices or even multiple MS Mail sites. To implement this, each postoffice must be configured to route messages through the Exchange MS Mail Connector. Each postoffice will have an indirect connection to the other postoffices through the MS Mail Connector backbone.

Directory synchronization can be configured to take advantage of the messaging backbone. Each postoffice passes new directory information to the Exchange site. The Exchange site contains, in effect, a master copy of the messaging system's directory, which it replicates to the individual postoffices. Figure 15.11 illustrates using an Exchange site as a messaging backbone for MS Mail.

FIGURE 15.11

Exchange as a messaging backbone for MS Mail

Accessing MS Mail Gateways from Exchange

As stated earlier, MS Mail includes optional software that enables an MS Mail system to exchange messages with foreign mail systems. That functionality can be leveraged by Exchange users. To do this, an Exchange server with the MS Mail Connector installed must also have the MS Mail Gateway Access Component installed. This setup allows Exchange users to send messages (through the MS Mail Connector) to an MS Mail gateway and to recipients on the foreign system. Figure 15.12 illustrates this process.

An Exchange server with the MS Mail Connector can also be configured to be the Gateway Postoffice. In this setup, all the other postoffices send foreign addressed messages to the Exchange server, which forwards them to the gateway computer. Figure 15.13 illustrates this procedure.

Accessing Exchange Connectors from MS Mail

Exchange users can utilize MS Mail gateways, and MS Mail users can utilize Exchange gateways (i.e., connectors). MS Mail users can address messages to X.400 or SMTP recipients and have those messages delivered through an X.400 Connector or Internet Mail Service installed in an Exchange site. The MS Mail messages enter the Exchange site through an MS Mail Connector, which passes them to the appropriate connector for delivery to the foreign mail system. MS Mail postoffices that need to send messages to the Exchange connectors must have the appropriate Gateway Access Component installed.

The steps and components involved in using IMS in place of a MS Mail gateway for SMTP are:

- Install IMS on a Microsoft Exchange Server.

- Install the Microsoft Mail Connector on the Microsoft Exchange Server.

- Add the Microsoft Mail Connector to the external postoffice list on each
  Microsoft Mail postoffice (this will be discussed later under the heading
  "MS Mail Postoffice Configuration").

- Reinstall the SMTP Gateway Access Component on the existing MS
  Mail postoffices. Specify the Microsoft Exchange Mail Connector as the
  gateway postoffice.

There are a couple of good reasons to use an Exchange connector instead
of an MS Mail gateway to access foreign mail systems. The Exchange connectors are Windows NT services that are 32-bit, multithreaded programs. They
can also run on a high-end server utilizing multiple processors and large amounts
of RAM. Using Exchange connectors also eliminates the need to use a dedicated computer for the MS Mail gateway. Figure 15.14 illustrates the use of
an Exchange connector as a gateway for MS Mail users.

Directory Synchronization Agent (DXA)

The MS Mail Directory Synchronization protocol has been incorporated in
other messaging products, like Exchange, permitting them to exchange directory information with MS Mail. The Exchange component that supports this

FIGURE 15.14

Using Exchange
connectors as gateways
for MS Mail users

protocol is the Directory Synchronization Agent (DXA). When this component
is used, Exchange can automatically exchange directory information with an
MS Mail system. Information about Exchange recipients is sent to the MS Mail
system, and information about MS Mail recipients is sent to the Exchange
Directory. MS Mail recipients are entered into the Exchange Directory as custom
recipients. Although the MS Mail Connector provides for message transfer
between the two systems, the DXA allows the users on each system to see the
directory information (e.g., e-mail addresses) of the other system.

The DXA enables an Exchange server to function as either a dirsync server
or dirsync requestor. Although it can assume either role, it can only perform
one of these roles at a time (i.e., the Exchange server cannot be a dirsync server
and a dirsync requestor concurrently). An Exchange site can have only one
Exchange server designated as a dirsync server, but a site is not required to have
a dirsync server. All Exchange servers in a site can be dirsync requestors using
an MS Mail postoffice as the dirsync server.

When configured as a dirsync server, an Exchange server will receive the
new directory information sent by the postoffices configured as dirsync
requestors and compile the Global Address List. This master list of directory
information is then sent to all requestor postoffices. Figure 15.15 illustrates
this configuration.

FIGURE 15.15

An Exchange server as a dirsync server

If configured as a dirsync requestor, an Exchange server will send its new directory information to the postoffice designated as the dirsync server and receive the Global Address List from that postoffice. Figure 15.16 illustrates this configuration.

FIGURE 15.16

An Exchange server as a dirsync requestor

One of the most useful administrative features of Exchange directory synchronization is the ability to select which Exchange recipients to synchronize to an MS Mail system. An Exchange administrator can prevent certain Exchange recipients from being sent to the MS Mail global address list. This can be implemented at two levels.

Each Exchange recipient has a property called *trust level,* which holds a value of 1–100. An Exchange dirsync servers, or requestor can be configured to only synch recipient objects with trust levels less than or equal to a specified value. For example, if an Exchange recipient named Bob has a trust level of 10, and the Exchange dirsync requestor is configured to synch objects with trust levels less than or equal to 3, then information about Bob will not be sent to the MS Mail dirsync server.

This feature can be applied at another level, the recipient container level. If there are many Exchange recipients that do not need to be synchronized, a separate Exchange recipients container can be created to hold these recipients. That container would not be included in the list of containers to send to the MS Mail system.

Creating a Global Distribution List

You may need to create a global distribution list containing all the Exchange recipients and all the MS Mail users. One way to do this is to create an Exchange DL that contains two members, an Exchange DL with all the Exchange recipients, and a custom recipient synched from MS Mail that represents an MS Mail DL which contains all the MS Mail users.

Schedule+ Free/Busy Connector

Schedule+ is a personal and group scheduling program. One of its many features allows users to view the free/busy schedule information of other users. MS Mail ships with Schedule+ version 1.0 and Exchange ships with Schedule+ version 7.5 (Schedule+ 7.5 is now called Outlook Calendar). Exchange includes the Schedule+ Free/Busy Connector to allow users with one version to view information from users of the other version. In the following two sections, we will discuss the elements and processes for sending scheduling information in both directions (i.e., from Exchange to MS Mail and from MS Mail to Exchange).

Sending Information from Exchange to MS Mail

All Schedule+ 7.5 free/busy information is stored in an Exchange public folder called Schedule+ Free Busy (found under the System Folders container in Exchange Administrator). The Schedule+ Free/Busy Connector uses a special mailbox agent (ADMINSCH) to translate and address that information for delivery to a designated distribution list (DL) on the MS Mail network. (When Exchange Server is installed, ADMINSCH is automatically created.) The MS Mail DL contains the administrative user accounts that are used to distribute free/busy information to the users of that network.

Sending Information from MS Mail to Exchange

On an MS Mail network, a program called SCHDIST.EXE can be used to collect free/busy information and send it in the form of a message to the ADMINSCH mailbox agent on the designated Exchange server. The Free/Busy Connector then translates it and places it in the Schedule+ Free Busy public folder. This information is available to Exchange clients using Schedule+ 7.5. Figure 15.17 illustrates the Schedule+ Free/Busy Connector architecture.

FIGURE 15.17

The architecture of the Schedule+ Free/Busy Connector

Now that we have covered the background for the Exchange components, we can move on to implementing these concepts and creating interoperability between Exchange and MS Mail environments.

Exchange and MS Mail Interoperability

This section discusses implementing the components necessary for the following types of interoperability between Exchange and MS Mail:

- Message exchange
- Directory synchronization
- Schedule+ information access
- Troubleshooting interoperability with Microsoft Mail

Message Exchange

The MS Mail Connector must be installed, configured, and started before messages can be exchanged between Exchange and MS Mail. MS Mail post-offices must be configured to route messages to the MS Mail Connector.

MS Mail Connector Installation

When you install Exchange Server, one of your options is to install the MS Mail Connector. If you choose this option, the MS Mail Connector will be installed and will appear in the Exchange hierarchy as an object in the site Connections container.

If the MS Mail Connector is not installed during the initial Exchange Server setup, it can be installed later by executing the Exchange Setup program (SETUP.EXE) and choosing the Add/Remove option. Highlight the Microsoft Exchange Server selection and click Change option. A dialog box appears permitting you to select the MS Mail Connector for installation.

MS Mail Connector Configuration

The MS Mail Connector configuration process can be organized into four main procedures:

1. Define and configure a physical connection to an external postoffice.

2. Define and configure message transfer.

3. Configure destination addresses.

4. Configure other settings.

These steps and procedures will be explained in the following sections. All of these procedures are executed through the Exchange Administrator program and configured on the MS Mail Connector object, found in the Connections container. You will configure an MS Mail Connector in Exercise 15.1.

Define and Configure a Physical Connection to an External Postoffice
To send and receive messages from an MS Mail postoffice, you must configure a physical connection on the Connections property page. As you learned earlier, three connection types can be used: LAN, Asynchronous, and X.25.

Some of the important attributes of each of these connections are listed here:

- **LAN Connection**   Only two pieces of information must be entered for this connection type:

    - **Postoffice path**   The network path to the shared directory on an MS Mail postoffice in which mail messages are stored. The path must be entered using the Universal Naming Convention (UNC). In a Microsoft networking environment, the path format would be \\computer_name\ share_name\directory_path. If the postoffice is located on a NetWare server, the path format would be \\server_name\volume_name\ directory_path.

    - **Connection attempts**   The number of times the MS Mail Connector will attempt to send a message before it returns the message to the sender with a Non-Delivery Report (NDR). The default is 3.

- **Asynchronous Connection (Async)**   Asynchronous connections require more settings than LAN connections. The primary settings are:

    - **Network name**   The name of the MS Mail network to which the MS Mail Connector is attaching.

    - **Postoffice name**   The name of a specific postoffice to which the MS Mail Connector will connect.

    - **Sign-on ID**   The serial number of the external postoffice to which a connection is being made.

- **Password** The password used at the external postoffice. This is an optional attribute at the external postoffice.

- **Connection attempts** The number of times the MS Mail Connector will attempt to send a message before it returns the message to the sender with a Non-Delivery Report (NDR). The default is 3.

- **Phone number** The phone number to the external postoffice.

- **Optional settings** Accessed by clicking the Options button.

- **X.25 Connection** For this connection option to be used, the X.25 protocol must already be installed and configured on the Exchange server. The X.25 option has many of the same properties as the async option, including network and postoffice name, sign-on ID, password, and connection attempts. The primary difference is that this connection type requires the X.121 address of the external postoffice. A 16-digit number identifies the computer on the X.25 network that contains the external postoffice.

Define and Configure Message Transfer Once a physical connection has been configured, you can define and configure message transfer. You must create one or more instances of the MS Mail Connector (PC) MTA. As you learned earlier, only one instance of the MS Mail Connector can exist on an Exchange server. However, that single instance of the MS Mail Connector can use multiple instances of the MS Mail Connector (PC) MTA to transfer messages. The Connector MTAs property page is used to create and configure an MTA.

To create a new Connector MTA instance, click the New button on the Connector MTAs property page. The main attributes to configure are:

- **Service name** The name that represents a particular instance of this MTA. This name is registered with the Windows NT operating system as a service which can be started and stopped with the Services applet in the Control Panel.

- **Polling frequency** Can be set to indicate how long this instance of the MTA waits before checking the external postoffice for new mail to be picked up. The default is 5 minutes.

- **Connection parameters** The MTA must use a physical connection to send and receive messages. That connection is chosen under Connection Parameters. The default is LAN.

After an MTA instance is created, you can determine the external postoffices with which it will exchange messages. This information can be entered after clicking the List button on the Connector MTAs property page.

If a particular MS Mail Connector (PC) MTA will use an async or an X.25 connection, additional properties need to be set for the MTA (such as the communication port and the modem timeout value).

Configure Address Spaces   Like other connectors, the MS Mail Connector is configured with the destination addresses to which it will route messages. These addresses are configured on the Address Space property page.

Four address templates can be used to enter addresses:

- X.400

- MS Mail

- Internet

- General (can be used to create any type of address)

Addresses can be to specific recipients on a foreign system, or they can be to an entire network of recipients. An example of an MS Mail address space is:

```
MS: Sprockets/Manufacturing/*
```

"MS" refers to the address space type (MS Mail in this example). "Sprockets" is the network name. "Manufacturing" is the postoffice name. The asterisk (*) is a wildcard, meaning all recipients.

Configure Other Settings   The General, Interchange, and Local Postoffice property pages contain other MS Mail Connector properties that can be configured:

- **General property page**   Use this page to set a maximum message size and indicate an administrative note for this connector.

- **Interchange property page**   Use this page to select an administrator's mailbox to receive information messages and alert notifications from this connector. Other properties on this page include the primary language used by clients accessing this connector and message tracking. If message tracking is enabled, information about messages sent through this connector will be written to the tracking logs.

- **Local Postoffice property page**   The MS Mail Connector allows an Exchange server to function as an MS Mail postoffice. As such, it must have a network and postoffice name. By default, the Exchange organization name is used as the network name, and the Exchange site name is used for the postoffice name. This page allows these values to be changed. The MS Mail Connector can also require a password to be used by external postoffices that are connecting to and sending messages to this connector. This page is where you enter this password.

Exercise 15.1 tells you how to configure the MS Mail connector. To perform this exercise, you must have an MS Mail system on your network.

EXERCISE 15.1

Configuring the MS Mail Connector

1. In Exchange Administrator, navigate to the Connections container and double-click on MS Mail Connector. The property pages for this object will appear.

2. On the Interchange page, designate one of your recipients as the administrator's mailbox.

3. On the Connections page, click Create to create a connection to an MS Mail postoffice. Choose the LAN connection parameter, and enter the UNC path to the MS Mail postoffice.

4. On the Connector MTAs page, click New to create a new Connector MTA instance. In the Service Name field, give this Connector MTA a name. Also choose the LAN option under Connection Parameters.

5. On the Address Space page, click New MS Mail to configure the addresses to which this connector will send messages. Enter the remote network and postoffice names in the template.

6. Click OK to save and exit these property pages.

7. In the Control Panel, run the Services applet. Scroll down until you see MS Mail Connector Interchange. Highlight that entry, and click Start. The MS Mail Connector will now start. (The service can also be stopped from this location.) Start the connector MTA service you created in Step 4.

MS Mail Postoffice Configuration

The previous procedures configured the MS Mail Connector to transfer messages to the external postoffices. Those postoffices also need to be configured to send messages to the MS Mail Connector. The primary information that must be entered at these postoffices is the network and postoffice name used by the MS Mail Connector. If the MS Mail Connector uses a password, it must also be configured on the MS Mail postoffices.

Microsoft ✓ *Exam* *Objective*

Configure synchronization of directory information between Exchange Server and other mail systems. Types of directory synchronization include:

- Manual
- Automatic

Directory Synchronization

The primary steps to implement directory synchronization between Exchange and MS Mail are:

1. Configuring and starting the DXA.

2. Use an Exchange server as a dirsync server,

   or

   Use an Exchange server as a dirsync requestor.

Each of these primary steps will be covered in the following sections.

Configuring and Starting the DXA

The Exchange DXA component is installed when the MS Mail Connector is installed. As a Windows NT service, it can be stopped and started through the Control Panel Services applet. It is represented by the Directory Synchronization object in the Exchange hierarchy. As with other Exchange objects, it has properties that can be configured.

Exchange Server as a Dirsync Server

To use an Exchange server as a dirsync server, the following procedures must be performed:

- **A dirsync server object must created and configured** In Exchange Administrator, choose File, New Other, Dirsync Server. (When you create this object, make your hierarchy context the Connections container.) Some of this object's properties are:

  - **Name** The directory name of this object.

  - **Dirsync administrator** The Exchange recipient that receives administration notifications pertaining to this object.

  - **Server** The name of the Exchange server that will function as the dirsync server.

  - **Schedule** A schedule can be defined to execute the T2 event, namely the compilation of the Global Address List and submission of it to the dirsync requestors.

- **Remote dirsync requestors must be created and configured** The Exchange server acting as a dirsync server must maintain the list of the dirsync requestors with which it will be communicating. This information is configured by the Exchange administrator by creating a remote dirsync requestor object for each MS Mail postoffice. These objects are created in Exchange Administrator by choosing File ➤ New Other ➤ Remote Dirsync Requestor. One of the most important properties of this type of object is the list of recipient containers that are to be exported to the remote requestor. This information is entered on the Export Containers property page. Attributes on this page include:

  - **Recipient containers** The Exchange recipient containers to export to this particular remote requestor. These containers can be located in any site.

  - **Trust level** The trust level used to select objects for synchronization with this remote requestor. All Exchange objects in the designated containers with a trust level less than or equal to this value will be synchronized.

- **Configure the MS Mail postoffices that are dirsync requestors** The MS Mail administrator must configure the dirsync requestors with information about the dirsync server.

Exchange Server as a Dirsync Requestor

If an Exchange server will be a dirsync requestor, the following procedures must be performed:

- **A dirsync requestor object must be created and configured** In Exchange Administrator, choose File ➤ New Other ➤ Dirsync Requestor to configure the dirsync requestor. (When you create this object, make your hierarchy context the Connections container.) The Dirsync Requestor object includes many of the same attributes as the dirsync server, such as name, server, and schedule. On the Export Containers property page you can designate which recipient containers to send to the dirsync server and which trust levels to use. On the Import Container property page you can designate the recipients container in which to create directory entries received from the dirsync server.

- **Configure the Mail dirsync server** The postoffice serving as the dirsync server must be configured with information about the Exchange server functioning as a dirsync requestor.

Schedule+ Information Access

Procedures must be performed in both the Exchange site and the MS Mail network for free/busy information to be accessible from one system to the other system. On the Exchange site, the following must be operational in order for the Schedule+ Free/Busy Connector to work:

- MS Mail Connector

- Directory synchronization between the Exchange site and MS Mail network

The Schedule+ Free/Busy Connector is installed when the MS Mail Connector is installed. If the MS Mail Connector was not installed at the initial Exchange Server setup, run the Exchange Server Setup program in maintenance mode and choose the Add/Remove option to install the MS Mail Connector.

Microsoft ✓ ***Exam*** ***Objective*** **Diagnose and resolve connectivity problems. Elements include:**

- Foreign connectivity
- Site-to-site connectivity
- Internet connectivity
- Connectivity within a site

Troubleshooting Interoperability with Microsoft Mail

Many troubleshooting situations related to interoperability with Microsoft Mail involve directory synchronization. For example, your Microsoft Exchange Server could be configured as a dirsync server with remote dirsync requestors defined. You configure the synchronization time on the Exchange server to Always. Three hours later, you notice that Microsoft Mail recipients have not yet replicated to your Exchange Global Address List. The solution to this problem is to run a utility named REQMAIN on the Microsoft Mail post-office. Running that utility with the Transmit option (i.e., reqmain –t) will force the postoffice to transmit its updates.

Lotus cc:Mail Connector

The Exchange Connector for Lotus cc:Mail provides both message exchange and directory synchronization between Exchange and cc:Mail systems. This connector is installed using Exchange Server Setup.

The Connector for Lotus cc:Mail uses two Lotus cc:Mail utilities, IMPORT.EXE and EXPORT.EXE. The connector and these two utilities are described here:

- **Lotus cc:Mail Connector** Transfers messages and synchronizes directories between Exchange and cc:Mail.

- **IMPORT.EXE** Imports information, both mail messages and directory information, into the cc:Mail environment.

- **EXPORT.EXE** Exports information, both mail messages and directory information, from the cc:Mail environment.

Figure 15.18 illustrates an organization using the Connector for Lotus cc:Mail.

FIGURE 15.18

The Connector for
Lotus cc:Mail

Summary

Exchange Server comes with the tools needed to interoperate, exchange messages, and perform directory synchronization with Microsoft Mail (MS Mail) and Lotus cc:Mail systems.

The MS Mail Connector enables message exchange between an Exchange system and an MS Mail system. This connector creates a temporary storage area (the MS Mail Connector Postoffice) for messages transmitted between Exchange and MS Mail. The MS Mail Connector is implemented as two Windows NT services (components), the MS Mail Connector Interchange and the MS Mail Connector (PC) MTA. The Interchange translates messages from the Exchange format to the MS Mail format, and vice versa. The MS Mail Connector (PC) MTA transfers messages between Exchange and MS Mail systems.

When the MS Mail Connector is installed, the Schedule+ Free/Busy Connector is also installed. The Schedule+ Free/Busy Connector permits the exchange of free/busy information generated by Exchange clients using Schedule 7.5 and MS Mail clients using Schedule+ 1.0.

Environments that contain both Exchange and Lotus cc:Mail can use the Connector for Lotus cc:Mail to enable both message exchange and directory synchronization between the two systems.

Review Questions

1. Your company has both Microsoft Exchange Server and Microsoft Mail. There will eventually be a migration from Mail to Exchange, but right now you need to come up with a coexistence strategy. Part of that strategy is to make a global distribution list available that contains recipients from both systems. How could you do that?

   A. Create both a Microsoft Mail distribution list that includes all Microsoft Mail users and a Microsoft Exchange distribution list that includes all Microsoft Exchange users. Create a Microsoft Exchange distribution list that includes the Microsoft Mail distribution list and the Microsoft Exchange distribution list.

   B. Create Internet mail connectivity between the two systems. Create SMTP custom recipients for each Microsoft Mail user. Create a distribution list that includes all Exchange users and all SMTP custom recipients.

   C. Configure directory synchronization between the two systems. After synchronization has taken place, create a master distribution list on the Microsoft Mail postoffice.

   D. Configure directory synchronization between the two systems. After synchronization has taken place, create a master distribution list on the Microsoft Exchange server.

2. A company uses a Microsoft Mail gateway for SMTP to exchange mail between its three Microsoft Mail postoffices and the Internet. This company has also just installed Microsoft Exchange Server. They have hired you as a consultant to outline the steps necessary to replace their current Mail gateway for SMTP with the Internet Mail Service. What are those steps? (Choose all that apply.)

   A. Install IMS on a Microsoft Exchange Server.

   B. Install the Microsoft Mail Connector on the Microsoft Exchange Server.

   C. Add the Microsoft Mail Connector to the external postoffice list on each Microsoft Mail postoffice.

D. Reinstall the SMTP Gateway Access Component on the existing MS Mail postoffices. Specify the Microsoft Exchange Mail Connector postoffice as the gateway postoffice.

E. Install the Gateway Access Component on the Microsoft Exchange Server to allow the Mail users to access Internet Mail Service.

3. You need to create directory synchronization between Microsoft Exchange Server and Microsoft Mail. Your Exchange Server has two recipient containers called Container-Albany and Container-Boston. You want only recipients in Container-Albany to be synchronized with Microsoft Mail. How could you set that up?

A. Remove the Microsoft Mail address space from all recipients in Container-Albany.

B. Remove all selected attributes in the DS Site Configuration object.

C. Configure the trust level of the recipients in Container-Boston to be higher than that of the DXA.

D. Configure the Microsoft Mail address space as the default address for all recipients in Container-Albany.

4. Your company currently uses Microsoft Mail. You have just added a Microsoft Exchange Server to the network. Management would like both systems to coexist and be able to exchange both messages and directory information. Management would also like to keep the current dirsync strategy. You consequently configure the Exchange server as a dirsync requestor. What other step must you do on the Exchange server?

A. Create a dirsync server on the Exchange server.

B. Configure the Microsoft Mail Connector on the Exchange server.

C. Create a directory replication bridgehead server.

D. Reinstall MTA.

5. Your network has three Microsoft Mail postoffices, named PO-1, PO-2, and PO-3. You replace PO-2 with a Microsoft Exchange Server and establish directory synchronization between the two mail systems. Management has asked if you could hide certain Exchange recipients from the two Microsoft Mail postoffices. They also want Exchange recipients to see all recipients from both systems. You decide to create two recipient containers, called Container-A and Container-B. You place all Exchange recipients that are to be hidden in Container-B. How should you configure the trust levels of these two containers?

   A. Configure the trust level of Container-A to be higher than that of the dirsync requestor. Configure the trust level of Container-B to be lower than that of the dirsync requestor.

   B. Configure the trust level of the recipients in Container-A to be lower than that of the dirsync requestor. Configure the trust level of the recipients in Container-B to be higher than that of the dirsync requestor.

   C. Configure the trust level of both containers to be higher than that of the dirsync requestor. Configure the trust level of Container-B to be lower than that of Container-A.

   D. Configure the trust level of both containers to be lower than that of the dirsync requestor. Configure the trust level of Container-B to be lower than that of Container-A.

6. Directory synchronization is configured between your Exchange site and a foreign mail system (i.e., a non-Exchange system). What is the best way to prevent certain Exchange recipients from being replicated to the foreign system?

   A. Mark as hidden the recipients you do not want replicated.

   B. Create a new recipients container. Move the recipients that you do not want to be replicated to this container.

   C. Create a dirsync distribution list. Add all the recipients that are to be hidden to this list.

   D. Configure the trust levels for the recipients that you do not want replicated to be higher than that of the connector.

7. Your company is made up of two domains, one includes Microsoft Mail and the other has Microsoft Exchange. Each domain and its message system has about half the users. There are no trust relationships between the two domains. A Microsoft Exchange recipient named Robert uses Microsoft Schedule+ 7.5 to create an appointment that includes a Microsoft Mail user named Shelley. When Robert views the Planner tab, he cannot see Shelley's availability. But Robert can send e-mail to Shelley. What do you need to do to allow Robert to view Shelley's availability?

   A. Establish a two-way trust between the domains.

   B. Delete and re-create the Microsoft Schedule+ Free/Busy public folder.

   C. Relocate the Microsoft Mail postoffice to the same machine as the Exchange server.

   D. Configure the Microsoft Schedule+ Free/Busy Connector.

8. Your Microsoft Exchange Server is configured as a dirsync server and has remote dirsync requestors defined. You configure the synchronization time on the Exchange server to Always. Three hours later, you notice that Microsoft Mail recipients have not yet replicated to your Exchange Global Address List. What is the solution to this problem?

   A. In Microsoft Mail, set the T1, T2, and T3 times to be the same.

   B. Set the T2 time on the Microsoft Exchange Server to be one hour later than the T2 time in Microsoft Mail.

   C. Run the Reqmain utility with the Transport option on the Microsoft Mail postoffice.

   D. Run the Reqmain utility with the Receive option on the Microsoft Exchange Server.

9. Your company uses a Microsoft Mail gateway for SMTP to transfer messages between its five postoffices and the Internet. Your company domain name is Plumbers.com. Your network is connected to the Internet through a filtered router. Management has had you install a Microsoft Exchange Server and configure the Microsoft Mail Connector. Management has the following mandatory and optional wishes:

Required Result: replace the Microsoft Mail gateway for SMTP with the Exchange Server.

Optional Result 1: POP3 clients being able to both send and receive messages.

Optional Result 2: prevent anonymous users on the Internet from using the Internet Mail Service as a relay host for other destinations.

Proposed Solution: to accomplish those results, one member of the network administration staff suggests the following actions:

- Install the Internet Mail Service.

- Reconfigure the Gateway Access Components on each Microsoft Mail postoffice to point to the MS Mail Connector postoffice as the downstream postoffice.

- Disable rerouting of SMTP messages.

- Make no changes to the router.

What results would the above proposal produce?

A. The proposed solution produces the required result and produces both of the optional results.

B. The proposed solution produces the required result and produces only one of the optional results.

C. The proposed solution produces the required result but does not produce either of the optional results.

D. The proposed solution does not produce the required result.

10. Which of the following does NOT relate to restricting Exchange objects from being synchronized with an MS Mail system?

A. Trust level of the object

B. Trust level of the Exchange dirsync server or requestor

C. The recipients container

D. EXPORT.EXE

11. Which of the following are required when using the Schedule+ Free/Busy Connector?

A. Directory synchronization with MS Mail

B. A Windows NT user account named FreeB

C. IMPORT.EXE running on the designated MS Mail postoffice

D. Both A and C

12. Schedule+ free/busy information exchanged between Exchange and MS Mail users is stored in the following:

A. A specially designated public folder

B. A specially designated mailbox

C. A specially designated DL

D. The Exchange Directory

13. The MS Mail directory synchronization parameter used by a dirsync server to recompile the Global Address List is:

A. T1

B. T2

C. Newsfeed push

D. T3

16

Migrating to Exchange

When an organization moves from its existing mail system to Microsoft Exchange, users' mailboxes, messages, address books, schedules, and other resources could need to be converted from the old system to Exchange. Exchange Server includes the tools needed to perform the *migration* (the move from the existing mail system to the new mail system).

This chapter will discuss the following topics:

- Migration strategies

- Migration tools

- Special migration issues

- Troubleshooting a migration

Migration Strategies

Although there are many different strategies that can be used to perform a migration, we will cover the primary two:

- Single-phase migration

- Multiphase migration

Single-Phase Migration

A single-phase migration moves all the user accounts and data to Exchange at once (see Figure 16.1). This strategy is the most appropriate under the following conditions:

- User accounts and mailboxes are the primary items to be migrated. Not much, if any, data needs to be migrated.

- All the necessary hardware and software is in place to accommodate the additions, including the necessary Exchange client software.

- The necessary personnel is available to complete the entire migration.

FIGURE 16.1

Single-phase migration

Multiphase Migration

A multiphase migration moves groups of user accounts and data to Exchange in different stages, over a period of time. This strategy is the most appropriate under the following conditions:

- Not all groups or departments can migrate at the same time.

- All the hardware or software requirements for the migration are not in place.

- There is not enough personnel to implement a single-phase migration within the acceptable downtime constraints.

Migration Tools

Three main tools are used to perform a migration:

- **Source extractors**   These programs can copy information from an existing mail system and place it in a format that can be migrated to Exchange at a later time.

- **Migration Wizard**   The Migration Wizard imports information into an Exchange environment. (It includes source extractors for Microsoft Mail and Lotus cc:Mail.)

- **Directory Import and Export**   These two commands can be accessed in Exchange Administrator to make bulk changes to Exchange recipients.

Source Extractors

A source extractor program can copy information out of an existing non-Exchange system and place that information in a format that can be imported into Exchange. The type of information that can be extracted from another mail system includes:

- Address information

- Distribution lists

- Mailboxes

- Messages

- Folders

- Schedule information

Exchange Server comes with source extractors for the following mail systems:

- Microsoft Mail for PC Networks, v3.*x*

- Microsoft Mail for AppleTalk Networks, v3.*x*

- Lotus cc:Mail (database version 6)

- DEC All-In-One, versions 2.3 and later

- IBM PROFS and OfficeVision

- Verimation MEMO MVS, version 3.2.1 and later

- Novell GroupWise

- Collabra Share

You will need to have administrator privileges on the foreign mail system that you will be extracting information from.

You can also create you own source extractor program. The Exchange SDK contains information on this process.

Extracted information is placed in a specific format in specific files. The Migration Wizard uses these files to import the information into the Exchange environment. The following three types of files are created by source extractors:

- **Primary files (*.PRI)**   These files contain the names of mailboxes or custom recipients, personal address book entries, and the message headers of messages being extracted. The format of this file is comma-separated value (CSV), which will be discussed in the next section.

- **Secondary files (*.SEC)**   These files contain the message bodies (content), message attachments, and scheduling data.

- **Packing list file (*.PKL)**   This file contains the filenames and other information pertaining to the information in the primary and secondary files.

Because the Migration Wizard uses all three file types, they are collectively referred to as the migration files.

Microsoft
✔ *Exam*
Objective

Import directory, message, and scheduling data from existing mail systems.

Migration Wizard

The Migration Wizard can extract information from a foreign mail system, or use information from another source extractor, and it can import that information into Microsoft Exchange. The Migration Wizard is executed from the Microsoft Exchange program group. This section will cover the following aspects of the Migration Wizard:

- Migration Wizard source extractors

- The two migration procedures

- Migration options

The term "export" is also sometimes used to refer to the process of extracting directory information from a foreign system.

Migration Wizard Source Extractors

Earlier in this chapter, we listed the names of the mail systems that source extractors exist for. The Migration Wizard itself is the source extractor for the following foreign mail systems:

- Microsoft Mail postoffices

- Lotus cc:Mail postoffices (database version 6 or 8)

- Novell GroupWise postoffices

- Collabra Share forums

The Migration Wizard can also use the extracted information collected by other separate source extractors.

The Two Migration Procedures

The Migration Wizard prompts the person running it to choose between two different migration procedures:

- One-step migration

- Two-step migration

Each will be discussed on the following page.

One-Step Migration   A one-step migration extracts information from a foreign mail system, and then imports it into Microsoft Exchange. Extraction and importation are performed in one step (at least from the perspective of the administrator). Some of the specific procedures and issues within a one-step migration will be discussed later under the heading "Migration Options."

Two-Step Migration   The two-step migration separates the extraction phase from the importation phase. In the first step, the Migration Wizard extracts directory information from the foreign mail system and places it into a CSV file (CSV stands for "comma-separated value"). The CSV file is also referred to as the "user list file." One of the reasons to perform a two-step migration is to modify the migrating users before they are actually imported into Microsoft Exchange. One way to do that is by editing the CSV file before it is imported into Exchange. For example, the display names of the migrating users might need to be modified to adhere to the naming convention used in the Exchange system. The foreign system might use "LastName FirstName," and the Exchange system might use "FirstName LastName." After the first step in the two-step migration, the administrator would open the CSV file with an application like Microsoft Excel and edit the migrating users' display names. After the necessary editing of the CSV file, the second phase of the migration can be initiated, namely the importing of the directory information and if desired, foreign data, into Microsoft Exchange. Editing the CSV file before the second step of a migration can be a very efficient way of modifying a large number of migrating users.

Migration Options

The Migration Wizard presents the person running it with a series of options relating to the extraction and importation of directory information and data. The topics these options relate to are listed below:

- **Selecting mailboxes to import**   An administrator can select the mailboxes to be imported during the migration. It is not necessary to migrate all the mailboxes of an existing system.

- **Creating mailboxes**   An administrator can create new Exchange mailboxes for each foreign mailbox being migrated or use existing Exchange mailboxes. The default is to create a new mailbox. Some of the additional options pertaining to new mailbox creation are:

  - **Recipient container**   The administrator can choose the recipient container in which to create the new mailboxes.

- **Templates**   The administrator can choose a mailbox template to use as the pattern for the new mailboxes. This allows an administrator to preconfigure each new mailbox with specific properties, like company name, mailbox storage restrictions, or other properties.

- **Passwords**   When the Migration Wizard is used to create Windows NT accounts, it can generate random passwords or use the alias name of the corresponding mailbox as the password.

- **Messages and folders**   Messages and folders can be migrated. All messages or only messages within a specified date range can be migrated.

- **Shared folders**   All shared folders can be migrated to the public folder container of the Exchange site.

- **Personal Address Books (PABs)**   The entries in users' Personal Address Books can be imported to Exchange mailboxes.

- **Calendar files**   Users' calendar files in the CAL directory on the postoffice can be imported to Exchange mailboxes.

Directory Import and Export

Once recipient objects have been migrated to Exchange, they can still be modified. Obviously, each recipient object can be individually modified by changing its properties. But if a large number of mailboxes need to be changed, changing them individually may be too labor intensive. A better way is to use the Directory Import and Export commands in Exchange Administrator (Tools menu). Directory Export can be used to copy the properties of a large number of Exchange recipients to a text file. This file can be imported into a word processor or spreadsheet program in order to edit its content. For example, a search-and-replace tool can be used to change one particular property of all mailboxes. Directory Import can then be used to import this file back into the Exchange Directory. These two utilities permit an administrator to perform bulk administration.

As another example, Microsoft Exchange could be connected to an SMTP backbone. One of the other systems connected to this backbone could be a large UNIX-based SMTP system of 26,000 users. The directory information about these users might be stored in a SQL database. If you wanted to add these 26,000 SMTP users as custom recipients to your Exchange directory, you could accomplish that through the Import utility of Microsoft Exchange Administrator.

Special Migration Issues

Any undertaking as potentially complicated as a migration can involve special situations.

Most of those situations can be grouped into the following five categories:

- Mail sent to migrated users

- Replies to migrated users

- Replies to migrated mail

- Preventing non-delivery reports

- Migrating distribution lists

Mail Sent to Migrated Users

Many migration scenarios will have only some of the foreign mail users migrating to Microsoft Exchange. That could be for a variety of reasons, such as a multiphase migration, where users are migrated at different times. An organization might also want the two mail systems to coexist. For various reasons, when some users are migrated and others are not, there can be problems with mail sent to migrated users. After a mailbox has been successfully migrated, the old mailbox could still receive mail that was in transit or sent from users who don't have the new address. This situation can be handled in a number of ways, as listed below

- **Forwarding feature.** If the foreign mail system has a forwarding feature, that feature can be implemented immediately after the migration.

- **Directory synchronization.** Directory synchronization can enable users in the foreign system to see and use the new addresses of the migrated users. The Microsoft Mail utility REQMAIN, which forces a postoffice to send its directory information to other peers, can even be run on the Microsoft Exchange server running the Mail Connector. This would serve to immediately send the new Exchange directory updates to the Microsoft Mail system. The directory synchronization option, if available, is probably the best option.

- **Use both mailboxes.** A third, and unattractive, option is for the migrated users to periodically log on to their old mailboxes and pick up any mail.

Two additional options require more explanation and are therefore found under the next two headings.

Maintaining Former E-Mail Addresses

Migrated users may need to keep their old e-mail addresses in order to receive mail sent to those addresses. Former e-mail addresses can easily be associated with a migrated user through the use of proxy addresses.

As you learned in Chapter 5, Exchange messages are addressed using names (the display name from the user's perspective, the DN from the system's perspective). However, an Exchange recipient may need to receive mail from a non-Exchange system; therefore, various e-mail addresses are automatically generated for each Exchange recipient. These addresses are also referred to as *proxy addresses*. Proxy addresses for MS Mail, Lotus cc:Mail, SMTP, and X.400 are created automatically for Exchange recipients.

If a migrated user needs to retain his or her old e-mail address, a current proxy address can be modified or a new one created. This can be done through the E-mail Addresses property page of an Exchange recipient. A recipient can even have two different addresses for the same address type. For example, suppose Bob Smith's new SMTP address is BobS@Chicago.Widget.COM and his previous SMTP address (before the migration) was bobsmith@widget.com. Other SMTP users will probably use his old address, and Bob will not receive his messages. The administrator can easily create a secondary SMTP address of bobsmith@widget.com so Bob will get all his mail.

The Microsoft Mail address format is referred to as the 10/10/10 format, which is shorthand for network/postoffice/userid. Sometimes the MS Mail proxy address of an Exchange recipient is referred to as a 10/10/10 address. Be aware of that for the Microsoft exams.

Editing the Alias File on an SMTP Relay Host

Some SMTP environments could be configured to take messages sent to an old address and route them to the new Exchange address, even without the use of proxy addresses. You can edit the alias file on an SMTP relay host to have the old e-mail address point to the new address. For example, incoming mail is received by an SMTP relay host. That host accesses its listing for that destination address and sees that the mail sent to that address is to be sent to a new address, in our case, a mailbox on an Exchange server.

Replies to Migrated Users

Another issue that relates to partial migrations is foreign mail users replying to migrated users. This is slightly different than sending mail to migrated users, which was discussed above. This situation arises when a foreign mail user has mail that was sent from a user before they were migrated. The return address on this mail points to the migrated user's old foreign mail address. When the current foreign mail user uses the "reply to sender" function to send mail to that user, they could receive a non-delivery report (NDR). For migrations from MS Mail, that result should not occur if the migrated user's postoffice has been migrated and deleted, if that user has the necessary proxy address (10/10/10 address), and if directory synchronization has taken place between the two systems. But if the above requirements are not met, then NDRs could be generated. For example, if users of a particular postoffice have been migrated, but that postoffice has not been deleted and is still found in the Microsoft Mail Connector, then replies to those migrated users will not be able to be delivered and would generate NDRs.

Replies to Migrated Mail

Another potential probelm situation is migrated users replying to migrated mail. A migration can include migrating foreign users' addresses, and/or, foreign mail. If mail is migrated, it could have a return address pointing to a user on the foreign mail system. Normally, when an Exchange user replies to a message, their MAPI address book provider tries to resolve the return address by referencing the Global Address List (GAL) or the user's Personal Address Book. But when the message being replied to is a migrated message, and the return address points to a foreign address, the MAPI address book provider will not find the return address. The easiest way to resolve that situation is to migrate all the users. In that scenario the address book provider will match the foreign return address to the new Exchange address. If that cannot be done, then custom recipients could be created for all "not yet migrated" users and that address can be used when replying to migrated mail. The Directory Synchronization Agent (DXA) can be used to create custom recipients for foreign mail users. One last method is to use "one-off" addressing when replying to migrated mail.

The above discussion on "Replies to Migrated Mail" is a generic explanation of this topic. Depending on the particular foreign mail system that you are coexisting with or migrating from, replying to migrated mail could be different.

Preventing Non-Delivery Reports

Some coexistence scenarios will create unwanted non-delivery report (NDR) messages. After describing one of those scenarios, we will also describe what can be done to prevent those unwanted NDRs.

Some organizations are connected to X.400 networks. In the course of a migration to Microsoft Exchange, an organization's current X.400 gateways could coexist with and be connected to a Microsoft Exchange X.400 Connector. Because the Exchange X.400 Connector will probably eventually replace the current gateway, the Exchange site could be configured with the same X.400 address space as the current X.400 gateway. It would also be normal to configure the current X.400 gateway to deliver all incoming X.400 messages to the Exchange X.400 Connector for delivery to the migrated users. A problem can arise when a message is forwarded to the Exchange X.400 Connector that is for a user who has not yet been migrated. That event would generate a non-delivery report (NDR).

To prevent unwanted NDRs the Exchange environment needs to know that it is sharing an X.400 address with another X.400 system. That lets Exchange forward to the other system any X.400 messages intended for non-Exchange recipients. Configuring Exchange for this situation is done through the Site Addressing object, General page, and by checking the "Share address space with other X.400 system" checkbox.

Migrating Distribution Lists

As stated earlier, a multiphase migration allows for both mail systems to be operational and resources to be gradually migrated. One of the most problematic issues with a multiphase migration relates to distribution lists (DLs). For example, a DL can be migrated to Exchange and remain operational on the existing system. If different changes are made to the two copies of that DL, problems can arise. Exchange recipients might be added to a DL after it has migrated to Exchange. Those recipients might not be added to the corresponding DL on the old system. At a later stage of the migration process, the older copy of that DL (still in use on the foreign system) might be migrated again and overwrite the existing one in the Exchange system. There are five basic methods for managing this situation:

- **Do not migrate the DL until the last phase**   You could decide not to migrate a particular DL until the last stage of a multiphase migration. But since mailboxes will be migrating over to Exchange during the different phases, constant modifications could be required for that DL.

- **Keep duplicate DLs on both systems**   You could have the same DL on both systems. This method would require coordinated changes between both copies of the DL.

- **Convert the DL to a public folder**   An MS Mail DL could be converted to an Exchange public folder. Users would then go to the public folder to view mail sent to the former DL.

- **Maintain the DL only on the Exchange system**   Because there would be only one copy of the DL, there is no problem with coordinating changes. But this method creates more traffic between the two systems. Whenever an existing user sends a message to the DL, the message is sent to the DL recipient in the Exchange system. An MTA then sends messages to the members of that DL, which could include recipients back in the existing system. (Remember, this is a multiphase migration. Both systems will be concurrent for a time.) In this situation, messages could be sent back to the network they originated in, thereby creating additional traffic.

- **Disable the DL on the existing system**   You could notify existing users that a particular DL is not going to be operational until after migration.

The following presents a scenario that allows you to choose from the above options. Your company has migrated about half of its Microsoft Mail users to Microsoft Exchange. The remaining half will continue to use Microsoft Mail. You would like to manage an existing Microsoft Mail distribution list from one application. You would also like Microsoft Mail users to be able to find the same addresses in the Microsoft Mail global address list that they used before the migration. Considering the above options, what would you do to meet these requirements? One solution is to not migrate the DL and configure dirsynch between the systems. That would allow Microsoft Mail users to view all the Exchange users in their address list, and would allow for the management of the DL from one system.

Another problem that can arise is an Exchange DL containing migrated users not synchronizing with a foreign mail DL. For example, your organization is in the middle of a multiphase migration from Microsoft Mail to Microsoft Exchange. Most of the migrated users are given proxy addresses that match their previous Microsoft Mail addresses. Microsoft Exchange DLs are created that include migrated users. You notice, however, that these DLs do not synchronize with the Microsoft Mail global address list. The probable cause of this problem is that some of the migrated users on the DL do not have proxy MS Mail e-mail addresses.

Synchronizing DLs in multiphase migration can be difficult. Be sure to plan for contingencies.

Microsoft ✓ ***Exam*** ***Objective***   **Diagnose and resolve migration problems.**

Troubleshooting a Migration

A migration, like any operation, can run into problems. The Windows NT Event Log, and the Migration Wizard error summary can be used to troubleshoot.

If problems occur during a migration, some of the probable causes are:

- The account used to perform the migration does not have administrator privileges in the existing system.

- The account used to perform the migration does not have administrator privileges on the Exchange server.

- The .PKL, .PRI, or .SEC files were edited improperly.

- The .PKL or .PRI files are missing.

- The .PKL or .PRI files are renamed.

- Network problems occurred during the migration.

- The Private Information Store ran out of space during the migration.

After using the Windows NT Event Log or the Migration Wizard error log to identify the cause of the problem, the administrator can resolve the problem by assigning the necessary permissions, editing the appropriate files, or making more disk space available.

While not actually a troubleshooting situation, you might want to limit the sizes of Microsoft Mail mailboxes before you migrate them to Microsoft Exchange Server. One way to do that is to run the MMFClean utility on the Microsoft Mail postoffice. Limiting the amount of data migrated could help prevent situations needing troubleshooting.

Performance can be an issue during a migration. It is possible to experience slow migration conversion rates. If that is the case, you could help performance by adding memory to the Microsoft Exchange server to decrease virtual memory paging on that server.

A situation you could encounter relates to migrating clients of Lotus cc:Mail Mobile for Windows. If you did not take these remote users into account and you performed the migration, you might not migrate messages stored on the remote computers. The solution is to have the mobile user copy the data files to a sharepoint so you can run the Migration Wizard against them.

Another troubleshooting situation involves being prevented from migrating Novell GroupWise mailboxes. The most likely cause of this problem is that the GroupWise account performing the migration has not been granted "proxy access" to the mailboxes. GroupWise mailbox owners must grant proxy access to their mailboxes to the account performing the migration. If they do not grant that access, their mailboxes will not be migrated.

Summary

A migration allows an existing non-Exchange mail system to be moved to an Exchange environment. Resources on the existing system (such as addresses, mailboxes, messages, folders, and schedule information) can all be imported into Exchange.

Special programs, called source extractors, prepare the resources on the existing system for inclusion in Exchange. Source extractors exist for many systems including: MS Mail, Lotus cc:Mail, and Novell GroupWise.

The Migration Wizard program imports the resources of an existing system into Exchange. The Migration Wizard can take information collected by a source extractor, or it can extract and import directly from an MS Mail, Lotus cc:Mail, Novell GroupWise, or Collabra Share system.

Review Questions

1. You are implementing a migration from Microsoft Mail to Microsoft Exchange. You have just completed the first step in a two-step migration. If you wanted to modify the existing naming convention during the second step in the migration, what file would you have to modify?

   A. Packing list file

   B. Primary file

   C. Secondary file

   D. Migration log file

2. Your Microsoft Mail system has 24,000 users. You will be migrating all of those users to Microsoft Exchange using the Migration Wizard and Exchange Administrator. What would be the most efficient way to pre-assign properties to the mailboxes being migrated?

   A. Modify the packing list file to include the desired properties.

   B. Edit the primary and secondary migration files.

C. Create a recipient with the desired properties. Use that recipient during an export and import procedure.

D. Create a mailbox with the desired properties. Designate that mailbox as the template mailbox during the migration.

3. The first step in a two-step migration has already taken place. The CSV file contains directory information on 2200 users. What would be the most efficient way to modify all of the recipient display names?

A. Complete the migration, and then use Microsoft Exchange Administrator to modify the display names.

B. Edit the CSV file, and then continue with the second phase of the migration.

C. Run the first step of the Migration Wizard again and this time modify the names.

D. Run the second step of the Migration Wizard and modify the names during that process.

4. Your Microsoft Exchange network is connected to an SMTP backbone. One of the other systems connected to this backbone is a large UNIX-based SMTP system of 26,000 users. The directory information about these users is stored in a SQL database. You would like to add these 26,000 SMTP users as custom recipients to your Exchange directory. How would you efficiently do that?

A. Manually create custom recipients for each SMTP user.

B. Configure directory synchronization between the two systems using Internet Mail Service.

C. Use LDAP to automatically import the SMTP users.

D. Use the Import utility of Microsoft Exchange Administrator.

5. You are importing an employee telephone list into your Exchange directory. You would like to keep the current directory information unchanged. X.400 addresses are one of the properties of your recipients. What Exchange object does the "o" in an X.400 address relate to?

   A. Organization name

   B. Site name

   C. Server name

   D. Domain name

6. There has been a partial migration of SMTP users to Microsoft Exchange Server. Both systems have their own connectors to the Internet for external mail access. The foreign system uses an SMTP relay host running on a UNIX server. You want the users who have migrated to still receive mail sent to their old SMTP addresses. What is the best way to do that?

   A. Move the SMTP relay host function to the Microsoft Exchange server.

   B. Configure a forward file on the SMTP relay host.

   C. Instruct each user to create a rule to forward mail to the old system.

   D. Update the alias file on the UNIX server acting as the SMTP relay host to point to the Microsoft Exchange server and mailbox.

7. The Microsoft Mail Connector is configured between Microsoft Exchange and Microsoft Mail systems. You use the Migration Wizard to migrate some of the Mail users over to Exchange. One of the migrated users, Marcy, can send mail to Microsoft Mail users, but cannot receive mail from those users. What is the most likely cause of her problems?

   A. Directory synchronization is not configured between the two systems.

   B. Marcy's original mailbox was deleted.

   C. Marcy's original mailbox was not deleted.

   D. The Microsoft Mail Connector was configured for sending not receiving.

8. Your Microsoft Mail system has multiple postoffices. You migrate one of the postoffices to Microsoft Exchange Server. After the migration, some of the migrated users report that they can send mail to Microsoft Mail users, but they cannot receive mail from those users. What could you do to remedy this situation?

   A. Delete the Microsoft Mail address space from the Site Addressing properties, and recalculate routing.

   B. Delete the obsolete Microsoft Mail mailboxes and assign a 10/10/10 address to the migrated users.

   C. Run the REQMAIN utility on the Microsoft Exchange server running the Mail Connector.

   D. Delete the Microsoft Mail address space for each migrated user.

9. Half of your company has migrated from Microsoft Mail to Microsoft Exchange. Users who have not yet migrated report that they are receiving non-delivery reports (NDRs) when they reply to messages that were sent by Microsoft Mail users before they had migrated. You check to see that the migrated users have the correct secondary proxy addresses, and they do. What is the most likely reason the Microsoft Mail users are receiving the NDRs?

   A. The migrated users' Microsoft Mail mailboxes are not deleted.

   B. Microsoft Mail site addressing is disabled.

   C. The Microsoft Mail address space for the migrated users is not enabled.

   D. The Microsoft Mail postoffice is still configured in the Microsoft Mail Connector.

10. You are implementing a multiphase migration from Microsoft Mail to Microsoft Exchange. During the migration, a Microsoft Mail Connector is delivering mail between the two systems. Microsoft Mail users report receiving non-delivery reports (NDRs). They receive the NDRs after they have replied to a message that was sent by a user before that user migrated. To troubleshoot this, you confirm that the Microsoft Mail e-mail address for both the original Microsoft Mail postoffice and the Microsoft Exchange connector are entered for each mailbox. You also confirm that all migrated users have been removed from their former Microsoft Mail postoffices. What should you do to ensure that message replies reach their new destinations?

A. Create SMTP address spaces for all users to use as the reply address.

B. Remove the original Microsoft Mail address space from each migrated mailbox.

C. Remove the Microsoft Exchange connector postoffice address space from each migrated mailbox.

D. Migrate all remaining Microsoft Mail users, and delete the postoffice.

11. Acme Inc. is migrating from an X.400 mail system to Microsoft Exchange. The migration is a multiphase migration. During the migration, the current X.400 gateway will be operational along with the Microsoft Exchange X.400 Connector. To allow for X.400 messages to be delivered to migrated users, the Exchange site is configured with the same X.400 address space as the current X.400 gateway. The current X.400 gateway is also configured to forward all X.400 mail to the Exchange X.400 Connector. Because all the users are not yet migrated, what could you do to prevent non-delivery reports (NDRs) for mail sent to Exchange for those non-migrated users?

A. Configure the external X.400 MTA to forward all X.400 messages for this organization to both the Exchange X.400 Connector and the current X.400 gateway.

B. Configure a custom recipient to have an X.400 proxy address that is identical to the address of the current X.400 gateway, and configure an inbox rule that routes all incoming mail to the X.400 gateway.

   C. Configure the Microsoft Exchange site addressing to have the same address as the current X.400 gateway, and to route all messages sent to non-Exchange recipients to the current X.400 gateway.

   D. During the migration, disable the X.400 address space in the Microsoft Exchange site addressing.

12. Sprockets Inc. is in the middle of a multiphase migration from Microsoft Mail to Microsoft Exchange. Each migrated user is given a proxy address that matches their previous Microsoft Mail address. Microsoft Exchange DLs are created that include migrated users. You notice, however, that these DLs do not synchronize with the Microsoft Mail global address list. What is the likely problem?

   A. Directory synchronization has not completed the T2 phase.

   B. The distribution lists contain recipients who do not have Microsoft Mail proxy e-mail addresses.

   C. The distribution lists contain addresses that are duplicates of existing Microsoft Mail addresses.

   D. The distribution lists contain names that are illegal.

13. HotChilis Inc. has migrated about half of its Microsoft Mail users to Microsoft Exchange. The remaining half will continue to use Microsoft Mail. There is an existing Microsoft Mail distribution list that you would like to manage from one application. You would also like Microsoft Mail users to be able to find the same addresses in the Microsoft Mail global address list that they used before the migration. How could you meet these requirements?

   A. Continue to manage the distribution list from Microsoft Mail, and configure directory synchronization between Microsoft Exchange and Microsoft Mail.

   B. Create a distribution list in Microsoft Exchange and include the original Microsoft Mail distribution list as a member of the new distribution list.

C. Create a distribution list in Microsoft Exchange, and assign the Microsoft Mail address of the new distribution list as a member of the original Microsoft Mail distribution list.

D. Configure directory synchronization between Microsoft Exchange and Microsoft Mail, and exclude all Microsoft Mail addresses from participation in directory synchronization.

14. You are migrating a Lotus cc:Mail system to Microsoft Exchange Server. Some of the clients are using Lotus cc:Mail Mobile for Windows. How would you access the remote message store of those clients during the migration?

   A. Copy all the remote e-mail data files to a network share point and run the Migration Wizard against those files.

   B. Use the Migration Wizard while each remote user is connected to the Lotus cc:Mail postoffice.

   C. Use the Migration Wizard while each remote user is connected to the Microsoft Exchange Server.

   D. Import all the remote data files into the Lotus cc:Mail postoffice and then run the Migration Wizard.

15. You attempt to migrate Novell GroupWise mailboxes to Microsoft Exchange Server. But you find that you are unable to migrate the mailboxes. What is the most likely cause of the problem?

   A. A password is configured for the mailboxes.

   B. The client computers are not running Client for Microsoft Networks.

   C. Proxy access has not been granted for each mailbox.

   D. The GroupWise mailboxes need to be created as custom recipients before the migration.

16. You are migrating a number of Microsoft Mail users to Microsoft Exchange Server. What could you do to limit the size of mailboxes you want to migrate?

A. Clean each mailbox with the MMFClean utility.

B. Run EDBUTIL.

C. Run Microsoft Exchange Performance Optimizer.

D. Set mailbox storage limits.

17. You have experienced slow migration conversion rates in the past. What factor would have the greatest effect on this problem?

A. Paging on the Microsoft Mail postoffice

B. Paging on the Microsoft Exchange Server

C. Processor on the Microsoft Mail postoffice

D. Processor on the Microsoft Windows NT workstation

18. Which property of an Exchange recipient can be used to allow a user to retain his or her pre-migration foreign addresses?

A. E-mail addresses (also called proxy addresses)

B. Protocol property

C. Custom attribute property

D. Advanced properties

19. Which of the following can be used to modify a large number of Exchange recipients in a bulk manner?

A. Performance Monitor

B. User Manager for Domains

C. Directory Import and Export

D. Event Viewer

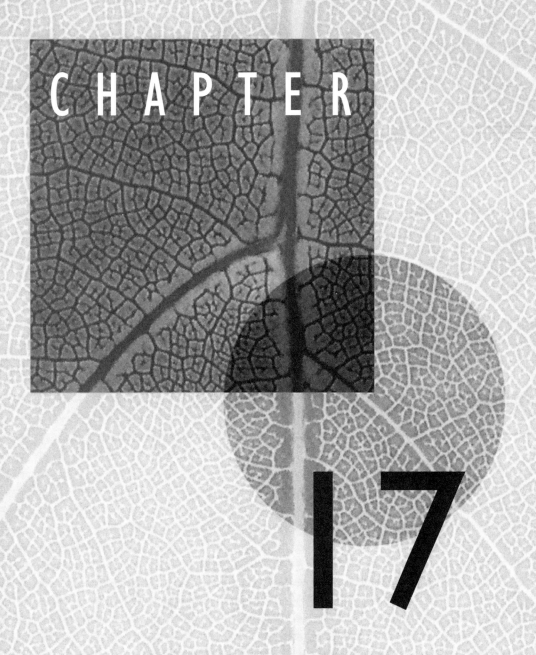

CHAPTER

17

Planning an Exchange Environment

areful planning leads to efficient and effective installation, configuration, and use of an Exchange system. Although Exchange is a highly powerful messaging tool, lack of planning can prevent its full potential from being unleashed. Someone once said that an ox cart is just as useful as a rocket, if you don't know where you are going.

This chapter is not a comprehensive "how-to" on Exchange planning. However, it will help prepare you for the Exchange exam by introducing you to planning issues. It will also help you plan real-world systems. We will discuss planning sites, servers, site connections, connections to non-Exchange systems, and migrations.

Planning the Exchange Topology

The first (and possibly most important) goal when planning your Exchange environment is to design the basic topology of your Exchange organization.

Planning the Exchange topology does not necessarily entail planning the specific properties of objects. Topology planning is mainly concerned with what objects (sites, number of servers, number and type of connectors, etc.) are needed, not how they will be configured. This planning stage focuses on the major organizational units of the Exchange organization. Once it has been determined what and where something is needed (e.g., a public folder for sales leads is needed on Server 1), the specific properties of that object can be planned later. The "big strokes" must be made before the "small strokes."

Three important questions to be addressed are:

- How many sites are needed?

- If you need more than one site, how will you connect them?

- Do you need to connect to non-Exchange systems?

But before answering these, you will need to collect some preliminary information.

What Preliminary Information Must Be Collected?

You need to collect a lot of information before you can begin to make planning decisions. You need information about your network, user needs, Windows NT servers, and non-Exchange mail systems.

Network Topology of Your Organization

A network topology is defined by the number, location, type, available bandwidth, and transport protocols of an organization's networks. Here is a list of some of the characteristics of a network topology:

- **Number of networks**   Networks are usually considered to be separated by a bridge or *router*. Each side of a bridge or router constitutes a network. Sometimes a specific physical network is also called a *network segment.*

- **Type and speed of network**   Ethernet/10 Mbps and Token Ring/4 and 16 Mbps are the most common. ARCnet/2.5 Mbps and ATM/155 Mbps are sometimes used.

- **Available bandwidth**   Use network traffic monitoring utilities in Microsoft Systems Management Server (SMS) or another packet sniffer program to determine the available bandwidth in a network. (A sniffer program is used to monitor activity on a network.)

- **Transport protocols**   For example, TCP/IP, NWLink, NetBEUI, etc.

Windows NT Domain Topology

A Windows NT domain is a group of computers that share the same user account database and security policies. You will need to have quite a bit of information about the domains, including the configuration of any trust relationships between domains, to properly plan your Exchange system.

User Needs

Many factors determine what Exchange resources will be available to users, and where those resources will be placed. You will need a lot of information about the users to efficiently and effectively make these decisions. Some of this information will already be collected in the network inventory. Some information may come from the current messaging system. Other information will need to come from estimates made by the users themselves or from managerial edicts. Here is a list of some of the major pieces of user information you will need to have:

- The network location of each user's computer, also referred to as the *network segment*. (This will be used to estimate performance.)

- The hardware resources of each computer. (Helps determine which Exchange client applications can be used and which computers need to be upgraded.)

- The operating system running on each computer. (Helps determine which Exchange client applications can be used and which computers need to be upgraded.)

- Whether or not each user has a Windows NT domain account. (A factor in determining site location.)

- The messaging services required (for both client and server configurations). Examples include:

  - Exchange Server

  - Microsoft Mail

  - Internet mail

  - Microsoft Fax

- The messaging configuration required (for both client and server configurations). Examples include:

  - Remote access

  - Read message options

  - Send message options

  - New message notification method

  - Advanced security

- The number of messages that will go through the system. (This is a factor in estimating system load.) Microsoft has defined three basic, message volume user profiles (see Table 17.1).

- The message storage requirements. (This will determine the server storage requirements and the number of servers needed.) Users' folders can be stored in either the Private Information Store (which is always located on an Exchange server) or in a personal folder store (which can be located on a user's local computer).

- Public folder planning. The following are some of the important issues involved in public folder planning:

  - Which public folders will be needed initially?

  - What is the estimated size of each public folder? This will help determine storage requirements.

  - Which users will need access to which public folders? This will help you decide on which servers to place specific public folders. For example, if a large number of users located on a single network need access to a particular public folder, you should create the public folder on a server on that network.

  - Based on storage requirements and an analysis of user access, which public folders will be created on which servers?

  - Will public folders need to be replicated across servers? If yes, which servers? Reasons for having multiple replicas of a public folder include load balancing, quicker user access across site boundaries, and fault tolerance.

  - If replication will be used, what replication schedule will be used?

  - Which users will be given permission to create top-level public folders?

  - Will there be individual configurations on specific public folders? Configuration options include user permissions, views, rules, forms, and size restrictions.

- The electronic forms that will be needed.

- The type of remote connections that will be needed to access mailboxes and public folders. You will need to know the number of users who will be remotely accessing Exchange resources, what type of connections they will be using, approximately when they will make those connections, and approximately how long they will need to be connected.

	Parameter	Light User	Medium User	Heavy User
TABLE 17.1 Message volume user profiles	Maximum inbox size (in messages)	20	125	250
	Old mail processing (per day)	5x	15x	20x
	Total sends per day (average)	7	20	39
	Total received per day (average)	20	56	119

Current Windows NT Servers

You need to have information about the current Windows NT servers, such as their hardware configurations, disk space, and RAM. Once you have determined the requirements for the number and configurations of servers, you can evaluate the current servers to see if you can use any of them or if you will need to install new servers.

Non-Exchange Mail Systems

You need to know if there are any non-Exchange mail systems (Microsoft Mail, Lotus cc:Mail, etc.) in an organization, and if they are to coexist with Exchange or be migrated to Exchange.

How Many Sites Are Needed?

Many small organizations will use a single Exchange site. Large and geographically dispersed organizations may require several sites. However, there are large, geographically dispersed organizations that use a single site. In this section, we will discuss requirements and other factors that help determine a site design.

Using all of the necessary factors, you can determine the number and location of the Exchange sites. If multiple sites will be used, you will also need to plan your intersite connections.

RPC Communication

A site's underlying network must permit RPC communication between clients and servers, and between all the servers in a site. To support RPC, a network must have permanent high-speed connections. The definition of high speed is somewhat arbitrary. Most designers do not recommend a bandwidth less than 128Kbps. Less than that would support only light traffic and would perform poorly. The recommended network speeds for a site are LAN speeds (such as ARCnet at 2.5Mbps, Token Ring at 4Mbps or 16Mbps, or Ethernet at 10Mbps). WAN connections over a T1 line at 1.5Mbps could also support a site, depending on load and other factors. (A T1 line is a leased network connection that provides fairly high bandwidth.)

An organization with six Ethernet networks connected by high-speed routers can support a single site. If this group of six networks also has a temporary low-bandwidth connection of 56Kbps to an additional remote network, two sites are required because the 56Kbps connection will not support RPC communication.

Factors other than RPC communication, like desired messaging performance, can dictate multiple sites. These factors will be discussed shortly.

Transport Protocols

Exchange supports TCP/IP, IPX/SPX, NetBEUI, and Banyan Vines. If a particular network does not support one of the supported Exchange transport protocols, it can not be part of a site.

Windows NT Domains

All of the Exchange servers in a site must use the same site service account for intrasite component communication. A single Exchange site can include more than one Windows NT domain, but all of the domains must be related by trust relationships. The Windows NT domains and the physical networks that make up a site determine the *site boundaries*.

Performance Requirements

You can estimate the performance difference for a single versus a multiple site topology by projecting estimated system loads of both topologies. Even if a network topology can support a single site, the estimated performance level might not meet the requirements.

Connecting Sites

The primary factor when choosing a site connector is the type of network infrastructure between the sites. If that infrastructure can support high-speed connections, the Site Connector is the obvious choice. Another message system can be used as a bridge between sites when there is no high-speed connection. SMTP and X.400 message systems can connect sites when the Internet Mail Service and X.400 Connector are used.

More than one connector can be used between sites in order to increase fault tolerance or balance loads. Each connector will have a cost associated with it so that the MTA's cost-based routing can function.

Connecting to Non-Exchange Systems

If an Exchange implementation will contain connections to non-Exchange systems, the sites that will make those connections can be designed at this stage. This will help determine site requirements, such as how many Exchange servers will be needed in a site, and their configuration.

Organizations should use standardized naming conventions. For example, mailbox names could be "first name last name" or "last name, first name." A general naming convention can be based on geography, company structure, building or floor numbers, etc. A good naming convention makes it easy to identify and add sites, servers, connectors, mailboxes, etc.

During the planning stage, you can also determine many fault tolerance and maintenance procedures. For example, backup routines, server and link monitors, and diagnostic logging can all be standardized.

Figure 17.1 illustrates some of the decisions that are made after the Exchange topology has been determined.

Microsoft ✓ Exam Objective

Develop security strategies.

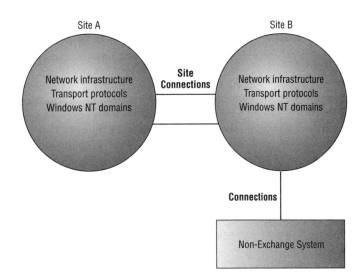

FIGURE 17.1

Decisions made after determining the Exchange topology

Planning Sites

After the number of sites and their locations have been determined, you can plan site-level messaging parameters that will be inherited by all of the servers in each site. Some of the site-wide parameters that you need to consider are listed in Table 17. 2.

TABLE 17.2	**Site-Level Object**	**Parameters**
Planning site-level configurations	DS site configuration	• The Tombstone lifetime (length of time information on deleted directory objects is preserved to notify other servers). The default is 30 days. • The Garbage collection interval (interval between the times expired tombstones are deleted). The default is 12 hours. • The Offline address book configuration. • Custom attributes.

	Site-Level Object	Parameters
T A B L E 17.2 (cont.) Planning site-level configurations	IS site configuration	• If message tracking is enabled or disabled for the IS. The default is disabled. • Top-level folder creation permissions. • Storage warnings schedule. • Public folder affinities.
	MTA site configuration	• If message tracking is enabled or disabled for the MTA. The default is disabled. • Messaging defaults (including RTS values, connection retry values, association parameters, and transfer timeouts).
	Site addressing	• E-mail addresses. • Routing calculation schedule.
	Encryption	• Advanced security use. • Preferred encryption algorithm. • Key Management Server location. • Key Management Server administration.
	Monitors	• Server Monitors. • Link Monitors.
	Protocols	• Which protocols will be enabled. • How protocols will be configured.

Connections and directory replication will be covered in the "Planning Site Connections" section.

Figure 17.2 provides an illustration of the main topics in site planning.

Planning Servers

You need to consider many important issues when you plan servers, including:

• Number and location of servers

FIGURE 17.2

Site planning main topics

- Server-level configurations

- Recipient configurations

- Exchange Server installation and configuration

- Exchange client installation and configuration

Microsoft ✓ *Exam* *Objective*   **Configure Server Locations.**

Number and Locations of Servers

The number of Exchange servers in a site will depend on factors such as network topology and speed, the number and locations of mailboxes, and performance and storage requirements. We will discuss each of these factors in the following text.

Microsoft
Exam
Objective

Choose an implementation strategy for Microsoft Exchange Server. Elements include:

- Server locations
- Address space

Develop an infrastructure for Exchange Server.

- Identify public folders, including server-side scripting.
- Identify private information stores.
- Plan Internet connectivity and access.

Server Locations and Network Segments

Performance is a critical factor in a messaging system. Placing Exchange servers on the best network segments for user access is very important for performance. This chapter is not a primer on network performance factors, but the following scenario provides one look at some network factors and Exchange. A company has four networks backboned on an Ethernet switch. Table 17.3 provides the speed of each segment and the number of Exchange users on it.

T A B L E   17.3

Network segments and users in case study

Segment	Speed	Users
A	100Mbps	0
B	10Mbps	125
C	10Mbps	75
D	10Mbps	150 remote

In the above scenario, it could make sense to put the Exchange servers on segment A because of that segment's high speed. Because servers are in a one-to-many relationship with clients, placing servers on a high speed segment could ensure better performance.

Number and Locations of Mailboxes

Determining the number of mailboxes and locating them on specific servers involves many factors. Some of these factors are:

- **Local delivery is a priority**   If the users who will frequently send information to each other are grouped together on the same server, message delivery will remain local to the server.

- **Local network traffic is a priority**   If all the users of a particular network segment are located on servers on that network segment, message transmission will be improved because messages will not have to travel over multiple network segments. (Be careful not to overemphasize this requirement and cause the physical network to be saturated.)

- **Fault tolerance increased through multiple points of failure**   If recipients are spread out between multiple servers, there will not be a single point of failure. (Don't put all your eggs in one basket.)

- **Fault tolerance increased by protecting a single point**   By placing your most important recipients on a single server, that server can utilize high-end fault tolerant features to protect those resources. (Put all your eggs in one basket, but guard that basket!)

Performance and Storage Requirements

In addition to the minimum hardware requirements for an Exchange Server installation (see Chapter 4), additional resources will probably be needed to accommodate the desired performance level, and mailbox and public folder storage needs.

Some of the factors that relate to server performance are:

1. Number of disks

2. Disk speed

3. Amount of memory

4. Processor speed and number of processors

5. Performance of network cards

Storage requirements can become unreasonable (users will try to save everything forever). The following policies can help control this problem:

- Set mailbox storage limits

- Set public folder storage limits

- Set age limits for items in public folders

- Set maximum message sizes

Microsoft ✓ ***Exam Objective***   **Develop the configuration of an Exchange Server computer.**

Server-Level Configurations

You need to examine many objects and properties when you plan server-level configurations. Table 17.4 lists some of the things you need to consider.

	Server-Level Object	Parameters
TABLE 17.4 Planning server-level configurations	Private Information Store	• Storage limits. • The server used to store public folders.
	Public Information Store	• Storage limits that cause a warning message to be sent to mailbox owners. • Storage limits that prevent mailbox owners from sending mail. • The server used to store public folders.
	Message Transfer Agent	• Message size limits. • Distribution list expansion. • Conversion of incoming messages to MS Exchange content.
	System Attendant	• Message tracking log file maintenance.

Recipient Configurations

When you planned the site servers, you decided which servers would house which recipients. Now we will discuss the configuration of the recipients.

The planning phase is a good time to decide which templates to use to create mailboxes, distribution lists, and custom recipients. Templates will make it easier to create and standardize these recipients later in the implementation phase. Some of the properties that can be specified in a template are listed in the following sections. You can also begin to plan the configurations of public folders.

Mailbox

The following are some of the critical properties of a mailbox. These should be carefully considered any time a new mailbox is created.

- Home server

- Hide from address book

- Message size limits

- Information store storage limits

- Distribution list membership

- Delivery restrictions

- Delivery options

- Advanced security

- Protocols

Distribution Lists

The following are some of the critical properties of a distribution list. These should be carefully considered any time a new DL is created.

- Members

- Delivery restrictions

- Message size limits

- Hide from address book

- Hide membership from address book

Custom Recipients

The properties of a custom recipient are basically the same as a mailbox, with the addition of the target (non-Exchange) e-mail address. Planning a custom recipient template entails determining the common properties for a group of foreign users. The target address of each custom recipient will be unique, so this field will not be part of the template.

Public Folders

When you designed the Exchange topology, you determined general information about groupware applications. At this planning stage, you need to design the intrasite related properties of public folders. Some of the properties you need to determine are:

- Intrasite replica locations

- Replication schedules

- Age limits

- Storage limits

- Server-side scripting

Microsoft ✓ ***Exam Objective***

Develop server-side scripting strategies.

If your organization could benefit from workflow applications, then server-side scripting strategies will need to be developed. That would include the processes to automate, the people involved in those processes, the developers needed to create the scripts, the development tools needed, and many other strategies.

Whether or not particular public folders will be replicated to other sites can be determined now or when you design the intersite configurations. We will do it later.

Exchange Server Installation and Configuration

Now that you have determined the number, network location, and configuration of the Exchange servers, you need to purchase the necessary copies and licenses for the Exchange Server product and schedule the installation of each server.

Microsoft ✓ ***Exam*** ***Objective***

Develop long-term administration strategies.

- Plan a backup strategy.
- Plan a disaster recovery strategy.
- Plan information store maintenance.
- Plan remote administration.
- Plan information retrieval strategies.

Exchange Server Maintenance

The Private Information Store and the Public Information Store are two important areas of an Exchange environment that need to be carefully maintained. Storage being used and public folder replication must be monitored to ensure an efficient and effective Exchange environment.

The Private Information Store permits an administrator to examine the storage levels of individual mailboxes. The Public Information Store permits the examination of individual public folder storage levels, folder replication status, and server replication status.

Server Backup Plan

Consider the following when creating an Exchange server backup:

- How frequently will backups be performed?

- What type of backup will be performed? Options include full, incremental, and differential.

- What time of day should backups be performed? A backup performed over the network can adversely affect network performance and probably necessitates performing the backup during off-hours.

- What device, or devices, will be used for backups?

- How will offsite storage of backup media be handled?

Microsoft ✓ *Exam* *Objective*

Choose Microsoft Exchange Client installation and integration strategies. Elements include:

- Network installation
- Client computer installation
- Scripted client installation
- Forms interoperability
- Schedule+ interoperability
- Calendar interoperability

Exchange Client Installation and Configuration

Earlier you collected an inventory of the user operating systems and computer hardware profiles. Now you can use that information to determine which Exchange client applications will be installed on which client computers.

You also collected messaging service requirements and common configuration requirements. Use that information to create default settings for the client setup program. That information can be placed in files such as EXCHNG .STF and DEFAULT.PRF if installing the Exchange Client, and in OUTLOOK .STF and OUTLOOK.PRF if installing the Outlook client. Those files, along with the setup files, can be placed at a network share point. Users can run the client setup program from that share point and utilize the default settings.

Planning Site Connections

Y ou have already determined the number of sites, their locations, and which connectors to use between the sites. Now you need to determine the properties of those connectors, the properties of the Directory Replication connectors, and the configuration of public folder replication to other sites. These topics are covered in the following sections.

Microsoft Exam Objective

Develop an infrastructure for Exchange Server.

- Identify public folders, including server-side scripting.
- Identify private information stores.
- Plan Internet connectivity and access.

NOTE Planning Internet connectivity and access is covered in this section, as well as in Chapter 14.

Microsoft Exam Objective

Choose an implementation strategy for Microsoft Exchange Server. Elements include:

- Server locations
- Address space

Connector Properties

Some of the common connector properties that need to be planned include:

- Address space

- Connector costs

- Remote sites with which to connect

- Remote servers with which to connect

If you will be using the Site Connector, you need to plan the following properties:

- Messaging bridgehead server

- Target servers

- Target server costs

If you will be using the X.400 Connector or the Dynamic RAS Connector, you need to plan these properties:

- Connection schedules

- Delivery restrictions

If you will be using the Internet Mail Service, the following decisions need to be made:

- Which Exchange server will run the IMS?

- What SMTP mail systems will be connected to and what are their address spaces?

- What type of connection will be used to connect to the Internet or other SMTP hosts?

- How will mail be sent? Your options include forwarding all messages to a single SMTP host or using DNS to resolve addresses and send messages to the recipients' hosts.

- What will be the site address used to generate SMTP e-mail addresses for Exchange users?

- Which recipient will receive IMS notifications?

Directory Replication Connector

Once you have designed your messaging connectors, your Directory Replication connectors can be planned. You need to determine the identity of the directory replication bridgehead servers (both local and remote), which sites to connect, and the replication schedule.

Public Folder Replication between Sites

If you decided that your Exchange topology will include public folder replicas in other sites, you must make plans for replication. Some of the properties that you need to plan to perform replication are the servers that will contain a replica, the schedule for folder replication, and the age limits of replicas.

Planning Connections to Non-Exchange Systems

In this section, we will plan a connection to a Microsoft Mail system. The two primary areas we will discuss are the Microsoft Mail Connector and the Directory Synchronization component.

Microsoft Mail Connector

To provide interoperability between an Exchange system and a Microsoft Mail system, the Microsoft Mail Connector is utilized. You must determine the following properties on this connector:

- Address space
- Interchange properties
- Local postoffice
- Connections
- Connector MTAs

Directory Synchronization Component

Your major decision for directory synchronization is determining which Exchange server will be involved in this process, and what role that server will play: Dirsync Server or Requestor.

If you decide to make your Exchange server a Dirsync Server, the names of the remote dirsync requestors must be collected, and a schedule for synchronization can be defined. If you decide to make the Exchange server a Dirsync Requestor, the name of the remote dirsync server must be known.

Directory synchronization must be coordinated with the administrator of the Microsoft Mail system.

Microsoft ✓ *Exam* *Objective*

Choose Microsoft Exchange Client installation and integration strategies. Elements include:

- Network installation
- Client computer installation
- Scripted client installation
- Forms interoperability
- Schedule+ interoperability
- Calendar interoperability

Schedule+ Free/Busy Connector

If Exchange users of Schedule+ 7.5 and Outlook want to share schedule and calendar information with MS Mail users of Schedule+ 1.0, the following components need to be included in the Exchange design plan:

- MS Mail Connector
- Directory synchronization between Exchange and MS Mail
- Schedule+ Free/Busy Connector

Although the previous scenario permits interoperability between the Exchange applications and MS Mail applications, some advanced features of Outlook are not available to Schedule+ 1.0 and 7.5 users. For example, Outlook nontabular views of calendar information are not available in Schedule+ 1.0 or 7.5. Some of the alternatives that can be used in this situation are:

- Manage a mixed environment. Because these applications can exchange information, a mixed environment can be used. Users simply need to understand that certain features of Outlook will not work for Schedule+ users.

- Configure Outlook to use the Schedule+ option for group scheduling.

- Migrate all clients to Outlook. Make sure users do not delete their Schedule+ files (.SCD and .CAL) because Outlook has an Import/Export Wizard that can import Schedule+ data.

Microsoft ✓ ***Exam Objective***

Develop long-term administration strategies.

- Plan a backup strategy.
- Plan a disaster recovery strategy.
- Plan information store maintenance.
- Plan remote administration.
- Plan information retrieval strategies.

Planning Long-Term Administration

You need to plan for more than just the installation and configuration of the Exchange environment. You also need to plan for the long-term care of the system. Some of the issues that you will need to address include:

- How many administrators will be needed? This will depend on the number of servers, sites, connectors, and recipients.

- Will remote administration be needed? If so, which sites and which remote computers will need to be configured? The relevant sites will need a RAS server, and the relevant remote computers will need the RAS client software installed and configured, as well as a local copy of the

Exchange Administrator program. User Manager for Domains and Server Manager are two additional programs that can also be installed on the remote computers if they are running Windows NT Workstation.

- Will there be specific administrators for particular Exchange functions or objects? (For example, in a large environment there might be an administrator for recipients and another administrator for connections to other sites and foreign systems.)

- Who will be the Exchange administrators? If they are not already trained, arrangements will need to be made to train them.

Planning a Disaster Recovery Strategy

Planning a disaster recovery strategy can involve a large number of considerations. Some of the major ones are listed here:

- What is your organization's definition of a disaster? A mere inconvenience (such as a connector being offline) at one organization can be a major catastrophe at another organization. An organization can define different degrees of disasters with different levels of response.

- What is your organization's definition of acceptable downtime for a particular disaster?

- What is the escalation process and who is to be notified and mobilized in the event of a disaster? How will they be notified (telephone, pager, e-mail, etc.)?

- What are the recovery steps for the defined disasters? These procedures should be written down and tested.

- Is there an inventory of the necessary resources for a recovery process? Resources include hardware (e.g., hard drive) and software (the Exchange Server CD).

Planning Migrations

Many organizations have existing messaging systems that are to be replaced by Exchange. Those existing systems already contain message data and address information that may need to be moved to the Exchange system. You need to determine if that is possible, and if so, how to perform the migration.

The following are some of the main steps for planning a migration:

1. Create a map and inventory of the current messaging systems. You need to know:

   - What systems are connected (so you will know what migrations are possible).

   - What resources are located in each system (so you will know what resources need to be migrated).

   - Which users are using which messaging client applications (so you will know which users need upgrades to their applications and which may need additional hardware).

2. A period of coexistence of the old messaging system and Exchange may be the best way to ease the pain of a migration. This period can be used to perform a phased migration where subsets of the users are migrated during each phase.

3. Design and plan user education. Users must be prepared for the migration and life with the new system.

4. Design and plan client software installation and upgrades.

5. Determine mailbox naming conventions. Decide what naming convention to use for the mailboxes being migrated.

6. Decide what resources will be migrated, such as mailboxes, distribution lists, personal address books, and schedule information.

7. Decide on the migration method, the single-phase or multiphase method.

8. Plan for contingencies. You need to have a fall-back plan if things do not go as planned.

Summary

The planning process is critical to implementing a successful, optimized Exchange organization topology. To plan properly, you will need to determine the number and location of Windows NT domains, and whether the organization will be connected to any non-Exchange systems.

You need to plan intrasite configurations (DS, IS, and MTA) and individual server configurations.

If multiple connected sites will be part of the Exchange organization, you will need to plan the number, types, and properties of the connectors.

Connecting an Exchange system to a non-Exchange system involves coordinated planning by personnel from both systems. When connecting to a Microsoft Mail system, for example, you will need to consider the properties of both the Microsoft Mail Connector and the Directory Synchronization component.

Planning is important when an existing non-Exchange system migrates its message data and address information to Exchange. Issues include what resources will be migrated and what type of migration method to be used. You also need to have a contingency plan in case the migration does not work.

Review Questions

1. You will be installing a Microsoft Exchange Server and must decide what network segment to place it on. There are four network segments (A, B ,C ,D), all backboned on an Ethernet switch. Segment A is at 100Mbps and has zero users. Segment B is at 10Mbps and has 125 users. Segment C is at 10Mbps and has 75 users. Segment C is at 10Mbps and has 150 remote users. What segment would you place the Exchange server on?

    A. Segment A

    B. Segment B

    C. Segment C

    D. Segment D

2. The hardware requirements of an Exchange server are affected by which of the following:

  A. Number of mailboxes

  B. Public folder storage

  C. Message traffic

  D. All of the above

3. Advanced security planning pertains to what object or objects?

  A. Mailboxes

  B. Connectors

  C. Sites

  D. Both A and C

4. Which of the following properties should be considered when planning a connector?

  A. Storage limits

  B. Scheduled connections

  C. Tombstones

  D. Both B and C

5. Which of the following is an important planning issue when interoperating with a non-Exchange system?

  A. POP3 configuration

  B. Mailbox cleanup

  C. Home server of the administrator

  D. Directory synchronization

6. Which of the following is NOT considered when planning a migration?

A. Assigning foreign users administrative rights

B. What resources will be migrated

C. Choosing a migration method (single-phase or multiphase)

D. Installing or upgrading client software

APPENDIX

A

Review Answers

Chapter I

1. The type of utility that would allow you to replace a foreign message system with Exchange is:

   A. Administrative tool

   B. Security utility

   C. X.500

   D. Migration tool

   Answer: D

2. This type of mail system has a passive server:

   A. Shared-file mail system

   B. Client/server mail system

   C. Host-based mail system

   D. Exchange Server

   Answer: A

3. Which of the following is NOT a feature of a client/server messaging system:

   A. Distributed processing

   B. Tight security

   C. Passive client application

   D. Reduced network traffic

   Answer: C

4. Microsoft Outlook is a desktop information manager application that runs on the following operating system:

   A. Windows 3.*x*

   B. Windows for Workgroups

   C. Windows NT

   D. 32-bit UNIX

   Answer: A, B, C

5. The following types of components can be used to connect Exchange to a foreign messaging system:

   A. Gateway

   B. Connector

   C. Directory Synchronization

   D. Key Management

Answer: A, B

6. The universal inbox is part of this software:

   A. Exchange Client

   B. SMTP clients

   C. POP3 clients

   D. LDAP clients

Answer: A

7. The following is an e-mail protocol:

   A. LDAP

   B. PNP

   C. PPP

   D. POP3

Answer: D

8. Which of the following could NOT be used as an Exchange e-mail client?

   A. Word processing program

   B. Web browser

   C. Internet e-mail program

   D. Microsoft Outlook

Answer: A

9. Which Exchange Client feature enables e-mail content to include multiple format types, such as fonts, sizes, and colors?

   A. WordPerfect

   B. This software cannot do this

C. Richman message content

D. Rich-text message content

Answer: D

10. This Microsoft technology enables the Exchange Client to create compound documents using drag-and-drop:

A. OLE

B. OOP

C. DLL

D. SNADS

Answer: A

11. Recalling a sent, but unopened, message is a feature of what program or programs?

A. Outlook

B. Exchange Client

C. Public folders

D. Forms

Answer: A

12. Which of the following relate to the performance of Exchange?

A. Load Simulator

B. 32-bit program

C. Multithreaded

D. Auditing

Answer: A, B, C

13. Since Exchange is scalable, it cannot be used in small to medium environments.

A. True

B. False

Answer: B

14. Exchange could use the Internet as part of its WAN design.

A. True

B. False

Answer: A

15. The following feature enables a Exchange client to create rules for processing incoming mail:

A. Search tool

B. Customized views

C. Universal inbox

D. AutoAssistants

Answer: D

16. What is the name of the mechanism when two Exchange components on the same machine pass instructions and data?

A. Remote procedure call

B. Remote instruction call

C. Local instruction call

D. Local procedure call

Answer: D

17. What is the name of the mechanism when a client-read instruction is sent to an Exchange server for execution?

A. Local procedure call

B. Local instruction call

C. Remote instruction call

D. Remote procedure call

Answer: D

Chapter 2

1. The following is NOT a core component of Exchange:

A. Internet Mail Service

B. System Attendant

C. Message Transfer Agent

D. Information Store

Answer: A

2. The Information Store is made up of these two databases:

   A. SQL and ODBC

   B. Message tracking log

   C. Private and public information store

   D. MTA and SA databases

Answer: C

3. This component generates new e-mail addresses:

   A. Directory Service

   B. System Attendant

   C. Global Address List

   D. Client components

Answer: B

4. This component is involved in advanced security:

   A. Directory Service

   B. Information Store

   C. Key Management

   D. Message Transfer Agent

Answer: C

5. This component builds routing tables:

   A. System Attendant

   B. Key Management

   C. Information Store

   D. Internet Mail Service

Answer: A

6. This component notifies clients of new mail:

   A. Directory Service

   B. Microsoft Mail Connector

   C. Information Store

   D. System Attendant

Answer: C

7. The Internet Mail Service relates to which protocol?

   A. X.400

   B. RPC

   C. OSF

   D. SMTP

Answer: D

8. Which of the following is NOT an example of a foreign system?

   A. An Exchange server in a different site

   B. IBM SNADS

   C. SMTP system

   D. Microsoft Mail system

Answer: A

9. This component calculates the route a message could take to its destination:

   A. System Attendant

   B. Message Transfer Agent

   C. Information Store

   D. Internet Mail Service

Answer: B

10. This standard is used as the pattern of the Exchange Directory:

   A. X.400

   B. SMTP

   C. LDAP

   D. X.500

Answer: D

11. The following object creates a transparent messaging environment for Exchange users:

   A. Site

   B. System Attendant

   C. Protocols

   D. INS

Answer: A

12. The Global Address List is contained in this object:

    A. Site

    B. Server

    C. Enterprise

    D. Organization

    Answer: D

13. Users must know the name of the server on which a public folder is homed in order to access the public folder.

    A. True

    B. False

    Answer: B

14. This component enables World Wide Web users to access Exchange resources:

    A. Outlook Web Access

    B. SNMP

    C. X.400

    D. X.500

    Answer: A

15. The Message Transfer Agent is based on this standard:

    A. SNMP

    B. SMTP

    C. X.500

    D. X.400

    Answer: D

Chapter 3

1. The IS communicates with this component to perform a remote delivery:

    A. SA

    B. IS on other server

    C. Key Manager

    D. MTA

    Answer: D

2. This component is referenced by other components when resolving an address:

   A. DS

   B. IS

   C. MTA

   D. SA

Answer: A

3. Intrasite Directory replication uses the MTA to route directory information.

   A. True

   B. False

Answer: B

4. The IS notifies clients of new messages.

   A. True

   B. False

Answer: A

5. This component assists in the implementation of advanced security:

   A. IS

   B. SA

   C. MTA

   D. DXA

Answer: B

6. The Outlook Web Access runs on this system:

   A. Microsoft Exchange server

   B. Web client

   C. Internet router

   D. Microsoft IIS server

Answer: D

7. The INS communicates with this component for the storing of USENET content:

   A. Microsoft IIS server

   B. DS

   C. SA

   D. IS

Answer: D

8. Connectors, such as the Connector for Lotus cc:Mail, CANNOT place foreign messages in the IS.

   A. True

   B. False

Answer: B

9. When routing a message, the MTA may communicate with this component for the physical transfer of the message:

   A. Connector or gateway

   B. MTA on another server

   C. Key Manager

   D. SA

Answer: A

10. The DS uses this information when performing a directory replication:

   A. Site number

   B. Update Sequence Number (USN)

   C. Server DS number

   D. Combination site and server number

Answer: B

11. The Link Monitor utility uses this component to send test messages:

   A. LDAP

   B. INS

   C. Key Security

   D. SA

Answer: D

12. To expand a distribution list, the MTA references this component:

A. IS

B. DS

C. Key security

D. SA

Answer: B

13. When addressing messages for delivery within an Exchange organization, this address format is used:

A. Distinguished Name

B. MS Mail name

C. Exchange lengthwise address

D. cc:Mail name

Answer: A

14. This component enables Web browser users to access Exchange resources.

A. MTA

B. Key Management

C. Web Browser Component

D. Outlook Web Access

Answer: D

15. The Information Store holds messages destined for foreign systems for transfer to this type of component:

A. Connector or gateway

B. DXA

C. DS

D. SA

Answer: A

16. This component is responsible for the delivery of messages when the recipient is homed on the same server as the sender.

A. Connector or gateway

B. MTA

C. DS

D. IS

Answer: D

17. When performing a directory replication with another Exchange server in the same site, a DS communicates with what component on the other server?

   A. MTA

   B. DS

   C. Directory Synchronization Agent (DXA)

   D. IS

   Answer: B

18. This component is involved in e-mail address generation and the logging of Exchange message tracking events.

   A. MTA

   B. DS

   C. SA

   D. IS

   Answer: C

Chapter 4

1. One of your company's locations contains an Exchange site with 25 users, each using Microsoft Outlook. You have purchased 25 client access licenses. The company hires 10 new employees that will connect to the site remotely. Five of the new users will be using POP3 applications, and five will be using HTTP applications. How many additional client access licenses must you purchase?

   A. 0

   B. 2

   C. 5

   D. 6

   E. 10

   F. 12

   Answer: E

2. You have upgraded your Exchange server by adding RAM and a hard disk. What should you do to make sure that Exchange will take maximum advantage of these changes?

   A. Run Microsoft Exchange Performance Optimizer.

   B. Run online maintenance.

   C. Run Microsoft Exchange setup again.

   D. Run the Migration Wizard.

   Answer: A

3. You manage two Microsoft Windows NT Server domains. The domains are named Personnel and Resources. The Personnel domain contains all user accounts, while the Resources domain contains all servers. You will be installing Microsoft Exchange Server into the Resources domain. You would like to use the Windows NT user accounts in the Personnel domain with mailboxes on the Exchange server. What type of trust relationship must be established between the two domains?

   A. No trust relationship is needed.

   B. The Personnel domain must trust the Resources domain.

   C. The Resource domain must trust the Personnel domain.

   Answer: C

4. The minimum amount of RAM needed by Microsoft Exchange Server is:

   A. 24

   B. 48

   C. 64

   D. 128

   Answer: A

5. The site services account must be configured:

   A. As a regular user account

   B. As a member of the Mail group

   C. After the Exchange installation

   D. As a member of the Domain Administrators global group

   Answer: A

6. Which file would be useful in a troubleshooting situation?

   A. Exchange Server Setup.LOG

   B. ERROR.LOG

   C. SETUP.EXE

   D. VIEWLOG

   Answer: A

7. The default location of the Exchange directory is:

   A. \EXCHANGE

   B. \MICROSOFT\EXCHANGE

   C. \EXCHSRVR

   D. \\EXCHANGE

   Answer: C

8. The Internet Mail Service requires this protocol to be running on the Exchange Server:

   A. NWLink

   B. Ethernet

   C. TCP/IP

   D. SNA

   Answer: C

9. This Windows NT-based program analyzes your Exchange Server machine and makes recommendations for better performance:

   A. Administrator program

   B. SETUP.HLP

   C. ANALYZER

   D. Performance Optimizer

   Answer: D

10. If there is a problem with the Exchange Server boot process, one action would be to view:

    A. The Event Log

    B. My Computer

C. Microsoft Explorer

D. Administrator Tools/User Manager for Domains

Answer: A

11. The following is one of the configuration requirements for the operating system that Microsoft Exchange Server uses:

A. Pagefile size equal to 50 plus the amount of RAM

B. NETBEUI

C. NWLink

D. Ethernet

Answer: A

12. Two sites, siteA and siteB, were both using version 4.0 of Exchange Server. The two sites also had directory replication configured between them. But after upgrading some of the servers in siteA to version 5.5, directory replication between the two sites stops working. Which of the following is a solution?

A. Uninstall version 5.5, and reinstall version 4.0.

B. Directory replication between sites cannot work until all servers have the same version.

C. Internet Mail Service must be used for directory replication.

D. Upgrade all directory bridgehead servers to version 5.5.

Answer: D

13. When adding a Microsoft Exchange Server to an existing site, which two pieces of information do you need to know?

A. The name of an existing Exchange Server in that site and the password for the site service account in that site.

B. Organization name and site name

C. Site name and administrator's user account

D. Organization name and administrator's user account

Answer: A

14. Which of the following is a requirement for Exchange Server 5.5 to work with Microsoft Cluster Server?

  A. The purchase of a 1000-user license

  B. Microsoft Windows NT Server version 5

  C. X.400 Connector

  D. The Enterprise Edition of Exchange Server 5.5

  Answer: D

15. Which Microsoft Windows NT Server 4.0 service pack is required to install Exchange Server 5.5?

  A. SP3

  B. SP2

  C. SP4

  D. SP5.5

  Answer: A

16. Which Exchange Server 4.0 service pack is needed to perform an upgrade to Exchange Server 5.5?

  A. SP3

  B. SP2

  C. SP4

  D. SP5.5

  Answer: B

Chapter 5

1. A user named Aaron leaves your company. Management would like a user named Bobbi to assume Aaron's responsibilities. What could you do so that Bobbi can receive Aaron's e-mail messages? (Select the best answer.)

  A. Make Bobbi's mailbox an alternate recipient for Aaron's mailbox.

  B. Disable Aaron's user account and give Bobbi profile permission to access Aaron's mailbox.

  C. Delete Aaron's mailbox and forward all undeliverable messages to Bobbi.

  D. Create a rule in Aaron's mailbox to forward all of Aaron's mail to Bobbi.

  Answer: A

2. You want to allow all the personnel in the technical support group to send and receive messages from the same mailbox. What can you do to enable this?

   A. Create a distribution list and designate the mailbox as the owner of the distribution list.

   B. Designate each technical support person as an owner of the mailbox.

   C. Allow each technical support person to send messages on behalf of the mailbox.

   D. Configure each technical support person's account as the primary Windows NT account for the mailbox.

   Answer: B

3. The aliases in your organization are formatted as first initial followed by last name. Management would like the format changed to last name followed by first initial. You also want all new aliases to use this new format. What must you do? (Choose all that apply.)

   A. Disable AutoNaming.

   B. Reset One-Off addressing.

   C. Modify all existing aliases.

   D. Modify alias name generation to be %Last%1First.

   Answer: C, D

4. Your company has two domains, Sales and Users. How would you ensure that new Windows NT user accounts that are created when a mailbox is created are placed in the Users domain, rather than the Sales domain?

   A. Use Directory Import to import a list of users from the Users domain.

   B. Add the administrator account in the Users domain to the permissions of the Recipients container.

   C. Create a template mailbox that has an account in the Users domain.

   D. Set the default Windows NT Server domain name to Users in the Microsoft Exchange Administrator program.

   Answer: D

5. You have created a distribution list called SalesDL. Whenever someone sends a message to SalesDL that requires a read receipt, the message sender only receives a receipt from the distribution list, not every member of the distribution list. What is the cause of the problem?

   A. The group membership is hidden from the address list.

   B. The distribution list is hidden from the address list.

C. The distribution list is configured to report to the owner of the distribution list.

D. The trust level of the distribution list is set higher than the recipients container.

E. The distribution list is configured to report to the message originator.

Answer: E

6. You have a distribution list with a large number of members. Whenever messages are sent to that distribution list the server experiences high CPU utilization. What could you do to minimize the performance loss on your server?

A. Remove all unnecessary address spaces from all recipients.

B. Move all members into their own recipients container.

C. Specify another server as the expansion server.

D. Move all recipients to another server.

Answer: C

7. What is one way to transfer mailboxes from one server to another server in the same site?

A. Designate a new home server for each mailbox.

B. Back up the Private Information Store on the existing server, and then restore the individual mailboxes on the other server.

C. Create new mailboxes on the second server that use the same display name as the mailboxes you want to move.

D. Drag-and-drop the mailboxes on the other server.

Answer: A

8. You need to move 10 mailboxes to another server in the same site. Each mailbox has five unique messages of 1 MB each. Each mailbox also has five single-instance messages of 1 MB each. After you move the mailboxes to the new server, how will the size of the Private Information Store on the new server change?

A. The Private Information Store will increase by 55 MB.

B. The Private Information Store will increase by 100 MB.

C. The size will not increase.

D. The size will decrease.

Answer: B

9. Two mailboxes have been moved to another server in a different site. After the move, neither user is able to use the Reply feature to successfully reply to messages that were sent by the other user prior to the move. But both users can send messages to other recipients. What is the most likely cause of the problem?

   A. Site affinity is not established between the two sites.

   B. Directory replication is not configured correctly.

   C. The two mailboxes need alternate recipients configured.

   D. The messages that are replied to refer to mailboxes that do not exist.

   Answer: D

10. You are using the import utility of Microsoft Exchange Administrator to modify a large number of existing mailboxes. You want to add an area code to the Telephone-Office2 field of each of these mailboxes. The export information of one of these recipients is listed below:

    ```
    Obj-Class,Alias Name,Display Name,Telephone-Office1,Telephone-Office2

    Mailbox,MPeterson,Mary Peterson,801-333-4343,333-5654
    ```

    Which field or fields must you include in your import file in order to add an area code to the Telephone-Office2 field? (Choose all that apply.)

    A. Mode

    B. Obj-Class

    C. Alias name

    D. Display name

    E. Telephone-Office1

    F. Telephone-Office2

    Answer: A, B, C, F

11. The following is an example of a mailbox attribute:

    A. Operating system

    B. Groups

    C. Server operating system

    D. Home server

    Answer: D

12. Permissions to a mailbox are assigned through:

A. Roles

B. UNIX permissions

C. Custom recipients

D. DLs

Answer: A

13. The following permits easy mass mailing:

A. A mailbox with multiple owners

B. Distribution list

C. A mailbox with multiple users

D. A mailbox set to forward messages

Answer: B

14. A foreign mail user would be this type of Exchange recipient:

A. Mailbox

B. A member of the Custom distribution list

C. Custom recipient

D. A mailbox with a foreign owner

Answer: C

15. Which of the following does NOT relate to a feature of a public folder?

A. Views

B. Rules

C. Permissions

D. Expansion Server

Answer: D

16. Copies of the same public folder located on several Exchange servers are called:

A. Clones

B. Clone folders

C. Folder images

D. Replicas

Answer: D

17. This menu option relates to selectively deleting messages in a mailbox:

A. Clean Mailbox

B. Purge Mailbox

C. Delete Mailbox

D. Remove Mailbox

Answer: A

18. This feature of a mailbox allows it to store and send messages containing formatting such as underlining, bolding, and fonts:

A. Font format

B. Word format

C. Rich-text format

D. Data compression

Answer: C

19. This type of program assists in the creating of mailboxes for NetWare users:

A. Extract tool

B. NetWare synchtool

C. Microsoft-NetWare synchronization tool

D. Cannot be done

Answer: A

20. The default permission for the primary NT account of a mailbox is:

A. Admin. role

B. Send as

C. Permissions Admin.

D. User

Answer: D

Chapter 6

1. You have created a Microsoft Exchange client network installation point on one of your servers. You want to predetermine the client settings in order to create a standard installation. What do you need to do to predefine the user settings of the Exchange client?

   A. Edit DEFAULT.PRF and copy this file to the installation share point.

   B. Edit DEFAULT.PRF and copy this file to each user's home directory.

   C. Edit TEMPLATE.PRF and copy this file to the installation share point.

   D. Edit TEMPLATE.PRF and copy this file to each user's home directory.

   Answer: A

2. Clients on your network use both IPX and TCP/IP. But for your Microsoft Outlook installation for 32-bit clients, you want them to only use IPX. What file would you have to modify?

   A. OUTLOOK.PRF

   B. DEFAULT.PRF

   C. EXCHNG.STF

   D. OUTLOOK.STF

   Answer: D

3. You have a standard PAB contained in the file MAILBOX.PAB and located at the network share point of G:\APPS\EXCHANGE. You also have a drive letter mapped to G: in your network login script that is used by all users. The Exchange Server service and PAB service are included in the OUTLOOK.STF at the installation point. There is also a DEFAULT.PRF file at the installation point. What is the final step in getting the PAB service installed during a scripted installation?

   A. Log on as the user before you install MS Outlook

   B. Log on as administrator before you install MS Outlook

   C. Place an empty mailbox.pab in every user's G:\EXCHANGE folder

   D. Log on as site service account before the installation

   Answer: A

4. Your network has hundreds of users. You have just installed Microsoft Exchange Server on five servers. You have also created an installation point on one of those servers. You would like clients to connect to this one server and perform an over-the-network installation. But you would like the clients to have the option during their installations to select any of the five Exchange servers. How would you do that?

   A. Leave the Exchange server field blank in DEFAULT.PRF

   B. Enter "any" in the Exchange server field in DEFAULT.PRF

   C. Delete the Exchange server field in DEFAULT.PRF

   D. Configure separate shares for each server and set the default in DEFAULT.PRF accordingly.

   Answer: D

5. The term used to describe the collection of MAPI configuration settings is:

   A. MAPI subsystem

   B. Service provider

   C. API

   D. Profile

   Answer: D

6. A PST file is also known as what type of message storage?

   A. Personal folder

   B. Private folder

   C. Offline folder

   D. Macintosh folder

   Answer: A

7. An inbox assistant is a:

   A. Secretary

   B. Temporary employee

   C. Permissions set on a mailbox

   D. A software agent that can apply rules to a mailbox

   Answer: D

8. Which of the following features enables Microsoft Outlook to place notices on messages to help prioritize them?

A. Message recall

B. AutoNameCheck

C. Voting

D. Message flags

Answer: D

9. Which of the following are two navigational aids in Microsoft Outlook?

A. Outlook Bar

B. Tabbed Windows

C. AutoDate

D. Message recall

Answer: A, B

10. The following line would be used to set up a shared installation point for Windows-based clients:

A. SETUP /A

B. INSTALL /N

C. INSTALL /A

D. SETUP /A /N

Answer: A

11. Microsoft Schedule+ enables the grouping of tasks into a:

A. Task commune

B. Task group

C. Project

D. Task community

Answer: C

12. If you wanted all new client installations to be configured to use IPX and not use TCP/IP, you would perform which action?

   A. Use Setup Editor to remove TCP/IP from the RPC binding order

   B. Do nothing, that is already the default

   C. This can not be done

   D. Run SETUP.EXE /A

Answer: A

13. You have created a Microsoft Schedule+ account for a conference room. You want to grant Joan permissions to read, create, and modify the schedule for the conference room, including information marked private. You also want all meeting requests for the conference room to be forwarded to Joan. How should you configure the permissions in the Set Access Permissions dialog box?

   A. Select Create in the User role box, and check the "User receives meeting requests sent to me" check box.

   B. Select Modify in the User role box, and check the "User receives meeting requests sent to me" check box.

   C. Select Delegate Owner in the User role box.

   D. Select Delegate in the User role box.

Answer: C

Chapter 7

1. A user named Jane uses Microsoft Outlook on both her office computer and her home computer. One night at home, Jane connects to her office server in order to read her mail. The next day at the office when Jane attempts to re-read the previous day's mail, there are no messages in her inbox. What is the most likely cause of this situation?

   A. Jane's mail was delivered to an OST file on her home computer.

   B. Jane's home computer is still logged on to the server.

   C. Jane did not synchronize her mailbox with the server.

   D. Jane's mail was delivered to a PST file on her home computer.

Answer: D

2. Patty has a laptop computer that she uses both at the office and when out of office doing work. Her laptop is configured with an OST file. She routinely synchronizes her laptop computer with the office server. Patty has identified a public folder that she would like to designate as an offline folder, but she does not see the Synchronization tab among the property pages of that public folder. What does she have to do to enable synchronization with that public folder?

A. The administrator must configure that public folder for synchronization.

B. The owner of the folder must configure it for synchronization.

C. Patty must designate the public folder as a Favorite folder.

D. Patty must logoff the server, and the folder will synchronize.

Answer: C

3. Lou has a laptop computer for doing work away from the office and a desktop computer at the office. Microsoft Outlook is installed on both computers. Lou would like to see all his messages while using either computer. The laptop computer does not have a continuous connection to the office server, but Lou would like to be able to read and compose messages while using the laptop offline. How should Lou configure his two computers?

A. Configure the laptop computer with an OST file, and the desktop computer to access his private folders in the Information Store.

B. Configure both computers with PST files.

C. Configure both computers to access his private folders in the Information Store.

D. Configure the laptop computer with a PST file, and the desktop computer to access his private folders in the Information Store.

Answer: A

4. You have configured Microsoft Outlook with an OST file. Your server suffers a major hardware failure. You also cannot recover Exchange data from your backup media. You reinstall Microsoft Exchange Server. What can you do to recover as much data as possible to your mailbox in the Private Information Store?

A. Copy the OST file to your server and synchronize your folders.

B. Copy the PST file to your server and synchronize your folders.

C. Rename the OST file with a PST extension and synchronize your folders.

D. While working offline, create a PST file and move the contents of your OST file to that PST file, then copy the contents of that PST file to your mailbox in the Private Information Store and synchronize your folders.

Answer: D

5. How would you group users by buildings from within the Microsoft Outlook Address Book?

   A. Create new recipient containers.

   B. Use AutoNaming.

   C. Create public folders for each building and add a listing of the people in those buildings.

   D. Create new Contacts folders for each building, designate those folders as part of the Outlook Address Book.

   Answer: D

6. Management has asked you to add another layer of security to the use of Microsoft Outlook. They would like users to have to enter their password at each startup of Microsoft Outlook. How could Outlook be configured to require a password?

   A. Configure each mailbox object to require a password.

   B. Clear the "Use network security during logon" checkbox in each user's profile.

   C. Configure "Required passwords" through Server Manager.

   D. Configure each home server to require a password.

   Answer: B

7. You are the administrator of a Microsoft Exchange site. A user named Chet wants to allow another user named Davina to read, and only read, items in his inbox. What should you do so Davina can read items in Chet's inbox?

   A. Designate Davina a delegate to Chet's mailbox.

   B. Instruct Chet to designate Davina the Reviewer role at the Mailbox and Inbox objects.

   C. Instruct Chet to designate Davina the Reviewer role at the Inbox object and the Exchange Server properties page.

   D. Add Davina's network account to Chet's mailbox.

   Answer: B

8. You will be using a scripted installation to setup a number of Microsoft Exchange Client applications. You will use Setup Editor to modify EXCHNG.STF. Even though all workstations use both TCP/IP and IPX, you want clients to use only IPX when connecting to their Microsoft Exchange servers. What should you do to accomplish that configuration?

   A. Remove TCP/IP from the RPC binding order in the installation script.

   B. Remove TCP/IP from all workstations.

    C. Unbind TCP/IP from workstation network adapters.

    D. Unbind TCP/IP from the Microsoft Exchange server network adapter.

Answer: A

9. Your network uses IPX as its only network protocol. Your Microsoft Exchange Server has two network adapters. One adapter is connected to the internal LAN and uses IPX. The other adapter is connected to an outside WAN and uses TCP/IP. Users on the internal LAN use Microsoft Outlook to connect to the Microsoft Exchange Server. When these users attempt to connect to the Microsoft Exchange Server, it takes up to 10 minutes to connect and to send mail. What can be done to reduce the time to connect and send mail?

    A. Bind TCP/IP to the network adapter of each client computer.

    B. Bind TCP/IP to the internal network adapter of the Microsoft Exchange Server.

    C. Change the RPC binding order on the Microsoft Exchange Server.

    D. Change the RPC binding order on each client computer.

Answer: D

10. Clients use Dial-Up Networking to access the Microsoft Exchange server. These clients would like to download only those messages that are smaller than 20 KB, and would like to do that without having to examine the size of each message. How could that be done? (Select the best answer.)

    A. Create a rule in the Out of Office Assistant that downloads only messages smaller than 20 KB.

    B. Create a rule in the Inbox Assistant that downloads only messages smaller than 20 KB.

    C. Configure the advanced filter options for remote mail to download only messages smaller than 20 KB.

    D. Configure a view based on size, and then download only those messages smaller than 20 KB.

Answer: C

11. You need to install Microsoft Exchange Server on a Novell NetWare network. You would like to use a network installation to setup Microsoft Outlook on all the clients. The network uses IPX as its only network protocol. What must you do to install Microsoft Outlook on each client and to enable them to connect to the Microsoft Exchange server? (Choose all that apply.)

    A. Create a network share point with Read permission for all clients.

    B. Create a network share point with Execute permission for all clients.

    C. Install and configure the SAP Agent on the Microsoft Exchange Server.

    D. Install and configure NWLink IPX/SPX Compatible Transport on the Microsoft Exchange Server.

    E. Install and configure TCP/IP on all client computers.

Answer: A, C, D

12. You are installing Microsoft Exchange Server to your Novell NetWare network. All client computers run Windows 95, Novell NetWare32 client, and Microsoft Outlook. What two actions must be done to enable these client computers to communicate with the Microsoft Exchange server? (Choose two.)

    A. Install the Client for Microsoft Networks on each client computer.

    B. Configure IPX Routing on the Microsoft Exchange Server.

    C. Install NWLink IPX/SPX Compatible Transport on each client computer.

    D. Install Gateway Service for NetWare on the Microsoft Exchange Server.

Answer: A, D

13. Which of the following is NOT a default information service in a messaging profile?

    A. Microsoft Fax

    B. Microsoft Mail

    C. Microsoft Exchange

    D. Both A and B

Answer: A

14. From which programs can the Send On Behalf Of permission be assigned?

    A. Microsoft Exchange Client

    B. Microsoft Outlook

    C. Microsoft Exchange Administrator program

    D. All of the above

Answer: D

15. Which of the following information files does SETUP look for when building a messaging profile?

    A. DEFAULT.PRF

    B. PROFILE.DAT

    C. PROFILE.PRF

    D. DEFAULT.DAT

Answer: A

16. What file contains the profile for an MS-DOS client?

   A. PROFILE.DOS

   B. PROF-MS.DOS

   C. EXCHANGE.PRO

   D. DOS.PRO

   Answer: C

17. Which of the following is NOT a feature of remote mail?

   A. PCMCIA cards

   B. Downloading only new messages

   C. Offline folders

   D. Working offline

   Answer: A

18. Which of the following relates to remote mail?

   A. Offline address book

   B. Scheduled connections

   C. ShivaRemote

   D. All of the above

   Answer: D

19. Which of the following file types can be imported by the Exchange Client?

   A. MMX

   B. GIF

   C. MMF

   D. Both B and C

   Answer: C

20. Exchange clients have which of the following as notification options for new mail?

   A. Play a sound

   B. Blinking screen

   C. Briefly change the pointer

   D. Both A and C

   Answer: D

21. Which of the following programs can be used to edit a messaging profile?

    A. WordPad

    B. PaintBrush

    C. Server Monitor

    D. The Mail and Fax applet in the Control Panel

    Answer: D

22. Which of the following is required for a folder to be designated for offline use?

    A. It must have a size limitation.

    B. It must have a password.

    C. It must not have a size limitation.

    D. It must be designated as a Favorite folder.

    Answer: D

Chapter 8

1. Various users in your organization need to use electronic forms while offline. To accommodate this scenario, you e-mail the necessary forms to these users while they are online. What else must be done for these users to use these forms while offline?

    A. Install Microsoft Visual Basic on each client computer.

    B. Install the forms into a public folder library.

    C. Install the forms into the organization forms library.

    D. Install the forms into a personal folder on each client computer.

    Answer: D

2. A form that is used to directly input information into a public folder is called:

    A. A Send form

    B. An Input form

    C. A Folder form

    D. A Post form

    Answer: D

3. The Exchange Client can send and receive Outlook forms.

   A. True

   B. False

   Answer: B

4. The following procedure makes forms available for use:

   A. Installing or publishing forms

   B. Customizing in Visual Basic

   C. Saving in the FRM format

   D. Saving to the Access database

   Answer: A

5. If a form needed wide availability, it would be installed in this location:

   A. Personal folder

   B. Organization forms library

   C. Administrator's mailbox

   D. A public mailbox

   Answer: B

6. Outlook can send and receive forms created in EFD.

   A. True

   B. False

   Answer: A

7. Which of the following is NOT a design feature of Outlook Forms Designer?

   A. AutoLayout

   B. Alignment

   C. Visual Basic scripting

   D. Lotus Notes formatting

   Answer: D

8. EFD saves form information in this database format:

   A. Microsoft Access

   B. SQL

   C. Paradox

   D. DB2

   Answer: A

Chapter 9

1. A user named Parry is the owner of a public folder named Research. Parry leaves your company and another administrator deletes Parry's user account. What would you as an administrator have to do to modify the permissions on the Research folder?

   A. Make the site service account the owner of the Research folder.

   B. Restore a backup tape of the server that was created before Parry was deleted.

   C. Designate your account as the owner of the Research folder.

   D. Grant your account the right to log on as a service.

   Answer: C

2. You want to create a public folder hierarchy that has both visible and hidden folders. You have created a distribution list called HR that contains the users who do need to view the hidden folders. What would be an efficient way of allowing the users who do need to view the hidden folder hierarchy the ability to do that?

   A. Give the List permission to the HR distribution list at each hidden folder.

   B. Give the Folder contact permission to the HR distribution list at each hidden folder.

   C. Create a root folder that contains all the hidden folders. Revoke all permissions for the Default user. Give Folder Visible permission to the HR distribution list at the root of the hidden folder hierarchy. Ensure that the HR DL has the Read items permission on each of the root's subfolders either explicitly or through the Default entry.

   D. Give the Create subfolders permission to the HR distribution list at each hidden folder.

   Answer: C

3. You own a public folder called Company Events. Because of the large number of comments about the events sent as replies, users have a hard time distinguishing the original postings from the replies. You decide to create a subfolder called Discussions that you want to hold the replies to the Company Events postings. What is the most efficient way to ensure all replies to Company Events go to the Discussions folder?

  A. Tell users to use the Discussions folder as a Cc recipient whenever they reply to Company Events.

  B. Configure a rule for Company Events that forwards everything to the Discussions folder except items from users that need to post company event items to the Company Events folder.

  C. Have all users make the Discussions folder a Favorite folder.

  D. Configure Company Events to delete everything it receives.

  Answer: B

4. What must be done to enable certain users to add scripts to public folders?

  A. Check the Enable Scripts box on each folder.

  B. Install the Scripting Agent on each user's computer.

  C. The Information Store database must be configured for a mirrored striped disk array.

  D. Each user must be given the Author role for the EventConfig folder.

  E. Each user must be given the Author role for each folder they need to add a script to.

  Answer: D

5. Which of the following relate to assigning rules to a public folder?

  A. Conditions

  B. Actions

  C. Folder Assistant

  D. All of the above

  Answer: D

6. Public folder permissions are grouped into predefined:

  A. Hives

  B. Clone sets

  C. Roles

  D. Sets

  Answer: C

7. If the recipient who is the owner of a public folder is deleted, what can be done in order to allow the administrator to grant permissions to other recipients?

A. Delete the public folder, and re-create it.

B. Designate the recipient used by the administrator as the owner.

C. Give the administrator account the "right to logon as a service".

D. Restore a backup tape that was made before the previous recipient was deleted.

Answer: B

8. What must you do to hide a subfolder from a particular recipient?

A. Revoke the Read Items permission from that recipient at the parent folder.

B. Revoke the Read Items permission from that recipient at that subfolder.

C. Hide the root folder above that subfolder.

D. A subfolder cannot be hidden, only its contents.

Answer: A

9. By default, all public folders can be seen in the GAL.

A. True

B. False

Answer: B

10. By default, all public folders are visible in the public folder hierarchy.

A. True

B. False

Answer: A

Chapter 10

1. You have just installed the Exchange Key Management server. During the setup, you chose to not use the floppy disk option for the KM service password. A few days later that server is shut down and restarted, but the Key Management server does not start. What is the likely cause of the problem?

A. The Microsoft Exchange Key Management service was started without the password as a startup parameter.

B. The Private Information Store is not started.

C. The SA was started without the password as a startup parameter.

D. The floppy startup disk was not inserted into the drive.

Answer: A

2. As administrator of a KM server, you receive a request to enable advanced security from a user named Alex. What must you do to accomplish that? (Choose all that apply.)

   A. Instruct Alex on how to use Windows NT domain logons.

   B. Enable advanced security as a property of Alex's mailbox.

   C. Instruct Alex how to perform person-to-person key exchange.

   D. Instruct Alex to configure his workstation as a certificate authority.

   E. Provide a security token to Alex and have him enter it in his Microsoft Outlook application.

   Answer: B,E

3. Your KM server is configured to use CAST-40 encryption. You now want to change the encryption protocol to CAST-64. What must you do to change and enable clients to use the new protocol? (Choose all that apply.)

   A. Reinstall KM server.

   B. Stop and restart the System Attendant.

   C. Configure each Exchange client application to use the new protocol.

   D. Change the preferred encryption protocol in the properties of the Encryption object.

   E. Recover the client encryption keys from all of the Exchange recipients.

   Answer: D,E

4. There can be only one KM administrator.

   A. True

   B. False

   Answer: B

5. Client software must be configured before a user's mailbox can be configured.

   A. True

   B. False

   Answer: B

6. Which program can create security tokens in a batch manner?

    A. SIMPORT.EXE

    B. BATCH.BAT

    C. BATCH.EXE

    D. SECADMIN.DLL

Answer: A

7. What program is used to revoke a user's keys and certificates?

    A. Exchange Administrator

    B. SIMPORT.EXE

    C. KM database

    D. REVOKE.EXE

Answer: A

8. The MS-DOS-based Exchange client, although slow, can perform signing and sealing operations.

    A. True

    B. False

Answer: B

9. CAST-64 cannot be used in the United States.

    A. True

    B. False

Answer: B

10. What core Exchange component is involved in the initialization of advanced security for a client?

    A. MTA

    B. IMS

    C. POP3

    D. System Attendant

Answer: D

11. What is the extension of the client-side file that stores a user's security information?

    A. .EPF

    B. .EFP

    C. .KMS

    D. .KM

Answer: A

12. Which of the following must an administrator do to enable advanced security for a user?

    A. Enable advanced security on the Security property page of that user's mailbox.

    B. Have the user first install and configure advanced security on their computer, then have the user inform the administrator of their configuration.

    C. Inform the user of their security token which will be used to configure their client software.

    D. Both A and C

Answer: D

Chapter 11

1. An IMAP4 client connects to your Exchange server and receives an error message stating that the message size is unknown. Which of the following should you do to fix this problem?

    A. Enable MCIS.

    B. Increase the Idle-Timeout.

    C. Use Plain-Text authentication.

    D. Clear the "Enable fast message retrieval" check box.

Answer: D

2. What are the requirements to allow an Exchange server to permit Web client access? (Choose four.)

    A. LDAP

    B. HTTP at the site

    C. HTTP at the server

    D. HTTP at the organization

E. HTTP at the mailbox

F. Active Server

Answer: B, C, E, F

3. How would you enable Web clients to access an Exchange server using the Windows NT Challenge/Response authentication method?

A. Internet Service Manager

B. HTTP properties

C. INS properties

D. POP3 properties

Answer: A

4. Your network includes an Active Server with Microsoft Exchange Outlook Web Access. The Webdata folder is a virtual directory on the IIS server with an alias of / Exchange. Your Exchange server has HTTP enabled. A Web client reports that when they attempt to connect to the Exchange server they receive an error stating "server is down or HTTP access is disabled." You check the OWA service and it is running. What is the problem?

A. HTTP is disabled at the organization.

B. HTTP is disabled at the mailbox.

C. The MTA is stopped.

D. HTTP should be disabled on the Exchange server, and only enabled on the Active Server.

Answer: B

5. Your organization contains two interconnected networks and corresponding Exchange sites named Accounting and Research. Both networks use IPX and TCP/ IP. The X.400 Connector is used to connect the two sites. No directory replication is configured between the sites. Your Exchange servers have LDAP enabled. The users in the Accounting site report that they cannot access the LDAP directory. You find out that all the users in the Accounting network use only IPX. What can be done to allow the Accounting users to access the LDAP directory?

A. Configure directory replication.

B. Configure the Site Connector.

C. Install TCP/IP on all the Exchange servers in the Accounting site.

D. Install TCP/IP on all the client computers in the Accounting site.

Answer: D

6. How can you restrict anonymous LDAP access to directory properties of recipients, but still allow Web clients with authenticated names to access those properties?

   A. Disable HTTP at the site.

   B. Disable anonymous access through the LDAP object.

   C. Define the Guest account as the anonymous account.

   D. Temporarily disable LDAP.

   Answer: B

7. You have enabled LDAP and allowed anonymous access. But you realize later that there are certain directory object attributes that you do not want to be viewed through anonymous access. What can be done to hide those attributes?

   A. Set LDAP to allow only initial substring searches.

   B. Remove those attributes from each object.

   C. Configure the trust levels of the containers.

   D. Clear the fields of those attributes in the DS Site Configuration object.

   Answer: D

8. Two organizations, Organization A and Organization B, need a long-term coexistence strategy. How could you allow LDAP clients to connect to Organization A and see the directories of both Organization A and Organization B?

   A. Directory replication

   B. Anonymous access

   C. Select Organization B as the default LDAP referral for Organization A.

   D. Select Organization A as the default LDAP referral for Organization B.

   Answer: C

9. A Microsoft Exchange user reports that several recently created newsgroups are not listed in your company's newsgroup hierarchy of public folders. What must you do so that those newsgroups will be listed?

   A. Accept the queued control messages.

   B. Download the newscr file from your ISP.

   C. Configure the newsfeed as a pull feed.

   D. Configure the newsfeed type as Outbound.

   Answer: A

10. Your company receives newsfeeds from your Internet Service Provider (ISP). You notice a folder within the newsgroup hierarchy that you do not want to receive. What must you do to permanently remove this folder from the hierarchy?

    A. Rename the folder.

    B. Exclude the folder from the newsfeed.

    C. Clear the folder's Folder Visible attribute.

    D. Delete the folder through Microsoft Outlook.

    Answer: B

11. Management has decided to allow company access to various newsgroups. Your Internet Service Provider can provide full newsgroup access, but they do not configure newsfeeds on a customer-by-customer basis. How would you configure the transfer of the newsfeeds?

    A. No transfer type is necessary.

    B. Configure it for both push and pull.

    C. Configure it for a push transfer only.

    D. Configure it for a pull transfer only.

    Answer: D

12. Your company provides newsfeeds to a subsidiary that retrieves news updates from your server. What would you have to do to enable your server to process those requests?

    A. Configure a pull transfer.

    B. Configure a push transfer.

    C. Include the relevant newsgroups in the Outbound property page.

    D. Enable newsreader support.

    Answer: C

13. You have assigned the chat account the access right of None. You have also permitted anonymous accounts to access your chat network. What type of access does the chat account have in this scenario?

    A. Channel host

    B. Channel spectator

    C. Channel participant

    D. None

    Answer: B

14. How would you prevent a certain user from accessing a particular channel on your chat network?

   A. Assign the user the None access right for that channel.

   B. Disable anonymous access.

   C. Delete that user on the ILS.

   D. Delete the chat service custom attribute for that user.

   Answer: A

15. How would you configure a custom recipient to receive Microsoft NetMeeting calls?

   A. Configure a new e-mail address type with the host name of the ILS server.

   B. Configure the LDAP properties with the IP address of the chat server.

   C. Configure a custom attribute with the IP address of the directory server.

   D. Configure the ILS server with an account name for the custom recipient and configure the custom recipient with the ILS server name and account name.

   Answer: D

16. How would you shut down one of five chat servers on your network without being noticed by users?

   A. You cannot do it.

   B. Smart-bleed the chat server.

   C. Execute StealthDown.

   D. Execute GracefulShutdown.

   Answer: B

17. Your network contains five chat servers. You would like to preserve the configuration of the chat network in the case of a disaster. What two things would you have to do? (Choose two.)

   A. Backup all servers.

   B. Export the Registry.

   C. Save the .rsp file.

   D. Use the ListConfig utility.

   Answer: A,C

18. You have just configured your Exchange server for IMAP4 client access. IMAP4 clients can be authenticated with either Basic (Clear Text), Windows NT Challenge/Response, or Windows NT Challenge/Response with SSL. You are informed by the administrator of your firewall that the firewall will allow traffic from SMTP (port 25), IMAP4 (port 143), and HTTP (port 80). What additional traffic must the firewall be configured to allow for your Exchange server IMAP4 configuration to be used?

A. IMAPS (993)

B. HTTPS (443)

C. NetBIOS (137)

D. RPC Endmapper (135)

Answer: A

19. A new Exchange server has been installed and configured for LDAP, HTTP, and POP3. The network project plan calls for allowing the following clients to access this server: LDAP, Web software using Windows NT authentication, POP3, and Microsoft Outlook using secure passwords. You refer to the current firewall configuration and see that it is open to DNS, HTTP, SMTP, and ports higher than 1023. What, if anything, must you do to enable the desired Exchange clients to pass through the firewall?

A. Open LDAP (389).

B. Open POP3 (110).

C. Open SSL.

D. Open port 135 for the RPC Endmapper service.

E. All of the above

Answer: A,B,D

20. Your Exchange server is using TCP/IP and is configured with LDAP, HTTP, and POP3. A firewall sits between your network and the Internet. Your Exchange server has its name and IP address entered into a public DNS server on the Internet.

Your network's firewall prohibits traffic on all ports that are not explicitly allowed. The ports that are open are port 25 (SMTP), port 53 (DNS), port 80 (HTTP), and all ports greater than port 1023.

Management would like users to be able to connect over the Internet to your Exchange server using Microsoft Outlook and LDAP applications. Policy dictates that passwords be transmitted in a secure manner.

Optional Results

While not required, management would like Web clients that do not support Windows NT Challenge/Response authentication to be able to connect to your Exchange server. Another wish is that POP3 clients could connect to the Exchange server and download their messages.

Proposed Course of Action

1. Assign port numbers to the Exchange Directory Service and Information Store. Then allow those ports through the firewall.
2. Configure LDAP on the Exchange server to allow anonymous access.
3. Configure the Exchange protocols to use SSL as an authentication method.
4. Allow SSL traffic through the firewall.
5. Allow LDAP traffic (port 389) through the firewall.
6. Allow RPC traffic (port 135) through the firewall.
7. Allow POP3 traffic (port 110) through the firewall.

What results does the proposed solution produce?

A. The proposed solution produces the required results and the optional results.

B. The proposed solution produces the required results and produces only one of the optional results.

C. The proposed solution produces the required results but does not produce either of the optional results.

D. The proposed solution does not produce the required results.

Answer: A

21. Your Exchange server is using TCP/IP and is configured with LDAP, HTTP, and POP3. A firewall sits between your network and the Internet. Your Exchange server has its name and IP address entered into a public DNS server on the Internet.

Your network's firewall prohibits traffic on all ports that are not explicitly allowed. The ports that are open are port 25 (SMTP), port 53 (DNS), port 80 (HTTP), and all ports greater than port 1023.

Management would like users to be able to connect over the Internet to your Exchange server using Microsoft Outlook and LDAP applications. Policy dictates that passwords be transmitted in a secure manner.

Optional Results

While not required, management would like Web clients that do not support Windows NT Challenge/Response authentication to be able to connect to your Exchange server. Another preference is for POP3 clients to connect to the Exchange server and download their messages.

Proposed Course of Action

1. Assign port numbers to the Exchange Directory Service and Information Store. Then allow those ports through the firewall.

2. Configure LDAP on the Exchange server to allow anonymous access.

3. Allow LDAP traffic (port 389) through the firewall.

4. Allow RPC traffic (port 135) through the firewall.

What results does the proposed solution produce?

A. The proposed solution produces the required results and the optional results.

B. The proposed solution produces the required results and produces only one of the optional results.

C. The proposed solution produces the required results but does not produce either of the optional results.

D. The proposed solution does not produce the required results.

Answer: D

22. Your Exchange server is configured for anonymous LDAP clients, but those clients that are outside your firewall report that they cannot access the directory. What is the problem?

A. The DS needs to be stopped and restarted.

B. Windows NT Challenge/Response needs to be enabled.

C. The LDAP port is not open on the firewall.

D. Clear Text authentication is needed.

Answer: C

23. If you wanted to prevent anonymous users using LDAP from seeing a particular Exchange attribute, like telephone numbers, where in the Exchange hierarchy would you have to go to prevent this?

A. Information Store Site Configuration

B. Encryption object

C. Directory Replication object

D. DS Site Configuration

Answer: D

24. If you wanted to reject certain IP addresses of Web clients from accessing your Exchange server, what program would you use?

A. Microsoft Exchange Administrator

B. Network applet in Control Panel

C. Internet Service Manager

D. Link Monitor

Answer: C

25. Which of the following is a reason why POP3 clients could not see e-mail messages in subfolders of their Inbox?

A. POP3 can only access messages in the Inbox, not subfolders of the Inbox.

B. LDAP is not enabled at the mailbox object.

C. NNTP is not enabled at the mailbox object.

D. The IIS computer is down.

Answer: A

26. Which of the following would have to be configured for an anonymous Web client to be able to read a public folder?

A. The Web client would have to log on using a Windows NT account.

B. The public folder would have to be listed in the Folders Shortcuts.

C. The folder owner would have to grant the Read permission to the anonymous user type.

D. Both B and C

Answer: D

27. For POP3 clients to be able to send Internet mail from their mailbox, what other component must be operational on the Exchange server?

A. LDAP

B. NNTP

C. Active Server Components

D. Internet Mail Service (IMS)

Answer: D

Chapter 12

1. You have installed Microsoft Exchange Server on a server that is heavily utilized. After installation, you notice that response times are slow and that the hard disk is constantly active. You use Windows NT Performance Monitor to collect the following statistics:

% Processor time = 70
% Disk free space = 60
Pages/sec = 40
Avg. Disk sec/Transfer = 0.02

What should you do to reduce disk activity and improve server response time?

A. Install more RAM.

B. Install a faster CPU.

C. Create additional swap files.

D. Install an additional hard disk.

E. Replace the hard disk with a faster hard disk.

Answer: A

2. Your organization had two sites that used the Microsoft Mail Connector for interconnection. Those two sites no longer need to be connected. You consequently try to delete the dirsync server on your server, but it remains visible in the hierarchy. When you attempt to delete it again, you receive a message stating that the object does not exist. How should you delete that object from the directory view?

A. Run Microsoft Exchange Setup with the Recovery option.

B. Perform a DS/IS consistency adjustment.

C. Run Setup to reinstall Exchange Server, and preserve existing settings.

D. Run Exchange Administrator in raw mode and delete the object.

Answer: D

3. Your organization has a single-master domain and a resource domain. The Exchange site service account is in the master domain, while your Exchange servers are in the resource domain. How can you simplify the procedure of assigning Exchange directory permissions to all Exchange administrators?

A. Create a recipients container for all administrators.

B. Create a distribution list that contains all administrators.

C. Create a Windows NT local group that contains all administrators.

D. Create a Windows NT global group that contains all administrators.

Answer: D

4. A site has two Exchange servers, Server A and Server B. All users in the finance department connect to Server A. All users in the marketing department connect to Server B. Each department has its own Exchange administrator. The site has only one recipients container. How would you allow the marketing administrator to manage recipients on both servers, but not manage any other objects in the hierarchy?

A. Assign permissions to the marketing administrator at the site object.

B. Assign permissions to the marketing administrator at the organization object.

C. Add the marketing administrator to the Domain Admins. group.

D. Assign the administrator role to the marketing administrator at the recipients object.

Answer: D

5. The password of the site service account gets changed in User Manager for Domains. When Exchange Server is shut down and restarted the Exchange services will not start. What can you do to prevent that situation?

A. Enter the account name and new password in the Services file in the ETC directory.

B. Run Microsoft Exchange Administrator in raw mode and designate the site service account again.

C. Assign the site service account the right to log on locally, then restart the computer.

D. Designate the new password in the site configuration properties.

Answer: D

6. You are running Microsoft Exchange Administrator from your Windows NT Workstation computer. Your computer is using both IPX and TCP/IP. Which naming convention can you use to connect to an Exchange server? (Choose all that apply.)

A. IP address

B. NetBIOS name

C. DNS host name

D. IPX network number

E. Media access control (MAC) address

Answer: A and B

7. Your Exchange recipients do not need a Microsoft Mail proxy address. How can you as the administrator disable the future creation of these addresses?

A. Delete the Microsoft Mail Connector.

B. Export the directory, remove the Microsoft Mail address space, then import the directory.

C. Disable the Microsoft Mail address space in the Site Addressing properties.

D. Create a blank entry in the address space for the Microsoft Mail Connector.

Answer: C

8. You have been asked as the Exchange administrator to set the default display names to LastName FirstName, such as Smith John. Where do you configure that setting?

A. The properties of each object

B. Only on the properties of individual mailboxes

C. Organization properties

D. Auto Naming property page of the Exchange Administrator program

Answer: D

9. A single site encompasses London and Tokyo. Three servers are in London, and two are in Tokyo. What can you do to ensure that users in London always access public folders in London before accessing replicas in Tokyo?

A. Configure site affinity between London and Tokyo.

B. Configure local address spaces for each public folder.

C. Set directory replication to use the Site Connector.

D. Set the location value so that servers in both cities are associated with each other.

Answer: D

10. You have a public folder that you do not want to be replicated or rehomed. How can you accomplish that?

A. Use the X.400 Connector between sites.

B. Set the site affinity number to 100.

C. Set the Replication Schedule property to "Never".

D. Disable the public folder.

Answer: C

11. Your organization has multiple Exchange servers. Currently, when users create public folders they are placed on Server A. After monitoring that server, you notice that its hard disk is almost full. You move all those public folders to Server B. How can you ensure that all future public folders will be created on Server B?

A. Delete all new replicas on Server A.

B. Configure Server B as the public folder server for all recipients on Server A.

C. Use Microsoft Exchange Performance Optimizer to configure Server A as only a private information store server.

D. Restrict top-level folder creation on Server A.

Answer: B

12. Your organization has four sites, each site consisting of two Exchange servers and 500 users. The four sites are connected with a 256K wide area network (WAN). The available bandwidth during the workday is less than 64K. While at night, the available bandwidth is 128K or more. You have created a public folder that contains 600MB of data that is not time critical. Users only access that folder approximately every fifteen minutes, and the folder data is only updated twice a week. On what servers should replicas be placed?

A. On every server

B. On each bridgehead server

C. Only on the server where the public folder was originally created

D. Only on domain controllers

Answer: B

13. Two servers, Server A and Server B, share public folder information across an unreliable WAN network. What can you do so that public folder information is synchronized on both servers?

A. Create public folders on both servers. Use a distribution list to transfer information between the servers.

B. Create public folders on both servers. Use a folder rule to transfer information between the servers.

C. Create a public folder on Server A. Designate Server B as an expansion server.

D. Create replicas of public folders on both servers.

Answer: D

14. You want to calculate the size necessary for your Private Information Store. You ascertain that the average size of each e-mail message on your server is 10 MB. You ask 10 users to track the type of messages they receive in one day. The users report back that they each received 10 messages. Five of those messages were sent using a local distribution list (i.e., the distribution list was an object on the same server as the message recipients). Two messages were sent to the 10 users by using a distribution list from another company that also uses Microsoft Exchange. Three messages were sent to the 10 users by using a distribution list from a company that does not use Microsoft Exchange. How many copies from the above scenario will be in the Private Information Store?

   A. 10

   B. 37

   C. 55

   D. 100

   Answer: A

15. Your Exchange server is backed up every night. Deleted item retention is set to 4 days. If you needed to enable users to restore all their messages what else would you need to do?

   A. Disable circular logging.

   B. Configure client profiles to not delete deleted items on exit.

   C. Configure Deleted item retention to not delete items until after the IS is backed up.

   D. Disable PST files on the local computers.

   Answer: C

16. Your network has 300 clients, each with a 100 MB storage limit, and with each message averaging 10 MB. If deleted item retention time was set to 7 days, and there were no single-instance messages, what would be the amount of disk space needed for the maximum storage limit of all mailboxes in the Private Information Store?

   A. 16 GB

   B. 27 GB

   C. 30 GB

   D. 33 GB

   Answer: C

17. A public folder has an "age limit" for messages of 90 days. The "Deleted item retention time" is set to 7 days. A particular item has been in this public folder for 87 days when a user deletes that item. Five days later, a user wants to recover that item. What can be done to recover that item?

   A. Nothing can be done.

   B. Run DS/IS consistency adjustment.

   C. Run Exchange Administrator in raw mode, and recover the item.

   D. Instruct the user to use the Microsoft Outlook Recover Deleted Item feature.

   Answer: D

18. A client uses an IMAP4 client while away from the office, and Microsoft Outlook while in the office. While using the IMAP4 client, the user deletes an item in their Inbox. On returning to the office, the user realizes the deleted item is still needed. How can the item be recovered?

   A. Use the Recover Deleted Items feature of Microsoft Outlook.

   B. It cannot be done.

   C. Execute ISINTEG –FIX.

   D. Log back in with the IMAP4 client and recover.

   Answer: D

19. Deleted Item Retention is enabled on a mailbox. What happens to items when they are deleted?

   A. They become hidden objects in the IS.

   B. They are placed in TEMP.EDB.

   C. They go to the Recycle bin on the local computer.

   D. They are placed in a Personal folder on the local computer.

   Answer: A

20. You have your Exchange server backed up using an offline backup procedure. After a hardware failure of that server, you restore the server using the offline backup tapes. But after the restore is complete, the IS will not start. What do you need to do?

   A. Run EDBUTIL.

   B. Run EDBUTIL with the consistency option.

C. Run SCANPST on each user's OST file.

D. Run ISINTEG –Patch.

Answer: D

21. A disk containing the IS databases reaches its storage capacity causing the IS to stop. What must you do before you can restart the IS?

A. Run ISINTEG with the fix option.

B. Run Setup with the recovery option.

C. Initiate online maintenance.

D. Run ISINTEG with the defragmentation option.

Answer: A

22. Your Exchange servers are scheduled for backup every evening at 1:00 A.M. The backup takes between three and four hours to complete. While you want IS maintenance to take place, you do not want it to conflict with the backups and you do not want it to impact server response time during regular business hours. How should you configure IS maintenance?

A. Schedule IS maintenance every 20 minutes.

B. Schedule IS maintenance to occur immediately before the backup.

C. Manually start and stop IS maintenance.

D. Run IS maintenance all day on weekends.

Answer: B

23. The Private Information Store on your server is approaching the capacity of its disk. Offline maintenance is not scheduled for another week. You do not want to impose space restrictions on users, but you do need to do something to slow the rate of growth of the Private Information Store. What can you do?

A. Run Microsoft Exchange Performance Optimizer on the Private Information Store.

B. Run MTACHECK.

C. Run the DS/IS Consistency Adjustment.

D. Perform online maintenance of the Private Information Store.

Answer: D

24. The connections between a Site A and Site B have been permanently removed. You notice that public folder replicas from Site A are still showing up in Site B. How can you remove those instances in the directory of Site B?

    A. Run EDBUTIL with the recovery option.

    B. Manually delete each replica in Site B.

    C. Perform a DS/IS Consistency Adjustment.

    D. Reinstall the site connectors, and then delete the replicas in Site B.

    Answer: C

25. You need to restore a mailbox that was accidentally deleted. The size of the mailbox was limited to 25 MB. The size of the Private Information Store is 500 MB. The size of the entire IS database is 1000 MB. In addition to the space needed for Microsoft Windows NT and Microsoft Exchange Server, how much space will be needed on the standby server in order to restore this deleted mailbox?

    A. 25 MB

    B. 500 MB

    C. 525 MB

    D. 1025 MB

    Answer: B

26. If you wanted to back up the Exchange database files to a disk, what files would you have to copy?

    A. PRIV.EDB

    B. PUB.EDB

    C. DIR.EDB

    D. EDB.CHK

    E. Transaction log files

    Answer: A,B,C

27. Your organization has an Exchange server with two disk controllers and hard drives. One hard drive contains the IS databases, the other hard drive has the transaction log files. Circular logging is disabled. One day one of the disk controllers malfunctions and corrupts the IS databases. You made a Full backup four days ago, and did three incremental backups since then. The hardware failure took place 12 hours after the last incremental backup. What information can be restored?

    A. Only the information stored after the last full backup but prior to the last incremental backup.

B. All information stored prior to the last time the logs were updated.

C. Only the information stored prior to the last full backup.

D. Only the information stored after the last incremental backup.

Answer: B

28. You are asked to create a backup strategy that will recover the most data in the event of a major hardware failure. Which of the following would be part of your strategy? (Select the best answer.)

    A. Install Micrsoft Exchange Server on a computer that is not a domain controller. Turn off circular logging.

    B. Install Microsoft Exchange Server on a computer that is not a domain controller. Turn on circular logging.

    C. Install Microsoft Exchange on a primary domain controller. Turn off circular logging.

    D. Install Microsoft Exchange on a primary domain controller. Turn on circular logging.

    Answer: A

29. Your organization performs a complete backup every weekend. You have been asked to add a plan to also backup the system every weekday evening with all the changes made since the weekend backup. You also want to minimize the time it takes to restore a system from the backups. How would you configure Microsoft Windows NT Backup?

    A. Set the weekend backup type to Normal. Set each weekday backup type to Incremental.

    B. Set the weekend backup type to Normal. Set each weekday backup type to Differential.

    C. Set the weekend backup type to Copy. Set each weekday backup type to Incremental.

    D. Set the weekend backup type to Copy. Set each weekday backup type to Differential.

    Answer: B

30. You are formulating a backup strategy for your company. The computer that will be your Exchange server has two hard drives of equal capacity, with one of the drives significantly faster than the other.

    Required result: A requirement of the backup strategy is to perform a complete backup every night.

    Optional Result 1: One optional result of the strategy is that the most recent database transactions can be recovered in the event of a hardware failure of the drive, or drives, housing the Exchange database files.

    Optional Result 2: Another optional result of the strategy is to minimize server response time for users.

    Proposed Solution: One proposed strategy includes: placing the IS transaction log files and the DS transaction log files on the faster hard disk, and the IS and DS database files on the slower hard disk; enabling circular logging; and performing a nightly backup.

    What results does this proposed strategy produce?

    A. The required result and both optional results

    B. The required result and only one of the optional results

    C. The required result and neither of the optional results

    D. Does not produce the required result

    Answer: B

31. You are formulating a backup strategy for your company. The computer that will be your Exchange server has two hard drives of equal capacity, with one of the drives significantly faster than the other.

    Required Result: A requirement of the backup strategy is to perform a complete backup every night.

    Optional Result 1: One optional result of the strategy is that the most recent database transactions can be recovered in the event of a hardware failure of the drive, or drives, housing the Exchange database files.

    Optional Result 2: Another optional result of the strategy is to minimize server response time for users.

    Proposed Solution: One proposed strategy includes: placing the IS transaction log files and the DS transaction log files on the faster hard disk, and the IS and DS database files on the slower hard disk; disabling circular logging; and performing a nightly backup.

What results does this proposed strategy produce?

A. The required result and both optional results

B. The required result and only one of the optional results

C. The required result and neither of the optional results

D. Does not produce the required result

Answer: A

32. You are formulating a backup strategy for your company. The computer that will be your Exchange server has two hard drives of equal capacity, with one of the drives significantly faster than the other.

    Required Result: A requirement of the backup strategy is to perform a complete backup every night.

    Optional Result 1: One optional result of the strategy is that the most recent database transactions can be recovered in the event of a hardware failure of the drive, or drives, housing the Exchange database files.

    Optional Result 2: Another optional result of the strategy is to minimize server response time for users.

    Proposed Solution: One proposed strategy includes: placing the IS database file and the IS transaction log files on the faster hard disk, and the DS database file and the DS transaction log files on the slower hard disk; enabling circular logging; and performing a nightly backup.

    What results does this proposed strategy produce?

    A. The required result, and both optional results

    B. The required result, and only one of the optional results

    C. The required result, and neither of the optional results

    D. Does not produce the required result

    Answer: C

33. You have created a standby Exchange server. You want to create a batch file that stops the primary Exchange server and copies all the necessary Exchange files to the standby server. Which of the following files would you include in the batch file copy process? (Select all that apply.)

    A. Directory file

    B. Checkpoint file

    C. Transaction log files

    D. PUB.EDB

    E. PRIV.EDB

    F. Personal Information Store

Answer: A,D,E

34. You need to configure a recovery server for your Exchange site. How should you configure the recovery server?

    A. Use the same NetBIOS name as the primary server. Join the existing site.

    B. Use the same organization name as the existing configuration. Use a new site name. Connect the new site to the existing site.

    C. Use the same organization name and site name as your existing configuration. Do not join the site.

    D. Use the same organization name and site name as your existing configuration. Join the existing site.

Answer: C

35. A user receives a message stating that their OST file is damaged. What should you tell them so they can access their messages without losing the unsynchronized changes in that file?

    A. Move the OST file to the server and run ISINTEG.

    B. Use the Migration tool to import the OST into a new mailbox.

    C. Rename the OST file with a PST extension and run SCANPST on the PST file.

    D. Run SCANPST on the OST file.

Answer: D

36. You want to take one of your Exchange servers offline, but you do not want that procedure to generate an error to Server Monitor. What can you do to prevent an error message?

    A. Pause Server Monitor.

    B. Stop Server Monitor.

    C. Use ADMIN /t n.

    D. Use the SHUTDOWN –NoError command.

Answer: C

37. You are running Microsoft Exchange Administrator from your work-station. You will be using Server Monitor to synchronize the clocks on ten Exchange servers. Whose clock will those servers be synchronized with?

   A. The server that is also a PDC

   B. The administrator's home server

   C. The administrator's workstation

   D. Any one of the ten servers

Answer: C

38. Because you have Web clients accessing your Exchange network, you feel the need to monitor the WWW Exchange service. What utility would best answer that need?

   A. Microsoft Exchange Link Monitor

   B. Microsoft Exchange Server Monitor

   C. Microsoft Exchange NT Event Viewer

   D. Microsoft Windows NT Performance Monitor

Answer: B

39. Your company has had problems with Exchange disk drives becoming full and stopping the IS service. What could you do to receive a warning before the IS reaches its limit again?

   A. Configure Microsoft Windows NT Performance Monitor to send you an email message when the Push Notification Cache Size has reached 100 percent.

   B. Configure Microsoft Windows NT Performance Monitor to send you an email message when the available disk space gets low.

   C. Configure Microsoft Exchange Server Monitor to send you a Microsoft Windows NT alert before the IS service stops.

   D. Configure Microsoft Exchange Server Monitor to send you an email message before the IS service stops.

Answer: B

40. Which of the following is NOT true for a differential backup of a database?

   A. Backs up new data since the last full backup

   B. Backs up modified data since the last full backup

   C. Takes progressively longer each day

   D. Takes less time than the incremental strategy

Answer: D

41. The diagnostic logging performed by Exchange services is written to this location:

A. Windows NT Event Log

B. \BIN

C. \exchsrvr\bin

D. \logging

Answer: A

42. Which of the following relates to information about a deleted Directory object?

A. RTS values

B. Retry timeouts

C. Bounce

D. Tombstone

Answer: D

43. Which of the following is required for single-seat administration of multiple Exchange sites?

A. RPC connections between sites

B. NNTP

C. POP3

D. X.400

Answer: A

44. Which of the following procedures could help recover significant disk space on an Exchange server?

A. MTACheck

B. Server Monitor

C. Online IS Maintenance

D. Performance Monitor

Answer: C

45. How would you use Exchange Administrator to group Exchange recipients by city?

A. Create an address book view container

B. Autonaming

C. You cannot group recipients

D. Delete the GAL and create Personal Address Books

Answer: A

Chapter 13

1. Two Exchange sites are connected through the Dynamic RAS Connector. Even though your WAN connection is expensive, it has frequent line errors causing long delays between connection retries. You want to reduce the delay between connection retries. What option would you modify in the properties of the Dynamic RAS Connector?

A. Checkpoint size (K)

B. Disconnect (sec)

C. Open interval (sec)

D. Max open retries

Answer: C

2. If two sites in two domains are using the same site service account and password, then what are the only two actions that have to be performed to configure the Site Connector? (Select two.)

A. Remote server name

B. Local server name

C. Account and password used to connect to remote site

D. Local site service account

Answer: A,C

3. You want to use an X.400 Connector to send messages to a foreign mail system (i.e., a mail system not part of your organization). The computer name of your X.400 Connector bridgehead is 16 characters in length. But the foreign mail will only accept names up to 8 characters in length. What can you do to remedy this situation on your server?

A. There is nothing you can do.

B. Specify a window size of 8.

C. Add a custom recipient to the X.400 Connector.

D. Enter an 8 character name in the Local MTA field on the Override page.

Answer: D

4. When configuring the X.400 Connector, what format could a remote host name be in if your network was using the Windows Internet Name Service (WINS)?

   A. Fully qualified domain name (FQDN)

   B. NetBIOS name

   C. IP address

   D. Media Access Control (MAC) address

   Answer: B

5. Two of your Exchange sites are connected over a low-speed wide area network (WAN) that experiences high latency (i.e., a long time for data to reach its destination) and packet loss. What two actions could you take to optimize performance given this scenario? (Select two.)

   A. Reduce the MTA checkpoint size.

   B. Increase the MTA message threshold.

   C. Use the Site Connector.

   D. Use the X.400 Connector.

   Answer: A, D

6. Two Exchange sites are connected over a WAN that charges for total bandwidth used and amount of time connected. How could you modify the MTA Messaging defaults to minimize your costs? (Select the best answer.)

   A. Reduce the checkpoint size (K).

   B. Reduce the recovery timeout interval (sec).

   C. Set the window size to zero.

   D. Increase the message threshold.

   Answer: B

7. The organization you work for has multiple Exchange sites. The site that you manage, named Research, engages in classified work. MIS management has asked you if there is a way to prevent other sites from seeing the directory information about the recipients in the Research site. But they also want the Research recipients to be able to view directory information from the other sites and be able to send and receive messages from those sites. Can you meet this requirement, and if yes, how?

   A. It cannot be done.

   B. Clear all directory replication attributes in the DS Site Configuration object.

C. Use the X.400 Connector and set directory attributes to hidden.

D. Configure the trust levels of all recipients in Research to a higher value than the other recipient containers in the other sites.

Answer: B

8. You need to configure directory replication between two sites. Those two sites do have LAN connectivity. What would you have to do?

   A. Configure directory export and directory import.

   B. Install a dirsync server and dirsync requestor.

   C. Install LDAP support on one server in each site.

   D. Define export containers and import containers on each site.

   E. Configure message transfer between both sites.

   Answer: E

9. Your company has asked you to design an Exchange environment. The company is in two buildings connected by a 33.6 Kbps dial-up connection. Building A has 100 users. Building B has 125 users. You find out that the vast majority of messaging will take place between users in their own building. You would also like to minimize directory replication traffic. What design would you use?

   A. A dual-site design, with one Exchange server in each building

   B. A single-site design, with one Exchange server in Building A

   C. A single-site design, with two Exchange servers in Building B

   D. A single-site design, with one Exchange server in each building

   Answer: A

10. Your Exchange site uses custom attributes that should not be replicated to other sites. How would you configure your site to accomplish that?

    A. Specify only the custom attributes in the DS Site Configuration object.

    B. Configure the trust level of your recipients container to be higher than the recipient containers in the other sites.

    C. Configure the permissions on the Directory Replication Connector to be only for the Domain Admins group.

    D. Specify all attributes except the custom attributes in the DS Site Configuration object.

    Answer: D

11. You will be installing two Exchange sites that will be connected with the X.400 Connector. You do not want administrators from one site to be able to administer the other site. What type of trust relationship, if any, would have to be established and what amount of account information exchanged between the two sites?

    A. Establish a two-way trust relationship. No account information needs to be exchanged.

    B. Establish a one-way trust relationship in either direction. Both accounts must have the same name and password.

    C. No trust relationship is needed. No account information needs to be exchanged.

    D. No trust relationship is needed. Account and password information must be exchanged.

    Answer: C

12. A company has brought you in as a network design consultant. The company currently has a host-based mail system with five remote locations. All locations are connected with a 56 Kbps network. This company will be migrating to Microsoft Exchange and wants you to recommend a design that will minimize network traffic during peak hours and yet optimize response time for users. Which of the following would you recommend?

    A. Install a Microsoft Exchange Server at each location. All servers replicate directory information with all other servers and use X.400 Connectors for message transfer.

    B. Install a Microsoft Exchange Server at each location. All servers replicate directory information with the main office and use X.400 Connectors for message transfer.

    C. Install a Microsoft Exchange Server at each location. All servers replicate directory information with the main office and use Site Connectors for message transfer.

    D. Install a single Microsoft Exchange Server at the main office. Clients connect by using remote mail or Web browsers.

    Answer: B

13. Your organization has 20 Exchange sites. They are connected by a wireless WAN that experiences high packet loss. You want to reduce the amount of redundant data that is sent over the WAN due to failed or interrupted connections. What two actions must you take with the MTA properties? (Choose two.)

    A. Set a high recovery timeout.

    B. Set a low recovery timeout.

C. Set a high checkpoint size.

D. Set a checkpoint value of zero.

E. Set a low checkpoint size that is greater than zero.

Answer: A, E

14. You have three remote Exchange sites. Those sites are connected by an unreliable network. The network protocol used is TCP/IP. You would like to schedule message transfer between the sites during off-peak hours. What connector would you use?

   A. Site Connector

   B. Microsoft Mail Connector

   C. Internet Mail Service

   D. X.400 Connector

   Answer: D

15. Your organization is made up of five Exchange sites. The five sites are connected using a mesh topology. X.400 Connectors are used to connect the sites. Each site also has an Internet Mail Service running. You want to make sure that all outgoing SMTP messages are only sent out of their sites through the IMS server, and not the X.400 Connector. Which of the following would accomplish this?

   A. Create an SMTP address space on each X.400 Connector. Assign a cost of 100 to each SMTP address space.

   B. Create an X.400 address space on each Internet Mail Service. Assign a cost of 1 to each X.400 address space.

   C. Create an X.400 address space on each Internet Mail Service. Assign a cost of 100 to each X.400 address space.

   D. Replace the existing address space on each Internet Mail Service with SMTP address space. Assign a cost of 100 to each SMTP address space.

   Answer: A

16. Your organization has two Exchange sites connected by a 1.54 Mbps leased line and backed up by a X.25 connection. An X.400 Connector called Connector A uses the 1.54 Mbps line, and another X.400 Connector called Connector B uses the X.25 line. What could you do to ensure that Connector B is used only if Connector A is not available?

   A. Assign an override value for the time-out of Connector A.

   B. Assign a cost of 100 to Connector A. Assign a cost of 1 to Connector B.

    C. Assign a cost of 1 to Connector A. Assign a cost of 100 to Connector B.

    D. Assign routing costs to all target servers.

Answer: C

17. Which of the following statements is NOT true for the X.400 Connector?

    A. Requires a high-speed network connection

    B. Can use TCP/IP

    C. Can be assigned costs

    D. Can connect through a public backbone

Answer: A

18. Which of the following is true for the Site Connector?

    A. Sends information between sites in a message format

    B. Can schedule connections

    C. Permits delivery restrictions

    D. Uses RPC

Answer: D

19. Using multiple messaging connectors between two sites can provide:

    A. Fault tolerance

    B. Load balancing

    C. A foundation for multiple directory replication connectors between the two sites

    D. Both A and B

Answer: D

Chapter 14

1. An IMS server sends mail to a Domain-A and a Domain-B. As IMS administrator, you begin to receive reports that Exchange e-mail attachments sent to Domain-B have been arriving as unreadable text. You investigate and find out that the problem does not exist with attachments sent to Domain-A. You also find out that Domain-A uses MIME while Domain-B uses UUENCODE. How would you fix this problem?

    A. Use the Internet Mail property page and designate UUENCODE as the encoding method for Domain-B.

B. Use the Internet Mail property page and designate MIME as the encoding method for Domain-A.

C. Configure Domain-B for SSL.

D. Configure IMS for SASL.

Answer: A

2. The Internet Mail Service is installed and configured on your network. Exchange recipients can send mail through IMS to SMTP users, but SMTP users cannot send mail to the Exchange recipients. You verify that your IMS server is accessible from the Internet. What is the most likely cause of the problem?

A. Your firewall is not open to port 110 (POP3).

B. Your firewall is not open to port 25 (SMTP).

C. Your client computers are not configured with TCP/IP.

D. Your client computers are not directly connected to the Internet.

E. Your domain has no MX record in DNS.

Answer: E

3. You want to restrict delivery of mail from your Internet Mail Service. You want only the recipient terry@retail.com to receive mail from your IMS. What address space would you add to the Internet Mail Service?

A. *

B. SMTP*@retail.com

C. SMTP *@retail.com

D. SMTP:terry@retail.com

Answer: D

4. You want to change the SMTP addresses of your Exchange recipients from <first name><last initial>@server1.com, to <first name><last name>@server1.com. How would you do that?

A. Address Space property page

B. Routing property page

C. Tools/Options and Auto Naming

D. One-Off addressing

Answer: C

5. The current fully qualified domain name (FQDN) of your site is server1.highfinance.com. The default Internet mail address for recipients is <alias>@server1 .highfinance.com. You need to change the default address to <alias>@highfinance .com. How would you do that?

   A. Use Directory Import.

   B. Modify the Site Addressing properties.

   C. Modify the One-Off Internet addressing template.

   D. Configure default alias name generation.

   Answer: B

6. Your Exchange environment uses IMS to send and receive SMTP mail with a company named Sockets & Wrenches. Sockets & Wrenches uses a host-based SMTP mail system. When users on your system send mail to the name of the host at Sockets & Wrenches, it is not delivered. But if those users use an IP address for addressing, the mail is delivered. You are informed that other systems can send mail to Sockets & Wrenches using a host name in the addressing. What should you do to enable your users to be able to send mail to Sockets & Wrenches using a host name in the addressing? (Select the best answer.)

   A. Configure a DNS server in the TCP/IP network configuration on your server.

   B. Configure a HOSTS file on each client.

   C. Configure an LMHOSTS file on each client.

   D. Configure IMS to forward all mail to Sockets & Wrenches.

   Answer: A

7. As administrator of an Exchange site with Internet Mail Service, you have been asked to have all outgoing SMTP mail sent to a single SMTP relay host. How should you configure the Internet Mail Service?

   A. Enter the SMTP relay host as an MX record in the DNS.

   B. Enter the SMTP relay host as a CN record in the DNS.

   C. Enter the SMTP relay host in the Internet Mail Service properties.

   D. Make the SMTP relay host the default gateway in the TCP/IP settings of your IMS computer.

   Answer: C

8. Your Internet Mail Service uses a dial-up connection to a remote SMTP server. How would you configure the dial-up connection so it could send messages at all times?

    A. Use the Internet Mail Service to configure the dial-up connection page and set the schedule to All Day.

    B. Use the RAS server with a schedule of Always.

    C. Use the Dynamic RAS Connector with a schedule of Always.

    D. Use the RASDial utility to have the connection open at startup.

Answer: A

9. You need the Internet Mail Service to connect two Microsoft Exchange sites over the Internet. These two sites also exchange mail with other SMTP servers on the Internet. How would you configure the connection between these two sites?

    A. In the Internet Mail Service, configure the sites as connected sites.

    B. Have both servers use the same relay host.

    C. Configure the Internet Mail Service to secure all outbound connections.

    D. Configure a Point-to-Point Tunneling protocol (PPTP) connection between the two sites.

Answer: A

10. Your site uses the Internet Mail Service to exchange messages with the Internet. After researching the topic of security, you decide you should take measures to prevent denial-of-service attacks. What two actions should you take?

    A. Use a relay host rather than DNS.

    B. Disable AutoReply to the Internet.

    C. Set size limits for all incoming messages.

    D. Restrict the users who can send outgoing messages.

    E. Configure your firewall to prevent all port 25 (SMTP) traffic.

    F. Reject connection attempts from unknown IP addresses.

Answer: C, F

11. You are the administrator of an Internet Mail Service. Some of your users report that their e-mail attachments sent to lawfirm.com arrive unreadable. Mail sent to other domains arrives intact and readable. You investigate and learn that the other domains are using MIME, and that lawfirm.com is using only UUENCODE. What can you do so that e-mail attachments sent to both lawfirm.com and other domains are readable?

    A. Use the E-Mail Domain option in Internet Mail Service to use MIME for all domains except lawfirm.com.

    B. Use the E-Mail Domain option in Internet Mail Service to use UUENCODE for lawfirm.com.

    C. All users who send attachments to lawfirm.com must add their destination addresses in their Personal Address Books and specify that only MIME is to be used.

    D. All users who send attachments to lawfirm.com must add their destination addresses in their Personal Address Books and specify that only UUENCODE is to be used.

    Answer: B

12. Your company, U.S. Water, has just replaced a UNIX-based POP3 and SMTP server with Microsoft Exchange Server and Internet Mail Service. The new server has the same IP address, domain name, and entry in DNS. POP3 clients can access their inboxes and retrieve mail. But when they try to also send mail, they get an error message. What is the most likely cause of the problem?

    A. The POP3 clients do not support Windows NT Challenge/Response.

    B. The POP3 clients do not support SSL.

    C. The Internet Mail Service uses a different address space than the POP3 clients.

    D. The Internet Mail Service is configured to not reroute incoming SMTP traffic.

    Answer: D.

13. You are the administrator of an Internet Mail Service computer. Users are reporting that messages they send to the Internet are not arriving. You decide to track some of these messages as a troubleshooting step. What Exchange components will you need to configure for message tracking? (Choose three.)

    A. Information Store

    B. Internet Mail Service

    C. Microsoft Exchange Connector for Lotus cc:Mail

    D. Microsoft Mail Connector

    E. Message Transfer Agent

    Answer: A, B, E

14. An Exchange user, Anita, sends a message through the Internet to another Exchange user named Brooks at Brooks@sprockets.com. Anita receives a non-delivery report (NDR) stating "Recipient Not Found: SPROCKETS.COM." You confirm that Brook's mailbox is configured with the e-mail address SMTP: Brooks@sprockets.com. What is the likely problem?

A. Anita's mailbox is not configured for TCP/IP.

B. Anita has exceeded her mailbox size.

C. Anita's Internet Mail Service has exceeded its licenses.

D. The host sprockets.com is not entered in DNS.

Answer: D

15. Which of the following is NOT a role of the IMS?

A. Automatically generate SMTP addresses for new Exchange recipients

B. Act as a DNS client

C. Act as an SMTP server

D. Act as a mail exchanger (MX)

Answer: A

16. The fully qualified domain name (FQDN) SALES.ACME.COM is in what root domain?

A. COM

B. SALES

C. There is no way to tell.

D. ACME

Answer: A

17. The IMS relies on which component to resolve addresses of Exchange recipients on inbound messages?

A. DNS

B. SMTP

C. Resolver program

D. DS

Answer: D

18. After a change is made to the IMS configuration, the following should be done:

    A. The IMS should be paused and restarted.

    B. The IMS should be reinstalled.

    C. The IMS should be stopped and restarted.

    D. The DNS server should be rebooted.

Answer: C

19. Which of these connections to an SMTP server or ISP does the IMS support?

    A. Permanent connection using TCP/IP

    B. A dial-up connection using PPP

    C. A dial-up connection using POP3

    D. Both A and B

Answer: D

20. Which of the following must be true for the IMS to use RAS for a dial-up connection?

    A. A SAP agent must be configured.

    B. RAS must be installed.

    C. An RAS phone book entry must be created for the remote SMTP server or ISP.

    D. Both B and C

Answer: D

21. Which of the following is the default Exchange naming convention for the domain name of a site?

    A. site.organization.com

    B. organization.site.com

    C. com.organization.site

    D. mailbox_name.site.organization

Answer: A

22. Which process maps domain names to IP addresses?

    A. Address encapsulation

    B. Name resolution

    C. IP wrapping

    D. Address spaces

Answer: B

Chapter 15

1. Your company has both Microsoft Exchange Server and Microsoft Mail. There will eventually be a migration from Mail to Exchange, but right now you need to come up with a coexistence strategy. Part of that strategy is to make a global distribution list available that contains recipients from both systems. How could you do that?

    A. Create both a Microsoft Mail distribution list that includes all Micro-soft Mail users and a Microsoft Exchange distribution list that includes all Microsoft Exchange users. Create a Microsoft Exchange distribution list that includes the Microsoft Mail distribution list and the Microsoft Exchange distribution list.

    B. Create Internet mail connectivity between the two systems. Create SMTP custom recipients for each Microsoft Mail user. Create a distribution list that includes all Exchange users and all SMTP custom recipients.

    C. Configure directory synchronization between the two systems. After synchronization has taken place, create a master distribution list on the Microsoft Mail postoffice.

    D. Configure directory synchronization between the two systems. After synchronization has taken place, create a master distribution list on the Microsoft Exchange server.

Answer: A

2. A company uses a Microsoft Mail gateway for SMTP to exchange mail between its three Microsoft Mail postoffices and the Internet. This company has also just installed Microsoft Exchange Server. They have hired you as a consultant to outline the steps necessary to replace their current Mail gateway for SMTP with the Internet Mail Service. What are those steps? (Choose all that apply.)

    A. Install IMS on a Microsoft Exchange Server.

    B. Install the Microsoft Mail Connector on the Microsoft Exchange Server.

    C. Add the Microsoft Mail Connector to the external postoffice list on each Microsoft Mail postoffice.

    D. Reinstall the SMTP Gateway Access Component on the existing MS Mail postoffices. Specify the Microsoft Exchange Mail Connector postoffice as the gateway postoffice.

    E. Install the Gateway Access Component on the Microsoft Exchange Server to allow the Mail users to access Internet Mail Service.

Answer: A, B, C, D

3. You need to create directory synchronization between Microsoft Exchange Server and Microsoft Mail. Your Exchange Server has two recipient containers called Container-Albany and Container-Boston. You want only recipients in Container-Albany to be synchronized with Microsoft Mail. How could you set that up?

   A. Remove the Microsoft Mail address space from all recipients in Container-Albany.

   B. Remove all selected attributes in the DS Site Configuration object.

   C. Configure the trust level of the recipients in Container-Boston to be higher than that of the DXA.

   D. Configure the Microsoft Mail address space as the default address for all recipients in Container-Albany.

   Answer: C

4. Your company currently uses Microsoft Mail. You have just added a Microsoft Exchange Server to the network. Management would like both systems to coexist and be able to exchange both messages and directory information. Management would also like to keep the current dirsync strategy. You consequently configure the Exchange server as a dirsync requestor. What other step must you do on the Exchange server?

   A. Create a dirsync server on the Exchange server.

   B. Configure the Microsoft Mail Connector on the Exchange server.

   C. Create a directory replication bridgehead server.

   D. Reinstall MTA.

   Answer: B

5. Your network has three Microsoft Mail postoffices, named PO-1, PO-2, and PO-3. You replace PO-2 with a Microsoft Exchange Server and establish directory synchronization between the two mail systems. Management has asked if you could hide certain Exchange recipients from the two Microsoft Mail postoffices. They also want Exchange recipients to see all recipients from both systems. You decide to create two recipient containers, called Container-A and Container-B. You place all Exchange recipients that are to be hidden in Container-B. How should you configure the trust levels of these two containers?

   A. Configure the trust level of Container-A to be higher than that of the dirsync requestor. Configure the trust level of Container-B to be lower than that of the dirsync requestor.

   B. Configure the trust level of the recipients in Container-A to be lower than that of the dirsync requestor. Configure the trust level of the recipients in Container-B to be higher than that of the dirsync requestor.

C. Configure the trust level of both containers to be higher than that of the dirsync requestor. Configure the trust level of Container-B to be lower than that of Container-A.

D. Configure the trust level of both containers to be lower than that of the dirsync requestor. Configure the trust level of Container-B to be lower than that of Container-A.

Answer: B

6. Directory synchronization is configured between your Exchange site and a foreign mail system (i.e., a non-Exchange system). What is the best way to prevent certain Exchange recipients from being replicated to the foreign system?

A. Mark as hidden the recipients you do not want replicated.

B. Create a new recipients container. Move the recipients that you do not want to be replicated to this container.

C. Create a dirsync distribution list. Add all the recipients that are to be hidden to this list.

D. Configure the trust levels for the recipients that you do not want replicated to be higher than that of the connector.

Answer: D

7. Your company is made up of two domains, one includes Microsoft Mail and the other has Microsoft Exchange. Each domain and its message system has about half the users. There are no trust relationships between the two domains. A Microsoft Exchange recipient named Robert uses Microsoft Schedule+ 7.5 to create an appointment that includes a Micro-soft Mail user named Shelley. When Robert views the Planner tab, he cannot see Shelley's availability. But Robert can send e-mail to Shelley. What do you need to do to allow Robert to view Shelley's availability?

A. Establish a two-way trust between the domains.

B. Delete and re-create the Microsoft Schedule+ Free/Busy public folder.

C. Relocate the Microsoft Mail postoffice to the same machine as the Exchange server.

D. Configure the Microsoft Schedule+ Free/Busy Connector.

Answer: D

8. Your Microsoft Exchange Server is configured as a dirsync server and has remote dirsync requestors defined. You configure the synchronization time on the Exchange server to Always. Three hours later, you notice that Microsoft Mail recipients have not yet replicated to your Exchange Global Address List. What is the solution to this problem?

A. In Microsoft Mail, set the T1, T2, and T3 times to be the same.

B. Set the T2 time on the Microsoft Exchange Server to be one hour later than the T2 time in Microsoft Mail.

C. Run the Reqmain utility with the Transport option on the Microsoft Mail postoffice.

D. Run the Reqmain utility with the Receive option on the Microsoft Exchange Server.

Answer: C

9. Your company uses a Microsoft Mail gateway for SMTP to transfer messages between its five postoffices and the Internet. Your company domain name is Plumbers.com. Your network is connected to the Inter-net through a filtered router. Management has had you install a Micro-soft Exchange Server and configure the Microsoft Mail Connector. Management has the following mandatory and optional wishes:

Required Result: replace the Microsoft Mail gateway for SMTP with the Exchange Server.

Optional Result 1: POP3 clients being able to both send and receive messages.

Optional Result 2: prevent anonymous users on the Internet from using the Internet Mail Service as a relay host for other destinations.

Proposed Solution: to accomplish those results, one member of the network administration staff suggests the following actions:

- Install the Internet Mail Service.
- Reconfigure the Gateway Access Components on each Microsoft Mail postoffice to point to the MS Mail Connector postoffice as the downstream postoffice.
- Disable rerouting of SMTP messages.
- Make no changes to the router.

What results would the above proposal produce?

A. The proposed solution produces the required result and produces both of the optional results.

B. The proposed solution produces the required result and produces only one of the optional results.

C. The proposed solution produces the required result but does not produce either of the optional results.

D. The proposed solution does not produce the required result.

Answer: B

10. Which of the following does NOT relate to restricting Exchange objects from being synchronized with an MS Mail system?

A. Trust level of the object

B. Trust level of the Exchange dirsync server or requestor

C. The recipients container

D. EXPORT.EXE

Answer: D

11. Which of the following are required when using the Schedule+ Free/Busy Connector?

A. Directory synchronization with MS Mail

B. A Windows NT user account named FreeB

C. IMPORT.EXE running on the designated MS Mail postoffice

D. Both A and C

Answer: A

12. Schedule+ free/busy information exchanged between Exchange and MS Mail users is stored in the following:

A. A specially designated public folder

B. A specially designated mailbox

C. A specially designated DL

D. The Exchange Directory

Answer: A

13. The MS Mail directory synchronization parameter used by a dirsync server to recompile the Global Address List is:

    A. T1

    B. T2

    C. Newsfeed push

    D. T3

    Answer: B

Chapter 16

1. You are implementing a migration from Microsoft Mail to Microsoft Exchange. You have just completed the first step in a two-step migration. If you wanted to modify the existing naming convention during the second step in the migration, what file would you have to modify?

    A. Packing list file

    B. Primary file

    C. Secondary file

    D. Migration log file

    Answer: B

2. Your Microsoft Mail system has 24,000 users. You will be migrating all of those users to Microsoft Exchange using the Migration Wizard and Exchange Administrator. What would be the most efficient way to pre-assign properties to the mailboxes being migrated?

    A. Modify the packing list file to include the desired properties.

    B. Edit the primary and secondary migration files.

    C. Create a recipient with the desired properties. Use that recipient during an export and import procedure.

    D. Create a mailbox with the desired properties. Designate that mailbox as the template mailbox during the migration.

    Answer: D

3. The first step in a two-step migration has already taken place. The CSVfile contains directory information on 2200 users. What would be the most efficient way to modify all of the recipient display names?

   A. Complete the migration, and then use Microsoft Exchange Administrator to modify the display names.

   B. Edit the CSV file, and then continue with the second phase of the migration.

   C. Run the first step of the Migration Wizard again and this time modify the names.

   D. Run the second step of the Migration Wizard and modify the names during that process.

Answer: B

4. Your Microsoft Exchange network is connected to an SMTP backbone. One of the other systems connected to this backbone is a large UNIX-based SMTP system of 26,000 users. The directory information about these users is stored in a SQL database. You would like to add these 26,000 SMTP users as custom recipients to your Exchange directory. How would you efficiently do that?

   A. Manually create custom recipients for each SMTP user.

   B. Configure directory synchronization between the two systems using Internet Mail Service.

   C. Use LDAP to automatically import the SMTP users.

   D. Use the Import utility of Microsoft Exchange Administrator.

Answer: D

5. You are importing an employee telephone list into your Exchange directory. You would like to keep the current directory information unchanged. X.400 addresses are one of the properties of your recipients. What Exchange object does the "o" in an X.400 address relate to?

   A. Organization name

   B. Site name

   C. Server name

   D. Domain name

Answer: B

6. There has been a partial migration of SMTP users to Microsoft Exchange Server. Both systems have their own connectors to the Internet for external mail access. The foreign system uses an SMTP relay host running on a UNIX server. You want the users who have migrated to still receive mail sent to their old SMTP addresses. What is the best way to do that?

A. Move the SMTP relay host function to the Microsoft Exchange server.

B. Configure a forward file on the SMTP relay host.

C. Instruct each user to create a rule to forward mail to the old system.

D. Update the alias file on the UNIX server acting as the SMTP relay host to point to the Microsoft Exchange server and mailbox.

Answer: D

7. The Microsoft Mail Connector is configured between Microsoft Exchange and Microsoft Mail systems. You use the Migration Wizard to migrate some of the Mail users over to Exchange. One of the migrated users, Marcy, can send mail to Microsoft Mail users, but cannot receive mail from those users. What is the most likely cause of her problems?

A. Directory synchronization is not configured between the two systems.

B. Marcy's original mailbox was deleted.

C. Marcy's original mailbox was not deleted.

D. The Microsoft Mail Connector was configured for sending not receiving.

Answer: C

8. Your Microsoft Mail system has multiple postoffices. You migrate one of the postoffices to Microsoft Exchange Server. After the migration, some of the migrated users report that they can send mail to Microsoft Mail users, but they cannot receive mail from those users. What could you do to remedy this situation?

A. Delete the Microsoft Mail address space from the Site Addressing properties, and recalculate routing.

B. Delete the obsolete Microsoft Mail mailboxes and assign a 10/10/10 address to the migrated users.

C. Run the REQMAIN utility on the Microsoft Exchange server running the Mail Connector.

D. Delete the Microsoft Mail address space for each migrated user.

Answer: B

9. Half of your company has migrated from Microsoft Mail to Microsoft Exchange. Users who have not yet migrated report that they are receiving non-delivery reports (NDRs) when they reply to messages that were sent by Microsoft Mail users before they had migrated. You check to see that the migrated users have the correct secondary proxy addresses, and they do. What is the most likely reason the Microsoft Mail users are receiving the NDRs?

A. The migrated users' Microsoft Mail mailboxes are not deleted.

B. Microsoft Mail site addressing is disabled.

C. The Microsoft Mail address space for the migrated users is not enabled.

D. The Microsoft Mail postoffice is still configured in the Microsoft Mail Connector.

Answer: D

10. You are implementing a multiphase migration from Microsoft Mail to Microsoft Exchange. During the migration, a Microsoft Mail Connector is delivering mail between the two systems. Microsoft Mail users report receiving non-delivery reports (NDRs). They receive the NDRs after they have replied to a message that was sent by a user before that user migrated. To troubleshoot this, you confirm that the Microsoft Mail e-mail address for both the original Microsoft Mail postoffice and the Microsoft Exchange connector are entered for each mailbox. You also confirm that all migrated users have been removed from their former Microsoft Mail postoffices. What should you do to ensure that message replies reach their new destinations?

A. Create SMTP address spaces for all users to use as the reply address.

B. Remove the original Microsoft Mail address space from each migrated mailbox.

C. Remove the Microsoft Exchange connector postoffice address space from each migrated mailbox.

D. Migrate all remaining Microsoft Mail users, and delete the postoffice.

Answer: D

11. Acme Inc. is migrating from an X.400 mail system to Microsoft Exchange. The migration is a multiphase migration. During the migration, the current X.400 gateway will be operational along with the Microsoft Exchange X.400 Connector. To allow for X.400 messages to be delivered to migrated users, the Exchange site is configured with the same X.400 address space as the current X.400 gateway. The current X.400 gateway is also configured to forward all X.400 mail to the Exchange X.400 Connector. Because all the users are not yet migrated, what could you do to prevent non-delivery reports (NDRs) for mail sent to Exchange for those non-migrated users?

A. Configure the external X.400 MTA to forward all X.400 messages for this organization to both the Exchange X.400 Connector and the current X.400 gateway.

B. Configure a custom recipient to have an X.400 proxy address that is identical to the address of the current X.400 gateway, and configure an inbox rule that routes all incoming mail to the X.400 gateway.

C. Configure the Microsoft Exchange site addressing to have the same address as the current X.400 gateway, and to route all messages sent to non-Exchange recipients to the current X.400 gateway.

D. During the migration, disable the X.400 address space in the Microsoft Exchange site addressing.

Answer: C

12. Sprockets Inc. is in the middle of a multiphase migration from Microsoft Mail to Microsoft Exchange. Each migrated user is given a proxy address that matches their previous Microsoft Mail address. Microsoft Exchange DLs are created that include migrated users. You notice, however, that these DLs do not synchronize with the Microsoft Mail global address list. What is the likely problem?

A. Directory synchronization has not completed the T2 phase.

B. The distribution lists contain recipients who do not have Microsoft Mail proxy e-mail addresses.

C. The distribution lists contain addresses that are duplicates of existing Microsoft Mail addresses.

D. The distribution lists contain names that are illegal.

Answer: B

13. HotChilis Inc. has migrated about half of its Microsoft Mail users to Microsoft Exchange. The remaining half will continue to use Microsoft Mail. There is an existing Microsoft Mail distribution list that you would like to manage from one application. You would also like Microsoft Mail users to be able to find the same addresses in the Microsoft Mail global address list that they used before the migration. How could you meet these requirements?

A. Continue to manage the distribution list from Microsoft Mail, and configure directory synchronization between Microsoft Exchange and Microsoft Mail.

B. Create a distribution list in Microsoft Exchange and include the original Microsoft Mail distribution list as a member of the new distribution list.

C. Create a distribution list in Microsoft Exchange, and assign the Microsoft Mail address of the new distribution list as a member of the original Microsoft Mail distribution list.

D. Configure directory synchronization between Microsoft Exchange and Microsoft Mail, and exclude all Microsoft Mail addresses from participation in directory synchronization.

Answer: A

14. You are migrating a Lotus cc:Mail system to Microsoft Exchange Server. Some of the clients are using Lotus cc:Mail Mobile for Windows. How would you access the remote message store of those clients during the migration?

   A. Copy all the remote e-mail data files to a network share point and run the Migration Wizard against those files.

   B. Use the Migration Wizard while each remote user is connected to the Lotus cc:Mail postoffice.

   C. Use the Migration Wizard while each remote user is connected to the Microsoft Exchange Server.

   D. Import all the remote data files into the Lotus cc:Mail postoffice and then run the Migration Wizard.

   Answer: A

15. You attempt to migrate Novell GroupWise mailboxes to Microsoft Exchange Server. But you find that you are unable to migrate the mailboxes. What is the most likely cause of the problem?

   A. A password is configured for the mailboxes.

   B. The client computers are not running Client for Microsoft Networks.

   C. Proxy access has not been granted for each mailbox.

   D. The GroupWise mailboxes need to be created as custom recipients before the migration.

   Answer: C

16. You are migrating a number of Microsoft Mail users to Microsoft Exchange Server. What could you do to limit the size of mailboxes you want to migrate?

   A. Clean each mailbox with the MMFClean utility.

   B. Run EDBUTIL.

   C. Run Microsoft Exchange Performance Optimizer.

   D. Set mailbox storage limits.

   Answer: A

17. You have experienced slow migration conversion rates in the past. What factor would have the greatest effect on this problem?

A. Paging on the Microsoft Mail postoffice

B. Paging on the Microsoft Exchange Server

C. Processor on the Microsoft Mail postoffice

D. Processor on the Microsoft Windows NT workstation

Answer: B

18. Which property of an Exchange recipient can be used to allow a user to retain his or her pre-migration foreign addresses?

A. E-mail addresses (also called proxy addresses)

B. Protocol property

C. Custom attribute property

D. Advanced properties

Answer: A

19. Which of the following can be used to modify a large number of Exchange recipients in a bulk manner?

A. Performance Monitor

B. User Manager for Domains

C. Directory Import and Export

D. Event Viewer

Answer: C

Chapter 17

1. You will be installing a Microsoft Exchange Server and must decide what network segment to place it on. There are four network segments (A, B ,C ,D), all back-boned on an Ethernet switch. Segment A is at 100Mbps and has zero users. Segment B is at 10Mbps and has 125 users. Segment C is at 10Mbps and has 75 users. Segment C is at 10Mbps and has 150 remote users. What segment would you place the Exchange server on?

A. Segment A

B. Segment B

C. Segment C

D. Segment D

Answer: A

2. The hardware requirements of an Exchange server are affected by which of the following:

A. Number of mailboxes

B. Public folder storage

C. Message traffic

D. All of the above

Answer: D

3. Advanced security planning pertains to what object or objects?

A. Mailboxes

B. Connectors

C. Sites

D. Both A and C

Answer: D

4. Which of the following properties should be considered when planning a connector?

A. Storage limits

B. Scheduled connections

C. Tombstones

D. Both B and C

Answer: B

5. Which of the following is an important planning issue when interoperating with a non-Exchange system?

A. POP3 configuration

B. Mailbox cleanup

C. Home server of the administrator

D. Directory synchronization

Answer: D

6. Which of the following is NOT considered when planning a migration?

    A. Assigning foreign users administrative rights

    B. What resources will be migrated

    C. Choosing a migration method (single-phase or multiphase)

    D. Installing or upgrading client software

    Answer: A

APPENDIX

B

Glossary

ActiveX The set of Microsoft protocols that specifies how software components can communicate with each other through the use of objects.

Address Encapsulation Placing a sender's native Exchange address in the form of a valid SMTP address. The encapsulated address is placed in the FROM field of the message.

Address Space The set of remote addresses that can be reached through a particular connector. Each connector must have at least one entry in its address space.

Address Space Scoping A property that restricts a connector to transferring messages sent from a specified scope. The scope can be the organization, a site, or the server location the connector resides within.

Age Limit A property that specifies the length of time a unit of data may remain in its container (e.g., public folder).

Anonymous Access Accessing a server without logging in with a Windows NT or other type of user account.

Application Programming Interface (API) A collection of programming commands (frequently called interfaces) that can invoke the functions of a program. Other programs can use a program's API to request services or communicate with that program. For example, Windows 95 contains an API referred to as the win32 API. For an application to request a service from Windows 95, it must issue that request using a win32 API.

Architecture The description of the components of a product or system, what they are, what they do, and how they relate to each other.

Attribute A characteristic of an object. Attributes of a mailbox include display name, primary Windows NT account, and storage limits. The terms *attribute* and *property* are synonymous.

Authentication A process whereby an object, such as a user, is allowed to access or use another object, such as a server or a protocol. For instance, the Microsoft Exchange Server POP3 protocol can be configured to only allow access to POP3 clients that use the Windows NT Challenge/Response authentication protocol.

AutoAssistants   A feature of a mailbox or public folder that can automatically carry out actions based on rules the user defines.

Back-End Program   A server application that provides services to front-end programs (client applications). Exchange Server is an example of a back-end program.

Bridgehead Server   A Microsoft Exchange server designated as a server to deliver data to another site.

Bulk Encryption Key   The random secret key generated by a client's security DLL used to seal messages.

Caching   Temporarily storing data in random access memory (RAM) where it can be accessed much faster than it could be from the disk.

Certification Authority (CA)   The central authority that distributes, publishes, and validates security keys. Exchange Server can be configured to perform this role. See also public key and private key.

Challenge/Response   A general term for a class of security mechanisms, including Microsoft-authentication methods that uses Windows NT network security and an encrypted password.

Chat   A real-time, text-based, conversation performed over a computer network or networks. See also Internet Relay Chat.

Checkpoint File   The file (EDB.CHK) that contains the point in a transaction log which is the boundary between data that has been committed and data that has not yet been committed to an Exchange database.

Ciphertext   Encrypted data.

Circular Logging   The process of writing new information in transaction log files over information that has already been committed. Instead of repeatedly creating new transaction logs, the Exchange database engine "circles back" and reuses log files that have been fully committed to the database. Circular logging keeps down the number of transaction logs on the disk. These logs can not be used to re-create a database because the logs do not have a complete set of data. The logs contain only the most recent data not yet committed to a database. Circular logging is the default setting of the Exchange Directory and Information Store databases.

Cleartext   Unencrypted data. Synonymous with plaintext.

Client Access License (CAL)   The license, purchased from Microsoft, that legally permits a client to access an Exchange server.

Cluster Server   A Microsoft software product that enables multiple physical servers to be logically grouped together for reasons of fault-tolerance.

Collaboration Data Objects   A Microsoft messaging API that can be used in applications to create messaging functionality. CDO could be used to create server applications that enable Internet client access to Microsoft BackOffice products through a Microsoft Internet Information Server.

Connector Cost   A numeric value assigned to a connector. The MTA uses connector cost as a criterion when it chooses between multiple connectors that support the same address space.

Connectors   Software that manages the transport of data between Exchange sites (e.g., the Site Connector) or between Exchange and a foreign message system (e.g., the X.400 Connector, Microsoft Mail Connector, and the Internet Mail Service). See also gateways.

Container Object   An object in the Exchange hierarchy that contains and groups together other objects. The organization object is a container object that contains the Folders, Global Address List, and Site objects.

Context Level   Refers to a level in the Exchange hierarchy that does not inherit permissions from other portions of the hierarchy. The three context levels are organization, site, and configuration. Administrative permissions must be assigned to users or groups individually at each of the three levels.

Cryptology   The study and implementation of hiding and revealing information.

Custom Recipient   An Exchange recipient object that represents a foreign message recipient. Custom recipients allow Exchange clients to address messages to foreign mail users.

Datagram   A packet that contains both data to be sent and information related to the transmission of the data, such as the network address of the packet's destination.

Decryption   Translating encrypted data back to plaintext.

Denial-of-Service Attack   A system shutdown cased by too many requests or too much data. Occurs when a computer system receives so many service requests or so much data that it becomes overwhelmed and effectively shuts down.

Desktop Information Manager   An application that can be used to manage many aspects of a user's activities, such as reading and sending e-mail, accessing calendar and scheduling information, and task management.

Digital Signature   A personal and unique number included with a message that proves the sender's identity.

Directory Replication   The transferring of directory information to other servers in a site (intrasite) or to another site (intersite). Intrasite directory replication is automatic, while intersite directory replication must be configured through the Directory Replication Connector.

Directory Replication Bridgehead Server   The Exchange server designated as the server that will send site directory information to another site. Only one server in a site can be assigned to replicate information with each remote site. There can be more than one directory replication bridgehead server in a site, but each must connect with a unique remote site. One server can, however, perform directory replication with multiple remote sites.

Directory Synchronization Protocol   The MS Mail protocol used to synchronize directory information between MS Mail postoffices. One server is designated as the dirsync server and the other servers are designated as dirsync requestors. The dirsync server maintains the master copy of a network's directory. The dirsync requestors send any new directory information to the dirsync server, and request a copy of the master directory.

Dirsync Requestor   A type of MS Mail postoffice that sends its new directory information to the designated dirsync server, and requests a copy of the master directory from the dirsync server. See also Directory Synchronization Protocol, T1, and T3.

Dirsync Server   A type of MS Mail postoffice that maintains the master copy of a network's MS Mail directory information. It also responds to requests by sending a copy of the master directory to dirsync requestors. See also Directory Synchronization Protocol and T2.

Discussion Thread   A collection of postings to a public folder related to a single subject.

Distinguished Name (DN)   An X.500-style address that denotes an object's location in the Exchange directory hierarchy. An example DN is: /o=widget/ ou=chicago/cn=education/cn=jayw.

Encryption   Scrambling data to make it unreadable. The intended recipient will decrypt the data into plaintext in order to read it.

ETRN   An SMTP authentication method used by SMTP clients using dial-up connections to request their queued mail from their SMTP server.

Expanding a Distribution List   The process of determining the individual addresses contained within a distribution list. This process is performed by the MTA.

Export Utility   A Microsoft Exchange utility that enables the copying (i.e., exporting) of the Exchange directory to a text file where it could be modified in a batch manner and then imported back into the directory. This utility is accessed through the Tools menu of Microsoft Exchange Administrator. See also Import Utility.

Extraction   The process of copying foreign message resources, such as mailboxes, messages, etc. and putting them in a format that can be imported into Exchange. See also source extractors.

Filtering   The ability to display only messages that meet various criteria, such as sender, subject, date, priority, and others.

Folder-Based Application   An application built within a public folder by customizing properties of the folder, such as permissions, views, rules, and the folder forms library to store and present data to users.

Foreign System   A non-Exchange message system.

Frame   The unit of information sent by a Data Link protocol, such as Ethernet or Token Ring.

Free/Busy   Terminology used in the Microsoft Schedule+ application to denote an unscheduled period of time (i.e., free) or a scheduled period of time (i.e., busy).

Front-End Program   A client application, usually running on a user's workstation, that communicates with the back-end program, usually running on a server computer. Outlook is an example of a front-end program for Exchange Server, the back-end program. See also back-end program.

Fully Qualified Domain Name (FQDN)   The full DNS path of an Internet host. An example is `sales.dept4.widget.com`.

Function Call   An instruction in a program that calls (invokes) a function. For example, MAPIReadMail is a MAPI function call.

Garbage Collection Interval   Interval of time between the deletion of expired tombstones. See tombstones.

Gateways   Third-party software that permits Exchange to interoperate with a foreign message system. See also connectors.

Gateway Access Component   The MS Mail software that permits a postoffice to send foreign addressed messages to a gateway postoffice for delivery.

Gateway Address Routing Table (GWART)   The routing table that contains all the address space entries for all the connectors in a site.

Gateway Postoffice   The MS Mail postoffice configured to receive messages to be delivered through a gateway.

Groupware   Any application that allows *groups* of people to store and share information.

GWART   See Gateway Address Routing Table.

Hierarchy   Any structure or organization that uses class, grade, or rank to arrange objects.

Home Server   The Exchange server on which an object physically resides.

HTML   See Hypertext Markup Language.

HTTP   See Hypertext Transfer Protocol.

Hypertext Markup Language (HTML)   The script language used to create WWW content. HTML can create hyperlinks between objects on the WWW.

Hypertext Transfer Protocol (HTTP)   The Internet protocol used to transfer information on the World Wide Web (WWW).

Import Utility   A Microsoft Exchange utility that enables the copying (i.e., importing) of directory information into the Exchange directory. This utility is accessed through the Tools menu of Microsoft Exchange Administrator. See also Export Utility.

Importing   The process of copying foreign message resources, such as mailboxes, messages, etc., into Exchange.

Inbox   The storage folder that receives new incoming messages.

Information Service   A group of service providers for a specific product or environment. The information service for Exchange Server includes service providers for an address book, message store, and message transport.

Internal Network Number   The network address of a Novell NetWare network.

Internet Locator Server (ILS)   A Microsoft server that monitors which users are online and available for collaboration, such as participating in a chat, a whiteboarding session, or even a videoconference.

Internet Message Access Protocol 4 (IMAP4)   An Internet retrieval protocol that enables clients to access and manipulate messages in their mailbox on a remote server. IMAP4 provides additional functions over POP3, such as access to subfolders (not merely the Inbox folder), and selective downloading of messages.

Internet Relay Chat (IRC)   An Internet protocol used to enable real-time, text-based conversations on a network or networks. Conversations are called chats or sessions, and the organization of a number of chats on a particular topic is called a channel.

Interoperability   The ability of different systems to work together (for example, the ability of two different messaging systems to exchange messages).

Interpersonal Messaging (IPM)   The X.400 standard for the format of an e-mail message.

Intersite   Transfer of information across site boundaries.

Intrasite   Transfer of information within one site.

Key   A randomly generated number used to implement advanced security, such as encryption or digital signatures. See also key pair, public key, and private key.

Key Pair   A key that is divided into two mathematically related halves. One half (the public key) is made public. The other half (the private key) is known only by one user.

Leaf Object   An object that does not contain any other objects. A mailbox object is an example of a leaf object.

Lightweight Directory Access Protocol (LDAP)   An Internet protocol used for client access to an X.500-based directory.

Local Delivery   The delivery of a message to a recipient object that resides on the same server as the sender.

Local Procedure Call (LPC)   When a program issues an instruction that is executed on the same computer as the program executing the instruction. See also Remote Procedure Call.

Location Transparency   Being able to access resources without knowledge of their physical location.

Lockbox   An encrypted secret key that is sent with a message.

Mailbox   The generic term referring to a container that holds messages, such as incoming and outgoing messages.

Mail Exchanger (MX)   The designation of an SMTP mail server in a DNS database.

Messaging Application Programming Interface (MAPI)   An object-oriented programming interface for messaging services, developed by Microsoft.

Messaging Bridgehead Server   An Exchange server designated to deliver messages to another site.

Microsoft Commercial Internet Server (MCIS)   A Microsoft suite of commercial-grade server applications marketed to Internet Service Providers, telecommunication carriers, cable network operators, etc. Applications include MCIS Mail Server, Chat Server, and News Server, among others.

Middleware   Software that serves to connect client software to server software.

Migration   Moving resources, such as mailboxes, messages, etc. from one messaging system to another. See also extraction, importing, and Migration Wizard.

Migration Wizard   An Exchange program that extracts data from a foreign message system and imports it into Exchange.

Mismatch   The situation when an Exchange server determines through the Knowledge Consistency Checker (KCC) that it does not have all the Exchange servers in the site in its Replication List.

Multimaster Model   A model where every server in a site has a copy of the site directory.

Multipurpose Internet Mail Extensions   An Internet protocol that enables the encoding of binary content within mail messages. For example, MIME could be used to encode a graphics file or word processing document as an attachment to a text-based mail message. The recipient of the message would also have to be using MIME to decode the attachment. MIME is newer than UUENCODE and in many systems has replaced it. See also UUENCODE.

MX   See Mail Exchanger.

Name Resolution   The DNS process of mapping a domain name to its IP address.

Network News Transfer Protocol (NNTP)   An Internet protocol used to transfer newsgroup information between newsgroup servers and clients (newsreaders), and between newsgroup servers.

NNTP   See Network News Transfer Protocol.

Newsfeed   The newsgroup data that is sent from one newsgroup server to other newsgroup servers.

Objects   The representation, or abstraction, of an entity. For example, each Exchange server is represented as an object in the Exchange Administrator program. As an object, it contains properties, also called attributes, that can be configured. For example, an Exchange server object can have properties that give certain administrators permission to configure that server.

Object Linking and Embedding (OLE)   The Microsoft protocol that specifies how programs can share objects and therefore create compound documents.

Offline Address Book (OAB)   A copy stored on a client's computer of part or all of the server-based Global Address List (GAL). An OAB allows a client to address messages while not connected to their server.

Offline Storage folder (OST)   Folders located on a client's computer that contain replicas of server-based folders. An OST allows a client to access and manipulate copies of server data while not connected to their server. When the client reconnects to their server, they can have their OST resynchronized with the master folders on the server.

One-Off Address   An e-mail address that does not exist in the Exchange GAL, but is specified as a message recipient by a user. One-off addresses are often used to send messages to Internet addresses that do not have corresponding custom recipients in the GAL.

Organization   The highest level object in the Microsoft Exchange hierarchy.

Originator/Recipient Address (O/R Address)   An X.400 address scheme that uses a hierarchical method to denote where on an X.400 network a recipient resides. An example is: c=us;a= ;p=widgetnet;o=widget;s=wilson;g=jay;.

Personal Address Book (PAB)   An address book created by a user and stored on that user's computer or a server.

Personal Storage folder (PST)   Folders created by a user and used for message storage instead of using their mailbox in the Private Information Store. PSTs can be located on a user's computer or on a server.

Plaintext   Unencrypted data. Synonymous with cleartext.

Point-to-Point Protocol (PPP)   An Internet protocol used for direct communication between two nodes. Commonly used by Internet users and their Internet Service Provider on the serial line point-to-point connection over a modem.

Polling   A process that queries a server-based mailbox for new mail.

POP3   See Post Office Protocol 3.

Port Number   A numeric identifier assigned to an application. Transport protocols like TCP use the port number to identify to which application to deliver a packet.

Post Form   A form used to send information directly to a folder without using messaging routing.

Post Office Protocol 3 (POP3)   An Internet protocol used for client retrieval of mail from a server-based mailbox.

Postoffice   An MS Mail server that stores messages.

Private Folder   A server-based folder that is part of a user's mailbox. Private folders are stored on an Exchange server in the private information store. The Inbox and Outbox are examples of private folders.

Private Key   The half of a key pair that is known only by one user and is used to decrypt data and to digitally sign messages.

Professional Office System (PROFS)   An International Business Machine (IBM) host-based messaging application.

Property   A characteristic of an object. Properties of a mailbox include display name, primary Windows NT account, and storage limits. The terms property and attribute are synonymous.

Proxy Address   A foreign e-mail address of an Exchange recipient. Proxy Exchange users (foreign mail users). It would be the proxy address the non-Exchange user uses to address mail to the Exchange recipient. Proxy addresses for SMTP and X.400 are automatically generated for Exchange recipients at their creation. If the connectors for MS Mail and cc:Mail were installed, then proxy addresses for those address types would also be automatically generated for Exchange recipients.

Public Folder Affinity   A numeric value that assigns a cost to another site. When clients need to connect to public folders in another site, affinity numbers are used to choose the site to connect to.

Public Folder Replication   The transferring of public folder data to replicas of that folder on other servers.

Public Key   The half of a key pair that is published for anyone to read and is used when encrypting data and verifying digital signatures.

Pull   A procedure where a user finds and retrieves information, such as when browsing a public folder. Users accessing a public folder containing a company's employee handbook is a type of pull communication.

Pull Feed   A procedure where a newsgroup server requests newsfeed information from another newsgroup server. The opposite of a push feed.

Public Folder   A folder used to store data for a group of users. Some of the features of a public folder are permissions, views, and rules.

Push   A procedure where information is sent (i.e., pushed) to users. Users do not need to find and retrieve (i.e., pull) the information. Exchange Server pushes incoming messages to MAPI-based Exchange clients.

Push Feed   A procedure where a newsgroup server sends information to another newsgroup server without requiring the receiving server to request it. The opposite of a pull feed.

Raw Mode   A specific operational mode of Microsoft Exchange Administrator that allows the viewing and manipulating of all the properties of Exchange objects. Can be initiated by running ADMIN /raw.

Recipient   An Exchange object that can receive a message. Recipients objects include mailboxes, distribution lists, public folders, and custom recipients.

Recovery Server   A server configured to be used in place of another server. If a server goes down because of a failure or is taken down for maintenance, a recovery server can be brought online to provide continued service to users. See also Standby Server.

Relay Host   An SMTP host designated to receive all outgoing SMTP mail. The relay host then forwards the mail to the relevant destination.

Replica   A copy of a public folder located on an Exchange server.

Replication   The transferring of a copy of data to another location, such as another server or site. See also Directory Replication and Public Folder Replication.

Remote Delivery   The delivery of a message to a recipient that does not reside on the same server as the sender.

Remote Procedure Call (RPC)   A set of protocols for issuing instructions that can be sent over a network for execution. A client computer makes a request to a server computer and the results are sent to the client computer. The computer issuing the request and the computer performing the request are remotely separated over a network. Remote procedure calls are a key ingredient in distributed processing and client/server computing. See also Local Procedure Call.

Replication Latency   The delay period (the latency) that occurs after a change to the directory before the DS begins the directory replication process. Latency allows multiple directory changes to be sent during directory replication. The default replication latency period is 300 seconds.

Resolver Program   Client software that queries a DNS database to map a domain name to its IP address.

Resolving an Address   The process of determining where (on which physical server) an object with a particular address resides.

Rich-Text Format (RTF)   A Microsoft format protocol that includes bolding, highlighting, italics, underlining, and many other format types.

Role   A group of permissions that define what activities a user or group can perform with regards to an object.

Scalable   The ability of a system to grow to handle greater traffic, volume, usage, etc.

Schema   The set of rules defining a directory's hierarchy, objects, attributes, etc.

Scripting Agent   The Microsoft Exchange Scripting Agent is a component that reads and executes a script attached to a public folder. It can carry out instructions by accessing databases, spreadsheets, gateways, and many other programs and services.

Sealing   The process of encrypting data.

Secret Key   A security key that can be used to encrypt data and that is only known by a sender and the recipients the sender informs.

Secure Sockets Layer (SSL)   An Internet protocol that provides secure and authenticated TCP/IP connections. A client and server establish a "handshake" whereby they agree on a level of security they will use, such as authentication requirements and encryption. SSL can be used to encrypt sensitive data for transmission.

Send Form   A stand-alone form that is sent from one user to another user.

Service Advertisement Protocol (SAP)   A Novell protocol that is used by servers to advertise their presence and services on a network.

Service Provider   A MAPI program that provides messaging-oriented services to a client. There are three main types of service providers: address book, message store, and message transport.

Shadow Postoffice   A postoffice without mailboxes. The Exchange MS Mail Connector Postoffice is referred to as a shadow postoffice because it does not contain user mailboxes and only temporarily stores incoming and outgoing MS Mail messages.

Signing   The process of placing a digital signature on a message.

Simple Authentication and Security Layer (SASL)   A protocol that provides authentication of SMTP client connections to an SMTP server.

Simple Mail Transfer Protocol (SMTP)   The Internet protocol used to transfer mail messages.

Simple Network Management Protocol (SNMP)   An Internet protocol used to manage heterogeneous computers, operating systems, and applications. Because of its wide acceptance and applicability, SNMP is well suited for enterprise-wide management.

Single-Instance Storage   Storing only one copy. A message that is sent to multiple recipients homed on the same server has only one copy (i.e., instance) stored on that server. Each recipient is given a pointer to that copy of the message.

Single-Seat Administration   The ability to manage a number of sites, servers, etc., from a single application on a single computer.

Site   A logical grouping of Exchange servers that are connected by a full mesh (every server is directly connected to every other server) and communicate using high-bandwidth RPC. All servers in a site can authenticate one another either because they are homed in the same Windows NT domain or because of trust relationships configured between separate Windows NT domains.

Site Services Account   The Windows NT user account that Exchange Server components within a site use to communicate with each other.

S/MIME   Secure MIME is an Internet protocol that enables mail messages to be digitally signed, encrypted, and decrypted.

Source Extractors   Software programs that can copy messaging resources, such as mailboxes and messages, from a foreign mail system and put the information in a format that can be imported into Exchange.

Standby Server   A server configured to be used in place of another server. If a server goes down because of a failure or is taken down for maintenance, a standby server can be brought online to provide continued service to users. See also Recovery Server.

Store-and-Forward   A delivery method that does not require the sender and recipient to have simultaneous interaction. Instead, when a message is sent, it is transferred to the next appropriate location in the network, which temporarily stores it, makes a routing decision, and forwards the message to the next appropriate network location. This process occurs until the message is ultimately delivered to the intended recipient, or an error condition causes the message to be returned to the sender.

Subsystem   A software component that, when loaded, extends the operating system by providing additional services. The MAPI program, MAPI32.DLL, is an example of a subsystem. MAPI32.DLL loads on top of the Windows 95 or Windows NT operating system and provides messaging services.

Systems Network Architecture Distribution Services (SNADS) An International Business Machines (IBM) store-and-forward protocol for the transmission of data. SNADS enables the sender and recipient to not have to be synchronized.

Target Server An Exchange server in a remote site that is designated to receive messages from the local site.

Token The packet of security information a certification authority sends to a client during advanced security setup. Information in the packet includes the client's public key and its expiration. A token is synonymous with a certificate.

Tombstone Information created by the DS about a deleted directory object. The tombstone is replicated to other Exchange servers in a site to inform them of the deletion.

Tombstone Lifetime The length of time a tombstone is kept before it is deleted.

Transaction Log A file used to quickly write data. That data is later written to the relevant Exchange database file. It is quicker to write to a transaction log file because the writes are done sequentially (i.e., one right after the other). Transaction log files can also be used to re-create data that has been lost in an Exchange database.

Trust Level A numeric value given an object that is used to determine if that object should be replicated to another location, such as a foreign directory.

T1 The interval used by dirsync requestors to send their postoffice address list to the designated dirsync server.

T2 The interval used by the dirsync server to compile a new Global Address List and to send that list to the dirsync requestors.

T3 The interval used by the dirsync requestors to rebuild their postoffice address list.

Uniform Resource Locator (URL) An addressing method used to identify Internet servers and documents.

Universal Inbox   One inbox folder that receives incoming items from all outside sources and of all types, such as e-mail, voice mail, faxes, pages, etc.

Update Sequence Number (USN)   A tracking device used during directory replication to ensure that all new changes to a directory are replicated throughout the site.

User Profile   A collection of information for MAPI client configuration that specifies the services a user wants to use and how MAPI client applications are to look and behave.

UUENCODE   Stands for UNIX-to-UNIX Encode, and is a protocol used to encode binary information within mail messages. UUENCODE is older than MIME. See also MIME.

Web   The World Wide Web.

Workflow Application   An application that can route electronic forms to users based on various criteria.

World Wide Web (WWW)   The collection of computers on the Internet using protocols such as HTML and HTTP.

WWW   See World Wide Web.

X.400   An International Telecommunications Union (ITU) standard for message exchange.

X.500   An International Telecommunications Union (ITU) standard for directory services.

Index

E

J

Job Candidate form, 274
Join an Existing Site option, 129
joining sites, 122–123, 129
Journal property page, 243
journals, 213–214, 243
JScript scripts, 68, 305

K

KCCs (knowledge consistency checkers), 98
Key Management Administrator Password dialog box, 328
Key Management components, 68
communication with, 88, 88
in security, 339–340
with System Attendant, 82–83
Key Management (KM) server
configuring, 327–330
installing, 320–322
operation of, 323–326, 324–326
starting, 322
troubleshooting, 342–343
upgrading, 322
Key Management Server Password dialog box, 329
Key Manager service, 323, 325, 329
Keyflow program, 11
keys, encryption
public/private pairs, 314–317, 314, 316–317
secret, 318–320, 319
KM database, 326, 329, 339–340

KM server. *See* Key Management (KM) server
knowledge consistency checkers (KCCs), 98

L

LANs
for MS Mail Connector, 576, 587
in shared-file computing, 12–14, 14
laptops
Exchange client installation on, 217
Outlook functions for, 213
latency, replication, 96
LDAP (Lightweight Directory Access Protocol), 36, 373–375
configuring, 352–353
port number for, 391
leaf objects, 51, 415
libraries
DLLs, 47, 131–132, 367
for forms, 271–272
licenses
as installation issue, 115–116, 116, 128–129
Registry entries for, 135
Lifetime setting in MTA, 454
Lightweight Directory Access Protocol (LDAP), 36, 373–375
configuring, 352–353
port number for, 391
Limit administrative access to home site option, 430
Limits property page, 156
Link Monitor utility, 23, 63, 82, 103–104, 458

N

O

Q

X

SYBEX BOOKS ON THE WEB

MCSE CORE EXAM NOTES™
FROM NETWORK PRESS®

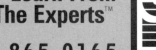

Official Microsoft Objectives for Exam 70-081: Implementing and Supporting Microsoft® Exchange Server 5.5

Exam objectives are subject to change at any time without prior notice and at Microsoft's sole discretion. Please visit Microsoft's Training & Certification Web site (www.microsoft.com/Train_Cert) for the most current exam objectives listing